W9-CEH-746

POINT COUNTERPOINT
EIGHT CASES FOR COMPOSITION

POINT COUNTERPOINT
EIGHT CASES FOR COMPOSITION

SECOND EDITION

THAYLE K. ANDERSON / KENT FORRESTER

Murray State University

Harcourt Brace College Publishers

Fort Worth   Philadelphia   San Diego
New York   Orlando   Austin   San Antonio
Toronto   Montreal   London   Sydney   Tokyo

Publisher	Ted Buchholz
Acquisitions Editor	Stephen T. Jordan
Developmental Editor	Sarah Helyar Smith
Senior Project Editor	Mike Hinshaw
Senior Production Manager	Annette Dudley Wiggins
Book Designer	Melinda Huff

Copyright © 1993, 1987 by Harcourt Brace Jovanovich, Inc.

All rights reserved. No part of this publication may be reproduced or transmitted in any form or by any means, electronic or mechanical, including photocopy, recording, or any information storage and retrieval system, without permission in writing from the publisher.

Requests for permission to make copies of any part of the work should be mailed to: Copyrights and Permissions Department, Harcourt Brace Jovanovich, Publishers, Orlando, Florida 32887.

Address for Editorial Correspondence: Harcourt Brace Jovanovich College Publishers, 301 Commerce Street, Suite 3700, Fort Worth, TX 76102.

Address for Orders: Harcourt Brace Jovanovich, Publishers, 6277 Sea Harbor Drive, Orlando, Florida 32887. 1-800-782-4479, or 1-800-433-0001 (in Florida).

ISBN: 0-15-500169-8

Library of Congress Catalog Card Number: 92-073716

Printed in the United States of America

3 1 0 090 9 8 7 6 5 4 3 2

For our parents:

Mark Kermit Anderson
Gwen Morrill Anderson

George Washington Forrester
Fern Milner Forrester

Table of Contents

1

USING OTHER PEOPLE'S IDEAS IN
YOUR WRITING

There's no end to the things you might want to do with the ideas you read in books. You might want to argue with them, mock them, explain them, or use them up to support your own ideas. Whatever your purpose is, you'll have to let your readers know what you're responding to by either summarizing or quoting those ideas.

Let's see how this works in practice. Let's say you want to respond to an idea by the seventeenth-century French cynic, the Duc de La Rochefoucauld. Here's how Rochefoucauld, in one of his frequent bad moods, described human nature:

The mind is always the dupe of the heart.

If you wanted to summarize Rochefoucauld's idea in your own words, you might write something like this and then follow it with your response:

The cynical Duc de La Rochefoucauld once wrote that people are always swayed by their emotions. As usual, Rochefoucauld was dead wrong. [Here you would elaborate on why Rochefoucauld was wrong, but we won't go into that now.]

If you wanted to get across the flavor of Rochefoucauld's words, you might want to quote his words, like this:

The cynical Duc de La Rochefoucauld once wrote, "The mind is always the dupe of the heart." As usual, Rochefoucauld was dead right. [Here you would elaborate on why Rochefoucauld was right.]

When you think about it, the ability to use the ideas of others is an essential skill in college. When you write an essay, take an essay test, respond in class, or put together a research paper, what you are really doing is summarizing and quoting—and then responding to—other people's ideas. Of course, you have to read before you summarize and quote—and we'll get to a lesson on reading shortly—but first you need to learn how to introduce those summaries and quotations—so that's where we'll begin.

INTRODUCING OTHER PEOPLE'S IDEAS

Once you've learned a few simple things about introducing sources, you can get on with the business at hand. Here, then, are those few simple things.

1. Move from your words to a summary or quotation by telling your reader that you are doing so. It's very hard for readers to keep track of who is speaking as they move down the page unless you introduce your sources. At the least, you ought to tell your readers the author's name or the title of the work. Sometimes you'll want to tell them even more. You might, for instance, want to identify the author, tell what century he or she lived in, and you may want to describe the relationship between your idea and the idea of your summary or quote. We'll discuss those matters in a moment, but for the time being here's what a few introductions look like:

> According to Abraham Lincoln, . . .
> Beatrix Potter, the author of *Peter Rabbit*, says, . . .
> A noted rocket scientist, Bob Darling, claims that . . .
> "Religion," Karl Marx claimed, "is the opium of the people."
> A *Wall Street Journal* editorial describes the inner city as . . .

Now we can go on to discuss the elements that make up an introduction to a source.

2. Identify the author when that identification communicates something relevant. Let's say you were going to summarize an idea from Donald Murray, who has taught writing at the college level, has won a Pulitzer Prize for editorial writing, and has published fiction, poetry, and writing textbooks. Obviously, here is a man who has some weight when it comes to the topic of writing. Notice how the writer below identifies Murray's expertise:

> Donald Murray, a Pulitzer Prize-winning editorialist, claims that one of the most important tasks for a writer is rewriting.

Also note that the writer didn't use *everything* he knows about Murray; that would have bogged down his writing. Instead, he selected only the most impressive or pertinent fact from Murray's credentials.

Of course, there will often be times when you won't know anything about the writer of the source you're using. Indeed, there will even be times when you won't even know the writer's name. In those cases, merely write something like this:

> In a *Christian Century* essay, the author argues that . . .
> In *Newsweek*, Sherry North claims that . . .

3. Use the present tense of the introductory verb unless you call attention to your source as a historical person. We can use the following passage from Donald Murray's *The Maker's Eye* to work on.

> Rewriting isn't virtuous. It isn't something that ought to be done. It is simply something that most writers find they have to do to discover what they have to say and how to say it. It is a condition of the writer's life.

If you're focusing on the ideas in this passage and those ideas seem in some way to be general truths, keep your verb in the present tense, like this:

Donald Murray says that one of the most important tasks for a writer is rewriting.

However, if you call attention to Murray as a historical person, you will have to shift to the past tense in your introductory verb, like this:

When he taught at the University of New Hampshire in 1985, Donald Murray said that one of the most important tasks for a writer was rewriting.

But enough of this. We could spend pages describing and redescribing exceptions and subtleties of the use of the introductory verb tense. But all of us would grow weary with that — and probably more confused. Just keep this general rule in mind: When you're focusing on the ideas in an essay rather than on your source as a historical person, keep your introductory verb in the present tense, and stay with that present tense until you're *forced* out of it. You'll make it easy on your reader if you do.

4. Use a verb that suggests the intent of the author. For instance, if the author is arguing, let your verb show that intent — like this:

In "Non-Violent Resistance," Mohandas Gandhi argues that passive resistance is not only the most moral form of resistance, but also the most effective.

In "Politics and the English Language," George Orwell contends that imprecise language is often used to hide base motives.

But when the author is merely describing, let that intent be known as well, like this:

In "The Preying Tree," Joseph Wheelwright, a professional woodworker, explains how he turned a tree into a statue.

In a chapter from *Under the Sea-Wind*, Rachel Carson, an early ecologist, *describes* the layers, or "horizontal communities," of ocean life.

Exercise: Introducing Sources

Instructions: Using the information in the footnotes that accompany the essays in this book, introduce quotes and summaries from these paragraphs. Look back at the advice given in the preceding section if you need help.

1. Introduce and quote the first sentence from paragraph 3 of James Fallows's "Language" (p. 303).
2. Introduce and quote the first sentence from paragraph 3 of Harold Edwards's "The Dour Critics of Advertising" (p. 202).
3. Introduce and summarize paragraph 3 in William Tucker's "Is Nature Too Good for Us?" (p. 58).

4. Introduce and summarize paragraph 1 of Eugene Rostow's "Our Worst Wartime Mistake" (p. 500).

READING AND SUMMARIZING

When you summarize an entire essay, what you're really after is a faithful rendering, in your own words, of the author's main idea. Our first bit of advice is this: Don't get lost in the details; a writer's main idea is sometimes obscured by a mass of words that twist and turn their way down the page.

Fortunately, there are places to go when you lose your way. Writers usually shine a light on their main idea in a few special locations in an essay: in the title, in the introduction, and in the conclusion. So slow up when you get to those three spots in the essay, because in each place you might find the author's summary of his or her work (in other words, a thesis statement). All you'll have to do, then, is translate a single statement of the source into a single statement of your own.

Reading a Title

Slowing up at the title might tell you more than you can get at a first glance. Here's a very explicit title by Barbara Lawrence:

Four-Letter Words Can Hurt You

Simple enough. All you have to do, once you've read the essay, is put Lawrence's title into your own words, perhaps something like this: "Barbara Lawrence argues that obscenity coarsens the relationship between men and women."

Of course, sometimes a title will tell you no more than the topic of the essay ("The Brown Wasps" by Loren Eiseley). But sometimes it will tell you what side of a controversial issue the author is on ("Viva Bilingualism" by James Fallows). And sometimes it will even add an extra dimension to the author's thesis. (Judy Syfers's attack on the disproportionate share of work that wives perform in a marriage is called "Why I Want a Wife.")

Reading an Introduction

If you can't find a main idea in a title, you'll likely find it in an introduction. The classic introduction consists of a single paragraph, with a thesis statement as its closing sentence — like this one:

My love for baseball began when I was a small boy. In addition to playing the game (with varied degrees of success!), I also loved reading about it. I read all sorts of baseball novels for boys, later graduating to reading biographies of ballplayers. But as I got older still, I read three baseball books that really changed my view of the sport.

Unfortunately for summarizers, not all introductions are so neat and clean. Some essays begin with an anecdote that covers three or four paragraphs; some begin with a series of examples that ends with a thesis; and a few begin ironically and never quite get around to a clear statement of the theme. But *almost* all essays contain an explicitly stated thesis (merely another name for a summary of the entire essay) somewhere early on. Look for it. It will make *your* summary easier.

Reading a Conclusion

You'll usually find a summary, or thesis, in an essay's conclusion. So if you can't find a thesis in the title and overlook it in the introduction, you still have one more chance to find it. Here, for instance, is the conclusion from an essay by Norman Chad called "Silence Can Be Golden," an essay that argues that television sports announcers ought to talk less:

> The only words announcers need to remember are two: Shut up.

Not many conclusions are so direct and simple as that one, but almost all will come back, in some way or another, to the thesis of the essay. So slow down when you hit the conclusion; you'll probably find a summary of the essay there.

Exercise: Summarizing an Essay

Instructions: Introduce and summarize the following short articles in a single sentence. If you need help, refer back to the preceding section.

1. "How to Tell Your Friends from the Japs" (p. 457)
2. "The Aggressors" (p. 277)
3. "An Alternative to Bilingualism" (p. 326)

SUMMARIZING AND PARAPHRASING A PARAGRAPH

Summaries are abbreviated versions of a source; paraphrases are longer. A ten-line paragraph that takes you a sentence to summarize might take you seven or eight lines to paraphrase. Here's a paragraph we can summarize and paraphrase:

> America and Britain have been unusual in leaving the curriculum so largely in the hands of teachers. Some form of national curriculum is used throughout Continental Europe, although the syllabus is typically not specified in as much detail as in Japan. And now Britain is changing course: legislation currently going through Parliament will introduce a national curriculum for England and Wales, with the principal subjects being English, math, science, technology, a foreign language, history and geography, and art, music, and design. It is envisioned that the new curriculum will take up approximately 70 per cent of teaching time, leaving the remainder free for optional subjects such as a second foreign language, or extra science.
> —from *Why Johnny Can't Read, but Yoshio Can* by Richard Lynn

A summary of that paragraph might go something like this:

> Richard Lynn says that the United States and Britain are almost alone among Western nations in allowing individual teachers, rather than national boards, to set curriculums.

As you see, a summary of a paragraph is little more than a restatement of the source's topic sentence. Not all paragraphs have a topic sentence, but enough do to make searching them out worthwhile.

Now here's a paraphrase of the same paragraph.

Richard Lynn says that the United States and Britain are almost alone among Western nations in allowing individual teachers to determine the subjects their students will study. By contrast, the educational curriculums of other Western nations are set by national educational boards (though, even here, their curriculums are not as standardized as those in Japan). Britain now seems likely to follow the Continental model; their Parliament is currently considering passing a law that will mandate a national curriculum. If that happens, the United States will be virtually alone in allowing teachers to set their own curriculums.

There are other things to keep in mind as you paraphrase:

1. Put paraphrases into your own words. When you don't, your paraphrase (or your summary) could be called, strictly speaking, plagiarism. You see, when you paraphrase, you are making a tacit claim that you have changed the original passage into *your* style, or idiom. The source is now in *your* diction and *your* sentence structure. When you summarize or paraphrase without changing the source to your style, it looks as though you're trying to pass off someone else's work as your own. To illustrate this point, we can use a sentence from *The Life and Death of Thomas Wolfe,* by Malcolm Cowley:

Wolfe was determined to be a great writer, like a thousand other boys of his age, but his determination was more ardent or obsessive and was based on a special sort of emotional need.

That's a fairly typical sentence of the sort one might paraphrase for a paper or test in a humanities class. Here's a case in which the paraphraser uses too much of the source's idiom:

Malcolm Cowley says that Thomas Wolfe, like so many other boys of his age, was determined to be a great writer; however, his determination was more ardent, and it was based on a sort of psychological need.

That just won't do. Good paraphrasers don't just move a word or two around and change a word or two. They translate the source's idiom into their own idiom. In this case. the paraphraser uses too many of the source's words. Look, for instance, at the word *ardent.* That obviously comes from the source. Very few people would choose just that word for just that situation. Be especially careful of carrying whole phrases intact into your paraphrase. (The bad paraphraser above carries the phrase *determination was more ardent* into his summary.) Of course, paraphrasers have to use *some* of the source's words. Prepositions, common nouns, transitional expressions, and even common verbs often have no synonyms. If your source, for instance, writes, "He blinked his eye," your summary will no doubt look much the same. (An overzealous paraphraser might come up with "He batted his orb.") But the principle remains: A paraphrase should be in your idiom. Here, then is an acceptable paraphrase of the Cowley sentence;

Malcolm Cowley says that Wolfe's drive to be a great writer was more "obsessive" than that of other young writers of his generation. Moreover, Cowley says, Wolfe's drive was fueled by psychological needs.

There is an easy way of avoiding plagiarism: Don't look at the source as you paraphrase or summarize; understand the source so well that you can put it aside and see if you can put it in your own words.

2. Remind your readers frequently that your paraphrases are not your ideas. As your readers work their way down a paper in which you shift back and forth between your ideas and the ideas of someone else, it's hard for them to keep track of who is speaking unless you tell them. And you'll have to tell them often, sometimes three or four times in a single paragraph. Here's what one of those paragraphs looks like (with the reminders in boldface):

In "Cruel Lib," **Keith Mano** says that it's a hard truth for many people to face, but most people are not very talented, pretty, or "charismatic." When they discover their real self, **Mano says**, they usually find that there's not much there. **Mano concludes** by saying that it's sometimes better for people to be limited — and thus protected from life's harsher realities — by the roles society expects them to play than have their inadequacies constantly exposed to the world.

Without those little reminders, your reader might think that some of the statements in a paraphrased paragraph are yours. By the way, don't worry about being repetitive. Those little reminders are as invisible to the reader as the *he saids* are in a novel.

Exercise: Paraphrasing a Paragraph

Paraphrase the following paragraphs. Refer back to the instructions preceding this exercise if you need help.

1. Introduce and paraphrase paragraph 1 of William A. Henry III's "Against a Confusion of Tongues" (p. 294).
2. Introduce and paraphrase paragraph 1 of Eric Gelman's "In Sports, 'Lions vs. Tigers'" (p. 237).
3. Introduce and paraphrase paragraph 1 of Eric Julber's "Let's Open Our Wilderness Areas" (p. 50).
4. Introduce and paraphrase paragraph 1 of David Gelman's "Just How the Sexes Differ" (p. 228).

QUOTING

To communicate the flavor of the source, you might have to do more than summarize; you'll probably have to use the source's actual words. In fact, when the source is ironic or vitriolic or funny — writing that depends on its tone — you'll *have* to quote to get across the flavor of the original. We can illustrate this point by using a satire of Thanksgiving by an anonymous letter writer to *The New Yorker:*

Consider for a moment the Thanksgiving meal itself. It has become a sort of refuge for endangered species of starch: sweet potatoes, cauliflower, pumpkin, mince (whatever "mince" is), those blessed yams. Bowls of luridly colored yams, with no taste at all, lying torpid under a lava flow of marshmallow! And then the sacred turkey. One might as well try to construct a holiday repast around a fish — say, a nice piece of boiled haddock. After all, turkey tastes very similar to haddock: same consistency, same quite remarkable absence of flavor. But then, if the *pièce de résistance* were a nice piece of boiled haddock instead of turkey, there wouldn't be all that fun for Dad when Mom hands him the sterling-silver, bone-handled carving set . . . and then everyone stands around pretending not to watch while he saws and tears away at the bird as if he were trying to burrow his way into or out of some grotesque, fowllike prison.

It just wouldn't do to say "The author criticizes the foods that we traditionally serve on Thanksgiving" and then stop. That doesn't communicate the humorous diction, the irony, and the comic exaggeration of the original. An essay of this sort depends almost entirely on the *way* it's written. To communicate that *way*, you'll use some of the words of the source, perhaps like this:

The author satirically describes the Thanksgiving meal as a "refuge for endangered species of starch," with a turkey that tastes like "a nice piece of boiled haddock."

Only stop to quote when your source's words are special in some way: funny, satirical, acid, vivid, clever, well put. If you quote commonplace words, it will look as though you couldn't understand the original well enough to put it in your own words. Here are some sentences that shouldn't be quoted. They're too commonplace.

We now know that a yeti track can be made by the sun melting the footprints of a small creature such as a fox or wild dog.
— "Epitaph to the Elusive Abominable Snowman" by Sir Edmund Hillary

A second example of these territorial instincts is, I think, in the Middle East today.
— "Two Imperatives in Conflict" by Richard Shoglow

You see the point, don't you? Don't quote the commonplace. Wait until the author says something in a special way.

You can lower your standards a little when you're quoting someone who is truly an authority in his or her field — someone like Willem de Kooning on modern art, Carl Sagan on extraterrestrials, Mae West on aging gracefully, Joseph Smith on Mormonism, Martin Luther King, Jr. on passive resistance, or Steve Jobs on computers. That is, when you run across an important authority, you can get away with quoting words that you wouldn't want to quote from a writer with less authority.

How Much to Quote

The most common mistake in quoting is quoting too much. Since it's always more work to summarize than to quote, writers who overquote look as though they haven't thoroughly assimilated the source — or, worse, were just plain lazy. Summarize most of the ideas that you use from other writers; quote only when the words are special.

Special Punctuation Related to Quotations

Surprisingly, some of the trickiest elements in quoting evidence from your sources involve punctuation. Let's review a few principles you will want to keep in mind as you quote your sources:

1. The two most frequently used punctuations, the period and the comma, go inside the closing quotation mark of your quoted passage.

> In a vigorous defense of contemporary advertising, Harold Edwards concedes that "Of course adwriters manipulate language to influence people," but, he insists, "so do all people who use language."

There is one exception to this rule: If you are using the widely accepted parenthetical documentation method (discussed in Chapter 10), your period goes *outside* the parentheses to make it clear that the parenthetical expression belongs with that sentence (rather than with the one that follows).

> In a vigorous defense of contemporary advertising, Harold Edwards concedes that "Of course adwriters manipulate language to influence people," but, he insists, "so do all people who use language" (165).

On the other hand, colons and semicolons, unlike periods and commas, always go *outside* the quotation mark:

> Advocating the multiple use principle for federally owned wilderness areas, Cynthia Riggs observes that most of this land "has little aesthetic or recreational value"; she insists that only small portions of these vast holdings have anything in common with our most beautiful or famous national parks (71).

Finally, the position of the other two end punctuations, the exclamation point and the question mark, depends on the following principle: If the question or the exclamation is contained within your quoted passage, the end punctuation belongs *within* the closing quotation mark.

> After pointing out the vast amounts of mineral resources locked up in federally protected wilderness areas, Cynthia Riggs asks, "Should America worry about the loss of energy resources?" Her answer is a resounding "yes!"

If, however, your quoted passage is only a part of the question you are posing or the exclamation you are making, your end punctuation belongs *outside* the closing quotation mark.

> After pointing out the vast amounts of mineral resources locked up in federally protected wilderness areas, Cynthia Riggs poses an important question: How concerned should we Americans be over "the loss of energy resources"?

2. Follow your introduction to quotations with a comma or colon (or move into the quotation with no punctuation at all). If your source introduction consists merely of a subject and a verb (usually one of utterance), set if off with a comma.

Al Goldstein, the publisher of various erotic magazines, admits, "It's a high profit business, pornography, but it's also high risk. My lawyers have made as much as I have."

If your source introduction consists of a dependent clause, set it off with a comma.

As James Cook observes in a *Forbes* essay, "The profit potential inherent in adult films is awesome."

If, on the other hand, your source introduction consists of a complete sentence, including a verb and a direct object, set if off with a colon.

In a *Forbes* essay, James Cook reveals the economic bottom line of the pornography business: "The profit potential inherent in adult films is awesome."

Al Goldstein, the publisher of various erotic magazines, is blunt about his operating expenses: "It's a high profit business, pornography, but it's also high risk. My lawyers have made as much as I have."

Sometimes you don't need any punctuation at all between your words and a quotation. For instance, if you are merely quoting a word or a phrase or if your sentence structure contains the subordinate conjunction *that*, move directly into your quotation without stopping for a punctuation mark.

According to a *Forbes* essay by James Cook, the bottom line in the pornography industry is simply that "The profit potential inherent in adult films is awesome."

Al Goldstein, the publisher of various erotic magazines, concedes that pornography is a "high profit business," but he insists that it is also a risky business. "My lawyers," he says, "have made as much as I have."

3. Set off quoted words or phrases within the passage you are quoting with single quotation marks.

Irving Kristol insists that ". . . pornography differs from erotic art in that its whole purpose is to treat human beings obscenely, to deprive human beings of their specifically human dimension. . . . To quote Susan Sontag: 'What pornographic literature does is precisely to drive a wedge between one's existence as a full human being and one's existence as a sexual being—while in ordinary life a healthy person is one who prevents such a gap from opening up.'"

Notice, incidentally, that if your source's quotation concludes your quotation, your period (or comma) goes inside *both* quotation marks.

Remember, too, that you do not use both the double and the single quotation marks if you quote only the exact words your source quotes.

In an effort to make his point, Irving Kristol quotes Susan Sontag: "What pornographic literature does is precisely to drive a wedge between one's existence as a full human being and one's existence as a sexual human being—while in ordinary life a healthy person is one who prevents such a gap from opening up."

4. If, as you write your essay, you estimate that the quotation you are about to record will exceed four lines of your regular text, set your quotation off by indenting the entire passage five spaces and by single-spacing it. The purpose of this indentation is to prevent your reader from losing track of the fact that you are quoting evidence from a source rather than presenting your own conclusions.

Remember to indent your longer quoted passage only five spaces from your left margin and to bring in your right margin approximately five spaces. Realize, too, that your indentation by itself sets off your passage as a quotation; you don't need to enclose it in quotation marks.

If your indented passage exceeds one paragraph, you can indicate paragraphs either by indenting the first lines of each paragraph (as usual) or by double-spacing between paragraphs. Choose either method, and then be consistent throughout your essay.

5. Indicate the fact that you have deleted irrelevant, redundant, or confusing words from your quotation with an ellipsis — three or four spaced periods. Three spaced periods indicate that you have deleted a word or phrase within a single sentence. Four spaced periods indicate either that you have deleted a passage that ends a sentence (and hence the fourth period is merely the sentence's end punctuation) or that you have deleted a full sentence or more from the passage you are quoting.

> One product of the wave of racist, anti-Japanese hysteria which swept across the nation immediately after the bombing of Pearl Harbor is a late-December 1941 *Time* essay entitled "How to Tell Your Friends from the Japs," which informs us that
>> "Japanese . . . are seldom fat: they often dry up and grow lean as they age. The Chinese often put on weight, particularly if they are prosperous. . . . the Chinese expression is likely to be more placid, kindly, open; the Japanese more positive, dogmatic, arrogant. . . .Japanese are hesitant, nervous in conversation, laugh loudly at the wrong time."

Incidentally, it is not necessary for you to use the ellipsis with individual words or phrases quoted from your source. And you will, moreover, begin a quoted passage with an ellipsis only when the partial sentence you have begun with could be construed by your reader to be a complete sentence in your source's text. Otherwise, go right to your quote without an ellipsis, as the author of the following passage does.

> In his *Harper's* essay, William Tucker concludes his case for the multiple use approach to federal wilderness reserves by arguing that if such areas "can be set aside for commercialism at no great cost, they should be," and that when areas are conducive to "primitive hiking and recreation . . . they should be maintained." Tucker insists, however, that if we think that we are serving ourselves or our posterity "by not developing resources where they exist . . . we are being very shortsighted." "Conservation, not preservation," he insists, "is once again the best guiding principle."

Remember, finally, that in deleting irrelevant material from your quotations, you must be careful not to abuse this device. Distorting your source's ideas with clever use of ellipses in order to conjure up support for your argument is blatantly dishonest and undermines the integrity and credibility of your essay.

6. If you need to interrupt your quoted passage with your own clarifying phrase or sentence, enclose your clarification in brackets. (Parentheses in this situation simply wouldn't do; your reader would attribute the parenthetical clarification not to you but to your source.) Here, then, is how brackets are used:

> In a letter to *The New Republic* in mid-1942, Ted Nakashima, an American citizen of Japanese descent who had been recently interned with his family in a relocation camp, was bitter in his description of his new environment: "The resettlement center [Camp Harmony, located at Puyallup, Washington] is actually a penitentiary — armed guards in towers with spotlights and deadly tommy guns, fifteen feet of barbed-wire fences, everyone confined to quarters at nine, lights out at ten o'clock."

If, incidentally, you need to specify the antecedent of a pronoun in your quoted passage, you can directly substitute the bracketed noun for the quoted pronoun without having to use an ellipsis to indicate your deletion. Here is an example of that.

> At one of many early-1942 California congressional hearings on what to do with California residents of Japanese descent, "[California Attorney General Earl Warren's] remarks at this point were confined to the Japanese alone: 'To assume that the enemy has not planned fifth column activities for us in a wave of sabotage is simply to live in a fool's paradise.'"

Finally, if, as you quote your source, you discover that the passage contains a typo or a grammatical or factual error, quote the error faithfully, but indicate to your reader that the error is not yours by inserting *sic* (Latin for "thus") in brackets immediately following the problem. Here is an example from the first edition of this book:

> A *Time* essay poses some intriguing questions: "Women playing lacrosse? Hockey? Women tackling each other in rugby and mixing it up in the scrum? Women running marathons? Small wonder that fathers, husbands and friends worry about the physical strains that the supposedly weaker six [*sic*] is undergoing these days."

Exercise: Quoting

Instructions: Use the suggestions in the section immediately above to introduce, punctuate, and select the words you quote.

1. In a single sentence, introduce and summarize paragraph 1 of "Just How the Sexes Differ" (p. 228). Then, in a second sentence, introduce a quotation from that same paragraph that supports your summary of it.

2. In a single sentence, introduce and summarize paragraph 1 of "The Language of Advertising claims" (p. 184). Within that sentence, quote an appropriate word or phrase.

3. In a single sentence, introduce and summarize the second paragraph in Susan Brownmiller's "Women Fight Back" (p. 404). Then introduce and quote a sentence to support your summary.

COMBINING SOURCES: SYNTHESIZING

Thus far we have only talked about using a single source at a time. In actual practice, of course, writers often have occasion to use more than one source. If you were writing a research paper, for instance, you might use the ideas of five or ten writers. In this section you'll learn how to move gracefully from source to source in a multisource paper.

We'll begin with a simple situation in which an author summarizes writer A in his first paragraph, and then moves, in his next paragraph, to a summary of writer B. Here is a passage from an essay called "The Reality of Death: What Happens When It Is Ignored?" In this first paragraph, Robert Head summarizes an attack on the funeral industry by Jessica Mitford.

In 1963 Jessica Mitford made little pretext at presenting a social scientific study [of the funeral industry], but relied heavily on satire to attract public readership. In this respect she was quite successful. Mrs. Mitford levied her attack both at the funeral industry and at the funeral itself and offered the conclusion that the best way to eliminate the latter was to exterminate the former. . . .

Now Head moves to his next paragraph, but note that he begins this paragraph by providing a transitional sentence that not only identifies the new source but also points out a small difference between the ideas of the first source and the ideas of the second source.

In the same year, Ruth Harmer published a more moderate yet critical study of the funeral service titled, *The High Cost of Dying*. Unlike Mrs. Mitford, Mrs. Harmer was willing to recognize that there was a connection between the funeral and the culture, but in a totally negative sense.

Easy enough. When you follow a paragraph that uses source A with a paragraph that uses source B, provide a transitional sentence that shows how A and B are related.

There will also be times when you'll need to combine two or more sources in a single paragraph. We can illustrate this point with an example from Donald Murray's "The Maker's Eye":

The writer, counsels novelist Nancy Hale, "should be critical of everything that seems to him most delightful in his style. He should excise what he most admires, because he wouldn't thus admire it if he weren't. . . in a sense protecting it from criticism." John Ciardi, the poet, adds, "The last act of the writing must be to become one's own reader. . . ."

Once again, note that the author shows us the relationship between his first source and his second through the use of the word *adds*. That simple little word points out that the second source confirms the idea of the first source.

The most important lesson in combining sources, then, is this: Let your reader know, as you introduce each source, how that new source is related to the source you've just used. Sometimes, as you see immediately above, the new source will merely further confirm, and thus add weight to, a point that your first source made.

But there will also be times when you will introduce a new source so that you can provide a counterbalancing opinion to a previous source or provide a slightly different slant on an idea your previous source raised. In each case provide a transition that shows the relationship between the two sources.

Exercise: Combining Sources

Instructions: If you need help with the following exercises, review the preceding section.

1. In a single paragraph of your own, combine a summary of the first two paragraphs of "Just How the Sexes Differ" (p. 228). Be sure to provide a transition between your first summary and your second.

2. In a single paragraph of your own, combine a summary of the first two paragraphs of "Myths About Advertising" (p. 189). Be sure to provide a transition from your first summary to your second.

3. In a single paragraph of your own, combine a summary of "Is Puffery Flummery?" (p. 175) and "Puffery Is Deception" (p. 177). Use a contrastive transition between the two summaries.

BEYOND NUTS AND BOLTS: REASONING AND RHETORIC

What we've been talking about thus far have been the techniques of handling other people's ideas. Now we would like to add a few suggestions about how to make your papers persuasive and logical.

Evaluating Your Sources

Before you read an article in this text, it's a good idea to read the source footnote to discover the periodical in which the article originally appeared. If you find a general-interest periodical there — *Newsweek, Atlantic, Saturday Review* — the writer's audience was the "common reader." "Common" readers, of course, include cat fanciers, joggers, recluses, high school graduates, Ph.D.s, vegetarians, and people with every other interest and appetite. But they don't come to a general-interest periodical to satisfy their special interest or political predilections. They go to *Vegetarian Times* and *The Village Voice* for those things.

If you find a specialized periodical in that footnote — *Christian Century, Commonweal, Libertarian Weekly*, and the like — you will likely notice a more personal tone, allusions to common beliefs, scorn for common enemies, easy generalizations. When a writer knows that his readers already agree with his position, he or she doesn't feel so much pressure to construct a heavily reasoned, fact-filled argument with every generalization qualified and validated. In fact, he or she sometimes merely writes to stir up the troops.

We're not saying that you should dismiss the arguments in these specialized journals, but we do suggest that you keep in mind the audience for which they were originally created. That's part of judging an argument. Read with your critical intelligence functioning.

Thinking About Your Audience

An audience influences the way a writer or speaker communicates. When Samuel Johnson heard that there was a woman preaching the gospel in eighteenth-century London, he huffed to his drinking companions, "Sir, a woman preaching is like a dog's walking on his hind legs. It is not done well, but you are surprised to find it done at all."

You women out there! How do you like Johnson's argument? Quite sound, don't you think? No? You mean to say that a woman preacher is not like a dog walking on its hind legs? You think Johnson's argument sexist, his analogy false? How can that be? His argument went over quite well indeed when he first uttered it to a bunch of like-minded eighteenth-century gentlemen, all of whom thought it splendid reasoning, unassailable really, and quite the best thing on the subject that they'd heard in a fortnight.

We suspect that if Johnson had been arguing with a group of eighteenth-century ladies, he probably would have constructed his argument somewhat differently, perhaps with polite deference to his listeners.

Writers who argue well keep their audience in mind. In "Does Life Begin Before Birth?", an essay that originally appeared in *Christianity Today*, John Stott argues that the fetus is very much a human being. He then goes on to quote the New Testament, which states that an expectant mother is a "woman with child." That biblical quotation no doubt worked well in *Christianity Today*, a magazine for readers who have a special interest in reading articles from a Christian viewpoint. Stott rightly assumed that biblical quotations would give a special kind of authority to his argument.

But that same biblical quotation wouldn't have worked as well in *Harper's*, a general-interest magazine. *Harper's* no doubt has Christian readers. But *Harper's* also has readers who are atheists, Buddhists, agnostics, Jews, and Druids. Because each special-interest group forms only a small part of the total audience, *Harper's* writers can't afford to make a special appeal to any single segment.

Unlike Stott's audience, your audience (unless your instructor tells you otherwise) will be that ill-defined, amorphous "common reader." You can't count on your common readers' knowledge of technical matters, but you can count on their knowledge of matters of general interest. They read the newspapers and a few magazines and books. See those people waiting at the bus stop? They're your audience.

Of course, they're ready to be interested in coins, cats, coffins, or arguments about birth control or euthanasia—if you can present the information in an interesting way. And if you're fair enough and persuasive enough, you might even get them to change their minds.

Or perhaps your instructor wants you to write for your peers. If that's the case, look around the classroom. See that student wearing New Balance running shoes and a Los Angeles Raiders sweatshirt. That's your peer.

Imagine an Individual

Even though a photograph of this "common reader" is hazy, that doesn't mean you can't have someone in particular in mind as you write. Indeed, you might imagine yourself talking to a friend. Look her in the face. Now try to clarify a point. Try to persuade her. Imagine what she'd say. Anticipate her objections and reactions to what you're saying. Your writing will probably be clearer and fresher if you can do this.

Stop to Explain

Because you have this generalized audience in mind (even when represented by a single person) your discussion can't be too technical — unless, of course, you stop to explain or define. What you stop for, of course, is a matter of judgment. You'll probably need to stop and explain what a double helix is, but you won't want to stop and explain what an electron microscope is. Once again, picture your friend. You would probably need to explain to her, for instance, why stylites had to get up on the right side of the bed. But for most references, you will have to use your best judgment. Would you need to describe a *danse macabre*? the Pentateuch? endorphins? Margaret Sanger? *Candide*? Dopey and Doc? C. S. Lewis? symbolism? satire? *Beauty and the Beast*? Think of your reader before making your decisions.

Definitions clog the flow of writing, so don't stop to define too often. Often the context of the reference will make it understandable.

Of course, when a definition lies at the heart of your argument, take all the time you need to explain it clearly. If you were writing on abortion, for instance, you would want to make absolutely clear to your readers the distinction between an embryo and a fetus. You don't have to do this formally ("We had better define our terms before we begin . . .). Nothing smothers a paper more thoroughly than beginning with a formal definition. But somewhere in your essay — probably early, perhaps even in a note — you'll have to make important distinctions clear.

When in doubt about whether to explain a reference, our advice is to assume your readers know more than they do. It's better to flatter your readers by assuming they recognize a reference rather than patronize them by assuming they don't.

Don't Antagonize Your Readers Needlessly

If you were writing for an audience that shared your quirks and politics, your writing would be shaped by that specialized audience. If you were, for instance, writing for *The New Republic*, you might drop a snide remark about George Bush. Your audience, composed of passionate liberals, would no doubt enjoy your good taste and wit.

However, if you were to drop that same snide remark on your "common reader," you'd likely turn off a whole pack of them. There are a lot of staunch Republicans, Yale alumni, and just plain folks out there who think that George Bush is one heck of a guy. So if you're really trying to persuade your readers rather than just blowing smoke, you'll have to keep your political passions and snide remarks in check. Save them for discussions with like-minded friends.

Work Hard to Hold the Common Reader's Attention

You'll have to work harder to interest a general audience than you would for a specialized audience. If you were writing for *Cat World*, a discussion of the relative merits of the brands of kitty litter may very well freeze your readers to their seats and leave them anticipating your next article, a comparative study of cat collars.

But when you're writing for a general audience, most of what you say about cats is boring—unless you make those cats come alive and leap off the page.

Fortunately, a good controversy, like the ones that many of you will be writing, usually produces lively prose. Just don't let your paper become too theory-laden. Stay close to earth. Be specific and concrete. Fill your paper with examples, case histories, real people.

Reasoning with Your Readers

Before You Begin Writing, Break Down Your Argument to Its Simplest Form

First write down your main idea, or thesis statement, perhaps something as simple as "We ought to ban advertising that is misleading." Underneath, list the reasons that led you to that main idea. Those are the topic sentences that support your thesis. You have just written a simple outline.

Don't Overgeneralize

On the street, our sweeping generalizations usually go unchallenged: "My mom is the best cook in the world." "The Republicans are trying to ruin the country." Fortunately, words that come from our mouths are as ephemeral as wisps of smoke, and listeners don't expect us to scrupulously support our generalizations. But they expect much more from us when we write.

Naturally, you don't have to qualify every generalization. Writers who do that sound pompous. But you do need to qualify those general statements that are conspicuously false, or those that are central to your argument. If you were to begin your paper with "Music is vital to everyone," your reader might very well respond, in his mind, with "Oh really? It's not to me." Here's that same statement, now qualified a number of ways:

Music is vital to *most* people.
Music is vital to *many* people.
Music is vital to *some* people.
Music is vital to a *few* people.
Music is vital *to me*.

The point is this: Know when you're making a generalization and ask yourself if it might strike your reader as a statement that needs to be qualified.

Don't Reduce Complicated Problems to a Single Cause

If you blame the ban on school prayer for poor discipline in schools, you have oversimplified the causes. These are complicated matters that shouldn't be reduced to single causes.

Of course, if you want to discuss only one cause, you can begin your argument by saying "There are various reasons for poor reading skills today—simplified textbooks, poor reading instruction, the pace of modern life, and so on — but I want to discuss what I feel is the most important reason: too much television watching."

Developing an Effective Writing Style

Most of the questions we argue can't be proved. Whether we *can* keep a patient alive after his heart has stopped is a matter that can be settled. But whether we *should* keep the patient alive, an ethical question, is arguable. Reasonable people can differ. And that is why all of us should be modest, tolerant, honest, and fair-minded. We should argue vigorously, but we should also be virtuous by arguing fairly. Here's how to do it.

Develop a Tolerant Tone

Truth, after all, comes in many forms and is usually found wavering somewhere on a line between two extremes. Under these circumstances, the best you can do is find your position on that line, and then do the best and fairest job you can of persuading others that the place you've chosen is reasonable.

If you're arrogant or intolerant, you'll get the expected knee-jerk reaction from those who already agree with you, but you'll antagonize those who are ready to be persuaded. Bring up the opposing arguments and treat them with respect. Go ahead and admit, if you can stand it, that the other side of the argument is not pure nonsense. That admission won't kill you. In fact, it might even leave your reader with the impression that you're a person who listens to all sides of the argument before making up your mind.

Develop a Reasoned Tone

Give your reader the impression that what you're after is the truth, not just a strong argument. If your source is contradicted by another source, comment on that fact. If the facts in the case are ambiguous, inform your reader of that ambiguity. You're a searcher after truth, wherever it lies. And avoid the word *prove*. Begin your contentions with words like these:

These arguments suggest that. . . .
These examples make it easy to believe that. . . .
Thus, there is good reason to believe that. . . .

Use the Middle Style When Writing for the "Common Reader"

Avoid the low. Avoid words that smack of hipness, like *unreal* and *gross*. If you feel proud about how hip or streetwise one of your words is, it's probably too low for your paper. Avoid the high. Let your writing speak simply, directly, honestly. Don't be afraid to let your personality come through. And don't be inhibited by counterfeit rules of grammar. You can begin sentences with coordinating conjunctions; you can end sentences with prepositions; and you can use contractions. Good writers have never paid attention to prissy rules of grammar.

Don't be afraid to sprinkle short, pithy sentences throughout your writing. Don't be too stiff or formal by stringing long, noun-laden, abstract sentences together. That makes your prose unreadable and pompous. If you've used a word in a sentence that you don't ordinarily use in daily conversation, be suspicious of it. Roll it around in your mouth. If it doesn't feel quite right, spit it out.

Try this: Read your prose aloud to someone. If you find yourself stumbling over words, it's likely your writing at that point is stiff and deserves revision. Loosen up. You'll do fine.

THE WILDERNESS: *Leave It Alone?*

Conservation and preservation may strike you as being synonymous, but don't tell that to a conservationist or a preservationist. They face one another — indeed, they often glare at one another — from the opposite sides of an ideological fence.

The issue centers on the huge real estate holdings of the U.S. government, which owns over 720 million acres (including over half of several Western states and three-fourths of Alaska). The Department of Energy estimates that these federally owned lands contain 85 percent of the nation's crude oil, 40 percent of its uranium, and 35 percent of its coal.

The conservationists and the preservationists have different ideas about how this federal land should be used. The conservationists say that public land should serve many of the competing needs of our society; it should serve the needs of the backpacker and the naturalist, but it should also serve the needs of industry and society at large.

The preservationists claim that these public lands should remain protected enclaves. Indeed, some of the preservationists see nature as a value independent of other human concerns — independent of humans themselves. To the preservationists, as to Ralph Waldo Emerson, "Beauty is its own excuse for being."

The ranks of the preservationists have grown through the twentieth century, and such groups as the Sierra Club and the Wilderness Society had by the 1960s become a powerful lobbying force. Their cause was fueled by the national concern over the vanishing resources and ecological balance of Island Earth. Small wonder, then, that preservationists were largely responsible for the landmark Wilderness Preservation Act of 1964 — and its rhetoric — in which Congress defined *wilderness* as "an area where the earth and its community of life are untrammeled by man, where man himself is a visitor but does not remain." The Wilderness Act of 1964 designated 9.1 million federally owned acres (in the lower forty-eight states) as wilderness areas in which only backpacking is allowed. The act also provided for more than 300 million additional acres of land to be withheld from multiple uses until the time when various federal agencies could determine whether these probationary lands should be added to the wilderness preserves. These agencies' studies of these additional lands resulted in an increase in the number of wilderness acres to 70 million by the early 1980s. If preservationists have their way, the number of wilderness acres will double in the near future.

In recent years, preservationists have also begun to worry about our heavily visited national parks. Convinced that the population density at national recreation areas may soon result in Winnebagos outnumbering trees, preservationists have tried to influence the National Park Service to limit public access by prohibiting convenience stores, asphalt parking lots, recreational vehicles, and, in some cases, even automobiles.

The ideological gains scored by the preservationists over the past two decades, however, have hardly driven the conservationists underground. And they too have called up the same image of Island Earth to support their claims. Our energy resources may be limited, they say, and thinking small may be the order of the day, but there are very real limits about how small an industrial society of over 250 million people can afford to think. Regardless of how successful our efforts to conserve our energy resources become, they say, our energy needs will remain immense, and we have yet to free ourselves from a heavy dependence on foreign sources. We thus need to begin to develop those energy resources that lie in the federally owned parts of the West and Alaska.

The conservationists often describe the preservationists as elitists. The federal government merely has stewardship over public lands, the conservationists say; its function is *not* to deny access to everyone who can't backpack into a rugged wilderness area. Like the preservationists, the conservationists don't want to see Yosemite turned into Cleveland, but they contend that some compromise must be made if Yosemite is to remain more than a source for inspiration for backpackers. Middle-class families in Winnebagos also enjoy beauty.

The hottest recent disputes have centered on Alaska, the site of the Exxon *Valdez* oil spill. In 1980 Congress created the Alaska National Wildlife Refuge, an area that constitutes over half of the huge state, and at that time 104 million acres of this refuge were designated as wilderness areas. The current dispute is over how much more of this refuge should be added to the nation's wilderness areas.

Another controversy was triggered in the Pacific Northwest by the discovery that the spotted owl has become nearly extinct. This battle pits preservationists' efforts to save the owl, along with the old-growth timber in which it lives, against the lumber industry's efforts to preserve thousands of lumbering jobs and to supply millions of board feet of lumber for the nation.

THE PONDS

Henry David Thoreau

As a kind of experiment in simple living, Henry David Thoreau, America's nine-teenth-century idealist and naturalist, once spent two years living on the shores of Walden Pond in Concord, Massachusetts. There he built a small cabin, read, ate vegetables from a garden he had planted, watched the seasons change the landscape, and walked in the woods. Walden (1854) is the book that came out of that experience.

In the "Ponds" chapter of Walden, Thoreau contrasts the physical and spiritual beauty of Walden Pond with the destruction of such beauty in neighboring Flint Pond. His sentiments here could have been written by late-twentieth-century pres-ervationists, most of whom, in one way or another, have acknowledged their debt to him.

. . . It is a soothing employment, on one of those fine days in the fall when all the warmth of the sun is fully appreciated, to sit on a stump on such a height as this, overlooking the pond, and study the dimpling circles which are incessantly inscribed on its otherwise invisible surface amid the reflected skies and trees. Over this great expanse there is no disturbance but it is thus at once gently smoothed away and assuaged, as, when a vase of water is jarred, the trembling circles seek the shore and all is smooth again. Not a fish can leap or an insect fall on the pond but it is thus reported in circling dimples, in lines of beauty, as it were the constant welling up of its fountain, the gentle pulsing of its life, the heaving of its breast. The thrills of joy and thrills of pain are undistinguishable. How peaceful the phe-nomena of the lake! Again the works of man shine as in the spring. Ay, every leaf and twig and stone and cobweb sparkles now at mid-afternoon as when covered with dew in a spring morning. Every motion of an oar or an insect produces a flash of light; and if an oar falls, how sweet the echo!

In such a day, in September or October, Walden is a perfect forest mirror, set round with stones as precious to my eye as if fewer or rarer. Nothing so fair, so pure, and at the same time so large, as a lake, perchance, lies on the surface of the earth. Sky water. It needs no fence. Nations come and go without defiling it. It is a mirror which no stone can crack, whose quicksilver will never wear off, whose gilding Nature continually repairs; no storms, no dust, can dim its surface ever fresh; — a mirror in which all impurity presented to it sinks, swept and dusted by the sun's hazy brush, — this the light dust-cloth, — which retains no breath that is breathed on it, but sends its own to float as clouds high above its surface, and be reflected in its bosom still.

A field of water betrays the spirit that is in the air. It is continually receiving new life and motion from above. It is intermediate in its nature between land and sky. On land only the grass and trees wave, but the water itself is rippled by the wind. I see where the breeze dashes across it by the streaks or flakes of light. It

Henry David Thoreau, "The Ponds," *Walden and Civil Disobedience* (Boston: Houghton Mifflin, 1906).

is remarkable that we can look down on its surface. We shall, perhaps, look down thus on the surface of air at length, and mark where a still subtler spirit sweeps over it. . . .

When I first paddled a boat on Walden, it was completely surrounded by thick and lofty pine and oak woods, and in some of its coves grape vines had run over the trees next the water and formed bowers under which a boat could pass. The hills which form its shores are so steep, and the woods on them were then so high, that, as you looked down from the west end, it had the appearance of an amphitheatre for some kind of sylvan spectacle. I have spent many an hour, when I was younger, floating over its surface as the zephyr willed, having paddled my boat to the middle, and lying on my back across the seats, in a summer forenoon, dreaming awake, until I was aroused by the boat touching the sand, and I arose to see what shore my fates had impelled me to; days when idleness was the most attractive and productive industry. Many a forenoon have I stolen away, preferring to spend thus the most valued part of the day; for I was rich, if not in money, in sunny hours and summer days, and spent them lavishly; nor do I regret that I did not waste more of them in the workshop or the teacher's desk. But since I left those shores the woodchoppers have still further laid them waste, and now for many a year there will be no more rambling through the aisles of the wood, with occasional vistas through which you see the water. My Muse may be excused if she is silent henceforth. How can you expect the birds to sing when their groves are cut down?

Now the trunks of trees on the bottom, and the old log canoe, and the dark surrounding woods, are gone, and the villagers, who scarcely know where it lies, instead of going to the pond to bathe or drink, are thinking to bring its water, which should be as sacred as the Ganges at least, to the village in a pipe, to wash their dishes with! — to earn their Walden by the turning of a cock or drawing of a plug! That devilish Iron Horse, whose ear-rending neigh is heard throughout the town, has muddied the Boiling Spring with his foot, and he it is that has browsed off all the woods on Walden shore; that Trojan horse, with a thousand men in his belly, introduced by mercenary Greeks! Where is the country's champion, the Moore of Moore Hall, to meet him at the Deep Cut and thrust an avenging lance between the ribs of the bloated pest?

Nevertheless, of all the characters I have known, perhaps Walden wears best, and best preserves its purity. Many men have been likened to it, but few deserve that honor. Though the woodchoppers have laid bare first this shore and then that, and the Irish have built their sties by it, and the railroad has infringed on its border, and the ice-men have skimmed it once, it is itself unchanged, the same water which my youthful eyes fell on; all the change is in me. It has not acquired one permanent wrinkle after all its ripples. It is perennially young, and I may stand and see a swallow dip apparently to pick an insect from its surface as of yore. It struck me again to-night, as if I had not seen it almost daily for more than twenty years, — Why, here is Walden, the same woodland lake that I discovered so many years ago; where a forest was cut down last winter another is springing up by its shore as lustily as ever; the same thought is welling up to its surface that was then; it is the same liquid joy and happiness to itself and its Maker, ay, and it *may* be to me. It is the work of a brave man surely, in whom there was no guile! He rounded this water with his hand, deepened and clarified it in his thought, and in his will bequeathed it to Concord. I see by its face that it is visited by the same reflection; and I can almost say, Walden, is it you? . . .

Flints', or Sandy Pond, in Lincoln, our greatest lake and inland sea, lies about a mile east of Walden. It is much larger, being said to contain one hundred and ninety-seven acres, and is more fertile in fish; but it is comparatively shallow, and not remarkably pure. . . . *Flints' Pond!* Such is the poverty of our nomenclature. What right had the unclean and stupid farmer, whose farm abutted on this sky water, whose shores he has ruthlessly laid bare, to give his name to it? Some skinflint, who loved better the reflecting surface of a dollar, or a bright cent, in which he could see his own brazen face; who regarded even the wild ducks which settled in it as trespassers; his fingers grown into crooked and horny talons from the long habit of grasping harpy-like; — so it is not named for me. I go not there to see him nor to hear of him; who never *saw* it, who never bathed in it, who never loved it, who never protected it, who never spoke a good word for it, nor thanked God that he had made it. Rather let it be named from the fishes that swim in it, the wild fowl or quadrupeds which frequent it, the wild flowers which grow by its shores, or some wild man or child the thread of whose history is interwoven with its own; not from him who could show no title to it but the deed which a like-minded neighbor or legislature gave him, — him who thought only of its money value; whose presence perchance cursed all the shore; who exhausted the land around it, and would fain have exhausted the waters within it; who regretted only that it was not English hay or cranberry meadow, — there was nothing to redeem it, forsooth, in his eyes, — and would have drained and sold it for the mud at its bottom. It did not turn his mill, and it was no *privilege* to him to behold it. I respect not his labors, his farm where every thing has its price; who would carry the landscape, who would carry his God, to market, if he could get any thing for him; who goes to market *for* his god as it is; on whose farm nothing grows free, whose fields bear no crops, whose meadows no flowers, whose trees no fruits, but dollars; who loves not the beauty of his fruits, whose fruits are not ripe for him till they are turned to dollars. Give me the poverty that enjoys true wealth. Farmers are respectable and interesting to me in proportion as they are poor, — poor farmers. A model farm! where the house stands like a fungus in a muck-heap, chambers for men, horses, oxen, and swine, cleansed and uncleansed, all contiguous to one another! Stocked with men! A great grease-spot, redolent of manures and buttermilk! Under a high state of cultivation, being manured with the hearts and brains of men! As if you were to raise your potatoes in the church-yard! Such is a model farm.

No, no; if the fairest features of the landscape are to be named after men, let them be the noblest and worthiest men alone. Let our lakes receive as true names at least as the Icarian Sea, where "still the shore" a "brave attempt resounds.". . .

White Pond and Walden are great crystals on the surface of the earth, Lakes of Light. If they were permanently congealed, and small enough to be clutched, they would, perchance, be carried off by slaves, like precious stones, to adorn the heads of emperors; but being liquid, and ample, and secured to us and our successors forever, we disregard them, and run after the diamond of Kohinoor. They are too pure to have a market value; they contain no muck. How much more beautiful than our lives, how much more transparent than our characters, are they! We never learned meanness of them. How much fairer than the poor before the farmer's door, in which his ducks swim! Hither the clean wild ducks come. Nature has no human inhabitant who appreciates her. The birds with their plumage and their notes are in harmony with the flowers, but what youth or maiden conspires with the wild luxuriant beauty of Nature? She flourishes most alone, far from the towns where they reside. Talk of heaven! ye disgrace earth.

CONSERVATION IS NOT ENOUGH
Joseph Wood Krutch

Joseph Wood Krutch, a professor of English at Columbia for many years, was also an ardent conservationist. In "Conservation Is Not Enough" (from The Voice of the Desert) *Krutch illustrates the grim consequences of man's efforts to "bring nature under control." He dismisses conservation as merely "a more knowledgeable variation of the old idea of a world for man's use only."*

Moralists often blame races and nations because they have never learned how to live and let live. In our time we seem to have been increasingly aware how persistently and brutally groups of men undertake to eliminate one another. But it is not only the members of his own kind that man seems to want to push off the earth. When he moves in, nearly everything else suffers from his intrusion — sometimes because he wants the space they occupy and the food they eat, but often simply because when he sees a creature not of his kind or a man not of his race his first impulse is "kill it."

Hence it is that even in the desert, where space is cheaper than in most places, the wild life grows scarcer and more secretive as the human population grows. The coyote howls further and further off. The deer seek closer and closer cover. To almost everything except man the smell of humanity is the most repulsive of all odors, the sight of man the most terrifying of all sights. Biologists call some animals "cryptozoic," that is to say "leading hidden lives." But as the human population increases most animals develop, as the deer has been developing, cryptozoic habits. Even now there are more of them around than we realize. They see us when we do not see them — because they have seen us first. Albert Schweitzer remarks somewhere that we owe kindness even to an insect when we can afford to show it, just because we ought to do something to make up for all the cruelties, necessary as well as unnecessary, which we have inflicted upon almost the whole of animate creation.

Probably not one man in ten is capable of understanding such moral and aesthetic considerations, much less of permitting his conduct to be guided by them. But perhaps twice as many, though still far from a majority, are beginning to realize that the reckless laying waste of the earth has practical consequences. They are at least beginning to hear about "conservation," though they are not even dimly aware of any connection between it and a large morality and are very unlikely to suppose that "conservation" does or could mean anything more than looking after their own welfare.

Hardly more than two generations ago Americans first woke up to the fact that their land was not inexhaustible. Every year since then more and more has been said, and at least a little more has been done about "conserving resources," about "rational use" and about such reconstruction as seemed possible. Scientists have studied the problem, public works have been undertaken, laws passed. Yet everybody

Joseph Wood Krutch, "Conservation Is Not Enough," *The Voice of the Desert* (New York: William Sloane Associates, 1954).

knows that the using up still goes on, perhaps not so fast nor so recklessly as once it did, but unmistakably nevertheless. And there is nowhere that it goes on more nakedly, more persistently or with a fuller realization of what is happening than in the desert regions where the margin to be used up is narrower.

First, more and more cattle were set to grazing and overgrazing the land from which the scanty rainfall now ran off even more rapidly than before. More outrageously still, large areas of desert shrub were rooted up to make way for cotton and other crops watered by wells tapping underground pools of water which are demonstrably shrinking fast. These pools represent years of accumulation not now being replenished and are exhaustible exactly as an oil well is exhaustible. Everyone knows that they will give out before long, very soon, in fact, if the number of wells continues to increase as it has been increasing. Soon dust bowls will be where was once a sparse but healthy desert, and man, having uprooted, slaughtered or driven away everything which lived healthily and normally there, will himself either abandon the country or die. There are places where the creosote bush is a more useful plant than cotton. . . .

To live healthily and successfully on the land we must also live with it. We must be part not only of the human community, but of the whole community; we must acknowledge some sort of oneness not only with our neighbors, our countrymen and our civilization but also some respect for the natural as well as for the man-made community. Ours is not only "one world" in the sense usually implied by that term. It is also "one earth." Without some acknowledgment of that fact, men can no more live successfully than they can if they refuse to admit the political and economic interdependency of the various sections of the civilized world. It is not a sentimental but a grimly literal fact that unless we share this terrestrial globe with creatures other than ourselves, we shall not be able to live on it for long.

You may, if you like, think of this as a moral law. But if you are skeptical about moral laws, you cannot escape the fact that it has its factual, scientific aspect. Every day the science of ecology is making clearer the factual aspect as it demonstrates those more and more remote interdependencies which, no matter how remote they are, are crucial even for us.

Before even the most obvious aspects of the balance of nature had been recognized, a greedy, self-centered mankind naïvely divided plants into the useful and the useless. In the same way it divided animals into those which were either domestic on the one hand or "game" on the other, and the "vermin" which ought to be destroyed. That was the day when extermination of whole species was taken as a matter of course and random introductions which usually proved to be either complete failures or all too successful were everywhere being made. Soon, however, it became evident enough that to rid the world of vermin and to stock it with nothing but useful organisms was at least not a simple task — if you assume that "useful" means simply "immediately useful to man."

Yet even to this day the *ideal* remains the same for most people. They may know, or at least they may have been told, that what looks like the useless is often remotely but demonstrably essential. Out in this desert country they may see the land being rendered useless by overuse. They may even have heard how, when the mountain lion is killed off, the deer multiply; how, when the deer multiply, the new growth of trees and shrubs is eaten away; and how, when the hills are denuded, a farm or a section of grazing land many miles away is washed into gulleys and made incapable of supporting either man or any other of the large animals. They may even have heard how the wonderful new insecticides proved so effective that fish and birds died of starvation; how on at least one Pacific island insects had to be reintroduced to pollinate the crops; how when you kill off almost completely a destructive pest, you run the risk of starving out everything which preys upon it and thus run the risk that the pest itself will stage an overwhelming comeback because its natural enemies are no more. Yet, knowing all this and much more, their dream is still the dream that an earth for man's use only can be created if only we learn more and scheme more effectively. They still hope that nature's scheme of checks and balances which provides for a varied population, which stubbornly refuses to scheme only from man's point of view and cherishes the weeds and "vermin" as persistently as she cherishes him, can be replaced by a scheme of his own devising. Ultimately they hope they can beat the game. But the more the ecologist learns, the less likely it seems that man can in the long run do anything of the sort.

"Nature's social union" is by no means the purely gentle thing which Burns imagined. In fact it is a balance, with all the stress and conflict which the word implies. In this sense it is not a "social union" at all. But it is, nevertheless, a workable, seesawing balance. And when it ceases to seesaw, there is trouble ahead for whatever is on the end that stays up, as well as for those on the end which went down.

Thus, for every creature there is a paradox at the heart of the necessary "struggle for existence" and the paradox is simply this: Neither man nor any other animal can afford to triumph in that struggle too completely. Unconditional surrender is a self-defeating formula — even in the war against insect pests. To the victor belong the spoils in nature also, but for a time only. When there are no more spoils to be consumed, the victor dies. That is believed by some to be what happened to the dominant carnivorous dinosaurs many millions of years ago. They became too dominant and presently there was nothing left to dominate — or to eat. It is certainly what happens to other creatures like the too-protected deer in a national forest who multiply so successfully that their herds can no longer be fed, or, more spectacularly, like the lemmings who head desperately toward a new area to be exploited and end in the cold waters of the North Sea because that area does not exist.

Curiously, the too tender-minded dreamed a dream more attractive than that of the ruthless exploiters but no less unrealizable. They dreamed of "refuges" and "sanctuaries" where the "innocent" creatures might live in a perpetually peaceful paradise untroubled by such "evil" creatures as the fox and the hawk. But it required few experiments with such utopias to demonstrate that they will not work. A partridge covey or a deer herd which is not thinned by predators soon eats itself into starvation and suffers also from less obvious maladjustments. The overaged and the weaklings, who would have fallen first victims to their carnivorous enemies, survive to weaken the stock, and as overpopulation increases, the whole community becomes affected by some sort of nervous tension — "shock" the ecologists call it — analogous to that which afflicts human beings crowded into congested areas.

No more striking evidence of this fact can be found than what happened when it was decided to "protect" the deer on the Kaibab Plateau in the Grand Canyon region. At the beginning of this century there was a population of about 4000 occupying some 127,000 acres. Over a period of years the mountain lions, wolves and coyotes which lived at its expense were pretty well exterminated. By 1924 the 4000 had become 100,000 and then calamity struck. In one year, 1924, 60,000 victims of starvation and disease disappeared and then, year by year, though at a decreasing rate, the population dwindled.

Wild creatures need their enemies as well as their friends. The red tooth and red claw are not the whole story but they are part of it, and the park superintendent with his gun "scientifically" redressing the balance is a poor but necessary substitute for the balance which the ages have established. We may find nature's plan cruel but we cannot get away from it entirely. The lion and the lamb will not — they simply cannot — lie down together, but they are essential to one another nonetheless. And the lesson to be learned is applicable far outside the field of conservation. It is that though the laws of nature may be mitigated, though their mitigation constitutes civilization, they cannot be abolished altogether.

So far as the problem is only that of the Kaibab deer, one common solution is the "open season" when man himself is encouraged to turn predator and hunters are permitted, as some conservationists put it, to "harvest the crop." To some this seems a repellent procedure and even as a practical solution it is far from ideal. Other beasts of prey destroy first the senile and the weaklings; man, if he selects at all, selects the mature and the vigorous for slaughter. The objection to this method is much the same as it would be to a proposal that we should attack the problem of human population by declaring an annual open season on all between the ages of eighteen and thirty-five. That is, of course, precisely what we do when a war is declared, and there are those who believe that the ultimate cause of wars is actually, though we are not aware of the fact, the overgrazing of our own range and the competition for what remains.

What is commonly called "conservation" will not work in the long run because it is not really conservation at all but rather, disguised by its elaborate scheming, only a more knowledgeable variation of the old idea of a world for man's use only. That idea is unrealizable. But how can man be persuaded to cherish any other ideal unless he can learn to take some interest and some delight in the beauty and variety of the world for its own sake, unless he can see a "value" in a flower blooming or an animal at play, unless he can see some "use" in things not useful?

In our society we pride ourselves upon having reached a point where we condemn an individual whose whole aim in life is to acquire material wealth for himself. But his vulgarity is only one step removed from that of a society which takes no thought for anything except increasing the material wealth of the community itself. In his usual extravagant way Thoreau once said: "This curious world which we inhabit is more wonderful than it is convenient; more beautiful than it is useful; it is more to be admired than it is to be used." Perhaps that "more" is beyond what most people could or perhaps ought to be convinced of. But without some realization that "this curious world" is at least beautiful as well as useful, "conservation" is doomed. We must live for something besides making a living. If we do not permit the earth to produce beauty and joy, it will in the end not produce food either. . . .

Here in the West, as in the country at large, a war more or less concealed under the guise of a "conflict of interests" rages between the "practical" conservationist and the defenders of national parks and other public lands; between cattlemen and lumberers on the one hand, and "sentimentalists" on the other. The pressure to allow the hunter, the rancher or the woodcutter to invade the public domain is constant and the plea is always that we should "use" what is assumed to be useless unless it is adding to material welfare. But unless somebody teaches love, there can be no ultimate protection to what is lusted after. Without some "love of nature" for itself there is no possibility of solving "the problem of conservation."

Any fully matured science of ecology will have to grapple with the fact that from the ecological point of view, man is one of those animals which is in danger from its too successful participation in the struggle for existence. He has upset the balance of nature to a point where he has exterminated hundreds of other animals and exhausted soils. Part of this he calls a demonstration of his intelligence and of the success which results from his use of it. But because of that intelligence he has learned how to exploit resources very thoroughly and he is even beginning to learn how to redress the balance in certain minor ways. But he cannot keep indefinitely just one step ahead of overcrowding and starvation. From the standpoint of nature as a whole, he is both a threat to every other living thing and, therefore, a threat to himself also. If he were not so extravagantly successful it would be better for nearly everything except man and, possibly therefore, better, in the longest run, for him also. He has become the tyrant of the earth, the waster of its resources, the creator of the most prodigious imbalance in the natural order which has ever existed.

From a purely homocentric point of view this may seem entirely proper. To most people it undoubtedly does. Is it not our proudest boast that we have learned how to "control nature"? Does not our dream of the future include a final emancipation from any dependence upon a natural balance and the substitution for it of some balance established by ourselves and in our exclusive interest? Is not that, in fact, what most people have in mind when they think of the final triumph of humanity?

But what every "practical" ecologist is trying to do is maintain the balance of nature without facing the fact that man himself is part of it, that you cannot hope to keep the balance unless you admit that to some extent the immediate interest of the human species may sometimes have to be disregarded. No other single fact is so important as man himself in creating the often disastrous imbalances which continually develop. It is not possible to reestablish them for long without undertaking to control the organism which has most obviously entered upon a runaway phase. Must we not recognize the fact that any real "management of resources" is impossible unless we are willing to sacrifice to some extent the immediate interests not only of certain individual men but also those of the human species itself? Most of us have reached the point where we recognize that the immediate interests of the lumberman or the rancher must sometimes be sacrificed to "the general good." Ultimately we may have to recognize that there is also a conflict between what is called the general good and a good still more general — the good, that is to say, of the whole biological community.

The more completely we bring nature "under control," the more complicated our methods must become, the more disastrous the chain reaction which is set up by any failure of wisdom, or watchfulness, or technique. We are required to know more and more and we are always threatened by the impossibility of achieving adequate knowledge, much less of adequate wisdom and virtue.

Every increase in the complexity of organization has made the situation more precarious at the same time that it has increased our comfort and our wealth. Until we learned to support a population far larger than would have been believed possible a century ago, there was no danger of general starvation, however disastrous and common local famines may have been, and though Malthus was obviously wrong in his estimates, it is by no means certain that he was wrong in his general principle. Until we increased the wealth of nations by linking them one with another we were not exposed to the danger of world-wide economic collapse. Until we learned how to "control" the atom there was no danger that atomic phenomena would get out of control and hence it is still not clear whether we are running machines or machines are running us. We have three tigers — the economic, the physical and the biological — by the tail and three tigers are more than three times as dangerous as one. We cannot let any of them go. But it is also not certain that we can hold all of them indefinitely. Many a despot has discovered that it was just when his power seemed to have been made absolute at last that the revolution broke out. And it may be that just about three hundred years was necessary to expose the fallacy of the ideal born in the seventeenth century.

If one is prepared to admit that there is a limit to the extent to which we can exercise a biological control exclusively in our own interest, then it is certainly worthwhile to ask how we might know when we are approaching that limit.

It will hardly do to say simply that the limit has been passed when a society is obviously sick. Too many different reasons have been given to explain that sickness, and several of them can be made to seem more or less convincing — indeed, several of them may be partially correct. But there is a criterion which it seems to me not wholly fanciful to apply.

Might it not have something to do with nature's own great principle, live and let live? Might it not be that man's success as an organism is genuinely a success so long, but only so long, as it does not threaten the extinction of everything not useful to and absolutely controlled by him; so long as that success is not incompatible with the success of nature as the varied and free thing which she is; so long as, to some extent, man is prepared to share the earth with others?

If by any chance that criterion is valid, then either one of two things is likely to happen. Perhaps outraged nature will violently reassert herself and some catastrophe, perhaps the catastrophe brought about when more men are trying to live in our limited space than even their most advanced technology can make possible, will demonstrate the hollowness of his supposed success. Perhaps, on the other hand, man himself will learn in time to set a reasonable limit to his ambitions and accept the necessity of recognizing his position as the most highly evolved of living creatures but not, therefore, entitled to assume that no others have a right to live unless they contribute directly to his material welfare.

The now popular saying, "No man is an island," means more than it is commonly taken to mean. Not only men but all living things stand or fall together. Or rather man is of all such creatures one of those least able to stand alone. If we think only in terms of our own welfare we are likely to find that we are losing it.

But how can man learn to accept such a situation, to believe that it is right and proper when the whole tendency of his thought and his interest carries him in a contrary direction? How can he learn to value and delight in a natural order larger than his own order? How can he come to accept, not sullenly but gladly, the necessity of sharing the earth?

As long ago as the seventeenth century, as long ago, that is, as the very time when the ambition to "control nature" in any large ambitious way was first coming to be formulated and embraced, a sort of answer to these questions was being given in theological terms. John Ray, one of the first great English biologists, formulated them in a book which was read for a hundred years, and what Ray had to say cuts two ways because it was directed against the egotism of man as expressed both by the old-fashioned theologians who thought that everything had been *made* for man's use and by the Baconians who assumed that he could at least *turn it* to that use.

"It is," Ray wrote, "a general received opinion, that all this visible world was created for Man; that Man is the End of Creation; as if there were no other end of any creature, but some way or other to be serviceable to man. . . . But though this be vulgarly received, yet wise men now-a-days think otherwise. . . . Creatures are made to enjoy themselves as well as to serve us." The greatest profit which we can get from the observation and study of other living things is, Ray went on to say, often not that we learn how to use them but that we may contemplate through them the wonders and the beauties of God's creation. What Ray was saying is precisely what Thoreau was restating in secularized form when he insisted that "this curious world which we inhabit . . . is more to be admired and enjoyed than it is to be used."

Since our age is not inclined to be interested in theological arguments, it is not likely to find Ray's exposition a sufficient reason for accepting gladly the continued existence on this earth of "useless" plants and animals occupying space which man might turn to his own immediate profit. Our generation is more likely to make at least certain concessions in that direction as the result of absorbing what the ecologist has to say about the impossibility of maintainaing a workable balance without a much more generous view of what is "useful" and what is not. But it is not certain that on that basis man will ever make quite enough concessions and it *is* entirely certain that he will not make them happily, will not find life pleasanter just because he makes them, unless he can learn to love and to delight in the variety of nature.

Perhaps, if we cannot send him as far back as the seventeenth century to be taught, we can at least send him back to the eighteenth. Pope, speaking half for metaphysics and half for science, could write:

> Has God, thou fool! worked solely for thy good,
> Thy joy, thy pastime, thy attire, thy food?
> ....
> Know, Nature's children all divide her care;
> The fur that warms a monarch, warmed a bear.

This is precisely what most men even two centuries later do not really understand.

POLEMIC: INDUSTRIAL TOURISM AND THE NATIONAL PARKS

by Edward Abbey

Edward Abbey worked for fifteen years as a park ranger for the National Park Service in the American West, and these experiences provided the basis for many of his books on America's wilderness areas. In this essay (a chapter in Desert Solitaire*) he attacks the conventional National Park Service's "the greatest good for the greatest number" policies in the typically tart, irreverent style that has made him one of the most widely read preservationists. You may want to contrast Abbey's arguments that public access to America's national parks should be tightly restricted with Eric Julber's arguments, later in this chapter, that public access should be relatively unrestricted.*

I like my job. The pay is generous; I might even say munificent: $1.95 per hour, earned or not, backed solidly by the world's most powerful Air Force, biggest national debt, and grossest national product. The fringe benefits are priceless: clean air to breathe (after the spring sandstorms); stillness, solitude and space; an unobstructed view every day and every night of sun, sky, stars, clouds, mountains, moon, cliffrock and canyons; a sense of time enough to let thought and feeling range from here to the end of the world and back; the discovery of something intimate — though impossible to name — in the remote.

The work is simple and requires almost no mental effort, a good thing in more ways than one. What little thinking I do is my own and I do it on government time. . . .

Yes, it's a good job. On the rare occasions when I peer into the future for more than a few days I can foresee myself returning here for season after season, year after year, indefinitely.

And why not? What better sinecure could a man with small needs, infinite desires, and philosophic pretensions ask for? The better part of each year in the wilderness and the winters in some complementary, equally agreeable environment — Hoboken perhaps, or Tiajuana, Nogales, Juarez . . . one of the border towns. Maybe Tonopah, a good tough Nevada mining town with legal prostitution, or possibly Oakland or even New Orleans — some place grimy, cheap (since I'd be living on unemployment insurance), decayed, hopelessly corrupt. I idle away hours dreaming of the wonderful winter to come, of the chocolate-colored mistress I'll have to rub my back, the journal spread open between two tall candles in massive silver candlesticks, the scrambled eggs with green chile, the crock of homebrew fermenting quietly in the corner, etc., the nights of desperate laughter with brave young comrades, burning billboards, and defacing public institutions. . . .

Romantic dreams, romantic dreams.

Edward Abbey, "Polemic: Industrial Tourism and the National Parks," *Desert Solitaire: A Season in the Wilderness* (New York: Ballantine Books, 1968).

For there is a cloud on my horizon. A small dark cloud no bigger than my hand. Its name is Progress.

The ease and relative freedom of this lovely job at Arches follow from the comparative absence of the motorized tourists, who stay away by the millions. And they stay away because of the unpaved entrance road, the unflushable toilets in the campgrounds, and the fact that most of them have never even heard of Arches National Monument. (Could there be a more genuine testimonial to its beauty and integrity?) All this must change. . . .

Arches National Monument has been developed. The Master Plan has been fulfilled. Where once a few adventurous people came on weekends to camp for a night or two and enjoy a taste of the primitive and remote, you will now find serpentine streams of baroque automobiles pouring in and out, all through the spring and summer, in numbers that would have seemed fantastic when I worked there: from 3,000 to 30,000 to 300,000 per year, the "visitation," as they call it, mounts ever upward. The little campgrounds where I used to putter around reading three-day-old newspapers full of lies and watermelon seeds have now been consolidated into one master campground that looks, during the busy season, like a suburban village: elaborate housetrailers of quilted aluminum crowd upon gigantic camper-trucks of Fiberglas and molded plastic; through their windows you will see the blue glow of television and hear the studio laughter of Los Angeles; knobby-kneed oldsters in plaid Bermudas buzz up and down the quaintly curving asphalt road on motorbikes; quarrels break out between campsite neighbors while others gather around their burning charcoal briquettes (ground campfires no longer permitted — not enough wood) to compare electric toothbrushes. The Comfort Stations are there, too, all lit up with electricity, fully equipped inside, though the generator breaks down now and then and the lights go out, or the sewage backs up in the plumbing system (drain fields were laid out in sand over a solid bed of sandstone), and the water supply sometimes fails, since the 3000-foot well can only produce about 5gpm — not always enough to meet the demand. Down at the beginning of the new road, at park headquarters, is the new entrance station and visitor center, where admission fees are collected and where the rangers are going quietly nuts answering the same three basic questions five hundred times a day: (1) Where's the john? (2)How long's it take to see this place? (3) Where's the Coke machine?

Progress has come at last to the Arches, after a million years of neglect. Industrial Tourism has arrived.

What happened to Arches Natural Money-mint is, of course, an old story in the Park Service. All the famous national parks have the same problems on a far grander scale, as everyone knows, and many other problems as yet unknown to a little subordinate unit of the system in a backward part of southeastern Utah. And the same kind of development that has so transformed Arches is under way, planned or completed in many more national parks and national monuments. I will mention only a few examples with which I am personally familiar:

The newly established Canyonlands National Park. Most of the major points of interest in this park are presently accessible, over passable dirt roads, by car — Grandview Point, Upheaval Dome, part of the White Rim, Cave Spring, Squaw Spring campground and Elephant Hill. The more difficult places, such as Angel Arch or Druid Arch, can by reached by jeep, on horseback or in a one- or two-day hike. Nevertheless the Park Service had drawn up the usual Master Plan calling for modern paved highways to most of the places named and some not named.

Grand Canyon National Park. Most of the south rim of this park is now closely followed by a conventional highspeed highway and interrupted at numerous places by large asphalt parking lots. It is no longer easy, on the South Rim, to get away from the roar of motor traffic, except by descending into the canyon.

Navajo National Monument. A small, fragile, hidden place containing two of the most beautiful cliff dwellings in the Southwest — Keet Seel and Betatakin. This park will be difficult to protect under heavy visitation, and for years it was understood that it would be preserved in a primitive way so as to screen out those tourists unwilling to drive their cars over some twenty miles of dirt road. No longer so: the road has been paved, the campground enlarged and "modernized," and the old magic destroyed.

Natural Bridges National Monument. Another small gem in the park system, a group of three adjacent natural bridges tucked away in the canyon country of southern Utah. Formerly you could drive your car (over dirt roads, of course) to within sight of and easy walking distance — a hundred yards? — of the most spectacular of the three bridges. From there it was only a few hours walking time to the other two. All three could easily be seen in a single day. But this was not good enough for the developers. They have now constructed a paved road into the heart of the area, *between* the two biggest bridges.

Zion National Park. The northwestern part of this park, known as the Kolob area, has until recently been saved as almost virgin wilderness. But a broad highway, with banked curves, deep cuts and heavy fills, that will invade this splendid region, is already under construction.

Capitol Reef National Monument. Grand and colorful scenery in a rugged land — south-central Utah. The most beautiful portion of that park was the canyon of the Fremont River, a great place for hiking, camping, exploring. And what did the authorities do? They built a state highway through it.

Lee's Ferry. Until a few years ago a simple, quiet, primitive place on the shores of the Colorado, Lee's Ferry has now fallen under the protection of the Park Service. And who can protect it against the Park Service? Powerlines now bisect the scene; a 100-foot pink water tower looms against the red cliffs; tract-style houses are built to house the "protectors"; natural campsites along the river are closed off while all campers are now herded into an artificial steel-and-asphalt "campground" in the hottest, windiest spot in the area; historic buildings are razed by bulldozers to save the expense of maintaining them while at the same time hundreds of thousands of dollars are spent on an unneeded paved entrance road. And the administrators complain of *vandalism.*

I could easily cite ten more examples of unnecessary or destructive development for every one I've named so far. What has happened in these particular areas, which I chance to know a little and love too much, has happened, is happening, or will soon happen to the majority of our national parks and national forests, despite the illusory protection of the Wilderness Preservation Act, unless a great many citizens rear up on their hind legs and make vigorous political gestures demanding implementation of the Act.

There may be some among the readers of this book, like the earnest engineer, who believe without question that any and all forms of construction and development are intrinsic goods, in the national parks as well as anywhere else, who virtually identify quantity with quality and therefore assume that the greater the quantity of traffic, the higher the value received. There are some who frankly and boldly advocate the eradication of the last remnants of wilderness and the complete subjugation of nature to the requirements of—not man—but industry. This is a courageous view, admirable in its simplicity and power, and with the weight of all modern history behind it. It is also quite insane. I cannot attempt to deal with it here.

There will be other readers, I hope, who share my basic assumption that wilderness is a necessary part of civilization and that it is the primary responsibility of the national park system to preserve *intact and undiminished* what little still remains.

Most readers, while generally sympathetic to this latter point of view, will feel, as do the administrators of the National Park Service, that although wilderness is a fine thing, certain compromises and adjustments are necessary in order to meet the ever-expanding demand for outdoor recreation. It is precisely this question which I would like to examine now.

The Park Service, established by Congress in 1916, was directed not only to administer the parks but also to "provide for the enjoyment of same in such manner and by such means as will leave them unimpaired for the enjoyment of future generations." This appropriately ambiguous language, employed long before the onslaught of the automobile, has been understood in various and often opposing ways ever since. The Park Service, like any other big organization, includes factions and factions. The Developers, the dominant faction, place their emphasis on the word *"provide for the enjoyment."* The Preservers, a minority but also strong, emphasize the words *"leave them unimpaired."* It is apparent, then, that we cannot decide the question of development versus preservation by a simple referral to holy writ or an attempt to guess the intention of the founding fathers; we must make up our own minds and decide for ourselves what the national parks should be and what purpose they should serve.

The first issue that appears when we get into this matter, the most important issue and perhaps the only issue, is the one called *accessibility*. The Developers insist that the parks must be made fully accessible not only to people but also to their machines, that is, to automobiles, motorboats, etc. The Preservers argue, in principle at least, that wilderness and motors are incompatible and that the former can best be experienced, understood, and enjoyed when the machines are left behind where they belong—on the superhighways and in the parking lots, on the reservoirs and in the marinas.

What does accessibility mean? Is there any spot on earth that men have not proved accessible by the simplest means—feet and legs and heart? Even Mt. McKinley, even Everest, have been surmounted by men on foot. (Some of them, incidentally, rank amateurs, to the horror and indignation of the professional mountaineers.) The interior of the Grand Canyon, a fiercely hot and hostile abyss, is visited each summer by thousands and thousands of tourists of the most banal and unadventurous type, many of them on foot—self-propelled, so to speak—and the others on the backs of mules. Thousands climb each summer to the summit of Mt. Whitney, highest point in the forty-eight United States, while multitudes of others wander on foot or on horseback through the ranges of the Sierras, the Rockies, the Big Smokies, the Cascades and the mountains of New England. Still more hundreds and thousands float or paddle each year down the currents of the Salmon, the Snake, the Allagash, the Yampa, the Green, the Rio Grande, the Ozark, the St. Croix and those portions of the Colorado which have not yet been destroyed by the dam builders. And most significant, these hordes of nonmotorized tourists, hungry for a taste of the difficult, the original, the real, do not consist solely of people young and athletic but also of old folks, fat folks, pale-faced office clerks who don't know a rucksack from a haversack, and even children. The one thing they all have in common is the refusal to live always like sardines in a can—they are determined to get outside of their motorcars for at least a few weeks each year.

This being the case, why is the Park Service generally so anxious to accommodate that other crowd, the indolent millions born on wheels and suckled on gasoline, who expect and demand paved highways to lead them in comfort, ease and safety into every nook and corner of the national parks? For the answer to that we must consider the character of what I call Industrial Tourism and the quality of the mechanized tourists—the Wheelchair Explorers—who are at once the consumers, the raw material and the victims of Industrial Tourism.

Industrial Tourism is a big business. It means money. It includes the motel and restaurant owners, the gasoline retailers, the oil corporations, the road-building contractors, the heavy equipment manufacturers, the state and federal engineering agencies and the sovereign, all-powerful automotive industry. These various interests are well organized, command more wealth than most modern nations, and are represented in Congress with a strength far greater than is justified in any constitutional or democratic sense. (Modern politics is expensive—power follows money.) Through Congess the tourism industry can bring enormous pressure to bear upon such a slender reed in the executive branch as the poor old Park Service, a pressure which is also exerted on every other possible level—local, state, regional—and through advertising and the well-established habits of a wasteful nation.

When a new national park, national monument, national seashore, or whatever it may be called is set up, the various forces of Industrial Tourism, on all levels, immediately expect action—meaning specifically a road-building program. Where trails or primitive dirt roads already exist, the Industry expects—it hardly needs to ask—that these be developed into modern paved highways. On the local level, for example, the first thing that the superintendent of a new park can anticipate being asked, when he attends his first meeting of the area's Chamber of Commerce, is not "Will roads be built?" but rather "When does construction begin?" and "Why the delay?"

(The Natural Money-Mint. With supersensitive antennae these operatives from the C. of C. look into red canyons and see only green, stand among flowers snorting out the smell of money, and hear, while thunderstorms rumble over mountains, the fall of a dollar bill on motel carpeting.)

Accustomed to this sort of relentless pressure since its founding, it is little wonder that the Park Service, through a process of natural selection, has tended to evolve a type of administration which, far from resisting such pressure, has usually been more than willing to accommodate it, even to encourage it. Not from any peculiar moral weakness but simply because such well-adapted administrators are themselves believers in a policy of economic development. "Resource management" is the current term. Old foot trails may be neglected, back-country ranger stations left unmanned, and interpretive and protective services inadequately staffed, but the administrators know from long experience that millions for asphalt can always be found; Congress is always willing to appropriate money for more and bigger paved roads, anywhere — particularly if they form loops. Loop drives are extremely popular with the petroleum industry — they bring the motorist right back to the same gas station from which he started.

Great though it is, however, the power of the tourist business would not in itself be sufficient to shape Park Service policy. To all accusations of excessive development the administrators can reply, as they will if pressed hard enough, that they are giving the public what it wants, that their primary duty is to serve the public not preserve the wilds. "Parks are for people" is the public-relations slogan, which decoded means that the parks are for people-in-automobiles. Behind the slogan is the assumption that the majority of Americans, exactly like the managers of the tourist industry, expect and demand to see their national parks from the comfort, security, and convenience of their automobiles.

Is this assumption correct? Perhaps. Does that justify the continued and increasing erosion of the parks? It does not. Which brings me to the final aspect of the problem of Industrial Tourism: the Industrial Tourists themselves.

They work hard, these people. They roll up incredible mileages on their odometers, rack up state after state in two-week transcontinental motor marathons, knock off one national park after another, take millions of square yards of photographs, and endure patiently the most prolonged discomforts: the tedious traffic jams, the awful food of park cafeterias and roadside eateries, the nocturnal search for a place to sleep or camp, the dreary routine of One-Stop Service, the endless lines of creeping traffic, the smell of exhaust fumes, the ever-proliferating Rules & Regulations, the fees and the bills and the service charges, the boiling radiator and the flat tire and the vapor lock, the surly retorts of room clerks and traffic cops, the incessant jostling of the anxious crowds, the irritation and restlessness of their children, the worry of their wives, and the long drive home at night in a stream of racing cars against the lights of another stream racing in the opposite direction, passing now and then the obscure tangle, the shattered glass, the patrolman's lurid blinker light, of one more wreck.

Hard work. And risky. Too much for some, who have given up the struggle on the highways in exchange for an entirely different kind of vacation — out in the open, on their own feet, following the quiet trail through forest and mountains, bedding down at evening under the stars, when and where they feel like it, at a time when the Industrial Tourists are still hunting for a place to park their automobiles.

Industrial Tourism is a threat to the national parks. But the chief victims of the system are the motorized tourists. They are being robbed and robbing themselves. So long as they are unwilling to crawl out of their cars they will not discover the treasures of the national parks and will never escape the stress and turmoil of the urban-suburban complexes which they had hoped, presumably, to leave behind for a while.

How to pry the tourists out of their automobiles, out of their back-breaking upholstered mechanized wheelchairs and onto their feet, onto the strange warmth and solidity of Mother Earth again? This is the problem which the Park Service should confront directly, not evasively, and which it cannot resolve by simply submitting and conforming to the automobile habit. The automobile, which began as a transportation convenience, has become a bloody tyrant (50,000 lives a year), and it is the responsibility of the Park Service, as well as that of everyone else concerned with preserving both wilderness and civilization, to begin a campaign of resistance. The automotive combine has almost succeeded in strangling our cities; we need not let it also destroy our national parks.

It will be objected that a constantly increasing population makes resistance and conservation a hopeless battle. This is true. Unless a way is found to stabilize the nation's population, the parks cannot be saved. Or anything else worth a damn. Wilderness preservation, like a hundred other good causes, will be forgotten under the overwhelming pressure of a struggle for mere survival and sanity in a completely urbanized, completely industrialized, ever more crowded environment. For my own part I would rather take my chances in a thermonuclear war than live in such a world.

Assuming, however, that population growth will be halted at a tolerable level before catastrophe does it for us, it remains permissible to talk about such things as the national parks. Having indulged myself in a number of harsh judgments upon the Park Service, the tourist industry, and the motoring public, I now feel entitled to make some constructive, practical, sensible proposals for the salvation of both parks and people.

(1) No more cars in national parks. Let the people walk. Or ride horses, bicycles, mules, wild pigs — anything — but keep the automobiles and the motorcycles and all their motorized relatives out. We have agreed not to drive our automobiles into cathedrals, concert halls, art museums, legislative assemblies, private bedrooms and the other sanctums of our culture; we should treat our national parks with the same deference, for they, too, are holy places. An increasingly pagan and hedonistic people (thank God!), we are learning finally that the forests and mountains and desert canyons are holier than our churches. Therefore let us behave accordingly.

Consider a concrete example and what could be done with it: Yosemite Valley in Yosemite National Park. At present a dusty milling confusion of motor vehicles and ponderous camping machinery, it could be returned to relative beauty and order by the simple expedient of requiring all visitors, at the park entrance, to lock up their automobiles and continue their tour on the seats of good workable bicycles supplied free of charge by the United States Government.

Let our people travel light and free on their bicycles — nothing on the back but a shirt, nothing tied to the bike but a slicker, in case of rain. Their bedrolls, their backpacks, their tents, their food and cooking kits will be trucked in for them, free of charge, to the campground of their choice in the Valley, by the Park Service. (Why not? The roads will still be there.) Once in the Valley they will find the concessioners waiting, ready to supply whatever needs might have been overlooked, or to furnish rooms and meals for those who don't want to camp out.

The same thing could be done at Grand Canyon or at Yellowstone or at any of our other shrines to the out-of-doors. There is no compelling reason, for example, why tourists need to drive their automobiles to the very brink of the Grand Canyon's south rim. They could *walk* that last mile. Better yet, the Park Service should build an enormous parking lot about ten miles south of Grand Canyon Village and another east of Desert View. At those points, as at Yosemite, our people could emerge from their steaming shells of steel and glass and climb upon horses or bicycles for the final leg of the journey. On the rim, as at present, the hotels and restaurants will remain to serve the physical needs of the park visitors. Trips along the rim would also be made on foot, on horseback, or—utilizing the paved road which already exists—on bicycles. For those willing to go all the way from one parking lot to the other, a distance of some sixty or seventy miles, we might provide bus service back to their cars, a service which would at the same time effect a convenient exchange of bicycles and/or horses between the two terminals.

What about children? What about the aged and infirm? Frankly, we need waste little sympathy on these two pressure groups. Children too small to ride bicycles and too heavy to be borne on their parents' backs need only wait a few years—if they are not run over by automobiles they will grow into a lifetime of joyous adventure, if we save the parks and *leave them unimpaired for the enjoyment of future generations*. The aged merit even less sympathy: after all they had the opportunity to see the country when it was still relatively unspoiled. However, we'll stretch a point for those too old or too sickly to mount a bicycle and let them ride the shuttle buses.

I can foresee complaints. The motorized tourists, reluctant to give up the old ways, will complain that they can't see enough without their automobiles to bear them swiftly (traffic permitting) through the parks. But this is nonsense. A man on foot, on horseback or on a bicycle will see more, feel more, enjoy more in one mile than the motorized tourists can in a hundred miles. Better to idle through one park in two weeks than try to race through a dozen in the same amount of time. Those who are familiar with both modes of travel know from experience that this is true; the rest have only to make the experiment to discover the same truth for themselves.

They will complain of physical hardship, these sons of the pioneers. Not for long; once they rediscover the pleasures of actually operating their own limbs and senses in a varied, spontaneous, voluntary style, they will complain instead of crawling back into a car; they may even object to returning to desk and office and that drywall box on Mossy Brook Circle. The fires of revolt may be kindled—which means hope for us all.

(2) No more new roads in national parks. After banning private automobiles the second step should be easy. Where paved roads are already in existence they will be reserved for the bicycles and essential in-park services, such as shuttle buses, the trucking of camping gear and concessioners' supplies. Where dirt roads already exist they too will be reserved for nonmotorized traffic. Plans for new roads can be discarded and in their place a program of trail-building begun, badly needed in some of the parks and in many of the national monuments. In mountainous areas it may be desirable to build emergency shelters along the trails and bike roads; in desert regions a water supply might have to be provided at certain points—wells drilled and handpumps installed if feasible.

Once people are liberated from the confines of automobiles there will be a greatly increased interest in hiking, exploring, and back-country packtrips. Fortunately the parks, by the mere elimination of motor traffic, will come to seem far bigger than they are now — there will be more room for more persons, an astonishing expansion of space. This follows from the interesting fact that a motorized vehicle, when not at rest, requires a volume of space far out of proportion to its size. To illustrate: imagine a lake approximately ten miles long and on the average one mile wide. A single motorboat could easily circumnavigate the lake in an hour; ten motorboats would begin to crowd it; twenty or thirty, all in operation, would dominate the lake to the exclusion of any other form of activity; and fifty would create the hazards, confusion, and turmoil that makes pleasure impossible. Suppose we banned motorboats and allowed only canoes and rowboats; we would see at once that the lake seemed ten or perhaps a hundred times bigger. The same thing holds true, to an even greater degree, for the automobile. Distance and space are functions of speed and time. Without expending a single dollar from the United States Treasury we could, if we wanted to, multiply the area of our national parks tenfold or a hundredfold — simply by banning the private automobile. The next generation, all 250 million of them, would be grateful to us.

(3) Put the park rangers to work. Lazy scheming loafers, they've wasted too many years selling tickets at toll booths and sitting behind desks filling out charts and tables in the vain effort to appease the mania for statistics which torments the Washington office. Put them to work. They're supposed to be rangers — make the bums range; kick them out of those overheated airconditioned offices, yank them out of those overstuffed patrol cars, and drive them out on the trails where they should be, leading the dudes over hill and dale, safely into and back out of the wilderness. It won't hurt them to work off a little office fat; it'll do them good, help take their minds off each other's wives, and give them a chance to get out of reach of the boss — a blessing for all concerned.

They will be needed on the trail. Once we outlaw the motors and stop the roadbuilding and force the multitudes back on their feet, the people will need leaders. A venturesome minority will always be eager to set off on their own, and no obstacles should be placed in their path; let them take risks, for Godsake, let them get lost, sunburnt, stranded, drowned, eaten by bears, buried alive under avalanches — that is the right and privilege of any free American. But the rest, the majority, most of them new to the out-of-doors, will need and welcome assistance, instruction and guidance. Many will not know how to saddle a horse, read a topographical map, follow a trail over slickrock, memorize landmarks, build a fire in rain, treat snakebite, rappel down a cliff, glissade down a glacier, read a compass, find water under sand, load a burro, splint a broken bone, bury a body, patch a rubber boat, portage a waterfall, survive a blizzard, avoid lightning, cook a porcupine, comfort a girl during a thunderstorm, predict the weather, dodge falling rock, climb out of a box canyon, or pour piss out of a boot. Park rangers know these things, or should know them, or used to know them and can relearn; they will be needed. In addition to this sort of practical guide service the ranger will also be a bit of a naturalist, able to edify the party in his charge with the natural and human history of the area, in detail and in broad outline.

Critics of my program will argue that it is too late for such a radical reformation of a people's approach to the out-of-doors, that the pattern is too deeply set, and that the majority of Americans would not be willing to emerge from the familiar luxury of their automobiles, even briefly, to try the little-known and problematic advantages of the bicycle, the saddle horse, and the footpath. This might be so; but how can we be sure unless we dare the experiment? I, for one, suspect that millions of our citizens, especially the young, are yearning for adventure, difficulty, challenge — they will respond with enthusiasm. What we must do, prodding the Park Service into the forefront of the demonstration, is provide these young people with the opportunity, the assistance, and the necessary encouragement.

How could this most easily be done? By following the steps I have proposed, plus reducing the expenses of wilderness recreation to the minimal level. Guide service by rangers should, of course, be free to the public. Money saved by *not* constructing more paved highways into the parks should be sufficient to finance the cost of bicycles and horses for the entire park system. Elimination of automobile traffic would allow the Park Service to save more millions now spent on road maintenance, police work and paper work. Whatever the cost, however financed, the benefits for park visitors in health and happiness — virtues unknown to the statisticians — would be immeasurable.

Excluding the automobile from the heart of the great cities has been seriously advocated by thoughtful observers of our urban problems. It seems to me an equally proper solution to the problems besetting our national parks. Of course it would be a serious blow to Industrial Tourism and would be bitterly resisted by those who profit from that industry. Exclusion of automobiles would also require a revolution in the thinking of Park Service officialdom and in the assumptions of most American tourists. But such a revolution, like it or not, is precisely what is needed. The only foreseeable alternative, given the current trend of things, is the gradual destruction of our national park system.

Let us therefore steal a slogan from the Development Fever Faction in the Park Service. The parks, they say, are for people. Very well. At the main entrance to each national park and national monument we shall erect a billboard one hundred feet high, two hundred feet wide, gorgeously filigreed in brilliant neon and outlined with blinker lights, exploding stars, flashing prayer wheels and great Byzantine phallic symbols that gush like geysers every thirty seconds. (You could set your watch by them.) Behind the fireworks will loom the figure of Smokey the Bear, taller than a pine tree, with eyes in his head that swivel back and forth, watching You, and ears that actually twitch. Push a button and Smokey will recite, for the benefit of children and government officials who might otherwise have trouble with some of the big words, in a voice ursine, loud and clear, the message spelled out on the face of the billboard. To wit:

HOWDY FOLKS. WELCOME. THIS IS YOUR NATIONAL PARK, ESTABLISHED FOR THE PLEASURE OF YOU AND ALL PEOPLE EVERYWHERE. PARK YOUR CAR, JEEP, TRUCK, TANK, MOTORBIKE, SNOWMOBILE, MOTORBOAT, JETBOAT, AIRBOAT, SUBMARINE, AIRPLANE, JETPLANE, HELICOPTER, HOVERCRAFT, WINGED MOTORCYCLE, ROCKETSHIP, OR ANY OTHER CONCEIVABLE TYPE OF MOTORIZED VEHICLE IN THE WORLD'S BIGGEST PARKING LOT BEHIND THE COMFORT STATION IMMEDIATELY TO YOUR REAR. GET OUT OF YOUR MOTORIZED VEHICLE, GET ON YOUR HORSE, MULE, BICYCLE OR FEET, AND COME ON IN. ENJOY YOURSELVES. THIS HERE PARK IS FOR *people*.

. . . Man is a gregarious creature, we are told, a social being. Does that mean he is also a herd animal? I don't believe it, despite the character of modern life. The herd is for ungulates, not for men and women and their children. Are men no better than sheep or cattle, that they must live always in view of one another in order to feel a sense of safety? I can't believe it.

We are preoccupied with time. If we could learn to love space as deeply as we are now obsessed with time, we might discover a new meaning in the phrase to *live like men.*

WILDERNESS LETTER
Wallace Stegner

In this letter to a California state legislator, Wallace Stegner, a Pulitzer Prize-winning novelist, historian, and the former director of Stanford's creative writing program, makes an impassioned plea for the preservation of wilderness areas. Notice that Stegner, like Thoreau (and like other nineteenth-century romantics such as Wordsworth, Emerson, and Whitman), sees in untainted natural beauty an almost transcendent spiritual value — a value worth preserving at all costs.

Los Altos, Calif.
Dec. 3, 1960

David E. Pesonen
Wildland Research Center
Agricultural Experiment Station
243 Mulford Hall
University of California
Berkeley, Calif.

Dear Mr. Pesonen:

I believe that you are working on the wilderness portion of the Outdoor Recreation Resources Review Commission's report. If I may, I should like to urge some arguments for wilderness preservation that involve recreation, as it is ordinarily conceived, hardly at all. Hunting, fishing, hiking, mountain-climbing, camping, photography, and the enjoyment of natural scenery will all, surely, figure in your report. So will the wilderness as a genetic reserve, a scientific yardstick by which we may measure the world in its natural balance against the world in its man-made imbalance. What I want to speak for is not so much the wilderness uses, valuable as those are, but the wilderness *idea*, which is a resource in itself. Being an intangible and spiritual resource, it will seem mystical to the practical-minded — but then anything that cannot be moved by a bulldozer is likely to seem mystical to them.

I want to speak for the wilderness idea as something that has helped form our character and that has certainly shaped our history as a people. It has no more to do with recreation than churches have to do with recreation, or than the strenuousness and optimism and expansiveness of what historians call the "American Dream" have to do with recreation. Nevertheless, since it is only in this recreation survey that the values of wilderness are being compiled, I hope you will permit me to insert this idea between the leaves, as it were, of the recreation report.

Something will have gone out of us as a people if we ever let the remaining wilderness be destroyed; if we permit the last virgin forests to be turned into comic books and plastic cigarette cases; if we drive the few remaining members of the wild species into zoos or to extinction; if we pollute the last clear air and dirty the last

Wallace Stegner, "Wilderness Letter," *The Sound of Mountain Water* (Garden City, N.Y.: Doubleday, 1969).

clean streams and push out paved roads through the last of the silence, so that never again will Americans be free in their own country from the noise, the exhausts, the stinks of human and automotive waste. And so that never again can we have the chance to see ourselves single, separate, vertical and individual in the world, part of the environment of trees and rocks and soil, brother to the other animals, part of the natural world and competent to belong in it. Without any remaining wilderness we are committed wholly, without chance for even momentary reflection and rest, to a headlong drive into our technological termite-life, the Brave New World of a completely man-controlled environment. We need wilderness preserved — as much of it as is still left, and as many kinds — because it was the challenge against which our character as a people was formed. The reminder and the reassurance that it is still there is good for our spiritual health even if we never once in ten years set foot in it. It is good for us when we are young, because of the incomparable sanity it can bring briefly, as vacation and rest, into our insane lives. It is important to us when we are old simply because it is there — important, that is, simply as idea.

We are a wild species, as Darwin pointed out. Nobody ever tamed or domesticated or scientifically bred us. But for at least three millennia we have been engaged in a cumulative and ambitious race to modify and gain control of our environment, and in the process we have come close to domesticating ourselves. Not many people are likely, any more, to look upon what we call "progress" as an unmixed blessing. Just as surely as it has brought us increased comfort and more material goods, it has brought us spiritual losses, and it threatens now to become the Frankenstein that will destroy us. One means of sanity is to retain a hold on the natural world, to remain, insofar as we can, good animals. Americans still have that chance, more than many peoples; for while we were demonstrating ourselves the most efficient and ruthless environment-busters in history, and slashing and burning and cutting our way through a wilderness continent, the wilderness was working on us. It remains in us as surely as Indian names remain on the land. If the abstract dream of human liberty and human dignity became, in America, something more than an abstract dream, mark it down at least partially to the fact that we were in subtle ways subdued by what we conquered.

The Connecticut Yankee, sending likely candidates from King Arthur's unjust kingdom to his Man Factory for rehabilitation, was over-optimistic, as he later admitted. These things cannot be forced, they have to grow. To make such a man, such a democrat, such a believer in human individual dignity, as Mark Twain himself, the frontier was necessary, Hannibal and the Mississippi and Virginia City, and reaching out from those the wilderness; the wilderness as opportunity and as idea, the thing that has helped to make an American different from and, until we forget it in the roar of our industrial cities, more fortunate than other men. For an American, insofar as he is new and different at all, is a civilized man who has renewed himself in the wild. The American experience has been the confrontation by old peoples and cultures of a world as new as if it had just risen from the sea. That gave us our hope and our excitement, and the hope and excitement can be passed on to newer Americans, Americans who never saw any phase of the frontier. But only so long as we keep the remainder of our wild as a reserve and a promise — a sort of wilderness bank.

As a novelist, I may perhaps be forgiven for taking literature as a reflection, indirect but profoundly true, of our national consciousness. And our literature, as perhaps you are aware, is sick, embittered, losing its mind, losing its faith. Our novelists are the declared enemies of their society. There has hardly been a serious or important novel in this century that did not repudiate in part or in whole American technological culture for its commercialism, its vulgarity, and the way in which it has dirtied a clean continent and a clean dream. I do not expect that the preservation of our remaining wilderness is going to cure this condition. But the mere example that we can as a nation apply some other criteria than commercial and exploitative considerations would be heartening to many Americans, novelists or otherwise. We need to demonstrate our acceptance of the natural world, including ourselves; we need the spiritual refreshment that being natural can produce. And one of the best places for us to get that is in the wilderness where the fun houses, the bulldozers, and the pavements of our civilization are shut out.

Sherwood Anderson, in a letter to Waldo Frank in the 1920's, said it better than I can. "Is it not likely that when the country was new and men were often alone in the fields and the forest they got a sense of bigness outside themselves that has now in some way been lost. . . . Mystery whispered in the grass, played in the branches of trees overhead, was caught up and blown across the American line in clouds of dust at evening on the prairies. . . . I am old enough to remember tales that strengthen my belief in a deep semi-religious influence that was formerly at work among our people. The flavor of it hangs over the best work of Mark Twain. . . . I can remember old fellows in my home town speaking feelingly of an evening spent on the big empty plains. It had taken the shrillness out of them. They had learned the trick of quiet . . ."

We could learn it too, even yet; even our children and grandchildren could learn it. But only if we save, for just such absolutely non-recreational, impractical, and mystical uses as this, all the wild that still remains to us.

It seems to me significant that the distinct downturn in our literature from hope to bitterness took place almost at the precise time when the frontier officially came to an end, in 1890, and when the American way of life had begun to turn strongly urban and industrial. The more urban it has become, and the more frantic with technological change, the sicker and more embittered our literature, and I believe our people, have become. For myself, I grew up on the empty plains of Saskatchewan and Montana and in the mountains of Utah, and I put a very high valuation on what those places gave me. And if I had not been able periodically to renew myself in the mountains and deserts of western America I would be very nearly bughouse. Even when I can't get to the back country, the thought of the colored deserts of southern Utah, or the reassurance that there are still stretches of prairie where the world can be instantaneously perceived as disk and bowl, and where the little but intensely important human being is exposed to the five directions and the thirty-six winds, is a positive consolation. The idea alone can sustain me. But as the wilderness areas are progressively exploited or "improved," as the jeep and bulldozers of uranium prospectors scar up the deserts and the roads are cut into the alpine timberlands, and as the remnants of the unspoiled and natural world are progressively eroded, every such loss is a little death in me. In us.

I am not moved by the argument that those wilderness areas which have already been exposed to grazing or mining are already deflowered, and so might as well be "harvested." For mining I cannot say much good except that its operations are generally short-lived. The extractable wealth is taken and the shafts, the tailings, and the ruins left, and in a dry country such as the American West the wounds men make in the earth do not quickly heal. Still, they are only wounds; they aren't absolutely mortal. Better a wounded wilderness than none at all. And as for grazing, if it is strictly controlled so that it does not destroy the ground cover, damage the ecology, or compete with the wildlife it is in itself nothing that need conflict with the wilderness feeling or the validity of the wilderness experience. I have known enough range cattle to recognize them as wild animals; and the people who herd them have, in the wilderness context, the dignity of rareness; they belong on the frontier, moreover, and have a look of rightness. The invasion they make on the virgin country is a sort of invasion that is as old as Neolithic man, and they can, in moderation, even emphasize a man's feelings of belonging to the natural world. Under surveillance, they can belong; under control, they need not deface or mar. I do not believe that in wilderness areas where grazing has never been permitted, it should be permitted; but I do not believe either that an otherwise untouched wilderness should be eliminated from the preservation plan because of limited existing uses such as grazing which are in consonance with the frontier condition and image.

Let me say something on the subject of the kinds of wilderness worth preserving. Most of those areas contemplated are in the national forests and in high mountain country. For all the usual recreational purposes, the alpine and forest wildernesses are obviously the most important, both as genetic banks and as beauty spots. But for the spiritual renewal, the recognition of identity, the birth of awe, other kinds will serve every bit as well. Perhaps, because they are less friendly to life, more abstractly nonhuman, they will serve even better. On our Saskatchewan prairie, the nearest neighbor was four miles away, and at night we saw only two lights on all the dark rounding earth. The earth was full of animals — field mice, ground squirrels, weasels, ferrets, badgers, coyotes, burrowing owls, snakes. I knew them as my little brothers, as fellow creatures, and I have never been able to look upon animals in any other way since. The sky in that country came clear down to the ground on every side, and it was full of great weathers, and clouds, and winds, and hawks. I hope I learned something from knowing intimately the creatures of the earth; I hope I learned something from looking a long way, from looking up, from being much alone. A prairie like that, one big enough to carry the eye clear to the sinking, rounding horizon, can be as lonely and grand and simple in its forms as the sea. It is as good a place as any for the wilderness experience to happen; the vanishing prairie is as worth preserving for the wilderness idea as the alpine forests.

So are great reaches of our western deserts, scarred somewhat by prospectors but otherwise open, beautiful, waiting, close to whatever God you want to see in them. Just as a sample, let me suggest the Robbers' Roost country in Wayne County, Utah, near the Capitol Reef National Monument. In that desert climate the dozer and jeep tracks will not soon melt back into the earth, but the country has a way of making the scars insignificant. It is a lovely and terrible wilderness, such a wilderness as Christ and the prophets went out into; harshly and beautiful colored, broken and worn until its bones are exposed, its great sky without a smudge or taint from Technocracy, and in hidden corners and pockets under its cliffs the sudden poetry of springs. Save a piece of country like that intact, and it does not matter in the slightest that only a few people every year will go into it. That is precisely its value.

Roads would be a desecration, crowds would ruin it. But those who haven't the strength or youth to go into it and live can simply sit and look. They can look two hundred miles, clear into Colorado; and looking down over the cliffs and canyons of the San Rafael Swell and the Robbers' Roost they can also look as deeply into themselves as anywhere I know. And if they can't even get to the places on the Aquarius Plateau where the present roads will carry them, they can simply contemplate the *idea*, take pleasure in the fact that such a timeless and uncontrolled part of earth is still there.

These are some of the things wilderness can do for us. That is the reason we need to put into effect, for its preservation, some other principle than the principles of exploitation or "usefulness" or even recreation. We simply need that wild country available to us, even if we never do more than drive to its edge and look in. For it can be a means of reassuring ourselves of our sanity as creatures, a part of the geography of hope.

Let's Open Our Wilderness Areas
Eric Julber

Eric Julber, a former Los Angeles attorney specializing in maritime law, a nature photographer, and an ardent hiker, testified before a congressional committee in the early 1970s, advocating maximum public access to federally owned parks and wilderness areas. This essay summarizes his testimony. Notice how sharply his arguments contrast with those of Edward Abbey in an essay that appears earlier in this chapter. Notice, too, the bottom line of Julber's arguments: Americans can become impassioned preservers of natural beauty only after they have had ample opportunities to experience this beauty; most of them, however, cannot experience it if access to parks and wilderness areas is stringently limited.

The prevailing philosophy with regard to the use of some 40 million acres of America's magnificent wilderness has become what I term "purist-conservationist." The purist is, generally speaking, against everything. He is against roads, campgrounds, ski lifts and restaurants. He has very strong ideas about who deserves to enjoy natural beauty and, ideally, would reserve beauty for those who are willing and able to hike, climb, crawl or cliffhang to achieve it. The purist believes that those who do not agree with him desire to "rape the landscape."

The purist standards were embodied in the Wilderness Act of 1964, which provides that in such areas there shall be "no permanent road . . . no temporary road . . . no mechanical transport and no structure or installation." The practical effect of this philosophy, thus frozen into federal law, has been to make many of the most beautiful areas of the United States "off limits" to anyone who is not willing and able to backpack into them. Statistics show that this means 99 *percent* of Americans.

In 1965, there were 1,475,000 visitors to the Wilderness areas. In 1970, the number of visitors had increased only to 1,543,000. This represents use by less than one percent of our population. Moreover, a survey on behalf of the President's Outdoor Recreation Resources Review Commission (ORRRC) showed, by statistical analysis, that the users are the intellectual and financial elite of our nation.

Reports the ORRRC: "In the sample of Wilderness users interviewed, more than 75 percent had at least a college degree, and a high proportion have done postgraduate work or hold advanced degrees. . . . Wilderness users are disproportionately drawn from the higher income levels. Professional and semiprofessional people, and those in white-collar occupations, account for approximately three quarters of those interviewed."

And what of ordinary Americans, those whose favorite recreations are driving, sightseeing, easy walking and camping? What of the too-old, the too-young, the timid, the inexperienced, the frail, the hurried, the out-of-shape or the just-plain-lazy, all of whose taxes acquired and maintain the Wilderness areas?

Eric Julber, "Let's Open Our Wilderness Areas," *Reader's Digest* May 1972.

For this group — 99 percent of the American population — federal agencies provide 73,700 acres of campgrounds and 39,100 acres of picnic sites: a total of 112,800 acres. And I believe that the areas provided to the common American are not the prime scenic areas; they are the fringes, the leftovers, the secondary scenic areas.

I feel I can speak with some authority as to purist philosophy, because I was once a purist myself. I have carried many a 50-pound pack; I've hiked to the top of Mt. Whitney, there to think beautiful thoughts; I've hiked the 200-mile length of California's John Muir Trail, running from Yosemite to Sequoia. And even in later years, when the press of law practice kept me physically away from the wilderness, in spirit I remained a purist. Keep those roads and crowds out, I said!

But no more. Recently I paid a visit to Switzerland. What I saw there made a non-purist out of me. Switzerland has, within the boundaries of a country half as large as South Carolina, one of the most astonishing concentrations of natural beauty on the face of the earth. Not only was I overwhelmed by Switzerland's beauty, but I was amazed to find that virtually every part of it was accessible and thoroughly used by people of all shapes and ages. It was, in fact, exploited to the ultimate — crisscrossed with roads, its mountain valleys heavily grazed and farmed, hotels and restaurants everywhere. Where the automobile cannot go, railroads take you; and when the going gets too steep for cogwheel trains, you catch an aerial tramway.

The most remarkable viewpoints in the country have been deliberately made accessible by some kind of comfortable transportation. People from all over Europe sit on Switzerland's restaurant patios, 10,000 feet high, admiring the magnificent views — views that in America would be excluded from 99 percent of our population without days of the most arduous struggle.

The Swiss philosophy says: Invite people in; the more the better. The purist says: Keep people out. The Swiss say: Let the strong climb if they choose (and many of them do), but let the children, the aged, the hurried or just-plain-lazy ride.

I, who have now done it both ways, say: My thoughts were just as beautiful on top of Switzerland's Schilthorn — 9,757 feet up; restaurant lunch of fondue, wine, strawberry pastry and coffee; reached by 30-minute tram ride — as they were on top of Mt. Lyell in America's Yosemite — 13,095 feet up; lunch of peanut-butter sandwich; reached by two-day hike. I conclude that the purist philosophy which keeps Americans out of their own land is an unwise misuse of our wilderness resources.

Let me propose an alternative philosophy. For want of a better term, call it an "access" philosophy. Consider as an example Muir Trail in California, with its magnificent Wilderness scenery — peaks, meadows, hundreds of lakes, streams, even glaciers. Its southern end is 212 miles from Los Angeles, its northern end 215 miles from San Francisco. Under present purist conditions, the Muir Trail is inaccessible to all except the hardiest, for only two roads touch it between its two ends. To reach its most beautiful parts you have to hike over mountain passes averaging 10,000 feet in height, packing supplies on your back.

Under the "access" philosophy, I would install aerial tramways at three or four locations within easy driving distance of Los Angeles. These tramways would have large gondola cars suspended from cables between towers that can be up to a mile apart; the cars would move silently high above the landscape. At the terminal of each tramway — after, say, an hour's ride — there would be restaurant facilities, picnic areas, observation points. A family could stay for a few hours or camp for weeks. General access would be year-round, as compared to the present 90-day, snow-free period.

Why not also put a tramway in Grand Canyon?

The visitor now cannot get from the South Rim to the North Rim (a distance of from 8 to 18 miles) without driving 217 miles around, and he cannot get to the bottom of the canyon (the most interesting part) except on foot or muleback. I would install an aerial tramway in an inconspicuous fold of the canyon, so that visitors could ride from the South Rim to the bottom, and from the bottom to the North Rim, thus getting a feel for its immense depths.

That brings up the ultimate argument that purists always fall back on: that the Swiss can do such things with taste, judgment and reverence for the landscape; that we Americans would botch it up. This is neither altogether true nor altogether false. We are capable of abominations, but we are just as capable of tasteful building as Europeans. Witness the beautiful aerial tramway at Palm Springs, Calif., which carries visitors to the slopes of Mt. San Jacinto. Built in 1963, after 15 years of battle with purists, this tramway has taken 2.5 million people to a lovely area which before was a full day's arduous climb away.

Surprisingly, the litter problem is often least great in precisely those areas where access is provided to beautiful spots. The Palm Springs aerial tramway, for instance, and Glacier Point in Yosemite are remarkably free of litter despite heavy visitation. This, I think, is because people will not litter when they feel others are watching; and also because purchasing a ticket on a tramway gives one a proprietary interest in keeping the premises clean.

It is my firm belief that if Americans were permitted access to Wilderness areas in the manner I have suggested, we would soon create a generation of avid nature lovers. Americans would cease to be "alienated" from their landscape, and would mend their littering tendencies. If you question any purist or wilderness buff, you will find that what initially "turned him on," in almost every case, was an experience in which he was provided access to natural beauty — be it in Glacier Park, Yellowstone, Grand Canyon or Yosemite (as in my own case) — by roads, bus or other similar non-purist means. Yet, if purists had had the influence 100 years ago that they have today, there would be no roads or other facilities in Yosemite Valley, and the strong probability is that neither I nor millions of other Americans would ever have seen its beauties, except on postcards.

I believe that the purist philosophy is unfair and undemocratic, and that an alternate philosophy, one of enlightened, carefully controlled "access," is more desirable and also ecologically sound. If the Swiss can do it, why can't we?

CONSERVATION AND THE ENVIRONMENTAL CRISIS
Charles F. Park, Jr.

Charles F. Park, Jr., the former dean of the school of Mineral Science at Stanford University, has long been one of the most widely recognized spokespeople for the multiple use of federal lands. In the following excerpt from Earthbound: Minerals, Energy, and Man's Future, *he argues that our national policies must accommodate our desperate need for energy resources as well as our need for natural beauty. He also asserts that the pollution of uninhabited areas by the mineral extraction industry is a thing of the past, and that, as these companies are acutely aware, their very economic survival depends on avoiding such incidents. (Can you see how the 1989* Exxon Valdez *incident both contradicts and affirms his argument?)*

Everyone sees the renewable resources of the earth, the flora and fauna, and most people are concerned about the preservation of scenery, primitive areas, and wildlife. Management of the large public domain is a fascinating, growing science. Seldom, however, until they are faced with shortages, problems of pollution, or unsightly change, do people think of conservation as applying to the other category of the earth's natural resources, those that are nonrenewable. Not often do they realize that renewable and nonrenewable resources are interrelated when it comes to conservation.

WHAT IS CONSERVATION?

Everyone expresses approval of the principle, but rarely do two people mean quite the same thing by *conservation*. To many people the word means *preservation* of the renewable resources—how to save lovely landscapes, how to prevent destruction and further reduction of the areas relatively unspoiled by our forefathers, how to maintain clean air and water, or how to protect or restore a diminishing wildlife species. The United States National Park Service considers itself an organization of conservationists. It encourages the preservation of large areas of unique public lands and natural wonders for recreation. No removal of or damage to vegetation or natural object is permitted, no privately owned mechanical equipment or industry (other than tourist facilities) is allowed to be installed within park boundaries.

The United States Forest Service also considers itself devoted to conservation. But conservation to the Forest Service, except in its mandated administration of the recently created Wilderness areas where entry is allowed only on foot, means *multiple use* of the land. It will permit within the national forests lumbering, grazing, mining, oil field development, hunting, and the leasing of summer home sites to the public.

Charles F. Park, Jr., "Conservation and the Environmental Crisis," *Earthbound: Minerals, Energy, and Man's Future* (San Francisco: Freeman, Cooper and Co., 1975).

Thus conservation means preservation to some, but multiple use to others, or something in between to still other groups. Peter Ellis says, "One sees in conservation what one wants to see." The subject is highly emotional; discussions about conservation are almost always lacking in objectivity. Opinions are stated with insufficient knowledge of the facts, which results in strongly biased viewpoints. Advocates of the preservationist point of view label anyone who uses the land in any way contrary to the preservationist belief as a destroyer of the wild and a killer of flora and fauna; extremists of the other side call these preservationists impractical dreamers, unfamiliar with the real world and willing to exaggerate conditions in order to create public sentiments favorable to their cause.

Like many extreme positions, that of the preservationists in some ways implies a lack of knowledge. For instance, opposition to fires in the wild, a part of the point of view of the strict conservationist, seems reasonable unless one knows that fire is a normal facet of the environment. Without fire to clear the land and provide a propitious environment, the reproduction of the California giant redwood is inhibited. The animals of the African plains could hardly maintain their life cycle without the fires that frequently sweep over grasslands and permit new grass to grow unimpeded.

The fervor of the preservationist attitude was well expressed by Ehrlich and Ehrlich when they said, "Each gain is temporary, but each loss is permanent. Species cannot be resurrected; places cannot be restored to their primitive state. Consequently, even if the conservationists were evenly matched against the destroyers, the battle would probably remain a losing one."

Who are these destroyers? Anyone who uses a sheet of paper, who drives an automobile, who has a telephone, a radio, a refrigerator. Anyone who owns a television set or uses artificial light. Anyone who heats a home, who applies paint, hammers a nail, or flushes a toilet. Even the staunchest of preservationists is such a destroyer. How can the preservationists expect their battle not to remain a losing one when those they are fighting include themselves? As Pogo put it, "We have met the enemy and he is us."

The problem of conservation stems directly from the pressure of growing numbers of people and the progressive reduction of amount of wild open space. This is recognized by everyone interested in maintaining an acceptable standard of living, clean air and water, a generally clean environment, and some regions of unspoiled wilderness. It is useless, however, to attempt to divorce man and his works from the rest of the environment because man is an integral part of the ecological system; he can no longer consider it something that exists only to serve him. "We abuse land because we regard it as a commodity belonging to us," said Aldo Leopold. "When we see land as a community to which we belong, we may begin to use it with love and respect."

Clearly man influences and changes the environment, but so does nature; otherwise the hairy mammoth and the dinosaurs would still be with us. Changes are inherent in nature, a fact well expressed by DuBridge: "The environment of this planet earth has been under continuous change for about 4.5 billion years. The earth never was in a stable state, for it has changed and evolved continually and radically through these many eons. In fact nature seems to abhor stability and to be in love with change."

Change cannot be avoided, although much of it can be directed. It is unrealistic to expect any family willingly to forgo the modern conveniences of life. It is unreasonable to expect people not to use deposits of needed minerals such as copper when the deposits are close at hand and their products help to lighten the burden of work. Civilized people want and must have raw materials, especially energy, at moderate prices; nations have gone to the extreme of war to obtain them. For this reason, if for no other, those who advocate the preservation of large wilderness areas known to contain valuable and necessary raw materials are not going to prevail. Actually, the minerals industries use a very small percentage of the land surface, and this use is temporary. Mineral extraction does not of necessity destroy the usefulness of land or its beauty, and many wilderness areas do not contain ore deposits or oil fields.

Here we use the term *conservation* as defined by Peter Ellis in a penetrating discussion: "Conservation is the effort to insure to society the maximum present and future benefit from the use of natural resources." We take conservation to mean, not the indefinite preservation of numerous large areas of unusable and inaccessible wilderness, to be visited only by the hardiest hikers, but maximum use for the benefit of the most people. This is not to say that primitive wilderness areas should not be established; they should be. But not all public land should be wilderness, any more than it should all be given over to mining. Either wilderness or mineral extraction represents only one use of the land. Conservation should mean its multiple use. . . .

EFFECTS OF THE EXTRACTIVE INDUSTRIES ON THE ENVIRONMENT

If land is to provide for society the maximum present and future benefit, no single use can be allowed to spoil it for other uses. Many examples can be cited of abandoned mining areas that have become unsightly, barren dumps, dusty tailing piles, heaps of rusty equipment, and dilapidated buildings. These places are ruined for recreation and esthetic enjoyment, and sometimes for wildlife. People say, bitterly, "This is what mining does to a lovely countryside."

Not all of these examples are old mines, unfortunately; a few have been abandoned recently. Also, all too often one sees ugly bulldozer cuts and unnecessary roads marring a landscape where mining is currently in progress. Legislation to prevent this type of destruction is overdue; proper regulation of industry, particularly on public lands, is a recognized and necessary function of government. If regulatory laws do not exist, they should be passed and enforced, even though such legislation may be difficult to formulate because frequently the destruction occurs on private property and takes place with the consent of the owner. Over twenty years ago Aldo Leopold pointed out a fact that is still too true: "When the private landowner is asked to perform some unprofitable act for the good of the community, he today assents only with outstretched palm." Ideally man should respect his environment to such an extent that he accepts personal responsibility for its care, instead of having responsibility forced on him by law.

In recent years the extractive industries have spent many millions of dollars in attempts to maintain an acceptable environment. In order to survive, they must cooperate with reasonable conservational and environmental objectives. All but a very few know this and have accepted these objectives as their own. Now is the time for closer cooperation between conservationists and industry, cooperation which could yield results that would be approved by all except the most extreme preservationist and the most shortsighted businessman. The goals of thinking people on both sides are now really not far apart.

Situations where the extractive industries have harmed the environment are for the most part in the past. However, situations where organizations devoted to the thesis of no further mineral development on public lands have caused the delay, for a time at least, or even the prevention of the development of mineral deposits are all in the present. These include the phosphate deposits along the shores near Savannah, Georgia; the molybdenum deposits at White Cloud, Idaho; the copper deposits on Plummer Mountain near Glacier Peak, Washington; and the chromium, nickel, and copper deposits of the Stillwater Basin in Montana. There are many others. One of the most interesting is a large copper deposit in Puerto Rico, where opposition to development has been organized by the Episcopal clergy in New York City, with the theme of preserving the culture of the poor, semiprimitive people in that part of the island. If this deposit were mined with careful protection of its environment, the culture of the local people would be changed by the addition of jobs and the improvement of their standard of living. Furthermore, the dependence of the United States upon foreign supplies would be decreased, as would inflation because of the beneficial effect on the balance of payments. Some people have suggested that the problem should be solved by pretending that the deposits do not exist, a desperate form of self-deception that would accomplish as much as a frightened ostrich does by burying its head in the sand. There must be a policy. What can it be except multiple use?

Approximately one third of the land area of the United States, most of it in Alaska, is owned by the federal government. The administration of this tremendous area is under the direction of various federal bureaus, such as the Bureau of Land Management, the National Park Service, the United States Forest Service, and the Department of Defense. To a lesser extent, overlapping control is exerted by others such as Fish and Wildlife, the Bureau of Indian Affairs, the Reclamation Service, the Bureau of Mines, and the Geological Survey. Some government bureaus are able to enforce regulations, others are not. The Forest Service can control the location of access roads and the cutting of timber; the Bureau of Land Management can prevent road building.

Additional amounts of land are owned by individual states and administered by various state bureaus.

Proper land management is a complex and enormous job. The conflicting goals of the many agencies and the needs of the public must all be taken into account. Maximum use of land for the most people cannot be achieved efficiently, and probably cannot be achieved at all, while numerous agencies with overlapping jurisdictions exercise varying amounts of control.

LAWS GOVERNING MINERAL RESOURCES ON PUBLIC LANDS

Laws governing mineral resources on public lands in the United States are highly complicated and variable. For oil, gas, and many of the nonmetallic minerals such as potash, a system of bidding and leasing is employed. For most metal deposits in solid rock, a system of mineral claims, based upon the land laws of 1872, is still in use. These mining claims have a maximum size of six hundred feet wide by fifteen hundred feet long. For *placers* (stream gravels and beach sands containing economic minerals) or gravel deposits, the claims contain up to a maximum of twenty acres.

Mineral land laws have been changed but little in recent years and many proposed changes have been vigorously opposed by most mining industrialists. They claim that the present system has been eminently workable, though they will admit to some abuses that need correction. Complete rewriting of the old law of 1872 has been advocated by others, who would like to extend the leasing system to cover all nonrenewable resources.

The leasing system has its drawbacks, particularly in the way it favors the larger operations and is apt to limit healthy competition. However, the leasing system is operating successfully in Australia, South Africa, Ireland, and elsewhere.

Four concepts are basic to any realistic and effective mining law:

- Prospecting for minerals should be encouraged by allowing individuals and companies maximum but nonexclusive access to public lands to search for ore deposits.

- A prospector or company having found evidence of the probable presence of a mineral deposit should be given exclusive exploration rights for a limited area for a limited time while he is focusing his exploratory activity on it.

- A person or corporation having discovered a valuable mineral deposit should have an exclusive right to develop and mine it, including the right to defer such development for a reasonable period of years until economic or technological conditions justify production.

- The law must provide the person or corporation with tenure for the duration of mining, on reasonable terms set in advance.

THE FUTURE

If one could foretell the future status of conservation of the environment, one would know the future of the human race. What we have to conserve is not one but all of our requirements of space, energy, and minerals. The environment we must protect is the entire earth, including its air and water. The awesome aspect of the situation is its magnitude, the interrelationship of its components, and the fact that it demands from man almost immediate action, objectivity, knowledge, wisdom, and cooperation. The hopeful aspect is that man has shown forethought about his future and is already trying to do something about the conservation of his environment.

Is Nature Too Good for Us?

William Tucker

In this essay William Tucker discusses the history of the conservationist-preserva-
tionist dispute in detail and then advocates a responsible stewardship of federal lands
rather than what he considers the elitist, unrealistic, and romantic policies of pres-
ervationists. Tucker points out, for example, that the most influential figures in the
preservationist movement are individualists who have spent prolonged periods living
in isolation in wilderness areas and that, while such experiences may have great
personal value, they do not qualify these preservationists to make public policy
decisions for the nation. Tucker also observes that preservationists want to freeze-
frame wilderness areas—to preserve them just as they were briefly in the late
nineteenth century after their indigenous human inhabitants, the Indian tribes, had
been removed—an arbitrary, artificial form of preservation, as far as Tucker is
concerned.

Probably nothing has been more central to the environmental movement than
the concept of wilderness. "In wildness is the preservation of the world," wrote
Thoreau, and environmental writers and speakers have intoned his message repeatedly. Wilderness, in the environmental pantheon, represents a particular kind of
sanctuary in which all true values—that is, all nonhuman values—are reposited.
Wildernesses are often described as "temples," "churches," and "sacred ground"—
refuges for the proposed "new religion" based on environmental consciousness.
Carrying the religious metaphor to the extreme, one of the most famous essays
of the environmental era holds the Judeo-Christian religion responsible for "ecological crisis."

The wilderness issue also has a political edge. Since 1964, long-standing preservation groups like the Wilderness Society and the Sierra Club have been pressuring
conservation agencies like the National Forest Service and the Bureau of Land
Management to put large tracts of their holdings into permanent "wilderness designations," countering the "multiple use" concept that was one of the cornerstones of
the Conservation Era of the early 1900s.

Preservation and conservation groups have been at odds since the end of the
last century, and the rift between them has been a major controversy of environmentalism. The leaders of the Conservation Movement—most notably Theodore
Roosevelt, Gifford Pinchot, and John Wesley Powell—called for rational, efficient
development of land and other natural resources: multiple use, or reconciling competing uses of land, and also "highest use," or forfeiting more immediate profits from
land development for more lasting gains. Preservationists, on the other hand, the
followers of California woodsman John Muir, have advocated protecting land in its
natural state, setting aside tracts and keeping them inviolate. "Wilderness area"
battles have become one of the hottest political issues of the day, especially in
western states—the current "Sagebrush Revolt" comes to mind—where large quantities of potentially commercially usable land are at stake.

William Tucker, "Is Nature Too Good for Us?" *Harper's* March 1982.

The term "wilderness" generally connotes mountains, trees, clear streams, rushing waterfalls, grasslands, or parched deserts, but the concept has been institutionalized and has a careful legal definition as well. The one given by the 1964 Wilderness Act, and that most environmentalists favor, is that wilderness is an area "where man is a visitor but does not remain." People do not "leave footprints there," wilderness exponents often say. Wildernesses are, most importantly, areas in which *evidence of human activity is excluded*; they need not have any particular scenic, aesthetic, or recreational value. The values, as environmentalists usually say, are "ecological" — which means, roughly translated, that natural systems are allowed to operate as free from human interference as possible.

The concept of excluding human activity is not to be taken lightly. One of the major issues in wilderness areas has been whether or not federal agencies should fight forest fires. The general decision has been that they should not, except in cases where other lands are threatened. The federal agencies also do not fight the fires with motorized vehicles, which are prohibited in wilderness areas except in extreme emergencies. Thus in recent years both the National Forest Service and the National Park Service have taken to letting forest fires burn unchecked, to the frequent alarm of tourists. The defense is that many forests require periodic leveling by fire in order to make room for new growth. There are some pine trees, for instance, whose cones will break open and scatter their seeds only when burned. This theoretical justification has won some converts, but very few in the timber companies, which bridle at watching millions of board-feet go up in smoke when their own "harvesting" of mature forests has the same effect in clearing the way for new growth and does less damage to forest soils.

The effort to set aside permanent wilderness areas on federal lands began with the National Forest Service in the 1920s. The first permanent reservation was in the Gila National Forest in New Mexico. It was set aside by a young Forest Service officer named Aldo Leopold, who was later to write *A Sand County Almanac*, which has become one of the bibles of the wilderness movement. Robert Marshall, another Forest Service officer, continued the program, and by the 1950s nearly 14 million of the National Forest System's 186 million acres had been administratively designated wilderness preserves.

Leopold and Marshall had been disillusioned by one of the first great efforts at "game management" under the National Forest Service, carried out in the Kaibab Plateau, just north of the Grand Canyon. As early as 1906 federal officials began a program of "predator control" to increase the deer population in the area. Mountain lions, wolves, coyotes, and bobcats were systematically hunted and trapped by game officials. By 1920, the program appeared to be spectacularly successful. The deer population, formerly numbering 4,000, had grown to almost 100,000. But it was realized too late that it was the range's limited food resources that would threaten the deer's existence. During two severe winters, in 1924–26, 60 percent of the herd died, and by 1939 the population had shrunk to only 10,000. Deer populations (unlike human populations) were found to have no way of putting limits on their own reproduction. The case is still cited as the classic example of the "boom and bust" disequilibrium that comes from thoughtless intervention in an ecological system.

The idea of setting aside as wilderness areas larger and larger segments of federally controlled lands began to gain more support from the old preservation groups. In part, this came from preservationists' growing realization, during the 1950s, that they had not won the battle during the Conservation Era, and that the national forests were not parks that would be protected forever from commercial activity.

Pinchot's plan for practicing "conservation" in the western forests was to encourage a partnership between the government and large industry. In order to discourage overcutting and destructive competition, he formulated a plan that would promote conservation activities among the larger timber companies while placing large segments of the western forests under federal control. It was a classic case of "market restriction," carried out by the joint efforts of larger businesses and government. Only the larger companies, Pinchot reasoned, could generate the profits that would allow them to cut their forest holdings *slowly* so that the trees would have time to grow back. In order to ensure these profit margins, the National Forest Service would hold most of its timber lands out of the market for some time. This would hold up the price of timber and prevent a rampage through the forests by smaller companies trying to beat small profit margins by cutting everything in sight. Then, in later years, the federal lands would gradually be worked into the "sustained yield" cycles, and timber rights put up for sale. It was when the national forests finally came up for cutting in the 1950s that the old preservation groups began to react.

The battle was fought in Congress. The 1960 Multiple Use and Sustained Yield Act tried to reaffirm the principles of the Conservation Movement. But the wilderness groups had their day in 1964 with the passing of the Wilderness Act. The law required all the federal land-management agencies — the National Forest Service, the National Park Service, and the Fish and Wildlife Service — to review all their holdings, keeping in mind that "wilderness" now constituted a valid alternative in the "multiple use" concept — even though the concept of wilderness is essentially a rejection of the idea of multiple use. The Forest Service, with 190 million acres, and the Park Service and Fish and Wildlife Service, each with about 35 million acres, were all given twenty years to start designating wilderness areas. At the time, only 14.5 million acres of National Forest System land were in wilderness designations.

The results have been mixed. The wilderness concept appears valid if it is recognized for what it is — an attempt to create what are essentially "ecological museums" in scenic and biologically significant areas of these lands. But "wilderness," in the hands of environmentalists, has become an all-purpose tool for stopping economic activity as well. This is particularly crucial now because of the many mineral and energy resources available on western lands that environmentalists are trying to push through as wilderness designations. The original legislation specified that lands were to be surveyed for valuable mineral resources before they were put into wilderness preservation. Yet with so much land being reviewed at once, these inventories have been sketchy at best. And once land is locked up as wilderness, it becomes illegal even to explore it for mineral or energy resources.

Thus the situation in western states — where the federal government still owns 68 percent of the land, counting Alaska — has in recent years become a race between mining companies trying to prospect under severely restricted conditions, and environmental groups trying to lock the doors to resource development for good. This kind of permanent preservation — the antithesis of conservation — will probably have enormous effects on our future international trade in energy and mineral resources.

At stake in both the national forests and the Bureau of Land Management holdings are what are called the "roadless areas." Environmentalists call these lands "de facto wilderness," and say that because they have not yet been explored or developed for resources they should not be explored and developed in the future. The Forest Service began its Roadless Area Resources Evaluation (RARE) in 1972, while the Bureau of Land Management began four years later in 1976, after Congress brought its 174 million acres under jurisdiction of the 1964 act. The Forest Service is studying 62 million roadless acres, while the BLM is reviewing 24 million.

In 1974 the Forest Service recommended that 15 million of the 50 million acres then under study be designated as permanent wilderness. Environmental groups, which wanted much more set aside, immediately challenged the decision in court. Naturally, they had no trouble finding flaws in a study intended to cover such a huge amount of land, and in 1977 the Carter administration decided to start over with a "RARE II" study, completed in 1979. This has also been challenged by a consortium of environmental groups that include the Sierra Club, the Wilderness Society, the National Wildlife Federation, and the Natural Resources Defense Council. The RARE II report also recommended putting about 15 million acres in permanent wilderness, with 36 million released for development and 11 million held for further study. The Bureau of Land Management is not scheduled to complete the study of its 24 million acres until 1991.

The effects of this campaign against resource development have been powerful. From 1972 to 1980, the price of a Douglas fir in Oregon increased 500 percent, largely due to the delays in timber sales from the national forests because of the battles over wilderness areas. Over the decade, timber production from the national forests declined slightly, putting far more pressure on the timber industry's own lands. The nation has now become an importer of logs, despite the vast resources on federal lands. In 1979, environmentalists succeeded in pressuring Congress into setting aside 750,000 acres in Idaho as the Sawtooth Wilderness and National Recreational Area. A resource survey, which was not completed until *after* the congressional action, showed that the area contained an estimated billion dollars' worth of molybdenum, zinc, silver, and gold. The same tract also contained a potential source of cobalt, an important mineral for which we are now dependent on foreign sources for 97 percent of what we use.

Perhaps most fiercely contested are the energy supplies believed to be lying under the geological strata running through Colorado, Wyoming, and Montana just east of the Rockies, called the Overthrust Belt. Much of this land is still administered by the Bureau of Land Management for multiple usage. But with the prospect of energy development, environmental groups have been rushing to try to have these high-plains areas designated as wilderness areas as well (cattle grazing is still allowed in wilderness tracts). On those lands permanently withdrawn from commercial use, mineral exploration will be allowed to continue until 1983. Any mines begun by then can continue on a very restricted basis. But the exploration in "roadless areas" is severely limited, in that in most cases there can be no roads constructed (and no use of off-roads vehicles) while exploration is going on. Environmentalists have argued that wells can still be drilled and test mines explored using helicopters. But any such exploration is likely to be extraordinarily expensive and ineffective. Wilderness restrictions are now being drawn so tightly that people on the site are not allowed to leave their excrement in the area.

What is the purpose of all this? The standard environmental argument is that we have to "preserve these last few wild places before they all disappear." Yet it is obvious that something more is at stake. What is being purveyed is a view of the world in which human activity is defined as "bad" and natural conditions are defined as "good." What is being preserved is evidently much more than "ecosystems." What is being preserved is an *image* of wilderness as a semisacred place beyond humanity's intrusion.

It is instructive to consider how environmentalists themselves define the wilderness. David Brower, former director of the Sierra Club, wrote in his introduction to Paul Ehrlich's *The Population Bomb* (1968):

> Whatever resources the wilderness still held would not sustain [*man*] in his old habits of growing and reaching without limits. Wilderness could, however, provide answers for questions he had not yet learned how to ask. He could predict that the day of creation was not over, that there would be wiser men, and they would thank him for leaving the source of those answers. Wilderness would remain part of his geography of hope, as Wallace Stegner put it, and could, merely because wilderness endured on the planet, prevent man's world from becoming a cage.

The wilderness, he suggested, is a source of peace and freedom. Yet setting wilderness aside for the purposes of solitude doesn't always work very well. Environmentalists have discovered this over and over again, much to their chagrin. Every time a new "untouched paradise" is discovered, the first thing everyone wants to do is visit it. By their united enthusiasm to find these "sanctuaries," people bring the "cage" of society with them. Very quickly it becomes necessary to erect bars to keep people *out*—which is exactly what most of the "wilderness" legislation has been all about.

In 1964, for example, the Sierra Club published a book on the relatively "undiscovered" paradise of Kauai, the second most westerly island in the Hawaiian chain. It wasn't long before the island had been overrun with tourists. When *Time* magazine ran a feature on Kauai in 1979, one unhappy island resident wrote in to convey this telling sentiment: "We're hoping the shortages of jet fuel will stay around and keep people away from here." The age of environmentalism has also been marked by the near overrunning of popular national parks like Yosemite (which now has a full-time jail), intense pressure on woodland recreational areas, full bookings two and three years in advance for raft trips through the Grand Canyon, and dozens of other spectacles of people crowding into isolated areas to get away from it all. Environmentalists are often critical of these inundations, but they must recognize that they have at least contributed to them.

I am not arguing against wild things, scenic beauty, pristine landscapes, and scenic preservation. What I am questioning is the argument that wilderness is a value against which every other human activity must be judged, and that human beings are somehow unworthy of the landscape. The wilderness has been equated with freedom, but there are many different ideas about what constitutes freedom.

In the Middle Ages, the saying was that "city air makes a man free," meaning that the harsh social burdens of medieval fuedalism vanished once a person escaped into the heady anonymity of a metropolitan community. When city planner Jane Jacobs, author of *The Death and Life of Great American Cities*, was asked by an interviewer if "overpopulation" and "crowding into large cities" weren't making social prisoners of us all, her simple reply was: "Have you ever lived in a small town?"

It may seem unfair to itemize the personal idiosyncrasies of people who feel comfortable only in wilderness, but it must be remembered that the environmental movement has been shaped by many people who literally spent years of their lives living in isolation. John Muir, the founder of the National Parks movement and the Sierra Club, spent almost ten years living alone in the Sierra Mountains while learning to be a trail guide. David Brower, who headed the Sierra Club for over a decade and later broke with it to found the Friends of the Earth, also spent years as a mountaineer. Gary Snyder, the poet laureate of the environmental movement, has lived much of his life in wilderness isolation and has also spent several years in a Zen monastery. All these people far outdid Thoreau in their desire to get a little perspective on the world. There is nothing reprehensible in this, and the literature and philosophy that emerge from such experiences are often admirable. But it seems questionable to me that the ethic that comes out of this wilderness isolation — and the sense of ownership of natural landscapes that inevitably follows — can serve as the basis for a useful national philosophy.

The American frontier is generally agreed to have closed down physically in 1890, the year the last Indian Territory of Oklahoma was opened for settlement. After that, the Conservation Movement arose quickly to protect the remaining resources and wilderness from heedless stripping and development. Along with this came a significant psychological change in the national character, as the "frontier spirit" diminished and social issues attracted greater attention. The Progressive Movement, the Social Gospel among religious groups, Populism, and Conservation all arose in quick succession immediately after the "closing of the frontier." It seems fair to say that it was only after the frontier had been settled and the sense of endless possibilities that came with open spaces had been constricted in the national con-sciousness that the country started "growing up."

Does this mean the new environmental consciousness has arisen because we are once again "running out of space"? I doubt it. Anyone taking an airplane across almost any part of the country is inevitably struck by how much greenery and open territory remain, and how little room our towns and cities really occupy. The amount of standing forest in the country, for example, has not diminished appreci-ably over the last fifty years, and is 75 percent of what it was in 1620. In addition, as environmentalists constantly remind us, trees are "renewable resources." If they continue to be handled intelligently, the forests will always grow back. As farming has moved out to the Great Plains of the Middle West, many eastern areas that were once farmed have reverted back to trees. Though mining operations can permanently scar hillsides and plains, they are usually very limited in scope (and as often as not, it is the roads leading to these mines that environmentalists find most objectionable).

It seems to me that the wilderness ethic has actually represented an attempt psychologically to reopen the American frontier. We have been desperate to maintain belief in unlimited, uncharted vistas within our borders, a preoccupation that has eclipsed the permanent shrinking of the rest of the world outside. Why else would it be so necessary to preserve such huge tracts of "roadless territory" simply because they are now roadless, regardless of their scenic, recreational, or aesthetic values? The environmental movement, among other things, has been a rather backward-looking effort to recapture America's lost innocence.

The central figure in this effort has been the backpacker. The backpacker is a young, unprepossessing person (inevitably white and upper middle class) who journeys into the wilderness as a passive observer. He or she brings his or her own food, treads softly, leaves no litter, and has no need to make use of any of the resources at hand. Backpackers bring all the necessary accouterments of civilization with them. All their needs have been met by the society from which they seek temporary release. The backpacker is freed from the need to support himself in order to enjoy the aesthetic and spiritual values that are made available by this temporary *removal* from the demands of nature. Many dangers—raging rivers or precipitous cliffs, for instance—become sought-out adventures.

Yet once the backpacker runs out of supplies and starts using resources around him—cutting trees for firewood, putting up a shelter against the rain—he is violating some aspect of the federal Wilderness Act. For example, one of the issues fought in the national forests revolves around tying one's horse to a tree. Purists claim the practice should be forbidden, since it may leave a trodden ring around the tree. They say horses should be hobbled and allowed to graze instead. In recent years, the National Forest Service has come under pressure from environmental groups to enforce this restriction.

Wildernesses, then, are essentially parks for the upper middle class. They are vacation reserves for people who want to rough it—with the assurance that few other people will have the time, energy, or means to follow them into the solitude. This is dramatically highlighted in one Sierra Club book that shows a picture of a professorial sort of individual backpacking off into the woods. The ironic caption is a quote from Julius Viancour, an official of the Western Council of Lumber and Sawmill Workers: "The inaccessible wilderness and primitive areas are off limits to most laboring people. We must have access. . . ." The implication for Sierra Club readers is: "What do these beer-drinking, gun-toting, working people want to do in *our* woods?"

This class-oriented vision of wilderness as an upper-middle-class preserve is further illustrated by the fact that most of the opposition to wilderness designations comes not from industry but from owners of off-road vehicles. In most northern rural areas, snowmobiles are now regarded as the greatest invention since the automobile, and people are ready to fight rather than stay cooped up all winter in their houses. It seems ludicrous to them that snowmobiles (which can't be said even to endanger the ground) should be restricted from vast tracts of land so that the occasional city visitor can have solitude while hiking past on snowshoes.

The recent Boundary Waters Canoe Area controversy in northern Minnesota is an excellent example of the conflict. When the tract was first designated as wilderness in 1964, Congress included a special provision that allowed motorboats into the entire area. By the mid-1970s, outboards and inboards were roaming all over the wilderness, and environmental groups began asking that certain portions of the million-acre preserve be set aside exclusively for canoes. Local residents protested vigorously, arguing that fishing expeditions, via motorboats, contributed to their own recreation. Nevertheless, Congress eventually excluded motorboats from 670,000 acres to the north.

A more even split would seem fairer. It should certainly be possible to accommodate both forms of recreation in the area, and there is as much to be said for canoeing in solitude as there is for making rapid expeditions by powerboat. The natural landscape is not likely to suffer very much from either form of recreation. It is not absolute "ecological" values that are really at stake, but simply different tastes in recreation.

At bottom, then, the mystique of the wilderness has been little more than a revival of Rousseau's Romanticism about the "state of nature." The notion that "only in wilderness are human beings truly free," a credo of environmentalists, is merely a variation on Rousseau's dictum that "man is born free, and everywhere he is in chains." According to Rousseau, only society could enslave people, and only in the "state of nature" was the "noble savage" — the preoccupation of so many early explorers — a fulfilled human being.

The "noble savage" and other indigenous peoples, however, have been carefully excised from the environmentalists' vision. Where environmental efforts have encountered primitive peoples, these indigenous residents have often proved one of the biggest problems. One of the most bitter issues in Alaska is the efforts by environmental groups to restrict Indians in their hunting practices.

At the same time, few modern wilderness enthusiasts could imagine, for example, the experience of the nineteenth-century artist J. Ross Browne, who wrote in *Harper's New Monthly Magazine* after visiting the Arizona territories in 1864:

> Sketching in Arizona is . . . rather a ticklish pursuit. . . . I never before traveled through a country in which I was compelled to pursue the fine arts with a revolver strapped around my body, a double-barreled shot-gun lying across my knees, and half a dozen soldiers armed with Sharpe's carbines keeping guard in the distance. Even with all the safeguards . . . I am free to admit that on occasions of this kind I frequently looked behind to see how the country appeared in its rear aspect. An artist with an arrow in his back may be a very picturesque object . . . but I would rather draw him on paper than sit for the portrait myself.

Wilderness today means the land *after* the Indians have been cleared away but *before* the settlers have arrived. It represents an attempt to hold that particular moment forever frozen in time, that moment when the visionary American settler looked out on the land and imagined it as an empty paradise, waiting to be molded to our vision.

In the absence of the noble savage, the environmentalist substitutes himself. The wilderness, while free of human dangers, becomes a kind of basic-training ground for upper-middle-class values. Hence the rise of "survival" groups, where college kids are taken out into the woods for a week or two and let loose to prove their survival instincts. No risks are spared on these expeditions. Several people have died on them, and a string of lawsuits has already been launched by parents and survivors who didn't realize how seriously these survival courses were being taken.

The ultimate aim of these efforts is to test upper-middle-class values against the natural environment. "Survival" candidates cannot hunt, kill, or use much of the natural resources available. The true test is whether their zero-degree sleeping bags and dried-food kits prove equal to the hazards of the tasks. What happens is not necessarily related to nature. One could as easily test survival skills by turning a person loose without money or means in New York City for three days.

I do not mean to imply that these efforts do not require enormous amounts of courage and daring — "survival skills." I am only suggesting that what the backpacker or survival hiker encounters is not entirely "nature," and that the effort to go "back to nature" is one that is carefully circumscribed by the most intensely civilized artifacts. Irving Babbitt, the early twentieth-century critic of Rousseau's Romanticism, is particularly vigorous in his dissent from the idea of civilized people going "back to nature." This type, he says, is actually "the least primitive of all beings":

> We have seen that the special form of unreality encouraged by the aesthetic romanticism of Rousseau is the dream of the simple life, the return to a nature that never existed, and that this dream made its special appeal to an age that was suffering from an excess of artificiality and conventionalism.

Babbitt notes shrewdly that our concept of the "state of nature" is actually one of the most sophisticated productions of civilization. Most primitive peoples, who live much closer to the soil than we do, are repelled by wilderness. The American colonists, when they first encountered the unspoiled landscape, saw nothing but a horrible desert, filled with savages.

What we really encounter when we talk about "wilderness," then, is one of the highest products of civilization. It is a reserve set up to keep people *out*, rather than a "state of nature" in which the inhabitants are "truly free." The only thing that makes people "free" in such a reservation is that they can leave so much behind when they enter. Those who try to stay too long find out how spurious this "freedom" is. After spending a year in a cabin in the north Canadian woods, Elizabeth Arthur wrote in *Island Sojourn:* "I never felt so completely tied to *objects*, resources, and the tools to shape them with."

What we are witnessing in the environmental movement's obsession with purified wilderness is what has often been called the "pastoral impulse." The image of nature as unspoiled, unspotted wilderness where we can go to learn the lessons of ecology is both a product of a complex, technological society and an escape from it. It is this undeniable paradox that forms the real problem of setting up "wildernesses." Only when we have created a society that gives us the leisure to appreciate it can we go out and experience what we imagine to be untrammeled nature. Yet if we lock up too much of our land in these reserves, we are cutting into our resources and endangering the very leisure that allows us to enjoy nature.

The answer is, of course, that we cannot simply let nature "take over" and assume that because we have kept roads and people out of huge tracts of land, then we have absolved ourselves of a national guilt. The concept of stewardship means taking responsibility, not simply letting nature take its course. Where tracts can be set aside from commercialism at no great cost, they should be. Where primitive hiking and recreation areas are appealing, they should be maintained. But if we think we are somehow appeasing the gods by *not* developing resources where they exist, then we are being very shortsighted. Conservation, not preservation, is once again the best guiding principle.

ACCESS TO PUBLIC LANDS: A NATIONAL NECESSITY

Cynthia Riggs

Cynthia Riggs, a geologist and a former writer for the American Petroleum Institute, points out that the 720 million acres of land owned by the federal government amounts to three acres for each of its citizens. She argues that for the vast majority of Americans, these three-acre parcels should be valued and used for other vital needs as well as for aesthetic beauty. Notice that she is indebted to Charles F. Park, Jr., whose essay appears earlier in this chapter, for some of her ideas. (Here is, indeed, a lesson for paraphrasers: Riggs uses and acknowledges ideas from Parks, but she expresses these borrowed ideas more effectively than did her source.)

Quick! Name America's largest landowner. No, not the King Ranch. No, not the Bank of America. No, Exxon isn't even in the running. The answer is the federal government. Of America's 2,271 million acres, 720 million belong to Uncle Sam. Add another 966 million underwater acres of the country's continental shelf, and you've got an impressive bit of real estate there.

In terms of the nation's resources, that vast range of public property represents enormous volumes of timber, grass, and minerals. Copper, zinc, gold, vanadium, tantalum, iron, and silver are among dozens of metallic minerals mined on federal lands. In energy minerals alone, government land may contain more than half the nation's remaining resources. According to the Department of Energy, this includes 85 percent of the nation's crude oil, 40 percent of natural gas, 40 percent of uranium, 35 percent of coal, 80 percent of oil shale, 85 percent of tar sands, and 50 percent of geothermal resources.

What does this mean to those of us who don't even own a 50- by 100-foot lot? Like others who visit national parks and camp in national forests and photograph national monuments, we consider these lands our heritage. Divide it among us, and we'd each have something like three acres apiece. Like all landowners, we'd like those three acres cared for, protected, preserved. It's nice to be a landowner. But there's the rub. Each of us also needs farmland for crops, rangeland for grazing, timber for homes, metals for machines, and energy for heat and fuel. For these, we must turn increasingly to those same public lands of ours where such resources are still to be found.

"No one can feel happy about intrusion upon the wilderness," writes Dr. Charles F. Parks, professor of geology at Stanford University, in his book, *Earthbound.* "It is justified only by the urgency of the need."

The need is urgent, and getting more so. Yet tens of millions of acres of public lands have been closed to mineral development by law or administrative actions. As

Cynthia Riggs, "Access to Public Lands: A National Necessity," *Exxon USA*, second quarter 1984.

of early 1983 only 162 million acres of federal onshore land and 13 million acres of offshore land were under lease for oil and natural gas exploration and production.

And the trend is away from development and toward preservation. In many cases the economic uses of land is prohibited in favor of a single-purpose use, such as preserving an area where a species of bird may nest, setting aside territory for grizzly bears, reestablishing a prairie ecosystem, or saving a historic site. From this clear need to protect a specific site, the drive for preservation has overwhelmed the concept of multiple use until today vast acreages of federal lands are permanently closed without reason or need, often without an evaluation of the land's aesthetic, biological, recreational, and economic resources. Would-be users — miners, skiers, cattle and sheep ranchers, farmers, campers, timber harvesters, energy firms — are affected.

Groups opposed to the multiple use of federal lands defend their stand in strong language: ". . . the industrial juggernaut must not further degrade the environment . . ." says an official of the Wilderness Society. Authors of the original law governing mineral extraction on federal lands are called a "rapacious gaggle of politicos" motivated by "cupidity and corruption." Under the appealing slogan, "Preserve the Wilderness," the society fights to keep federal lands out of the hands of the "destroyers."

Who are the destroyers?

"Anyone who uses a sheet of paper, who drives an automobile, who has a telephone, a radio, a refrigerator," Dr. Parks says. "Anyone who owns a television set or uses artificial light. Anyone who heats a home, who applies paint, hammers a nail, or flushes a toilet. Even the staunchest of preservationists is such a destroyer."

Are environmentalists hypocritical, then?

Not really. Most hold their convictions with the best of intentions and genuine good will. They fear that without the strongest of safeguards, all public lands would be subject to indiscriminate development. They see bulldozers coming over every horizon. Yet most federal lands have no potential for mining or oil. Mineral lodes and oil- and gas-bearing structures are not common. Their very rarity is what gives their development such high priority. The U.S. Geological Survey has identified 260 million of its onshore acres in the lower 48 states as worth exploring for petroleum, which is a small percentage of the total acreage of federal lands. Of that, oil or gas deposits might lie beneath no more than one out of 10 of those acres. Were oil exploration encouraged to the fullest, few Americans would ever see signs of it. Nor would development, as conducted under today's environmental regulations, result in more than temporary change to the land.

Nonetheless, some environmental professionals continue to insist that more land should be set aside as wilderness. Robert Cahn, Washington editor for *Audubon Magazine*, writing of land within Alaska Wildlife Refuges, says that "the national interest might be served better by wilderness than by development." Cahn praises the Alaska National Interest Lands Conservation Act (which added 10 new national parks, 44 million acres to the National Park, and 56 million acres to the National Wilderness Preservation System) as "the greatest land-protection law in modern history."

And so it is. Yet land withdrawals of such magnitude must inevitably have serious implications for the American economy. "Civilized people want and must have raw materials, especially energy, at moderate prices," emphasizes Dr. Parks. "Nations have gone to the extreme of war to obtain them. For this reason, if for no other, those who advocate the preservation of large wilderness areas known to contain valuable and necessary raw materials are not going to prevail."

Other scientists confirm this view. Dr. William Conway, director of the New York Zoological Society and Bronx Zoo, advises, "It is absolutely impractical to imagine that the human race will not develop the undeveloped lands that remain on this earth." And he calls for a collaborative effort for development and conservation.

Similarly, public officials worried for America's welfare deplore extremes in the name of the environment. John B. Crowell, Jr., Assistant Secretary of Agriculture for Natural Resources and Environment, speaking at an Audubon Society meeting on pressures on the land, told his audience, "We are concerned that additions to the wilderness system be made with careful consideration of the costs . . . of foregoing the long-term availability of resources such as timber, minerals, oil and gas, geothermal power, developed recreation, and forest production."

The wilderness of which he speaks is one of several categories of the federal land system, which includes national parks and national monuments. The former now encompasses 68 million acres of land of exceptional natural, historic, or recreational value; the latter, a much smaller volume, covering the smallest area compatible with proper care or management. National monuments may be single buildings, such as Ford's Theatre in Washington, D.C. or an area of special geologic interest such as the 211,000-acre Dinosaur National Monument in Utah and Colorado.

Mineral extraction is prohibited in national parks and national monuments.

Wildlife preserves account for almost 90 million acres of federal lands. Almost 54 million acres were added in 1980, all in Alaska. Petroleum exploration and production is permitted by law on wildlife refuges, provided proper environmental precautions are taken. In practice, however, few leases have been granted for such activities in these areas.

Wild and scenic rivers comprise another one million acres in the 49 states other than Alaska, and five million acres in Alaska. This relatively small percentage of federal lands has a large impact on energy development because it limits access to other lands. Seismic or exploration crews cannot work across or near scenic rivers, and pipeline rights of way are restricted. Another federal land designation that limits economic use is that of National Grasslands and Wetlands. Petroleum operations are permitted legally, but administrative delays in granting leases drag on for months and even years. Military reservations make up another 30 million acres, and on these lands, public use of all kinds is tightly restricted. Indian lands generally have not presented an access problem, and tribal councils have worked with oil companies to make oil exploration and production compatible with Indian use — and economically desirable.

Two land programs particularly inhibiting to economic development are the Wilderness Preservation System, set up in 1964, and the Endangered Species Act. Together, these programs present a tangle of confusing and sometimes contradictory regulations.

The Wilderness Act defines wilderness as "an area where the earth and its community of life are untrammeled by man, where man himself is a visitor who does not remain." A wilderness area must be at least 5,000 acres in area, roadless, and unimproved. The wilderness program has grown from nine million acres to 80 million acres. If land now under study is added to the system, the wilderness area could be doubled to 167 million acres. The wilderness designation puts land off limits to all but a few users, such as backpackers. Motorized vehicles are prohibited, and road and permanent facilities are not allowed.

Some groups feel this is the way it should be. "Just because (land) is there, it's important, whether you or I or anyone else can get at it or not," says Stephen Chapman, of Minnesota's Clean Air, Clean Water Unlimited. "Perhaps (the land) is even better because we can't get to it."

Of wilderness, an article in *Harper's* magazine explains that "The wilderness concept appears valid if it is recognized for what it is—an attempt to create what are essentially 'ecological museums' in scenic and biologically significant areas of the lands. But 'wilderness' in the hands of environmentalists has become an all-purpose tool for stopping economic activity as well."

Conveniently ignored in all of this is the fact that most government land is not suitable for the "wilderness" category proposed for it. It has little aesthetic or recreational value. It has nothing in common with those spectacular parks such as Yellowstone, Yosemite, the Grand Canyon, or the Grand Teton. When land of scientific and recreational value is subtracted from the total, hundreds of millions of acres remain that can and should contribute to the national welfare through practical use. Its value as a source of raw materials far exceeds its value for recreation or science. Yet these lands, too, are often locked up with the rest.

Ignored, too, is the fact that the environmental impact of such economic activities as oil and gas extraction is slight, temporary, and carried out under strict guidelines that allow the land to revert eventually to its natural state. Yet it continues to be an article of faith among environmental activists that oil and gas activities equate with wholesale and permanent destruction which can be prevented only by prohibiting access to areas where the presence of hydrocarbons is suspected.

The Endangered Species Act is another law that has been widely used to stop economic activity. The story of the snail darter is well known. This small, minnow-sized fish, found in an area about to be inundated by construction of the Tellico Dam, a part of the TVA system, was pronounced an endangered species. As a result, construction of the multimillion-dollar dam was delayed for years at immense cost while scientists studied the possibility of relocating the fish to a new habitat. Eventually, it was discovered that snail darters are not all that uncommon, and the species was removed from the endangered list. But not until millions of dollars and valuable time had been lost.

Even private land is not exempt from the government's land policies. According to the Chase Manhattan Bank, about 30 percent of private land in the lower 48 states "has been effectively withdrawn by the need to comply with mind-boggling environmental laws and regulations. All this without any explicit analysis of the energy loss associated with alternate land uses."

Should Americans worry about the loss of energy resources? Some say no. We have enough oil and gas now, goes the argument. Let's lock up the land until we need its raw materials.

Yet the argument collapses in the face of the facts:

- America imports one-third of its oil at a cost of $50 billion a year.
- America consumes two barrels of oil from its reserves for each barrel of new oil found.
- On today's oil search, tomorrow's energy security depends.

Oil development is a long-range proposition. From the time a decision is made to prospect for oil, some 10 years may be needed to go through the lengthy process of looking for, finding, testing, developing, and producing oil into the nation's supply system. If the oil search is not pressed today, there won't be enough to go around tomorrow.

This reality lends a sense of urgency to the need to resolve a growing impasse over access to public lands. Arbitrary barriers to exploration and development of minerals on most public lands are neither wise nor necessary. A policy of careful, orderly, and steady development is preferable to one of nothing today followed by a crash program tomorrow when the awful truth sinks in.

Isn't that what you would prefer for your three acres? Should you be among the few to claim three acres in the Grand Canyon, you would certainly vote to protect it. But if you are among the many with three parched acres of sagebrush, tumble-weed, and alkali dust in Nevada's Basin and Range Province, or in the frozen bleak and barren tundra of North Alaska, your decision might well be, "Let's see if there isn't some badly needed oil under that land."

A Forest of Manmade Threats Descends on Yellowstone

James F. Coates

James Coates, a Chicago Tribune *staff writer, reports on the myriad problems currently confronting the nation's first and most famous national park. Coates suggests that our good-faith efforts to facilitate heavy tourist traffic and commercial activities in areas of great natural beauty inevitably create greater problems than the ones such efforts were intended to solve. His assessment of Yellowstone's dilemmas (made before the devastating forest fires of 1988) serves as another example that supports the preservationists' argument that multiple use and maximum public access policies have abysmal track records.*

INSPIRATION POINT, Wyo. — Millions of Americans have come here to gaze in awe over the rim of the Yellowstone Canyon at the pencil-thin green strand at the bottom of the abyss that is, in fact, the 75-foot-wide Yellowstone River.

From there, their eyes travel up past towering cliffs of yellow and red rock pocked with steam-belching geysers to the thundering Yellowstone Falls, where white water churns off a 308-foot precipice.

As chief administrator of Yellowstone National Park, Robert Barbee looks at that stunning scene each day and becomes troubled about ever-more-vexing signs that modern society is slowly — but most measurably — ruining one of its few remaining natural treasures.

Copper foundries 900 miles away in Arizona and even across the border in Mexico send chemicals into the air, which come out of the skies as acid rain over Yellowstone Lake, which feeds the falls.

Barbee said a recent rainfall acidity pH reading of 4.4 was similar "to the worst" recorded in Canada when many lakes were said to have "died" because they turned acid.

"We don't view this as at the crisis stage, at least not yet," Barbee said. "But it's something we are watching very closely.

"We're watching a lot of things closely, it seems," he added ruefully.

A private group, the Greater Yellowstone Coalition, has outlined 88 threats to Yellowstone that its experts warn could mean the loss of many of the natural wonders that still are commonplace here in America's first national park.

Among these threats are:

- Oil companies pressuring to drill gas wells just across the park's boundaries in areas where grizzly bears feed when their food in the park gives out. The bears will not seek food so close to humans, and the result could be eradication of the park's estimated 350 grizzlies.

James Coates, "A Forest of Manmade Threats Descends on Yellowstone," *The Chicago Tribune* 19 May 1985, sec. 1.

- Developers planning to build a ski resort called Ski Yellowstone just across the park's border at West Yellowstone, Mont., in the path of major elk and bear migration routes.

- Cattle and sheep ranchers who graze their animals in national forests alongside the park demand that buffalo be shot when they wander outside the park. Last winter 88 bison were shot by the Montana Department of Game and Fish near Gardiner, Mont.

- Korean businessmen hire American poachers to sneak into the park and shoot bear for their gall bladders and elk for their antlers, both of which are sold for high profits as aphrodisiacs in Korea and China.

- Timber companies have obtained permits to clear cut logs in watersheds that environmentalists warn will ruin fly fishing by causing mud to collect in the waters of the awesome Yellowstone, Madison and Henry's Fork Rivers.

- Several state and federal dam projects near the park's boundaries pose similar threats to fly fishing because the projects will stem the migration of fish.

As park officials put the finishing touches on plans to handle the annual influx of tourists, Barbee noted that virtually every well-known aspect of Yellowstone appears threatened by the ever-more-populous world that presses in from every direction.

Last year, for example, there were more incidents in which human beings ran afoul of grizzly bears in the park than ever before.

One tourist, Britt Fredenhagen, 25, was killed by a grizzly and a dozen people were mauled with varying degrees of severity. There had been only three previous cases of bears killing humans in the park since 1916.

"We just have ever more people who want to enjoy the same country where the bears range, and that means more contacts and more problems," the park chief said.

After the attacks began last summer, the Montana Game and Fish Department suggested opening a limited hunting season for grizzlies but abandoned the idea, at least temporarily, after protests from environmentalists.

"I think we could solve our grizzly bear problem if we could hunt two or three a year," Don Bianchi, public information officer for the department, said at the time.

But, Barbee noted, the idea of shooting bison when they cross the park boundary remains "an active one because the animals carry a disease called brucellosis, which causes ranchers' cows to abort their calves.

"There is brucellosis all over the place besides from buffalo," he said. "Elk carry it. So do rodents and even some insects."

Montana's shooting of the 88 bison that wandered outside the park last winter created controversy when it was learned that because of a bureaucratic snafu the carcasses were allowed to rot in a warehouse instead of being used for food, as the state had planned.

Barbee noted that there even has been speculation — which he discounts — that oil and gas wells near the park have tapped into thermal areas, throwing Old Faithful's schedule of eruptions off by 10 minutes and causing other geysers to stop erupting altogether.

A major study by biologists, chemists, geologists and other experts with the Greater Yellowstone Coalition concluded that unexpected pressures on the national forests, mountains and farm and ranch country that surround the 2 million-acre national park are threatening to change park conditions that are close to the way they were before the first settler—white or Indian—arrived.

Bob Anderson, executive director of the coalition, said in an interview: "We look at many projects or policies and we see great danger from their cumulative effects.

"Any one of them could be tolerated, but taken together, they will destroy this national treasure."

WE CAN HAVE BOTH OIL AND
WILDLIFE PROTECTION
Frank H. Murkowski

*In 1980 Congress passed the Alaskan National Interest Lands Conservation Act,
which set aside nearly a third of the largest state in the Union as federally protected
wilderness or potential wilderness areas. This landmark preservation measure triggered a firestorm of protest from many Alaskan residents. Frank Murkowski, a
Republican senator from Alaska, is addressing pending congressional legislation that
would permit oil exploration on portions of these preserved areas. His arguments
reflect those of many angry Alaskans in response to what they consider heavy-
handed, imperious efforts by outsiders to subvert the commercial interests of those
who live in the state to the aesthetic concerns of the occasional, elitist visitor.*

It seems to be the case in the United States that officials never put a traffic light
on the corner until *after* someone's been hurt. Unfortunately, this has been our
nation's approach to the questions surrounding our long-term energy needs. We
never seem to ask ourselves, where will the oil come from? Until, that is, we're in
the midst of an oil crisis. Then we seem to ask, where did it go?

The 100th Congress has a historic opportunity to reverse that trend and take a
major step toward ensuring that our nation remains less dependent on foreign oil.
In the coming months, we will begin debate on what will probably be the largest
energy-related decision of the late 20th century — oil exploration inside the Arctic
National Wildlife Refuge (ANWR).

Some environmental organizations argue that Alaska's environment would be
destroyed if oil exploration took place in the refuge. These arguments have a familiar
ring. Less than 20 years ago, the same organizations were leading the charge with
the same issues against the Alaska pipeline. They said the same things back then,
and were subsequently proved very wrong.

Oil has been produced on Alaska's North Slope at Prudhoe Bay now for 10 years.
Each day, nearly 2 million barrels is shipped through the 800-mile trans-Alaska
pipeline — across Alaska's tundra and permafrost — without damage to the ecology.
That oil amount accounts for about 25 percent of the total US production — a key
component of the country's energy security.

Those who attempt to exploit fear over the well-being of caribou that live in
ANWR ignore the Prudhoe Bay experience. The commonly heard assertion that
caribou cannot survive alongside prudent oil development is simply not true. There
were about 3,000 caribou in Prudhoe Bay in 1972. Today that number has increased
fivefold, to nearly 14,000. There is no either/or choice. We can have both oil and
wildlife protection.

Opponents of exploration in the refuge also fail to mention that we are talking
about opening only 1.5 million acres of an 18 million-acre refuge that already has 8

Frank H. Murkowski, "We Can Have Both Oil and Wildlife Protection," *The Christian Science Monitor*
17 March 1987.

million acres of designated wilderness. Even if the Coastal Plain were at full development, less than 0.0001 percent (1/1,000 of 1 percent) of the reserve would be touched.

There is little question that our country's crude oil needs must be met. But surprisingly, amid the fighting in Iraq, attacks on oil tankers in the Persian Gulf, and a serious downturn in US domestic oil exploration, there are still those expressing the sentiment that the nation no longer needs Alaskan oil.

Keep in mind the reason the US needs oil from Alaska. Our dependence on imported oil has jumped from 27 percent to 40 percent. That is significantly greater than the level of our dependence on imported oil in the '70s, which precipitated the energy crisis.

The US must have a balanced energy policy to help us meet energy needs in the 21st century. But we cannot rely solely on energy conservation and development of alternative sources of energy. Although there are enough petroleum reserves on earth to meet worldwide needs for at least the next 75 years, three-quarters of those reserves are in the volatile Middle East. The nations of that area have the ability to price their oil at a level that will be expensive for US consumers, yet not high enough to make development of alternative sources economically feasible. Without question, new sources of oil must be found.

Remember also that currently we are talking only about exploring for oil. There is no guarantee that any will be found; and even if Congress gave the go-ahead today for oil exploration to begin in ANWR, it would be 10 to 15 years before oil would be on line and ready to be delivered to US consumers.

The US has the strongest environmental laws in the world, and Alaskans are dedicated to maintaining clean air, water, and that special Alaska life style. Our laws will ensure that exploration in the reserve will be consistent with the protection of the other resources, like caribou, that are important to our national heritage.

The US proved with the Alaska pipeline that development could be done right. I am confident ANWR can be explored with the same success.

Let's not wait until the next energy crisis — when we are all once again standing in gas lines and blaming the government — to worry about our nation's energy future. Our security depends on Congress acting wisely and doing so now.

Close the Arctic National Wildlife Refuge to Oilmen

Morris K. Udall

Morris K. Udall, a longtime Democratic congressman from Arizona and the former chairman of the House Interior and Insular Affairs Committee, has long been an ardent defender of federal wilderness preservation policy. Like Frank Murkowski in the previous essay, he is reacting to pending congressional legislation that would permit oil exploration in certain potential wilderness areas protected by the 1980 Alaskan National Interest Lands Conservation Act. His arguments reflect those of many preservationists against expanding commercial development in a state that remains America's last frontier — and a frontier of spectacular natural beauty.

Above the Arctic Circle, in the remotest corner of the United States, is a land of stark beauty between Alaska's Brooks Range and the Beaufort Sea. The coastal plain of the Arctic National Wildlife Refuge (ANWR), often thought of as a barren expanse of nothingness, actually nurses life astounding in its diversity, richness, and wildness.

Much attention focuses on the Porcupine caribou herd, the largest in the US, whose annual trek across the continent is a source not only of wonder but of food, clothing, and livelihood to many native peoples. But many other creatures depend on this fragile swath of permafrost as well — polar bears, brown bears, musk oxen, wolves, wolverines, Arctic foxes, seals, 108 species of birds, and numerous species of fish — and together they display the magnificent pageantry of life in this hostile and delicate world.

Although the term "wildlife refuge" is arguably a misnomer where animals are hunted and habitat disturbed, here it speaks with forceful eloquence. Of the more than 1,000 miles of Alaskan coastline above the Arctic Circle, the 100 miles of ANWR coastal plain is the only coastline not now available for commercial exploitation. This, indeed, is a last, true refuge for Arctic wildlife in America.

These facts are beyond dispute. But if the Reagan administration, the oil companies, and their supporters have their way, even this last haven will be sacrificed to the insatiable thirst for more oil. True to form, they tell us we can exploit this distant, sensitive land for all its industrial worth without disturbing the wildlife that has inhabited it for millennia. If the two fundamental assertions of development forces were true — that the coastal plain harbors vast oil resources and that they could be developed without risk — their argument might be compelling. But their assertions are at best highly speculative, and at worst deeply in error.

Is there a lot of oil beneath the coastal plain? The most honest answer is that no one knows. Only the most preliminary geophysical work has ever been conducted, and only one well has ever been drilled. But a legally mandated draft study issued by the Reagan administration itself provides some insight.

Morris K. Udall, "Close the Arctic National Wildlife Refuge to Oilmen," *The Christian Science Monitor* 17 March 1987.

In Alaska especially, it matters far less how much oil is "in place" than how much is economically recoverable. Alaskan oil is extremely expensive to find, produce, and transport. Only supergiant fields are feasible, and then only under favorable economic conditions.

So, tucked away in the footnotes is the real news of this bullish report. Even if we had oil prices of $33 per barrel and 6 percent inflation, there would be an 81 percent probability that no economically recoverable reserves of any amount will be found on the coastal plain. Even if we are lucky enough to hit on the 1-in-5 chance that we might find any such reserves, the strongest likelihood is that we could produce only about 6 percent of Prudhoe's 10 billion barrels; odds of producing about 25 percent are about even.

It is outrageous for an administration that has actively engaged in dismantling a broad, sensible energy policy to claim that we need to open this area up in the name of national security. If our national security is at stake, why has the administration destroyed funding for conservation and alternative energy strategies, pushed hard for relaxation of fuel economy standards, vetoed legislation to set energy efficiency standards for major appliances, and opposed many other rational energy policies, any one of which alone would replace the energy that could conceivably be produced from ANWR?

Whenever constructive steps like these are proposed, the Reagan administration always says there is something more important, from budget cuts to free-market theories. When it comes to private development of public resources, however, the US has an energy crisis.

Industry also has a way of continually arguing that the one area it is restrained from exploring is the one area where it really has to explore. It was not long ago that Congress was told in no uncertain terms that to restrict activity in the National Petroleum Reserve-Alaska to the west of Prudhoe Bay was unthinkable because of its vast potential. A few years and a few dry holes later, NPRA is yesterday's forgotten energy cookie jar.

Perhaps you think that even another drop of oil is worth it if it can be produced without risk to the environment. Certainly, the industry is not shy about pointing to its record at Prudhoe Bay and issuing assurances that all will be well in ANWR. But Prudhoe Bay and ANWR are not that much alike. The coastal plain is a much narrower strip between mountains and sea and provides habitat for far more wildlife than Prudhoe.

Moreover, the industry has had only some 15 years' experience with wildlife in the Arctic. To come to grand conclusions about the long-term effects of development on wildlife from such a brief period is self-serving and foolish. Recently published studies of wildlife populations around national parks in the Lower 48 provide very sobering data on the damaging effects of even simple human constructions — fences and roads — over periods of 30 to 50 years.

And again, the administration's own report offers data that damn the conclusions they seek to draw from it. For example, the report estimates that 20 to 40 percent of the Porcupine caribou herd would be eliminated or disturbed by development. Yet the administration argues in its conclusion that all effects on wildlife can be mitigated. Similar destruction of other species could be expected, according to the administration report.

We would not think of putting dams in the Grand Canyon or tapping Yellowstone's Old Faithful, even though the chances of producing useful energy this way are 100 percent. Before the developers convince me that we should take an enormous gamble with the one-of-a-kind resource we have on the coastal plain of the Arctic National Wildlife Refuge, they are going to have to come up with far better policies and arguments.

THE BATTLE FOR THE WILDERNESS
Michael Satchell

Michael Satchell, a writer for U.S. News & World Report, surveys the nature and extent of the preservationist-conservationist controversy in late-twentieth-century America. Notice that the furor swirls around two basic issues: (1) how uninhabited, federally owned lands should be used for long-term public welfare and (2) how much access the public should be allowed to federal wilderness areas or national parks. Because this essay is replete with examples of arguments from both sides of these two issues, you would do well to read it early in your research on this topic.

Two centuries ago, America's wilderness was a vast frontier to be tamed and developed by a young and burgeoning Republic. Today, it is a resource that conservationists seek to preserve and nurture for present and future generations. Protecting the best of our outdoor heritage is an enduring American ethic reaching deep into the national psyche. Yellowstone, for example, was established as the first national park in 1872 even as sodbusters were plowing up the prairie and land-hungry settlers were rolling west in Conestogas. But today's wilderness advocates are approaching a crucial stage in their preservation struggle. "Our wild lands," says former Senator Gaylord Nelson of Wisconsin, counselor to the Wilderness Society, "are our most important endangered species."

In 1991, President Bush is expected to send to Congress his recommendations for protecting primitive areas administered by the federal Bureau of Land Management (BLM) in 11 Western states. The nation has 90.7 million acres designated by Congress as federally protected wilderness. This amounts to 1.8 percent of the land in the Lower 48 states, or 4 percent of the country's 2.2 billion acres if Alaska is included. Two congressional bills would add 11.5 million more acres in California and Utah, and hearings on the California measure begin this month on Capitol Hill. The BLM is also studying 25 million acres of its holdings for inclusion in the system.

SHRINKING OPPORTUNITY

Because of the rapid pace of development, it will almost certainly be the last opportunity to add significant tracts of pristine federal land to the nation's wilderness mosaic. The likely outcome of the congressional proposals and the BLM recommendations will be a compromise — somewhere between 10 and 15 million acres — that will hearten but not placate environmentalists. They would like to see the nation's wilderness acreage doubled.

The battle pits preservation groups against myriad motorized-recreation and commercial interets. The conservationists' creed is that pristine areas, once developed, are lost forever as wilderness. The environmentalists won a major victory last week

Michael Satchell, "The Battle for the Wilderness," *U.S. News & World Report* 3 July 1989.

when a U.S. court of appeals strengthened their ability to block commercial development on 180 million acres of BLM land in 17 Western states. The ruling gives the groups standing to sue the BLM in development cases because of their recreational interest in these lands. But the antiwilderness coalition will fight adding even a single acre. The trinity of their argument is that wilderness designation prevents access, wastes resources and costs jobs.

This growing conflict is a clash of cultures often divided by history and geography: Rural Westerners whose pioneer forebears settled, developed and sometimes died for these lands, and mostly urban environmentalists, many from the East, who came late to the scene to demand a voice in how this virgin terrain is administered. The basic issue is whether to open up pristine land for what the federal government terms "multiple use" activities. These include mining, logging, livestock grazing, oil, gas and geothermal development, off-road-vehicle recreation and other commercial ventures. In protected wilderness, you can hike, backpack, ride a horse, canoe, fish and—except in national parks and selected wildlife refuges—hunt. Roads, motorized vehicles, permanent structures and almost all commercial ventures are prohibited.

"The next five years are going to be critical for protecting the land," says Paul Pritchard, president of the National Parks and Conservation Association, whose wish-list agenda includes establishing 46 more national parks. Among the possibilities are a tall-grass prairie park in Kansas or Oklahoma, a preserve in Big Sur, Calif., and a park in the Florida Keys. But Charles Cushman, the determinedly antiwilderness executive director of the Multiple-Use Land Alliance, says the conservationists are being greedy. "How much do these selfish, single-purpose, special-interest preservationist groups want?" he asks. "When will they be satisfied?"

In some areas, the issue has raised passions beyond a civil exchange of differences. At the Escalante Sawmill in Escalante, Utah, workers sport baseball caps and pickups bear bumper stickers reading "SUWA Sucks," a reference to the Southern Utah Wilderness Alliance, whose agenda includes more-restrictive logging in the nearby Dixie National Forest. Some local preservationists, afraid to reveal their membership in the alliance, ask to receive their SUWA literature in unmarked envelopes.

At the heart of the conflict are 250 million acres of both multiple-use and unprotected lands administered by the BLM in the Western states of the Lower 48. They include vast roadless territories in the deserts of new Mexico and Arizona, the dunes and mountains of the Southern California desert and the red-rock buttes and slick-rock canyons of southern Utah. The stunning diversity of ecosystems includes shorelines, wetlands, wild rivers, grasslands, cactus plains, alpine meadows, forests, volcanic craters and towering snowcapped mountain ranges. These lands are also the federal government's most diverse and expansive wildlife habitat, supporting bear, antelope, elk, bighorn sheep and scores of threatened or endangered species including grizzlies, golden eagles and desert tortoises. Beyond providing hunting, fishing and backpacking, they offer watershed protection, archaeological-study areas, bioscience resources and such intangible values as scenic beauty, solitude and spiritual renewal.

LANDS WORTH SAVING

The BLM was founded in 1946 primarily to manage grazing and other commercial development on public lands in the West. In 1976, Congress passed a law that reorganized the agency and ordered it to survey its land holdings and recommend by 1991 those worthy of wilderness status. In 1980, the BLM chose 25 million of these 250 million acres as potential wilderness that met the criteria for protection: Lands that were roadless and undeveloped and offered outstanding opportunities for recreation and solitude. The antiwilderness forces want provisions that will prevent further consideration of BLM lands for protection beyond the agency's 1991 recommendations. Conservationists, who believe the BLM's wilderness-study areas should be triple the 25 million acres, accuse the agency of caving in to development proponents. And based on BLM's preliminary recommendations, they fear the agency will list only a fraction of those 25 million acres for protection. In California, the BLM is slated to recommend only 2.3 million of its 17.1 million acres for protection and 1 million of its 12.2 million acres in Arizona. Former Governor Bruce Babbitt, an avid environmentalist, calls Arizona's proposed allocation "pathetic."

Nationwide, urban residents with financial means are increasingly moving to unspoiled areas, particularly those offering scenic beauty and upscale recreation amenities like golf and skiing. Jackson Hole, Wyo., at the foot of the Grand Tetons, is one of the most popular sites. But conservationists charge that burgeoning condominium developments in such environmentally critical areas are aesthetic blights that often have a severe impact on wildlife. The Spring Creek ranch development at Jackson Hole, for example, not only straddles a ridge and mars a sublimely scenic vista but also occupies traditional winter range used for millenniums by mule deer.

Does the nation really need more primal land for breathing space? Spurring the protectionist drive is the fact that many of our major outdoor resources are gradually being compromised and degraded, just as South America's tropical rain forests are being leveled and Africa's wildlife is being decimated. National parks from Maine to California are overcrowded. Conservationists cite excessive logging, mining, road building, grazing, off-road-vehicle use and commercial development in national forests and on BLM lands. These provide buffer zones for the hard-pressed crown-jewel parks and are themselves an often overcrowded recreational resource. The result is air, water and noise pollution, soil erosion, wildlife-habitat destruction and a loss of scenic values. Consider:

- All of the big national parks face serious threats. At Grand Canyon, for example, the number of visitors has increased from 2.5 million to 3.9 million in the past three years, often bringing to the park's south rim automobile gridlock that is reminiscent of the bumper-to-bumper traffic that jams Yosemite Valley. For an average of 42 days each winter, canyon tourists must peer into its awesome depths, or across to the other rim, through a murky soup of air pollution. Florida's Everglades, America's premier wetland and its most endangered national park, is drying up as water is diverted for cities and agriculture. Pesticide pollution has killed off 90 percent of the park's wading-bird flocks, and nesting bald eagles have declined 70 percent. In North Carolina and Tennessee, Great Smoky Mountains National Park, the most popular big preserve with over 10 million annual visitors, is looking for protective relief from urban encroachment and logging in adjacent national forests. Bills to set aside 467,000 of the park's 519,000 acres as protected wilderness, to prevent new road construction and assure future pristine integrity, have languished in Congress for 12 years.

- Two million acres of open land are lost to commercial development annually. More than half of the nation's 215 million acres of environmentally critical wetlands have been destroyed since the 1950s. Only 10 to 14 percent of the ancient forests in the Pacific Northwest, where today's trees were saplings when Columbus sailed for America, remain standing, and many are falling to the loggers' chain saws. In Kansas and Oklahoma, just 1 percent of the original tall-grass prairie remains.

- New England's major forests, owned by paper-and-pulp companies, offer the nation's only opportunity to reclaim substantial tracts of additional wild lands from private holdings. As the industry declines regionally, attempts by groups like the Wilderness Society to purchase and preserve some of these forests are threatened by land speculators and a vacation-home-building frenzy. There are only 192,000 acres of protected federal wilderness in the Northeastern states from Maine to Maryland, yet almost a quarter of the nation's population lives there.

AN AMERICAN FASCINATION

The modern emphasis on preserving rather than exploiting primitive land began in political earnest just a quarter of a century ago. This September will mark the 25th anniversary of the 1964 Wilderness Act, which initially set aside 9.1 million acres of national forests to remain forever in their natural state. Rugged, unfettered and challenging, wilderness has long been a romantic metaphor for the American spirit, just as its heroic cowboy figure exemplifies the mythic best of the American character. As cities continue to expand, population increases and the daily grind grows more fractious and tense, wilderness offers a respite far from the madding crowd. When oil befouls a landscape, medical wastes wash ashore and toxic dumps pollute neighborhoods, just the thought of a pristine wilderness haven to reflect upon, perhaps to flee to, is for many a deeply reassuring idea.

Getting away from it all means different things to different people. For the Bell family of Long Beach, Calif., wilderness relaxation means an exhilarating 70-to-100-mile weekend motorcycle race across the desert. Sam and Dana Bell, along with their three daughters, ages 10, 9 and 7, pilot their own motorcycles, and a 5-year-old son rides along with his father. They feel that wilderness designation threatens their hobby. Environmentalists have petitioned the U.S. Department of the Interior to have the California desert tortoise declared an endangered species. "Desert wilderness should be recreation land for people," says Dana Bell. "Now they want to deny us our favorite activity. It doesn't make sense."

The catalog of preservationist fears over threatened wild lands does little to convince multiple-use advocates that more wilderness is a wise investment in America's outdoor future. The broad, loosely knit antiwilderness coalition includes livestock and extractive industries, hunters and outfitters, off-road-vehicle (ORV) enthusiasts and the ORV industry, motor-home campers, local governments and business and civic organizations. Lining up with them are such national groups as the American Farm Bureau Federation, the National Grange and the National Rifle Association.

THE OPPOSITION ORGANIZES

Unlike the nation's powerful, sophisticated and well-financed conservation organizations such as the Sierra Club and the National Wildlife Federation, groups like the Multiple-Use Land Alliance and the Blue Ribbon Coalition are only now beginning to organize effectively. They are pulling together dozens of disparate local and regional special-interest groups from desert motorcycle racers to rockhounds, miners to woolgrowers. The once disjointed movement now has a coast-to-coast computer network; holds national conventions; stages press conferences in Washington, D.C.; lobbies Congress, and presses its antiwilderness message on self-produced cable-television programs.

Dr. Loren Lutz, a semiretired dentist in Pasadena, Calif., is an avid hunter and fervent wildlife conservationist. As founder of the Society for the Conservation of Bighorn Sheep, one of his continuing interests is building wildlife drinking fountains called guzzlers. These are often located in the desert and are supplied by rainwater gathered in dammed-up arroyos. The water sustains game animals in barren areas. "I support wilderness, but too much land under protection is counterproductive," he contends. "It means closing roads and preventing access by off-road vehicles. No access means we can't build or service our guzzlers. No guzzlers mean no wildlife."

The antiwilderness agenda is philosophically rooted in a longstanding anger at the federal government's control of vast areas in the Western states. For example, 85 percent of Nevada, 64 percent of Utah and Idaho, half of Wyoming and Oregon and 46 percent of California are technically owned, though hardly controlled, by the American taxpayer. This is a particularly nettlesome issue in Utah, where taming the wilderness and reaping its bounty are the historical foundation of a Mormon theocracy that abhors allowing any land to lie fallow and commercially unproductive. "Residents out West resent federal interference like the Brazilians resent foreigners telling them what to do with the Amazon," says Wallace Stegner, an author, lecturer and elder statesman of the environmental movement.

In this preservation-vs.-multiple-use wrangle, one person's environmental desecration is another's economic development. The financial health of many rural communities is tied to the boom-bust cycle of the West's extractive industries such as coal, oil, natural gas, timber, uranium, and synfuels. Before falling world oil prices triggered the collapse of the energy boom in the early 1980s, Exxon estimated that the West held $860 billion worth of coal and oil-shale reserves that would provide 870,000 new jobs. But these are lean times. A recent study for the Western Governors' Association found that 1 in 3 rural Western counties is losing population, jobs and income. In the search for answers, or perhaps scapegoats, environmentalists are often blamed for these economic woes. The conservationists in turn argue that most wilderness areas do not contain significant, economically viable reserves of minerals.

A DWINDLING ACTIVITY

"Jobs or woodpeckers" is the usual thrust of the multiuse argument, with wilderness advocates often portrayed as elitist outsiders eager to lock up valuable lands for their exclusive use. Recent studies have handed the multiple-use forces fresh ammunition. Backpacking into wild areas, as measured by permits, sales of lightweight camping equipment and ranger observations, is slowly declining as the baby-boom generation ages. Last year, 1.6 million backpackers camped in wilderness areas, compared with 2.4 million a decade ago.

Calvin Black is an example of rural Westerners who view wilderness designation as an economic blow to local communities. A Blanding, Utah, business entrepreneur and politician, Black scorns conservationists' claims that wilderness boosts local tourism economies. As evidence, he cites a 50 percent population drop in the last four decades, a continuing erosion of jobs and moribund economies in three southern Utah counties located near five national parks. "The backpacking crowd characterizes the wilderness issue as protection or destruction, but that is not a fair debate," Black says. "You can protect the values of the land and still have multiple use. We are good stewards."

Today's fight over public-land use recalls the brief and inconclusive Sagebrush Rebellion of the late 1970s, when some conservative Westerners sought to persuade the federal government to relinquish control of its lands to the states. The movement, which fizzled along with the Western energy boom, viewed federal land control as economic socialism. This anti-Washington sentiment spawned a generation of prodevelopment advocates including former President Reagan, Interior Secretaries James Watt and Donald Hodel and BLM chief Robert Burford. All were firmly committed to intensive economic use of the Western wild lands, and their legacy continues. While George Bush's preservation commitment has yet to undergo a conclusive test, his Interior Secretary, Manual Lujan, Jr., is regarded by the conservation lobby as prodevelopment and insensitive to preservation issues. Environmental leaders who met recently with Lujan were startled when he told them he favored livestock grazing in the national parks and characterized BLM lands as "a place with a lot of grass for cows." Lujan says he was joking, but his nomination of several Watt–Hodel-era disciples to key Interior slots is expected to bolster the multiuse movement.

The extent of Western antipreservation sentiment was dramatically demonstrated last fall when Montana's incumbent Democratic senator, John Melcher, was unexpectedly defeated. Melcher was the author of a painstakingly crafted, 2.2-million-acre wilderness bill for his state that sailed through both houses of Congress. Just before the November election, former President Reagan vetoed the bill, contending it would cost the state jobs. It was only the second time a President has refused to sign a wilderness measure. Republican Conrad Burns, a virtual unknown, exploited the issue in the logging communities, Melcher's substantial lead quickly evaporated, and Burns won by 13,000 votes.

As the countdown to the congressional deadline of 1991 continues, some hard-line preservationists like Susan Tixier, associate executive director of the Southern Utah Wilderness Alliance, vow to fight for every acre and refuse to compromise. Others believe that future economic growth in the rural West must be tied to environmental principles. Areas dependent on livestock, mining, oil, timber and gas, they say, need assistance to develop alternative jobs if potential resource lands are set aside. The strongest allies of the multiple-use forces are the BLM and the Forest Service, whose mandate and policies have historically favored resource development over preservation.

In this modern incarnation of the range wars fought a century ago by cattlemen, sheepherders and farmers, millions of acres are again the prize. But this time, as 1991 approaches and each side presses its campaign to influence Congress and the public, far more is at stake than homesteads, water and grazing rights. Hard-pressed rural Western communities tied to extractive industries face this new conflict in terms of a fight for economic survival. Those who exult in a roar of unleashed horsepower with their wilderness experience seek the freedom to continue their recreational lifestyle. And for preservationists, the outcome will determine the essence of the great outdoors experience for millions of Americans who seek the traditional wilderness sojourn of primal scenery, physical challenge and perfect solitude.

In Alaska, the Future Is Now

Michael Roger

Michael Roger reports on the ongoing controversy over the vast tracts of federal lands (consisting of most of the largest state in the Union) that came to a boil with the passage of the Alaskan National Interest Lands Conservation Act in 1980. You will want to compare the arguments cited in this essay with those expressed by Murkowski and Udall in essays appearing earlier in the chapter.

Alaskans call us Outsiders—or worse. When environmentalists temporarily blocked the lucrative Alaskan oil pipeline in the early 1970s, a popular bumper sticker in the state was "Let the Bastards Freeze in the Dark." Now bumpers proclaim: "We Don't Give a Damn How They Do It Outside." The xenophobia is authentic, but the phrase is bravado. For, like it or not, Alaskans will continue to take orders from the Outside because while they live there, the land is *ours*. The sea into which the Exxon Valdez hemorrhaged is *ours*. The national forests that are being harvested belong to *us*. The frozen tundra along the Arctic Ocean, which may cover a vast vault of oil, doesn't belong to the oil companies or the Eskimos: it's *yours*. Fully 60 percent of the state is owned by the federal government; most of it is wilderness and the decisions about the future of our last frontier are the legitimate concern of every American.

The next great battle will be fought over the fate of the Arctic National Wildlife Refuge. ANWR is a Maine-size piece of real estate hundreds of miles above the Arctic Circle, chill even in August. This is a place where humans can look up from their campsite breakfast to see two dozen buff-brown caribou trot by, pursued moments later by five wolves, pale gray and black, loping silently up the treeless valley. It includes stretches of the stark, snow-topped Brooks Range, cut by blue-gray rivers that stream down from glaciers into the forbidding Beaufort Sea. Much of ANWR is flat, green marshy tundra, home to herds of caribou, hordes of mosquitoes and occasional hulking musk oxen—but near impassable terrain for humans.

ANWR is also the precise distillation of the competing forces that shape the 49th state; geologists believe it is home to America's last great untapped reservoir of crude oil. The refuge could satisfy, at best, a year of the nation's oil needs. But at present prices, that's worth about $60 billion, and $10 billion in royalties for Alaska and the federal government. Oil development would directly impact only a tiny percentage of the massive wildlife refuge's land area. And millions of Americans would burn that oil, compared to the handful of wilderness buffs who will ever view wolves and caribou in what is arguably the most expensive tourist destination in the United States. "The day you see gas lines in the Lower 48," says one oil-company representative, "ANWR will open to us."

Congress will decide whether to permit drilling. Environmentalists will lobby hard to keep ANWR pure wilderness—but not so most Alaskans. "We're 96 percent de facto wilderness," says Gov. Steven Cowper. "And economic opportunities are

Michael Roger, "In Alaska, the Future Is Now," *Newsweek* 18 September 1989.

hard to come by." At $8 to $10 billion a year in revenue, oil dwarfs the second-place fishing industry, which earns little more than $1 billion. Every Alaskan over six months of age receives a yearly tax-free oil dividend that will approach $900 in 1989; for some rural families, that's as much as a third of their cash income. But by the year 2000, the existing oil fields will yield only half their current flow, and so, for Alaska, oil from ANWR would be a short-term salvation.

ANWR reflects a basic truth of the far north: Alaskans may love wilderness, but they also need to make a living. Choosing sides on an environmental controversy may depend on whether one has a job or not. Such basic economics inform every major decision facing Alaska. The issues range from the future of national forest land to the prospect of rearranging Alaska's awe-inspiring landscape to get at the coal reserves that lie beneath the surface.

- The Tongass National Forest is an immense rain forest in southeastern Alaska, a dense green sprawl of spruce and hemlock with wildlife ranging from deer to grizzly bear. For three decades, the animals have shared the woods with commercial woodsmen; by now, parts of the Tongass have been so heavily logged that hikers and kayakers are often startled when they find themselves wandering into stark expanses of clear-cut forest. The intense logging — about 300,000 acres out of a total forested 5.5 million have been cut thus far — is a legacy of the '50s, when the U.S. Forest Service granted unusually generous 50-year contracts to help a local wood-pulp industry take root.

    Environmentalists contend that the clear-cutting of the Tongass is both bad conservation and bad business. The federal government pays millions in subsidies each year to keep the industry competitive in the world market. Recent Japanese acquisitions in the pulp trade add an international element. "The Tongass is now being cut for Japanese rayon and cellophane," says Jack Hession, Alaska representative of the Sierra Club. "Why should Japan remain 20 percent forested while we scalp our last remaining temperate rain forest?" Last spring the House of Representatives passed a bill protecting the most valuable wilderness areas of the Tongass; the Senate will take up the issue this fall.

- Alaska remains this nation's primary source of extractable minerals. Aside from oil and gold, however, few of these deposits have been tapped. Developers are already planning to pipe trillions of cubic feet of natural gas from the North Slope, to be liquefied for shipment to Pacific Rim markets. Since this project will probably use the existing pipeline corridor, environmental impact should be minimal. But arctic Alaska also holds two thirds of this nation's remaining coal; the energy-hungry Pacific nations may someday make its extraction profitable. Environmentalists fear that once oil and gas are exhausted, widespread mining could disfigure the landscape far more than the oil industry ever has.

- The 1980 Alaskan National Interest Lands Conservation Act, the most sweeping conservation measure ever assembled by Congress, designated 104 million acres of Alaskan land as wilderness. While some Alaskans feared that the state's economic future had been sacrificed to environmentalism, the Lands Act had less impact on Alaska's economy than did the subsequent sag in oil prices. But the Act has loopholes; the prospect of oil exploration in the Arctic National Wildlife Refuge was specifically left open. A more subtle issue is the extensive private "inholdings" on wilderness land—often mining claims made before wilderness status was granted. One such inholding has already resulted in a private lodge constructed in the middle of Denali National Park. Congress will soon inventory Alaskan inholdings, but the options may be limited: the cost of purchasing those lands could be as much as $100 million.

- The 1971 Alaska Native Claims Settlement Act, resolving Indian and Eskimo land claims, was the most radical native treaty in this nation's history. Rather than establishing reservations, ANCSA created 13 native regional corporations, which received both cash and land to develop. Individual natives received shares in the corporations. If the corporations succeed, Alaska natives will prosper for generations. But the corporate nature of the settlement puts the fate of native lands at the mercy of the marketplace. During the '90s, some native corporations may permit their members to sell shares on the open market; a takeover artist or a Tokyo bank could someday buy up control of native lands.

No force as powerful as the oil boom is likely to strike Alaska again— but that's not necessarily good news for the Alaskan wilderness. The erosion of wilderness often occurs in small steps. The trans-Alaskan oil pipeline, for example, was the largest private construction project in history, on a scale more befitting war than commerce. Yet the pipeline itself, a silver ribbon four feet wide and 800 miles long, is a model of environmental caution, with minimal impact on its surroundings.

Not so its accompanying construction road, which cuts through the heart of the Brooks Range, forever opening Alaska's remote North Slope to development. Environmentalists urged that the road should never be opened to the public; today, while a permit is required for passage, the road is essentially open, its shoulders sometimes dotted with trash. There is already one truck stop; more signs of civilization will appear unless the federal and state governments act to control development.

The local urge to develop reflects the pioneer's view of wilderness. This is, after all, a state where one can hunt in the national parks, a heresy written into the law to protect those Alaskans who still bag a moose to help the family through the winter. Such attitudes assume that there's always new ground just over the next hill, but even Alaska's huge reserves of land are finite.

Many Alaskans are well aware of that. Like arctic flora, the state's environmentalists are hardy and persistent—a mix of grass-roots organizers and computer networks rated one of the most sophisticated environmental movements in the world. Alaskan activists seem to sue at the drop of a leaf, functioning nearly as another branch of government. "A lot of our litigation just tries to get existing laws enforced," says Lauri Adams of the Sierra Club Legal Defense Fund in Juneau. "It's like shooting fish in a barrel. Every time we look at what an agency is supposed to be doing, we find big holes."

These "greenies" have finally earned some social acceptability. Pollution now affects enough Alaskans, from Fairbanks and Anchorage to the once pristine Kenai Peninsula, that a politician can stump for clean air and water and not be laughed out of town. And after the Valdez spill, Denny Wilcher, president of the Alaska Conservation Foundation, received his first $1,000 donations from residents of the state.

Environmentalists also have tentative allies in the native corporations. Sealaska Corporation, in southeastern Alaska, derives substantial income from cutting timber in the Tongass National Forest. Yet the corporation has supported additional controls on timber harvesting. "Our long-term economic future will be determined not so much by extraction of natural resources, but maintenance of natural beauty," says Byron Mallot, the chief executive of Sealaska. "We always feel we have a higher level of responsibility than other organizations: our people live here."

There is no call for Outsiders to be smug. We need to heed a truth Alaskans have long understood: pure wilderness is a luxury that requires sacrifice and, in return, just sits there. Why, then, should we bother? In the end a decision to leave alone an area like ANWR will not turn on how many caribou, if any, might be harmed, or what, if any, damage the tundra might suffer. The ultimate justification must be a leap of faith, a belief that it's worth keeping wild land untouched simply so we will know it is there. But in a world of diminishing resources, just saying no to development may be a gesture we no longer choose to afford. If that proves the case, then both Alaskans and Outsiders will be the poorer—for wilderness is one luxury that, once sold, can never be regained.

SUGGESTIONS FOR WRITING

Informal Essays

1. Using a personal experience and a passage or two from one of the essays in this chapter, conclude that we should or should not restrict automobiles from a national park of your choice.

2. After reading a few essays in this chapter, write a personal essay on the value that you derive from your favorite natural setting.

3. Write a personal essay in which you show why you prefer the "unnatural" environment of towns and cities over the "natural" environment of rocks and trees. Approach the topic ironically or humorously if you wish.

Short Documented Papers

1. Contrast one or two of the strongest arguments on each side of the issue concerning access to national parks. You might begin by reading the contrasting ideas of Edward Abbey and Eric Julber.

2. Contrast one or two of the strongest points on both sides of the issue concerning the use of federal lands for oil and mineral exploitation. You

might start by reading a survey essay like Michael Satchell's "The Battle for the Wilderness."

3. Describe two or three of the arguments of either the preservationist's or the conservationist's side of the issue of wilderness use.

4. Write a paper on Alaska's land-use controversy.

Longer Documented Papers

1. Write a research report in which you describe three or four of the strongest points made by proponents in the controversy concerning multiple use versus preservation.

2. Write a research argument in which you take a side in the controversy. As you argue, don't fail to take the other side's argument into account.

3. Make the well-developed case for limiting or expanding access to national parks.

LAST RITES: *Meaningful Tradition or Tasteless Extravagance?*

The tableau is familiar: The lid of the metallic gray casket is open, and the corpse lies face up, deep in the embrace of a soft mattress. Her face is thick with rouge and her hair is silver and stiffly coiffed. Her head rests on a plump, silken pillow, and her mouth has been curled up in the slightest trace of a smile. In back of the casket, surrounded by a mass of flowers, the minister describes the virtues of the deceased. After the service, the mourners file by the casket to view the remains. Later they will say how natural she looked. Such is the American way of death.

A controversy has been boiling, off and on over the past century or so, about whether the American way of death is a meaningful tradition or a tasteless and expensive ritual.

The critics of the traditional funeral, of course, say that it's a tasteless extravagance. The money that the survivors spend on airtight coffins, embalming, flowers, ornate headstones, and other accouterments of the traditional funeral could be spent, the critics say, on more practical things. It's a pathetic sight, the critics say, to see a widow spend a thousand dollars on an engraved metal casket (one day on show before it's buried) when she could have used the money to buy clothing for the children. This kind of criticism is nothing new, of course. Back in the nineteenth century, both Mark Twain and Charles Dickens laughed at the traditional funeral. "Why do we spend more on a death than a birth?" asks Mr. Mould, the undertaker of Dickens's *Martin Chuzzlewit*.

The "show" of the American funeral, its detractors add, is also distasteful. Too often, they say, the funeral merely encourages the survivors to spend money to put on a show for the living, some of whom come to see if Martha "did right" by Jack by burying him in style. Americans are natural conformists, the critics say, and this is nowhere more evident than in their slavish devotion to an empty rite.

Behind the funeral, the critics usually point out, is a businessman whose profits depend on selling coffins and needless "services" such as embalming. Funeral directors are too often little more than unctuous casket salesmen, the critics say, who prey on people when they are at their most vulnerable. In *The American Way of Death*, Jessica Mitford, a longtime critic of morticians, quotes a lawyer in Ohio: "It has long been my belief that American funeral directors exploit the grief of a bereaved family, as well as empty their pockets."

"Nonsense!" the defenders of the traditional funeral say. It's shallow to look only at the trappings of a funeral. "The heart hath reasons," as Pascal once said, "which Reason itself doth not know."

The price of the funeral is a small price to pay, the defenders say, for what it does for the hearts of the living. The American funeral allows mourners the opportunity to purge their grief, and it encourages them to face up to the fact of death. In "Funerals Are Good for People" (reprinted in this chapter) a psychiatrist, William Lamers, Jr., claims that the traditional funeral eases the mourner's grief by providing a setting in which they can work through their traumatized feelings about the death of their loved ones.

The traditional American funeral, some of its defenders add, is also an important rite within our Judeo-Christian tradition. Paul Irion (whose essay "The Perspective of Theology" is reprinted in this chapter) claims that the American funeral represents a view of death that is "consonant with the understanding of life and death in Christian theology."

The controversy surrounding the American way of death may seem a bit macabre, but it goes beyond the question of how to treat the corpse. When we think about how we want our last rites to take place, we are actually thinking about how we want our lives to take place. And like all good controversies, the questions it raises don't lead to dead-certain answers. We grope to find a way of handling death, just as we grope to find a way of handling life.

THE BIER BARONS
Al Morgan

Sometimes the target of a writer's satire is so goofy that a writer only has to faithfully describe it to mock it. That's basically what Al Morgan does in "The Bier Barons," a description of the funeral business in Southern California. Morgan begins with a look at the selling of death in Hollywood, and then focuses his attention on that "Paradise of Burying Ground," Forest Lawn Cemetery.

Morgan isn't alone in finding the Southern California funeral industry an inviting target. In 1948, twelve years before Morgan's essay appeared in Playboy, Evelyn Waugh made fun of pet cemeteries and Forest Lawn in his novel The Loved One. Indeed, it's probably hard for such a satirist to keep his wit in check when he contemplates the hard-sell, sometimes tasteless Southern California funeral business, where you can arrange to have music and air conditioning piped into the coffin of the dearly departed, and where a parakeet-shaped urn for the ashes of your feathery friend will set you back twenty-five hundred dollars.

"Show me the manner in which a people bury their dead and I shall measure with mathematical exactness the degree of civilization attained by these people." The gent who uttered these ringing lines was British Prime Minister Gladstone, and it is a crying shame that we will never have the benefit of his mathematical measurement of the level of civilization of a certain city in the Western portion of the United States, in the sixth decade of the Twentieth Century.

That city is Hollywood, California, justly famous as a world-wide symbol of glamor and make-believe, and now equally famous for another major industry, the packaging and peddling of that most unsalable of all commodities: death.

The mortuary business has become a whopping industry, ranking just behind the making of motion pictures and the sale of used cars. The merchants of death — the plot salesmen, the tombstone hustlers, the embalming parlor proprietors — have turned what once was a quiet, necessary service and a solemn religious rite into a streamlined, klieg-lighted multi-billion-dollar industry. The hustlers of death, who have run an embalming school diploma, six feet of dirt plus the ethics of a snake-oil salesman into a bonanza, can give your old corner undertaker cards and spades in the business of merchandising his product, a product described in unctuous tones in Hollywood radio commercials as "the one purchase we must all make."

The facts of death, to even the casual tourist, are as inescapable as the facts of life in Hollywood. Billboards on all the major highways proclaim the virtues of one or another of the mortuary establishments competing for the death buck.

"We treat every woman like our sister. Every man like our brother or son. Female attendants!"

"Funerals on credit. As little as $2.85 a week. Nothing down."

"Spend Holy Week at Forest Lawn."

"Utter-McKinley — the only funeral home in the entire world located on internationally famous Hollywood Boulevard, near Vine."

Al Morgan, "The Bier Barons," *Playboy* June 1960.

around in the area on my own, I was unable to obtain any estimate for similar services lower than $500. . . .

Last year Charles V. Gates, an engineer in San Luis Obispo, California, found that the mere threat of using a funeral society's services toppled prices for him by 50 per cent. His experience started when he began shopping around, at the insistence of his ninety-year-old parents, for a mortician who would take care of their cremation after death. Gates found that the local crematory would not accept his parents' remains unless they were embalmed and placed in caskets. The lowest estimate was $510 for each person. This price struck the elderly couple as senseless. Since they planned to be cremated, they could see no point to either embalming or a casket.

Finally, in frustration, the son told the mortician involved that he planned to write the Bay Area Funeral Society to see if they could help him. The undertaker then said he'd be happy to donate a coffin if Mr. Gates would forget the whole thing. Later, when the society arranged to handle all details for a total of $232 each, the San Luis Obispo mortician offered to meet the competition. The son refused. When his parents die, they will be transported to the Bay Area for cremation. There is, incidentally, no California law requiring a casket when people are cremated. . . .

The Bay Area group has attracted a number of zealous cohorts, but none more dynamic than Jessica Treuhaft, a born rebel at heart, a seeker after causes and a member of the famous English family of Mitfords. . . .

When I called on her in her Oakland house one afternoon, I found her sipping tea and quietly enjoying the latest issue of *Mortuary Management*. "This is a lovely magazine," she said. "Did you know that Dorothy Parker, when she was a magazine editor, used to subscribe to it and tack up articles on her bulletin board to entertain the staff?"

I picked up one of the back copies on her coffee table. My eye fell on an advertisement for a mortuary college in Boston. Two curvaceous majorettes, with dimpled knees, were beckoning the reader to join a seminar on such courses as "Color in the Funeral Service," "Embalming Problems" and "Tax Planning for Tangible Savings."

Over the teacups, Jessica Treuhalf revealed her experiences as an ardent researcher for the society. She had telephoned or visited in widow's weeds many funeral establishments to inquire about prices. In one place, having been shown a $515 casket, she tearfully asked the owner if he had something less expensive. She was told that he did have a "flattop," if she'd care to come out to the garage to look at it. "But I assure you," he added with distaste, "that you wouldn't be caught dead in it!"

On another occasion she played the role of a hard-as-nails relative shopping for a funeral for a "sister-in-law," who, she explained, was a terminal-cancer case in the hospital. She asked for the minimum price without a casket, since the sister-in-law was to be cremated. Three morticians she visited implied that it was illegal to cremate bodies without using a coffin. To a fourth she said that she planned to pick up the sister-in-law in her station wagon and take her personally to the crematory. "Is that legal?" she asked, knowing full well that it was.

There was a long pause. Finally the funeral director spluttered. "Madame," he said, "the *average* lady has neither the inclination nor the facilities to be carting dead bodies about."

In addition to being a tireless recruiter for the society, Mrs. Treuhaft has been a writer and speaker on the subject of the American funeral and a careful reader of the professional trade journals.

By subscribing to the publication, *Successful Mortuary Operation and Service*, she got a look at the high-powered salesmanship that lies behind the sedate facade of many funeral homes. In a series of selling tips this publication gave Jessica Treuhaft a few hints on how to sell a coffin.

"Never say to a client, 'I can tell by the fine suit you're wearing that you appreciate fine things and will want a fine casket for your father,'" advises the publication. Instead, it urged that the funeral director say, "Think of the beautiful memory picture you will have of your dear father in this beautiful casket." On another page it suggested, "After quoting a price, continue talking for a moment or two. And never use the dollar sign on a price tag!" Before appearing on the famous TV debate, Mrs. Treuhaft had read *Mortuary Management* so thoroughly that she was able to disconcert the opposition by quoting from the publication to show that a lively conflict exists between clergymen and morticians on the subject of keeping down the cost of funerals. The magazine had recently published a series of suggestions from funeral directors on how to handle clergymen who tried to influence parishioners to purchase less expensive caskets.

It was suggested by one mortician that the minister be invited into the mortician's office for coffee while the family is left in the show-room to make a selection. "This works *part* of the time," he wrote.

Another contributor reported, "We have this same problem of nosy clergymen in our town, and I am convinced there is nothing that can be done about the situation. We tried."

Statistical proof that such a cleavage does exist between clergymen and morticians was indicated in a poll that Dr. Robert L. Fulton, well-known Los Angeles State College sociologist, conducted for the industry in 1959. The poll revealed that a majority of Protestant ministers and 41 per cent of Catholic priests believed "American funeral directors exploited or took advantage of a family's grief in selling funeral services."

Some of the complaints made by clergymen were that funerals were "too solemn," "too expensive" and that there was too much "pagan display" with too little of the "meaning of death." Said the late Rev. Dr. Bernard Iddings Bell, the noted Episcopal clergyman, "By a conspiracy of silence and pretense, we make our funerals as unlike funerals as possible. . . . I have even seen the faces of corpses rouged. All this is macabre, morbid, indecent."

One of the most passionate critics of morticians was the late W. W. Chambers, a Washington, D.C., funeral director. The firm that bears his name conducts more funerals in the nation's capital than does any other firm and has handled five of them in the White House.

Testifying before a congressional committee in 1948 against a proposal to license undertakers, the late Mr. Chambers said, "The business is a mighty sweet racket."

He said he got into it when he was working in a livery stable and saw a "poor broken widow" being sold a seventeen-dollar casket for $250. "It has the horse business beat a mile," he declared. During his testimony, Mr. Chambers made coast-to-coast headlines by insisting he could embalm an elephant for $1.50.

FASHIONS IN FUNERALS
Jessica Mitford

Nothing has ever upset those in the funeral business quite the way that Jessica Mitford's The American Way of Death *did when it was published in 1963. For years following its publication, funeral trade publications were still smarting from the arrows that Mitford had shot their way.*

It's not surprising that The American Way of Death *had such an impact. Mitford is a deliciously wicked and clever writer, and she so obviously savors the tasteless and macabre, of which the traditional American funeral offers so much. In the course of Roul Tunley's research into the high costs of funerals (see preceding essay) he visited Mitford's home in San Francisco and found her sipping tea and enjoying the latest issue of* Mortuary Management.

This excerpted chapter, "Fashions in Funerals," describes the origins of some of our burial practices and shows off Mitford's rapier wit.

> *. . . disposal of the dead falls rather into a class with fashions, than with either customs or folkways on the one hand, or institutions on the other . . . social practices of disposing of the dead are of a kind with fashions of dress, luxury and etiquette.*
> "Disposal of the Dead" by A. L. Kroeber.
> *American Anthropologist* (New Series)
> Volume 29:3, July-September, 1927

One of the interesting things about burial practices is that they provide many a clue to the customs and society of the living. The very word "antiquarian" conjures up the picture of a mild-eyed historian groping about amidst old tombstones, copying down epitaphs with their folksy inscriptions and irregular spelling, extrapolating from these a picture of the quaint people and homey ways of yore. There is unconscious wit: the widow's epitaph to her husband, "Rest in peace—until we meet again." There is gay inventiveness:

> Here lie I, Master Elginbrod.
> Have mercy on my soul, O God,
> As I would have if I were God
> And thou wert Master Elginbrod.

There is pathos: "I will awake, O Christ, when thou callest me, but let me sleep awhile—for I am very weary." And bathos: "'Tis but the casket that lies here; the gem that fills it sparkles yet."

For the study of prehistory, archeologists rely heavily on what they can find in and around tombs, graves, monuments; and from the tools, jewels, household articles, symbols found with the dead, they reconstruct whole civilizations, infer entire systems of religious and ethical beliefs.

Jessica Mitford, "Fashions in Funerals," *The American Way of Death* (New York: Simon & Schuster, 1963).

Inevitably some go-ahead team of thirtieth-century archeologists will labor to reconstruct our present-day level of civilization from a study of our burial practices. It is depressing to think of them digging and poking about in our new crop of Forest Lawns, the shouts of discovery as they come upon the mass-produced granite horrors, the repetitive flat bronze markers (the legends, like greeting cards and singing telegrams, chosen from an approved list maintained at the cemetery office) and, under the ground, the stamped-out metal casket shells resembling nothing so much as those bronzed and silvered souvenirs for sale at airport gift shops. Prying further, they would find reposing in each of these on a comfortable mattress of innerspring or foam rubber construction a standardized, rouged or suntanned specimen of Homo sapiens, U.S.A., attired in business suit or flowing negligée according to sex. Our archeologists would puzzle exceedingly over the inner meaning of the tenement mausoleums the their six or seven tiers of adjoining crypt spaces. Were the tenants of these, they might wonder, engaged in some ritual act of contemplation, surprised by sudden disaster? Busily scribbling notes, they would describe the companion his-and-her vaults for husband and wife, and the approved inscription on these: "TOGETHER FOREVER." For purposes of comparison they might recall the words of Andrew Marvell, a poet from an earlier culture, who thus addressed his coy mistress:

The grave's a fine and private place,
But none, I think, do there embrace.

They might rashly conclude that twentieth-century America was a nation of abjectly imitative comformists, devoted to machine-made gadgetry and mass-produced art of a debased quality; that its dominant theology was a weird mixture of primitive superstitions, superficial attitudes towards death, overlaid with a distinct tendency towards necrophilism. . . .

Where did our burial practices come from? There is little scholarship on the subject. Thousands of books have been written describing, cataloguing, theorizing about the funeral procedures of ancient and modern peoples from Aztecs to Zulus; but about contemporary American burial practices almost nothing has been written. . . .

The major Western faiths have remarkably little to say about how funerals should be conducted. Such doctrinal statements as have been enunciated concerning disposal of the dead invariably stress simplicity, the equality of all men in death, emphasis on the spiritual aspects rather than on the physical remains.

The Roman Catholic Church requires that the following simple instructions be observed: "1) That the body be decently laid out; 2) that lights be placed beside the body; 3) that a cross be laid upon the breast, or failing that, the hands laid on the breast in the form of a cross; 4) that the body be sprinkled with holy water and incense at stated times; 5) that it be buried in consecrated ground." The Jewish religion specifically prohibits display in connection with funerals: "It is strictly ordained that there must be no adornment of the plain wooden coffin used by the Jew, nor may flowers be placed inside or outside. Plumes, velvet palls and the like are strictly prohibited, and all show and display of wealth discouraged; moreover, the synagogue holds itself responsible for the arrangements for burial, dispensing with the services of the Dismal Trade." In Israel today, uncoffined burial is the rule, and the deceased is returned to the earth in a simple shroud. The Church of England Book of Common Prayer, written several centuries before burial receptacles came into general use, makes no mention of coffins in connection with the funeral service, but rather speaks throughout of the "corpse" or the "body."

What of embalming, the pivotal aspect of the American funeral? The "roots" of this procedure have indeed leaped oceans and traversed centuries in the most unrootlike fashion. It has had a checkered history, the highlights of which deserve some consideration since embalming is (as one mortuary textbook writer puts it) "the very foundation of modern mortuary service — the factor which has made the elaborate funeral home and lucrative funeral service possible."

True, the practice of preserving dead bodies with chemicals, decorating them with paint and powder and arranging them for a public showing has its origin in antiquity — but not in Judaeo-Christian antiquity. This incongruous behavior towards the human dead originated with the pagan Egyptians and reached its high point in the second millennium B.C. Thereafter, embalming suffered a decline from which it did not recover until it was made part of the standard funeral service in twentieth-century America.

While the actual *mode* of preservation and the materials used differed in ancient Egypt from those used in contemporary America, there are many striking similarities in the kind of care lavished upon the dead. There, as here, the goal was to outmaneuver the Grim Reaper as far as possible.

The Egyptian method of embalming as described by Herodotus sounds like a rather crude exercise in human taxidermy. The entrails and brain were removed, the body scoured with palm wine and purified with spices. After being soaked for seventy days in a saline solution the corpse was washed and wrapped in strips of fine linen, then placed in a "wooden case of human shape" which in turn was put in a sepulchral chamber.

Restorative art was by no means unknown in ancient Egypt. The Greek historian Diodorus Siculus wrote: "Having treated [the corpse], they restore it to the relatives with every member of the body preserved so perfectly that even the eyelashes and eyebrows remain, the whole appearance of the body being unchangeable, and the cast of the features recognizable. . . . They present an example of a kind of inverted necromancy." The Egyptians had no Post Mortem Restoration Bra; instead they stuffed and modeled the breasts, refashioning the nipples from copper buttons. They fixed the body while still plastic in the desired attitude; they painted it with red ochre for men and yellow for women; they emphasized the details of the face with paint; they supplemented the natural hair with a wig; they tinted the nails with henna. A mummy of the XVIIIth Dynasty has even been found wearing some practical burial footwear — sandals made of mud, with metal soles and gilded straps.

Egyptian preoccupation with preservation of the body after death stemmed from the belief that the departed spirit would one day return to inhabit the earthly body; that if the body perished, the soul would eventually perish too. Yet although embalming was available to all who could pay the price, it was by no means so universally employed in ancient Egypt as it is today in the U.S.A. The ordinary peasant was not embalmed at all; yet, curiously enough, his corpse comes down to us through the ages as well preserved as those of his disemboweled and richly aromatic betters, for it has been established that the unusually dry climate and the absence of bacteria in the sand and air, rather than the materials used in embalming, are what account for the Egyptian mummies' marvelous state of preservation.

The Greeks, knowing the uses of both, were no more likely to occupy themselves with the preservation of dead flesh than they were to bury good wine for the comfort of dead bodies. They cremated their dead, for the most part, believing in the power of flame to set free the soul. The glorious period that conventional historians call the Golden Age of Greece is for historians of embalming the beginning of the Dark Ages.

The Jews frowned upon embalming, as did the early Christians, who regarded it as a pagan custom. Saint Anthony, in the third century, denounced the practice as sinful. His impassioned plea, recorded by Athanasius, might well be echoed by the American of today who would like to avoid being transformed by the embalmer's art and displayed in a funeral home:

"And if your minds are set upon me, and ye remember me as a father, permit no man to take my body and carry it into Egypt, lest, according to the custom which they have, they embalm me and lay me up in their houses, for it was [to avoid] this that I came into this desert. And ye know that I have continually made exhortation concerning this thing and begged that it should not be done, and ye well know how much I have blamed those who observed this custom. Dig a grave then, and bury me therein, and hide my body under the earth, and let these my words be observed carefully by you, and tell ye no man where ye lay me. . . ."

Mummification of the dead in Egypt was gradually abandoned after a large part of the population was converted to Christianity. . . .

The two widely divergent interests which spurred the early embalmers—scientific inquiry, and the fascination and financial reward of turning cadavers into a sort of ornamental keepsake—were to achieve a happy union under the guiding hand of a rare nineteenth-century character, "Dr." Thomas Holmes. He was the first to advance from what one funeral trade writer jocularly calls the "Glacier Age"—when preservation on ice was the undertakers' rule—and is often affectionately referred to by present-day funeral men as "the father of American embalming." Holmes was the first to popularize the idea of preserving the dead on a mass scale, and the first American to get rich from this novel occupation.

Holmes developed a passionate interest in cadavers early in life (it was in fact the reason for his expulsion from medical school; he was forever carelessly leaving them around in inappropriate places) and when the Civil War started, he saw his great opportunity. He rushed to the front and started embalming like mad, charging the families of the dead soldiers $100 for his labors. Some four years and 4,028 embalmed soldiers later (his own figure), Holmes returned to Brooklyn a rich man.

The "use for everyone of a casket that is attractive and protects the remains" (*attractive* seems an odd word here) is a new concept in this century, and one that took some ingenuity to put across. Surprisingly enough, even the widespread use of any sort of burial receptacle is a fairly new development in Western culture, dating back less than two hundred years. Until the eighteenth century few people except the very rich were buried in coffins. The "casket," and particularly the metal casket, is a phenomenon of modern America, unknown in past days and in other parts of the world.

As might be expected, with the development of industrial technique in the nineteenth century, coffin designers soared to marvelous heights. They experimented with glass, cement, celluloid, papier-mâché, India rubber; they invented Rube Goldberg contraptions called "life signals"—complicated arrangements of wires and bells designed to set off an alarm if the occupant of the coffin should have been inadvertently buried alive.

The newfangled invention of metal coffins in the nineteenth century did not go unchallenged. An admonition on the subject was delivered by Lord Stowell, Judge of the Consistory Court of London, who in 1820 was called upon to decide a case felicitously titled Gilbert vs. Buzzard. At issue was the right to bury a corpse in a newly patented iron coffin. The church wardens protested that if parishioners were to get into the habit of burying their dead in coffins made proof against normal decay, in a few generations there would be no burial space left.

Said Lord Stowell, "The rule of law which says that a man has a right to be buried in his own churchyard is to be found, most certainly, in many of our authoritative text writers; but it is not quite so easy to find the rule which gives him the rights of burying a large chest or trunk in company with himself." He spoke approvingly of attempts to abolish use of sepulchral chests "on the physical ground that the dissolution of bodies would be accelerated, and the dangerous virulence of the fermentation disarmed by a speedy absorption of the noxious particles into the surrounding soil." . . .

The production of ever more solid and durable metal caskets has soared in this century, their long-lasting and even "eternal" qualities have become a matter of pride and self-congratulation throughout the industry—and this in one area of manufacture where built-in obsolescence might seem (as Lord Stowell pointed out) to present certain advantages. As we have seen, the sales of metal caskets now exceed sales of the old-fashioned wooden types. A brand-new tradition has been established; how deep are the roots, Messrs. Habenstein and Lamers?

Mourning symbols have run the gamut. In medieval England and in colonial America, the skull and crossbones was the favored symbol, making its appearance on everything connected with death from tombstone to funeral pall to coffinmaker's sign. Funerary extravagance took the form of elaborate mourning clothes, the hiring of mutes (or paid mourners), tremendous feasting sometimes of many days' duration, and gifts to the living, who were showered with rings, scarves, needlework, books and, most customarily, gloves.

Funeral flowers, today the major mourning symbol and a huge item of national expenditure, did not make their appearance in England or America until after the middle of the nineteenth century, and only then over the opposition of church leaders.

From colonial days until the nineteenth century, the American funeral was almost exclusively a family affair, in the sense that the family and close friends performed most of the duties in connection with the dead body itself. It was they who washed and laid out the body, draped it in a winding sheet, and ordered the coffin from the local carpenter. It was they who carried the coffin on foot from the home to the church and thence to the graveyard, and who frequently—unless the church sexton was available—dug the grave. Funeral services were held in the church over the pall-covered bier, and a brief committal prayer was said at the graveside. Between the death and the funeral, the body lay in the family parlor where the mourners took turns watching over it, the practical reason for this being the ever-present possibility that signs of life might be observed.

The first undertakers were drawn mainly from three occupations, all concerned with some aspect of burial: the livery stable keeper, who provided the hearse and funeral carriages, the carpenter or cabinetmaker who made the coffins, and the sexton, who was generally in charge of bell-tolling and grave-digging. In some of the larger cities midwives and nurses advertised their services as occupational layers out of the dead, and were so listed in city directories. The undertaker's job was primarily custodial. It included supplying the coffin from a catalogue or from his own establishment, arranging to bring folding chairs (if the service was to be held in the home, which was often the case), taking charge of the pallbearers, supervising the removal of the coffin and loading it into the hearse, and in general doing the necessary chores until the body was finally lowered into the grave.

Shortly before the turn of the century, the undertaker conferred upon himself the title of "funeral director." From that time on, possibly inspired by his own semantics, he began to *direct funerals*, and quietly to impose a character of his own on the mode of disposal of the dead.

Some of the changes that were in store are foreshadowed in *The Modern Funeral* by W. P. Hohenschuh, published in 1900. Hohenschuh may have been the first to put into words a major assumption that lies behind modern funeral practices: "There is nothing too good for the dead," he declares. He goes on to advise, "The friends want the best that they can afford. . . . A number of manufacturers have set an excellent example by fitting up magnificent showrooms, to which funeral directors can take their customers, and show them the finest goods made. It is an education for all parties concerned. . . . It is to be commended." Hohenschuh's injunctions about funeral salesmanship, although vastly elaborated over the years, remain basic: "Boxes must be shown to sell them. By having an ordinary pine box next to one that is papered, the difference is more readily seen than could be explained, and a better price can be obtained for the latter." And on collections he warns, "Grief soon subsides, and the older the bill gets, the harder it is to collect."

In 1900 embalming was still the exception rather than the rule and was still generally done in the home — although Hohenschuh mentions a new trend making its appearance in California, that of taking the body to the funeral parlor after death for dressing and embalming. He proposes an ingenious approach to selling the public on embalming: "It may be suggested that bodies should be embalmed in winter as well as in summer. It may be a little difficult to have people accept this idea, but after having tried it a few times, and people realize the comfort to themselves in having the body in a warm room, this preventing them against colds, besides the sentimental feeling against having the body in a cold room, it is an easy matter to make the custom general." However, the most profitable aspect of the modern funeral — that of preparing the body for the public gaze — seems to have escaped this astute practitioner, for he opposes the open casket at the funeral service, and remarks, "There is no doubt that most people view the dead out of curiosity."

It was still a far cry from these early, hesitant steps of the emerging funeral industry to the full-fledged burlesque it has become.

Requiem for Everyman
Ruth Mulvey Harmer

The year 1963 was a very bad one for funeral directors. In that year two books savaged the funeral industry: Jessica Mitford's The American Way of Death *and Ruth Harmer's* The High Cost of Dying.

Harmer's book, full of arguments and statistics, is more indignant. Where Harmer fumes, Mitford savors the ridiculous and stifles a laugh. Funeral directors tolerated Harmer's book; they despised Mitford's book.

In this excerpt from Harmer's final chapter, she attacks the notion (so beloved by its defenders) that the traditional American funeral serves a valuable purpose by providing a set of ceremonies that ease the psychological trauma to the survivors. She concludes by suggesting alternatives to the traditional funeral.

In our Western culture, most persons are agreed that some kind of final acknowledgement is fitting and proper. For who, indeed, is so unworthy that his passing should go unnoticed, unmourned, unmarked? A funeral is not, of course, the only alternative. There are other ways in which death may offer the means of achieving dignity. If prisoners, who are generally characterized by feelings of insecurity about themselves, are able to realize a moral and emotional elevation by risking their lives to participate in medical and scientific experiments without thought of personal gain, would it not be more practical and meritorious for others to make such a contribution rather than to attempt to acquire status through a costly funeral and burial? To help the advancement of medical science in a general way would certainly be to end life on a commendable note. More personally, to make contributions of sight, of health, of life itself — through such agencies as eye, bone, artery, and blood banks — would be to express in the highest sense of the word that *magnanimity*, that large-souled generosity, that is the mark of a noble man and the goal of a civilized one.

Not all, of course, are willing to do that. Many feel that some kind of funeral ceremony is necessary. And it must be conceded that a funeral can be of value; it does provide during a period of crisis a set of customs and rituals that minimize the traumatic effect of the experience and offer other members of the group an opportunity for spiritual and secular communion. Bereavement for all who genuinely feel grief is a shock that disrupts and disturbs and devastates; for some, it is such an intolerable experience that their incoherent response may be suicide or moral and emotional disintegration. Funerals can help to alleviate the pain of individuals affected by offering a series of actions that must be performed and by offering the solace that grief is shared by others. The social unit — the family, the tribe, and nation, and even, as in the case of Mrs. Roosevelt's funeral, the community of

Ruth Mulvey Harmer, "Requiem for Everyman," *The High Cost of Dying* (New York: Collier-Macmillan, 1963).

nations — gains a feeling of cohesiveness and fraternity from participating in an affecting ritual.

Unfortunately, current funeral practices do not serve those ends, but negate them. They encourage irrational responses by enhancing the feeling of unreality survivors often experience when death occurs. By forcing bereaved persons to play publicly their parts as chief mourners during the first terrible wave of grief, funerals intensify their emotional shock and dislocation. The social value has also been minimized because the undertakers, the entrepreneurs, have appropriated the members' traditional roles and usurped their functions. Even though a number of mourners may show up somberly clad for the ceremony, they have surrendered to the florist the expression of their thoughts and feelings and to the mortician the expression of their ritualistic gestures. The occasion, therefore, merely isolates and alienates them from other members of the group. Spiritually, death is the one human event that makes us most acutely conscious of the dignity and divinity of man and most completely aware of the folly of our preoccupation with getting and spending. But a theatrical production starring a theatrically made-up corpse enhances the illusion of the importance of the world and the flesh and makes the spiritual realities of the occasion as remote as any Grade B motion picture does — all at tremendous cost to the living.

A first step has already been taken by many religious leaders to simplify the funeral service and strip it of its pagan emphasis on the material: the extravagant casket, the heaps of floral offerings, the embalmed corpse decked out brighter than life with fancy garb and layers of cosmetics. Most religious groups in the country have endorsed the idea that the funeral should be conducted in a church rather than in a commercial establishment and that the spiritual implications once again be emphasized so that the occasion may, as the Psalmist wrote, "teach us to number our days, that we may apply our hearts unto wisdom." Many churches are now precluding elaborate ceremonies conducted by fraternal organizations. A considerable number have also, like the Los Angeles Episcopal diocese, made it mandatory that the casket be closed before the beginning of the service on the grounds that it is pagan, just as parading past the open casket "is an ugly survival of paganism, when the mourners danced around the funeral pyre, beating their tom-toms."

Although some religions do not adapt themselves to the practice, many churches are encouraging the substitution of memorial services for elaborate funerals. At a specified time — a week, two weeks, or a month after death has occurred — members of the family and friends meet at the church or home to commemorate the person who has died. The delay is held important since it gives the persons most deeply affected an opportunity to appreciate the gathering of friends to honor the dead at a time when they are less likely to indulge in uncontrollable emotional outbursts. At the service, whatever is appropriate in the way of homage is paid to the person as an individual. "What is important," one Unitarian minister said, "is to express something true about the person, to acknowledge death as a deep break in the experience of the living. . . . In the frank acknowledgment of the meaning of death and in identifying the person who has died, what may be achieved is a celebration of life in its full dimension."

Squandering money on flowers that cannot be enjoyed by the recipient has become so repugnant to many that it has now become common practice to urge that instead of sending floral offerings to the funeral home or cemetery a check be sent to some worthwhile organization. Opportunities to make one's death a contribution to the living are numerous, although not all are of equal value since many of the charity promoters can put the funeral entrepreneurs to shame in the matter of exploiting decent human emotions. The most satisfactory solution is for the donor to select a charity he knows and approves. Although the family of the deceased may have specified the _____ Fund, there is nothing to prevent the mourner from sending the five or ten or fifteen or more dollars he might have spent on flowers to the principal of a nearby school, for example, to be used to help some youngster achieve his goal. Such a gift could only add to the stature of the person thus commemorated.

If funeral services were simplified and limited to relatives and closest friends, the living might be better served. Grief and anguish are not buried with the corpse, and during the long period of adjustment that inevitably follows the day of the funeral, life might be made more bearable for the survivors by having those who would normally have attended the funeral spend that amount of time with them. By restricting attendance at the funeral, the persons closest to the dead would be freed from the obligation of putting on a show designed to impress casual on-lookers. Economically as well as emotionally the saving would undoubtedly be great; many an otherwise sensible person has indulged in extravagance against his or her better judgment and at great cost to the members of the family merely to protect the memory of the dead against the accusations of neighbors whose only standard of measurement about death as life is "How much did it cost?"

Post-funeral activities may also be simplified in the interests of the living and the dead. The bomb-proof vaults and elaborate air-tight caskets with and without hospital beds are an essential blasphemy — a denial of all of our philosophical and religious beliefs. To accept that dust shall be returned to dust is to commit ourselves to what we call our deepest beliefs — an acceptance that enables us to feel, like Socrates, that "neither in life, nor after death, can any harm come to a good man."

One of the great values of the memorial societies and the funeral cooperatives is that they encourage us to think in a realistic way about the practical aspects of death. By concerning ourselves with the economics, we are led to question the worth. From there, it is not a long step to making pertinent and ultimate inquiries about the meaning of death. When we have answered them in a reasonable way, we shall have gone far toward establishing the meaning of life and toward the establishment of a satisfactory conduct of life for ourselves and the world we live in. To do that is really to have lived.

The Perspective of Theology
Paul E. Irion

Critics of the traditional American funeral usually point to the macabre and tasteless attention given to the corpse. By contrast, Paul Irion says that this focus on the corpse is consistent with the Christian hope of the Resurrection. Christianity, Irion says, has always seen humans as body and soul, and since the body must someday be raised from the dead, it is entirely reasonable that funeral rites would give attention to the corpse itself. "If death brings total annihilation to all of man's being," Irion says, "and if the concept of man as a whole is taken seriously, can we assume that the body of the deceased is any less a part of him than his spirit?"

Funeral practices have been from the earliest times religious in nature. The investigations of cultural anthropology have been able to follow the course of development of a cult of the dead from early, even prehistoric times. "Since of all the mysterious, disintegrating and critical situations with which man has been confronted throughout the ages death appears to have been the most disturbing and devastating, it is hardly surprising that the earliest traces of religious belief and practice should center in the cult of the dead." Studies of intentional interments from as early as the Middle Paleolithic age show the emergence of particular patterns for ceremonial treatment of the dead.

According to archaeological investigation it would appear that practices followed in development of the cult of the dead had as their major function provision of a way for dealing with the mystery of death. Efforts were made to provide for the well-being of the one who had died and to sustain the survivors in their fear and awe as they faced death.

James advances the hypothesis that "when modes of burial begin to be stereotyped by tradition they may tend to influence beliefs about the locality and nature of the next life." This hypothesis would affirm that primitive man recognized the radical dislocation created by death. He was unable to penetrate the mystery of this event, but he did seek ways to deal with it and with his own fear of it. As these coping rituals assumed more stable form and structure they became the basis for more abstract notions of what death was and what happened to the individual in death. Man's emotional needs in the face of the crisis created by death, according to James's hypothesis, produced ritualistic satisfaction which in turn produced abstract ideas and beliefs about the nature of life and death.

James, as an anthropologist, does not really need to be concerned with the question of whether this process is founded on objective reality or whether it is totally subjective. From his point of view this is not really an important issue. But for the one who seeks to approach the funeral theologically the question is crucial. The theological perspective will not deny the validity nor the importance of subjective experience. However, at the same time it will not assume that the answer which has been found is merely the product of man's striving or reflection but will affirm

Paul E. Irion, "The Perspective of Theology," *The Funeral: Vestige or Value?* (Nashville: Abingdon Press, 1966).

that it is founded upon objective reality. Even the fact that empirical validations cannot be given to this reality does not necessarily indicate that it is totally subjective in nature.

Although we have no desire to baptize the status quo as automatically Christian, it does seem evident that in the main the American understanding of the funeral has been religious. At least in principle, if not always in practice, the major emphases of the funeral have represented the Judeo-Christian heritage of the majority of the American population.

By this we mean that the formal intention and content of the American funeral service, regarded in optimum terms, represents a view of death, of the body of the deceased, of the resources available for meeting the needs of the mourners which is consonant with the understanding of life and death in Christian theology. Certainly it would be ridiculous to assert that the modern funeral in actual practice is totally in harmony with the understanding of Christian theology. There are numerous practices in vogue today which obviously do not meet that criterion. However, this does not mean that the funeral itself cannot be defined theologically.

We should note here again that the perspective from which we view the funeral will be that of Protestant Christian theology. We cannot presume to speak from the viewpoint of Judaism or Roman Catholicism. This delineation represents no judgment on other points of view but is a deliberate narrowing of the scope to enable more intensive treatment.

Speaking now of the funeral in terms of its best form and usage, let us see how it represents adequately this theological position. The funeral, thus considered, does bear witness to an understanding of death which sees this phenomenon realistically. The very occurrence of the funeral signifies that death has taken place, life as we know it has drawn to a close. This is an irreversible and irrevocable event. It is a part of man's human condition, for although he can delay death he cannot avoid it ultimately. Man can be truly man only as he faces up to these facts and confronts the reality of death. One of the functions of the funeral is to help him do just this.

Furthermore, the funeral represents a theological understanding of the body of the deceased. Here there must be a concern for proportion. It is possible to have too much or too little regard for the body of the one who has died. From the point of view of the New Testament it is incorrect to see man's existence solely in terms of his physical body. Thus the Christian funeral is not intent upon centering all attention on the corpse, making of it an object of reverence, seeking to maintain the existence of the person by preserving the body ad infinitum. At the same time, the body is regarded as a part of the created order. In the language of Paul, the Christian sees it as the temple of the Holy Spirit. Even in death it represents part of the total person, in no less sense than the nonphysical elements of man. Thus the Christian funeral is not intent upon ignoring the body nor despising it, getting it out of sight or thought as quickly as possible. The Christian funeral seeks to put the body in perspective as a part of the total person who has died.

According to its best understanding the funeral presents resources which the faith offers to meet the needs of the bereaved. It brings a faithful confidence in the present concern and abiding love of God for both living and dead into confrontation with the sense of painful loss, fear, guilt, and confusion in the mourners. The funeral bears witness to the Christian hope for new life beyond death, to the sustaining love of God even amid suffering, and to the strength which God provides for the facing and accepting of reality. This witness is made not only verbally but in the activity of the Christian community, the church, ministering to the bereaved.

The Protestant theological rationale for the funeral contains at least two major themes. First of all the funeral is intended to be a benediction on the deceased, his person and his life. Some churches, particularly in the Anglican and Roman Catholic traditions, interpret this as an occasion for intercessory prayer for the deceased. The prayers for the dead are intended to petition for the salvation of the individual's soul and the improvement of his state beyond death. Most Protestant churches would understand this element of benediction as a passive commitment of the deceased to the mercy of God rather than as active intercession.

One purpose of the funeral defined as benediction involves the respectful and dignified disposition of the body. The mode of disposition is irrelevant at this point. The fact that the funeral has as one of its functions a ceremonial accompaniment for separating the body of the dead from the community of the living is an act of benediction because the body is not summarily discarded. This is in no sense a matter of fearing reprisal from the spirit of the deceased if the body is not buried, as was the case among the ancient Greeks or even the people of the Middle Ages. Rather it is an endeavor to symbolize the ending of a life by enabling the dissolution of the physical matrix in which that life was lived while still indicating an abiding concern and affection for the total person of the deceased. The commitment of the whole person to God is the act of blessing which constitutes one portion of the theological understanding of the purpose of the funeral.

The funeral can be understood as an act of benediction because it stands in the context of the Christian hope for the resurrection. Commending the deceased to God is an act which can be undertaken only in the confidence in the resurrection. The disposition of the body is a symbol of separation from this life, but it is not a consignment to oblivion because of this hope. Actually, it is the confident hope in resurrection which makes it possible to conceive the funeral in terms of benediction.

The second major theme in the theological rationale for the funeral is that of coping with death. The funeral provides a means for dealing with death both in terms of the death of a loved one and of one's own death.

The funeral is, in part, a ritual which seeks to lay a basis for confronting the mystery of death. The emotional trauma that accompanies the death of one with whom we have had a meaningful relationship is quite evident. Coupled with this is a search for some sort of explanation or interpretation which will begin to yield the meaning of death. Death very often brings intense suffering to the bereaved. Suffering becomes more tolerable when we can find some meaning in it. This need for explanation and meaning can be observed in the statements very often made by mourners in the early phases of their bereavement. These statements become so common that one sometimes suspects that they are little more than clichés. "His time had come." "It's God's will." "He's better off now."

The funeral offers a way in which meaningful interpretation of the suffering that comes through loss can be presented. Although the element of mystery cannot be removed from the future, witness can be borne to the faith that the future, like the present, is within the scope of God's power and concern. In spite of the necessary search for answers there can be the confidence that both life and death exist within a structure of meaning.

This coping process is founded upon the hope for the resurrection which is central to the Christian confrontation of death. Although the pain of separation is not allayed, death is a less formidable antagonist when it is seen in the light of the promise of new life. As the funeral bears witness to the Christian hope, the bereaved gain perspective upon the death of their loved one.

The other dimension of the coping process deals with the potency of reflecting upon one's own death. The universality and inevitability of death is never truly shaded by either subtlety or secrecy. Bereavement brings these facts home forcefully. Thus it is that the funeral has the task of assisting the individual to confront this reality.

Herman Feifel has pointed to the way in which the capacity to grasp the concept of a future and of inevitable death is a unique part of human nature. Man does not confront this future with total equanimity. "Death is something that happens to each one of us. Even before its actual arrival, it is an absent presence. Some hold that the fear of death is a universal reaction and that no one is free from it." If this reaction is part of our common humanity, it seems entirely reasonable that such feelings would come closest to the surface when death has caused personal bereavement. Thus the ceremonial context of death and bereavement would have as one of its focuses the possibility for coming to terms with death, even in relationship to one's own death.

This theme has particular reference to the place which the body of the deceased often plays in the funeral ritual. Assuming that the New Testament is correct in pointing out that man is really a totality rather than a composite of separable parts, the place of the body in the funeral is affected. This is not to say that belief in the resurrection of the whole man dictates any particular practice involving the body, but it does most certainly shape attitudes toward the body, the corpse of the deceased.

Even some of the more traditional forms of the concept of resurrection have been implicitly dualistic. As we have already seen, a popular notion among Christians has been that body and soul separated at the time of death, the spirit lived on while the body perished, then the immortal spirit and the resurrected body were rejoined at the end of time. This belief can have one of two effects upon the way in which the body is regarded. On the one hand, because it is seen as the perishable part of the person it can be disregarded and virtually ignored. This attitude is commonly held in Protestant churches. On the other hand, if this body will someday be raised from the grave, it must be highly regarded. Thus, for example, one finds the Roman Catholic Church resisting cremation because it is an unnatural form of dissolution which is not regarded as proper for the body of a Christian.

If, however, one accepts the biblical position that the resurrection involves the whole man, a new perspective emerges. That which we call man's body is no less a part of him than that which we call his spirit. Death touches radically the total man, so that one part cannot be lightly discarded while another is brought to its fulfillment. There are those who have felt that minimal attention given to the body of the deceased enhanced the spiritual aspect of his nature and therefore was proper Christian perspective. But we must ask if the New Testament understanding of resurrection, with its elements of continuity and discontinuity cutting across the totality of man's being, does not call this assumption into question. If death brings total annihilation to all of man's being, and if the concept of man as a whole is taken seriously, can we assume that the body of the deceased is any less a part of him than his spirit? In fact, from our human perspective, one needs to question earnestly whether or not the body, by virtue of its tangible presence before the funeral, is not a proper and adequate representation of the person, so long as it is fully and realistically acknowledged that he is dead.

The tension between continuity and discontinuity that the concept of resurrection contains also has implications for the preservation of the body. The element of discontinuity certainly indicates that the concept of resurrection provides no warrant for the long-term preservation of the body. There is no Christian basis for practices similar to those of the Egyptians, who sought to preserve and reanimate the body in order to assure its survival beyond death. To assume that embalming or shielding the corpse from the elements is in any way connected with the hope for resurrection lacks foundation.

At the same time, although it should not be asserted that the concept of resurrection demands it, the theme of continuity provides some rationale for the short-term preservation of the corpse as an intermediate stage in the separation process. Totally to ignore or even to depreciate the body, the medium through which the individual has been known, may well be an ignoring of the element of continuity. This is not to say that the actual dead physical body is the continuing factor. This is not the case, for the corpse is already involved in the process of dissolution. But, in spite of its transient nature, even its temporary presence after death can symbolize the conviction that somatic identity is reestablished and that there is a sense in which the continuity of personhood pertains in the resurrection.

Two thousand years of theological reflection have made the resurrection no less a mystery than it was in the first century of our era. Yet it has persisted as one of the central meanings of the Christian faith enabling the confrontation with death. The unique quality of the Christian funeral rests on this meaning.

De Mortuis
J. H. Plumb

In the first half of his essay, J. H. Plumb joins other writers in mocking some of the more bizarre and tasteless aspects of the American funeral. But then he introduces something new into the dialogue about American funerals: a historical perspective. The American funeral, Plumb suggests, serves the same emotional and psychological purposes for us as ancient and exotic burial rites did for our distant ancestors. It's all a matter of perspective: "What is tasteless and vulgar in one age," Plumb says, "becomes tender and moving in another."

The British have hilarious fun over the quaint funerary habits of the Americans. The death of Hubert Eaton, the world's greatest entrepreneur of death, and the recent discovery of a funeral home for pets, by a wandering British journalist, released another gale of satirical laughter in the English press. The mockery was hearty and sustained; yet was it deserved? Well, certainly much of Mr. Eaton's Forest Lawn is hard to take — the wet, nursery language for the hard facts of dying ("the loved one" for the corpse, "leave taking" for burying, and "slumber" for death), the cosmetic treatment (the contortions of death waxed away, replaced by rouge and mascara and fashionably set hair) — all of this is good for a gruesome joke. The place names of Forest Lawn appall — Lullabyland, Babyland. The piped guff, the music that flows like oil, and the coy fig-leaved art give one goose flesh.

One turns, almost with relief, to a harsh fifteenth-century representation of the dance of death — livid corpses, jangling bones, and skulls that haunt. How wholesome, after Hubert Eaton, seem the savage depictions by Bonfigli of the ravages of plague, or even the nightmares of death painted by Hieronymus Bosch. And how salutary in our own age to turn from Forest Lawn to the screaming, dissolving bodies of a Francis Bacon painting, for surely this is how life ends for most of us, in pain, in agony.

And if Forest Lawn nauseates, what of the Pets Parlor? "Blackie" combed and brushed, stretched out on the hearth rug before a log fire, waits for his sorrowing owners. The budgerigar is wired to its perch. The Ming Room houses the Siamese cats, and if you want to do your kitty proud, you can spend three hundred dollars or so on a stately laying out, a goodly coffin (if you're worried about its fun in the afterlife, you can put an outsize rubber mouse in with it), and naturally a special plot in Bide-A-Wee, the memorial park for pets. Vice-President Nixon's dog, Checkers, had the treatment: he lies among the immortals in Bide-A-Wee, like Hubert in Forest Lawn.

However, this will become a mere second-class death if deep-freezing really catches on, as it shows every sign of doing. The Life Extension Society is spreading, and the entrepreneurs have smelled the profit in immortality. As soon as the breath goes, get yourself encapsulated in liquid nitrogen and stored in one of the specially constructed freezers that are springing up all over America from Phoenix to New

J. H. Plumb, "De Mortuis," *Horizon* Spring 1967.

York. And so wait for the day when they can cure what you died of, or replace what gave way — the heart, the brain, the liver, or the guts — or rejuvenate your cells.

None of this is cheap: the capsule costs four thousand dollars, and then there are the freezing costs and who knows what they may be in fifty years, so it would be imprudent not to make ample provision. Forest Lawn may be death for the rich; this is death for the richer, death for the Big Time. But in America there are a lot of very rich, so maybe soon now, outside all the large cities, there will be refrigerators as huge as pyramids, full of the frozen dead. This surely must be a growth industry.

Perhaps by the year 2000 Hubert Eaton will seem but a modest pioneer of the death industry, for who does not crave to escape oblivion? The rich have always tried to domesticate death, to make death seem like life. The American way of death is not novel: seen in proper historical perspective it reaches back not only down the centuries but down the millenniums, for it is a response to a deep human need.

Some of the earliest graves of men, dating from paleolithic times, contained corpses decked out with bits of personal finery and sprinkled with red ocher, perhaps the symbol of blood and life, done in the hope of a future resurrection. After the neolithic revolution, which created much greater resources and considerable surplus wealth, men went in for death in a very big way. Doubtless the poor were thrown away, burned or exposed or pushed into obscurity, back to the anonymous mind from which they came.

The rich and the powerful, high priests and kings, could not die; they merely passed from one life to another. Because the life hereafter was but a mirror image of life on earth, they took with them everything they needed — jewels, furniture, food, and, of course, servants. In the Royal Graves at Ur, some of the earliest and most sumptuous of tombs ever found, a row of handmaidens had been slaughtered at the burial — death's necessities were life's. No one, of course, carried this elaboration of funerary activity further than the Egyptians. And the tombs of Pharaohs and the high officials of the Egyptian kingdom make Forest Lawn seem like a cheap cemetery for the nation's down-and-outs.

What should we think of vast stone mausoleums outside Washington, stuffed with personal jewelry from Winston's, furniture from Sloane's, glassware by Steuben, food from Le Pavillon, etc., etc., and in the midst of it all the embalmed corpse of a Coolidge or a Dulles? We should roar with laughter. We should regard it as vulgar, ridiculous, absurd. Pushed back three millenniums, such habits acquire not only decorum but also majesty, grandeur, awe.

The Egyptians were as portentous in death as in life, and their grave goods only occasionally give off the breath of life, unlike the Etruscans, who domesticated death more completely and more joyously than any other society. A rich caste of princes built tombs of singular magnificence, filling them with amphorae, jewels, and silver. And they adorned their walls with all the gaiety that they had enjoyed alive. There was nothing solemn about their attitude to death. In their tombs they hunted, played games, performed acrobatics, danced, feasted; their amorous dalliance was both wanton and guiltless. Deliberately they banished death with the recollected gusto of life. No society has brought such eroticism, such open and natural behavior, to the charnel house. But in the annals of death, Etruscans are rare birds.

How different the grandiose tombs of medieval barons, with their splendid ala-baster of marble effigies. There they lie, larger than life, grave, portentous, frozen in death, a wife, sometimes two, rigidly posed beside them, and beneath, sorrowing children, kneeling in filial piety, the whole structure made more pompous with heraldic quarterings. Yet these are but another attempt to cheat death, to keep alive in stone what was decaying and crumbling below. And even here a breath of life sometimes creeps in. The Earl and Countess of Arundel lie side by side, dogs beneath the feet, pillows under the head, he in armor, she in her long woolen gown. But, movingly enough, they are holding hands. The sons of Lord Teynham cannot be parted, even in death, with their hawk and hound. Nor were these tombs so cold, so marmoreal, when they were first built. They were painted, the faces as alive with color as the corpses in the parlors of Forest Lawn.

Seen in the context of history, Forest Lawn is neither very vulgar nor very remarkable, and the refrigerators at Phoenix are no more surprising than a pyramid in Palenque or Cairo. If life has been good, we, like the rich Etruscans, want it to go on and on and on, or at the very least to be remembered. Only a few civilizations have evaded expensive funerary habits for their illustrious rich, and these usually poverty-stricken ones. For all their austerity, the Hindus, burning bodies and throw-ing the ashes into the Ganges, have maintained distinction in their pyres. Not only were widows coaxed or thrown onto the flames, but rare and perfumed woods were burned to sweeten the spirit of the rich Brahman as it escaped from its corrupt carapace. Cremation à la Chanel!

What is tasteless and vulgar in one age becomes tender and moving in another. What should we say if we decorated our tombs with scenes from baseball games, cocktail bars, and the circus, or boasted on the side of our coffins of our amatory prowess, as erect and as unashamed in death as in life. And yet when the Etruscans do just these things, we are moved to a sense of delight that the force of life could be so strong that men and women reveled in it in their graves.

So the next time you stroll through Forest Lawn, mildly repelled by its silly sentimentality, think of those Etruscans; you will understand far more easily why seven thousand marriages a year take place in this California graveyard. After all, like those Arundels, Eros and Death have gone hand in hand down the ages. The urge to obliterate death is the urge to extend life, and what more natural than that the rich should expect renewal. How right, how proper, that Checkers should be waiting in Slumberland.

FUNERALS ARE GOOD FOR PEOPLE
William M. Lamers, Jr.

According to William Lamers, a California psychiatrist, the traditional American funeral, usually with an open coffin, satisfies deep human needs of the mourners. Although critics of the traditional funeral usually point in disgust to the custom of "viewing the remains," Lamers says that mourners need to confront the reality of death; indeed, it is through that confrontation that they can release their grief. Traditional funerals, Lamers says, "do a therapeutic job, and in most cases they can do it for a lot less money than we psychiatrists could."

While attending a medical meeting about a year ago, I ran into a fellow I'd known in residency. "What are you doing here, Bill?" he asked. "Giving a talk on the responses to death," I replied. "It will cover the psychological value of funerals as well as—"

"Funerals!" he exclaimed. "What a waste *they* are! I've made it plain to my wife that *I* don't want a funeral. Why spend all that money on such a macabre ordeal? And why have the kids standing around wondering what it's all about?"

"Look, Jim," I said patiently, "I've seen case after case of depression caused by the inability of patients—young and old—to work through their feelings after a death. I've found that people are often better off if they have a funeral to focus their feelings on. That lets them do the emotional work necessary in response to the loss." My friend still looked doubtful. And, as we parted company, I wondered how many other physicians are also overlooking the psychological value of funerals.

Their value is brought home time and time again in my own practice. Consider the woman who called me recently after making a suicide attempt. She was a divorcée and the mother of three sons, the youngest of whom had died of encephalitis about two months before. She was very much attached to her sons and highly dependent on them emotionally. The youngest had been her pet, and her grief at his loss was overwhelming.

Well-meaning friends persuaded the woman to have an immediate cremation and memorial service rather than go through the pain of a funeral. As a result, within a few hours after the boy's death, his body was cremated. Two weeks later a memorial service was held. The mother went around smiling to show people how well she'd adjusted to the boy's death. There was a small rock 'n' roll band and several poetry recitations. It was very pleasant and happy and likely provided some beautiful memories. Yet it was all only frosting on an underbaked cake.

Within a few weeks the mother became extremely depressed. She was afraid to express her true feelings from fear of offending the friends who had planned the memorial service. She didn't want them to feel it wasn't good enough, and she tried to cover up her tremendous unresolved grief. All that was a prelude to her suicide attempt. This woman still had doubts that her son was dead. I'm convinced that, had she gone through a formalized funeral experience and been allowed to vent her grief, her son's death would have held some finality for her. And her feelings wouldn't have healed superficially while the core still continued to fester.

I see constant evidence that the problems resulting from a serious separation—through death, divorce, or other means—can have great psychological impact. If these problems remain unresolved, grave emotional trouble can result later. That's what happened to a patient I saw several years ago. She'd been married and divorced four times, each time to men at least 20 years older than she. And all were men who were gone from home most of the time—sea captains, traveling men, and the like.

She began to develop ulcers, high blood pressure, and had made several suicide attempts. When referred to me, she was about to divorce her fifth husband and marry a sixth. Apparently she also went through psychiatrists as fast as husbands: I was the fourth she'd seen. In consultation she told me she couldn't remember anything before the age of 10. Two or three sessions with her brought no results. Finally, trying to get at her early childhood through the back door, I said, "Tell me about your mother and father." She told me she'd been brought up in Europe and that her father had died in the early days of World War II.

Slowly, more of the story came out. One day, her father came back from the mountains—he was a guerrilla leader—to a triumphant reception in the village. Apparently he was also under strong suspicion of collaborating with the Germans. He'd been home less than an hour when some of his soldiers came and, on a ruse, took him away. Minutes later, my patient painfully recalled, she and her mother were summoned to the village square. There, with no explanation from the villagers, her father was shot before her eyes.

In that village it was the custom for villagers to file through the home to view the body and express condolences. Then there would be a funeral service, a procession, and a gathering afterwards. In this instance, however, my patient and her mother were carted away to another town. No one knows what happened to the father's body, but there was no funeral. Possibly as a direct result, my patient had never been able to accept emotionally the fact of her father's death.

In my office she finally wept. The extent of her reaction indicated that at last she was beginning to express the feelings that might have been more properly handled about 20 years earlier. From then on, she was gradually able to understand that, in marrying older men who were away most of the time, she'd been searching for her father. Today, she's settled down considerably. But I can't help believing that a funeral, with its acknowledgement of death, would have contributed to her emotional well-being years earlier.

When a death occurs, most people feel a need to *do* something. And the doing can come out in several ways—in crying, in the funeral and burial, perhaps in informing others that the death has occurred, perhaps in assuring themselves that what was seen and heard was, in fact, a true happening. The funeral makes these things easier by providing the setting in which people can begin to resolve their feelings about death.

Children, of course, are especially vulnerable to the suffering that results from unresolved grief situations. So we do them a tremendous injustice when we don't let them know the facts or we lie—describing "the trip" Grandfather has gone on, for example. We need to answer their questions about death in a straightforward manner and give them the opportunity to talk about death and to express their feelings toward it. Many parents don't seem to understand this. They're not doing their children a favor by sheltering them.

A case in point is that of a 7-year-old girl whose mother brought her to me shortly after the death of the father. The little girl had become despondent, and her mother couldn't understand why. As the mother explained it, she'd done everything to protect her daughter's feelings. She'd kept almost all knowledge of the death from the child and hadn't allowed her to participate in the services or the burial.

Their first visit to me occurred about a week before President John F. Kennedy's assassination. Shortly after the assassination, the mother called to tell me her daughter had run away. Desperately, she asked me what to do, but I couldn't be of much help.

A few days later the girl returned home. She'd been at a friend's house where for the entire weekend she'd watched the Kennedy funeral on TV — a steady, continuous ritual of mourning. When the little girl came home, she told her mother: "Everything's O.K. now. I know what happened to Daddy."

Are there any satisfactory funeral substitutes — a memorial service, for example? In my opinion, there aren't. Though a memorial service is a response to loss and can be extremely satisfying for many, it's not ideal because it lacks several basic elements. First, a memorial service usually doesn't take place when feelings are most intense, which is shortly after the death. Second, members of the family aren't involved in communication, participation, and repeated exposure to the fact that death has occurred. These things force people to acknowledge the reality of loss. Finally, a memorial service doesn't include the presence of the body, which means people aren't given as great an opportunity to fix the fact of death in their minds.

In contrast to the memorial service, which is a one-time gathering, the traditional funeral as we know it in this country is a continuum of things. It includes visitations at the funeral home, usually with the remains lying in state. Frequently, there are religious services there as well as in the church, a procession to the place of burial, and committal service. Afterward, there's often a gathering of close friends and relatives. Throughout these events there's a repeated acceptance of condolences, acknowledgement of the fact of death, sharing of grief feelings, and encouragement for the future.

Since I'm so profuneral, you may wonder how I feel about those attacks on the funeral profession in recent years. Let me make it plain that I don't own a funeral home. Some funeral directors *are* guilty of abuse and of taking advantage of the public. I contend, however, that they're in the minority and that criticism of the funeral business has been blown out of proportion. In time of need, the majority of the directors provide an effective means of helping families through a lot of turmoil.

What can we, as physicians, do to steer families of dying patients in the right direction? Naturally, we can't actively impose our beliefs on others. In other words, it's unwise to steer a family toward a particular kind of funeral or service. If they prefer to have a memorial service held, then this may well be the most satisfactory for them.

On the other hand, a family that's avoiding the reality of death, trying to seal it over without allowing normal emotional responses to come to the surface, may need guidance. In that case, we doctors have an obligation to point out the possible consequences and to make ourselves available to discuss the situation. We do patients a disservice when we oversedate or overtranquilize them so that they're unaware of what's happening or unable to experience normal feelings of grief.

In short, we should encourage the practice of something as psychologically economical as funerals. They do a therapeutic job, and in most cases they can do it for a lot less money than we psychiatrists could.

THE ROLE OF THE MORTICIAN

Richard Huntington and Peter Metcalf

Huntington and Metcalf, anthropologists, argue that the traditional American fu-neral has been remarkably uniform and stable over the past centuries, and that fact tells us that Americans tacitly approve of its rites. Huntington and Metcalf further defend the traditional funeral by citing a study that suggests that mourners often receive comfort and help from funeral directors. In fact, the widows in the Boston study they cite actually received more comfort from funeral directors than they did from clergymen and physicians. Americans, these two anthropologists suggest, ap-prove of the "American way of death."

As the critics have shown, funeral directors have not failed to exploit their position in order to make a profit. [Ruth Harmer's *The High Cost of Dying* and Jessica Mitford's *The American Way of Death*] are full of examples of such opportunism. For example, Mitford describes how funeral directors regularly play upon the emotional state of their customers in order to get them to purchase a more expensive coffin than they had intended. As she points out, the morticians' customers are almost by definition "impulse buyers." . . . Again, cemetery landscapers are in a particularly favorable position vis-à-vis their customers: They collect payment on plots that they will not have to provide for perhaps many years, leaving themselves with interest-free capital in the interim. . . .

The National Funeral Directors Association has frequently exercised a powerful political influence. It maintains well-financed lobbies in Washington and the state capitals. Occasionally it has been able to secure legislation favorable to the business interests of its members. For instance, the association has steadily opposed crema-tion, and in some states has supported laws that make it unnecessarily expensive by requiring that a coffin be provided and burned up with the corpse. . . .

However, in comparative perspective the proportion of available resources com-mitted to death ritual does not seem exceptional: Certainly the Berawan and the Malagasy use up more. Moreover, the amount spent each year on funerals in the United States is considerably less than the amount spent on weddings, yet few condemn the materialism of weddings. Charges of exploitation are not leveled at the dressmaking industry, or the Brewers' Association of America on the grounds that they make a profit out of these festive events. . . . Presumably this is because the critics regard weddings as socially useful and funerals as useless. But who is to judge the value of a ritual?

The same kind of overstatement has occurred in connection with conspicuous consumption at American funerals. Certainly, commercialism is noticeable, but it is not unlimited. For example, sumptuous flower arrangements surrounding the coffin are a feature of the "viewing," and it could be argued that the mourners

Richard Huntington and Peter Metcalf, "The Role of the Mortician," *Celebrations of Death* (New York: Cambridge University Press, 1979).

compete to display their affluence in such gifts. However, very nice distinctions of status govern the size of floral tributes. It would be entirely tactless for a mere acquaintance or a distant relative to offer too large a wreath. In general, the impression is of a striving to find the *correct* level of expenditure in funeral accoutrements, rather than the most *impressive*. . . .

The same tendency is noticeable in the funeral cavalcade. Although it is common for close relatives to request that the hearse drive past the deceased's former residence or work place, the display at such times is modest by comparison with, say, nineteenth-century England. In *The Victorian Celebration of Death*, J. S. Curl presents a remarkable photograph from England of a six-horse hearse, heavily draped in black crepe, the horses decorated with black-dyed ostrich feathers, and attended by a dozen or so equerries. The striking feature of the picture is the obvious poverty of the neighborhood to which this apparition has been summoned. By comparison, the dark American hearse and line of cars is positively spartan. In grave markers also, the prevalent trend is toward simple horizontal tablets. Clearly, wealth and social class *are* expressed in funerals, as they are in other phases of American culture, such as housing, clothing, and automobiles. However, there is little evidence of the manipulation of the dead for status-climbing purposes.

Considering the economic explanation as a whole, there is no doubt that the existence of a tightly organized group of specialists who control every phase of the disposal of corpses is the most significant single feature of American funerals. It explains why funerals cost what they do, and why nonspecialists, such as kin and clergy, appear only in passive roles.

But it does not explain everything about them. Why do they have the ritual form they do? There are other things that could be done to the corpse that would be just as expensive and therefore just as profitable. The very uniformity of funeral rites places limits on the economic explanation because merchandisers usually try continually to add new products to tickle the fancy of consumers. There has been, it is true, some gimmickry in the funeral industry — drive-in funeral parlors are a recent example — but the overall form of the rites has remained remarkably stable for several decades.

Moreover, it is clear that Americans are not just passive consumers of the only services available to them; they actively approve of them. A survey in several midwestern cities revealed that a majority of respondents felt that contemporary funerals are appropriate, and that the funeral director has an important role to play in comforting the bereaved. . . . P. Silverman concludes in "Another Look at the Role of the Funeral Director" (1974) that the widows she worked with in Boston received more help and comfort from the funeral director than from either physician or clergyman. This tacit approval is also manifest in the limited success of movements to reform funeral practices. Nonprofit funeral and memorial societies have had some success, and certainly provide much cheaper funerals, but their membership remains small. Some unions have established funeral plans for members, but their experience has been that the cheapest variety does not sell. Their blue-collar clientele still demands all the elements found in the commercial funeral. . . .

A final piece of evidence: Modern-style embalming, with its associated rites, has been practiced for nearly a century now. During that time, the United States has continued to receive immigrants from many different cultural backgrounds. The statistics quoted in the preceding section indicate that the majority have adopted American deathways, just as they have absorbed other aspects of national culture. Had it been otherwise, institutions would surely have sprung up to cater to their needs. This shows that funerals somehow fit into a peculiarly American ideology; that funerals express something. Economics is powerless to explain what.

The Lost Art of Dying
Graham Turner

In the following essay, Graham Turner seems to regret the decline of traditional funeral practices in England. The English try to sweep death under the carpet, Turner says, by ignoring the rituals of death—and this is due in large part to the atrophy of Christianity itself. Turner quotes Dr. Zaki Badawi, a British Muslim, ". . . the real trouble with people in [Britain] is that they are materialistic, don't believe in God, and so feel that death is the end of everything."

Dr. Robert Twycross, director of the Michael Sobell Center for the terminally ill in Oxford, says that he recently met a woman of 70 whose husband was dying at home from a brain tumor. The man probably was not going to live for more than 24 hours, yet "that dear woman insisted that he be brought in here immediately. She couldn't face the idea of him dying at home because, at the age of 70, she had never seen a corpse!"

She is not unusual. In the nearby Churchill Hospital, a woman of 71 sitting beside a desperately sick husband confided to the chaplain that she simply did not know what to say to him, because she had never been near anyone who was dying, let alone dead.

We belong to a unique generation for which the sight of death and the experience of dealing with it have become alien even to the elderly. As Dr. Richard Lansdown, chief psychiatrist at a children's hospital, remarks sadly, "Death has become a foreign country where we don't know how to behave."

Gone are the days when the face of death was a familiar, domestic presence. A century ago, only 5 percent of the population died in a hospital. The dying were cared for at home. Their deaths did not cause families to shrink from their very presence. Today, more than 70 percent of us die in a hospital. Very few relatives of those who die at home want to keep the body in the house before burial.

And there are many people who are so determined to shield their children from death that they will not even allow them to attend Grandma's funeral. Fewer than half of the customers of one of York's leading funeral directors now want to view the bodies of their dead relatives in the firm's chapel. In our times, those two mighty taboos, sex and death, have changed places. People now shriek about sex from rooftops, and it is from death that we seek to distance ourselves.

Indeed, we flee from any intimation of mortality. Chris Weaver, an undertaker, says that half of the married people whose funerals he has handled have never told their spouses whether they want to be buried or cremated. Only one person in three has made a will.

The more we have sought to keep death at arm's length, the more perfunctory its rituals have become. In 1945, only 9 percent of those who died were cremated. Now 75 percent are, often without any church ceremony. "Seven times out of 10," says Chris Weaver, "people will say to me, 'I hope the vicar won't go on; we don't want a long service.'"

Graham Turner, "The Lost Art of Dying," *The Sunday Telegraph* 26 Feb 1989.

Among the native British, there is also very little weeping these days. Gone are the floods of tears and graveside collapses that marked Victorian and Edwardian funerals. Gone are the widow's mourning weeds. And the vast majority of today's mourners opt for music of the "Abide with Me" variety, but others settle for renderings of popular folk songs. The ashes are usually scattered in a garden of remembrance.

As the rituals of death have atrophied, so have the rituals of mourning. All too often the deceased are kept in cold storage before they are consigned to the flames. The bereaved are given the cold shoulder afterward. "How do we treat them?" asks Dr. Tom West, medical director of St. Christopher's Hospice in London. "By crossing the road and walking down the other side of the street." The reason people cross the road, says Richard Lansdown, is that they no longer know what to say. There is no longer any language of religious consolation in our society.

We have also grown accustomed to such superficial relationships that we shy away from the deep involvement that joining people in their grief implies. Even parents of dead children often complain that their friends expect them to overcome their misery within a very short time. This quite specifically means not speaking about the person who has died. "I think we've lost the art of dealing with the relatives" of the dead, says the bishop of Lewes, Peter Ball.

The changing demography of death may go some way toward explaining our attitudes. In 1900, 143,000 British babies died before they were a year old. Now, the figure is 6,000. Even more startling, there are only 155,000 deaths a year of people under the age of 70. The fact that death has become the monopoly of the aged has totally changed our perception of it, says Eric Midwinter, director of Britain's Center for Policy on Aging. When the Grim Reaper struck at random and took a baby, a nursing mother, or a breadwinner, it left great rifts in the social fabric, and rites of passage were designed to help heal them. Now, because the vast majority of people enjoy a normal span of life, death is "sort of all right" — often seen as more of a blessing than a disaster.

Yet the death rituals of Jews and Moslems in Britain are not nearly so cursory. Jews, says Rabbi Julia Neuberger, divide the period of mourning into three clear stages, which go on for 11 months and mirror the stages of natural grief. The first, *shiva*, lasts for seven days. During that time, there are evening prayers at the chief mourner's house, and members of the community come to console the bereaved family.

Moslems also have fixed periods of mourning. "The family grieves for three days," says Dr. Zaki Badawi, chairman of the Council of Imams and Mosques, "then again on the seventh and 40th days, while a widow would mourn for four months and 10 days. If we see bereaved persons in the street, far from trying to avoid them, we cross the road to offer them the ritual greeting. 'May God accept him — or her — in His mercy, give you the strength to endure the loss, and compensate you for it.'

"Westerners seem to fear death as if it were a creature from Mars. But the real trouble with people in [Britain] is that they are materialistic, don't believe in God, and so feel that death is the end of everything." The evidence offered by those who work in hospitals and hospices suggests that perhaps 80 percent of those facing death [in Britain] are nominal Anglicans, with 10 percent committed Christians and the rest atheists. Not many seek the consolations of religion.

Sometimes, according to Mother Frances, an Anglican nun who runs an Oxford home for children with life-threatening illnesses, busybodies come to the home to tell the parents of the sick children, "If you really prayed and had faith, your child would be well." She notes, "I've known a case where a mother—who had already had one child die, had another dying, and was ill herself—was told by this 'Christian' that if she had a real faith, she wouldn't be grieving!" Yet Christians do not seem to die better deaths than unbelievers. And the "more affluent you are," says Dame Cicely Saunders, the pioneer of the hospice movement, "the more angry and frightened you will be at death."

It saddens John Baker, bishop of Salisbury, that as a society we sweep death under the carpet. "We should think about death far more," he says, "because it sharpens one's priorities as very few other stimuli can. It makes you say, 'What are the really important things I should be doing with my life, not just selfishly but also for other people? Are there quarrels I'd like to heal, relationships I should mend, something I'd like to do for somebody but kept putting off?' What we're doing by pushing the thought of death away is robbing ourselves of its power to make our lives what they are meant to be."

Hot Tombs

Michael Specter

Michael Specter, writing for The New Republic, *was the first to spot a new Yuppie trend: status after death. BMWs while alive, a tony burial plot while dead. "If you struggle all your life to get good jobs and the best apartments and to send your children to Harvard," one anonymous Yuppie says, "why the hell should you want to spend 3,000 years lying under a highway in Queens?" Specter even has a theory to account for this sudden desire for nice burial plots: It's the "Roots" thing. Yuppies move around so much while alive, Specter says, that they yearn for something nice and permanent.*

It's late sunday afternoon and you are savoring a final few moments on the peaceful deck of your summer home. The Volvo's in the shop, so your wife packs the children, the basil and a few carefully selected baby eggplants into the back of the Saab. Although traffic can be difficult on the long trip home, that doesn't usually bother you. But today is different. This was the weekend you had promised yourself you would see about getting the family a plot in that perfect little cemetery just down the road. Driving by, you notice a fresh grave has just been cut near the historic stone gatehouse. Damn.

After all, the place has been filling up for 200 years, and prime space doesn't last forever. It's not as if you expect to occupy a plot anytime soon, of course, but could there be a better time than now, in leisure and in health, to make what surely will be the most permanent decision of your life? Both the houses are in good shape, and thanks to your personal trainer, so are you. The kids made it into the private schools of your choice, and the latest nanny is working out better than either you or your wife had hoped. Perhaps some people would find it morbid to dwell on death at the height of one's vitality, but let's face it, the '60s, the '70s—even the '80s— are over. Eternity is just around the corner.

All of a sudden, a generation taught first to trust nobody over 30, and then to seek fulfillment through accumulated goods, has stumbled over the notion of its eventual demise. And how is it reacting to the first real intimations of mortality? Not with the defiance you might have expected of the Woodstock generation. Not with the hedonistic blinders of the '70s, or the amused contempt of the '80s. Baby boomers are buying cemetery plots in record numbers. From sea to shining sea, smart young couples are edgily sizing up the nation's cemeteries, from the gaudiest memorial parks to the clubbiest little churchyards. And you'd better grab these plots while they're hot, because whether it's a duplex apartment with a Park view and a private elevator or a box tomb in a meadow crowned by the simplest stela, real estate is real estate.

Yuppies have seen the future, and it is death. According to the Pre-Arrangement Association, which represents funeral directors, cemeterians, and other suppliers to the death care industry, successful young people with little else to worry about have

Michael Specter, "Hot Tombs," *The New Republic* 11 September 1989.

become the driving engine of the growing multibillion-dollar death business. They are out there hustling for the "right" cemetery spot in much the same way they have scoured the nation for the most sophisticated cabernets, the most authentic Italian espresso machines, and the best Aprica strollers.

"Pre Need" — as opposed to "At Need," which is how the industry refers to the shortsighted people who die before they find a cemetery — is clearly going gangbusters. Before 1960 it was rare to find any healthy young person searching for his own grave. During the '60s only ten percent of all such purchases were made far in advance. But according to the PAA, the figure grew to 20 percent in the '70s and 40 percent in the '80s. And nobody sees any end soon to this bull market.

In most ways, trends in cemeteries parallel those that exist above ground. Grave sites in major cities are difficult to come by and cost thousands of dollars. "Rich or yuppie people with large ways and means are always able to buy a more expensive casket or a more impressive burial lot," says Dayne Sieling, the PAA's executive vice president. "So naturally they gravitate to the more prestigious cemeteries." In rural America the price drops drastically. Americans of the 20th century are still among the first people routinely to die far from where they were born. So naturally we are among the first to go house-hunting for our sacred resting place.

In tony locales such as Georgetown's Oak Hill Cemetery or Pine Lawn in Long Island, most of the truly desirable spots are already taken, though like the finest restaurateurs, smart cemetery proprietors always reserve a little room in case somebody special should pop by. But the careful grave-watchers at the American Cemetery Association don't expect the real land crunch to hit until the year 2000, when most boomers will have hit 50, the age of no return. That's less than 11 years away, gang. So if you don't see how you survived so far without decent life insurance, and you wonder whether risk equity stocks are really the right instrument for your 401k retirement plan, is it that stupid to start thinking about a grave when you're 40?

"It makes great sense if you're willing to admit it," says a physician from New York City, who is willing to admit it but not to be quoted by name. He recently acquired for himself, his wife, and two sons a fine patch of pricey Long Island hillside. "If you struggle all your life to get good jobs and the best apartments and to send your children to Harvard, why the hell should you want to spend 3,000 years lying under a highway in Queens?"

He's got a point. And as the folks from the Pre-Arrangement Association, and allied groups such as the Casket Manufacturers Association of America, constantly remind anyone who will listen, dying isn't getting any cheaper. "In any competitive situation, economics plays a factor," says the PAA's Dayne Sieling, describing what must be the ultimate layaway plan. "Why not use today's dollars to pay tomorrow's prices?" Enough said.

But even today's prices can be hefty. Unless you are willing to shell out the minimum entry fee of about $15,000, for example, you can forget about getting into Westwood Village Memorial Park in Los Angeles, the final (and perhaps only) resting place of Marilyn Monroe. (For less than a third of that you can still lie within musket shot of Jefferson Davis, Gen. J. E. B. Stuart, and other members of the Confederate pantheon in Richmond's Hollywood Cemetery.)

At Abel's Hill Cemetery in Chilmark, one of the exclusive towns on Martha's Vineyard, you can bury your whole family at the bargain basement cost of $210, but only if you already own a house there — which shouldn't run you much more than a million dollars or so. "We've always been able to take whoever comes," says Basil Welch, the superintendent of Abel's Hill, a shabbily genteel cemetery where, through what could only be a harmonic convergence, Lillian Hellman and John Belushi somehow managed to end up together for the rest of time. (Although Hellman lived on Martha's Vineyard, she wasn't a resident of Chilmark, and her friends had to move heaven to get her into that piece of earth.) But even this deal isn't going to last forever. "There's been a stream of young people making plans in the past few years," Welch adds. "You don't want to be buried standing up, do you?"

Maybe the nomadic existence of so many people in a country linked principally by people like Oprah Winfrey and Willard Scott accounts for the sudden desire to be securely planted in terra firma for a few millennium. Maybe it's part of that "Roots" thing. But the only segment of the market that is moving nearly as fast is cremation. More than 25 percent of all people who die in California now go up in smoke. In the rest of the country it's a smaller but growing figure.

Somehow, though, for the yuppies of this world — whether they are religious or not — cremation doesn't seem to hold much appeal. "Most people want to be remembered," said Harvey Geller, of Columbia Memorial Park in the planned city of Columbia, Maryland. "And they want to be visited. It's just harder for most people to see the grandchildren gathering around the urn than around a more traditional grave." Like everything else in Columbia — which is Maryland's version of Singapore — everything in Geller's cemetery has been planned, down to the size of the tree trunks. All sections will be separated by judiciously placed trees or ponds. Even the exact angles of the roads have been laid out to match the town.

The choices can seem staggering. There are roomy lots and crypts and vaults and urn areas for cremation. And most cemeteries offer a range of prices. "Something to suit every purse and give rein to every social aspiration" was the way Jessica Mitford put it in her classic 1963 text, *The American Way of Death*. Cemeteries are splayed out like cities, and as we know, most cities have more than one side of the tracks.

But for people of means, people who know the difference between a single malt whiskey and a muddied blend, who can choose correctly between a vacation in Aspen or Vail or whether to use chorionic villi sampling rather than amniocentesis, why not the best when it comes to eternal repose? Sharon Memorial Park, just outside Boston, is considered one of the Northeast's prestige burial sites. It is big and lush and quiet. In a rare display of institutional decorum, its managers decided tombstones were vulgar, so they use bronze plaques instead. At $800 per regular grave ($1,500 for a couple and $2,300 for four), it's a comparative bargain, particularly when you realize that ten percent of the costs go to a perpetual care fund that pretty much guarantees that weeds won't crowd you out of eternity. "Landscapewise, it's magnificent," says Sharon's Glenna Goldstein. "Beautiful and elegant. When people in this part of the country start thinking about Jewish cemeteries, they start thinking about Sharon Memorial Park."

The death business couldn't have become as successful as it is without the shrewd sales tactics of its leaders. Cemetery owners, taking full advantage of the deregulation of their industry, now use phone marketing, direct mail, and personal visits in their attempts to sign new recruits. "I've been in this business since 1956, and God, how it's changed," said Columbia's Geller. "We send out brochures now and people can return cards if they are interested. Telemarketing has become a major part of recruiting and so have neighborhood canvasses, print ads, and billboards." Spring Grove Cemetery, in Cincinnati, has a walking tour that takes two hours, and the route covers less than a fifth of the property, but as its brochure points out. "It surveys the richness of 19th-century material culture, and emphasizes Spring Grove's character as a built environment."

Cemeteries traditionally have been repositories of class structure. In Europe it wasn't until a few hundred years ago that they were even acceptable for upper-class burials. Until then the sacred and the noble were buried in the church. The dregs got dumped in the fields. Although most cemeteries still break down along religious, ethnic, or class lines, the distinctions are often far more subtle these days. If you have gone off the American dream lately, you might be surprised to find that, to some degree at least, in death American democracy remains happily intact. There, after all, everyone has the right to do with himself as he sees fit.

As Philippe Aries notes in *The Hour of Our Death*, if you cannot afford an "estate" in life, it is a lot easier, and cheaper, to simulate one in the hereafter. You might be poor while you're breathing, but if you care enough to scrimp for a few years, most people can still manage to reach new heights in death. Money might not get you into Harvard anymore, but it can still get you buried next to its alumni.

Of course, none of this matters to the truly informed sophisticate, for he or she is no doubt a cryonicist, and has no intention of going quietly into the good night. These people are the true avant-garde. When they die, they fork over about $125,000 to have their bodies frozen and dipped in liquid nitrogen. Then they are stored in stainless steel capsules and hooked up to a variety of electronic equipment that makes sure they keep their cool. From then on they lie around like extras from "Star Trek" for a few hundred years until some scientist with nothing better to do figures out how to defrost them. It's not for everyone, of course, but what is?

GRAVE MISUNDERSTANDINGS

Bruce Bower

In this short article from Science News, *Bruce Bower summarizes the theories of Aubrey Cannon, an archeology professor at the University of Toronto. Cannon claims that competition among the mourners for social status determines the ornateness of the burials of their loved ones, with poor people often spending lavishly on grave site memorials as they try to emulate the ornateness of burials among the upper classes. Unfortunately for the lower classes, when rich people see that the poor are emulating their financial outlay on burials, the rich recover their status by reverting to simple and frugal burials. And thus the cycle continues.*

Dead men tell no tales, but their graves—and those of their female compatriots—utter intriguing stories to archaeologists. Traditional theories hold that an elaborate burial site containing an elegantly appointed corpse signifies the deceased belonged to a privileged social class. Ostentatious graves also supposedly illuminate a society's reverence for the dead. On the other hand, archaeologists tend to associate simple burial trappings with lower social classes and an unsentimental attitude concerning death.

But it may be time to write an epitaph for these seemingly self-evident interpretations, says archaeologist Aubrey Cannon of the University of Toronto. Mortuary practices, like tastes in clothes and etiquette, follow fads and fashions, Cannon asserts. Depending on the historical circumstances, a body in a fancy casket topped by a monumental headstone is as likely to have been a working stiff as a nobleman.

From ancient Greece to Victorian England, funerals have offered mourners an occasion to express their social status, or at least the status to which they aspire, Cannon proposes in the August-October *Current Anthropology.* Typically, in his view, the well-placed and wealthy have distanced themselves from the masses by devising magnificent funerals and graves for their kin. In turn, lower classes and even downright poor people made great sacrifices to mimic the extravagant displays when their own loved ones died, sparking a competition among social classes to devise the most stunning funeral pageantry. At some point, the wealthy threw in the towel and reverted to simple funerals as the clearest way to distance themselves socially from the masses.

Thus, status competition leads to historical periods during which mourners favor either elaborate or simple funerals, Cannon says. Fundamental shifts in beliefs about death, he contends, seem largely irrelevant to burial styles.

Consider 19th-century Victorian England. The growing affluence of farmers in the early 1800s led them to emulate the urban gentry in fashions of house building, household goods, clothing and funerals. In a study of 3,500 19th-century grave monuments from 50 rural villages in England, Cannon finds the diversity of monument shapes increases until the middle of the century, then markedly declines. Higher social classes tended to employ certain monument styles before they peaked

Bruce Bower, "Grave Misunderstandings," *Science News 136* 1989.

in popularity, Cannon asserts, whereas lower-status individuals were often memorialized by monuments that were fast becoming unfashionable with the trend-setting upper crust.

Historical records of British undertakers document an increasing restraint in funeral arrangements among the upper classes as early as 1843, he notes. The lower classes gradually followed suit. Today, only a minority of the poorest segment of British society prefers elaborate funerals, and civic and church authorities promote simple burials.

Similar shifts in funeral fashion occurred throughout the history of ancient Greece, Cannon maintains. For example, the number and types of metal offerings placed in Greek graves increased significantly from 1125 B.C. to 760 B.C., followed by a sharp decline initially appearing in the graves of socially elite individuals. Early Athenian ceramic-vase grave markers first emerged around 900 B.C., and their flamboyant features probably reflect the search for new status symbols among upper-class mourners, Cannon says.

Cycles of burial fashion also occur in societies lacking complex economic and political hierarchies, he adds. In the early 17th century, Iroquois living in what is now the northeastern United States began to pack graves with beaver-skin robes, shell beads, axes and other items of value. The practice was eventually adopted even by those who endured great hardship to come up with appropriate offerings. But tribal fashions quickly changed in the 18th century, when simple graves and restrained funeral ceremonies gained favor. Simplicity still holds sway among the Iroquois, who today prohibit burial with glass beads or anything red.

Cannon's contention that status competition produces historical trends in how people of diverse cultures are buried deserves careful testing, says Curtis Runnels of Boston University. If the theory holds up, he notes, it suggests societies do not simply evolve from primitive to more complex forms, but instead share general historical trends in the use of goods and possessions.

Cannon correctly emphasizes the status and aspirations of mourners rather than the social position of the deceased, remarks Richard Bradley of the University of Reading in England. "The dead did not bury themselves, yet attempts to read social position from grave goods often seem to suggest otherwise," he says.

However, some archaeologists argue that Cannon oversimplifies burial practices.

A burial is only one link in a chain of related ceremonies, including body preparation, ritual services and mourning, asserts Brad Bartel of San Diego State University. To confirm Cannon's contention, he says, researchers must study historical evidence concerning each link.

Status competition is not the only important influence on burial practices, Bartel adds. As populations grow, shifts in family structure and living arrangements inevitably alter burial arrangements, he contends.

Another problem for Cannon's theory is that the decorative aspects of a grave are not the only status symbols available to the upper classes, says Jeffrey Quilter of Ripon (Wis.) College. For example, the Victorian elite may have been buried more frequently in family vaults, in exclusive cemeteries or even in "better" sections of public cemeteries.

And while the historical pattern described by Cannon characterizes the simple burials of Greece during the 7th century B.C., frugal funerals again appeared in the

5th century B.C. as a result of laws reserving monumental tombs for the war dead, maintains Ian Morris of the University of Chicago.

Future research will help determine whether general historical forces such as status competition outweigh specific cultural influences in determining how people are buried, Cannon says.

For now, however, the Canadian investigator has struck a scientific nerve. Even is his theory has flaws, Morris remarks, "it remains a major contribution to the archaeology of death."

THE LAST PERSON WHO WILL EVER TOUCH YOU

C. Ray Hall

When a funeral directors' convention came to town, C. Ray Hall, a feature writer for Louisville's The Courier-Journal Magazine, *took the opportunity to interview four of the undertakers. As it turns out, the undertakers don't come across as glinty-eyed and greedy as writers like Jessica Mitford and Roul Tunley (whose work is reprinted in this chapter) make them out to be. Indeed, they look like small-town businesspeople everywhere: They're proud of their work, they'd like to make more money, and they worry about what people think of them. Surprisingly, all four admit to occasionally crying at the funerals they arrange.*

Upwards of 7,000 people are descending on Louisville this week for the convention of the National Funeral Directors Association. Doubtless they will endure countless gibes about handing out *dour* prizes and generally painting the town gray while leaving a skeleton crew back home.

What are the funeral directors doing in Louisville, of all places? Resting up, probably: Next year, their convention will be in Las Vegas.

This afternoon, the conventioneers will loll about Millionaires' Row at Churchill Downs. Later this week, they will be entertained by political satirist Mark Russell and singer Lee Greenwood.

These folks aren't exactly like other conventioneers. As they talk shop, the word "cremains" may reverberate — in a dignified way — through the corridors of the Galt House East. They can gaze at vendors' exhibits that include $60,000 hearses, $13,000 caskets, shampoo-bottles of pink embalming fluid and trocars — the thin, spear-like implements used to siphon fluids from the torsos of the recently departed.

Like many other well-dressed conventioneers, these folks worry about corporate takeovers. About 4 percent of American funeral homes are now owned by conglomerates. They also fret over changing demographics: People live longer; they're more mobile, leaving behind their extended families and old rituals, such as traditional funerals; many people in this long-living, rootless generation embrace cremation, a procedure that causes one Kentucky funeral director to say, "If somebody can tell me how to make money on cremation, I'd love to hear it."

That utterance came at the Kentucky Funeral Directors' meeting last winter, in which one of the speakers proclaimed, "This is an exciting time for the funeral business!"

With so many funeral directors in our midst, we thought it would be a good time to find out what all the excitement is about. Or, failing that, to find out why undertakers do what they do and what it does to them. For example: Have you ever asked an undertaker how he or she felt? Or said, "I'm glad to see you."

We thought not.

C. Ray Hall, "The Last Person Who Will Ever Touch You," *The Courier-Journal Magazine* 28 October 1990.

In that spirit, we have undertaken to speak with five Kentucky funeral directors, whose comments enliven the following pages.

IN THE BEGINNING . . .

"When I was 6 years old, I can vividly remember my father teaching me the different vessels to raise in embalming. I wanted to be around him so much, and I would ask questions. He would tell me, and I would look and watch. If he would get called out in the middle of the night, I would hear the phone ring, and I'd go and beg him to just take me with him. I just wanted to go. It was so interesting to me.

"I would get upset if they would have a body come in that had tuberculosis and he would tell me I couldn't be in the preparation room because the bacteria that causes tuberculosis is spore-borne and it doesn't die with the human remains. Very dangerous for the embalmer. So he wouldn't let me be around.

"He wouldn't let me be around a person that had been decomposed or a person that had been in a serious accident. He would try to shield those things from me. He didn't want that to really shock me. So when he would leave, I would go back in there to look at them anyway, because I found it so interesting. . . .

"The men that worked at the funeral home — they sort of spoiled me, let me have my way . . . when I was a child, even when I wasn't dressed to go on funerals, the fellows would sneak me in the hearse, and when I got to a funeral and my father saw me, it was too late. He couldn't take me back. I've been on so, so many funerals. Thousands. Thousands."

— Woody Porter

" All I ever wanted to do was be a funeral director. So at 12 and 13 I wanted a little suit, and they bought me one, and I'd open the door. . . . I liked that opening the door and putting on a lady's jacket as she was going out."

— Mark Engle

"When we were little, we would play funeral. Woody would be the funeral director and the preacher, and us four girls would be the choir and the mourners. He would convince us that, yes, we did want to play funeral."

— Marie Porter

"I don't think there was a black preacher in Louisville I couldn't mimic. . . .

"My father tells me one time — I don't remember it — I had my next door neighbor, a friend of mine, laid out in my little wagon, and I had him just like he was a deceased person, and I was taking him down the street to 'bury' him — and his mother just went totally off."

— Woody Porter

WHAT STRANGERS THINK OF YOU

"I don't think anyone likes to think of their own mortality, and that's what, in essence, it is when you meet your funeral director. You're coming face to face with your own mortality.

"When you're sitting down having a conversation with someone and all of a sudden they find out you're a funeral director, they get the nervous giggles. I mean, because it surprised them and they are now facing their mortality.

"It always surprises me when that happens, but it shouldn't, because it happens every day."

— Alan Beard

"Women, when they find out what I do, I get an increased feeling of respect for who I am. When men find out what I do . . . if it's a social setting, I feel men draw back a little bit. I'm a professional woman and I think that's OK for a lot of men; there are a lot of professional women out here. But they're not sure — funeral business, what kind of person are you?"

— Marie Porter

WHAT LITTLE BROTHERS THINK OF YOU

"My brother couldn't stand it. I mean, if I was embalming a body and he wanted to borrow money for a Pepsi, after he was a teen-ager, I had to come out and hold my hands up and let him get the money out of my pockets. He wouldn't come in, nor would he touch me — or let me touch the money and touch him.

"So I think he picked the right profession — the legal profession."

— Mark Engle

A TALE FROM THE CRYPT

"They disinterred a man that had been in the ground for 20 years and were going to send him to Florida; his wife had moved to Florida. I'd have been about 8 . . . and I heard them all talking about it. I wanted to see what that fellow looked like. By myself, 8 or 9 o'clock at night, I went down and opened up the casket lid. He had a double-breasted blue suit and a paisley tie. He was in a sealer casket in a vault, and he looked good. All his skin was gone up here [around his nose], and it looked dark, but that's all that was hurt on him. I could have waxed his nose, cosmetized him and shown him again. . . .

"Nothing holds true in all cases, but a good embalming job, a sealer casket and a vault, you ought to be the best you can be."

— Mark Engle

THE UNDERTAKER AS PAGEANT DIRECTOR

"I'm bit on pageantry and so forth. So, the more funeral I can put on, that's just the way I am. I like ceremony, I like pageantry, I like big weddings, I like big funerals. I like all the white cars I can line up.

"And so I plead guilty to that. It could be argued that some of that is unnecessary, and I guess it is, but it's not unnecessary when you go to that house after the service and they are happy and they are pleased and you have helped them with that loss."

— Alan Beard

ANOTHER TALE FROM THE CRYPT

"Apparently the men at the cemetery had a new operator of their backhoe equipment. He dug the grave too long. Instead of being 8 feet long, it was like 12 feet long. And we, too, had a new man handling cemetery equipment. He goes out and sets up the cemetery equipment. . . . We had the service and the minister was standing at the head of the grave and stepped away. And I stepped almost in the exact same spot and went completely down into the grave. I disappeared.

"They had taken the grass and covered up the end of the hole that was not covered with the casket or vault. I stepped into it and went down into the hole.

"And I fall down in there, and I said, 'This is the way you catch wild animals — dig a hole in the ground and cover it up where you can't see it!' A lot of people standing around heard the undertaker hollering. . . .

"How do you get out of a 6-foot hole with dignity? I guess the beauty of it was the family had already started moving to the cars and didn't hear it."

— Alan Beard

THE DOWN SIDE OF UNDERTAKING

"When I was growing up, all I really knew was people died, and they came to the funeral home, and they were embalmed, and they had the funeral. I can remember the smell of flowers — that intense smell of flowers — and I never saw anything except the sad parts of it. I was never around when any arrangements were being made, so I never could see how you interacted with people. I also knew that my father worked long, long hours. Growing up, I can remember one vacation we took as a family, and we were teenagers by the time we took a vacation."

— Marie Porter

"The hardest part of being in this business for years, for me, was the hours. I have one daughter, and I missed her first Christmas because I was working at the funeral home. . . . It was necessary at the time, but it's not necessary now. I wouldn't do that today."

— Woody Porter

IF YOU'RE SO WELL-DRESSED, WHY AREN'T YOU RICH?

"It's hard for you to go out because they think you have plenty, plenty of money and you can afford to set up people and do all kinds of things for them. They tell you, 'Man, you buried my family. I know you've got money.' They fail to realize, to be successful, how much of your income has to go back into your business because the overhead in the funeral industry is tremendous.

"Everybody wants to be a funeral director. Why? They think you make plenty of money; they see you drive a big car, dressed up in a suit every time they see you. And they say, 'Wow, they don't seem like they're working too hard.'

"That big car is a necessity, because when people pay their money for livery services, they want to be in a big car. And I guarantee you if you're going to pay X amount of dollars for a vehicle to ride in, you're going to choose the vehicle that is the most luxurious."

— Woody Porter

"I thought I could make a comfortable living — and I have. By no means am I wealthy, but I have made a comfortable living. I guess I'm real lucky in that most people I talk to, if they had a choice, they would not be where they are doing what they're doing. And I can't say that. I'm doing exactly what I want to do where I want to do it. And how can things be any better than that?"

— Alan Beard

THE LAST HOUSE CALL

"We just buried the last person — I guess — that we'll ever take to a home. This lady, everybody that died in her family, we took to her house. And she just died this year, Miss Katy, bless her heart, and she would always have fried chicken ready for my father and me after we got the person laid out in the living room.

"It was difficult getting the body in there — had to get carpet and stuff to put it up on its end so you wouldn't damage the casket. . . . And then once we got everything set up, we'd go get Miss Katy, and she'd come in for her approval, and then she'd take my father and me back to the kitchen for our fried chicken.

"We've taken a body home — when I was in high school — had to go through a window in order to get in because the doors were too narrow. We've had some pretty difficult times. . . .

"It used to be rough taking bodies home. You damage your equipment. I know I dropped a glass shade to a lamp that's there at the head of the casket. A mistake. Coming up the street, in the station wagon — I was about 16 years old — to get another shade, I cried because I really let my father down. He wasn't even there."

— Woody Porter

GOING GENTLY INTO THAT GOOD EUPHEMISM

"It always irritates me when a funeral director will not say 'death.' You watch 'em. 'He passed away.' He didn't just pass away: he *died*. The public does it, and that's understandable. But for a funeral director to not say 'death' and 'body' and 'funeral,' to me, well, it's just — interesting.

"Engage 'em in conversation and you will almost never hear 'em say 'death.' They will skirt that issue from now on. . . .

"Instead of saying we had X number of funeral services this year, or we have X number of bodies this year, we say we have so many 'calls.' You don't ever go get a 'body'; you always make a 'first call.' The first call is going to where the person died and bringing them back to the funeral home.

"It just amuses me that funeral directors shy away from saying 'death.' It amazes me. You'll be making funeral arrangements and you'll need to know, for the newspaper notice or for your own record, what time the man died. And it comes across as, 'What time did it happen?' Or, 'Was the coroner there? What time did the coroner say this occurred?' You never say, 'What time did he die?'"

— Alan Beard

"Death is a very realistic image. So 'death' is a good word. We don't want to lose that word as far as depicting what has taken place. But 'passing on' is a term we shouldn't lose track of either . . . death to the body, the passing on of the spirit."

— Tony Ratterman

CONFLICTS OF INTEREST

"I don't think it's proper for an active funeral director to be coroner of the county if there are other funeral homes in the county. Ninety-nine percent of them do it well. They go out of their way to be sure that not only is there nothing wrong but there's no perception that it's wrong.

"But I still don't think it's a good idea; I'm not criticizing those that do it; I'm just saying that, for me, when I came into a market where there was more than one funeral home, I got out [of being coroner].

"The other side of that is: It is difficult. It is very difficult when a family that you're serving wearing one hat as a funeral director says, 'Don't tell the newspaper Daddy shot himself.' As a funeral director, I don't have to tell them. . . . As the coroner, as a public official, I have an obligation to tell them if they ask. So I was never able to reconcile those kinds of things."

— Alan Beard

ARE FUNERALS DIFFERENT IN THE SOUTH?

"Families are what makes the difference in the South since they revere, respect, want a full-blown kind of ceremony for their family. That's why I have a hard time going to these national meetings . . . you get frustrated at them not realizing that they're there to serve that family. . . .

"I think the families in the South want more pomp and ceremony and want it to mean something for them, whereas some other places: 'The life's over; I did all I could do. Now let's get through the smallest ceremony we can and go on about our lives.'"

— Mark Engle

DUST TO DUST, ASH TO CASH

"I wanted to be a funeral director. The industry forced me to be a businessman. My dad did not get charged interest and did not have to pay a casket supplier, fluid supplier, vault supplier until he got the money. . . .

"Well, when you've got lax collections and don't make them sign contracts, then you suddenly learn you're going to have to try something. That's forced us to be business people. . . . So now when we finish being a nice guy and helping you through the casket room, we have to say, 'How did you want to take care of this?'

"And that goes against everything that we as rural funeral directors were trained to do. It was, 'Whatever you want . . . everything will be all right; we'll be right here to help you.' Now you have to do that and sort of get a little firm, and that hurts.

"I never have a problem after that by saying, 'You promised me this, and you didn't keep your promise.' So I'm strong at that point, but I'm real weak at that, because you're crying, your kids are crying and I'm upset with you and for you, and I'm wanting to just help you, but I remember, you know, the last time I had a guy just like [this], he didn't pay me; I'd better sew this one up. . . .

"My dad didn't understand that. He couldn't understand why I would come in here and have to make them have to sign a contract. I said, 'Daddy, I don't want to; I agree with you. And we may lose them. But I'd rather do 100 funerals and get paid for 'em than do 200 and get paid for 150. You're not going to make any money, and you're working yourself to death.'"

— Mark Engle

"In order to start this funeral home from scratch . . . it would cost $960,120. And then you would have no operating capital. So, a minimum of $40,000 in operating capital, you're talking about, to start this firm from scratch, it would take $1 million. Well, if I had $1 million, I would put it in the bank in secured certificates and live off the interest. I wouldn't put it in the funeral home and go to work every day. . . .

"I think that funeral homes in the future — and I'm talking about 10 years from now — you're either going to have to be an acquirer or you're going to be acquired. . . . You're going to have to get bigger, or you're going to be swallowed up.

"When I was in school, they used to talk about publish or perish. I think we're either going to have to purchase or perish.

"I would be less than candid if I didn't tell you that I see opportunity there. . . .

"An independent, I think, can operate more efficiently, probably, than a large acquisition firm can, but they don't have the resources and the capital to put into it. If we weren't lean and mean, so to speak, we wouldn't be here at all."

— Alan Beard

"I guess Woody wondered if I was too soft for this business.

"The first time I realized [I wasn't was when] I could ask somebody to be paid for my services. I thought, 'Well, now, Marie, do you want to get paid? You can't give the shop away. . . .

"I've heard Woody say, 'Well, now sugar' — he's got this real folksy way about him — he'll say, 'My sister collects the money and she won't let you pay on this $10 a month.'

"And I tell him, 'That's right. Make me the bad guy.'"

— Marie Porter

THE VIEW FROM THE EMBALMING ROOM

"You can embalm better than we do . . . if you just wanted to preserve a body and didn't care how it looked. Arsenic is better than formaldehyde. But, see, the definition of embalming in America is: disinfection, preservation and restoration to a lifelike appearance.

"I mean, you could mummify them just about — but they start to shrivel. I actually embalm too strong. . . . But I'd rather cover that up than to have somebody not smell good. . . . Well, I have to think covering up a brown spot is a lot easier than covering up a smell. I get sick on the smell. I'm a gagger. There's different philosophies. Neither one of those are wrong."

— Mark Engle

"Most people, I'll tell you, they don't want to deal with the embalming part. I've had many an employee come through here and stay just a couple of days. They go down there and help in that preparation room, and they can't take it, because it's pretty rough.

It's a hazardous occupation, an embalmer. Just as hazardous, if not more so, than [being] a pathologist. The diseases you subject yourself to are just unreal. Thank God technology did not pass the embalming profession by. Technology has enabled them to manufacture things that better protect you. . . . I can remember when I started doing it, I never heard of a mask. Now you have breathing apparatuses . . . the ventilation systems are so much better.

"I can stay in there now and breathe in the most would-be uncomfortable situations. But before, mucus was coming out of your nose, you're coughing, you're breathing all these hazardous chemicals. A few years ago, when I first got out of embalming school, the average age at death for a person who embalmed [exclusively] was 49. Formaldehyde is a cancer-causing chemical. You were closed up in a poorly ventilated room, breathing hardening compounds, powders and formaldehyde fumes all day long; it's very, very hazardous."

— Woody Porter

"It's always been amazing to me how much younger people look after they've been embalmed. And the reason for that, of course, is the embalming fluid is the color of blood. . . . Through light cosmetics and embalming fluid, color is put back into our skin. Plus, the capillaries are filled with this 'blood' so that it tends to bulge us out a little bit and to expand us so that we look more robust. And, of course, if we've lost a lot of weight, under our clothing, that can be padded, with cotton, and so a person can appear very much at ease and look very good. Through cosmetics, a person can look very acceptable."

— Tony Ratterman

"I embalm, and the way I can tell you're [well] embalmed, I can tell by color, but the biggest way is by feel. So if you're firm, then I know I've done a good job because it's going to continue to dry and it's going to continue to preserve; therefore, it can only get better. 'Course, at a certain point, it's the best it can be, and it starts downhill. But there are times you embalm, and they're still sort of mushy, and there's not a whole lot you can do. . . .

"If you are swelling them where they don't look good, then you've got to leave them soft. Back to that restoration to a lifelike appearance.

"It's your career. When you put that body out, it's you. So if you can say [to the family], 'Gee, you need to bury him day after tomorrow and not three days, we need to because the embalming didn't do well' and you can tell them they're starting to swell.

"That's what amazes me. I tell the truth. . . . A lot of funeral directors are afraid to tell the families the facts. I want to make it as soft as I can, but I tell them the facts: 'He's still embalmed, but not as well as I would like because he was beginning to swell, and I know you wanted him to look good.' That's pretty simple, and I don't see how it could get you in trouble."

— Mark Engle

"I do it all except do the hair. Sometimes I've done that, but normally not. I pride myself in cosmetics. I've gone to seminars that beauticians go to because, to me, the challenge is to make that person look more living. The [cosmetic] products that are made for deceased people do not make them look that way. I have very few cosmetics that are made by embalming-chemical companies. Most things I use are made for the living. Most cosmetics for the dead are made to cover up mistakes. That's the difference. . . ."

— Woody Porter

"I am no better embalmer than anybody on this staff. In fact, our two younger men are much better embalmers than I am because they have had later training. . . . However, a lot of people in this community think I am a wonderful embalmer. It's a false perception because they come in here, they see someone, they look good, they assume I embalmed that body when I did not. And that comes, too, from the fact that I came from a very small place where I did all the work. . . ."

— Alan Beard

"When I embalm today, I'm in seventh heaven. I just enjoy doing that. And I've been blessed, I think. I have some good hands. I think I probably would have been a pretty good surgeon, because I have a pretty good touch with what I'm doing.

"You've got to have a feel about it. You have to know the human body, the features of people. I observe living people so closely. I see you. Just the few minutes I've been with you, I close my eyes and I can see you. That's a blessing. That's something God has given you, you were born with."

— Woody Porter

"Embalming is the most important thing that takes place for the family's sake at a funeral home. If the deceased person looks like themselves, and if their appearance is acceptable, and therefore comforting to the family, then the family's biggest fears are dissipated.

"Last summer [1989], my wife passed away. She had had cancer. And she lost some weight, but it didn't take away from her appearance. She always looked pretty in spite of the fact that she had lost some weight. But my greatest fear, my greatest anxiety, was what was she going to look like?

"Would she look like my wife, the girl that I loved? And it meant so much to me when I saw her. She was always a beautiful person, and the fact that she looked beautiful to me as she was laid out was very appropriate, I thought. She deserved that."

— Tony Ratterman

A MYTH UNCOVERED

"A lot people think you don't put pants on them [corpses]. Educated people. Adults think like kids when they're ignorant of a subject, in my opinion. And kids will ask you. . . . Not long ago, a young man died. He had two small boys, and they wanted to see their daddy's legs. They had heard you cut their legs off. I said, 'Honey, they can see anything they want. We're not here to hide anything.' So I went into the visitation room, took the flower spray off, raised the lid and let them see. They were happy, but, you know, there were some relieved adults, too. There really were."

— Mark Engle

WHO COUNTS?

"Quite frankly, most funeral directors—unless somebody's being unusually skimpy that has money—probably don't notice the price of a funeral. What I mean by that is people buy their level. As long as you're buying your level, nobody thinks anything of it either way. . . .

"The average funeral is probably $3,500 to $4,200, something like that."

—Mark Engle

DEALING WITH AIDS . . .

"I had to come to grips with that pretty quick . . . probably four or five years ago. I sent a man to Lexington to pick up a body, and this lady had called and said, 'Will you pick up my baby? I said, 'Yes, ma'am.' So I had an embalming service in Lexington pick him up and embalm him. I did not know the cause of death.

"I sent a guy down. . . . He called me everything he could lay his tongue to. I said, 'I didn't know. I promise you I didn't know it was an AIDS case.'

"So they were all up in arms. What would they do? Well, it was my call. They were saying direct burial, 'we're not going to touch it, we're refusing. . . .'

"I went over to my house, and I sat about two or three hours. I think it was a Sunday morning. I called the Kentucky exec [the executive director of the Kentucky Funeral Directors], and I got a number for the Centers for Disease Control in Atlanta. I asked the exec, 'What's been your experience? What have these other guys been telling you?' We'd had some seminars, but I thought, 'That's not going to be in Hazard.' (We've had three, by the way.)

"At any rate, I called the CDC, and all I kept thinking was, 'That's that woman's son. I don't believe in that. I can't condone that. I can't believe in it, but I'll get the body ready myself if I have to.'

"The Centers for Disease Control [recommended] double gloves, put a mask on— of course the body's embalmed, it's pretty well safe at this point, and so I just said, 'Guys, if you don't want to do it, I will. That's that woman's son, and the Centers for Disease Control says the body's safe.'

"The danger is in the embalming, predominantly; you've got to be careful.

"Now, I don't want to embalm one. And if we get one here, we would probably send it to this guy in Lexington. Charges $500. That's OK. It just makes us feel better. . . .

"But I would embalm one. You'd just be careful, extra careful. . . . You're supposed to treat it roughly like tuberculosis.

"I buried that woman's son with dignity. I thought we owed her that."

—Mark Engle

WHEN A CHILD DIES . . .

"After you've been working with it for a long time, it doesn't affect you as deeply as it did before. After a while, there's a realization that death happens at all ages, and at whatever age it happens, for the person who died, it's a very beautiful thing: The passing on to the next life is a beautiful thing. Death is not beautiful, but the passing on . . . is a beautiful thing.

"A funeral director must somehow insulate himself from becoming overly sensitized to all this, and so you simply accept the premise that death happens at all ages . . . and so your job is really to make the people comfortable, to help them to deal with this reality. . . .

"And so you try to plant seeds of hope. . . .

"For stillborn children, in its essence, it's a very sad outcome to a beautiful event, and yet, forever and ever, it's like a little secret that's shared intimately by the mother and father. It was a relationship that was never really ever shared with any other people. For people to know that they have something very special that's unique to them can be very comforting to them. Knowing that the spirit that they helped create lives forever, and that they will see that spirit someday can be very comforting, too. To get people to focus in on the eternal side . . . is the only way to resolution of this issue because if you focus in on the death side of it, it can only lead you to loneliness and despair."

— Tony Ratterman

"No one can look on the face of a child in a casket and not be moved. . . . However, my faith is such that I know in my mind that that child is all right. . . . To me, a real tragedy would be the death of a child's parents. I know that that child is taken care of, but when a child's parents are killed, then distant family members or friends or society has to take care of that child during life. To me, that is a much greater tragedy than the death of a child."

— Alan Beard

DEATH WITHOUT BENEFIT OF CLERGY

"There is a situation that I always find to be strange. I came from Crofton; we're here in the heart of the Bible Belt. I'll never forget the first time that I dealt with a family that . . . didn't believe in God.

"To me, a person that didn't believe in God was a heathen. This man was prominent, of great stature; he was an atheist. I have never become accustomed to a funeral service . . . without religion, without any statement of faith involved."

— Alan Beard

THE FIRE LAST TIME

"We don't do many cremations. Not many at all. I think it's because this is a fairly conservative area and the traditional values still pretty much hold. . . .

"I once discussed the idea I thought cremation was OK. I still wanted a traditional funeral service, but maybe cremation was all right as a method of final disposition. Woody said, 'Are you crazy?' And Daddy said, 'Well, not if I have something to do with it — you won't be cremated.'

"Woody said, 'You need to come sometime and watch the actual cremation process. Then let me know whether you still want to be cremated.'"

— Marie Porter

IS IT ALL RIGHT FOR A FUNERAL DIRECTOR TO CRY?

"One of the ways I used to deal with my own grief over the death of friends—and I guess I'll sound like the village idiot here—but I used to talk to them. While I was preparing the body, I talked to them. That's when I laughed and that's when I cried and that's when I said things to them I should have said while they were living, and didn't.

"And then when I dealt with the family, I could be professional, because I had already done that. I had already purged myself. In that regard, I faced the grief; I went on and got my grieving over with before I dealt with the family. . . .

"With a friend, you know how he's going to respond, and you can carry on a conversation with him whether he's there or not. That's the way I dealt with it. We 'talked' about things we had in common or things we did together or going to a ballgame, those kinds of things.

"I've never admitted that before to anybody, but that's the way I used to deal with it. . . .

"People see me in town and they ask me the same thing they asked me yesterday, because what else do they know to say, really? That's why when you make close friends, you really cherish them. I don't know, maybe that's why I talked to them."

— Alan Beard

"There's a couple of churches in town, they call me the crying funeral director, because I cry. . . . That happens to you sometimes, especially when you're feeling blue, you're sitting there listening to the minister and you're hearing the people cry and you say, 'Wow, what if that's my mama? Or what if that's my daddy? How would you feel? You'd feel hurt.' And little babies. Gosh. After my daughter was born, and before she was a year old, I couldn't embalm a baby. I would have to let somebody else do it, because when a child's an infant—babies look alike. I would see my daughter all the time. I couldn't do it."

— Woody Porter

"There was a minister here, his wife died of cancer. . . . At the time I was a 21- or 22-year-old funeral director. . . . At the funeral, instead of having 'The Old Rugged Cross' or something sad, he had a youth choir sing the 'Hallelujah' chorus. He just sat there nodding and smiling while they were singing. Tears were running down my cheeks, and he wasn't shedding one. He was in his heart, but he just had that deep a conviction."

— Mark Engle

"Many times I've identified emotionally with what the family's going through, and my voice has cracked, I've become teary, and I know that's OK. It's just something that happens and you can't help yourself.

"I don't mean to give the impression that a good funeral director normally becomes emotionally involved, because you really don't. . . .

"I'll never forget the time that a girl had been killed in a traffic accident, and the boy that was driving the car was put in a wheelchair, and he came to the church from the hospital. The church was filled with people. At the time for the sharing of a sign of peace, the girl's mother and father came back and embraced the young boy who was driving the car.

"I became really teary about that, just because, on one hand, it showed such utter forgiveness and, on the other hand, the sense of understanding that existed between the parents. And when you see those deep emotions being communicated and accepted, it's just so beautiful that you can become overwhelmed.

"And it's one of the good sides of this business—because you see people at their very best and very worst. But you see the total baring of human emotions and at times very beautiful, deep things take place. . . . Owners of funeral homes don't become calloused to those deep, beautiful exchanges that go on between human beings."

—Tony Ratterman

SUGGESTIONS FOR WRITING

Informal Essays

1. After reading the introduction to this chapter and Ruth Harmer's "Requiem for Everyman," describe a funeral you have attended and show that it was either a traditional or a nontraditional funeral.
2. Analyze the effect that a funeral had on you. Was the ceremony emotionally satisfying, or did you instead see it as a needless extravagance?
3. Describe the kind of funeral you would like to have—and why.

Short Documented Papers

1. After reading the introduction and two or three essays from this chapter, argue that the traditional American funeral is either a tasteless extravagance or an emotionally valuable experience.
2. Write a paper in which you attack the argument you consider the weakest of the arguments on either side of the controversy concerning the American way of death.
3. Analyze Paul Irion's argument in "The Perspective of Theology." How *exactly* is the traditional American funeral a Christian experience?
4. Write a short paper in which you sum up the arguments of either those who defend the traditional American funeral or those who attack it.
5. Describe the alternatives to the traditional American funeral. Begin by reading Ruth Mulvey Harmer's "Requiem for Everyman."
6. Draw what conclusions you can about funeral traditions from your reading of Jessica Mitford's "Fashions in Funerals."

Longer Documented Papers

1. Write a report in which you contrast the two sides of the controversy concerning the American way of death.

2. Write a paper in which you argue one of the sides of the controversy concerning the traditional American funeral. During the course of your argument, be sure to bring up the other side's arguments.

ADVERTISING: *Is It More Than Harmless Puffery?*

A single page of advertising in a national magazine costs a company about sixty thousand dollars. A single minute of advertising during the Super Bowl costs about a million dollars.

With so much at stake, advertisers are naturally going to use all of the resources of art and language to influence our buying habits. In fact, the air seems thick at times with a barrage of commercially seductive images and manipulative language. Sometimes advertisers even hire psychologists to explain the deep urges that drive a consumer to purchase Corn Crispies rather than Crispie Corns.

We are being seduced, the critics of advertising say. With all that money to spend for artists, copywriters, producers, models, and motivational researchers, advertisers have got us where they want us, and we are almost powerless to resist their pleas.

Those who defend advertising say that the effectiveness of motivational research in advertising is vastly overrated and that consumers are not so weak-willed as the critics of advertising would have people believe. Besides, the defenders add, in a free society advertisers should be able to use language in the same ways that the rest of us use it. The use of a rhetorical technique in advertising, they say, is as fair as its use in novels, essays, and newspaper columns.

Sometimes the issue of fairness comes down to this crucial question: Does a particular ad *intend* to deceive? Unfortunately, it's not always easy to tell. For one thing, an ad can be untruthful without being deceptive. Do you remember those television ads with the little happy-faced brushes that scrubbed a sink clean? That ad was untruthful, but it wasn't deceptive. That is, the soap company obviously wasn't trying to persuade us that cute little living brushes helped their soap do its job; they were trying to say that their soap worked *as if* little brushes were at work. Unfortunately, it's not always so clear when an image is used to illustrate a point; images used as metaphors (like the little brushes) can easily shade off toward deception.

But if we consumers have little difficulty recognizing visual metaphors, we have a harder time recognizing puffery (those exaggerated claims that advertisers make). In fact, it's sometimes next to impossible to tell where hyperbole ends and deception begins. What about the restaurant that claims that its pizza is the best in town? Or the mattress company that claims that you'll sleep like a baby on its individually wrapped springs? Is puffery deceptive? Or is it instead a part of the conventional language of advertisers that no one takes seriously — and was never meant to be taken seriously?

A more serious question is this: Is advertising a healthy or unhealthy influence on society? The charges and countercharges are familiar enough. Advertising, the critics say, encourages a materialistic life-style. (Advertising keeps the economy healthy, the defenders reply.) Advertising, the critics contend, warps our sense of reality because no one can live up to the handsome people and happy faces of advertisements. (Ads encourage our wish-fulfillment fantasies, the defenders reply, and thus help make life more bearable.)

A final question is this: Even if we do find advertising misleading and unhealthy, do we want to regulate it more than it is now? Blatant deception in advertising is now illegal. Should the Federal Trade Commission step in to regulate the language of advertising even further? Should, for instance, the FTC clamp down on puffery, those ambiguous and exaggerated claims that advertisers like to make for their products?

The critics of advertising like to quote Thomas Wolfe's idea that advertising consists of "fat, juicy, sugar-coated lies for our great Boob public to swallow." Advertising's defenders prefer Robert Louis Stevenson's comment that "Everyone lives by selling something."

. . . And the Hooks Are Lowered
Vance Packard

In ". . . And the Hooks Are Lowered," an excerpt from The Hidden Persuaders, *Packard both describes and criticizes. It's a description of the kinds of motivational research that lie behind an advertising campaign. But Packard also obviously disapproves of this kind of research. Packard suggests that deep motivational research is unfair because the consumer is nearly defenseless at the hands of psychologists, sociologists, and other experts hired by a company trying to sell a product.*

Vance Packard specializes in writing analyses of popular culture for a wide audience. His books include The Wastemakers *(an analysis of America's consumer culture),* The People Shapers *(an analysis of the uses of motivational research in many aspects of American culture), and* The Status Seekers *(an analysis of the ways people seek status by buying things).*

The techniques used for probing the subconscious were derived straight from the clinics of psychiatry, for the most part. As Dr. [George Horsley] Smith advised marketers in his book on motivation research, "Different levels of depth are achieved by different approaches" [*Motivational Research in Advertising and Marketing*].

I shall summarize here some of the more picturesque probing techniques put to use by the depth probers of merchandising. For this Dr. Smith's authoritative book has been a helpful guide.

One of the most widely used techniques for probing in depth is what is called the "depth interview." When 1,100 of the nation's top management men met at a conference in New York in early 1956 (sponsored by the American Management Association), they were treated to a closed-circuit TV demonstration of an actual depth interview, with psychologists doing the probing.

These interviews in depth are conducted very much as the psychiatrist conducts his interviews, except that there is no couch since a couch might make the chosen consumer-guinea pig wary. (Many of these consumers are induced to co-operate by the offer of free samples of merchandise. Others apparently just enjoy the attention of being "tested.") Typically the psychologist, psychiatrist, or other expert doing the probing tries, with casualness and patience, to get the consumer into a reverie of talking, to get him or her musing absent-mindedly about all the "pleasures, joys, enthusiasms, agonies, nightmares, deceptions, apprehensions the product recalls to them," to use Dr. Smith's phrase.

Sometimes these depth interviews take place with whole groups of people because, oddly, the group reverie often is more productive. Many people tend to become less inhibited in a group than when they are alone with the interviewer in the same way that some people can only warm up at a party. As Dr. Smith explains it, "What happens is that one member makes a 'daring,' selfish, or even intolerant statement. This encourages someone else to speak in the same vein. Others tend to

Vance Packard, ". . . And the Hooks Are Lowered," *The Hidden Persuaders* (New York: David McKay, 1957).

sense that the atmosphere has become more permissive and proceed accordingly. Thus we have been able to get highly personalized discussions of laxatives, cold tablets, deodorants, weight reducers, athlete's foot remedies, alcohol, and sanitary napkins. On the doorstep, or in the living room, a respondent might be reluctant to discuss his personal habits with a stranger."

Much of the depth probing by marketers is done with what Professor Smith calls "disguised," or indirect, tests. The person tested is given the impression he is being tested for some other reason than the real one. Most are what psychiatrists call "projective" tests. In this the subject is presented with a drawing or other stimulus that doesn't quite make sense. Something must be filled in to complete the picture, and the subject is asked to do that. In doing this he projects a part of himself into the picture.

One of the most widely used is the famed ink-blot test developed by the Swiss psychiatrist Hermann Rorschach. Here a series of ten cards on which are printed bisymmetrical ink blots is used. They are ambiguous forms representing nothing whatever. The subject sees in the picture what he "needs" to see, and thus projects himself into it — his anxieties, inadequacies, conflicts.

Many of the depth probers of merchandising however prefer the so-called TAT to the Rorschach. The TAT (Thematic Apperception Test) in its pure clinical form consists of a series of printed pictures chosen carefully from magazine illustrations, paintings, etc. Merchandisers, however, make adaptations by including pictures of their own, pictures they are thinking of using in ad copy.

Again the subject is encouraged to project himself into the picture so that the probers can assess his impulses, anxieties, wishes, ill feelings. Suppose that in a series of pictures every single one shows some fellow in an embarrassing jam with some obvious figure of authority, such as boss, teacher, cop, parent. The testee is asked to tell a story about each picture. If in his stories the underling usually kills or beats up or humiliates the authority figure, we have one kind of character; if he builds a secure and comfortable dependence with the authority figure, we have quite a different story.

A variation is the cartoon-type test where the testee can write in words in a "balloon" of the cartoon left empty. In the Rosenzweig picture-frustration test, for example, one of the figures says something that is obviously frustrating to the other person pictured, and the subject is invited to fill in the frustrated person's response. In one cited by Dr. Smith a man and woman were standing near their parked car as the man hunted through his pockets for his keys. The wife exclaimed, "This is a fine time to have lost the keys!" What would the man reply?

One of the most startling of the picture tests used by market probers is the Szondi test. It is, as one research director of an advertising agency told me, "a real cutie." He has used it with whisky drinkers. The assumption of this test is that we're all a little crazy. The subject being probed is shown a series of cards bearing the portraits of people and is asked to pick out of them the one person he would most like to sit beside if he were on a train trip, and the person pictured that he would least like to sit beside. What he is not told is that the people shown on the cards are all thoroughly disordered. Each suffers severely from one of eight psychiatric disorders (is homosexual, sadist, epileptic, hysterical, catatonic, paranoid, depressed, or manic). It is assumed that we will sense a rapport with some more than others, and that in choosing a riding companion we will choose the person suffering acutely from the same emotional state that affects us mildly.

The ad agency in question used this Szondi to try to find why people really drink whisky. Among its ad accounts are major whisky distillers. The agency was interested in diagnosing the personality of the heavy drinker for a thoroughly practical reason: heavy drinkers account for most of the whisky consumed (85 percent of the volume is consumed by 22 percent of the drinkers). In using the Szondi on heavy whisky drinkers, it tested the subjects before they had a drink and then tested them after they had had three drinks. The research director relates: "A change takes place that would make your hair stand on end!"

Why does a man drink heavily? Here is his conclusion: "He wouldn't drink unless he got a change in personality that was satisfying to him." Some of these people undergo extremely surprising changes of personality. Meek men become belligerent, and so on.

In other tests instruments are used to gauge the subjects' physiological responses as clues to their emotional states. The galvanometer, better known as lie detector, has been used by the Color Research Institute and *The Chicago Tribune*, to cite just two examples. A subject's physiological reactions are clocked while he sees images and hears sounds that may be used in trying to promote the sale of products. James Vicary, on the other hand, employs a special hidden camera that photographs the eye-blink rate of people under varying test situations. Our eye-blink rate is a clue to our emotional tension or lack of tension.

Hypnosis also is being used in attempts to probe our subconscious to find why we buy or do not buy certain products. Ruthrauff and Ryan, the New York ad agency, has been employing a prominent hypnotist and a panel of psychologists and psychiatrists in its effect to get past our mental blockages, which are so bothersome to probers when we are conscious. The agency has found that hypnosis sharpens our power to recall. We can remember things that we couldn't otherwise remember. One place they've been using it is to try to find why we use the brand of product we do. An official cited the case of a man who under hypnosis told why he preferred a certain make of car and always bought it. This man, under hypnosis, was able to repeat word for word an ad he had read more than twenty years before that had struck his fancy. The agency is vague as to whether it is at this moment using a hypnotist. However, it does uphold the fact that the results to date have been "successful" to the degree that "we believe in years to come it may be employed as a method."

One ad man I talked with revealed he had often speculated on the possibility of using TV announcers who had been trained in hypnotism, for deeper impact.

The London Sunday Times front-paged a report in mid-1956 that certain United States advertisers were experimenting with "subthreshold effects" in seeking to insinuate sales messages to people past their conscious guard. It cited the case of a cinema in New Jersey that it said was flashing ice-cream ads onto the screen during regular showings of film. The flashes of message were split-second, too short for people in the audience to recognize them consciously but still long enough to be absorbed unconsciously.

A result, it reported, was a clear and otherwise unaccountable boost in ice-cream sales. "Subthreshold effects, both in vision and sound, have been known for some years to experimental psychologists," the paper explained. It speculated that political indoctrination might be possible without the subject being conscious of any influence being brought to bear on him.

When I queried Dr. Smith about the alleged ice-cream experiment he said he had not heard of it before and expressed skepticism. "There is evidence," he agreed, "that people can be affected by subthreshold stimulation; for example, a person can be conditioned to odors and sounds that are just outside the range of conscious awareness. However, this is rarely done in one instantaneous flash. . . ." When I questioned *The London Sunday Times* about its sources a spokesman reported: ". . . Although the facts we published are well attested, the authorities in question are unwilling to come any further into the open." Then he added: "There have, since publication of this article, been two programmes dealing with the subject on the B.B.C. Television, when experiments of a similar nature were tried on the viewing public; but although some success was claimed, it is generally agreed that such forms of advertising are more suitable for the cinema than for the slower television screen."

Although each depth-probing group has its own favorite techniques, it may use many others when appropriate. The research director at Young and Rubicam, for example, states: "In research at Y.&R. we like to think we practice 'eclectism,' a frightening word which simply means 'selecting the best.' We are willing to experiment with depth interview, word association, sentence completion, Minnesota multiphasic personality inventories (which incidentally turn up things like inward and outward hostility) and even Rorschach and Thematic Apperception Tests. . . ."

Our subconscious attitudes, of course, are far from being the whole explanation of our buying behavior, even the depth probers are quick to acknowledge. A sale may result from a mixture of factors. Dr. Wulfeck, of the Advertising Research Foundation, points out: "A consumer may have an internal hostility toward a product, and he may still buy it because of other facts such as advertising, distribution, dislike of competing brand, and so on."

Even the advertising agencies most devoted to motivation research still carry on exhaustively the two mainstay kinds of research: market research (study of products, income levels, price, dealers, etc.) and copy research (the testing of specific layouts, phrases, etc.).

There appears to be abundant evidence, however, that by 1957 a very large number of influential marketers were trying to use this new depth approach in some of their work. It was here to stay.

When in the chapters that follow we enter into the wilderness of the depth manipulators by getting down to cases, you may occasionally find yourself exclaiming that only the maverick and extremist fringe of business would embrace such tactics. Here, briefly, is the evidence to the contrary, showing that the depth approach — despite the fact that it still has admitted limitations and fallibilities — has become a very substantial movement in American business. Some of the journals most respected by America's leading marketers had this to say during the mid-fifties:

Printer's Ink: "Overwhelmingly a group of top-drawer advertising agencies and advertising executives, representing many of the nation's outstanding advertisers, favor the increased use of social sciences and social scientists in . . . campaign planning." (February 27, 1953)

Tide: "Some of the nation's most respected companies have sunk millions of dollars into ad campaigns shaped at least in part by analysis of consumer motivations." (February 26, 1955) It reported making a study that found that 33 per cent of the top merchandisers on its "Leadership Panel" were getting M.R. surveys from their ad agencies. (October 22, 1955)

Wall Street Journal: "More and more advertising and marketing strategists are adapting their sales campaigns to the psychologists' findings and advice." It said Goodyear Tire and Rubber, General Motors, General Foods, Jewel Tea, and Lever Brothers were only a few of the large outfits that had made M.R. studies. (September 13, 1954)

Sales Management printed one estimate that $12,000,000 would be spent by marketers in 1956 for research in motivations. (February 1, 15, 1955)

Advertising Age: "The big news in research during 1955 was M.R., its advocates and critics." (January 2, 1956)

Fortune: "Of the $260,000,000,000 spent on consumer products last year (1955) a full half probably went to industries in which one or more major manufacturers had tried M.R." It is estimated that nearly a billion dollars in ad money spent in 1955 came from the big corporations that had used M.R. directly or through their ad agencies, and added that M.R. had been responsible for some major shifts in advertising appeals. (June, 1956)

Are Advertising and Marketing Corrupting Society? It's Not Your Worry

Theodore Levitt

Levitt's article is a defense of advertising against all those who say that it "debases" American society. Basically, Levitt argues that advertising is a neutral activity, and that an advertiser has no business trying to decide for us what is good or bad. The businessman, Levitt says, is there to make a profit for the company. And when he does this he performs a valuable service for a capitalist society: He creates jobs and he gives satisfaction through the products he sells. Leave it to the reformers and saints, Levitt says, to change society. Business and advertisers are doing their job when they sell a product.

At the time Theodore Levitt wrote this article he was a marketing and economic consultant.

It's natural enough for people now and then to think about the consequences of their actions. It shows that they have compassion, which is a good thing.

In our more abstracted and contemplative moments we all ask ourselves some pretty basic questions. Even the most self-assured entertain doubts. Is it all worth while? Isn't what we do for our daily bread pretty trite, superficial, banal, or even downright corrosive in its general consequences?

If you happen to sell antibiotics, maybe you feel good about what you do, although it may occasionally bother you that a lot of needy people can't afford your asking price. On the other hand, if you sell switch-blade knives, you need a stronger stomach.

ARE YOU A "HIDDEN PERSUADER," SELLING WHAT PEOPLE DON'T NEED?

But what about the in-between cases? The man who sells mud packs to aging matrons in search of youth? Or, what if you push chemises on ladies who were perfectly satisfied wth the styles they reluctantly bought last year? What if you pay big money to the "hidden persuaders" so you can manipulate people into buying things they don't need, can't afford, and are of doubtful utility? What will your soul-searching ruminations yield then?

Or, suppose you're a solid, devoted, church-going family man in the automobile business. How do you feel, knowing that the car has debased American life and morals, facilitating crime, vice, infidelity, adultery and unchastity?

Whatever your business, it is possible to see its wholesale contribution to decadence, self-indulgence, materialism, cynicism, irresponsibility, selfishness — a swell-

Theodore Levitt, "Are Advertising and Marketing Corrupting Society? It's Not Your Worry," *Advertising Age* 8 October 1958.

ing galaxy of assorted social, economic, human, cultural, psychological, moral and ethical evils. There is no escape. The more successful the quest of your particular business — whatever it may be — the more evil it generates.

This can be said even if, let's assume, you produce and distribute such an apparently neutral commodity as electric power. Electricity runs the factories that produce all the gadgets that are ruining people's sense of values and the barbaric weapons that will destroy us all. Electricity keeps the night clubs operating, and everybody knows what happens in their opaque illumination.

WHERE IS BUSINESS LEADING US?

On what logical grounds can you say that people who argue this way, who perhaps want to return to a more primeval way of life, have any less legitimate claim to truth, wisdom, or common sense than you? Maybe they're right. After all, what is the business man's headlong quest leading to? After you have all the gadgets, all the living space, all the deodorants, all the Bermuda shorts, and all the steaks you can possibly use — what then, little man?

We are discussing the general topic of management's mission in the new society . . . and the specific question of certain dangers that may accompany the success of its marketing effort. To set the stage for our discussion, Professor Bursk has asked these questions:

"Suppose . . . we can succeed in endowing consumers with all the material goods — necessities, conveniences, luxuries — that our factories can produce and our stores can handle? There still are grave questions. What will happen to people as human beings? Will they lose their dignity, their culture, their appreciation of spiritual values? Will their standard of living be higher just because they can afford to obsolete their possessions quicker, continually buying new fancy models at the expense of economic waste? What is the psychology of unbounded satisfaction? What are the effects of manipulation — whether it be blatant persuasion, or subtle motivation like the hidden persuaders? Will we become a nation of robots with mechanical appetites?"

These are vital questions. They show a necessary and commendable feel for the real deep-down juice of life. Society needs always to be asking itself where it is going. Otherwise it won't know what road to take. Somebody must think and do something about these questions. But it is the thesis of my remarks today that whoever that somebody is, it should not be the business man.

DOES THE BUSINESS MAN HAVE THE RIGHT TO DECIDE WHAT'S GOOD FOR US?

The cultural, spiritual, social, moral, etc. consequences of his actions are none of his occupational concern. He is in business for his own personal edification — neither to save nor to ruin souls. His job is perfectly neutral on these matters. Besides, the minute he becomes preoccupied with the deeper purposes and consequences of what he does, he becomes a conscious arbiter of our lives. He will be trying consciously to decide what is good or bad for us; what we should or should not have; should or should not see, hear, read, think, or do. He will have thrown the mighty weight of his great economic power behind the community-wide implementation of his own private values and tastes. And even if these are the highest expression of God's will, I submit the result could be nothing less than evil.

Nobody can know better than the adult individual himself what his values and tastes should be, even if he is a congenital idiot. The fact that we put idiots away is beside the point. The point is this: the business man exists for only one purpose, to create and deliver value satisfactions at a profit to himself. He isn't, and shouldn't be, a theologian, a philosopher, or a sort of Emily Post of commerce. His job is ridiculously simple. The test of whether the things he offers do indeed contain value satisfactions is provided by the completely neutral mechanism of the open market.

If what is offered can be sold at a profit (not even necessarily a long-term profit), then it is legitimate. The consumer has cast a favorable economic ballot. He wants it. If enough other consumers don't agree and cast their more powerful political ballots against the commodity or practice in question, that is okay, too. That is the veto of democratic politics over democratic economics. And this ranking is precisely the desirable and necessary order of their importance.

If the business man becomes preoccupied with all the involved normative questions that his activities raise, he will fail to perform his greatest responsibility: to succeed as a business man. The business man should pursue his own sense of workmanship with a singular purpose, unburdened by peripheral considerations that drain his vitality or cloud his objectives. He should be free to probe wherever his instincts and talents lead, just as scientists and philosophers should be free to do in their fields. When it comes to the scope and direction of their jobs, they should be true only to the bedrock purposes of their respective functions — as neutral about the outcome as the goddess of justice.

Everything inseparably has good and bad consequences, depending in part on your values. And every thinking person should try to be aware of both. But what we should want is less, not more, concern with the consequences of successful marketing. We should get away from normative considerations entirely. The reason is purely functional. It is the same one as applies when we say that the scientist should leave dogma and personal preference at the door when he enters his lab. Dogma restricts scientific development, just as much as scientific development undermines dogma. Dogma also restricts top marketing development and performance. And for my part, with special reference to business men, their self-conscious preoccupation with elevating the public is potentially very dangerous.

When you consciously use your product to affect the spiritual, cultural, aesthetic, and home lives of your customers, then you are playing God. It is bad enough that you intimately affect our private lives in the random process of doing your job as business man. To affect them intentionally and in a clearly manipulative fashion that has nothing to do with the object of selling as such, to do that is a compounded evil. There are already too many institutions and individuals tyrannizing us with their own special versions of God's will. We don't need any more.

DO LUXURIES REALLY CORRUPT?

If capitalism learns to distribute and sell goods as well as it can produce them, if really hot-shot marketing becomes successful enough to create a sort of commercial

Frankenstein loading people up with redundant goods, creating superficial and vulgar wants, and generating the kind of opulence that turns luxuries into necessities and necessities into ceremonial rather than substantive values — if this happens, perhaps we will get soft and decadent and finally drift down into the quagmire of decay that was Rome's fate.

But let's not go overboard in an orgy of moral self-flagellation. A lot of this viewing with alarm is an irrational Puritan reaction against the good life. We shrink from having really uninhibited good times. We still associate virtue with work and idleness with vice. Deep down inside we can't shake off the guilt of Adam's fall. "In the sweat of thy face shalt thou eat bread." Things must not be too easy. That leads to the degradation of the spirit. Spiritual purity is equated with hard work and physical discomfort. . . .

WHAT BREEDS MORE CULTURE — PLUSH LIVING, FRONTIER ADVERSITY?

I ask you, which capitalist society is culturally and technologically more creative — opulent U.S. or hand-to-mouth Spain? Which condition has produced more statesmen, business leaders, writers, poets, scientists, and clergymen — the well-heeled breeding of the Churchills, the Huxleys, the Rockefellers, and the Adamses, or the mountaineer adversity of the Hatfields and the McCoys? Which soldiers fought more successfully during World War II — the pampered, almost undisciplined Americans with their chewing gum and fleece-lined shoes, or the arrogant Germans goose-stepping in ice-cold leather boots after their intoxicating dream of historic mission?

And what is better, for our wives to spend endless drudging hours scrubbing clothes half-clean on corrugated washboards and serving us half-done, half-digestible cakes they proudly made from scratch, or for the hidden persuaders to have banished their Puritan guilt feelings about using automatic washing machines and pre-mixed flour?

Everybody is a hidden persuader of sorts. Every statement addresses itself to a customer. Every act covets an objective. The fact that some people are getting more efficient than they used to be is entirely beside the point.

To get all excited about the social and human consequences of so-called successful marketing is a sort of know-nothing hysteria. It defies the facts. Are things really as bad as seems always to be implied? After all, last year more Americans attended live performances of serious music than went to professional baseball and football games combined. More books — good books — are being read per capita today than 50 years ago. Our taste in furniture is certainly superior to mid-Victorian monstrosities and the overstuffed Grand Rapids eyesores that dominated our living rooms not so long ago. Magazines like *Harper's Bazaar*, *Playboy*, *Esquire*, and *Holiday* that cater to the so-called people of means (the idle rich?) regularly publish some of the best authors writing in the English language today — people like the late Joyce Carey, Kenneth Tynan, William Sansom, A.B. Guthrie Jr., Anthony West, Sylvia Wright, Eudora Welty and others.

And as for conformity, whatever we have today, we've always had it abundantly. The abiding quality of conformity during some of history's most flowering times of creative uniqueness—whether in music, art, literature, science, or business—is illustrated in a brief passage in Aubrey Menen's wonderfully witty and serious book, "The Prevalence of Witches."

It tells about a group of Englishmen living in the mythical jungle colony of Limbo. One of the older men who'd been there since God knows when always carries a whippy stick. A new arrival, fresh from the Home Office, asks why. The answer: "Everybody who knows how to live in the jungle carries a whippy stick." "What for?" "To break the backs of snakes." "Have you ever broken the back of a snake?" "Never. Whenever I see one I run like hell. But if you're going to be accepted here you'll have to carry a whippy stick. It's like swinging a tennis racket in the suburbs of London on a Saturday afternoon. You must do the proper thing. . . ."

MATERIAL GAIN MEANS SPIRITUAL LOSS—OR DOES IT?

The quest for perfection is a nice ideal. But when individuals generalize their own notions of the beautiful and the true, when they turn into inspired spokesmen intent on making converts—then we are treading on dangerous ground, especially when the effort is sustained by the business man's great secular powers.

Who has the right to say so confidently that spiritual values (whatever they are) are so much worth having? If we invented a super tranquilizer that could be given to babies, like smallpox shots, to make them forever lead lives of spiritual contemplation and withdrawal, like St. Augustine, or even Thoreau—if we could do that, should we administer it? Would that produce the best of all possible worlds? I doubt it, as certainly St. Augustine did in his "Confessions." It seems to me he wrote particularly nostalgically about his carefree Manichaean days when yielding to the temptations of the flesh provided many happy hours of youthful diversion. And it is well to remember that Thoreau stayed at Walden Pond less than two years. He voluntarily returned to a world we perversely celebrate him for having rejected. . . .

SPIRITUAL VALUES FOR BOARD CHAIRMEN

Once you begin to second guess the non-material consequences of the soundly materialistic functions of business, you get involved in an endless and fruitless rhetoric. If you are at all serious about these bigger issues, they will keep you from doing the workmanlike job that your business demands. Anyone who seriously dabbles with the higher values during business hours inevitably finds that they engulf him. That is why successful operating men generally leave them alone. No wonder this is the province of the chairman of the board—the elder statesman who is tapering off and now cultivates a garden that promises a different, more elevating kind of yield.

It is true, you cannot as business man serve two masters, God and mammon. As a business man I suggest you serve business and yourself. That is your only function. Saving souls, promoting or preserving spiritual values, elevating taste, cultivating human dignity and consumer self-respect—these high-priority objectives are other people's business if that is what they want to do. The business man's job is to do the things that are the pure, undiluted objectives of business—to satisfy the materialistic and related ego objectives of those who run it. . . .

THE GOLDEN FLEECE
Joseph J. Seldin

Joseph Seldin begins with a summary of three charges that have been leveled against the advertising industry: Advertising, despite what its defenders say, does not expand the market; advertising creates artificial wants; and advertising spreads unhealthy values.
Seldin agrees with all three charges. The solution is simple, according to Seldin: The Federal Communications Commission and the Federal Trade Commission should get tough by clamping down on the advertising industry.

The odd thing about all the criticism of advertising is that nobody has suggested doing away with it. At least not since the depressed thirties has anyone seriously suggested it. Instead, in the postwar period, advertising has been accorded wide recognition by critics as a handmaiden of abundance. They point out that advertising is not specially needed in economic depression, when lack of money makes consumers automatically immune to advertising's persuasion. But when consumers have the money and willingness to buy, advertising then serves a vital purpose by manufacturing consumption to match the manufacture of production. Advertising is the one force relied on to dispose of the mountains of goods that a remarkably prolific economy is capable of turning out.

Needless to say, however, the critics do not view advertising as an unmixed blessing.

First, they are doubtful that advertising actually fulfills the classic economic function claimed by its evangelists — expanding the market, thereby lowering costs of production, leading to lower consumer prices. By and large it works that way with useful consumer goods that do not have wide distribution, but with scores of advertisers today selling almost identical products in markets approaching saturation, advertising's clamorous persuasion tends more to get consumers to switch brands. Expanding an almost saturated market is, to say the least, more difficult and costly.

Moreover in such basic industries as auto, steel, petroleum, pharmaceuticals, prices are no longer set by the forces of supply and demand but by administrative decision. The "administered price" is the reality in many sectors of the economy. A U.S. Senate subcommittee, after hearings on the workings of the administered price in the auto industry, concluded that whereas advertising expanded the market in the early days of the auto industry this might not be true today, with the auto so endemic in U.S. life. The subcommittee estimated that advertising accounts for more than $100 of the retail price of the average car, and observed: "This is not an insignificant cost which the buyer must assume for the dubious privilege of having the merits of the different makes thrust upon him." The subcommittee also estimated that the $100 on a $2,000 car would "tend to reduce annual sales by several hundred thousand cars," raising the startling possibility thereby that in certain sectors of the economy advertising may have come full circle and might in reality

Joseph J. Seldin, "The Golden Fleece," *The Golden Fleece: Selling the Good Life to Americans* (New York: Macmillan, 1963).

be acting more as a brake than a spur to consumption. It would be of major illumination, if not in the national interest, for some nonpartisan group to study the many-faceted impact of advertising on today's national economy.

Second, the critics decry as needless and wasteful the manner in which the full force of advertising creates artificial wants and aggrandizes their satisfactions while so many of the real needs of the people remain unfulfilled. They object, as artifice and diversion, to the way advertising prods consumers relentlessly to pile up personal material possessions in the face of "large ready-made needs for schools, hospitals, slum clearance, sanitation, parks, playgrounds," as John K. Galbraith suggested in *The Affluent Society*. The critics see as a pressing need the redressing of the growing imbalance between our affluent private lives and our impoverished public lives.

Third, the critics are particularly anguished by the *modus operandi* of advertising which selects, from the enormous range of human impulses of which man is capable, primarily the discreditable ones, because they have been found to be the most profitable. Fear, jealousy, envy, ambition, snobbery, greed, lust, and other appeals antithetical to society, are incessantly played up in popular ads to the disfigurement of human values. Such concepts as love, manliness, femininity, friendship are portrayed as though the very real human values they represent are attainable through the purchase of a new shaving lotion, a new deodorant, a new car. Man is conditioned by the ads to regulate his conduct in large measure by external considerations. As Henry Steele Commager wrote in *The American Mind*, "He read books to make conversation, listened to music to establish his social position, chose his clothes for the impression they would make on business associates, entertained his friends in order to get ahead, held the respect of his children and the affection of his wife by continuous bribery." According to the portrayal of Americans in ads, they are decadent, yet few truly believe this. And statesmen who know the American character "appealed to higher motivations, and not in vain. The problem remained a fascinating one, for if it was clear that advertisers libeled the American character, it was equally clear that Americans tolerated and even rewarded those who libeled them." This condition results from advertising's steady devaluation of the quality of man's experience and the stereotyping of his capacity for social response.

These, in brief, are the three main areas of criticism of advertising as it operates today, without diminishing any recognition of it as the historic vehicle of abundance. Yet, oddly, so thin-skinned is the advertising community that any criticism is quickly interpreted as a full-fledged attack on the institution of advertising itself. This is remote from the truth. The critics are concerned because advertising wields such enormous influence in the shaping of popular standards and yet has no social goals. Unlike the school and the church, with which advertising has been compared in magnitude of social power, advertising has no "social responsibilities for what it does with its influence," as David M. Potter wrote in *People of Plenty*. Whereas the school and the church are self-conscious about their roles as guardians of the social values, seeking to improve man by teaching qualities of social usefulness, advertising lacks such social values "unless conformity to material values may be so characterized." Whereas the school and the church exert their influence in the direction of beliefs and attitudes held to be of social value, advertising turns its energies to the stimulation and exploitation of emulative anxieties and material accumulations, imposing them as standards of social value.

The advertising community is not unmindful of lack of social purpose to balance social power, and even those of its practitioners unfreighted by a social conscience recognize the patent danger in too freebooting an operation which would only serve to add to the ranks of influential critics and raise the level of popular criticism. The advertising trade press is distinguished by recurring articles and editorial pleas for a greater show of public responsibility. At trade meetings the same plea is heard. As Donald S. Frost, newly elected chairman of the Association of National Advertisers, told that group, the industry had to set its house in order, "If we don't, someone else is going to do it for us."

Most of the industry's efforts are bent toward the elimination of the obvious friction areas with the public. Advertisers are asked to exercise self-control in their ads. Patently only one automobile can provide more gasoline mileage than the rest, only one cigarette can filter best, only one soap can produce the whitest wash. Advertisers are asked to steer clear of the raw depiction of pain, suffering, sex, fear, and other human emotions; to refrain from pounding commercials, screaming jingles, and inopportune blackouts of the TV screen at dramatic moments. To reinforce these strictures the industry abounds in instruments of self-regulation so that the proliferating organizations of advertisers, ad agencies, and media all bristle with high-sounding codes of conduct. The broadcast codes, for instance, effectively outlaw ads for fortune-telling, occultism, spiritualism, astrology, phrenology, mind reading, tip sheets, character reading, few of which, of course, are thriving businesses today. They keep hard liquor ads off the air, out of deference to the strongly organized "dry" sentiment in the country, permit beer and wine ads only when modestly presented (nobody is ever shown drinking beer or wine on the TV screen). They require products of a "personal" nature — laxatives, deodorants, toilet tissue, corn removers, headache and cold remedies, and intimate garments — to be treated with special concern for the sensibilities of the public.

But the ineffectual nature of the codes is apparent to any TV viewer who is treated seven nights a week to elementary courses in physiology, replete with hammered brains, animated intestines, mist-filled lungs, burbling stomach juices, choked sinus cavities and nasal passages. The codes are no more than framed wall decorations in the executive offices of advertisers, agencies, and networks when it comes to big business. As *Advertising Age* observed: "Codes of practice and ethics are all too often just pleasant mouthings of pious committees, without real effect in their industries." There is even disagreement in the advertising community as to who bears the final responsibility for good conduct, the advertiser, the agency, or the media. Some say the advertiser who O.K.'s and pays for the ads, some say the agencies whose persuasive skills are often so overzealously employed on his behalf, and some say the media which should act as the final backstop of good conduct for the industry. Each of the participants admits to a share in the responsibility but none wants to take on the whole job. In this piecemeal approach to responsibility each tends to say, "Let George do it," but by that no one means any of the government regulatory agencies. The government, as one adman put it, represents an "outside interfering hand."

It would be visionary, of course, to expect to sell sweetness and light to the advertising community unless it could be established at the same time that sweetness and light sell goods. The advertising community says its job is to sell the world, not to save it; the saving it leaves to education and religion. And the selling job is so important to the continuation of the nation's prosperity that it invests the advertising community with a special license to indulge in small and medium-sized built-in selling deceptions. Regrettable as it is to have to proceed by these somewhat shabby methods, it is considered a small price indeed for the citizenry to pay for their material well-being.

It is doubtful, however, that certain changes in the law for the greater protection of the citizenry will place their well-being in jeopardy. The James M. Landis report to the President in 1960, for instance, recommended more regulatory power for the Federal Trade Commission and the Food and Drug Administration so that they could operate more effectively and more commensurately with today's marketing realities. The report noted that "inordinate delay characterizes the disposition of adjudicatory proceedings before substantially all of our regulatory agencies." So far as the FTC is concerned, since the burden of proof rests on it to disprove advertising claims, which it often lacks the manpower, the laboratory facilities, and the funds to do, the inevitable result is to bog the FTC down in lengthy hearings. To cite an extreme example, it took 16 years and nearly 12,000 pages of testimony before the FTC could pin a cease and desist order on Carter's Little Pills which required the toning down of product claims. Customarily cases drag on for years before the successive administrative remedies open to advertisers are exhausted. Even to disprove the claim that "four out of five doctors" recommend a product imposes on the FTC the burden to amass considerable evidence. This burden "significantly emasculates the Commission's power to deal with the spate of deceptive advertising that floods our newspapers, our periodicals and our air waves." The report recommends a sanction more effective than those presently possessed by FTC: "The interlocutory cease and desist order appealable to a court would be a first step."

It is true, of course, that under the Wheeler-Lea Act the FTC is empowered to obtain temporary court injunctions when it can establish that the advertising of foods, drugs, cosmetics, or devices threatens to inflict irreparable injury on the public. But in actual practice the FTC has found that the courts demand such extensive proof before they will issue temporary injunctions that the court hearings on the injunctions are no less burdensome than full FTC trials of the cases.

The upshot is that, since an ad runs until conclusively proved false, all too many advertisers promote deceptive campaigns and rely on administrative remedies to block FTC action until the campaigns have run their course. Frequently, before the FTC gets to the point where it issues a cease and desist order, the campaign is over and the advertiser is off on a new one. The chase then begins anew. Given the power to issue an interlocutory cease and desist order on the basis of a prima facie showing, however, the FTC could freeze the campaign indefinitely while the cumbersome process of taking evidence and reaching a decision unfolds. The public would gain the full measure of benefit.

The Food and Drug Administration also needs additional regulatory power. This was expressed dramatically by Abraham Ribicoff, former Secretary of Health, Education and Welfare, who told a Congressional hearing that "the time has come in the U.S. to give American men, women and children the same protection we have been giving hogs, sheep and cattle since 1913." He argued that "until we are allowed to require that a drug be proven effective before it is marketed, we must say to the American people: a hog is protected against worthless drugs, but you are not." He referred to the Virus-Serum-Toxin Act of 1913 which forbids worthless biologicals for the treatment of domestic animals but which, until 1962, had no counterpart with respect to drugs for human consumption. According to the law prior to 1962 the FDA was required to approve a new drug if it was safe even if it was totally or partially ineffective for the claims made for it. Only when placed on the market could FDA attack it, and then only by contending that it was improperly labeled. It was a matter of common practice, however, for advertisers to skirt FDA jurisdiction by using an innocuous label on the drug and making strong advertising claims for it in the mass media. As President John F. Kennedy observed in his special message to Congress on the need for more consumer protection: "There is no way of measuring the needless suffering, the money innocently squandered, and the protraction of illness resulting from the use of such ineffective drugs."

As a result of the unfortunate use of thalidomide, which caused countless deformities in babies, however, the law was amended in 1962 by an aroused Congress to require new drugs to be proved effective and safe before FDA approved their distribution. Nonetheless, since the overwhelming majority of drugs on the market are not new drugs, and require no FDA approval, the situation is only slightly improved. The needless suffering, the money innocently squandered, and the protraction of illness goes on apace.

Another law that requires retailoring to modern marketing realities is the packaging law. Hearings before a special Congressional subcommittee have demonstrated what many consumers already know, that food labels and packages are often far less trustworthy than they appear. Here again, in matters of safety, the FDA has swift legal recourse. But its authority over "economic cheats" is another matter. The quarter-century-old labeling law, which has never given more than a soupçon of protection to consumers, needs revision to give FDA specific power to crack down on cheats who "slack fill" containers, and who so obscure the facts about size, weight, and contents of packages as to make informed consumer selection difficult if not impossible.

The Landis report reserved its strongest language for the Federal Communications Commission, charging that it has "drifted, vacillated and stalled in almost every major area." The available evidence also indicates that the FCC, "more than any other agency, has been susceptible to ex parte presentations, and that it has been subservient, far too subservient, to the subcommittees on communications of the Congress and their members. A strong suspicion also exists that far too great an influence is exercised over the Commission by the networks."

Central to the problem is the manner in which the FCC grants radio and TV station licenses based on proposed programming in the public interest, which bears little or no resemblance to the actual programming after the station is licensed. "The Commission knows this but ignores these differentiations at the time when renewal of licenses of the station is before them. Nevertheless, it continues with its Alice-in-Wonderland procedures."

Hence in return for a promise to broadcast in the public interest, the licensee has handed over to him at no charge a public air channel for his private profit. Failure to live up to his promise means nothing, since the FCC has never revoked the license of a single station for this reason. At license renewal time, every three years, the FCC rubber-stamps renewals, only very occasionally applying what has become known in the broadcast trade as the "raised eyebrow" technique to improve programming. Although the broadcaster, as a matter of law, owns nothing but a revocable license, as a matter of practice, as James L. Fly, a former FCC commissioner, remarked at a Fund for the Republic discussion, he "has just as much permanence as a fee simple deed to the Empire State Building."

In 1961 the National Association of Broadcasters was reminded by newly elected FCC chairman Newton N. Minow that it was not enough to cater to the public's whims: "You must also serve the nation's needs. . . . Your obligations are not satisfied if you look only to popularity as a test of what to broadcast." The public interest was not merely what interested the public. He invited each broadcaster to "sit down in front of your television set when your station goes on the air and stay there without a book, magazine, newspaper, profit and loss sheet or rating book to distract you — and keep your eyes glued to that set until the station signs off. I can assure you that you will observe a vast wasteland."

It consisted of "a procession of game shows, violence, audience participation shows, formula comedies about totally unbelievable families, blood and thunder, mayhem, violence, sadism, murder, western badmen, western good men, private eyes, gangsters, more violence, and cartoons. And, endlessly, commercials — many screaming, cajoling and offending. And most of all, boredom. True, you will see a few things you will enjoy. But they will be very, very few. And if you think I exaggerate, try it." He said, in closing: "Gentlemen, your trust accounting with your beneficiaries is overdue."

The speech shocked the broadcasters. "No one has talked to them like that," observed *Advertising Age*, "since the dear dead days when the then FCC chairman, James Lawrence Fly, stirred the breezes in the ballroom of the Jefferson Hotel in St. Louis with his charge that the National Association of Broadcasters, whose convention he was at the moment addressing, was like mackerel in the moonlight — 'it both shines and stinks.'"

The FCC implemented its warning to the broadcasters by granting short-term renewals in 1961 to 20 radio stations which allegedly failed to match performance with promise. As the "wasteland" speech made press headlines around the nation many stations discovered that considerable numbers of their listeners and viewers had become pen pals of the FCC.

The FCC might also take into account at the time of license renewal deliberations the deceptive advertising carried by stations in disregard of official notification of FTC findings in this regard. Is this not also in the public interest?

Congress might amend the broadcast law so that the networks are regulated. As the law now stands, the networks are not a fact of life and FCC exercises control over them only through control over the stations.

Lastly the task of the stations to meet their public service responsibility will be made easier if the control that advertisers have over program content is ended. There is no compelling reason, other than the commercial, for advertisers to control both commercials and programming. The principle that applies in the print media, that the advertiser controls the advertisement and the newspaper or magazine controls the editorial matter needs extension to the broadcast media. In an editorial urging advertisers to "get out of show business," *Advertising Age* said, "As long as the end-aim of all programming is to achieve a high rating, and as long as advertisers can associate their commercial messages with high-rated programs and refuse to associate them with lower-rated programs, stations and networks can attain truly balanced programming in the public interest only at great economic risk."

Admittedly these suggestions are only starters, and the road back to more rational national values is a long one, but to the extent that the grip of the advertisers is relaxed on the nation's media and citizens the nation can begin to look elsewhere for its lost national purpose. "With the supermarket as our temple and the singing commercial as our litany," as Adlai Stevenson wrote in his chapter on *The National Purpose*, "are we likely to fire the world with an irresistible vision of American's exalted purposes and inspiring way of life?" It may not be easy to restore a national purpose, but it is always helpful to know where not to look.

Should Advertising Be Eliminated?

Samm Sinclair Baker

Samm Sinclair Baker, who has worked as a copywriter, advertising consultant, and advertising agency president, recognizes that the industry has its bad apples and that it needs to reform itself. But Baker concludes that advertising does more good than harm, and we'd better be careful lest we throw out the baby with the bath water. Besides, Baker suggests, advertising comes with its own checks and balances. He tells the story of a piemaker whose business was almost ruined when he advertised his bad-tasting pies. Advertising bad products only hastens their demise.

In the light of all the flaws and fraudulent aspects of advertising, should it be eliminated? Absolutely not. In spite of its evils, advertising embodies many indispensable benefits. There are lots of bright, able admen who are concerned about the public welfare as well as their own. But there is urgent need to change today's pervading immoral approach to advertising. Preferably this regeneration should be created by admen themselves.

It is most doubtful that such self-reform will be instituted and carried through adequately by the advertising industry. The many failures in the past have proved that self-regulation is almost impossible, as the few representative samples in this book have disclosed. There are hundreds more examples left untold because of space limitations.

In the spirit of self-regulation, the Association of National Advertisers and the American Association of Advertising Agencies jointly set up the Committee for the Improvement of Advertising Content. The purpose was to seek out complaints about ads. In two years, *only ten advertisements* were found to be in bad taste by the committee.

The auto companies knew for years that their cars had safety flaws, whether or not they were actually "unsafe at any speed." They had many warnings to adopt safety devices and regulations. After long delays in needed reforms, they still didn't take unified action. The government finally had to impose laws to *force* manufacturers to incorporate minimum safety features for every car.

Is there undue stress in this book on the reprehensible practices of advertising? Why not emphasize the honest ads? Because ads, like people, *should* be honest and truthful. When ads, like people, are dishonest, they must be criticized and exposed. That, unfortunately, covers a very large percentage of advertising.

Delivering the provost's lecture at Michigan State University, Prof. John W. Crawford said: "Advertising is an instrument in the hands of the people who use it. If evil men use advertising for base purposes, then evil can result. If honest men use advertising to sell an honest product with honest enthusiasm, then positive good for our kind of capitalistic society can result."

Samm Sinclair Baker, "Should Advertising Be Eliminated?," *The Permissible Lie: The Inside Truth About Advertising* (New York: World Publishing, 1968).

It was not until I was away from day-to-day advertising activity for over a year that I could look at Madison Avenue objectively. Then I realized (recognizing fully my own participation in such a course for decades) that the general approach of admen is based on *the permissible lie.*

Often without being specifically conscious of it, most admen tackle the selling of goods from the viewpoint of seeking to get away with whatever they can — *to the boundary of being punished legally.* The usual belief is that this course is necessary and therefore excusable.

Honest, interesting, informative advertising can be the most productive for the advertiser and agency over the long run. The benefits of advertising a good product can be enormous for all, as well as disastrous for an inferior product, as illustrated by a short short story:

Once there was a baker who baked very poor pies. Naturally he sold very few pies. He decided that he could sell more by advertising. So he placed an appealing ad in the local newspaper; he was a very able adman but an inferior baker.

Soon after he opened his shop the next morning, crowds of women attracted by the ad started pouring in for his pies. His wife was delighted. But suddenly the baker yelled, "Lock the door! Don't let in any more customers!"

When the store had been emptied, he placed a sign on the door: "Sold out of pies." His wife complained, "But we still have dozens of unsold pies."

"I know," said the baker, "but I suddenly realized that if so many people find out how bad our pies are, they'll tell their friends. *Nobody* will ever come to our shop again. We'll be ruined. Before I advertise any more, I'll have to learn how to bake better pies."

That's just one of the important benefits of advertising: It tends to raise the quality of products offered for sale. Nothing fails faster than a poor product that has been boosted by heavy advertising.

For good or evil, advertising — as noted in a *Life* editorial — is a vital part of "the engine of the American economy." It's an essential activity of our economic system. Without advertising, our superior forms of manufacturing, marketing, and distribution which contribute to producing the highest average standard of living in the world could not exist.

The Gross National Product — which is the amount paid out annually in the U.S.A. for goods and services — is about $630 billion at this writing. That's about $112 billion gain in the past three years on record, and it's climbing (expected to be $1.2 trillion in 1975). Translated into terms of human consumption, about $90 billion is now spent just on food each year. The average big supermarket offers about 7,500 different food items. In a single market there is a choice of twenty-two kinds of baked beans.

Some critics of advertising and marketing contend that twenty-two different types and labels of baked beans are too many, creating waste. Is it really too wide a choice for the thousands of families shopping in a giant supermarket? Would 220 kinds of baked beans, or 2,200 be too many brands for almost 200 million people?

It has been said that "what critics call the wastefulness of advertising is really the price that has to be paid for freedom of choice." Furthermore there *is* plenty of choice between advertised and unadvertised labels, so the advertiser is not in the driver's seat.

Some social critics, although very much concerned about material gains and comforts for themselves, attack advertising indiscriminately, failing to realize and acknowledge that it is "the showcase of business" — controlled by business. Along with the evils, the benefits of both must be considered.

It is easy to forget that advertising functions on the smallest, most fundamental terms, as well as the largest. Not every ad is on costly TV programs or full color pages in print. This little sign tacked on a factory bulletin board is an ad for safety: "Girls, if your sweater is too large for you, look out for the machines. If you are too large for your sweater, look out for the machinists."

A simple letter can be a potent ad, such as this one: "Dear Mr. Walker. . . . In case you haven't noticed, we are busy painting at 19 Pine Lane, around the corner from you. We take great pride in our work, and want the finished job to reflect an attractive, well-kept neighborhood. While our men are at hand, we can offer you savings on a paint job that you may have planned for the near future. Why not drive over and see the work we do, then call us. Yours for a friendly handshake. . . . John Baraglia."

Mr. Walker was thinking about a paint job. He looked at Mr. Baraglia's work. He liked it. John's competitive bid won. Both of them gained through timely, honest, informative advertising.

It is fitting to have some leading practicing admen tell you of its benefits. "Art" (not Arthur) Tatham, board chairman of Tatham-Laird and Kudner Agency, said: "Advertising plays one of the most important roles in providing people with the opportunity freely to that right [freedom of choice]. The exercise of choice depends on information. Advertising provides it . . . much of the task of good advertising is to portray as clearly and intimately as possible the way the product fits into the lives of the particular people it can best serve."

In a message addressed to "bright young men and women," the American Association of Advertising Agencies stated:

> The biggest objection to advertising seems to be that it makes people want things they *really don't need* . . . such things as refrigerator-freezers, air conditioners, movie cameras, sports cars, dishwashing machines, clothes dryers, frozen foods, instant foods, vitamins, new synthetic fibers for lightweight clothing, TV sets, stereo, hi-fi, *two* automobiles, more leisure time and the equipment to enjoy it: boats, skis, fishing and hunting equipment, fast travel by jet — just to name a few.
>
> Sure . . . we could get along without most of these "unnecessary" adjuncts to modern living — and we really wouldn't miss them if we turned back the clock to the days *before you were born*. For as you may or may not realize, most of these things came into real distribution *only during your young lifetime*. And *Advertising* helped make them all possible. So, in a broad sense . . . . a *good part* of the *good life* you take for granted today has been stimulated by Advertising over the past twenty years. (The italics are the advertiser's.)

Challenged on this point of "unnecessary adjuncts," an adman was asked, "What in the world, for example, would a woman want with ten new dresses?" He answered quickly, "Ten new hats."

Lord Thomson, English newspaper magnate, wrote in *The Advertising Quarterly*: "Advertising is not expendable. It is not a garnishment of business, but an essential ingredient in our economy. . . . It makes jobs; it reduces selling costs; it helps increase our standard of living. Effectively and properly used, it increases productivity and makes possible the only security a company and its labor forces can hope to have in an uncertain world."

Again note the key phrase in the foregoing: Advertising "effectively and properly used." Most of the objections to advertising are on the score of prevailing *improper* usage.

Does advertising lower prices? The cost reduction process generally operates simply in this sequence:

1. Advertising informs you of the product and its availability.
2. If you try the product and like it, you buy more and tell others about it (unless offensive advertising then sells you off the product).
3. With increased sales, production goes up, cost per unit goes down. You get the benefit usually in lower prices.

Contrary to the belief of many, the more money spent on advertising by a company as sales increase, usually the lower the ad cost per unit. With autos, for example, according to Advertising Publications, Incorporated, the five top companies—American Motors, Chrysler, Ford, General Motors, and Studebaker—in one year increased their total advertising expenditures 5.6 percent. In the same year sales climbed 8.7 percent. Ad cost per car dropped 2.8 percent.

Several dozen people were asked how much of the average $3,000 they paid for their cars was advertising expense. Their guesses ranged from $200 to $500. They were influenced by the tremendous total advertising expenditures for cars—about $250 million in advertising in one year for the top five makers alone.

They were astonished to learn that the average advertising cost for the cars they bought was under $35. Chevrolet, which spent the most—about $65 million—sold over 2.1 million cars, with an ad cost of under $30 per car. On the other hand, Studebaker, which spent about $5.5 million sold about 65,000 cars—with an ad cost of about $85 each; this high cost was subsequently an ingredient in its downfall.

Advertisers keep trying to improve products. This is not due to a sense of public service but because each competitor is trying to outperform the other.

The non-advertiser can operate this way: He sells stores his X-label peas, usually by providing a price advantage and possibly (not necessarily) reducing quality. His product quality is more likely to vary since he has no large advertising investment in X-label to protect. He can profit until customers find X-label peas unsatisfactory. He then changes the name only, offering the same product as Y-label peas. He can continue under different labels, serving different stores.

The brand advertiser can't operate this way. If his quality falters, the public stops buying it. His brand dies, and perhaps his business with it.

The retailer in some instances displays and pushes the private label (unadvertised) product because he may make an eight-cent profit on the twenty-five-cent package, compared with a five-cent profit on the advertised brand. Other retailers give best display to the advertised brand because they found that they sell ten packages at a five-cent profit for a total fifty-cent profit. In the same period of time, they sell five packages of the unadvertised label at eight-cents profit each—a total forty-cent profit—ten cents less total profit than on the advertised brand.

How much profit per package the retailer makes doesn't concern you, of course.

You choose — you decide. It's so simple: You buy a can of Del Monte peaches for fifty-three cents. You see unadvertised Delbel peaches for forty-nine cents for the same size can. You try both. If you find Delbel as good as Del Monte, you'll keep buying it and saving four cents per can. Not $1 billion spent on advertising could force you to buy Del Monte against your wishes.

The advertised brand has the advantage of familiarity. Henry Slesar, head of Slesar and Kanzer agency, wrote a famous ad for McGraw-Hill magazines. It showed a stony-faced man staring coldly out at the reader. He was saying: "I don't know who you are. I don't know your company. I don't know your company's product. I don't know your company's reputation. Now — what is it you wanted to sell me?"

Advertising makes it easier for you to *sample* a product and decide for yourself. The largest single order to date in the history of the Cedar Rapids, Iowa, post office was from Quaker Oats cereal mill. It consisted of thirty-five boxcars of 5.7 million sample boxes of Cap'n Crunch pre-sweetened corn and oats cereal. The postage alone cost Quaker Oats about $180,000. People liked the samples and bought the big boxes in stores, scoring a quicker success for Quaker.

Many of the big advertised brands — Daffodil Farm Bread, Vicks Formula 44, Baggies, Yuban Instant Coffee, Kraft dressings, and thousands more — owe some of their success to free or cut-price sampling. Is this any way to run a business, spending a half million dollars and more in one shot to give away your advertised product *free*?

You bet it is — if the product is good.

But — like the baker's pies — if the product is bad, each ad dollar added will kill it quicker.

Is Puffery Flummery?

Sid Bernstein

Sid Bernstein is, as he says in his opening sentence, "unalterably and completely in favor of puffery in advertising." Puffery, according to Bernstein, is merely advertisers' attempts to make their products look as good as possible. Innocent puffery occurs when a car dealer claims "They Don't Call Us the Best Dealer for Nothing." Deception is entirely different, Bernstein says. Deception occurs when that car dealer claims that he has the lowest prices in the city when he doesn't.

At the time he wrote this article Bernstein was the president of Advertising Age, *which bills itself as the "National Newspaper of Advertising."*

I am squarely, unalterably and completely in favor of puffery in advertising. And so, I've just discovered to my pleasure, is our decade-old unabridged Webster's International dictionary, which contains this definition:

puffery: flattering publicity; extravagant commendation esp. for promotional purposes; *specif*: ADVERTISING.

I am not sure that I would go so far as to classify all advertising as puffery, but I certainly visualize advertising as designed to present "a rose colored vision of loveliness," rather than a cataloging of good and bad features. That is advertising's function — to make the best possible case for its sponsor's product or service. It's important that this basic function be understood by everyone — by practitioners, public, legislators, regulators. At the same time:

I am squarely, unalterably and completely opposed to false, deceptive or misleading advertising.

But I think there is a difference between deception and puffery, and that *fact* and *intent* are the really important elements. Plus the application of common sense.

In Wisconsin, no dealer can now headline an ad, "They Don't Call Us the Best Dealer for Nothing," as one did before the new code went into effect. Presumably, he is also forbidden to invite people to visit his "beautiful" showroom, or to talk to his "most courteous" sales people, or to aver that his cars come in "gorgeous" colors, or will "make you feel like a million dollars" if you buy and drive one.

Horse radish.

That's innocent puffery — and not only advertising, but every form of written and spoken communication is going to suffer if it is circumscribed.

On the other hand, it is definitely not innocent puffery if this dealer says, "Our prices are the lowest in the state," or "Nobody will give you as good a trade-in," or "$1,000 off on our brand new models."

Statements like these are subject to strict factual tests, and they should be rigidly applied. If they are true, fine; if they are untrue or only partly true or true only part

Sid Bernstein, "Is Puffery Flummery?," *Advertising Age* 2 October 1972.

of the time, zap the advertiser and zap him hard. He's not guilty of puffery; he's lying and cheating.

But let the advertiser — the company whose money is being spent — be the only one who worries seriously about whether "State Farm is all you need to know about life insurance," or "Ford has a better idea" or "The instrument of the immortals" are statements that have meaning or value in their advertising.

Most of us still have far more serious things to worry about than statements like these.

Puffery Is Deception
Ivan Preston

Ivan Preston, a journalism professor and member of the editorial board of Journalism Quarterly, *claims that an advertiser's extravagant and unprovable claims (puffery, in other words) are deceptive and ought to be banned by the Federal Trade Commission. Preston claims that even innocent-sounding ads like "You Meet the Nicest People on a Honda" are deceptive enough to require intervention by the FTC. And most cosmetics ads ought to be banned. "Cosmetics promise much," Preston says, and "deliver nothing. . . ."*

. . . Puffery deceives less than the maximum, but it still deceives materially and substantially. It implies false facts which affect purchasing decisions detrimentally for a substantial portion of the public. The fact that people don't complain about it does not prove otherwise. . . .

"Blatz is Milwaukee's finest beer" certainly deceives, . . . even though it does not deceive absolutely. No one would think that all the world, including Blatz's competitors, universally affirms that Blatz is Milwaukee's best. But consumers, while not insisting on that ultimate literal meaning, must think the claim means something! They must think it means that more people than just the Blatz owners and employees think Blatz is the best. They must think there is some specific criterion which the product meets in order to merit the claim of "finest." The truth is that Blatz has offered no such criterion, and to the best of my knowledge none exists. Therefore the belief implied by the claim of "finest" is false and deceptive to the public, and materially so because it affects purchasing decisions negatively.

"You'll meet the nicest people on a Honda," I've already conceded, is not interpreted by people as an absolute guarantee that they'll make the greatest friends they could ever hope to make — or their money back. Of course they won't think that, and as a result the advertiser may insist there's no important element of deception in the claim. But why then does the advertiser use that sort of claim? Undoubtedly it's because he thinks the consumer will be inclined to accept *some* aspect of belief about the relationship between social satisfaction and Honda ownership. If the claim doesn't work it won't be used; if it's used it must be thought to be working. And if it works it must be because the consumer believes *to some extent* that the cycle company is guaranteeing to contribute *in some way* to his social life. His belief may be vague — he may not know exactly how he thinks the cycle will contribute — but he believes for a fact that it will.

And when the consumer believes any such thing he has been materially deceived, because the cycle company is guaranteeing no such thing whatever. There is a vast difference between an ad implying "We'll put you on the road" and one implying "We'll put you into the fun." The manufacturer can give you the physical, tangible product which he can guarantee will put you on the road. He can give you nothing

Ivan Preston, "Puffery Is Deception," *The Great American Blow-up: Puffery in Advertising and Selling* (Madison: University of Wisconsin Press, 1975).

which will guarantee you'll get into the fun. Yet he uses the social-psychological type of misrepresentation because the consumer will treat it to some extent as something guaranteed.

An insidious aspect of this sort of claim is that the consumer may never learn the implied guarantee is phony. If he gets on the road today but doesn't get into the fun, he figures the fun will come tomorrow. If it doesn't come tomorrow there's always another day. He never reaches the point where he knows it's not to be. Perhaps this explains why people don't complain about deception — they have to find out about it first, and the subtlety of puffery's deception helps prevent discovery. That is the magic in cosmetic advertising, which deals heavily in social guarantees yet probably plays an infinitesimal role in actual satisfactions. Cosmetics promise much, deliver nothing, and sell like hot cakes for years on end with the same customers. The public couldn't have discovered the deception if it keeps on buying like that.

Keeping the truth hidden is more critical to the cosmetics business than the motorcycle business because its sales consist of small purchases repeated frequently. If the consumer becomes disillusioned with his Honda he will already have afforded the company a good profit on an expensive item which was intended to last for quite a while. The company wouldn't have expected to make a re-sale very soon, anyway. In cosmetics, however, the initial purchase is a small matter, and profit expectations depend significantly upon a great volume of repeat purchases by the same individual. Under these conditions the falseness of the implied promise must be kept hidden through the course of its constant failures, or there will be no point in using it in the first place. The cosmetics people need that kind of concealment, and there is every reason to believe they get it.

The conclusion from such illustrations — and many more could be offered — can only be that puffery deceives the public materially and substantially and should be prohibited. If the law has not yet agreed it is probably because the regulators have not yet sufficiently adapted their thinking to encompass deception which is subtle and indirect rather than direct and absolute. The regulators are accustomed to asking what *specific* false claim is stated or implied to the consumer so that he believes it and is therefore deceived. They are accustomed to concluding that if no *specific* falsity can be definitely identified, then there is no deception in a legal sense.

In order to get action on puffery's deception, we must get the regulators out of that habit. With puffery the consumer usually does not believe some specific claim which is false, but he believes that there is *something* specific which must be true. With Blatz, for example, the consumer does not believe any precise claim about what "finest" means, but he believes it must mean something about fineness. He doesn't believe something specifically, but he specifically believes that there's something. And if in truth the term "finest" means nothing about fineness, then the implication that it means *something* should be regarded by the regulators as a specific falsity and charged as such. Admittedly it's a more vague charge than the regulator is accustomed to handling, but surely it's a sound enough criterion to work with.

Startlingly, there occurred in 1972 a solitary regulatory incident which confirms this line of thinking. The National Advertising Review Board found General Motors to be potentially deceptive in its use of a puffery claim consisting of the symbol "GM" and the phrase "Mark of Excellence" superimposed on a square resembling a small plaque. The Review Board felt the claim's use would be acceptable only if restricted to employment as a company signature or trademark in the corner of a print ad or at the end of a broadcast commercial. But using the claim as a primary part of the company's sales story would be deceptive "in view of the recent spate of recalls of cars because of defects constituting possible safety hazards."

This decision amounted to an admission that "Mark of Excellence" meant something to consumers. It was considerably different from the usual ruling about a phrase so vague. For once, the regulators did not insist on knowing precisely what it would imply, but were content with knowing something it wouldn't imply. It wouldn't imply the sloppy workmanship that has resulted in recalls; it wouldn't imply the dangers to life and limb caused by defects not recalled. Whatever "Mark of Excellence" did mean, it certainly didn't mean those things.

The decision was noteworthy because it used subtle means to interpret subtle deception. It's too bad it wasn't made by the FTC. The National Advertising Review Board is an industry self-regulating organization composed of fifty appointees from advertisers, ad agencies, and the public. Its decisions do not have the force of law and do not constitute legal precedents. Still the ruling was a step in a new direction and contributed strongly toward rejecting the idea that puffery's deception is trivial because it is not absolute.

THE SOCIAL CRISES OF THE MASS CULTURE

Stuart Ewen

Stuart Ewen's essay comes from his book The Captains of Consciousness, *a harsh, broad attack on America's "consumer culture."*

Ewen comes to the task of attacking the advertising industry from the point of view of the radical left. As a result, Ewen posits a kind of conspiracy of manufacturers and advertisers to subvert the finer ideals and values of Americans. Advertising is little more than a tool of a "repressive corporate order," and its purpose is the creation of a "dependable mass of consumers required by modern industry. . . ."

In the years following World War II, the trend toward cultural mobilization reached epic proportion. Television was carrying corporate culture into what was to become a vast majority of American homes. The expansion of bureaucracies and of service industries was defining an increasing sector of the social processes according to a centralized corporate logic. More than pervasive, the injection of corporate bonding into the interstices of existence was altering and attempting to safely standardize the common perception of daily life. While heralding a world of unprecedented freedom and opportunity, corporations (in concert with the state apparatus) were generating a mode of existence which was increasing regimented and authoritarian. If consumer culture was a parody of the popular desire for self-determination and meaningful community, its innards revealed the growing standardization of the social terrain and corporate domination over what was to be consumed and experienced.

While the decade of the fifties was largely one of containment, a time of social and political petrification, the explosive years that followed revitalized the domain of public opposition and militancy. Ironically, as the cultural apparatus attempted to compensate for the confinements of the productive society, it was in the realm of the culture that growing resistance focused most sharply. From different fronts within an increasingly corporatized society came indications that the cultural apparatus of consumerism provided a rich soil for discontent as well as complacency.

First, the social landscape was attacked and disrupted by those who were most ignored in its parameters. While during the Depression scarcity had conformed to a multiracial ideology, creating a kind of "We're all in this thing together" mentality, the culture of the fifties reiterated the notion of class along the lines of *who could* and *who could not* buy their way to *happiness*. Industry was moving South, agriculture was stagnating or being mechanized, and on both fronts it was the black population that was bearing the brunt of the transformation. The postwar movement among blacks—first in the South, then continuing and extending into the cities of the North—represented a beginning of resistance that came from that part

Stuart Ewen, "The Social Crises of the Mass Culture," *Captains of Consciousness: Advertising and the Social Roots of the Consumer Culture* (New York: McGraw-Hill, 1976).

of the population which was most noticeably being ignored on the level of gainful employment and by the social program of consumerization.

If black resistance was related to an exclusion from the corporate social network, other resistance was born of familiarity. It grew among those for whom the cultural web of consumerism was being most elaborately and intricately spun: the children and women of the *consumer culture*. Where for their grandparents and parents it had been the productive apparatus, its fragmentary routines and standardization, which gave ground to discontent, the standardization of culture, flourishing after World War II, broadened alienation even more. As corporately determined patterns tempered the realm of daily existence, the degradation of labor gave way to a broad degradation of social life *per se*. The commercialization of culture, attempting to reproduce corporate priorities in the wide social realm, tended also to broaden the scope of opposition.

Within the advertised life style, young people and their mothers had been the *social principles* of the consumer ethic. Men were expected to act out corporate commands primarily in job-defined ways. For women and children, the corporate ideal was geared toward a definition of home and community life. If "home" was a man's refuge from the work-a-day world, for mothers and children it was expected to be a place where their own form of commitment to that world was acted out. Daily life was expected to be carried out according to the conformities of consumption. Amidst a promise of unlimited possibilities, women and children confronted limited and predigested realities. Among the children and women whose lives were encased by the commercialized democracy, the competitiveness, obedience and confinement implied in the corporate version of social life took its most definite toll.

Within the student movement of the 1960s and the rebirth of feminism that followed lay the sense that the social realm, the realm in which life reproduces life, was becoming increasingly authoritarian and repressive. Integral to the politics of the New Left was a recognition that social space was severely circumscribed by a repressive corporate order. In the twenties, advertising and consumerism had stood as a corporate alternative to what had been a chronically oppressive industrial situation. For the youth culture of the sixties, advertising posed no such alternative. Raised within the all-pervasive aura of mass consumption, students in the "movement" confronted advertised culture as their common memory, their basic definition of corporate life itself. The New Left confronted the "quality of life" beyond the industrial factory, out in the broader social realms which corporate organization was set on conquering.

The reemergence of feminism in the late 1960s betrayed parallel developments. The tension between the imagery of "housewife" and the growing involvement of women in the job market had been irritating in the twenties. In the fifties and sixties this irritation had erupted into a festering wound. With more women than ever employed in clerical work and service activities (corporate housekeeping and nurturing roles), "wifely" personae that encouraged isolation and a sense of social irrelevancy persisted, even as the domestic realm was steadily being devaluated within the priorities of the broad, corporate society.

Women's politics, the critique of sexual objectification and of "male chauvinism," became focused on the home situation. The home was a seeming anachronism, being reproduced and reinforced by the unresponsive corporate vision. The "home," the "husband," became a shorthand for the social denigration of women within corporate society.

Within the robotized veneer of the fifties lay the heart of the resistance that was to emerge. Beginning with a perception of the "one-dimensionality" and "loneliness" of social existence, today the critique has come full circle, confronting the world of work. As evidenced by our recent history, the barbarity and boredom of working conditions has been dramatized in the widespread opposition to corporate regimentation. Strikes and job actions against speed-up and enforced overtime are united with a critique of consumerism; both working conditions and consumption stand inadequate to meet the expression of human needs.

From the late sixties on there has been a proliferation of cultural movements which have expanded the scope of opposition. As resistance has mounted, however, the captains of consciousness have hardly thrown in the towel. Appropriating the lingo and styles of the New Left, the counterculture, feminism, neo-agrarianism, ethnicity, drug-vision and other phenomena, the advertising industry, seeking markets, has generated a mass culture which reflects the spirit but not the cutting edge of this resistance. While advertising of the twenties spoke against the deprivations of scarcity, an increasing amount of today's advertising and product imagery speak to the deprivations of what has been called "abundance." Within advertising, the social realm of resistance is reinterpreted, at times colonized, for corporate benefit. Ads mirror the widespread judgment that mass-produced goods are junky and unhealthy. Products are advertised as if they contain this anticorporate disposition — praised for their organic naturalness and their timeless quality. Modes of anticorporate resistance and sentiment reappear in the ads themselves, miraculously encased within the universal terms of the market. General Mills reinforces corporate hegemony in the name of natural cereals — a harkening to a precorporate, idealized past. The automobile industry offers machines for wish fulfillment — at the same time hoping to contain those wishes within the domain of the cash nexus. From the oil industry comes a more authoritarian image to confront the loci of resistance. Oil industry ads are singular in their ability to say, "We know you don't like things as they are, but we're the boss and that's the way it is!" Most other ads tend, however, to offer a way out of the corporate bummer. On both the material and psychological levels, advertising offers refuge from an overly managed and infiltrated social space.

As we are confronted by the mass culture, we are offered the idiom of our own criticism as well as its negation — corporate solutions to corporate problems. Until we confront the infiltration of the commodity system into the interstices of our lives, *social change* itself will be but a product of corporate propaganda. There have been the beginnings of a politics of daily life. This politics has already been subjected to the ironies of that which it opposes. As the politics of domestic government is linked to the politics of daily life, there must be an unrelenting vigilance against and rejection of the corporation mode of amelioration.

The triumph of capitalism in the twentieth century has been its ability to define and contend with the conditions of the social realm. From the period of the 1920s, commercial culture has increasingly provided an idiom within which desires for social change and fantasies of liberation might be articulated and contained. The cultural displacement effected by consumerism has provided a mode of perception that has both confronted the question of human need and at the same time restricted its possibilities. Social change cannot come about in a context where objects are invested with human subjective capacities. It cannot come about where commodities contain the limits of social betterment. It requires that people never concede the issue of who shall define and control the social realm.

The Language of Advertising Claims

Jeffrey Schrank

In "The Language of Advertising Claims" Jeffrey Schrank analyzes the claims that advertisers make for their products. These claims, according to the author, a full of what he calls "pseudo-information" and they "balance on the narrow line between truth and falsehood. . . ."

Jeffrey Schrank, once a high school English teacher, is now a writer and the president of the Learning Seed Company.

High school students, and many teachers, are notorious believers in their immunity to advertising. These naive inhabitants of consumerland believe that advertising is childish, dumb, a bunch of lies, and influences only the vast hordes of the less sophisticated. Their own purchases are made purely on the basis of value and desire, with advertising playing only a minor supporting role. They know about Vance Packard and his "hidden persuaders" and the adwriter's psychosell and bag of persuasive magic. They are not impressed.

Advertisers know better. Although few people admit to being greatly influenced by ads, surveys and sales figures show that a well-designed advertising campaign has dramatic effects. A logical conclusion is that advertising works below the level of conscious awareness and it works even on those who claim immunity to its message. Ads are designed to have an effect while being laughed at, belittled, and all but ignored.

A person unaware of advertising's claim on him or her is precisely the one most defenseless against the adwriter's attack. Advertisers delight in an audience which believes ads to be harmless nonsense, for such an audience is rendered defenseless by its belief that there is no attack taking place. The purpose of a classroom study of advertising is to raise the level of awareness about the persuasive techniques used in ads. One way to do this is to analyze ads in microscopic detail. Ads can be studied to detect their psychological hooks, they can be used to gauge values and hidden desires of the common person, they can be studied for their use of symbols, color, and imagery. But perhaps the simplest and most direct way to study ads is through an analysis of the language of the advertising claim.

The "claim" is the verbal or print part of an ad that makes some claim of superiority for the product being advertised. After studying claims, students should be able to recognize those that are misleading and accept as useful information those that are true. A few of these claims are downright lies, some are honest statements about a truly superior product, but most fit into the category of neither bold lies nor helpful consumer information. They balance on the narrow line between truth and falsehood by a careful choice of words.

The reason so many ad claims fall into this category of pseudo-information is that they are applied to parity products, products in which all or most of the brands

Jeffrey Schrank, "The Language of Advertising Claims," *Teaching About Doublespeak* (Urbana, IL: National Council of Teachers of English, 1976).

available are nearly identical. Since no one superior product exists, advertising is used to create the illusion of superiority. The largest advertising budgets are devoted to parity products such as gasoline, cigarettes, beer and soft drinks, soaps, and various headache and cold remedies.

The first rule of parity involves the Alice in Wonderlandish use of the words "better" and "best." In parity claims, "better" means "best" and "best" means "equal to." If all the brands are identical they must all be equally good, the legal minds have decided. So "best" means that the product is as good as the other superior products in its category. When Bing Crosby declares Minute Maid Orange Juice "the best there is" he means it is as good as the other orange juices you can buy.

The word "better" has been legally interpreted to be a comparative and therefore becomes a clear claim of superiority. Bing could not have said that Minute Maid is "better than any other orange juice." "Better" is a claim of superiority. The only time "better" can be used is when a product does indeed have superiority over other products in its category or when the better is used to compare the product with something other than competing brands. An orange juice could therefore claim to be "better than a vitamin pill," or even "the better breakfast drink."

The second rule of advertising claim analysis is simply that if any product is truly superior, the ad will say so very clearly and will offer some kind of convincing evidence of the superiority. If an ad hedges the least bit about a product's advantage over the competition you can strongly suspect it is not superior — maybe equal to but not better. You will never hear a gasoline company say "we will give you four miles per gallon more in your car than any other brand." They would love to make such a claim, but it would not be true. Gasoline is a parity product.

To create the necessary illusion of superiority, advertisers usually resort to one or more of the following ten basic techniques. Each is common and easy to identify.

1. The Weasel Claim

A weasel word is a modifier that practically negates the claim that follows. The expression "weasel word" is aptly named after the egg-eating habits of weasels. A weasel will suck out the inside of an egg, leaving it appear intact to the casual observer. Upon examination, the egg is discovered to be hollow. Words or claims that appear substantial upon first look but disintegrate into hollow meaninglessness on analysis are weasels. Commonly used weasel words include "helps" (the champion weasel); "like" (used in a comparative sense); "virtual" or "virtually"; "acts" or "works"; "can be"; "up to"; "as much as"; "refreshes"; "comforts"; "tackles"; "fights"; "come on"; "the feel of"; "the look of"; "looks like"; "fortified"; "enriched"; and "strengthened."

Samples of Weasel Claims

"*Helps control* dandruff *symptoms* with *regular use.*" The weasels include "helps control," and possibly even "symptoms," and "regular use." The claim is not "stops dandruff."

"Leaves dishes *virtually* spotless." We have seen so many ad claims that we have learned to tune out weasels. You are supposed to think "spotless," rather than "virtually" spotless.

"Only half the price of *many* color sets." "Many" is the weasel. The claim is supposed to give the impression that the set is inexpensive.

"Tests confirm one mouthwash *best* against mouth odor."

"Hot Nestlés' cocoa is the very *best*." Remember the "best" and "better" routine.

"Listerine *fights* bad breath." "Fights" not "stops."

"Lots of things have changed, but Hershey's *goodness* hasn't." This claim does not say that Hershey's chocolate hasn't changed.

"Bacos, the crispy garnish that tastes just *like* its name."

2. The Unfinished Claim

The unfinished claim is one in which the ad claims the product is better, or has more of something but does not finish the comparison.

Samples of Unfinished Claims

"Magnavox gives you more." More what?

"Anacin: Twice as much of the pain reliever doctors recommend most." This claim fits in a number of categories but it does not say twice as much of what pain reliever.

"Supergloss does it with more color, more shine, more sizzle, more!"

"Coffee-mate gives coffee more body, more flavor." Also note that "body" and "flavor" are weasels.

"You can be sure if it's Westinghouse." Sure of what?

"Scott makes it better for you."

3. The "We're Different and Unique" Claim

This kind of claim states that there is nothing else quite like the product advertised. For example, if Schlitz would add pink food coloring to its beer they could say "There's nothing like new pink Schlitz." The uniqueness claim is supposed to be interpreted by readers as a claim to superiority.

Samples of "We're Different and Unique" Claim

"There's no other mascara like it."

"Only Doral has this unique filter system."

"Cougar is like nobody else's car."

"Either way, liquid or spray, there's nothing else like it."

"If it doesn't say Goodyear, it can't be polyglas." "Polyglas" is a trade name owned by Goodyear. Goodrich or Firestone could make a tire exactly identical to the Goodyear one and yet couldn't call it "polyglas" — a name for fiberglass belts.

"Only Zenith has chromacolor." Same as the "polyglas" gambit. Admiral has solarcolor and RCA has accucolor.

4. The "Water Is Wet" Claim

"Water is wet" claims say something about the product that is true for any brand in that product category, (e.g., "Schrank's water is really wet.") The claim is usually a statement of fact, but not a real advantage over the competition.

Samples of "Water Is Wet" Claim

"Mobil: the Detergent Gasoline." Any gasoline acts as a cleaning agent.

"Great Lash greatly increases the diameter of every lash."

"Rheingold, the natural beer." Made from grains and water as are other beers.
"SKIN smells differently on everyone." As do all perfumes.

5. The "So What" Claim

This is the kind of claim to which the careful reader will react by saying "So What?" A claim is made which is true but which gives no real advantage to the product. This is similar to the "water is wet" claim except that it claims an advantage which is not shared by most of the other brands in the product category.

Samples of the "So What" Claim

"Geritol has more than twice the iron of ordinary supplements." But is twice as much beneficial to the body?

"Campbell's gives you tasty pieces of chicken and not one but two chicken stocks." Does the presence of two stocks improve the taste?

"Strong enough for man but made for a woman." This deodorant claim says only that the product is aimed at the female market.

6. The Vague Claim

The vague claim is simply not clear. This category often overlaps with others. The key to the vague claim is the use of words that are colorful but meaningless, as well as the use of subjective and emotional opinions that defy verification. Most contain weasels.

Samples of the Vague Claim

"Lips have never looked so luscious." Can you imagine trying to either prove or disprove such a claim?

"Lipsavers are fun — they taste good, smell good and feel good."

"Its deep rich lather makes hair feel good again."

"For skin like peaches and cream."

"The end of meatloaf boredom."

"Take a bite and you'll think you're eating on the Champs Elysées."

"Winston tastes good like a cigarette should."

"The perfect little portable for all around viewing with all the features of higher priced sets."

"Fleischmann's makes sensible eating delicious."

7. The Endorsement or Testimonial

A celebrity or authority appears in an ad to lend his or her stellar qualities to the product. Sometimes the people will actually claim to use the product, but very often they don't.

Samples of Endorsements or Testimonials

"Joan Fontaine throws a shot-in-the-dark party and her friends learn a thing or two."

"Darling, have you discovered Masterpiece? The most exciting men I know are smoking it." (Eva Gabor)

"Vega is the best handling car in the U.S." This claim was challenged by the FTC, but GM answered that the claim is only a direct quote from *Road and Track* magazine.

8. The Scientific or Statistical Claim

This kind of ad uses some sort of scientific proof or experiment, very specific numbers, or an impressive sounding mystery ingredient.

Samples of Scientific or Statistical Claims

"Wonder Bread helps build strong bodies 12 ways." Even the weasel "helps" did not prevent the FTC from demanding this ad be withdrawn. But note that the use of the number 12 makes the claim far more believable than if it were taken out.

"Easy-Off has 33% more cleaning power than another popular brand." "Another popular brand" often translates as some other kind of oven cleaner sold somewhere. Also the claim does not say Easy-Off works 33% better.

"Special Morning—33% more nutrition." Also an unfinished claim.

"Certs contains a sparkling drop of Retsyn."

"ESSO with HTA."

"Sinarest. Created by a research scientist who actually gets sinus headaches."

9. The "Compliment the Consumer" Claim

This kind of claim butters up the consumer by some form of flattery.

Samples of "Compliment the Consumer" Claim

"We think a cigar smoker is someone special."

"If what you do is right for you, no matter what others do, then RC Cola is right for you."

"You pride yourself on your good home cooking. . . ."

"The lady has taste."

"You've come a long way, baby."

10. The Rhetorical Question

This technique demands a response from the audience. A question is asked and the viewer or listener is supposed to answer in such a way as to affirm the product's goodness.

Samples of the Rhetorical Question

"Plymouth—isn't that the kind of car America wants?"

"Shouldn't your family be drinking Hawaiian Punch?"

"What do you want most from coffee? That's what you get most from Hills."

"Touch of Sweden: could your hands use a small miracle?"

Myths About Advertising
John Crichton

*In his essay John Crichton, a past president of the American Association of Adver-
tising Agencies, answers some of the criticisms of those who attack the advertising
industry. For instance, he disputes the critics' charge that ads are almost universally
misleading and that the "acquisitiveness" that advertising promotes is necessarily a
bad thing.*

. . . In recent years various occult powers have been imputed to advertising.
These are deeply-held concerns about "subliminal" advertising, or "motivational
research." The first suggests that advertising can be successful by operating beneath
the ordinary level of comprehension; the second suggests that systematic exploration
of the psyche can produce advertising which successfully manipulates people because it is directed toward their most susceptible areas of mind and personality.

Alas for the fable! The human mind is remarkable, and eye and memory can be
trained to receive and retain and identify messages or objects flicked on for a split-
second. The aircraft identification techniques of World War II are a good example.
There is no recorded research which testifies in any respect to the successful use of
subliminal advertising in selling. It remains in fact one of those hideous nonsense
notions which haunt our fear-filled society.

The motivation research story is more complex. Research will reveal that products, services, and institutions have a personality. Their users and non-users have
opinions about the products, sometimes from experience, sometimes from conversations with other users (particularly family and friends); there are publications
specializing in analysis of products and their performance, like *Consumer Reports*;
some magazines and newspapers have analytical columns which test and review new
products.

In short, experience with and opinions about products may be formed from many
influences other than advertising.

It is, however, a marketing axiom that people buy satisfactions, not products. As
Professor Levitt of the Harvard Business School has said, people don't buy quarter-
inch drills, they buy quarter-inch holes. By extension, they don't buy soap, they buy
cleanliness; they buy not clothing, but appearance. It is both efficient and ethical
to study the public's perception of a product, and to try to alter or to reinforce it,
and it may frequently lead to product reformulation or improvement in order to
effect the desired change in attitude, buying, and satisfaction leading to repurchase.

There remain three areas which are usually items of vehement discussion with
regard to advertising, and its morals and ethics.

The first is *advocacy*. Advertising always advocates. It pleads its case in the
strongest and most persuasive terms. It is neither objective nor neutral. It makes its
case, as dramatically as possible, with the benefit of words, pictures, and music. It
asks for attention, absorption, conviction, and action.

John Crichton, "Myths About Advertising," *Ethics, Morality, and the Media*, ed. Lee Thayer (New York:
Hastings House, 1980).

This disturbs critics, who feel that advertising ought to be objective, informative, and dispassionate. They wish advertising not to be persuasive, but informative. Their model for advertising is the specification sheet, and they have to some degree confused *advertising*, which must interest large numbers of people, with *labeling*, which is for the instruction of the individual purchaser, and performs a much different function.

If morals and ethics stem from public attitudes, it may be interesting that the public both perceives and appreciates the advocacy of advertising. It understands clearly that "they are trying to sell me something," and their attitude is appropriately intent and skeptical. Typically they are well-informed about the product and its competitors. It is a useful attitude in a democracy.

Research tells us that the public is both interested in and derisive about advertising. It is interested in the products which are being sold. It finds elements of the selling process entertaining. The public is, however, quickly bored and inattentive when the products or the way they are sold are unattractive to them.

The second problem area is *accuracy*, used here instead of "truth" because its elements are somewhat easier to define. Most advertising people believe advertising should be accurate; that is, they believe the product should not be sold as something it is not, nor should promises be made for its performance which it cannot fulfill.

In general, advertising's accuracy is good. The dress one sees advertised in the newspaper is available in the sizes and colors listed, and at the price advertised. The headache remedy will alleviate headache pain. It could hardly have been on the market for five decades if it did not. The orange juice looks and tastes like fresh orange juice. The instant coffee cannot be distinguished in blindfold tests from ground coffee which has been percolated. The anti-perspirant reduces perspiration.

Beyond accuracy, the question is often one of perception. It is true that the dress in the advertisement is available in the sizes, colors and price advertised—but will the dress make the purchaser look like the slim young woman in the ad? Answer, only if the purchaser looks like her already. There is no magic in advertising, and no magic in most products. The satisfaction with that dress cannot be literal, and most research suggests that in the public mind no such literal translation exists. It is not expected that the purchase of the dress will make the purchaser look like the person in the ad.

And while frozen orange juice may look and taste like fresh orange juice, it will not have the pulpy texture of freshly-squeezed juice, and therefore to many people will never be its equivalent. Therefore the purchaser must decide whether the texture means enough to him to squeeze the oranges. But the accuracy is not the question, it is the extended perception of what the words mean, so that accuracy becomes equivalency.

The third area is *acquisitiveness*. It is felt by many critics that advertising is a symbol of the preoccupation of our society with material things, and that preoccupation preempts the most important spiritual values. It is felt by critics that the steady drum-fire of advertising and advertising claims, the constant parade of products and services, serve to bewitch and beguile the viewer and reader, who gradually is corrupted into being either a hedonist or a consumptionist.

Of this criticism, two things should be said. The first is that the more material a society has, the greater its support for matters and institutions of the mind and spirit. It is the affluent societies of history to which one must look for the art, architecture, music, universities, hospitals, and cathedrals.

The second is that man is acquisitive. Plato again, as the Athenian, speaks: "Why, Clinias my friend, 'tis but a small section of mankind, a few of exceptional natural parts disciplined by consummate training, who have the resolution to prove true to moderation when they find themselves in the full current of demands and desires; there are not many of us who remain sober when they have the opportunity to grow wealthy, or prefer measure to abundance. The great multitude of men are of a clean contrary temper: what they desire they desire out of all measure; when they have the option of making a reasonable profit, they prefer to make an exorbitant one. . . ."

It is difficult to imagine that without advertising one would have an elevated society, one in which acquisitiveness had gradually disappeared. What one knows about such diverse tribes as the Cheyennes and the Kwakiutl of the Northwest is that both took individual wealth seriously, whether in stolen horses or in gifts to be given ostentatiously in a Potlatch. Acquisitiveness is innate, as Plato suggested; what advertising does is to channel it.

Daniel Bell, in "The Cultural Contradictions of Capitalism," argues that advertising is a sociological innovation, pervasive, the mark of material goods, the exemplar of new styles of life, the herald of new values. It emphasizes glamour, and appearance. While Bell concedes that a society in the process of quick change requires a mediating influence, and that advertising performs that role, he also sees that "selling became the most striking activity of contemporary America. Against frugality, selling emphasized prodigality; against asceticism, the lavish display." It is his judgment that "the seduction of the consumer had become total," and he believes that with the abandonment of Puritanism and the Protestant Ethic, capitalism has no moral or transcendental ethic, and he points to the conflict between the workaday habits which require hard work, career orientation, and delayed gratification, and the private life in which (in products and in advertisements) the corporation promotes pleasure, instant joy, relaxing, and letting go. "Straight by day," and a "swinger by night," in Bell's capsule summary.

But Bell also sees "in Aristotle's terms, *wants* replace *needs* — and wants, by their nature, are unlimited and insatiable."

Probably no more haunting problem exists for society than motivating people. The system of motivation and rewards within a society is critical to the kind of society it will ultimately be, and to the welfare and happiness of the people in it. The drive for material goods which characterizes most Western societies may be less admirable than a different kind of reward and motivation set of goals. The fact is that the system works, and that it does both motivate and reward people. If it appears to critics that the motivations are inferior, and that the rewards are vulgar, it must be remembered that at least the people have their own choice of what those rewards will be, and observation tells us that they spend their money quite differently. It is essentially a democratic system, and the freedom of individual choice makes it valuable to the people who do the choosing. One man's color television set is another man's hi-fidelity system; one man's summer cottage is another man's boat; and one man's succession of glittering automobiles is another man's expensive education of his children. In each case, the choice of the distribution of rewards is individual.

Advertising as Capitalist Realism

Michael Schudson

Michael Schudson is not a knee-jerk critic of the advertising industry. In the acknowledgment section of the book from which our excerpt is taken, Advertising, the Uneasy Persuasion, *Schudson mentions that as a boy he worked for his father, a copywriter. And though he didn't go into business himself (he became a professor), he says that his experience in the advertising business has never allowed him to "share the academy's contempt for business enterprise."*

In the excerpt we have chosen, however, Schudson discusses the negative effect that advertising and the consumer culture have on the values of those who live under their influence. Advertising, Schudson says, is "capitalist realism."

In a fundamental sense the basic source of the drive toward higher consumption is to be found in the character of our culture. A rising standard of living is one of the major goals of our society. Much of our public policy is directed toward this end. Societies are compared with one another on the basis of the size of their incomes. In the individual sphere people do not expect to live as their parents did, but more comfortably and conveniently. The consumption pattern of the moment is conceived of not as part of a way of life, but only as a temporary adjustment to circumstances. We expect to take the first available chance to change the pattern.

That sounds like a world advertising would love to create, if it could. But it also sounds like the world Tocqueville described in 1830, well before advertising was much more than long gray lists of patent medicine notices in the newspapers. It sounds as much like a world likely to invent modern advertising as a world that modern advertising would like to invent.

Then what does advertising do?

Advertising might be said to lead people to a belief in something. Advertising may make people believe they are inadequate without Product X and that Product X will satisfactorily manage their inadequacies. More likely, it may remind them of inadequacies they have already felt and may lead them, once at least, to try a new product that just might help, even though they are well aware that it probably will not. Alternatively, advertising may lead people to believe generally in the efficacy of manufactured consumer goods for handling all sorts of ills, medical or social or political, even if a given ad fails to persuade that a given product is efficacious. There is the question of belief in a small sense—do people put faith in the explicit claims of advertisements, change their attitudes toward advertised goods, and go out and buy them? And there is the question of belief in a larger sense—do the assumptions and attitudes implicit in advertising become the assumptions and atti-

Michael Schudson, "Advertising as Capitalist Realism," *Advertising, the Uneasy Persuasion: Its Dubious Impact on American Society* (New York: Basic Books, 1984).

tudes of the people surrounded by ads, whether or not they actually buy the advertised goods?

Social critics have argued that the greatest danger of advertising may be that it creates belief in the larger sense. It has been common coin of advertising critics that advertising is a kind of religion. This goes back at least to James Rorty who wrote of the religious power of advertising, holding that "advertising . . . becomes a body of doctrine." Ann Douglas has written that advertising is "the only faith of a secularized consumer society." In more measured tones, Leo Spitzer relates advertising to the "preaching mentality" in Protestantism and says that advertising "has taken over the role of the teacher of morals." The advertiser, "like the preacher" must constantly remind the backslider of "his real advantage" and "must 'create the demand' for the better."

Others have observed that many leading advertisers were the children of ministers or grew up in strict, religious households. The trouble with these remarks, and others like them, is that they fail to establish what kind of belief, if any, people actually have in advertisements. And they fail to observe that advertising is quintessentially part of the profane, not the sacred, world. Marghanita Laski has observed of British television that neither religious programs nor royal occasions are interrupted or closely juxtaposed to commercial messages. This is true, though to a lesser degree, with American television—the more sacred the subject, the less the profanity of advertising is allowed to intrude. If it does intrude, the advertiser takes special pains to provide unusually dignified and restrained commercials. If the advertiser fails to make such an adjustment, as in the commercial sponsorship of a docudrama on the Holocaust in 1980, public outrage follows.

So I am not persuaded by the "advertising is religion" metaphor, on the face of it. But the problem with seeing advertising as religion goes still deeper: advertising may be more powerful the *less* people believe in it, the less it is an acknowledged creed. This idea can be formulated in several ways. Northrop Frye has argued that advertisements, like other propaganda, "stun and demoralize the critical consciousness with statements too absurd or extreme to be dealt with seriously by it." Advertisements thus wrest from people "not necessarily acceptance, but dependence on their versions of reality." Frye continues:

> Advertising implies an economy which has some independence from the political structure, and as long as this independence exists, advertising can be taken as a kind of ironic game. Like other forms of irony, it says what it does not wholly mean, but nobody is obliged to believe its statements literally. Hence it creates an illusion of detachment and mental superiority even when one is obeying its exhortations.

Literary critics have been more sensitive than social scientists to the possibility that communications do not mean what they say—and that this may be the very center of their power. There has rarely been room for the study of irony in social science but irony is a key element in literary studies. Leo Spitzer, like Frye, observes that ads do not ask to be taken literally. In a Sunkist oranges ad he analyzed, he found that the ad "transports the listener into a world of Arcadian beauty, but with no insistence that this world really exists." The ad pictures "an Arcady of material prosperity," but Spitzer holds that the spectator "is equipped with his own criteria, and subtracts automatically from the pictures of felicity and luxury which smile at him from the billboards."

According to Spitzer, people are detached in relation to advertising. They feel detached, disillusioned, and forcibly reminded of the tension between life as it is lived and life as it is pictured. This is a characteristic attitude toward precious or baroque art. In this attitude, no condemnation of the excess of the art is necessary because one is so firmly anchored in the matter-of-fact reality that contradicts it.

For Spitzer, people are genuinely detached in relation to advertising. They view it from an aesthetic distance. For Frye, in contrast, people have only "an illusion of detachment." For Frye, it is precisely the belief people have that they *are* detached that makes the power of advertising all the more insidious. Advertising may create attitudes and inclinations even when it does not inspire belief; it succeeds in creating attitudes because it does not make the mistake of *asking* for belief.

This corresponds to the argument of a leading market researcher, Herbert Krugman, of General Electric Co. research. He holds that the special power of television advertising is that the ads interest us so little, not that they appeal to us so much. Television engages the audience in "low-involvement learning." Krugman's argument is that the evidence in psychology on the learning and memorization of nonsense syllables or other trivial items is very much like the results in market research on the recall of television commercials. He draws from this the suggestion that the two kinds of learning may be psychologically the same, a "learning without involvement." In such learning, people are not "persuaded" of something. Nor do their attitudes change. But there is a kind of "sleeper" effect. While viewers are not persuaded, they do alter the structure of their perceptions about a product, shifting "the relative salience of attributes" in the advertised brands. Nothing follows from this until the consumer arrives at the supermarket, ready to make a purchase. Here, at the behavioral level, the real change occurs:

> . . . the purchase situation is the catalyst that reassembles or brings out all the potentials for shifts in salience that have accumulated up to that point. The product or package is then suddenly seen in a new, "somehow different" light although nothing verbalizable may have changed *up to that point.*

Consumers in front of the television screen are relatively unwary. They take ads to be trivial or transparent or both. What Krugman suggests is that precisely this attitude enables the ad to be successful. Were consumers convinced of the importance of ads, they would bring into play an array of "perceptual defenses" as they do in situations of persuasion regarding important matters.

Any understanding of advertising in American culture must come to grips with the ironic game it plays with us and we play with it. If there are signs that Americans bow to the gods of advertising, there are equally indications that people find the gods ridiculous. It is part of the popular culture that advertisements are silly. Taking potshots at commercials has been a mainstay of *Mad* magazine and of stand-up comedians for decades. When Lonesome Rhodes meets Marsha Coulihan, station manager for a country radio station, in Budd Schulberg's story, "Your Arkansas Traveler," he says to her: "You must be a mighty smart little gal to be handlin' this here radio station all by yourself." She replies: "My good man, I am able to read without laughing out loud any commercial that is placed before me. I am able to pick out a group of records and point to the guy in the control room each time I want him to play one. And that is how you run a rural radio station."

If advertising is the faith of a secular society, it is a faith that inspires remarkably little professed devotion. If it is a body of doctrine, it is odd that so few followers would affirm the doctrine to be true, let alone inspired. Christopher Lasch has seen this problem. He argues that the trouble with the mass media is not that they purvey untruths but that "the rise of mass media makes the categories of truth and false-hood irrelevant to an evaluation of their influence. Truth has given way to credibil-ity, facts to statements that sound authoritative without conveying any authoritative information." But this analysis will not do for the problem of advertising. People are not confused about the importance of truth and falsity in their daily lives. It is just that they do not regularly apply judgments of truth to advertisements. Their rela-tionship to advertisements is not a matter of evidence, truth, belief, or even credibility.

Then what is it? Whether Krugman's formulation is right or wrong, his view at least leads us to ask more pointedly what kind of belief or nonbelief people have in relation to advertising. Again, this is in some sense a question about religion. The form of the question of whether or not people believe advertising messages is like the question of whether or not people believe in and are affected by religious teachings. On the latter question, anthropologist Melford Spiro has distinguished five levels at which people may "learn" an ideology:

1. Most weakly, they may *learn about* an ideological concept.
2. They may learn about and *understand* the concept.
3. They may *believe* the concept to be true or right.
4. The concept may become salient to them and inform their "behavioral environment" — that is, they may not only believe the concept but orga-nize their lives contingent on that belief.
5. They may internalize the belief so that it is not only cognitively salient but motivationally important. It not only guides but instigates action.

Tests of the effectiveness of advertising are most often tests of "recall"; ads are judged by the market researchers to be "effective" if they have established Level 1 belief, learning about a concept. Advertisers, of course, are more interested in Levels 4 and 5, although their ability to measure success at these levels is modest. Most theories of advertising assume that the stages of belief are successive, that consumers must go through Level 1 before Level 2, Level 2 before Level 3, and so on. What Krugman argues and what Northrop Frye can be taken to be saying, is that one can reach Level 4 without ever passing through Level 3. The voices of advertising may inform a person's "behavioral environment" without inspiring belief at any time or at any fundamental level. The stages are not sequential. One is independent from the next.

"What characterizes the so-called advanced societies," Roland Barthes wrote, "is that they today consume images and no longer, like those of the past, beliefs; they are therefore more liberal, less fanatical, but also more 'false' [less 'authentic'] . . ." Barthes is right about the present but very likely exaggerates the break from the past. A few years ago I saw a wonderful exhibit at the Museum of Traditional and

Popular Arts in Paris, dealing with religion in rural France in the nineteenth century. The exhibit demonstrated that religious imagery was omnipresent in the French countryside. There were paintings, crucifixes, saints, and Bible verses adorning the most humble objects — plates, spoons, cabinets, religious articles of all sorts, especially holiday objects, lithographs for the living room wall, greeting cards, illustrated books, board games for children, pillowcases, marriage contracts, painted furniture for children, paper dolls, carved and painted signs for religious processions, and so forth. Of course, the largest architectural monuments in most towns were the churches, presiding over life crises and the visual landscape alike. And, as French historian Georges Duby has argued, the grandeur of church architecture was intended as a form of "visual propaganda."

None of this necessarily made the ordinary French peasant a believing Christian. There were pagan rites in nineteenth-century rural France, as there are still today. Nor, I expect, did this mass-mediated reinforcement of Christian culture make the peasant ignore the venality of the church as an institution or the sins of its local representatives.

Still, the Church self-consciously used imagery to uplift its followers and potential followers, and there was no comparable suffusion of the countryside by other systems of ideas, ideals, dreams, and images. When one thought of salvation or, more modestly, searched for meanings for making sense of life, there was primarily the materials of the Church to work with. It has been said that languages do not differ in what they can express but in what they can express *easily*. It is the same with pervasive or official art: it brings some images and expressions quickly to mind and makes others relatively unavailable. However blatant the content of the art, its consequences remain more subtle. Works of art, in general, anthropologist Clifford Geertz has written, do not in the first instance "celebrate social structure or forward useful doctrine. They materialize a way of experiencing; bring a particular cast of mind into the world of objects, where men can look at it." Art, he says, does not create the material culture nor serve as a primary force shaping experience. The experience is already there. The art is a commentary on it. The public does not require the experience it already has but a statement or reflection on it: "What it needs is an object rich enough to see it in; rich enough, even, to, in seeing it, deepen it."

Capitalist realist art, like socialist realism, more often flattens than deepens experience. Here I judge the art and not the way of life it promotes. Jack Kerouac may deepen our experience of the road and the automobile, but the advertising agencies for General Motors and Ford typically flatten and thin our experience of the same objects. This need not be so. The AT&T "Reach Out and Touch Someone" commercials for long-distance telephone calling sentimentalize an experience that genuinely has or can have a sentimental element. If these ads do not deepen the experience they at least articulate it in satisfying ways.

There is another side to the coin: if an ad successfully romanticizes a moment, it provides a model of sentiment that one's own more varied and complicated experience cannot live up to. Most of our phone calls, even with loved ones, are boring or routine. When art romanticizes the exotic or the exalted, it does not call our own experience into question, but when it begins to take everyday life as the subject of its idealization, it creates for the audience a new relationship to art. The audience can judge the art against its own experience and can thereby know that the art idealizes and falsifies. At the same time, the art enchants and tantalizes the audience with the possibility that it is *not* false. If it can play on this ambiguity, art becomes less an imitation of life and turns life into a disappointing approximation of art.

The issue is not that advertising art materializes or "images" certain *experiences* but, as Geertz says, a *way of experiencing.* The concern with advertising is that this way of experiencing — a consumer way of life — does not do justice to the best that the human being has to offer and, indeed, entraps people in exploitative and self-defeating activity. But what can it really mean to say that art materializes a way of experience? What does that *do*? Why should a social system *care* to materialize its way of experiencing? The individual artists, writers, and actors who put the ads together do not feel this need. They frequently have a hard time taking their work seriously or finding it expressive of anything at all they care about.

Think of a smaller social system, a two-person social system, a marriage. Imagine it to be a good marriage, where love is expressed daily in a vast array of shared experiences, shared dreams, shared tasks and moments. In this ideal marriage, the couple continually make and remake their love. Then why, in this marriage, would anything be amiss if the two people did not say to each other, "I love you"? Why, in a relationship of such obviously enacted love, should it seem necessary to say out loud, "I love you"?

Because, I think, making the present audible and making the implicit explicit is necessary to engage and renew a whole train of commitments, responsibilities, and possibilities. "I love you" does not create what is not present. Nor does it seal what is present. But it must be spoken and respoken. It is necessary speech because people need to see in pictures or hear in words even what they already know as deeply as they know anything, *especially* what they know as deeply as they know anything. Words are actions.

This is also true in large social systems. Advertising is capitalism's way of saying "I love you" to itself.

The analogy, of course, is not perfect and I do not mean to jump from marriage to market with unqualified abandon. But in social systems writ large — and not just capitalism but all social systems — there are efforts both individual and collective to turn experience into words, pictures, and doctrines. Once created, these manifestations have consequences. They become molds for thought and feeling, if one takes a deterministic metaphor, or they become "equipment for living" if one prefers a more voluntaristic model or — to borrow from Max Weber and choose a metaphor somewhere in the middle, they serve as switchmen on the tracks of history. In the case of advertising, people do not necessarily "believe" in the values that advertisements present. Nor need they believe for a market economy to survive and prosper. People need simply get used to, or get used to not getting used to, the institutional structures that govern their lives. Advertising does not make people believe in capitalist institutions or even in consumer values, but so long as alternative articulations of values are relatively hard to locate in the culture, capitalist realist art will have some power.

Of course, alternative values *are* available in American culture. In some artistic, intellectual, and ethnic enclaves, one can encounter premises and principles that directly challenge capitalism and the expansion of the market to all phases of life.

In contrast, the mainstream news and entertainment media operate within a relatively circumscribed range of values. But even in this narrower discourse, there is often criticism of consumer values or of the excesses of a consumer society. I came upon attacks on materialism, suburbia, conformity, and advertising in the 1950s as a student in social studies classes in a public junior high school and high school. Only a few years ago, people spoke contemptuously of the "me generation" and President Jimmy Carter diagnosed a national "crisis of confidence," opining that "we've discovered that owning things and consuming things does not satisfy our longing for meaning." Recent lampooning of "Preppies" and "Yuppies" (young, upwardly-mobile professionals) betrays anxiety about, if also accommodation to, consumption as a way of life. So I do not suggest that advertisements have a monopoly in the symbolic marketplace. Still, no other cultural form is as accessible to children; no other form confronts visitors and immigrants to our society (and migrants from one part of society to another) so forcefully; and probably only professional sports surpasses advertising as a source of visual and verbal clichés, aphorisms, and proverbs. Advertising has a special cultural power.

The pictures of life that ads parade before consumers are familiar, scenes of life as in some sense we know it or would like to know it. Advertisements pick up and represent values already in the culture. But these values, however deep or widespread, are not the only ones people have or aspire to, and the pervasiveness of advertising makes us forget this. Advertising picks up some of the things that people hold dear and re-presents them to people as *all* of what they value, assuring them that the sponsor is the patron of common ideals. That is what capitalist realist art, like other pervasive symbolic systems, does. Recall again that languages differ not in what they can express but in what they can express *easily*. This is also true in the languages of art, ideology, and propaganda. It is the kind of small difference that makes a world of difference and helps construct and maintain different worlds.

LAISSEZ-FAIRE ADVERTISING
George Griffin

At one time, George Griffin thought that the advertising industry needed more regulators and regulations to stamp out misleading and tricky advertising. But he no longer feels that way. Now he thinks that unless there is gross misrepresentation, "a promoter ought to be allowed to promote." What should be stepped up, Griffin says, is education. High schools should do a better job of analyzing the language of advertising.

How do I really feel about advertising?

Tell the truth, now. How do you feel about it? Do you think it's a positive force in the American system? Does it make capitalism better or worse? Where would we be without advertising?

Where would I be—not only do I write about it, sometimes I actually try my hand at creating some of the stuff. So, I'm as glued to it as you are.

If you're in the graphic arts industry some or much of your income is advertising-connected. Thus, you're an advocate, right? Should we draw any lines at all? I think it's a good question.

There was a time when I thought that some controls would be in the public's interest. Certain restrictions on the advertising of tobacco, liquor, and similar products made sense to me and still do, and I'm sure there's a need for limits on the so-called "outdoor advertisers" which can be visual pollution for the public. I'm not real fond of advertising which invades my perception without invitation. Except for these few named exceptions, however, I'm more and more in favor of letting advertisers do just about anything they wish.

NEGATIVE OPTION

I once thought that various types of tricky advertising should be illegal. There are certain come-on's which are so effective the unwily consumer hardly has a chance. Choice among such techniques are "negative option" promotions such as those used by book and record clubs. Some of the double truck, full color ads that are used to romance such clubs are so powerful I almost pick up a pen or dial a number myself. Telemarketing is now as much a part of direct marketing as is the mail. I can become a member the Best Value Record and Video League (a fictitious example) by simply sending in a coupon or dialing a number, and I'll get 33 records or tapes of my favorite recording star as a BONUS for acting before midnight of July 15, 1995. Of course, the "negative option," usually described in small type nowhere near the main ad copy, will tell me that I'll receive a frequently published member magazine, which will contain the name of the current selection. If I don't return the card saying "No," they'll assume that I've said "Yes" and ship the record or tape

George Griffin, "Laissez-Faire Advertising," *Graphic Arts Monthly* October 1985.

to the address I specified and charge my account. How would you like to sell printing on such a basis?

It's tricky, tricky, tricky. Maybe not to you and me. We're sophisticates in this field. We know about the hidden terms and conditions. We know the magic of the word, "Free." We know how to resist temptations of this kind. But the typical consumer, especially the young one, doesn't understand the tricks. Many actually believe they're going to get a flock of free gifts without spending any money. You and I know better, but there are millions who answer these ads each year and industry records prove that consumers go along with the negative option system for enough months to rack up impressively profitable purchases. Many spend over $100 a year for merchandise they did not order. There was a time when I thought such advertising should be stopped.

I used to think that ads such as "This Is an Advertising Test" or "We Will Sell Not More Than Two Inflatable Doll Houses to Each Person Who Sends Just $3 Each Before Dec. 3!" should be outlawed along with most of the weight loss and exercise scams, but I no longer feel that way. I now tend to feel that unless there is patent misrepresentation or fraud, a promoter ought to be allowed to promote.

EDUCATING CONSUMERS

At the same time, I think there should be greatly stepped-up efforts by educators to see to it that by the time a person has graduated from high school he or she knows about the more familiar come-ons and tricks of advertising and is well aware of the industry's ability to invent new, ever craftier techniques to hoodwink consumers. The tricks work best on people who aren't aware of how they work. Advertisers will stop using such techniques when aware consumers simply don't respond to them.

Anyway, that's my theory and its occurrence in my mind synchronizes with my shift toward loosening up on controls. Let advertising be laissez-faire. If it isn't then it's almost a contradiction in terms. Of all literary or creative expressions, advertising, in particular, needs to be free or its efficiency may be dampened too much to justify the effort.

If informed buyers refuse to support tricky advertising, won't it tend to disappear? I hope so. They still sell snake oil in undeveloped countries where many of the people are superstitious and illiterate. But snake oil sales drop off sharply in regions where people are better educated and know that it isn't a cure-all. If there are legitimate uses for snake oil, let's hear them and I, for one, will consider purchasing some.

TRUTH IN ADVERTISING

My own experiences with advertising strongly suggest that the most effective ads simply tell the truth in an interesting way. And this is precisely why I think advertising needs to be free. Let the worst of it fail and the truth prevail.

One day I will develop an almost perfect analogy between the art/science of fishing and the craft known as salesmanship (including advertising.)

Experienced fishermen know that the smarter (and older) fish are the hardest to fool. Perhaps they have been hooked before. Some fish apparently reach a point at which they no longer strike at anything artificial. They save their energy for the real thing—their natural food. Informed buyers are the same way. Eventually they become immune to unstraight offers, come-ons, and hypes. The greater the number of such buyers, the more incentive there is and will be to give them what they demand: good reasons for buying.

CREATIVITY

I hope that no reader will think that I mean advertising should be any less creative, colorful, or promotional. To the contrary. Advertising that relies on hype substitutes falsehood for imagination, and programs which depend on tricks to get their sales are anything but creative! Indeed, many such ads and campaigns are almost carbon copies of their snake oil predecessors. The negative option of 1985 is so different than what it was 20 years ago. P.T. Barnum is credited with the maxim about a sucker being born every minute, but it looks to me like times are changing. I don't think the tricksters and hucksters will have an easy go of it in the future. There may be just as many suckers being born as ever, but they're wising up in the process of consuming, and that's a good trend.

So, the challenge is to be more imaginative, not less. Take the facts and build on them. Amplify them. Color them. Make them as interesting as they can possibly be. The "America Today" Gannet series on public television recently aired an interview with "real" archaeologists at a dusty dig in the U.S. Southwest. "Is it as exciting as the Indiana Jones version of archaeology?" the diggers were asked. Their answers were almost yes. Of course it's hard to compete with fantasy, but the scientists agreed that the ever-present possibility of turning up artifacts many thousands of years old is a thrill and a mystique which makes the profession stimulating and enjoyable.

The truth can be fascinating. Facts can be illustrated, enhanced, and dramatized. In advertising, there should be no need for fiction. If a product or service's marketability is so "borderline" that hype and tricks must be resorted to then what's the justification for even putting the thing on the market? Switch strategies. Find something the buyer wants on its own merits.

PRINTING

We don't have to invent the demand for printing. It already exists and is growing. We don't have to pretend that printing is a valuable service—it demonstrates its worthy skills on a daily basis. And there's no point in a printer's exaggerating the firm's capabilities. No one can fake good printing. It must be the real thing or it's recognized for what it isn't as much as what it is. We're lucky, for there's no end to how we can say: Printing serves many needs and interests.

With fun-to-read copy and photographs that stop the eye and cause the mind to pause, we can make our printing services the most interesting subject the prospect has encountered. We can get the consumer's attention, perhaps even keep it, and demonstrate in the process why the printing being offered is something the buyer should buy. . . .

THE DOUR CRITICS OF ADVERTISING
Harold Edwards

Harold Edwards defends advertising by attacking its detractors. While advertising's critics want the various governing agencies to exercise more power by clamping down harder on advertising, Edwards answers by saying that that would only lead to an "unworkable tangle of laws," and its only benefit would be to "fatten the swarms of lawyers who think their job is to protect us against ourselves."

According to Edwards, the charge that we need to be protected from advertising is "pure nonsense."

The young lady with surprisingly fleshy lips desires us more than anything else in the world. Shoehorned into a tight and diaphanous dress, her eyes full of lust, she looks out at us and purrs, "I like all my men wearing English Leather — or nothing at all."

Pretty harmless nonsense, isn't it? Or were you taken in? Did your unconscious rise up and whisper to you, "Henry, Henry, if you buy English Leather, diaphanously-dressed women will purr to you"? Were you seduced so thoroughly by the ad that you were *forced* to buy a bottle of English Leather?

A number of critics of advertising believe that we *are* too weak to resist the appeals of advertisers. In *The Hidden Persuaders*, for instance, Vance Packard, a persistent critic of the advertising industry, argues that consumers are virtually powerless at the hands of advertising agencies and their hired hands, the motivational researchers. The advertisers know us, Packard says. They have burrowed into our psyches and have discovered our secret fears and desires, and now they use our weaknesses to seduce us into buying English Leather.

Packard isn't alone in claiming that we are weak and they are strong. Jeffrey Schrank, writing for the National Council of Teachers of English, claims that "Advertisers delight in an audience which believes ads to be harmless nonsense, for such an audience is rendered defenseless by its belief that there is no attack taking place."

"Rendered defenseless." Hmm. What a high opinion of the power of advertising. And what a low opinion of mankind. In fact, a patronizing attitude is never far below the surface of the arguments of those who scorn advertising. They, the aristocrats of reason and clear thinking, can of course see through the wiles of the advertisers. We, the confused and irresponsible peasants, need to be protected. It's for our own good, they say.

Indeed, like all bureaucratic busybodies, the critics of advertising want to protect us against ourselves. We might buy the wrong product (the wrong product, of course, according to their lights). We might be illogical. We might be confused about the competing claims of products. In fact, some of the critics think we're so defenseless that they want the Federal Trade Commission, like a big brother, to step in and protect us against the sweet nothings that advertisers whisper into our ears.

Harold Edwards, "The Dour Critics of Advertising." This essay appears by permission of the author.

We don't need protection. While the language of a soap advertisement may be rhetorically suspicious, the motives of soap sellers are as clear and as pure as a soap bubble: They want to sell soap. We may not always be able to discern the motives of politicians, educators, and newspaper columnists, but no one above the age of five was ever fooled by the motive of a soap company. *Of course* ad writers manipulate language to influence people. So do all people who use language — from government politicians to newspaper columnists. And so do essayists who want to persuade us that the language of advertising is unfair.

At least the motives of advertisers are out in the open. The copywriters for Spring Morning Soap may imply in their ads that, after lathering with their soap, you'll be accosted by strangers who will beg to touch your lovely skin. But we're not as gullible as the critics say. We've learned to take advertising, like political speeches, with a grain of salt. Besides, *Consumer Reports* (a strong proponent of more regulations) will tell us, if we really want to know, about the merits of one soap over another (and they inevitably pick the cheapest, most "reasonable" bar of soap.)

Most of us don't even want to have our purchases pre-approved by the men and women in the labs of *Consumer Reports*, much less by government regulators. We continue to buy Oil of Olay, diet pills, tummy tighteners, new and improved detergents, and two-hundred dollar Reebok tennis shoes. We like to get a little crazy every now and then and buy a soap dream instead of a soap bar.

The art of persuasion — for that is what the language of advertising really is — goes back at least to the Greeks, who called it rhetoric and used it to embellish political speeches in the forum. One suspects, though, that the artful use of words soon moved out into the Greek marketplace. It's easy to imagine an eager Greek sandal salesman's spiel: "Comfiest shoe in Heathendom! Plato wears 'em!" (And no doubt there was also a busybody Greek dogooder who immediately leaped up and "exposed" the salesman: "No fair. Celebrity testimonial.")

Modern critics of advertising continue to warn us against celebrity testimonials, and some of the more radical critics want the government to step in and forbid the advertisers from seducing us with colorful words, fuzzy words, and exaggerated words.

They would have advertisers make their ads as grey and as unappetizing as a legal document or a page of bureaucratic prose. In "The Language of Advertising" Joseph Seldin even objects to the "unrelieved cheerfulness" of ads. Apparently he would prefer that the models scowl occasionally so that the advertisement will resemble real life.

In fact, the critics of advertising seem to lack a sense of humor. They don't laugh. They get into snits. They take every ad seriously, even when humor and exaggeration are obviously at work. When a football player steps up to sell Brut cologne, clinging women drinking in his every word, the dour critics can only see a celebrity hawking perfume. Offended because the ad fails to appeal to their Reason and Intellect, the critics pounce, "Ah hah! EMOTIONAL APPEAL # 3: CELEBRITY TESTIMONIAL."

Lacking a sense of humor, the critics solemnly construct their long lists of FALSE CLAIMS AND EMOTIONAL APPEALS, where we are told that advertisements not only hoodwink us with testimonials of famous people, but they fool us with weasel words, swindle us with glittering generalities, and cozen us with incomplete comparatives.

One critic of advertising warns us, in MISLEADING TECHNIQUE # 6: THE VAGUE CLAIM, that we ought to watch out for these devious uses of language:

Fleischmann's makes sensible eating delicious.

For skin like peaches and cream.

Take a bite and you'll think you're eating on the Champs Elysées.

The end of meatloaf boredom.

Oh dear me, what ever shall we do? We are being seduced by Hamburger Helper, who claims that its product is the end of meat loaf boredom. Let's call in the FTC, the FCC, and the NAB to stamp out these outbreaks of advertising nonsense, these assaults on our logic and good sense.

It bothers the critics of advertising no end when people aren't as logical as they are. Remember the rush to buy pet rocks a few years back? The critics of advertising were outraged. "Who's to blame?" they asked. "How could people be so silly," they fumed, "as to be seduced into buying slickly-packaged rocks?"

"Who's to blame?" That's not the right question. Consumers thought the pet rock idea was cute, so they exercised a basic right in a free economy: They pulled out their wallets and bought the rocks. *No one* is to blame when people choose to buy pet rocks — or pet toadstools or pet grass or pet anything. The appropriate question in a free market is this: How can we encourage more people to come up with new ideas?

After reading a number of these attacks on the advertising industry, I get the distinct impression that their hostility toward advertising goes deeper than their dislike of its seductive power — that it really stems from their dislike of the free marketplace. To the critics of advertising, to try to make a profit is, well, not quite a reputable motive. Besides we consumers don't need all of the choices that the American marketplace offers us. To its critics, their noses in the air, the system of free enterprise needs more rules written by people like them.

At any rate, they hold the language of advertising to a standard that doesn't exist anywhere else in our society outside of a legal contract. For instance, linguists nowadays tell us that language change is not only inevitable, but usually a good thing. Change, they say, refreshes the language. Yet when advertisers use neologisms — or even usages that reflect current usage — we are told that they are wrecking the language. In *Strictly Speaking*, for instance, Edwin Newman fusses (ironically and superciliously, of course) about the "assaults" on our language when products like Easy-Off, Arrid, and Fantastik cleaner use unorthodox spelling. And Winston used to cause the critics intense pain with the ungrammatical claim that their cigarettes "taste good like a cigarette should."

When a careful essayist qualifies his statements, we are told he is being logical. When advertisers qualify their statements, we are told that they are using "weasel" words. To the critics of advertising, a rose by another name doesn't smell as sweet. Jeffrey Schrank, for instance, calls it "weaseling" (rather than "qualifying") when an advertiser says that his product "*helps* control dandruff." (Actually, it's rather difficult to see what alternative the advertiser had. If he had said instead that his product "*controls* dandruff," Schrank and his fellow nitpickers would have jumped up to holler, "FALSE CLAIM!")

When we agree with the emotionally-loaded words of a speaker at a dinner, a politician on the stump, a crusading columnist, we admire his command of the resources of the language, his "rhetoric." When advertisers use those same emotionally loaded words, the critics say that they are being unfair by seducing our unconscious.

Of course advertisers use the resources of language and rhetoric to persuade us to buy their products. Ads are full of weasel words, nonce words, vague words, celebrity's words, humorous words, and sometimes outrageously exaggerated words. (Look at those great ads for breast enlargement creams in the back pages of the *National Enquirer*.)

Anyone with a sense of humor or a sense of the absurd ought to sit back and enjoy the color and noise — and the occasional absurdity — of the "literature of commerce." (D. H. Lawrence once wrote that "some of the cunningest American literature is to be found in advertisements of soap suds.")

It's probably no coincidence that some of the harshest criticism of the language of advertising comes from members of the educational establishment, who are insulated against the noise — and the risks — of the marketplace. Indeed, one of the most persistent critics is the National Council of Teachers of English. From their lofty position above the hurly-burly, the Council members look down contemptuously on the dirty little business of buying and selling.

Down below, the language of advertising, like the free market itself, is noisy, impudent, and independent. And the critics don't like it. Like all busybodies who know what's best for us, they want some government agency, the Federal Trade Commission in this case, to intervene even more forcefully than they do now to curtail some of this noisy advertising.

But that would only lead to an unworkable tangle of laws. Besides, we don't need more lawyers defending us against misleading metaphors and pernicious personifications. Do things *really* go better with Coke? Is Schlitz *really* the kings of beers? Are we *really* flying friendly skies when we fly United? Let us figure it out, not a hoard of lawyers.

Right now, nowhere is freedom of speech more strictly curtailed than in the world of business. Advertising in particular is fair game for all kinds of free speech restrictions, restrictions that would elicit howls of complaints if they were imposed on other areas of American society. Indeed, the same people who use the First Amendment to defend pornography see no problem at all in shutting off all kinds of advertising speech.

The rest of us ought to worry about the tendency to turn governmental agencies into language police. We are already in the habit of denying First Amendment rights to advertisers; as a result, we are perhaps less likely to hesitate the next time we find that people are using language in other ways that we don't like.

Aldous Huxley, whose *Brave New World* is a warning against the tendencies of governments to become our all-knowing big brothers, enjoyed the language of advertising — and its freedom. In fact, he saw a connection between the language of advertising and a free society. "The art of advertisement writing," he wrote "has flowered with democracy. The lords of industry and commerce came gradually to understand that the right way to appeal to the Free Peoples of the World was familiarly, in an honest man-to-man style."

To insist that the language of advertising is unfair and that we need to be protected from it is pure nonsense.

Government Injunction Restraining Harlem Cosmetic Co.

Josephine Miles

Josephine Miles is a poet who has written numerous scholarly studies of poetry and poetic diction, including Style and Proportion: The Language of Prose and Poetry *(1960). She is also a former literature professor at the University of California. In "Government Injunction," Miles suggests that government regulations that try to take "ineffectual" products off the market sometimes miss the point. "The heart has reasons," Blaise Pascal once wrote, "that reason itself does not know."*

They say La Jac Brite Pink Skin Bleach avails not,
They say its Orange Beauty Glow does not glow.
Nor the face grow five shades lighter nor the heart
Five shades lighter. They say no.

They deny good luck, love, power, romance, and inspiration
From La Jac Brite ointment and incense of all kinds,
And condemn in writing skin brightening and whitening
And whitening of minds.

There is upon the federal trade commission a burden of glory
So to defend the fact, so to impel
The plucking of hope from the hand, honor from the complexion,
Sprite from the spell.

Josephine Miles, "Government Injunction Restraining Harlem Cosmetic Co.," *Poems: 1930–1960* (Bloomington: Indiana University Press, 1960).

BARBIE DOLL
Marge Piercy

Marge Piercy is both a writer of fiction (including Fly Away Home, 1984) *and poetry* (Stone, Paper, Knife, 1983). *"Barbie Doll" comes from her collection of poetry,* Circles on the Water.

In "Barbie Doll" Piercy's criticism goes beyond advertising to the consumer culture itself. Piercy's heroine in the poem, the "girlchild" of the first line, just can't measure up to the images of beauty that advertising, or "society," disseminates. That is, she can't measure up until a mortician performs plastic surgery on her corpse.

This girlchild was born as usual
and presented dolls that did pee-pee
and miniature GE stoves and irons
and wee lipsticks the color of cherry candy.
Then in the magic of puberty, a classmate said:
You have a great big nose and fat legs.

She was healthy, tested intelligent,
possessed strong arms and back,
abundant sexual drive and manual dexterity.
She went to and fro apologizing.
Everyone saw a fat nose on thick legs.

She was advised to play coy,
exhorted to come on hearty,
exercise, diet, smile and wheedle.
Her good nature wore out
like a fan belt.
So she cut off her nose and her legs
and offered them up.

In the casket displayed on satin she lay
with the undertaker's cosmetics painted on,
a turned-up putty nose,
dressed in a pink and white nightie.
Doesn't she look pretty? everyone said.
Consummation at last.
To every woman a happy ending.

Marge Piercy, "Barbie Doll," *Circles on the Water* (New York: Knopf, 1982).

SUGGESTIONS FOR WRITING

Informal Essays

1. After reading a few essays from this chapter, write an essay in which you discuss an ad or two that touched you in some way. Perhaps an ad for GI Joe dolls made you hunger for GI Joe dolls. Perhaps an ad for a perfume touched your inner being.
2. After reading Jeffrey Schrank's essay, "The Language of Advertising Claims," write an essay in which you analyze the various rhetorical devices and emotional appeals of a magazine advertisement of your choice.
3. Defend advertising by describing the clever and creative nature of advertising. Be sure to point to specific ads.

Short Documented Papers

1. Argue with one of the essays in this chapter, buttressing your argument with examples from at least two other essays that agree with you.
2. Contrast Bernstein's "Is Puffery Flummery?" with Preston's "Puffery Is Deception." Keep out of the argument yourself.
3. Analyze what you consider the weakest argument on either side of the controversy.
4. Analyze the strongest argument made on either side of the controversy.

Longer Documented Papers

1. Argue that the language of advertising is unfair.
2. Defend the language of advertising.
3. Argue that advertising is a pernicious (or a benign or healthy) influence on society. Take into account the opposing side's arguments.
4. Argue that the government should step up its efforts at policing advertising.
5. Argue that the government should keep its hands off advertising.
6. Write a research report in which you describe both sides of the controversy concerning the healthy or unhealthy influence of advertising on society.
7. Write a research report in which you contrast aspects of each side of the controversy over whether advertising is fair.

SEX DIFFERENCES: *Innate or Acquired?*

One thing is certain: Men and women will be arguing about what causes the differences between male and female behavior long after this generation has passed away. (One book on sex differences is appropriately titled *The Longest War.*) It's too interesting a controversy, and too basic to what we are, to go away soon.

Although the issue ebbs and flows, right now it seems to be more heated than ever. And it's occurring not just where we would expect it to occur, in magazines like *Harper's, National Review,* and *Ms.* — magazines whose lifeblood depends upon a monthly transfusion of controversy. It also pops up with some frequency in magazines that usually avoid controversy — magazines like *Runner's World* and *Good Housekeeping.*

Differences in the behavior of men and women are, of course, everywhere apparent. Men commit most violent crimes. According to most studies (including one in this chapter), men's speech is usually direct and factual; women's speech is usually indirect, supportive, and social. Men are more promiscuous than women.

Differences in ability and health are equally apparent. Men excel in sports that require explosive strength, in particular upper-body strength; women excel in small motor coordination, which is why some manufacturers hire women to assemble small electronic parts. Young females demonstrate greater verbal abilities in achievement tests; young males score higher on mathematic achievement tests. Men have more heart attacks; women suffer more attacks of depression. Women's immune systems are more efficient. Women live longer.

But what has fueled a new sexual controversy is not so much the dispute over such differences, but instead over the contradictory conclusions about what causes them. It's the old nature-nurture controversy all over again. For centuries, sex differences have usually been explained as the result of "nature" that is innate and unalterable. Women, men typically argued, were physically weak and psychologically submissive (and, some men argued, intellectually feeble) by nature. God made them that way.

During this century, by contrast, the "nurturists" have carried the day, and their argument has become central to the feminist movement. The social environment, feminists say, is by far the strongest influence on our behavior. Men and women differ only in one significant way: their reproductive functions. Virtually all other differences are merely the result of social conditioning. This argument contributes a compelling logic to the feminist cause. And of course, women's current highly visible and successful presence in the gym, the classroom, the laboratory, and the boardroom has contributed an undisputable credibility to the argument that the environment determines our sexual behavior.

But lately the "nature" side has rejoined the argument. And the nature, or environmental, arguments are not coming from quarters that feminists might dismiss as know nothings. They are coming from the biologists, neurologists, psychologists, and other members of the intellectual community — many of them women. These conclusions, although they are by no means unanimous, suggest that the influence of the environment simply doesn't tell the whole story of sex differences — that those old commonsensical notions about the reasons for the differences between men and women are often accurate.

Many sociobiologists, for example, now conclude that different male and female traits have evolved over millions of years. These sex differences were originally dictated by men's and women's reproductive and social roles in primitive human societies back along the evolutionary chain. Recent research in other scientific fields corroborates the sociobiologists' claims that the differences between the sexes stem largely from heredity. Neurologists, for example, have presented evidence that the male hormone, testosterone, dramatically alters the brain development of the male fetus and thus accounts for some typically male behavioral patterns.

Many feminists view such research as a pretentious new guise for the same old sexism, and they are not impressed by the fact that women seldom come off as the more flawed sex in these studies. Such research, they insist, can have only an insidious effect on the political and social climate of a culture that is just now, they say, emerging from its long history of female subjugation.

And so the "conversation" continues.

THE PSYCHOLOGY OF
SEX DIFFERENCES
Eleanor E. Maccoby and Carol N. Jacklin

Eleanor E. Maccoby and Carol N. Jacklin are Stanford University psychologists whose The Psychology of Sex Differences, *an analysis of nearly fourteen hundred sex-difference studies, has been widely recognized by other writers and researchers in the field. The following excerpt is drawn from the last chapter of their book.*

SUMMARY OF OUR FINDINGS

Unfounded Beliefs About Sex Differences

1. *That girls are more "social" than boys.* The findings: First, the two sexes are equally interested in social (as compared with nonsocial) stimuli, and are equally proficient at learning through imitation of models. Second, in childhood, girls are no more dependent than boys on their caretakers, and boys are no more willing to remain alone. Furthermore, girls are not more motivated to achieve for social rewards. The two sexes are equally responsive to social reinforcement, and neither sex consistently learns better for this form of reward than for other forms. Third, girls do not spend more time interacting with playmates; in fact, the opposite is true, at least at certain ages. Fourth, the two sexes appear to be equally "empathic," in the sense of understanding the emotional reactions of others; however, the measures of this ability have so far been narrow.

Any differences that exist in the "sociability" of the two sexes are more of kind than of degree. Boys are highly oriented toward a peer group and congregate in larger groups; girls associate in pairs or small groups of age-mates, and may be somewhat more oriented toward adults, although the evidence for this is weak.

2. *That girls are more "suggestible" than boys.* The findings: First, boys and girls are equally likely to imitate others spontaneously. Second, the two sexes are equally susceptible to persuasive communications, and in face-to-face social-influence situations (Asch-type experiments), sex differences are usually not found. When they are, girls are somewhat more likely to adapt their own judgments to those of the group, although there are studies with reverse findings. Boys, on the other hand, appear to be more likely to accept peer-group values when these conflict with their own.

3. *That girls have lower self-esteem.* The findings: The sexes are highly similar in their overall self-satisfaction and self-confidence throughout childhood and adolescence; there is little information about adulthood, but what exists does not show a sex difference. However, there are some qualitative differences in the areas of functioning where the two sexes have greatest self-confidence: girls rate themselves higher in the area of social competence; boys more often see themselves as strong, powerful, dominant, "potent."

Eleanor Emmons Maccoby and Carol Nagy Jacklin, *The Psychology of Sex Differences* (Stanford, CA: Stanford University Press, 1974).

Through most of the school years, the two sexes are equally likely to believe they can influence their own fates, rather than being the victims of chance or fate. During the college years (but not earlier or later), men have a greater sense of control over their own fate, and greater confidence in their probable performance on a variety of school-related tasks that they undertake. However, this does not imply a generally lower level of self-esteem among women of this age.

4. *That girls are better at rote learning and simple repetitive tasks, boys at tasks that require higher-level cognitive processing and the inhibition of previously learned responses.* The findings: Neither sex is more susceptible to simple conditioning, or excels in simple paired-associates or other forms of "rote" learning. Boys and girls are equally proficient at discrimination learning, reversal shifts, and probability learning, all of which have been interpreted as calling for some inhibition of "available" responses. Boys are somewhat more impulsive (that is, lacking in inhibition) during the preschool years, but the sexes do not differ thereafter in the ability to wait for a delayed reward, to inhibit early (wrong) responses on the Matching Familiar Figures test (MFF) or on other measures of impulsivity.

5. *That boys are more "analytic."* The findings: The sexes do not differ on tests of analytic cognitive style. Boys do not excel at tasks that call for "decontextualization," or disembedding, except when the task is visual-spatial; boys' superiority on the latter tasks seems to be accounted for by spatial ability (see below), and no sex differences in analytic ability are implied. Boys and girls are equally likely to respond to task-irrelevant aspects of a situation, so that neither sex excels in analyzing and selecting only those elements needed for the task.

6. *That girls are more affected by heredity, boys by environment.* The findings: Male identical twins are more alike than female identical twins, but the two sexes show equivalent amount of resemblance to their parents.

Boys are more susceptible to damage by a variety of noxious environmental agents, both prenatally and postnatally, but this does not imply that they are generally more influenced by environmental factors. The correlations between parental socialization techniques and child behavior are higher for boys in some studies, higher for girls in others. Furthermore, the two sexes learn with equal facility in a wide variety of learning situations; if learning is the primary means whereby environmental effects come about, sex equivalence is indicated.

7. *That girls lack achievement motivation.* The findings: In the pioneering studies of achievement motivation, girls scored higher than boys in achievement imagery under "neutral" conditions. Boys need to be challenged by appeals to ego or competitive motivation to bring their achievement imagery up to the level of girls'. Boys' achievement motivation does appear to be more responsive to competitive arousal than girls', but this does not imply a generally higher level. In fact, observational studies of achievement strivings either have found no sex difference or have found girls to be superior.

8. *That girls are auditory, boys visual.* The findings: The majority of studies report no differences in response to sounds by infants of the two sexes. At most ages boys and girls are equally adept at discriminating speech sounds. No sex difference is found in memory for sounds previously heard.

Among newborn infants, no study shows a sex difference in fixation to visual stimuli. During the first year of life, results are variable, but neither sex emerges as more responsive to visual stimuli. From infancy to adulthood, the sexes are highly similar in interest in visual stimuli, ability to discriminate among them, identification of shapes, distance perception, and a variety of other measures of visual perception.

Sex Differences That Are Fairly Well Established

1. *That girls have greater verbal ability than boys.* It is probably true that girls' verbal abilities mature somewhat more rapidly in early life, although there are a number of recent studies in which no sex difference has been found. During the period from preschool to early adolescence, the sexes are very similar in their verbal abilities. At about age 11, the sexes begin to diverge, with female superiority increasing through high school and possibly beyond. Girls score higher on tasks involving both receptive and productive language, and on "high-level" verbal tasks (analogies, comprehension of difficult written material, creative writing) as well as upon the "lower-level" measures (fluency). The magnitude of the female advantage varies, being most commonly about one-quarter of a standard deviation.

2. *That boys excel in visual-spatial ability.* Male superiority on visual-spatial tasks is fairly consistently found in adolescence and adulthood, but not in childhood. The male advantage on spatial tests increases through the high school years up to a level of about .40 of a standard deviation. The sex difference is approximately equal on analytic and nonanalytic spatial measures.

3. *That boys excel in mathematical ability.* The two sexes are similar in their early acquisition of quantitative concepts, and their mastery of arithmetic during the grade-school years. Beginning at about age 12–13, boys' mathematical skills increase faster than girls'. The greater rate of improvement appears to be not entirely a function of the number of math courses taken, although the question has not been extensively studied. The magnitude of the sex differences varies greatly from one population to another, and is probably not so great as the difference in spatial ability. Both visual-spatial and verbal processes are sometimes involved in the solution of mathematical problems; some math problems can probably be solved in either way, while others cannot, a fact that may help to explain the variation in degree of sex difference from one measure to another.

4. *That males are more aggressive.* The sex difference in aggression has been observed in all cultures in which the relevant behavior has been observed. Boys are more aggressive both physically and verbally. They show the attenuated forms of aggression (mock-fighting, aggressive fantasies) as well as the direct forms more frequently than girls. The sex difference is found as early as social play begins — at age 2 or 2½. Although the aggressiveness of both sexes declines with age, boys and men remain more aggressive through the college years. Little information is available for older adults. The primary victims of male aggression are other males — from early ages, girls are chosen less often as victims.

Open Questions: Too Little Evidence, or Findings Ambiguous

1. *Tactile sensitivity.* Most studies of tactile sensitivity in infancy, and of the ability to perceive by touch at later ages, do not find sex differences. When differences are found, girls are more sensitive, but such findings are rare enough that we cannot have confidence that the difference is a meaningful one. Additional work is

needed with some of the standard psychophysical measurements of tactile sensitivity, over a range of ages. Most of the existing studies in which the data are analyzed by sex have been done with newborns.

2. *Fear, timidity, and anxiety.* Observational studies of fearful behavior usually do not find sex differences. Teacher ratings and self-reports, however, usually find girls to be more timid or more anxious. In the case of self-reports, the problem is to know whether the results reflect "real" differences or only differences in the willingness to report anxious feelings. Of course, the very willingness to assert that one is afraid may lead to fearful behavior, so the distinction may not turn out to be important. However, it would be desirable to have measures other than self-report (which make up the great bulk of the data from early school age on) as a way of clarifying the meaning of the girls' greater self-attribution of fears and anxiety.

3. *Activity level.* Sex differences in activity level do not appear in infancy. They begin to be seen when children reach the age of social play. During the preschool years, when sex differences are found they are in the direction of boys' being more active. However, there are many instances in which sex differences have not been found. Some, but not all, of the variance among studies can be accounted for by whether the measurement situation was social. That is, boys appear to be especially stimulated to bursts of high activity by the presence of other boys. But the exact nature of the situational control over activity level remains to be established. Activity level is responsive to a number of motivational states—fear, anger, curiosity—and is therefore not a promising variable for identifying stable individual or group differences. More detailed observations are needed on the vigor and qualitative nature of play.

4. *Competitiveness.* When sex differences are found, they usually show boys to be more competitive, but there are many studies finding sex similarity. Madsen and his colleagues find sex differences to be considerably weaker than differences between cultures and, in a number of studies, entirely absent. Almost all the research on competition has involved situations in which competition is maladaptive. In the Prisoner's Dilemma game, for example, the sexes are equally cooperative, but this is in a situation in which cooperation is to the long-run advantage of both players and the issue is one of developing mutual trust. It appears probable that in situations in which competitiveness produces increased individual rewards, males would be more competitive, but this is a guess based on commonsense considerations, such as the male interest in competitive sports, not upon research in controlled settings. The age of the subject and the identity of the opponent no doubt make a difference—there is evidence that young women hesitate to compete against their boyfriends.

5. *Dominance.* Dominance appears to be more of an issue within boys' groups than girls' groups. Boys make more dominance attempts (both successful and unsuccessful) toward one another than do girls. They also more often attempt to dominate adults. The dominance relations between the sexes are complex: in childhood, the sex segregation of play groups means that neither sex frequently attempts to dominate the other. In experimental situations in which the sexes are combined, the evidence is ambiguous on whether either sex is more successful in influencing the behavior of the other. Among adult mixed pairs or groups, formal leadership tends to go to males in the initial phases of interaction, but the direction of influence

becomes more sex-equal the longer the relationship lasts, with "division of authority" occurring along lines of individual competencies and division of labor.

6. *Compliance.* In childhood, girls tend to be more compliant to the demands and directions of adults. This compliance does not extend, however, to willingness to accept directions from, or be influenced by, age-mates. Boys are especially concerned with maintaining their status in the peer group, and are probably therefore more vulnerable to pressures and challenges from this group, although this has not been well established. As we have seen in the discussion of dominance, it is not clear that in mixed-sex interactions either sex is consistently more willing to comply with the wishes of the other.

7, *Nurturance and "maternal" behavior.* There is very little evidence concerning the tendencies of boys and girls to be nurturant or helpful toward younger children or animals. Cross-cultural work does indicate that girls between the ages of 6 and 10 are more often seen behaving nurturantly. Within our own society, the rare studies that report nurturant behavior are observational studies of free play among nursery school children; sex differences are not found in these studies, but the setting normally does not include children much younger than the subjects being observed, and it may be that the relevant elicitors are simply not present. Female hormones play a role in maternal behavior in lower animals, and the same may be true in human beings, but there is no direct evidence that this is the case. There is very little information on the responses of adult men to infants and children, so it is not possible to say whether adult women are more disposed to behave maternally than men are to behave paternally. If there is a sex difference in the tendency to behave nurturantly, it does not generalize to a greater female tendency to behave altruistically over varying situations. The studies of people's willingness to help others in distress have sometimes shown men more helpful, sometimes women, depending on the identity of the person needing help and the kind of help that is needed. The overall finding on altruism is one of sex similarity.

In Chapters 5 and 6, we raised the question of whether the female is more passive than the male. The answer is complex, but mainly negative. The two sexes are highly similar in their willingness to explore a novel environment, when they are both given freedom to do so. Both are highly responsive to social situations of all kinds, and although some individuals tend to withdraw from social interaction and simply watch from the sidelines, such persons are no more likely to be female than male. Girls' greater compliance with adult demands is just as likely to take an active as a passive form; running errands and performing services for others are active processes. Young boys seem more likely than girls to put out energy in the form of bursts of strenuous physical activity, but the girls are not sitting idly by while the boys act; they are simply playing more quietly. And their play is fully as organized and planful (possibly more so), and has as much the quality of actively imposing their own design upon their surroundings as does boys' play. It is true that boys and men are more aggressive, but this does not mean that females are the passive victims of aggression — they do not yield or withdraw when aggressed against any more frequently than males do, at least during the phases of childhood for which observations are available. With respect to dominance, we have noted the curious fact that while males are more dominant, females are not especially submissive, at least not to the dominance attempts of boys and girls their own age. In sum, the term "passive" does not accurately describe the most common female personality attributes.

Returning to one of the major conclusions of our survey of sex differences, there are many popular beliefs about the psychological characteristics of the two sexes that have proved to have little or no basis in fact. How is it possible that people continue to believe, for example, that girls are more "social" than boys, when careful observation and measurement in a variety of situations show no sex difference? Of course it is possible that we have not studied those particular situations that contribute most to the popular beliefs. But if this is the problem, it means that the alleged sex difference exists only in a limited range of situations, and the sweeping generalizations embodied in popular beliefs are not warranted.

However, a more likely explanation for the perpetuation of "myths," we believe, is the fact that stereotypes are such powerful things. An ancient truth is worth restating here: if a generalization about a group of people is believed, whenever a member of that group behaves in the expected way the observer notes it and his belief is confirmed and strengthened; when a member of the group behaves in a way that is not consistent with the observer's expectations, the instance is likely to pass unnoticed, and the observer's generalized belief is protected from disconfirmation. We believe that this well-documented process occurs continually in relation to the expected and perceived behavior of males and females, and results in the perpetuation of myths that would otherwise die out under the impact of negative evidence. However, not all unconfirmed beliefs about the two sexes are of this sort. It is necessary to reconsider the nature of the evidence that permits us to conclude what is myth and what is (at least potentially) reality. . . .

The Longest War: Sex Differences in Perspective

Carol Tavris and Carole Offir

In this excerpt from The Longest War: Sex Differences in Perspective *(1977), Carol Tavris and Carole Offir discuss long-documented differences between male and female attitudes toward premarital and extramarital sex, and they review various explanations of the causes of these differences. As you will discover, the authors tend to favor the environmental rather than the biological explanations. You might want to contrast their conclusions with those drawn by John Lincoln Collier in an essay appearing later in this chapter. Tavris and Offir are professors at San Diego Mesa College.*

the scientific study of sex

In 1938, Indiana University selected Alfred C. Kinsey to teach a new course in sex education and marriage. Kinsey was not an obvious choice for the job. He was a biologist who had devoted his career to the study of gall wasps, which reproduce asexually, without insemination of the female by the male. But Kinsey was an extremely conscientious man, so he set out to rectify his lack of knowledge about people by consulting the library. Surprised at the lack of reliable information there, he decided to gather the data himself. Kinsey had spent twenty years collecting and categorizing several million gall wasps; now he applied the same painstaking approach to collecting sexual statistics. For the next eighteen years, he spent his mornings, noons, and nights talking to people about their sex lives. . . .

In 1948 Kinsey and his associates published *Sexual Behavior in the Human Male*, based on their interviews with 5,300 American men. This volume was followed in 1953 by *Sexual Behavior in the Human Female* (with Wardell B. Pomeroy, Clyde E. Martin, and Paul H. Gebhard) based on data from 5,940 females. The basic conclusion of the two books was that many of the sexual practices and "perversions" prohibited since Victorian times were actually common, and some were nearly universal. The smaller statistical surveys done since Kinsey have on the whole confirmed his findings.

Because of the work of Kinsey and later sex researchers, our knowledge of human sexuality has taken a great leap forward in just a few decades. It turns out that in almost every area of sexual behavior women are far from being as sexless as the Victorians hoped, but neither are they as sexy as the Victorians feared. Men are more active than women by all measures of sexual activity—number of partners, frequency of orgasm, homosexual encounters, sexual fantasies, masturbation. Some people take this to mean that men have a stronger sex drive than women. Others say the reason for the difference is that men have been freer than women to act on their sexual impulses. Before trying to decide between these two explanations, let's take a closer look at the data. . . .

Carol Tavris and Carole Offir, *The Longest War: Sex Differences in Perspective* (New York: Harcourt Brace Jovanovich, 1977).

premarital sex

Kinsey found that while most women born before 1900 (86 percent) had been virgins on their wedding nights, by the 1950s virginity was honored more in word than in deed. Nearly half of the married women in Kinsey's sample had coitus before they were married. (The figures for men were even higher: 98 percent of those with a grade-school education, 85 percent of high-school graduates, and 68 percent of those with some college had had premarital intercourse.) On the other hand, Kinsey did not find that premarital sex had become a casual matter for women. Over half of the women who had sex before marriage had only one partner, almost always the fiancé. A third had two to five partners, and only 13 percent had more than five. For most of the women Kinsey interviewed, premarital sex occurred in the context of a serious relationship.

During the 1960s discussion flourished about whether premarital sex was still on the increase. Some sociologists argued that since the 1920s behavior had not changed nearly so much as attitudes about sex; people were not acting differently, they were simply talking more openly and tolerantly (Reiss 1960, 1969; Bell 1966). This view eventually gave way before mounting evidence of real behavioral change during the 1960s. Two separate studies revealed a striking increase in premarital sex among college women between 1958 and 1968 (Bell and Chaskes 1970; Christensen and Gregg 1970). A national study of over 4,000 young unmarried women found that by the age of nineteen almost half were no longer virgins (40 percent of the white women and 80 percent of the blacks), compared with 18 or 19 percent in the Kinsey sample (Kantner and Zelnik 1972).

The trend away from female virginity continued into the seventies. A national study commissioned by the Playboy Foundation in 1972 and reported by Morton Hunt (1974) found that among married people, the younger the person, the greater the likelihood that intercourse had occurred before marriage. In the youngest group, 81 percent of the women said they were not virgins when they married.

In a 1974 sex survey of 100,000 *Redbook* readers, nine out of ten wives under the age of twenty-five reported having premarital sex (Levin and Levin 1975). Although the sexual behavior of *Redbook* readers is not necessarily representative of the whole country, the inescapable conclusion, from many studies of many different groups of women, is that the virgin bride is following the route of the buffalo and becoming a statistical rarity. Men are still more likely than women to have sex before marriage, but the gap is narrowing.

But merely counting virgins can be misleading. When you go beyond these general numbers, you find that many important differences between men and women are still alive. For example, though fewer women today require engagement before having premarital sex than used to, the majority of women who have sex before marriage still do so with the one, or maybe two, they love; men are more likely to sleep with the many, or any, they like. In the *Playboy* survey, the median number of premarital partners reported by males was six. In contrast, over half of the married women who had premarital sex had only one partner, just as in Kinsey's study. In a national sample of teenagers, Robert Sorensen (1973) found that one quarter of the boys were what he called "sexual adventurers" — they preferred to have many sexual partners, concurrently or in rapid succession. In contrast, only 6 percent of the girls were sexual adventurers. Young black women have somewhat fewer partners than young white women (Kantner and Zelnik 1972).

The first experience with intercourse often has a different meaning for males and females. In a survey of the sexual attitudes and experiences of 20,000 *Psychology Today* readers (Athanasiou, Shaver, and Tavris 1970), 66 percent of the women but only 41 percent of the men said that their first partner had been a spouse, fiancé(e), or steady date. Fifteen percent of the men but only 6 percent of the women reported that their first partner was a casual acquaintance or stranger. Similarly, Harold Christensen and Christina Gregg (1970) found in a 1968 study of midwestern college students that 86 percent of the women but only 53 percent of the men had their first premarital experience with a steady or fiancé(e). Other studies have found similar results.

So more women are having premarital sex than ever before, but they are not necessarily motivated to seek sexual adventure in itself as often as men are. Christensen and Gregg reported that 23 percent of the college women they questioned said that during their first premarital experience they had yielded because of force or a sense of obligation rather than personal desire. Only 2.5 percent of the men questioned said the same. When Judith Bardwick (1971) asked some college women why they made love, she got answers like the following:

"He'd leave me if I didn't sleep with him."
    "Right now to please him."
    "Well, a great strain not to. Fairly reluctant for a while, but then I realized it had become a great big thing in the relationship and it would disintegrate the relationship . . . I wanted to also."
    "Mostly to see my boyfriend's enjoyment."
    "I gave in to Sidney because I was so lonely."

Few of Bardwick's interviewees said that they made love because *they* wanted to and because they physically enjoyed sex. Bardwick thinks most of them accepted sex as the price of a romantic relationship, or as a way to prove their love. Whereas previous generations of women said no to premarital sex because they feared they would lose the man if they said yes, Bardwick's work suggests that today many young women say yes because they fear they will lose the man if they say no. At any rate, that is what they tell interviewers.

In an effort to discover the sexual concerns of young men and women, psychologist Carol Roberts asked her community college students, most of them unmarried, to list any problems they had with "any aspect of sexual functioning — psychological, physiological, or social." She has been doing this for several years and has a remarkable set of replies.

The women speak mostly of insecurities, guilts, and fears:

Fear of pregnancy
Fear of rape
Being conquered and of no further use
Being rejected if one says no
Masturbation — accepting it

Fear that one's partner is physically repulsed by you
Fear of loss of self-respect
Fear of becoming too attached when the feeling is not mutual
Guilt feelings about premarital sex
Pressure to have sex even when one doesn't want to
Fear of not satisfying one's partner
Embarrassment or concern over not being orgasmic

But many of the men's comments are complaints about women rather than expressions of their own conflicts or worries:

Finding a partner who is open to varying sexual experiences
Having to be always on the hunt
Not being able to have sexual relations when one wants to
Women who tease, without wanting to engage in sexual activity
Women's refusal to take responsibility for their own sexuality
Women who use their sexual attractiveness in a manipulatory fashion
The excessive modesty of women (they want the lights off)
Passive women
Aggressive women
Necessity to say you love the woman even if it isn't true
Being expected to know all about sex
Inability to communicate feelings or needs during the sex act

These responses imply that many couples in bed together might as well be on separate planets, for all the similarity of their perceptions and purposes. (This generalization applies mainly to unmarried people in their late teens or early twenties. Older single men and women are probably much more alike in outlook than younger ones.) The sex-and-love tangle may be the factor that is most responsible for such misunderstandings. Women, more often than men, use sex to get love; men use love to get sex. In a recent survey on sex roles, more than half of the men but only 15 percent of the women said they had told a sex partner they cared more for her or him than they really did in order to have sex (Tavris 1973). In contrast, a fourth of the women but very few of the men admitted they had used sex to bind a partner into a relationship.

It's clear that among young people, stated attitudes and actual behavior have changed almost as rapidly as the cost of living, but sexual motives and concerns have changed far less. Some old, familiar themes can still be heard, especially when the issue is whether sex can be separated from love, or ought to be. Men, more often than women, regard sex and love as unconnected experiences. In the *Playboy* survey, 60 percent of the males and 37 percent of the females thought premarital coitus was all right for men even without strong affection, but only 44 percent of the men and 20 percent of the women gave the same privilege to women. The double standard has been weakened, but it is not gone.

extramarital sex

Kinsey found that men were more likely than women to have sex not only before marriage but outside of it. Though he did not present exact statistics, he estimated that about half of the husbands he interviewed had intercourse with a woman other than their wives at some time during their married lives. In contrast, only about one-fourth of the wives had sex with someone other than their husbands. Even this percentage of women is inflated because Kinsey included a disproportionate number of divorced women in his calculations, and they were more likely than never-divorced wives to have had extramarital sex. When Hunt recomputed Kinsey's statistics, taking this overrepresentation into account, he estimated that the incidence of extramarital sex in Kinsey's time was closer to one woman in five.

People have always been fascinated with adultery even as they condemn it. In recent years Americans have become more tolerant about extramarital sex. While only a few believe it should be encouraged, an equally small number think it is always wrong under all circumstances. Studies find that the majority of people regard extramarital sex the way they regard eating garlic. It's fine for them, but they don't want anyone near them to do it — especially their spouses.

The most dramatic change in attitudes toward extramarital sex, and in behavior, has come from young women. In Kinsey's time, only some 8 percent of the married women under age twenty-five had had extramarital sex, but today the estimated figure has jumped to 24 percent (Hunt 1974). A generation ago, only a third as many young wives as husbands reported an extramarital experience, but today three-fourths as many young wives as husbands do. "The change," says Hunt, "is not a radical break with the ideal of sexual fidelity but a radical break with the double standard."

Although as many women as men may soon be having extramarital sex, differences between men and women in number of partners and in motives remain. In the *Psychology Today* survey, twice as many males as females reported six or more extramarital partners (14 percent to 7 percent), a finding supported in other surveys as well. It could be that men have more partners because they have more opportunities; the *Redbook* report found that employed wives are more likely to have sexual affairs than unemployed wives (though some smaller studies have found the opposite). But it is also possible that women enter extramarital liaisons, like premarital ones, less for lust than for love. For women, having sex outside marriage is still strongly correlated with marital dissatisfaction (Levin and Levin 1975). Men are more likely to try to distinguish emotionally the casual encounter for sex's sake from the marriage. Thus husbands are initially more enthusiastic than wives about unconventional forms of extramarital sex. Hunt found that among couples under age twenty-five, 5 percent of the husbands but only 2 percent of the wives had tried mate-swapping — which is often called wife-swapping, with good reason: all the available studies show that when the wife first participates it is often at the husband's instigation or insistence. In the *Psychology Today* survey, 41 percent of the husbands but 22 percent of the wives expressed an interest in swapping. . . .

biology and learning

Both women and men are biologically equipped to enjoy sexual arousal and orgasm regularly throughout their lives. But for all the talk about women's multiple orgasms, men have more orgasms than women — per episode, per month, per whatever. Kinsey found that by the time the average man married, he had had 1,523 orgasms, compared to 223 for the average women. The gap may be narrower today, but still it is a rare man who never has orgasms (in addition to the spontaneous emissions that result from sperm accumulation), while many women are years into a relationship before they reach orgasm during intercourse and a surprisingly large number—ranging to 20 percent—never do. In this society, sex seems to be more important to men than to women. On survey after survey they say they like it more, do it more, think about it more.

Many explanations have been offered for the sex difference in sexual activity, generally emphasizing one of two perspectives. Biological and evolutionary views argue for programed differences in sex drive between the sexes. Some people, such as Mary Jane Sherfey, think that women have the stronger sex drive but that it had to be suppressed long ago so that the family unit could survive. Others think that men developed the stronger sex drive because promiscuity was a necessary and efficient way to keep women pregnant and the tribe expanding. Learning explanations, on the other hand, maintain that the inborn sexual impulses of men and women are probably equal and that differences in behavior and attitudes result from the ways these impulses are shaped and directed.

Today, most social scientists think that both perspectives have something to offer and avoid taking an either-or stance. For example, John Gagnon and William Simon (1969, 1973) have set forth in some detail an explanation of sexual behavior that emphasizes learning but also illustrates the complex interplay between biology and culture. Like many other sex researchers, Simon and Gagnon believe that adult sexuality is conditioned to a large extent by adolescent experiences with masturbation and that sex differences in sexuality are linked to the fact that boys masturbate more often than girls. The increase of male hormones at puberty causes a boy to have frequent erections even when he is not preoccupied with erotic activities or thoughts, so his attention is directed to his genitals. At the same time, the social demands of the American masculine role, which emphasize aggressiveness, achievement, conquest, and potency, encourage the boy to experiment. For most boys, experimentation begins with masturbation, a purely physical experience detached from images or feelings of romantic love. Boys commonly masturbate in front of other boys—the one who ejaculates first may even win a prize—and many learn about masturbation from friends before they try it. The encouragement of his peers motivates a boy to experiment some more. Sex becomes a device for confirming one's status among other males, especially for working-class boys.

For girls, Simon and Gagnon say, anatomy and cultural rules produce another pattern entirely. It is much easier for a girl to ignore her genitals and to remain ignorant about them. The sign of male arousal, an erect penis, cannot be misinterpreted, but women often need time to learn to recognize signs of their own arousal. Girls are less likely to discover and practice masturbation; if they do, they usually make the discovery on their own and talk about it to no one. For many girls, the vagina and clitoris are untouchable, even unmentionable. (Many women refer only to a vague area "down there"; men have many words to call their genitals, and none of them are vague.)

For both anatomical and social reasons, then, Simon and Gagnon think that girls are less likely to learn about physical sexuality and orgasm. What they do learn about is romance, attractiveness, and the importance of catching a mate: "While boys are learning physical sex, girls are being trained in the language of love and the cosmetic values of sexual presentation through training in dress, dancing and other display behavior. . . . At no point is sexual expression valued in itself, independent of the formation of families" (Simon and Gagnon 1969). Boys, we might add, are more likely than girls to take communal showers and nude swimming lessons, to try group masturbation, and to have conversations about sex, experiences that give them different associations with sex from the ones girls learn. In short, most boys learn to think of sex as an achievement while many girls learn to think of it as a service to the male.

Biological and societal explanations also overlap to explain the well-known observation that boys reach their sexual peak in their late teens, women not until their mid-thirties. One line of reasoning is that hormones are responsible for the number of orgasms adolescent males have, which declines with age; impotence, we hear, is a "natural" occurrence in middle and old age. The explanation for the delayed peak in women is that they mature sexually only with pregnancy and childbirth, which increase the capacity of the pelvic area for engorgement and sexual tension. Kinsey, too, often attributed the sex differences he observed to biological causes. He thought men, like bumblebees, were designed to pollinate as many female flowers as they can.

But major social differences between men and women also could account for the discrepancy in sexual peaks. Young males are encouraged to sow their oats, women to hoard them. Women are taught to inhibit their sexuality all through adolescence, waiting for love as well as orgasm. It may therefore take a long-term relationship with a husband or lover before they feel self-confident enough, and trusting enough, to express their sexuality fully. In addition, because women do not masturbate as much as men, it takes them longer to learn (and tell their partners) what pleases them. But the belief that sexuality is governed by biological rules sets up expectations about "normalcy" that may create self-fulfilling prophecies. If men expect their performance to decline with age, they are not surprised if it does — and their expectation may contribute to the decline. If women think they are going to be sexiest in their thirties, they may finally let themselves go, which contributes to their sexual pleasure.

the mangaian example

Perhaps the best way to appreciate the impact that social conventions can have on sexual behavior is to break out of our cultural cage for a moment. Donald S. Marshall, an anthropologist, spent a year in Mangaia, a tiny Polynesian island in the South Pacific. Mangaians of both sexes love sex, Marshall reports (1971), and their example suggests a high human capacity for sexual pleasure. Just as the Eskimos have many words for snow in all its various forms, the Mangaians have lots of words for intercourse and for the sexual organs. They have several descriptive words for clitoris alone, which suggests that they devote somewhat more attention to female anatomy than Americans do.

Mangaians start their sex lives early. Girls begin to have intercourse with orgasm at twelve or thirteen, and they have several lovers before marriage with no negative sanction from the community. From the start girls expect their lovers to satisfy them sexually. Boys entering puberty learn about sex from older women, who teach them coital techniques, cunnilingus, foreplay, and how to bring a girl to several orgasms before they have their own. Mangaians all say that a girl must learn to have orgasms and that a good man teaches her how. Both sexes agree that a good man will be able to continue penetration for fifteen to thirty minutes or more, while a good woman moves her hips like "a washing machine." "A 'dead' partner who doesn't move," notes Marshall, "is universally despised."

Although Marshall did not collect detailed sexual histories from everyone on Mangaia, he found consistent, striking differences between Americans and Mangaians in sexual attitudes and frequencies. The Mangaian experience suggests that the two sexes are much more alike in terms of sexual potential than American performance statistics indicate, and that there is little biological inevitability to "premature ejaculation" or "frigidity." Young Mangaian couples typically reach climax three to five times a night — both sexes — but they are not overly concerned about orgasm, presumably because everyone achieves it. American girls link love and sex more readily than American boys do, but Mangaian girls happily take lovers for sexual pleasure. In Mangaia, the sexes do not have radically different "sexual peaks," and sexual frequency remains high for both sexes throughout life. No one is too old or too ugly to have a partner.

For years, physicians and poets chatted knowingly about sex without benefit of the physiological facts. Since Masters and Johnson, people chat more knowledgeably about the physiological facts but rarely put them into a psychological context. Sex is more than a matter of hydraulics. Masters and Johnson, so often accused of making sex mechanical, have said that when you treat sex as an exercise to be performed according to a set of directions, "you are dissecting and removing and depersonalizing the whole sexual experience." Sexual liberation is not just a question of dispelling physical hang-ups and freeing the body to respond. It is also a question of freeing the mind, so that one can enjoy — or reject — sex on the basis of choice, not coercion.

Works Cited

Athanasiou, Robert; Shaver, Phillip; and Tavris, Carol. 1970. Sex. *Psychology today* 4 (July):37–52

Bardwick, Judith M. 1971. *Psychology of women: a study of bio-cultural conflicts*. New York: Harper & Row.

Bell, Robert R. 1966. *Premarital sex in a changing society*. Englewood Cliffs, New Jersey: Prentice-Hall.

Bell, Robert R., and Chaskes, Jay B. 1970. Premarital sexual experience among coeds, 1958 and 1968. *Journal of marriage and the family* 32:81–84.

Christensen, Harold T., and Gregg, Christina F. 1970. Changing sex norms in America and Scandinavia. *Journal of marriage and the family* 32:616–27.

Gagnon, John H., and Simon, William. 1969. They're going to learn in the streets anyway. *Psychology today* 3 (July):46–47ff.

Gagnon, John H., and Simon, William. 1973. *Sexual conduct: the social sources of human sexuality*. Chicago: Aldine.

Hunt, Morton. 1974. *Sexual behavior in the 1970s*. Chicago: Playboy Press.

Kantner, John F., and Zelnik, Melvin. 1972. Sexual experience of young unmarried women in the United States. *Family planning perspectives* 4 (October):9–18.

Kinsey, Alfred C.; Pomeroy, Wardell B.; and Martin, Clyde E. 1948. *Sexual behavior in the human male*. Philadelphia: Saunders.

Kinsey, Alfred C.; Pomeroy, Wardell B.; Martin, Clyde E.; and Gebhard, Paul H. 1953. *Sexual behavior in the human female*. Philadelphia: Saunders.

Levin, Robert J., and Levin, Amy. 1975. Sexual pleasure: the surprising preferences of 100,000 women. *Redbook* 145 (September):51–58. [See also Tavris, Carol, and Sadd, Susan, *The Redbook report: the sexual preferences of American women*, New York: Delacorte, in preparation.]

Marshall, Donald S. 1971. Too much in Mangaia. *Psychology today* 4 (February):43–44ff.

Masters, William H., and Johnson, Virginia E. 1966. *Human sexual response*. Boston: Little, Brown.

———. 1970. *Human sexual inadequacy*. Boston: Little, Brown.

Reiss, Ira L. 1960. *Premarital sexual standards in America*. Glencoe, Illinois: The Free Press.

———. 1969. Premarital sexual standards. In *The individual, sex, and society*, eds. Carlfred B. Broderick and Jessie Bernard, pp. 109–18. Baltimore: The Johns Hopkins Press.

Simon, William, and Gagnon, John H. 1969. Psychosexual development. *Trans-action* 6 (March):9–18.

Sorensen, Robert C. 1973. *Adolescent sexuality in contemporary America (the Sorensen report)*. New York: World Publishing.

Tavris, Carol. 1973. Who likes women's liberation and why: the case of the unliberated liberals. *Journal of social issues* 29(4):175–94.

JUST HOW THE SEXES DIFFER
David Gelman

David Gelman, a staff writer for Newsweek, *presents a comprehensive survey of the controversies that have developed in biological and behavioral sex research. Gelman's survey is laced with studies, conclusions, and pronouncements both from researchers who feel that most sex differences are accounted for by environmental conditioning and from researchers who insist that many basic sex differences are genetic. You would do well to read this overview relatively early in your perusal of this chapter.*

Captain to Laura: ". . . If it's true we are descended from the ape, it must have been from two different species. There's no likeness between us, is there?"
— *"The Father," by August Strindberg*

So it has begun to seem, and not only in the musings of a misogynist Swedish playwright. Research on the structure of the brain, on the effects of hormones, and in animal behavior, child psychology and anthropology is providing new scientific underpinnings for what August Strindberg and his ilk viscerally guessed: men and women *are* different. They show obvious dissimilarities, of course, in size, anatomy and sexual function. But scientists now believe that they are unlike in more fundamental ways. Men and women seem to *experience* the world differently, not merely because of the ways they were brought up in it, but because they feel it with a different sensitivity of touch, hear it with different aural responses, puzzle out its problems with different cells in their brains.

Hormones seem to be the key to the difference—and an emerging body of evidence suggests that they do far more than trigger the external sexual characteristics of males and females. They actually "masculinize" or "feminize" the brain itself. By looking closely at the neurochemical processes involved, investigators are finding biological explanations for why women might think intuitively, why men seem better at problem-solving, why boys play rougher than girls.

Whether these physiological differences destine men and women for separate roles in society is a different and far more delicate question. The particular way male brains are organized may orient them toward visual-spatial perception, explaining—perhaps—why they are superior at math. Women's brains may make them more verbally disposed, explaining—possibly—why they seem better at languages. Males of most species appear to be hormonally primed for aggression, pointing—it may be—to the long evolutionary record of male dominance over women.

But few of these presumed differences go unchallenged. And whether they imply anything more—about leadership capacities, for example, or that men are biologically suited for the workplace and women for the hearth—is another part of the thicket. The notion that biology is destiny is anathema to feminists and to many

David Gelman, "Just How the Sexes Differ," *Newsweek* 18 May 1981.

male researchers as well. It is their position that sexual stereotyping, reinforced by a male-dominated culture, has more bearing on gender behavior than do hormones. "As early as you can show me a sex difference, I can show you the culture at work," insists Michael Lewis, of the Institute for the Study of Exceptional Children.

The new research has thus revived, in all its old intensity, the wrangle over whether "nature" or "nurture" plays the greater part in behavior. At the same time, it has become a fresh battle ground for feminism, a continuation of the sex war by other means. Spurred by the women's movement, large numbers of female scientists have moved into an area of inquiry once largely populated by men and by male ideas of gender roles. Both male and female investigators have been challenging male-fostered notions of female passivity and submissiveness. But because some are also acknowledging the role of biology, they are catching flak from hard-core feminists, who fear such findings will be used — as they have been in the past — to deny women equal rights.

Some researchers now refuse to be interviewed, or carefully hedge their assertions. "I found myself being screamed at — this time by the very people whose cause I had supported," wrote sociologist Alice Rossi, after she landed in hot water for talking about the "innate predisposition" of women for child-rearing. "People are being really hounded," agrees anthropologist Sarah Blaffer Hrdy, who found she could not even hypothesize about men's math abilities without provoking feminist wrath.

The research comes under indictment on another count: since possibilities for experimentation with humans are limited, it leans heavily on animal studies. Complains Stanford psychologist Eleanor Maccoby, who reviewed the literature on sex differences: "People look at this and say it is all biological. They generalize wildly from a little monkey research." But most researchers are cautious about making the leap from lower primates to Homo sapiens. Human evolution involved a huge increase in brain flexibility that gave rise to human culture. And over the long course of that evolution, humans have become much less the creatures of their hormones than are rats or rhesus monkeys.

Even so, the researchers are providing some fascinating new glimpses into the biology of behavior. Among their odd assortment of laboratory subjects are male canaries whose song repertoire is imprinted, like a player-piano roll, in a cluster of brain cells; virginal female rats that go through the motions of nursing when confronted with rat pups, and young girls who turn "tomboyish" because they were exposed to male hormones before birth.

There are also enough anomalies — male marmosets that tenderly nurture their young, female langurs that fight ferociously for turf — to cast doubts on some firmly entrenched beliefs about gender behavior. But these contradictions, too, are providing new insights into the essential nature of the sexes.

The everyday perception of sexual differences is a mélange of fact and assumption. That men, for the most part, are larger and stronger than women is something that anyone can see and physiologists can verify. There are also clear-cut differences in primary sexual functions: menstruation, gestation and lactation in women, ejaculation in men. Beyond that, observes Harvard biologist Richard Lewontin, "we just don't know any differences except the plumbing features that unambiguously separate men from women." Other presumed distinctions provide a continuing source of strife for both sexes. For example, the proposition that men are naturally more competitive than women seems increasingly debatable as women move into male jobs and sports, where they often prove as combative as men. In any case, the average differences that exist between men and women leave plenty of room for individual variations in the sexes. Not all males in a given group are more aggressive or better at math than all females; not all women are more adept at learning languages. "Women and men both fall along the whole continuum of test results," notes neuropsychologist Eran Zaidel of the University of California, Los Angeles.

Like most behavioral traits, competitiveness is hard to measure objectively, harder yet to attribute to innate causes. Scientists have been trying to zero in on those traits that *can* be measured, by way of psychological tests and brain and hormone studies. A few years ago Diane McGuinness, of the University of California at Santa Cruz, made a study of the vast body of technical literature that has sprung up in the field. She concluded that from infancy on, males and females respond in ways that provide significant clues to their later differences in behavior.

McGuinness believes that girl infants are more alert to "social" cues. They respond more to people, read facial expressions better and seem better able to interpret the emotional content of speech even before they can understand words — a clue to the proverbial "women's intuition." Boy infants are more curious about objects and like to take them apart — the beginning, perhaps, of their superior mechanical aptitude. As infants, they are awake longer and more active and exploratory.

Girls, notes McGuinness, have a "superior tactile sensitivity," even in infancy. They excel in fine-motor coordination and manual dexterity, suggesting why they are better at such tasks as typing and needlework — or neurosurgery. This same affinity for precision and detail seems to account for girls' greater verbal ability. They speak earlier and more fluently and, perhaps aided by superior auditory memory, carry a tune better. (McGuinness doubts a connection, but it has been shown in some studies that mothers tend to carry on more "conversations" — talking and singing — with girl infants than with boy babies.)

Boys stutter more than girls, spell worse and are classified far more often as "learning disabled" or "hyperactive" — quite possibly, McGuinness argues, because the early stress on reading and writing favors girls. But boys have a clear advantage in visual-spatial orientation, marked by a lively interest in geometric forms and in manipulating objects. At an early age boys and girls are about equal in arithmetic, but boys pull ahead in higher mathematics. Their faster reaction time and better visual-spatial ability appear to give them an edge in some sports.

Are these differences real and could they be biologically based? Stanford's Maccoby is skeptical. She and an associate, Carol Jacklin, reviewed more than 1,400 studies of sex differences and concluded that only four of them were well established: verbal ability for girls and visual-spatial ability, mathematical excellence and aggression in boys. Maccoby also contends, as many researchers do, that sex typing and the different set of expectations that society thrusts on men and women have far more to do with any differences that exist — with their divergent abilities — than do genes or blood chemistry. Diane McGuinness, on the other hand, believes there is "compelling" evidence that sex differences are a result of biological determinism, and her colleague, Karl Pribram, agrees. Pribram suspects that men and women may be "programed" differently from the beginning. "We don't know why these things are true," says Pribram. "But it's very difficult to say culture is predisposing males to fail at English and females at math."

To get some inkling how this programming might come about, anthropologists turn to evolutionary scenarios derived from the study of primitive cultures. The most familiar accounts center on hunter-gatherer societies, the prototype of human social organization. There was a clear division of labor along sexual lines in these societies. The risky business of hunting and fighting fell to the males, presumably because they were more expendable: it required only one male to impregnate many females. Thus, males may have evolved the larger musculature, faster reactions and greater visual-spatial acuity for combat, for hurling spears, for spotting distant prey. As an evolutionary result, even today they are more competitive, more at risk. They experience more stress, die younger than women in maturity and suffer more accidental deaths in childhood.

Females were the gatherers and the first agriculturalists. Limited to less venturesome roles by successive pregnancies and the need to care for infants, they may have developed close-to-the-nest faculties of touch and hearing, perhaps even a greater facility for speech as they interacted with their offspring and other females. According to Darwinian theory, these adaptively advantageous traits would then be passed on in the gene pool. Anthropologist Donald Symons carried this thinking a controversial step further in a 1979 book contending that males are predisposed to sexual promiscuity, while females are prone to constancy. His reasoning: a male's reproductive success was determined by the number of females he could impregnate. Females, he said, feared the wrath of jealous stronger mates and found monogamy more conducive to raising offspring — their own measure of reproductive efficacy.

Symons's thesis, wrapped in all its sociobiological trappings, impressed some scientists and infuriated others. In addition, the subject is an explosive one for feminists. If men are driven by testicular fortitude, women reject the notion that they are limited by a kind of ovarian docility. Anne Petersen, director of the adolescent laboratory at Chicago's Michael Reese Hospital, supports this view: "When women really needed to keep making babies because so many died and women themselves didn't live very long, their work was of a different nature and needed to be related to reproduction. That's not true anymore."

Evolutionary evidence does suggest that with the advent of weapons, some physical distinctions between males and females became less necessary. Differences in size and strength have greatly diminished over the millennia, perhaps, according to University of Michigan paleoanthropologist Milford Wolpoff, because "the physical requirements of the male and female roles have become more similar." The main anatomical trend, Wolpoff says, "has been for males to become more feminized."

Harvard's Sarah Blaffer Hrdy is one of the new generation of social scientists who are trying to debunk the concept of female passivity. In a forthcoming book, "The Woman That Never Evolved," Hrdy argues that female territoriality — the aggressive protection of turf — has been overlooked by most anthropologists. "The central organizing principle of primate social life is competition between females, and especially female lineages," she writes. In such matrilinear societies, she argues, "the basic dynamics of the mating system depend not so much on male predilection as on the degree to which one female tolerates another."

Hrdy's work has encouraged other researchers to look beyond the evolutionary stereotypes. Until now, she contends, most such studies have focused on males arranging themselves in order to take advantage of females. "We've really been ass-backwards in trying to understand the primate social organization by looking only at males," asserts Hrdy.

By shifting the anthropological focus, the Hrdy breed of researchers hopes to show that gender roles are not unalterably determined by biology; instead, they may be the product of particular cultures. Even so, the evidence for an inborn masculine "aggression factor" seems inescapable. It is widely agreed that in the majority of animal species, males are more prone to fighting than are females. Biologists trace this to the hormone testosterone, secreted in the testes of the male fetus during a critical period in its development. Although the sex of a fetus is basically determined by its genetic coding (XX chromosomes for females, XY for males), any fetus has the chance of developing either male or female characteristics, depending on the hormones it is exposed to. Testosterone and other male hormones "masculinize" a fetus, differentiating its genitalia from the female's. At the same time, the male hormones prevent the development of ovaries, which secrete female hormones that would stimulate the growth of feminine characteristics.

Scientists first got on the trail of testosterone in 1849. Experiments showed that roosters became less aggressive and lost their sexual drive after they were castrated, then regained their "roosterhood" when extracts from the testes were implanted in them. A century later, in 1959, physiologists Robert Goy and William Young conducted a study still considered a landmark in the field. First they injected pregnant female guinea pigs with massive doses of testosterone. The result: the genetically female offspring in the brood had both male genitalia and ovaries. When the ovaries were removed and the aberrant females were given a fresh dose of testosterone, they behaved like males, even "mounting" other females — the gesture of male dominance in many species.

Goy, now with the University of Wisconsin's Primate Research Center, has confirmed the effects of testosterone in experiments with rhesus monkeys over the past decade. Not only is female behavior partly masculinized by prenatal testosterone, he says, but the robustness and vigor of males depend on how long they have been exposed to the hormone. "The different kinds of behavior that you see young male monkeys display," Goy asserts, "are completely, scientifically and uniquely determined by the endocrine conditions that exist before birth."

To see if hormones play a similar role in human behavior, John Money of Johns Hopkins University and Anke Ehrhardt of Columbia studied one of nature's own experiments — children exposed to abnormally high levels of androgens (male hormones) before birth because of adrenal-gland malfunctions. Among other effects discovered, the researchers at Johns Hopkins found that girls born with this disorder exhibited distinctly "tomboyish" behavior, seldom played with dolls and began dating at a later age than other girls.

The much-cited Money-Ehrhardt research has provided a classic context for the nature-nurture debate. Some scientists maintain that the tomboyism was a clear result of the hormone exposure, and they bolster their argument by noting the scores of animal experiments that demonstrate similar effects. But others criticize the study for failing to emphasize that girls with congenital adrenal hyperplasia do not *look* like normal girls at birth; they often require corrective surgery to restore normal female genitals. Thus, the argument goes, they may be treated differently as they grow up, and their behavior could be more the result of an abnormal environment than of abnormal blood chemistry.

The debate rages back and forth. But at least one scientist who has been on both sides, Rutgers psycho-endocrinologist June Reinisch, recently found evidence to buttress the hormonal argument. Over a period of five years Reinisch studied 25 boys and girls born to women who had taken synthetic progestin (a type of androgen) to prevent miscarriages. When the scientist compared them with their unexposed siblings by giving each child a standard aggression test, she found significant differences between the groups. Progestin-exposed males scored twice as high in physical aggression as their normal brothers; twelve of seventeen females scored higher than their unexposed sisters. "This result was so striking," says Reinisch, "that I sat on the data for a year before publishing."

Reinisch has by no means renounced her belief in the importance of environment. Like many of her colleagues, she suspects that hormones act to "flavor" an individual for one kind of gender behavior or another. But how the individual is brought up is still an important factor. As Robert Goy explains, "It looks as though what the hormone is doing is predisposing the animal to learn a particular social role. It isn't insisting that it learn that role; it's just making it easier. The hormone doesn't prevent behavior from being modified by environmental and social conditions."

As to how the initial "flavor" comes about, researchers now believe that hormones change the very structure of the brain. Some variations in the brains of males and females have been observed in animals. They were found mainly in the hypothalamus and pre-optic regions, which are closely connected to the reproductive functions. In those areas males are generally found to have more and larger "neurons"—nerve cells and their connecting processes. Experiments conducted by Dominique Toran-Allerand of Columbia University using cultures of brain cells from newborn mice have shown that neuronal development can be stimulated by hormones, and this suggests a key to the sexual mystery. Says animal physiologist Bruce McEwen of Rockefeller University: "Growth, as the primary event caused by hormones, could account for the observed differences in brains."

The clearest evidence to date of the brain-hormone link is in songbirds. Several years ago Rockefeller researchers Fernando Nottebohm and Arthur Arnold discovered sex differences in certain clusters of brain nuclei that control the singing function in canaries. The nuclei, they found, are almost four times as large in males as in females—apparently explaining why male songbirds sing and females don't. Singing is part of the mating ritual for the birds, and Nottebohm demonstrated that the size of the nuclei waxed and waned with the coming and going of the mating season. When he treated female songbirds with testosterone, the singing nuclei doubled in size and the females produced malelike songs. "This was the first observation of a gross sexual dimorphism in the brain of a vertebrate," Nottebohm told a scientific meeting last November.

Many scientists are now convinced that hormones "imprint" sexuality on the brains of a large number of animal species by changing the nerve-cell structure. "Even the way dogs urinate — that's a function that is sex different and is determined by hormones," says Roger Gorski, a UCLA neuro-endocrinologist who has done important experiments with animal brains.

But what about humans? So far, no one has observed structural differences between the brains of males and females in any species more sophisticated than rats. In humans, the best evidence is indirect. For years researchers have known that men's and women's mental functions are organized somewhat differently. Men appear to have more "laterality" — that is, their functions are separately controlled by the left or right hemisphere of the brain, while women's seem diffused through both hemispheres. The first clues to this intriguing disparity came from victims of brain damage. Doctors noticed that male patients were much likelier than females to suffer speech impairment after damage to the left hemisphere and loss of such nonverbal functions as visual-spatial ability when the right hemisphere was damaged. Women showed less functional loss, regardless of the hemisphere involved. Some researchers believe this is because women's brain activity is duplicated in both hemispheres. Women usually mature earlier than men, which means that their hemispheric processes may have less time to draw apart. They retain more nerve-transmission mechanisms in the connective tissue between the two hemispheres (the corpus callosum) and can thus call either or both sides of the brain into play on a given task.

On the whole, women appear to be more dominated by the left, or verbal, hemisphere and men by the right, or visual, side. Researchers McGuinness and Pribram speculate that men generally do better in activities where the two hemispheres don't compete with, and thus hamper, each other, while women may be better able to coordinate the efforts of both hemispheres. This might explain why women seem to think "globally," or intuitively and men concentrate more effectively on specific problem-solving.

A few enterprising researchers have tried to find a direct connection between hormones and human-brain organization. UCLA's Melissa Hines studied 16 pairs of sisters, of whom one in each pair had been prenatally exposed to DES (diethylstilbestrol), a synthetic hormone widely administered to pregnant women during the 1950s to prevent miscarriages. Using audiovisual tests, Hines found what appeared to be striking differences between the exposed and unexposed sisters.

First, Hines played separate nonsense syllables into the women's right and left ears. Normally, the researcher explains, most people — but especially males — report more accurately what they hear with the right ear. In her tests, the hormone-exposed women picked the correct syllable heard with the right ear 20 percent more often than their unexposed sisters. A test of their right and left visual fields produced comparable results. The implication was that the women's brains had been masculinized. "It is compelling evidence that prenatal hormones influence human behavior due to changes in brain organization," says Hines.

Differences in brain organization may have practical implications for education and medicine. Some researchers believe that teaching methods should take note of right-left brain differences, though past attempts at such specialized teaching have been ineffective. Other scientists predict clinical benefits. It is useful to know, for example, that females who are brain-damaged at birth will cope with the defects better than males. Columbia's Toran-Allerand suggests that certain types of infertility might be corrected once scientists understand how hormones mold the reproductive structures of the brain. "I'm interested in clinical applications," she says, "but all these questions get lost in the furor over behavioral differences."

The furor may be inevitable. The very mention of differences in ability between men and women seems to imply superiority and inferiority. Women researchers in the field have had the toughest going at times. Some have found themselves under Lysenkoist pressure to hew to women's-liberation orthodoxy, whatever their data show. University of Chicago psychologist Jerre Levy, a pioneer in studies of brain lateralization, withdrew from public discussion of her work after she was bombarded with hostile letters and phone calls. Harvard's Hrdy recalls sitting on a panel that was cautiously examining the "hypothesis" of male math superiority when a feminist seated next to her whispered, "Don't you know it's evil to do studies like that?" Says Hrdy: "I was just stunned. Of course it's not evil to do studies like that. It's evil to make pronouncements to say they're fact."

From the time women began moving—rather aggressively—into male-female studies, many researchers have grown wary of making such pronouncements. It has become increasingly difficult to find any statement that is not assiduously qualified. One reason is that differences among members of the same sex are far greater than average differences *between* sexes. Monte Buchsbaum of the National Institutes of Health conducted tests of electrical activity in the brain showing that women tend to have a larger "evoked potential" than men—an indication of greater sensitivity to certain stimuli. But, he cautions, "individuals can vary over about a fivefold range. The variation between the sexes is only about 20 to 40 percent." Harvard's Richard Lewontin notes that the average male-female differential in math scores is only "half a standard deviation. That's rather small." The math dispute is "just silly," scoffs Lewontin, and assertions about "who's most aggressive or who's most analytical are just the garbage can of barroom speculation presented as science."

Many researchers contend that a child's awareness of gender is more decisive than biology in shaping sexual differences. "The real problem for determining what influences development in men and women is that they are called boys and girls from the day they are born," says biologist Lewontin. He cites the classic "blue, pink, yellow" experiments. When a group of observers was asked to describe newborn infants dressed in blue diapers, they were characterized as "very active." The same babies dressed in pink diapers evoked descriptions of gentleness. When the babies were wearing yellow, says Lewontin, observers "really got upset. They started to peek inside their diapers to see their sex."

It is clear that sex differences are not set in stone. The relationship between hormones and behavior, in fact, is far more intricate than was suspected until recently. There is growing evidence that it is part of a two-way system of cause-and-effect—what Lewontin calls "a complicated feedback loop between thought and action." Studies show that testosterone levels drop in male rhesus monkeys after they suffer a social setback and surge up when they experience a triumph. Other experiments indicate that emotional stress can change hormonal patterns in pregnant females, which in turn may affect the structure of the fetal brain.

By processes still not understood, biology seems susceptible to social stimuli. Ethel Tobach of New York's American Museum of Natural History cites experiments in which a virgin female rat is presented with a five-day-old rat pup. At first, her response is vague, says Tobach. "But by continuing to present the pup, you can get her to start huddling over it and assuming the nursing posture. How did that come about? There's obviously some biochemical factor that changes . . . When you have the olfactory, visual, auditory, tactile input of a five-day-old pup all those days, it can change the blood chemistry."

A more enigmatic example, says Tobach, is found in coral-reef fish: "About six species typically form a group of female fish with a male on the outside. If something happens to remove the male, the largest female becomes a functional male, able to produce sperm and impregnate females. It has been done in the lab as well as observed in the natural habitat."

The human parallels are limited. No one expects men or women to undergo spontaneous sex changes, and millennia of biological evolution aren't going to be undone by a century of social change. But it is now widely recognized that, for people as well as animals, biology and culture continually interact. The differences between men and women have been narrowing over evolutionary time, and in recent decades the gap has closed further.

Perhaps the most arresting implication of the research up to now is not that there are undeniable differences between males and females, but that their differences are so small, relative to the possibilities open to them. Human behavior exhibits a plasticity that has enabled men and women to cope with cultural and environmental extremes and has made them — by some measures — the most successful species in history. Unlike canaries, they can sing when the spirit, rather than testosterone, moves them. "Human beings," says Roger Gorski, "have learned to intervene with their hormones" — which is to say that their behavioral differences are what make them less, not more, like animals.

In Sports, "Lions vs. Tigers"
Eric Gelman

Eric Gelman, a reporter for Newsweek, *discusses the extent to which women have closed the gap that once yawned between male and female performances in athletic competition. He also points, however, to basic physiological facts that make it clear that while female athletes have narrowed this gap dramatically, they cannot close it. The sex differences really at issue in this essay, incidentally, are those of physiological strength and endurance (as manifest in athletic performance) between males and females. Compare Gelman's conclusions with those of John Nicholson in an essay later in this chapter.*

When Don Schollander swam the 400-meter freestyle in 4 minutes, 12.2 seconds at the 1964 Olympics, he set a world record and took home a gold medal. Had he clocked the same time against the women racing at the 1980 Moscow Games, he would have come in fifth. In the pool and on the track, women have closed to within 10 percent or less of the best male times, and their impressive gains raise an intriguing question: will men and women ever compete as equals?

Athletics is one area of sex-difference research that generates little scientific controversy. Physiologists, coaches and trainers generally agree that while women will continue to improve their performances, they will never fully overcome inherent disadvantages in size and strength. In sports where power is a key ingredient of success, the best women will remain a stroke behind or a stride slower than the best men.

A man's biggest advantage is his muscle mass. Puberty stokes male bodies with the hormone testosterone, which adds bulk to muscles. A girl's puberty brings her an increase in fat, which shapes her figure but makes for excess baggage on an athlete. When growing ends, an average man is 40 per cent muscle and 15 per cent fat; a woman, 23 per cent muscle, 25 per cent fat. Training reduces fat, but no amount of working out will give a woman the physique of a man. Male and female athletes sometimes try to build bigger muscles by taking anabolic steroids — artificial male hormones that stimulate muscle growth — even though physicians consider them dangerous and all major sports have outlawed them.

Bulging muscles alone can't make a woman as strong as a man. Men have larger hearts and lungs and more hemoglobin in their blood, which enables them to pump oxygen to their muscles more efficiently than women can. A man's wider shoulders and longer arms also increase his leverage, and his longer legs move him farther with each step. "A female gymnast who puts her hands on a balance beam and raises herself up is showing a lot of strength," says Barbara Drinkwater, a physiologist with the University of California at Santa Barbara, Calif. "But a woman won't throw a discus as far as a man." Although highly conditioned women can achieve pound-for-pound parity with men in leg strength, their upper-body power is usually only one-half to two-thirds that of an equally well-conditioned male athlete.

Eric Gelman, "In Sports, 'Lions vs. Tigers,'" *Newsweek* 18 May 1981.

A few sports make a virtue of anatomy for women. Extra body fat gives a female English Channel swimmer better buoyancy and more insulation from the cold, and narrow shoulders reduce her resistance in the water. As a result, women have beaten the fastest male's round-trip Channel crossing by a full three hours. In long-distance running contests, women may also be on equal footing with men. Grete Waitz's time of 2 hours, 25 minutes and 41 seconds in last year's New York City Marathon was good enough to bring her in ahead of all but 73 of the 11,000 men who finished the race. "Women tend to do better relative to men the longer the distance gets," says Joan Ullyot, author of "Running Free." "On races 100 kilometers and up, it may turn out that women are more suited to endurance than men." Under the body-draining demands of extended exertion, a woman's fat may provide her with deeper energy reserves. Satisfied that women can take the strain, the International Olympic Committee has authorized a women's marathon for the 1984 Games. In previous years the longest Olympic race for females was 1,500 meters — less than a mile.

Women athletes have dispelled the myths about their susceptibility to injury. The uterus and ovaries are surrounded by shock-absorbing fluids — far better protected than a male's exposed reproductive equipment. And the bouncing of breasts doesn't make them more prone to cancer, or even to sagging. As for psychological toughness, Penn State physiologist and sports psychologist Dorothy Harris says that "if you give a woman a shot at a $100,000 prize, you discover that she can be every bit as aggressive as a man."

Going one-on-one with a man is not the goal of most women in sports. "It's like pitting lions against tigers," declares Ullyot. "Women's achievements should not be downgraded by comparing them to men's." But as organized women's sports grow up, they will have to face up to at least one serious masculine challenge. According to Ann Uhlir, executive director of the Association for Intercollegiate Athletics for Women, when a college starts taking its women's sports program seriously, it tends to put a man in charge.

IT IS DIFFERENT FOR WOMEN

James Lincoln Collier

In this article James Lincoln Collier discusses the conclusions researchers have drawn from studies on male and female attitudes toward sexual intercourse. This essay complements and updates Carol Tavris and Carole Offir's discussion, which appears earlier in this chapter; but, unlike these authors, Collier clearly favors the biological, rather than the environmental, explanations of the causes of such differences.

"Shortly after our culture said to women, 'You may have orgasms,' it began saying, 'You *must.*'"

So states Dr. John Francis Steege, assistant professor of obstetrics-gynecology at Duke University Medical Center. Contrary to current cultural wisdom, he maintains that orgasm is not inevitably a part of sex for women; indeed, for some women it is not even terribly important.

Dr. Steege is one of a growing number of experts who are saying that sex for women should not be judged by male standards. Investigators in universities and clinics around the country have concluded that males and females do not bring all of the same needs to sex, or experience it in the same way. Although it may be true, as some researchers have reported, that there is little physical difference between male and female orgasm, its *meaning* appears to be different for a woman than for a man.

For almost two decades women have been taught that they can and should have orgasms as easily as men — indeed, more easily, because they have the capacity for multiple orgasms which men lack. Despite all this "consciousness raising," however, many women have more difficulty than men do in achieving orgasm in intercourse. According to a study by Michigan clinicians Dana Wilcox and Ruth Hager, "Our findings challenge the theory that it is pathological for a woman to be unable to experience orgasm from intercourse." They say that less than half (41.5 percent) of women regularly experience orgasm through intercourse alone, without additional stimulation. Instead, some women (33 percent) regularly choose to experience orgasm during foreplay, and a smaller percentage after intercourse.

Why *don't* the majority of women achieve orgasm in intercourse as easily as men? A number of researchers, including Wardell Pomeroy, academic dean of the Institute for the Advanced Study of Sexuality, look to evolution for an answer. So far as we know, in no other species of mammal do females experience orgasm. This is probably because male orgasm is necessary for reproduction, while female orgasm is not. According to one theory, human females have begun to evolve the capacity for orgasm for reasons not fully understood. But the development is still uneven, existing in a greater degree in some women than in others.

Whatever the cause, most women do have a higher "threshold" of orgasmic response than men. That is to say, it takes more to trigger it. Unfortunately, many

James Lincoln Collier, "It *Is* Different for Women," *Reader's Digest* January 1982.

women have come to believe that they could always be orgasmic during sex if they could only relax, or try a different technique, or *something*. As a result, says William Kephart, professor of sociology at the University of Pennsylvania, "these women feel inadequate if they don't regularly have orgasms."

All of this makes it sound as if women who have difficulty in achieving orgasm find sex frustrating. In fact, they don't. Surveys have shown repeatedly that such women can and usually do enjoy sex. One study, made at Pennsylvania State University by psychologist David Shope, discovered that a high percentage of women who didn't have orgasms felt complete relaxation following intercourse anyway.

If orgasm is not the central goal of intercourse for many women, what *is*? One thing, apparently, is a state which has been referred to as "arousal." In a study at the University of California, Prof. Uta Landy concludes that arousal is very important. "Physiologically," says Landy, "arousal seems to be a pulsing, a push, a throbbing throughout the entire pelvic region which means a readiness for intercourse. The feeling is spread much wider throughout the body than it is in men, where it is usually concentrated in the sex organ."

What men fail to understand — and find puzzling when they do — is that for many women this feeling of arousal is not just a stage on the road to orgasm, but an end in itself. For some women it is a pleasant, "tingly" experience; for others it is almost ecstatic. "It's as if I were bursting with sunshine," says one woman.

Moreover, the state of arousal is not merely physical. Feelings of affection and closeness to the sex partner are also involved. Nor does it necessarily lead to orgasm. When most men achieve a certain level of arousal, they are impelled to go to orgasm. This is not always so for women. Says Shope, "It is evident that petting techniques capable of producing a state of high sexual arousal in women do not ensure the continuation of this state in coitus." Indeed, arousal is more commonly experienced by women in petting or foreplay. When the shift to intercourse comes, in many instances the woman's arousal level may actually *drop*, rather than rise.

And yet for most women intromission — the feeling of the male inside her — constitutes an important part of sex. Most women, in fact, do not feel that the sex act is complete until this happens. According to Shope's study, desire for intromission was strong in 85 percent of the women who were orgasmic, and moderate to strong in 90 percent of the non-orgasmic ones. Even when women did not expect to achieve a climax, nearly all of them wanted intromission anyway.

"This is an interesting point," says Landy, "because, as studies show, intercourse is not necessarily the best way for a woman to achieve orgasm. It suggests that intromission has a meaning of its own for women."

Another point, long held by folk wisdom and now supported by the new studies, is that women are less promiscuous than men. With the new freedoms of the past decade, many women have felt that they ought to be as free as men to seek sex wherever they can find it. Yet it turns out that most women aren't all that interested in casual sex. According to studies by Judith Bardwick, professor of psychology at the University of Michigan, females still have fewer sex partners than do males — even though the rate of non-monogamous sexual relations among women is rising.

Researchers like sociobiologist Richard Dawkins of Oxford University in England and anthropologist Donald Symonds of the University of California at Santa Barbara have an intriguing explanation for this phenomenon, based on the different "sexual strategies" generally pursued by male and female animals throughout evolutionary history. For a male, in order to reproduce himself most successfully, and thus win the evolutionary competition with other males, the idea has been to mate with as many females as possible.

This strategy has been possible because, for males, there is little energy involved in reproduction. For females, however, a great deal of time and energy goes into producing an offspring. So the human female strategy has been to make sure that the father is sufficiently attached to her to help protect and feed the child. Therefore, she naturally prefers to have sex with somebody she believes loves and cares for her, rather than with somebody who will depart the next morning.

Whether all women — or men, for that matter — will accept these explanations of male and female sexual behavior, one thing seems abundantly clear: we must begin to rethink a lot of accepted notions about sex. For men and women, it *is* different.

THE PERILS OF PAUL, THE PANGS
OF PAULINE

Jo Durden-Smith and Diane DeSimone

This Playboy *essay is a condensed version of Jo Durden-Smith and Diane DeSimone's book,* Sex and the Brain *(1983). It contains this chapter's most comprehensive discussion of the brain-hemisphere theory—which, the authors conclude, accounts for numerous differences in intellectual skills, social behavior, and physiological vulnerabilities between males and females. Needless to say, the authors don't think that environmental conditioning tells the whole story about sex differences. Compare their conclusions with those drawn by John Nicholson, Constance Holden, and Melvin Konner in their essays elsewhere in this chapter.*

The back pages of the paper contain some amazing items these days: There's almost always something such as "GENE FOUND FOR DEPRESSION"; "CRIMINAL BEHAVIOR THOUGHT TO BE INHERITED"; "MURDERESS AQUITTED: PSYCHIATRIST POINTS TO PREMENSTRUAL TENSION"; "BRAIN CHEMICAL TIED TO SCHIZOPHRENIA." And: "IS THERE A GENE FOR MATH?"

We read the items separately, not seeing how they hang together. And so we fail to realize that, buried in those small headlines, there is a revolution going on—a revolution that will soon change, once and for all, the way we think about human behavior. . . .

What does that mean for men and women? It means that at precisely the time we're most avidly rushing to psychiatrists and other practitioners of the spirit, science is quietly announcing that the game is off, a new die is cast, the rules have changed. We're not the purely "psychological" creatures we thought we were, fraught with psychological problems that, if they are to be cured, demand psychological understanding. Instead, we are the creatures, to an extent not yet fully known, of *biological* forces. Our mood disorders, our madness and, perhaps, even our crime are biological in both origin and expression—in the brain. That goes for not only the major problems that bedevil this society—the one percent of people who suffer from schizophrenia, the five percent who are crippled by illnesses of mood, the two percent who commit almost all of the crime and the billions of dollars such aberrations cost each year. It goes for the minor problems that bedevil our families and our relationships—the mood swings of parents, the hyperactivity and aggressiveness of children, and come-and-go depressions of women and the irritability and instability of men. At the mysterious heart of *all* these things lies biology—set up by the genes, mediated by the sex hormones and expressed in a different chemistry in the ultimate home of our personality, our brain.

For the moment, then, forget psychology—all the assumptions you've learned about a mind that you inhabit and that you alone can control. Ignore the effects of the environment on who you are and the way you behave. Fix your gaze, instead, on the biological and genetic core of yourself, as a member of one sex of the human

Jo Durden-Smith and Diane DeSimone, "The Perils of Paul, the Pangs of Pauline," *Playboy* May 1982.

species — differently made, differently programed, differently wired and with a different chemical design, differently "juiced," as one scientist recently put it. For, if you do, you'll begin to see why the small newspaper headlines combine into a radically new view of men and women. You'll begin to piece together the causes of many of the misunderstandings and tensions between us. And you'll begin to understand, as science is just beginning to, why the bewildering strengths and weaknesses of each one of us, man and woman, seem to come packaged together. Why a woman's immune system is superior to a man's but more likely to attack the body it's supposed to protect. Why men, in general, are superior in math reasoning but are much more likely to be sexual deviants or psychopaths. Why women are strong in areas of communication but are preferentially attacked by phobias and depression. And why there are more males at both ends of the intellectual spectrum — more retardates but *also* more geniuses.

If you think that psychiatrists, psychologists and all those who've made a professional commitment to the effects of the environment will be horrified by this altered gaze of yours, you're right. But if you think that their spiritual father, Sigmund Freud, would be equally horrified, you're wrong. Freud treated all sorts of personalities and disorders, among them psychosomatic illnesses, schizophrenia, hysteria and depression. And he said many times that despite all his theories, one day a "constitutional predisposition" would be found to be responsible for our problems. "A special chemism," he predicted, would be discovered at their heart. And he was right. By inference and indirection, such a chemism has been found at the core of our nature as men and women. And we are at the beginning of a road through that chemism that will lead us to a full explanation of why we are differently gifted, differently protected and differently at risk. For the complete story, you'll have to wait 20 years or so; 20 years marked — if one can judge by present signs — by controversy, battle, arguments about free will and radical new approaches to education, health and the treatment of violence, mood and madness. In the meantime, here are the landmarks — and the paths that science is tracing between them.

Let's start with heart disease and heart attacks. Forty million Americans have some form of heart disease, and this year, about 1,500,000 will have heart attacks. The majority in both categories are men. "Ah-ha!" the men among you will no doubt say. "That's the environment. That's stress. Just wait until the same number of women go out into the world and start pulling the same weight that we do. They'll soon be dropping like ninepins from the effects of stress, just as *we* are."

Sorry, guys. That's almost certainly untrue. The connections between the stresses of the brain and the problems of the heart aren't well understood — and that's something you'll have to remember throughout this article, that science knows not a lot but very little. From what science *does* know, however, three things stand out. First, working women are healthier, in general, than their nonworking sisters. Second, women are protected against the most common form of heart disease by their primary sex hormones, the estrogens. And, third, they seem to respond to stress — both chemically and behaviorally — quite differently from men.

Human responses to stress are mediated by a group of brain structures known to control emotion and what scientists fondly call "the four Fs" — feeding, fleeing, fighting and . . . sex. Those structures direct the body's immediate responses to danger — the accelerated heartbeat, the heightened senses, the rush of adrenaline, the raised blood pressure, the preparation for a quick burst of energy. During stress, the hormonal mechanisms by which they do this become more or less continuously activated. A little stress isn't bad for you — it's a necessary part of life and it may, indeed, be pleasurable. But, in the long term, it can have several nasty effects. It can make the body less resistant to infections and, conceivably, to certain forms of cancer. (The dim connection between stress and the defensive immune system should be borne in mind for later.) It can cause heart disease, because the heart, among other things, is forced to work too hard. And it can so excite a center high in the brain that the heart is sent by it into a fatal overdrive — a fibrillation, a full-blown attack. Whether or not those things happen seems to depend on the individual's genetic make-up.

But it also depends on gender. So-called Type-A people — who have a chronic urgency about time and are hard-driving, competitive, extroverted and aggressive — are said to be particularly at risk from the damaging effects of stress. But it's now beginning to appear that this is true of only Type-A *males.* Studies in Sweden have recently shown that Type-A females, when solving work-related problems, simply don't show the increase in heart rate, blood pressure and adrenaline flow that Type-A males do. Even when their over-all health picture is the same, they don't have as many heart attacks.

That doesn't mean, of course, that women aren't responsive to stress. It simply means that their chemistry is different in some way. They seem to find different things stressful, and they seem to react in a different way to the stress in their environment. If there is a word that can sum up this difference in their make-up, it's emotion. Women tend to be put into stress by the emotional coloration of their lives — not by paper problems but by people and communication problems. And when they experience setback, failure or emotional pressure, they don't go into overdrive the way men do. They respond emotionally or fall back into depression. You may not like that, ladies, but it's probably a good thing. It certainly doesn't cause as much wear and tear on the body.

The next question is, *Why* should there be that over-all difference? And the answer is really anybody's guess. It probably has to do with the different evolutionary pressures that affected the development of men and women — men, the hunters and competitors for sex, were more likely to need elaborate stress mechanisms in the presence of danger; and women, the nurturers and centers of social groups, were more likely to need fine-tuned emotional responses and skills. Depression and the effects of continuous stress may be the different prices men and women pay for those legacies — an integral part of our maleness and femaleness.

That that is true — at least for poor males — is suggested by a few pieces of evidence. Scientists working with male laboratory animals have shown that dominance (sexual success and the successful maintenance of a large piece of turf) is associated with high blood pressure and hardening of the arteries, telltale signs of the effects of stress. But they've also found that the animals at the top of the heap have high levels of testosterone, the hormone most essential to maleness. The plot thickens. For it's testosterone that makes hardening of the arteries such a problem in *human* males. It causes the production of a liver protein that ties up cholesterol in the arteries' lining, causing the formation of fat deposits called plaques. The bigger those plaques, the more difficulty the heart has in pumping blood. The more difficulty the heart has, the greater the risk of heart disease.

Findings of this sort are, again, only landmarks in an otherwise empty landscape. But they make it plain that in stress, behavior, emotion, genes, sex hormones, the body and the brain are all interlinked. And they point the way toward the discovery of a more general connection between emotion and disease, the brain and the immune system. For the moment, there are only a few curious straws in this area. Laboratory animals, for example, don't get the hardening of the arteries scientists try to inflict on them if they're handled a lot — if they're loved. And married people are generally happier and healthier than unmarried ones. They have less heart disease. So it goes.

Having left the men among you deeply worried about an area in which you seem to be at a disadvantage, let's turn the tables on the women — let's move upstairs to an area in which *women* seem to be at a disadvantage. It, too, involves anxiety, and it involves an ability — mathematical-reasoning ability. Is that, too, part of a special chemism?

"There you go again," you women will no doubt say. "Everyone knows that's the environment. Girls are taught from the beginning that math is for boys. They're given no encouragement. They have no role models, no expectations, no self-confidence and no support. And a lot less is demanded of them. It's no *wonder* that they become anxious about math. And it's no wonder that they seem to be less good at it than boys."

Sorry, ladies. But that, too, is almost certainly untrue — and it surely isn't the end of the story. Do you begin to see how controversial this theorizing about the differences between men and women can get? Johns Hopkins' Camilla Persson Benbow and Julian Stanley most assuredly do. Three months after those scientists merely *suggested* that there might be real, "endogenous" differences in math ability, they were seen at a conference looking pale and haggard — drained by the often-unreasonable attacks launched against them in the wake of their December 1980 report.

"You have to understand," Benbow says softly, with a distant trace of a Scandinavian accent, "that we didn't start out looking for sex differences in mathematical ability. The Johns Hopkins Study of Mathematically Precocious Youth — S.M.P.Y. — simply conducted six talent searches in the mid-Atlantic states between 1972 and 1979. We were looking for gifted seventh and eighth graders who, though they hadn't usually been taught any higher mathematics, could still manage a very high score on the math part of the Scholastic Aptitude Test — a test designed for bright, college-bound high school seniors. What we were looking for, in other words, was a natural aptitude for mathematical reasoning. We found about 10,000 children in those six years.

"But we also found something that rather shocked us: There were more boys than girls among our kids. On the average, the boys scored much higher than the girls. And on no occasion was a girl tops on the test. Well, we were bound to ask why. So we studied the boys and girls on every variable available that could possibly account for the discrepancy — preparation in mathematics, liking for math, the encouragement given them, and so on. And we could find no difference at all —

except the one in over-all ability, mathematical-reasoning ability. Since 1979, we've looked at another 24,000 children and have found the same sex difference in ability. And we've conducted a nationwide talent search for children at the top end of the scale. We found 63 boys — and no girls."

Benbow, a striking woman in her mid-20s, is clearly still surprised, a year after the publication of her and Professor Stanley's paper, by the controversy it generated. She's reluctant to say that the chemistry governed by the sex chromosomes is at the root of that sex difference, and she would love, she says, to find an environmental difference that has been overlooked, to find it and correct it. But she quotes a follow-up study completed on a group of girls who were specially taught and specially encouraged. And even *that*, she says, seems to have made no ultimate difference. At the root, still, is the difference in mathematical-reasoning ability. When the time comes for girls to use it formally in class — in calculus, differential equations and analytical geometry, for example — they seem to fall even further behind the boys, even when they're gifted and have no anxiety about the subject.

"All this," says Benbow carefully, "suggests that there may be a biological basis to the difference, after all. And, if so, then it's likely to be connected to the male's right-hemisphere superiority in visual-spatial tasks. You see, females tend to use their stronger *left* hemisphere — their superior verbal skills — in their approach to problems. I know I do. And there's a certain level at which the verbal approach is inefficient in math — look at the way mathematicians are forced to talk to one another, via symbols on a blackboard. Now, that approach may be something that actually *suits* males. From the beginning, they're less verbally oriented than females — more oriented to things, to objects in space. They're less dependent on context. They're more abstract.

"This may help explain, too, I think, why men are overrepresented in certain disciplines in science — something we've also been studying. To be a good physicist or engineer, for example, requires not only mathematical-reasoning ability but also skill in three-dimensional visual imagery. And that probably makes most women unfit. To be a good scientist at all, in fact, seems to require a set of qualities more characteristic of men than of women — spatial ability, independence, a low social interest and an absorption in things. Let's face it, human males like to manipulate *things* — from Tinkertoys to the cosmos." She laughs. "Females are more dependent, more communicative, more sensitive to context and more interested in people. Perhaps that's why there are so many women in psychology. Like me."

How mathematical-reasoning ability and stress are interconnected may not be clear at first sight. There are, however, a number of threads that do, in fact, connect them. One can be seen intuitively, at the level of personality and problem solving: independence versus interdependence; absorption in abstract problems — things — versus absorption in people; fixated men versus emotional, communicative and less stress-prone women. Another can be seen at the level of the sex hormones. For from various bits and pieces of evidence, men's superior visual-spatial — and, hence, math — ability seems to be related to their testosterone, just as are a number of their problems in stress. Chemism lies at the heart of both and, therefore, may explain why there have been many more male composers and painters — not to mention architects and town planners — in history. Hormones, visual-spatial ability, application, abstraction. *For every strength, there is weakness, though.* Visual-spatial men are better organized on the right side of their brain, verbal women on the left. But they are both comparatively weak on the side where the other is strong.

That fact takes us deeper into the differences between us. It takes us to the embattled core of our civilization. To crime. To mood. To sudden changes in personality. To madness. And to the problems of our children.

If you've ever given a party for four-and-five-year-olds (or even 11-and-12-year-olds), you may remember that you've known instinctively that girls develop faster and are more mature than boys. They're less shy, more verbal and readier to join the group. They have puberty earlier. And, until then — to use a favorite Monty Python phrase — they're "all-round less weedy." The reason, as you probably sensed at the time, has nothing to do with environment or with the circumstances of your party. It is that boys, *from the beginning*, are more precarious — an altogether more iffy proposition — than girls.

To begin at the beginning: Sperm carrying the male sex chromosome seem to swim faster and have more staying power than sperm carrying the female sex chromosome. That's good. And between 120 and 140 males are conceived for every 100 females. Also good. From there on in, though, it's downhill all the way. More males are spontaneously aborted during pregnancy, and although they retain a slight edge at the time of birth — 106 to 100 — the decline continues. More males than females are born dead. Thirty percent more males than females die in the first months of life. And 70 percent of all birth defects are associated mainly with males. The result is that by the time of puberty, the head start achieved by the male sperm has been lost. And the population of men and women has become about equal — at a considerable cost to males.

The reason is, again, anybody's guess. Some sociobiologists say it has to do with the higher value of the male in a polygamous species. Whatever the ultimate cause, though, there is an immediate one much nearer to hand. For the fact is, the male has to go through many more elaborate transformations in the womb than the female. More can go wrong, so more males die in the womb. And, as a result of all the hormonal toings-and-froings to which they're exposed, they are born less mature, less sturdy and less ready for the world than girls. Like all premature babies, they're more at risk after birth — both in the body and in the brain.

For example, the slightest brain damage — occurring during or after birth — has a far more debilitating effect on boys than it does on girls. What's more, it virtually always strikes boys in the hemisphere in which they're less well organized — the left. It's not male visual-spatial abilities, secure in their right hemisphere, that suffer. It's language skills and language controls, in the left. Boys' left hemisphere, in other words, faces a sort of double indemnity. And the result is that they're four or five times as likely to suffer from language disorders and disabilities as any girl. Boys are more likely (five to one) to stutter when the left hemisphere loses control during speech. They're more likely to be austistic (four to one), often with a complete absence of left-hemisphere language. They're more likely to be what's called an *idiot savant* (figures unknown) — language-damaged and incapacitated but with some narrow, brilliant mathematical skill. (Ah-ha!) And boys are more likely to suffer from two so-called developmental disorders: aphasia, or extreme difficulty learning to talk (five to one); and dyslexia — extreme difficulty with reading and writing (up to six to one). Nelson Rockefeller had dyslexia, so we know the company's good. And, recently, Albert Galaburda of Boston's Beth Israel Hospital found direct evidence that at least one type of dyslexia is caused by early language-area brain damage—damage, when it happens in girls, that has less effect on their more developed and better organized left hemisphere.

But hang on, guys—your problems with your left hemisphere only *start* here. And those problems strike, in a very mysterious way, right to the heart of the male personality. Men commit almost all the violent crime, and the so-called antisocial personality at the root of most of it seems to be caused by poor functioning of the left hemisphere. Men are the sexual deviates—the pedophiles, the fetishists, the exhibitionists and the homosexual sadists. Here, too, something has gone wrong with the way the left hemisphere governs behavior. For *all* the other problems that afflict men and boys much more than they do women and girls, it's almost certainly the same old left-hemisphere story. Hyperactivity, alcoholism, mania and early-onset schizophrenia: left hemisphere. And if you think those things don't concern you personally, you're wrong. Hyperactivity, for example, affects more than 2,000,000 boys in this country. It's not a problem that is, by any means, always outgrown—hyperactive children often grow up to become alcoholics or child abusers, hot-tempered, aggressive and unable to keep a job. As for schizophrenia, you should know this: For every full-blown schizophrenic in this society, there are between three and ten more walking around with lesser but related disorders.

Your first reaction to that news may be, "Yes, but that really *is* the environment, isn't it? That's too many toys, too much stimulation. It's diet. It's a terrible home. It's crazy parents. It's a bad upbringing." Unfortunately, it simply isn't that easy. That it isn't brings us right back to the special chemism we've been talking about all along, the chemistry that distinguishes man and woman. First, those largely male disorders can't be cured by psychiatric hand-holding methods—"understanding" the patient's problem or the environment that "caused" it. Second, the only therapy that ultimately works on such disorders is the use of drugs or anti-hormones that alter the chemistry of the brain. And, third, for all those abnormalities, scientists have recently found just what Freud predicted for his "mental" illnesses—a constitutional predisposition, a *genetic* element.

"The genetic studies," says psychiatrist Pierre Flor-Henry, "have looked not just at how much these things run in families. "They've looked at identical twins. And—most important—they've looked at what happens in *adoption.* Is a child, adopted early, more likely to follow the pattern of his real parents than the pattern of his adoptive parents—in crime, hyperactivity, schizophrenia, and so on? The answer is yes, he is. It's not just the environment, then. Nature, a predisposition, is at work in some way we don't yet fully understand. Equally important, there's also a *connection* between some of them, a genetic connection. For example, alcoholism, hysteria and antisocial personality seem to cluster in the same families."

Flor-Henry is a slight, dapper Franco-Hungarian in his 40s: clinical professor at the University of Alberta, director of admission services at the Alberta Hospital and a man who spends much of his research time trying to pull together into one over-all picture all that is now being discovered about the two brain hemispheres, the chemistry and the disorders of men and women. "There's not much to go on," he says. "We still know so little. But genes are responsible for the body's chemistry.

So the predisposition is a chemical one, perhaps triggered into expression by damage of some kind or by an event or series of events in the world. It's not guaranteed. But the damage or the events, if they happen, may preferentially affect and alter the chemical organization, in males, of their brain's weaker left hemisphere.

"And the genetic defect then comes into its own, resulting in behavior that's deranged or unstable in one way or another. The behavior—and the brain—can then be treated only with drugs that, either directly or indirectly, put the left hemisphere back into balance. In schizophrenia, that involves drugs affecting the supply of a brain chemical called dopamine. In hyperactivity, it involves drugs that affect the dopamine supply in a *reverse* direction. In sexual deviance—and, perhaps, in antisocial personality, violent crime, it involves drugs that block the action of the main male sex hormone."

If you men are thinking that your comparative left-hemisphere weakness makes you a variable, deviant, hit-or-miss sex, then you're right. Nature doesn't seem to have taken out much insurance on you—especially where the social and verbal left hemisphere is concerned. You are less well protected against your own excesses, just as in stress. If it's any consolation, Flor-Henry believes it's because you evolved as the sex-*seeking* gender. He thinks that the human *right* hemisphere developed in such a way that visual-spatial skills were linked in it to mood, movement and sexual fulfillment. And because the male was the one to go after sex—rather than just being able to sit and wait for it—the organization of the male right hemisphere became particularly pronounced. Males became lopsided—they put all their eggs in the right-hemisphere basket. Females evolved in a more balanced way. Because females were the pursued rather than the pursuers, they were able to develop verbal skills and verbal controls in the left hemisphere that were much more stable, secure and efficient. That goes some way toward explaining why women tend not to become psychopaths and violent criminals. Women, remember, don't go into over-drive when under stress. They tend to become depressed. And their pattern of crime is quite different. They don't act out against people. Antisocial males, on the other hand, virtually *always* attack people. And Flor-Henry thinks they're out of control of the verbal and social left hemisphere. Instead, they're exaggerated, out-on-a-limb, right-hemisphere males using all their visual and spatial skills for aggression.

If this evolutionary dispensation seems profoundly unfair to you males, then all we can do is remind you of the delicate balance between strengths and weaknesses. In the words of an old joke, "With a Bernstein diamond comes the Bernstein curse." And the same rule goes for women. This time, though, they're at risk somewhere else—just where males are strong. In the right hemisphere.

There are three things you can say with certainty about depressed people. One, they don't jump around. Two, they tend to lose all sexual interest. And, three, they're mostly women. Every year, 40,000,000 Americans suffer, to one degree or another, from depression. Two thirds of them are women.

Of course, you can sing the old song about the environment. "Girls are taught from the beginning not to express their anger. They turn their anger inward. When they become women, they find themselves in a rotten, male-dominated society. Men don't give them what they want. They stifle and ignore all women's emotional subtlety. No wonder women are depressed."

The last part of the song is probably true. And, of course, there *are* real environmental causes for depression. If you've set your heart on being a concert pianist and can't even manage *Chopsticks*, you're likely to be depressed. And if you've lost a father, mother, husband, wife, child or friend, you shouldn't be expected to be happy. But that still doesn't explain why so many more women than men are afflicted by a disorder that affects mood, movement and sex drive in their right hemisphere. And it certainly doesn't explain why, though nothing on the surface of a woman's life is wrong, she can suddenly be sent into a terrible tail spin. Psychological explanations of that sort of depression are useless, and such psychiatric treatment of it is, at best, a waste of money and of time — women may simply become even more entrenched in their despair. No, the only way to understand so-called *vital* depression (which women have to endure five times more often than men), as well as phobias (which cripple women at least twice as often), is through women's chemism — genes, hormones and brain chemistry. Again, it lies right at the heart of the female personality. And it can tell us a lot about the human female's emotional vulnerability, her more general swings in mood that break up relationships and leave men feeling left out, unsympathetic and confused.

"Depression and the phobias obviously hang together," says Flor-Henry. "They attack the hemisphere in which the organization of the female brain is more precarious — the right hemisphere. The phobias — they should be called the panics — are panics about heights, open and closed spaces, water, and so on. And they obviously have to do with mood, movement and visual-spatial skill — right hemisphere. The same things are affected in vital depression — *plus*, of course, sexual drive. Again, right hemisphere. There are two other things, too, that yoke them together. First, the only *really* effective treatment for both is with antidepressants — not Valium or Librium but two classes of drugs that have no effect at all, except maybe an unpleasant one, on normal people. And, second, both seem to involve a genetic predisposition, just as the predominantly *male* disorders do. Not much is yet known about the phobias. But work done in Belgium has shown that adopted children with depression are more likely to have that depression in common with their *real* parents rather than with their adoptive parents.

"So," says Flor-Henry, spreading his fingers on the table. "Genetic. Biological. Chemical. Right hemisphere. We don't know how those things interconnect. And we don't know how they relate to the milder forms of depression and mood disorder in women. My guess is, though, that all those things are part of one evolutionary package — affecting the weaker right hemisphere and involving the sex hormones."

The sex hormones — here they are again. They're somewhere at the core of a man's response to stress, and they're also at the heart of the chemistry of a woman's moods. The evidence isn't hard to find. It comes from routine parts of ordinary life — from puberty, childbirth, the menstrual cycle, menopause, the pill. And the upshot of it is this: Alter the level of a woman's sex hormones, in large or even in small ways, and she'll be likely to suffer from subtle and not-so-subtle changes in mood and personality. Sometimes, she'll no longer be in control of her own personality — her hormones will be.

We haven't space here to go into the problems of puberty and menopause, but you should know this: About seven percent of new mothers suffer for weeks, even months, from severe depression — complete with loss of sexual interest — at precisely the time when their hormone levels have been abruptly altered by the births of their children. And an unknown percentage of women on the pill report a bewildering variety of side effects, including lowered sex drive, irritability and, yes, depression. Those things are all too often looked on — by lover, husband, doctor, even the woman herself — as psychological in origin. Her responsibility. And they can lead to the breakup of relationships and marriages. How many new mothers have you known whose husbands left them within 15 months of the baby's birth?

Then there's premenstrual tension. Before you guys walk away or chuckle, you should know that you, too, may have your "time of the month" — that's how new this science is — and it may be marked by the same irritability and tension. If it exists, however, it seems also to be unpredictable and irregular. And that means that you'll have to abandon all your old assumptions about "women's problems." Who, after all, would you want doing skilled and responsible jobs — flying a plane, performing brain surgery, and so on? Someone whose switches in mood are predictable or someone whose switches in mood are *un*predictable?

British psychiatrist Katharina Dalton believes that premenstrual tension affects four out of ten women to some extent, and for eight days — before and during menstruation — it *seriously* affects the life of one of those four. Being on the pill, says Dalton, actually makes the condition worse. Not only do the symptoms include brooding, lethargy, depression, loss of memory and emotional control; they also include, she says, an increased incidence of quarrels, accidents, suicides, baby battering and crime.

In November 1981, Dalton appeared in court as a witness for the defense of one of her patients, a 29-year-old English barmaid named Sandie Smith. You may have read about that case, for its implications haven't gone unnoticed by the press. Smith had had 30 previous convictions — for arson and assault, among other offenses — and she was already on probation for having stabbed another barmaid to death in 1980. This time, she was charged with threatening to kill a policeman. Dalton, however, was able to demonstrate that all her crimes were connected by a 29-day cycle — and by premenstrual tension. And Smith was given three years' probation.

The very next day, November tenth, the very same defense — premenstrual tension — was brought up by Dalton in the case of another woman, Christine English, who had had an argument with her lover and had run over him with a car. English was discharged — conditional for a year — after pleading guilty to manslaughter. The court ruled that at the time of her crime, she had "diminished responsibility."

Those are examples of where the new discoveries about the chemistry of men and women can lead, and there's no doubt that the same defense will soon be used in a case in the United States. It will call into question, in a public way, everything we now presume about personal responsibility and the effects of the environment. Is a woman suffering from premenstrual tension responsible for what she does? Is a man responsible for his reaction to stress? Is a male criminal responsible for his crimes or does the responsibility lie with his testosterone level and his lopsided brain organization?

These are revolutionary new questions. Revolutionary in law. Revolutionary in the home. Revolutionary in the way we think about ourselves and about one another. And if we are to find answers for them, we will have to think very carefully, not only about the chemistry of the brain but also about our place in nature and the way in which our biological evolution may now be at odds with our cultural evolution.

Take phobias, for example. They usually appear in women only during the child-bearing years. And, you'll notice, they involve fears of everything that might have been dangerous in the environment in which we evolved — heights, open and closed spaces, water, snakes, and so on. Such phobias weren't a bad idea then — especially if you had to protect a child.

What about depression? Well, for most of our evolutionary history, isolated women could not survive. They *had* to be interdependent members of social groups. Indeed, they were the necessary glue that held those groups together. A woman's tendency to depression, then, may have been a mechanism that reinforced her interdependence and accelerated her back into the group by producing the cry for help. In today's society, of course, there aren't many close-knit social groups. There is a cry for help, but no help comes — and we have a major problem with depression.

Each one of the landmarks in this science of men and women brings us nearer to a picture of the whole landscape of ourselves. In 1981, for example, scientists located for the first time an actual gene that they think is involved in depression. And it's in a very odd place: It's either very close to or actually among a group of genes that govern the development of the human immune system — our defense against diseases. And it's the neighbor of a gene that's responsible, when expressed, for masculinizing female fetuses in the womb.

Maleness and femaleness, mental illness, hormones, hemispheres and diseases: This is the final mystery and our final port of call. What is there at the heart of our nature that gives us not only different strengths and weaknesses but a proneness to such different diseases? How can that be added to the picture?

One thing about organic diseases — they're physical, not "environmental." Either you get them or you don't. So there probably will be no complaints about this part of our story — except, perhaps, from you guys. Because here, again, you're at a disadvantage. You're just not as well protected as women. As if dying in the womb, being born "weedy" and maturing more slowly weren't enough, you're more likely to have inherited one of the whole rash of diseases from which the human female is shielded — including diseases in which your immune system doesn't work properly or hardly works at all. You're also generally more at risk from the whole sea of viruses and bacteria in which we swim.

The truth is, the male's immune system is just not as good as the female's. The reason (here we come to chemism again) has something to do with his Y sex chromosome and his main male sex hormone, testosterone. Little is known about this yet — there are few landmarks in this particular part of the landscape. But testosterone, when given from the outside, seems to act in all humans as a depressor of their immune system; estrogen, the female sex hormone, seems to have the reverse effect. Testosterone, too, is probably also responsible for the fact that men don't produce as much immune-globulin M — a blood protein important to the body's defenses — as women do. That is part of the reason men are more likely to contract such illnesses as hepatitis, respiratory ailments and legionnaire's disease. Estrogen seems to beef up production of immune-globulin M — and it seems, in some mysterious way, to be involved in a process by which a woman's immune defenses, like her hormone levels, actually fluctuate during the menstrual cycle.

The question, of course, is, Why should men be worse off — less well defended — than women? Why should the person standing next to you have a superior immune system, modulated and monitored by her sex hormones? The answer is — and she may not like it — babies. When a woman becomes pregnant, she has to do something truly amazing. For nine months, she has to support inside herself, and *not reject*, as she would a graft, a bundle of tissue that is antigenically different from hers, because of the father's contribution to its genetic make-up. At the same time, she has to protect herself *and* this bundle of tissue against any infections. How does she do that amazing thing? No one really knows. But, to do it, she must have inherited something that works for her throughout her life, a much more sophisticated immune system than any man's, one capable of finer tuning. That is likely to be the gift of her two X chromosomes. On them, she has a double set of immune-regulating genes.

End of story? Not quite. Having been evenhanded with men and women throughout this article, we can't quite leave it here. The moral throughout, for men and women, is that for every advantage, there's a disadvantage; for every plus, there's a minus. And the case of the female immune system is no exception. So efficient is it that it sometimes becomes *overefficient* and attacks the body it's supposed to be protecting. Women suffer much more than men from the so-called autoimmune diseases — from such well-known ones as multiple sclerosis, juvenile-onset diabetes and rheumatoid arthritis to even more mysterious ones, such as Graves' disease, in which the glands, the hormones, the brain and behavior are all affected. The most interesting — and most mysterious — disease in this last category is one called systemic lupus erythematosus (S.L.E.). And it's worth looking at S.L.E. just for a moment, because it suggests how intricately intermeshed the chemistry at the heart of personality is. And it shows, in a sense, how men and women can help each other.

"Systemic lupus affects about 500,000 people in this country, more than 450,000 of them women," says Robert Lahita, a leading S.L.E. researcher and assistant professor of immunology at The Rockefeller University in New York. "It's often extremely hard to diagnose. And it produces in a percentage of people many of the symptoms of depression, obsessional neurosis or schizophrenia. One of the few *visible* symptoms — and it doesn't always occur — is a rash on the cheeks, which in the 19th Century was thought to make the face look wolflike. That's why it's called *lupus* — the Latin for wolf. Basically, it's a disease in which the body mounts an attack on the genetic and protein-making machinery inside the cells of its own tissues.

"Now, why is this disease so extraordinarily interesting? Well, first, because it may be brought on by *stress*, and there's some evidence that it flares up after emotional upsets. So stress and the brain are involved from the beginning. Second, males born with *two* X chromosomes, as well as their usual Y, can get it more often than normal males. Third, women who have it are made much worse when on the pill; it usually starts at puberty, with few cases after menopause, and its symptoms are often aggravated during menstruation. So the female sex hormones are obviously involved.

"It's the abnormal female-hormone pattern that we've been investigating at Rockefeller. And what we've found out is that two things seem to have gone profoundly wrong in these S.L.E. patients. Their estrogen is being processed in a very odd way: They're making too many by-products that have strong hormonal effects and too few by-products that don't have hormonal effects but *do* seem to act as chemical messengers in the brain. In a sense, they're making too little brain-active estrogen.

At the same time, though, they may have much less active *testosterone* than they should have. And the approach through testosterone looks like it may be the best treatment we can offer for this mysterious disease. Stress, emotion, sex chromosomes, sex hormones, a deranged immune system and mental disorder — who knows what truths about men and women the study of S.L.E. will help uncover? But, for the moment, the irony is that to treat it in women, doctors will soon be borrowing from men something that lies at the root of *their* response to stress, their left-brain weakness and their immune inferiority."

Borrowing. It is this, perhaps, that gives the gathering science of men and women its special interest. What is it, for example, that makes women more sensitive to pain than men? What is it that makes their brains more responsive to stimuli than men's? What is it that makes men's — but not women's — blood coagulate when they're given aspirin? Perhaps these principles can be borrowed from one sex and given to the other. Perhaps, above all, whatever mysterious principle allows women to live longer than men can *also* be borrowed.

As 20th Century men and women, we're at the beginning of a new age. For the first time, science has tools delicate enough to probe the central mysteries of our behavior and our personality. And, in a sense, all the separate disciplines of science are beginning to come together into one — the science of men and women. Already, that science is burrowing at the roots of madness, stress, mood and lethal physical and mental disorders. And, in the process, it is bringing back from the vast continent of its general ignorance news that all too often we don't want to hear. As is usual with science, that news is both good and bad. Good because it promises new treatments and new cures — and a gradual abandonment of the long-haul tinkering of psychiatry. Bad because it will force us to alter radically the way we think about ourselves — about our minds, our personal responsibility, our free will.

It is also bringing back news that we're going to have to face sooner or later about our separate inheritances as men and women. The news is that we're far older than we think we are. And who we are today is simply the current expression of the long history of our coming to this place. We were, and still are, designed by nature for the purposes of that travel, purposes that are still reflected in our strengths and weaknesses alike. Women are still protected for the purpose of motherhood — whether or not, as individuals, they want to have children. Men are still geared to be hunters and sex seekers — whether or not, as individuals, they hunt and seek sex. Men are also less stable and more various than women. "They're the sex through which nature experiments," says Flor-Henry. "In the large scale of things, you see, individual males don't matter very much. They're throwaways. So that has left nature free to experiment with them. That's why there are more sexual deviants among men. That's why there are more mental retardates among men. And that's why there are more *geniuses* among men."

Pluses and minuses — they belong together at the heart of Freud's special chemism in men and women, making us complementary and necessary to each other. Neither is better, neither is worse. It is not a competition, and we have to learn to understand that. "I think it's rather unfair," says Camilla Benbow, "that when men have a problem, everybody's willing to accept the fact that it's genetic, it's brain damage, it's biological. But when women have a problem, oh, no, it can't be any of those things. It's the environment. I think that's unreasonable."

Tired of Arguing About Biological Inferiority?

Naomi Weisstein

Naomi Weisstein, a professor of psychology at the State University of New York at Buffalo and a founding member of the Chicago Women's Liberation Union, has long been an influential figure in the contemporary feminist movement. In this Ms. essay, she launches a formidable attack on longstanding biological assumptions about male aggression and dominance throughout the primate world, assumptions that have served as a basis for the conclusion that human males are genetically programmed to dominate and control their social orders. Contrast Weisstein's arguments about male dominance and aggression with those of David Gelman, Jo Durden-Smith and Diane DeSimone, and Melvin Konner in other essays in this chapter.

In the past 15 years, primatologists, many of them women like Thelma Rowell, Jane Lancaster, Alison Jolly, Dian Fossey, Jane Goodall, and Biruté Galdikas, have found that female status in the primate world is often high, ranging from assertive to clearly dominant.

"By concentrating on prosimians [for instance, lemurs and indri], one can argue that female dominance is the primitive and basic condition, for among all the social lemurs ever studied, this is so," says anthropologist Sarah Blaffer Hrdy in her delightful and brilliant tour through female primate behavior, *The Woman That Never Evolved* (Harvard University Press). Alison Jolly's *Lemur Behavior: A Madagascar Field Study* (University of Chicago Press) describes dominance in a prosimian. Females grab food from males, push them out of the way (to "displace them," they often don't even push — males just get up and leave if a female approaches), and hit them upside the head when they get cranky. Not that males don't play "typical" aggressive games. They wave their tails at each other in "stink fights," establishing a threat hierarchy presumably by who smells the worst. The females couldn't care less. A female will "bound up to the dominant male (established by the stink wars), snatch a tamarind pod from his hand, cuffing him over the ear in the process." Similar female dominance is observed in other more advanced species — from squirrel monkeys in South and Central America (New World monkeys, still fairly primitive) to the talapoin in Africa (an Old World monkey, not very primitive).

Perhaps more interesting than out-and-out female dominance is the peaceable kingdom of the monogamous primates who share child-rearing. Marmoset fathers carry their offspring except when suckling. A siamang father carries his offspring after the first year of their lives. Defense is also usually shared. One of the more fascinating aspects of monogamous primate life is the duetting, or combined territorial calls of the harmonious pair. In the early morning in the forests of Malaysia, a female gibbon will begin her hour's long great call with her mate supplying backup

Naomi Weisstein, "Tired of Arguing about Biological Inferiority?," Ms. November 1982.

vocals. As distinct from more hierarchical species, fights among mates are rarely observed (although pairs are intensely territorial and do attack invaders). Rather, monogamous primates seem to spend a great deal of time just digging each other, grooming, hugging, and huddling together. Interestingly, sex is relatively infrequent, a corrective to the widespread caveman theory—argued, for instance, by Donald Johanson and Maitland Edey in *Lucy* (Simon & Schuster)—that human females abandoned estrus cycles and developed continuous sexual receptivity in order to keep the male monogamous and faithful.

Monogamy is not infrequent in primates, from some prosimians (for example, indri) all the way up to the lesser apes, gibbons, and siamangs. Many species are downright romantic. Titi monkey mates will sit for hours pressed close together, their tails entwined; male marmosets will patiently feed their mates (as will 14 species of New World monkeys).

Even among the "classics," the hierarchal species of Old World monkeys like baboons and macaques, the picture has changed. While every male member of a troop of Amboseli baboons outranks every female member, each has a specific social position that depends on the rank of the *mother*. Knowing the rank of the mother, claims Glenn Hausfater (as quoted in Hrdy), allows you to predict much of an Amboseli baboon's daily life: its diet, the amount of spare time spent foraging and resting, even the average number of parasite ova emitted in a stool (an indication of the quality of the food it gets)—as well as its ability to displace other animals, and the amount of time it will be groomed, deferred to, or harassed—all indications of "dominance." With Japanese macaques, the social organization revolves around grandmothers, mothers, daughters, and sisters. The highest-ranking or "alpha" male outranks the highest ranking female in terms of specific behaviors like displacing others, or taking their food, but his power requires acceptance from influential females.

The emerging picture, then, for females in the primate world, is almost diametrically opposed to what is commonly believed. Female primate behavior is tough, assertive, and socially central. But—here is where interpretation comes in—the variations described are *between* species, and it is possible that each species inherits its specific social behavior. If so, humans, by extension, could be argued to have inherited a rare and virulent form of male dominance. What is more interesting, therefore, is to go back over the data and examine the variations *within* species or between closely related ones. Here, variations in social behavior will most likely be environmental, not genetic.

Among a group of Japanese macaques (Arashiyama west) imported to Texas, the original "alpha" female was deposed by a middle-ranking female and her female relations, reported Harold Gouzoules in *Primates*. A new dominance hierarchy was established and the former alpha and her kin were lowered in rank. Similarly, peasant revolt was reported for a troop of savanna baboons, where the once dominant females were pushed to the bottom of the hierarchy. Parallel rebellions have been observed in a variety of other baboon and macaque species.

These are important data. The overthrow of lineages in hierarchical Old World monkeys upsets the sociobiological belief that dominance or other specific behavioral traits are fixed by the genes. What really seems to be inherited is a lot of political acumen plus the specific social structure of rank. When, through politics, this structure is overturned, behavior turns with it. These data indicate that what's in the genes is not a *specific* social behavior like dominance, but a *general* social understanding: an ability to figure out when to strut your stuff, when to rebel, and when to lie low. (Upsets in rank also suggest that among monkeys, submission is not gladly borne. That's a very different message from the idea that an animal is "naturally" submissive, as some sociobiologists want us to believe.)

The rise and fall of lineages within a generation means that dominance *per se* is not inherited. So do the facts of sexual selection, which turn out to be more complex than previously believed. For instance, a stock-in-trade of comic-book biology is the most tyrannical male winning out in the mating season, thereby reproducing his own shady character and eventually making it a species-wide trait. But observations show that among such species as chimps, females often neglect the most dominant male (as established in threat or fight hierarchies) in favor of the more sociable and less disruptive males. Since rape is virtually unknown among nonhuman primates (subadult orangutans appear to be the one exception), this means the most dominant male doesn't necessarily get the breeding advantage.

Dominance would thus appear to be neither a fixed trait (that is, one always expressed because it is "inherited") nor one assured through the process of sexual selection. But this conclusion applies to individual animals. How about whole sexes? Here, too, there is some reason to believe that dominance can depend just as much on the environment as on the genes. Perhaps the most impressive example of a turnabout in male behavior is in a species of monogamous langur on the Mentawei islands off the coast of Sumatra. All other known langurs are polygamous, highly aggressive, and male dominant (although here, too, as with other Old World monkeys, dominant males are transient and females form the coherent social nucleus of the troop). Life for most langurs is hell. Females fight each other; males kill each other. By contrast, however, the Mentawei island langurs appear to exhibit the harmonious relations of monogamous pair bonds.

What has happened? Since they are genetically so close to their warring cousins, something in the environment of these langurs has radically altered their behavior. The speculation is that human hunting pressure drove the Mentawei island langurs into the protection of monogamy. But what is more important than *why* they got there is *that* they got there. If nearly the same genes produce male tyrants in one environment and gentle companions in another, then genes alone don't determine these specific behaviors in primates. What behaviors will be expressed may depend, in much larger part than previously thought, on what primates are faced with, *not* what they're born with.

The evidence is piling up. Females are generally assertive and central to many primate social organizations. Relations between sexes can change radically with changes in the environment. All these observations should figure critically in the contemporary view of male and female "nature"; and yet, they usually don't. The data come in, but much contemporary evolutionary theory doesn't change. Why?

It is important to understand how profoundly, pervasively, and totally, bias can affect something as purportedly "scientific" as biology. You need much more than evidence to bring down as cherished a notion as male dominion. Whenever privilege is at stake, theories justifying privilege will linger on well after the evidence has overturned them.

It isn't necessarily a conscious conspiracy. Rather, the new data are not acknowledged, or they are treated as trivial, or appropriate implications from them are overlooked. The data don't act to influence the theories, and so the theories remain the same.

This is nowhere more comically evident than in the strangely Victorian accounts of the evolution of human female sexuality. The human female orgasm, according to Donald Symons's 1979 book, *The Evolution of Human Sexuality* (Oxford), is a "byproduct of selection for male orgasm." (And Symons's work was hailed by zoologist E.O. Wilson as "the most thorough and persuasive account of human sexual behavior thus far that incorporates a professional understanding of sociobiology.") Symons claims that women have orgasms as a service to men, not because orgasms would be independently pleasurable and useful to women. Furthermore, orgasms are not assumed to be a part of our evolutionary history and thus found in lower primates as well. As David Barash also writes in *Sociobiology and Behavior* (Elsevier), "The female orgasm seems to be unique to humans."

Since females don't ejaculate, orgasm *is* harder to document in them. But since the late 1960s (well before the Symons and Barash works were published), females in a number of species — rhesus monkeys, stumptail macaques (Suzanne Chevalier-Skolnikoff has provided a wealth of data here), Japanese macaques, orangutans, chimps, baboons — have been observed during sexual activity doing something that really could be nothing else. At a certain point they clutch their partners (frequently, other females), freeze, then pant, moan, open their mouths in a particular way, and make involuntary spasmodic body gestures. Maybe they're faking it? Actual physiological measurements in laboratory studies performed by Frances Burton show that rhesus monkeys go through at least three similar stages of the four that Masters and Johnson describe for women.

I would suggest that difficulty in establishing orgasm among lower female primates has nothing to do with the evidence and everything to do with the androcentric bias that can't imagine why females of any species would develop orgasmic capability independent of males. Sexuality still means male-defined sexuality. (After all, it wasn't until Masters and Johnson's pioneering studies of sexuality in the human female that we ourselves went beyond the male-defined notions. It is hardly surprising that behavioral biology hasn't got there yet.)

Perhaps the most telling example of bias concerns the famous juvenile female, Imo, a Japanese macaque living with her troop at Koshima Islet. Scientists provisioned the troop there with sweet potatoes. Imo discovered that washing sweet potatoes got the sand off. Her discovery quickly spread among the other juniors in the troop, who then taught their mothers, who in turn, taught their infants. Adult males never learned it. Next, scientists flung grains of wheat in the sand to see what the troop would do. Rather than laboriously picking the wheat out of the sand grain by grain, Imo discovered how to separate the wheat from the sand in one operation. Again this spread from Imo's peers to mothers and infants, and, again, adult males never learned it. The fact that these Japanese macaques had a rudimentary culture has been widely heralded. But what are we to make of the *way* culture spread in this troop?

If Imo had been male, we would never have heard the end of the "inventive" capacities of primate males, and since generalization spreads like prairie fire when the right sex is involved, no doubt their role in the evolution of tool use and — why not?—language as well. But the urge to grand theory withers when females are the primary actors, and when the task relates to food—at least food without killing. Imo has been described as "precocious" and left at that. (Precocious, indeed! How would you get the sand out of wheat?)

The lesson of Imo's fate is important. Bias is as much a matter of what is put into theory as what is observed in the first place.

So what does primate biology imply—apart from bias—about our human possibilities? When we look at all the data, and try to interpret them without androcentric bias, what do we have?

"Primates live in pairs, harems, unisex bands, multimale troops, as solitaries, as flexible communities that group and split, and as small subunits which attach to and disengage from very large associations. Females can be dominant, subordinate, equal, or not interested. Virtually every known social system except polyandry (one female, several males) is represented," writes Blaffer Hrdy. That means we belong to an order remarkable for its flexibility, its capacity to adapt to changing environments, needs, and ideas. Except for one species of baboon around the horn of Africa, females are not subordinate in the primate world to anything like the degree intimated by mainstream behavioral biology. Indeed if we derive the meaning of the word "natural" from lower primates, we must conclude that human female subjugation is anything but natural. It is an abomination on nature.

This *does* leave us with a problem, however. If biology tells us that female subjugation is unnatural, how did we get into the patriarchal mess we're in?

Enter Man the Hunter. It has been argued that humans evolved in especially murderous, male-dominant ways because of the exigencies of our particular prehistory. "We are uniquely human even in the noblest [sic] sense because for untold millions of years, we alone killed for a living," writes Robert Ardrey in his 1976 apologia for male privilege, *The Hunting Hypothesis* (Atheneum). But, popular as this view is, it is as wrong as the biological view of male domination. Humans started out small, uncoordinated, with crude tools and a rudimentary language. "A more vulnerable state for a hominid, fresh from the boondocks, in competition with the full paid-up carnivores of the grasslands is hard to imagine" writes John Napier in criticizing Ardrey's statement. "There is absolutely no evidence," said Richard Leakey in a recent televison interview, "that we became human through hunting." "Up until very recent times," he explained, "there's no record at all of human aggression. If you can't find [it] in the prehistoric record, why claim it's there?"

In fact, it's more likely that it was Woman the Gatherer who led the procession down the evolutionary pike. The stone tools found with fossil evidence from some 2 million years ago are small and crude. The most damage these could have done would have been to chop roots into small tough salads, and the evidence overwhelmingly points to gritty roots and tubers as our primary diet for the millions of years we ranged over the dry and inhospitable African savannas. Females would have been under most pressure to gather these roots and tubers because they had to provide not only for themselves but for their young. Anthropologist Nancy Tanner, in her book *On Becoming Human* (Cambridge University Press), argued that mothers and young, learning and gathering in a social environment of growing cognitive and communicative proficiency, were the central actors in our evolution. (Suggestive of Imo's talents, chimp females use food-gathering tools with greater frequency than males—as is also described by William McGrew in *The Great Apes*). According to Tanner (and to Adrienne Zihlman in a recent article in *Signs*), socializing, communicating females took us into the present.

It is now thought likely that the subjugation of women did not start until some 12,000 years ago when hunting and gathering were replaced with domesticated plants and animals. Current hunter-gatherer societies (for example, the !Kung and the Mbuti) give us some idea of how we may have lived in much of our human history; and in these societies, women are most fully equal to men and often supply the major portion of food. But as anthropologist Eleanor Leacock has shown in *Myths of Male Dominance* (Monthly Review Press), even where women aren't the main food-getters (for instance, in the hunting-fishing-and-trapping Montagnais-Naskapi of the Labrador Peninsula), equality between the sexes still prevails. Indeed, Leacock has argued that equality persisted well into early horticulture, and anthropologist Connie Sutton dates the subjugation of women to the development of the state.

Wherever women's troubles started, hunter-gatherers are of utmost importance to our understanding of our genetic legacy. They tell us that male dominance is not in our genes. It is not something we inherited in becoming human, along with the big brain and the small canines. It emerged afterward. It is a specific *cultural legacy*.

But culture carries with it a capacity to change it, and this is the really awesome part of our evolutionary story. Male dominance is one kind of cultural legacy. The vision of a just and equal society is another. What biology has bequeathed to us in those millions of years of gathering on the plains is the capacity to choose between specific cultures, to evaluate our lives, to intervene in our own fate. Biology has provided us with the ability to explore our possibilities, to change what is in the present and try something we would like better for the future. Our biological legacy is the ability to choose how we would like to live.

Rather than a curse against women, biology is a promise to us. Biology shows us that the subjugation of women is anything but natural and fixed. It seems to be a late human invention not likely to have been in the transitional ape-human populations, nor evident in what may well have been the social organization of human society for much of the time that we have been human.

Even without our capacities to create and change specific cultures, biology tells us that we belong to an order stunningly flexible in its social arrangements and capable of great change within species. With this cultural capacity, possibilities expand. Biology tells us that there is nothing genetic stopping us from having full sexual and social expression.

Biology tells us, finally, to get to work.

MEN AND WOMEN: HOW DIFFERENT ARE THEY?

John Nicholson

John Nicholson, the author of A Question of Sex: The Differences Between Men and Women *(1979), conducts seminars on sex differences at Bedford College, London University. In the following excerpts from his book* Men and Women: How Different Are They? *(1984), he discusses environmental influences on the emerging sexual identities of children, physiological differences between males' and females' strength and endurance capacities (as manifest in athletic performances), and the significant differences in male and female vulnerability to death and disease. You will want to compare Nicholson's arguments with those made by David Gelman, Eric Gelman, and Jo Durden-Smith and Diane DeSimone in other essays in this chapter.*

GENDER ROLES AND CULTURE

. . . How do children become aware of their gender and start thinking in terms of masculinity and femininity? The obvious assumption is that their parents tell them about it or else allow them to deduce the importance of gender from the fact that boys and girls are treated very differently. But it is not as simple as this. Parents do not actively instruct children in gender roles by saying this is how boys/girls behave; you are a boy/girl, so this is how you should behave. Nor is there much evidence to suggest that parents shape boys and girls into behaving in the ways we think of as masculine and feminine by rewarding different behaviour in the two sexes.

It does not seem to be the case that boys are more aggressive than girls because parents tolerate or even encourage aggression in boys but not in girls. In fact, research shows that it is equally discouraged in children of both sexes, and that boys are actually more often punished for displaying it than girls are (boys generally receive more punishment than girls). But parents do of course draw children's attention to gender by dressing boys and girls differently after the first year or so, and they encourage them to develop different interests and perhaps different behaviour by providing them with different sorts of toys. Even the harmless old tradition of blue for boys, pink for girls reflects a bias in favour of boys, because it used to be popularly believed that blue wards off evil spirits!

Of course parents aren't the only source of information young children are exposed to on the subject of the significance of gender. Other children are an important influence, especially older brothers and sisters: young children of both sexes become more masculine if they have an older brother and more feminine if they have an older sister. Nor should the influence of the media be underestimated. According to one American calculation, the typical four-year-old has already watched some 3,000 hours of television (the figure must be smaller in countries

John Nicholson, *Men and Women: How Different Are They?* (New York: Oxford University Press, 1984).

without all-day TV broadcasting). Analysis of the contents of TV programmes — and most children's books, for that matter — leaves no doubt about the message the media convey.

As a general trend, heroes outnumber heroines by something like three to one. More specifically, a study carried out in America as recently as 1980 confirmed that the old stereotypes are very much alive in the minds of those who make television programmes. Men are still portrayed at work more often than women, while women tend to be shown at home and, more often than not, in emotional distress! TV males are more likely to solve their own problems, while females, though proficient at dealing with other people's troubles, usually require assistance to handle their own.

A British study, carried out at roughly the same time, found that the position was no better during the commercial breaks. An analysis of 170 British TV advertisements produced predictable results. Whereas men were typically portrayed as authoritative, autonomous and knowledgeable, women tended to be shown as ignorant, impulsive buyers, concerned with the social desirability of a product rather than whether or not it was practical or represented good value. As an indication of the bias in TV ads, the researchers pointed out that although more than 40 per cent of adult women in the UK were in paid employment at the time they carried out their survey, they represented only 13 per cent of the central roles in the commercials being studied.

The role which television plays in inculcating sexual stereotypes in children is hard to assess. Expert opinion seems to have swung quite sharply away from the once popular view that children are not much affected by what they see on the screen. On the other hand, there do seem to be some grounds for cautious optimism about the willingness of at least some TV directors to present a less biased view of the adult world. For example, another survey of American TV commercials carried out at the end of the 1970s found that women were more often shown working in traditionally masculine jobs than in earlier studies. However, men were never shown in traditionally feminine occupations outside the home, and although they were sometimes seen to be cooking and cleaning, this was invariably being done under the supervision of their wife, usually to make a humorous point.

Where children's books are concerned, we might expect the media to exert a more liberal influence. But this does not seem to be the case, at least where the USA is concerned. Researchers who investigated how men and women were depicted in nineteen prize-winning children's picture books published between 1972 and 1979 detected few signs of the considerable changes which had taken place in sex roles in the real world. Comparing these books with prize-winners from the period 1967–1971, they found that although the ratio of male to female pictures had changed dramatically (from 11:1 to 1.8:1, for human characters), the authors, regardless of their own sex, still seemed to be locked into traditional sex-typing when it came to what the characters actually did. Almost without exception, the female characters were presented as warm, caring and affectionate, but dependent and incidental to the plot. The male characters, on the other hand, were tough, self-sufficient and aggressive, and it was around them that the stories revolved.

How much children are actually affected by what they see and have read to them is still a vexed question. But we know that they are not indifferent to the message of the media, and the only lesson they can learn about sex roles is that men and women are very different and unequal beings. Surprisingly, there is considerable controversy about the extent to which parents or other adults are instrumental in instilling sexual stereotypes. It has long been assumed that young children imitate the behaviour of their same-sexed parent. But this has not proved easy to demonstrate convincingly in the laboratory. Recently, however, Australian psychologists have provided clear evidence that by the time they are eight or nine, children of both sexes can be swayed in their preferences by observing the choice made by young adults of their own sex.

But researchers have been surprised by how little overt sex-typing children experience from their parents. They are very rarely told to behave in a way appropriate to their sex, though they may be actively discouraged from engaging in behaviour thought to be appropriate only for the opposite sex. This is particularly so for boys. Little girls are allowed to get away with quite a lot in the way of masculine behaviour—no one minds a tomboy although parents are less concerned about boys getting their clothes dirty than girls—but parents, especially fathers, are swift to stamp out signs of effeminacy in their sons. . . .

Since children are surrounded by adults with preconceptions about masculine and feminine behaviour, it is tempting to assume that they first become aware of gender as something adults seem to think is important. But some theorists have suggested that children would take on a gender role without any outside assistance, as an inevitable consequence of the biological differences between the sexes, specifically in their genitals. Psychoanalysts claim that there is a connection between people's genitals and their personality. The fact that the penis is an organ which intrudes into the world is said to lead to men being outgoing, adventurous and aggressive, while the internal reproductive system of a woman is alleged to make her passive, receptive and peaceful. When parents talk to their children about the difference between their genitals, they sometimes give the impression that girls are people who lack penises. According to Freud, this leads to the condition of penis envy, which he claimed is one of the most powerful influences on the developing female personality, and at the root of women's feeling that they are inferior to men. But while it is true that children are keenly interested in their genitals and anxious to understand why there are two different models available, we shall soon see that the psychoanalytic explanation of the development of gender roles cannot account for all the facts.

An alternative explanation is that masculinity and femininity develop in the same way as the physical differences between the sexes we shall be discussing in the next chapter, as a result of the action of the sex hormones which circulate in our bodies. The problem with this explanation is that children start responding to gender at a time when the overall production of sex hormones is at a low ebb, and when there is very little difference between the sexes in hormonal activity.

In fact, when children of different ages are asked questions to discover what they think about masculinity and femininity, it transpires that the concept of gender is not something which just becomes clearer and clearer as the child grows up. On the contrary, the willingness of children to accept gender roles seems to wax and wane as their thought processes change, and no single principle—whether of biology or learning—can explain what actually happens. Instead we are confronted with a complicated mixture of biological change, the influence of parents' and teachers' views about boys and girls, and a child's own determination to make sense of the world and of other people's attitudes and behaviour. . . .

STRENGTH

There are two different kinds of muscle fibre, one of which (red fibre) enables us to perform feats of endurance such as long-distance running or mountain-climbing, while the other (white fibre) is involved in sudden bursts of physical exertion like sprinting or weight-lifting. How much of either fibre an individual has is what determines how good he or she is at the two sorts of activity. Most people have an equal balance between the two and so excel at neither activity, but some have an excess of one or other type of muscle fibre. These are the people who become outstanding sprinters or marathon runners, and an imbalance between the two fibres occurs much more often amongst men than amongst women. However, there are ways in which women's muscles give them strength denied to men. Because of her menstrual cycle, a woman must have muscles which are equipped to survive in a constantly changing chemical environment in which hormone levels rise and fall and the amount of water retained varies according to the time of the month. Male muscles exist in a comparatively (though not entirely) stable environment, and as a result seem less able to cope when the body's chemical balance is unexpectedly disturbed, for example by illness. This may be one reason why men feel shaky and are more likely to complain of aches and pains when they get flu.

Scientists are still arguing about the difference between men's and women's muscles, but it probably has to do with the red fibres (those concerned with endurance tasks). The suggestion is that men's red fibres use oxygen more efficiently, with the result that they can work harder than women. However, as they use up oxygen, men's red fibres also build up the body's natural pain agents. Women's muscles may use oxygen less efficiently, but they do not build up these pain inducers, so women may actually be able to carry on performing an endurance task after men have been stopped by the pain barrier.

Men also develop larger hearts and lungs, higher blood pressure, a lower resting heart-rate, and a greater capacity for transporting oxygen through the bloodstream coupled with greater ability to get rid of the chemical products of physical exercise. Men and women differ even in the composition of their blood, because at adolescence boys acquire more red blood cells and haemoglobin (the pigment which carries oxygen from the lungs to the muscles) whereas girls do not. Not only are the lungs of the average man larger than those of the average woman, but they can also take in one and a half times as much oxygen as hers. All these differences have an effect on our powers of endurance, since we can only go on being active as long as our muscles get the oxygen they use as fuel. If men have larger lungs which can take in more oxygen, more powerful hearts to pump that oxygen round and more haemoglobin to carry it to the muscles, it is hardly surprising that the average adult male has more stamina than the average woman.

EXERCISE AND ATHLETICISM

. . . We know that ordinary, untrained men and women have very different physical capabilities, and we have a pretty good idea why they are different. But what about trained athletes, who regularly drive themselves to the limit of their physical capacity and so presumably realize their full physical potential? If you look at the record books and see what progress the fastest men and women in the world have made over the last forty years or so, you can get a clear indication of the extent to which women's physical inferiority stems from cultural expectations rather than from biology. Take the 800 metres track race, for example. The first time women competed in this event at the Olympic Games was in 1928, when many of the competitors were overcome by exhaustion. The event therefore disappeared from the Olympic programme until 1960, on the grounds that it was clearly dangerous for women to run so far. But Table 2, which lists the occasions on which world records for the 800 metres were broken between 1939 and 1981, reveals that women's fastest times have improved by more than eighteen seconds over this period, while the best performance by a man has improved by only three seconds. Men can still run the 800 metres faster than women, but the gap between the fastest man and the fastest woman has been cut from twenty-five to less than twelve seconds, as more women have become involved in athletics and as people have come to realize that there is nothing astonishing about a woman running half a mile. . . .

In swimming events, the difference is even smaller (it averages out at less than 8½ per cent), and it is startling to realize that the woman who holds the world record for the 400 metres free-style at the time of writing (1982) would have beaten Mark Spitz in the 1972 Olympics. When it comes to long-distance swimming — crossing the English Channel, for example — women are actually faster than men, which makes it somewhat ironic that the organizers of international swimming meetings rarely include 800- or 1500-metre races for women. No doubt they are still haunted by the fifty-year-old memory of those elegantly clad ladies collapsing in the half-mile track event.

There are two other aspects of a woman's biology which might be expected to have deleterious effect on her performance as an athlete — the menstrual cycle and pregnancy. However, these seem to be less of a handicap than you might suppose, if the results of the Olympic Games are anything to go by. At the 1976 Olympics an American swimmer won three gold medals and broke a world record while at the height of her period. And so far as pregnancy is concerned, the Russians revealed after the 1964 Games that no fewer than ten of their twenty-six female champions were pregnant when they earned their medals!

Feminists may find all this very encouraging, but there is a snag. Women can certainly narrow the gap in physical performance between themselves and men, but they do so by making themselves more like a man. Successful female athletes reach a state of physiological fitness in which they bear a closer resemblance to male athletes than to non-athletic members of their own sex. As a result of training, women athletes can reduce the proportion of their body which is fat to less than 10 per cent, compared with 25 per cent for the average unfit woman and 12 per cent for the average unfit man, and they are also able to tip the balance between the red and white fibres in their muscles in favour of the sprinting, but not the endurance, fibres.

However, other anatomical and physiological factors make it very unlikely that women will ever become men's equals in sprinting. The size and shape of their pelvis and hips and their less favourable leg- to body-length ratio are problems that no amount of training can overcome (successful female athletes tend to be born and to remain a rather 'masculine' shape), while the greater ability of a man's muscles to break down lactic acid and so avoid cramp is another factor which must always handicap women over a short sprint.

There can be little doubt that women will come nearer to matching men's athletic performance, as long as attitudes continue to change, more women are attracted to the sport, and the necessary additional facilities are made available to them. Regulations like that restricting women under twenty-one to races of four miles or less might also be reconsidered in the light of what we now know about women's physical capabilities. It is ironic that some of the most determined opposition to the cause of female athleticism still comes from athletics officials. A spokesman for the International Olympic Committee, the most prestigious body in athletics, gave a fair indication of their thinking on the subject when explaining why the IOC were rejecting a suggestion that the 1980 Olympic programme should include a woman's 3,000 metres event: it was, he asserted, 'a little too strenuous for them.' At the time that he was speaking, the percentage difference between the men's and women's world records for the marathon stood at 12.8; two years later, a woman ran the marathon in a time which would have won her a gold medal in every Olympic men's marathon up to 1948; and forty-five years *earlier*, a young South African schoolmistress, the legendary Miss Geraldine Watson, had finished sixth in an otherwise all-male field competing in the Durban 100-mile race! . . .

Other writers who have reached this conclusion have gone on to claim that as the cultural barriers come down, the differences in athletic performance between men and women will eventually disappear. Trends . . . have led to some bold and startlingly specific predictions: for example, that female track stars will be competing on equal terms with men by the year 2077, top swimmers by 2056, and the best women cyclists by 2011.

Such claims seem to me to be based on bad biology as well as doubtful mathematics. I say this because when you look at the differences between trained men and women, they often turn out to be *greater* than those between untrained, unfit Mr. and Mrs. Average. For example, if you take the average untrained couple out jogging, the man will pump 100 millilitres of oxygenated blood with every heartbeat, compared to the woman's 75 millilitres. After training, however, he will be pumping 160 millilitres to her 110, so that the difference between them has actually doubled. The same thing applies to the efficiency with which the lungs extract oxygen from the blood. Before training, the average man's muscles can extract 50 millilitres for every kilo he weighs, while a woman's take 40. But when they are both fit, he will be able to extract 84 to her 70. The performance of her muscles has actually improved by a slightly greater percentage than his, but this cannot compensate for the fact that the absolute gap between them has widened.

These are the sorts of observation which gave rise to the remark of the exercise physiologist quoted at the beginning of the chapter: nature has built man as a four-litre, and woman as a three-litre car. A three-litre car can be tuned up to run better than a four-litre when the larger vehicle is not firing properly, but it cannot keep up when both are operating at maximum efficiency. This is a crude analogy, and there is every reason why women should make the most of their physical potential (it is estimated that the average unfit adult woman could become 10 to 20 per cent stronger in a month if she did proper exercises, and up to 40 per cent fitter if she kept on with them subsequently). However, it illustrates why I for one am unconvinced by the more extreme claims which are based on the progress that women athletes have made towards narrowing the gap between the sexes in athletic achievement. . . .

HEALTH, SICKNESS AND DEATH

As I have described them so far, the physical differences between men and women all seem to operate to the male's advantage. But like all good stories, this tale has a sting in it. Men may be better at lifting dumb-bells or running races, but when it comes to sheer ability to survive, women have a definite edge on them. Perhaps it is no more than elementary justice that the very features which put women at a disadvantage in feats of strength work in their favour when the going gets really rough. If food is scarce, the larger stores of fat which hold a woman back as an athlete now provide her with more to live on, and her small frame ensures that she loses less heat than the bulkier male when the climate becomes very cold. Similarly, the fact that women burn up food and oxygen more slowly means that they require less of both to keep going. It seemed reasonable to describe the less dynamic metabolism of a woman as inefficient when we were talking about athletic performance, but things look very different when the prize is survival rather than a new world record.

Of course, survival is rarely a pressing concern to those of us who live in the Affluent Society, so you may think that the fact that women are better equipped for it than men is a matter of purely academic interest. Nothing could be further from the truth. There is abundant evidence that even in societies like ours, where starvation is virtually unknown and people very rarely freeze to death, men are physically much more vulnerable than women from the moment they are conceived until they die.

Consider the following statistics. For every 100 females conceived, there are estimated to be between 107 and 124 males. But the male embryo is more likely to abort spontaneously, perhaps by a factor of 135 to 100. As a result, only 106 boys are actually born for every 100 girls. This figure varies slightly from year to year, place to place, season to season and even according to time of day: more males are born in the periods before sunrise and sunset, more females around midnight and noon. The parents' age and the size of the existing family are also significant factors: the older a woman, and the more children she has already, the less likely it is that she will give birth to a boy. Fascinating though these findings are, the mechanism behind them remains a mystery. However, the fact that boy babies are also more likely to succumb to perinatal complications such as lack of oxygen may explain why they originally became more highly valued than girls, while the fact that girls were more often the victims of infanticide in societies which used this form of birth control was perhaps the price they paid for being easier to replace.

Of course, most males survive birth, but their problems are only just beginning. A new-born boy is more likely than a girl to die before he is one year old, is more susceptible to infection, and has a greater chance of being born with some congenital illness or of suffering from the kinds of brain disorder which lead to epilepsy, cerebral palsy or febrile convulsions. In our society, those who live through the first year have an excellent chance of reaching the age of thirty-five. But the majority of those who fail to make it are men. During these years men are more likely to die in accidents — particularly on the road — and they continue to be more susceptible to fatal infectious diseases. They are also more prone to heart attacks and ulcers. And despite the fact that more young women try to commit suicide, more young men succeed in doing so. As a result, by the age of thirty-five there are roughly the same number of men and women left alive.

It is after forty that fatal diseases really begin to take their toll. Women are more likely than men to suffer from cancer of the reproductive organs and from various diseases related to the hormones, like diabetes and thyroid disorders, but men are far more susceptible to most other forms of serious illness. For example, they are four times more likely to get lung cancer, three times more likely to contract heart-disease, and they are also significantly more prone to suffer strokes and disorders of the respiratory system like bronchitis and emphysema. In consequence, the numerical balance between the sexes, which was originally weighted so heavily in favour of the male, now tips the other way, and by the time we get to seventy, there are two women for every man still surviving. At the time of writing, the average British woman can expect to live until she is seventy-six. The average man, however, has no statistical justification for anticipating any more than the allotted biblical lifespan of three score years and ten. Amongst the 4,000 centenarians alive in Britain today, women outnumber men by four to one.

What is it about men that makes them superior in trials of strength but worse at the ultimate test of staying alive? The first thought that comes to mind is that men and women have different life-styles, and it may merely be that men's lives are more dangerous. Perhaps the fact that more men die in car crashes just means that they spend more time on the road (it may also have something to do with the difference between men's and women's driving styles). When trying to explain why men suffer more from lung cancer and other diseases of the respiratory system, we obviously cannot ignore the fact that they smoke more than women. We hear a lot about executive stress these days, and it is generally assumed that men are more likely than women to have jobs which either involve physical danger (being a deep sea diver, for example) or else are so demanding in terms of mental energy, heavy responsibility and long hours that they endanger a person's health. But I suspect that the hazards of executive life are exaggerated: some studies have found that workers on the shop-floor are more prone to stress illnesses than executives. Moreover, we shall see later in the book that the two jobs which are the woman's traditional lot — having babies and being a housewife — can both endanger her health, so it looks as though differences in life-style do not tell the whole story of women's superior survival ability.

Any lingering doubts about this are dispelled by the findings of a team of researchers who had the inspired idea of investigating the actuarial prospects of 40,000 monks and nuns. These were all white, unmarried, native-born Americans, doing the same job — teaching. None of them smoked or drank alcohol; all had the same diet and were equally free from the stresses of family or business life. But in spite of their similar life-styles, by the age of forty-five the nuns could expect to live an average of five and a half years longer than the monks. In fact, the difference in life-expectancy between the sexes in this group, who did not indulge in any of the excesses of modern living, was actually greater than in the general American population at the time. This may seem very unfair to non-smoking teetotallers who thought they might be notching up some extra years by their abstemiousness — especially strong-minded husbands who were hoping to steal a march on wives who smoke and drink. It also means that we must once again turn to the biological differences between the sexes for an explanation of why men and women differ in their susceptibility to disease and in their ability to survive.

Various theories have been put forward and, as you might expect, it looks as though chromosomes and sex hormones are involved. So far as inherited diseases and childhood infections are concerned, the answer appears to lie in the twenty-third pair of chromosomes, where the presence or absence of a Y chromosome determines a person's sex. Unlike the Y chromosome, which carries little if any genetic information and whose only positive effect is to lead to maleness, the larger X chromosome contains a lot of information about how we develop. For example, its instructions can affect the colour of the eyes, composition of the blood, and skin texture. Occasionally the X chromosome is flawed: it may contain too little information for a certain part of the body to develop properly, or perhaps the message is jumbled up. When this happens, all is lost for the male. He has only one X, and to the extent that it is at fault, some aspect of his development must necessarily be faulty. His body has no choice but to obey the faulty instructions on his single X chromosome, and as a result he is born with an abnormality. But females have a second X, carrying duplicate information, and so long as this is not damaged in the same way, it will be able to supply the relevant information in the correct form, and thus cancel out the effects of the defective chromosome. A female only suffers if both her X chromosomes have identical faults. Since they come from two different donors (her two parents), the odds against this happening are obviously much greater than the chances of the male's single X being flawed. There are a number of what are known as X-linked diseases, including colour-blindness, haemophilia, rickets, diabetes, immunoglobin deficiency and hyperthyroidism, all of which are more common amongst boys than amongst girls. Colour-blindness, for example, affects more than one man in twelve but less than one woman in a hundred. However, when a man is colour-blind, it is always as a result of receiving a faulty X chromosome from his mother. A woman who is a carrier has an even chance of passing it on to her child who, if male, will inevitably be colour-blind.

The X chromosome may also be responsible for regulating the antibodies which fight off infection. Infections rarely prove fatal now that antibiotics are available. But when deaths do occur it is usually in the first year of life, when boys are more likely to die than girls. Some scientists have suggested that the extra genes provided by a second X chromosome give women a chemical back-up system which men lack. This may help to keep women's bodies on an even keel chemically, and hence make them less vulnerable than men to all kinds of biochemical disturbance. The reason for thinking that sex chromosomes can affect the balance of the whole body is that when there is something wrong with a baby's sex chromosomes, not only its sexual development but also its intelligence and general health tend to be affected.

This line of reasoning is pleasantly straightforward, but unfortunately it is incompatible with a second, equally compelling hypothesis which has been put forward to answer another of the questions raised by the genetic differences between males and females: given that women have two X chromosomes, and men have only one, why aren't the two sexes more different? Many biologists believe that the best way to explain this is to make the assumption that a woman's second X chromosome is inactive, in the sense that the information it contains is not acted upon. But the theory we have been discussing assumes that it *is* active. Both theories cannot be right: at present, however, we simply don't know which needs to be replaced.

As for sex hormones, if they are involved in the differences between the reactions of the two sexes to disease, it is not at all certain what the connection is. Doctors used to think that there was something about female sex hormones which gave women extra protection against all the diseases that seem to favour men as their victims. However, the incidence of these diseases amongst women does not suddenly rocket up after the menopause, when production of the sex hormones drops. This theory has therefore fallen into disrepute, to be replaced by a new idea: rather than women being protected by their sex hormones, men may be killed off by theirs. In support of this suggestion, there is some evidence that men who are given extra male hormones are more likely to die from an early heart attack. This ties in with the results of rather a bizarre piece of research, which relates to the days when being a patient in a mental hospital was a more hazardous business than it is today. Examination of the medical records of one such hospital in America shows that male patients who had been castrated tended to live an average of thirteen years longer than those who had not. It is difficult to know how much weight we should attach to this evidence, since all the patients, whether their genitals were intact or not, tended to die much younger than people in the general population and from atypical causes. But it is at least suggestive that men deprived of their main source of sex hormones may live longer than those who are not. . . .

Advances in medical science may also go some way towards narrowing the gap between the sexes in their susceptibility to illness and in life expectancy. But biology is a powerful force for conservatism, and I have the feeling that these differences — though they may be reduced — are no more likely to disappear altogether than any of the other physical differences between men and women.

FEMALE MATH ANXIETY
ON THE WANE
Constance Holden

Constance Holden, a staff writer for Science, *summarizes numerous recent studies on male and female achievement-test performance differences in mathematics, and she surveys various social environmentalists' efforts to account for these differences. Compare the conclusions of the studies Holden details here with those drawn by the Eleanor Maccoby and Carol Jacklin essay and the Jo Durden-Smith and Diane DeSimone essay elsewhere in this chapter. This particular difference in abilities, incidentally, has sparked more controversy in the last decade than has any other issue in sex-difference research. Two studies conducted by Camilla Persson Benbow and Julian C. Stanley at Johns Hopkins University (summarized in* Science *in 1980 and 1983) provided a mass of data suggesting that twelve-year-old, mathematically gifted males consistently scored significantly higher on the math portion of the SAT examination than did their twelve-year-old, mathematically gifted female counterparts. Benbow's and Stanley's conclusions that environmental conditioning was really not evident in this difference drew a firestorm of protest from a number of feminists, educators, and researchers who insisted that any such difference is merely a product of sexual social roles.*

At the recent annual meeting of the American Educational Research Association, no fewer than 25 sessions dealt with male-female differences in achievement and interest in mathematics and science.

The topic is undeniably provocative. On the one hand, it appears that "math anxiety," the much touted explanation for girls' lower achievement in the 1970s, is no longer much in evidence. But despite this, boys are doing significantly better than girls in the upper reaches of scores from standardized tests in math, science, and even history.

The apparent decline of math anxiety was documented in a presentation by Frank Besag of the University of Wisconsin (Milwaukee), who surveyed the school records of 7500 students from grades 9 through 11 and gave them the MARS test on math anxiety and a test measuring their self-esteem. He and Maureen Wahl found few sex differences on course participation, grades, or dropout rates, and found no differences between boys and girls on math anxiety or self-esteem. "It would certainly seem to me that some of it [math anxiety] has been overcome," said Besag.

The impression given from several of the sessions was that if math anxiety still exists for girls, it kicks in relatively late, since they have better grades than boys do on all subjects through elementary school. The problem is that the sexes begin to diverge in science and math interest and achievement in high school, and the divergence becomes more pronounced in higher education.

Constance Holden, "Female Math Anxiety on the Wane," *Science* 236(8 May 1987).

Much of this disparity has to do with divergent interests. Linda K. Zimmerer and Susan M. Bennett of the California Assessment Program reported that a survey of high school students throughout the state showed that "boys have more positive attitudes toward science," even though girls got better grades. Boys spent more time than girls studying 9 of the 12 topics surveyed. On achievement tests, boys scored significantly higher in 25 of 33 categories. Girls did better on two: laboratory safety and observation (telescopes and microscopes were their favorite instruments). Girls did better on reading, memory, and comprehension, and boys on science vocabulary. Girls were good at inferring; boys at predicting. The researchers concluded that the differences were "a reflection of more than simply classroom instruction."

This seemed to be borne out in observations by Sharon Rallis of Rhode Island College who said the "differential course work hypothesis may be inadequate to explain differences in achievement and career choice" between males and females.

Rallis and her colleagues selected two groups from 2200 Rhode Island 12th graders: those who were "academically prepared" for science careers, with course work including calculus and physics, and those expressing an intent to have a science career. The "most striking revelation" was the small number of prepared girls who indicated a career interest in engineering, science, or technology — 11 of 59, compared with 47 of the 74 "prepared" males.

Why the difference? Rallis said teachers and counselors insisted there were no relevant differences between males and females as a group. But they would also make statements such as, "girls don't like mechanical stuff as much as boys." Prepared females were more likely to be interested in other professional fields such as business, medicine, and law; yet pay was mentioned as a factor in career choice twice as often by boys. Half the students said their parents were influential in their choices. The researchers concluded that information and encouragement (from sources outside school) were more important for girls than boys in choosing science as a career.

Camilla Benbow of Iowa State University, who is involved in the Johns Hopkins University Study of Mathematically Precocious Youth (SMPY), had a similar message. She reported that of 2000 mathematically gifted students, 63% of the males and 35% of the females chose to major in math or science. She also said males were twice as likely as females to choose research careers. "Attitudes towards science" emerged as the most powerful variable, followed by "family support for goals" and the educational levels of subjects' fathers. Irene T. Miura of San Jose State University, who compared science interests between the sexes in high and low socioeconomic groups, also concluded that the sexes "did not differ on variables most likely to be influenced by schools."

Marlaine Lockheed of the World Bank suggested that sex differences stem more from affective (emotional) differences than from "a reasonably nonexistent cognitive deficiency." She noted that there have been "major changes" in course participation by females and that "as courses become required there are fewer and fewer differences."

This observation, however, does little to explain the findings that have been emerging from the group at Johns Hopkins, headed by Julian Stanley. The findings from SMPY suggest that sharp sex discrepancies exist at the extreme end of the achievement spectrum in many subjects.

The Johns Hopkins group has been looking at thousands of youths who score 700 or above on the mathematical portion of the Scholastic Aptitude Test by the age of 13. The sex ratio at this level is 12.9 males to every female. At 451 (the male mean), they found the ratio to be 1.5:1. This increases to 2:1 at 500 and 4:1 at 600.

The group has been analyzing national data from a variety of standardized aptitude and achievement tests, and has found that males consistently score higher in the quantative domains than do females. They compared gender differentials among tests by estimating the "effect size," which is computed by dividing the difference between the male and female means by the standard deviation of the scores. An effect size of 0.8 is large, and 0.2 or below is small.

In the Differential Aptitude Test, for example, 8th-grade females show a modest superiority in numerical ability, abstract reasoning, and verbal reasoning, but this disappears by the 12th grade. Males, on the other hand, show an effect size of 0.66 on mechanical reasoning, which goes up to 0.89 by the 12th grade. The male effect size for space relations goes from 0.13 in 8th grade to 0.22.

The general pattern is similar for high school students taking the American College Testing Program, where male effect sizes range from 0.23 to 0.40 in social studies, math, and natural sciences. In College Board Achievement tests, females did slightly better in English and composition, but males showed intermediate effect sizes in biology, math, chemistry, and European history. Graduate Records Examinations revealed two of the largest effect sizes favoring males — 0.79 in political science, and 0.71 in math.

Graduate and professional school entrance examinations tell the same story. Effect sizes are negligible only in the Law School Admissions Test, which is the most difficult in terms of logic and reasoning but contains no quantitative questions. The largest effect size favoring females was 0.19, on the verbal portion of the management test.

Although many of the effect sizes are not large, Stanley said they can result in severe discrepancies in the upper scores. For example, the male advantage in spatial relations (0.22) translates to a male-female ratio of almost 2 to 1 in the top 10% of scores. The male effect size of 0.63 in European history in 1985 corresponds with a 10 to 1 ratio among the highest scorers.

Stanley observed that females are overall better students from kindergarten through graduate school, and that they do better on course-related exams than on standardized tests. He characterized women as being more oriented to social interaction and aesthetics, while men go for the quantitative, the abstract, "power and control." He did not hazard any explanations for this — "we've tried to firm up the whats so that other researchers may pursue the whys."

It remains a matter of debate whether observed sex differences in math and science achievement are significant, and whether they represent a problem to be solved. Some cling to the view that the discrepancies can be explained by differential course-taking; others believe that they stem from factors as yet unmeasured. Some think the subject has been blown all out of proportion. Said Susan F. Chipman of the U.S. Office of Naval Research: "People are just *too* interested in this topic."

Girl Talk—Guy Talk
Alfie Kohn

Alfie Kohn, a contributing editor of Psychology Today, *summarizes the conclusions of several different studies regarding the differences between male and female speech mannerisms, inflections, and social attitudes in conversation. Are the implied causes of the sex differences in conversation a matter of genetics or social conditioning? Can you detect any relationship at all between the female left-hemisphere strength, according to the brain hemisphere theory of sex differences, and the conclusions drawn by the studies cited in this essay?*

"Hey, y' know what?"

"Mmmm?"

"I was walking near that, um, new construction site? Near the bank?"

"Yeh."

"Well, this kinda crazy guy comes up to me, you know? I'm, like, ready to run for the bank."

"Huh."

"It's really *amazing* that these people approach you in broad daylight, don't you think?"

"I know. I was at the movies once and some bum started asking me for money."

"Really? What happened?"

With this imaginary dialogue, enter the stereotypical world of men's and women's speech, in which men tend to dominate conversations, interrupt or shift the topic to one they prefer, and in which women—by adopting a questioning, tentative tone—work hard to gain men's attention.

In fact, a decade's worth of research has shown that men and women in our culture use distinctive styles of speech and also tend to play different roles when talking with one another. More recently, researchers have moved away from examining men's and women's language in the abstract, preferring to scrutinize the actual settings, such as courtrooms and physicians' offices, in which conversation takes place. Although some researchers now suggest that speech patterns are as much a function of social status as of gender, studies have confirmed definite sex differences in diverse situations.

Boston College sociologist Charles Derber has studied the roles that men and women take on in conversation and has found that men often shift conversations to their preferred topics, whereas women are more apt to respond supportively. In a study of married couples, Derber found that the wife gave more active encouragement to her husband's talk about himself, while the husband "listened less well and was less likely to actively 'bring her out' about herself and her own topics."

In fact, men often interrupt outright, and they do this far more frequently than women do, several studies have shown. Candace West and Don Zimmerman, sociologists at the University of California, recorded a number of two-party conversa-

Alfie Kohn, "Girl Talk—Guy Talk," *Psychology Today* February 1988.

tions. When men spoke with men or women with women, there were relatively few interruptions, and those that did occur were balanced between the two speakers. When men conversed with women, however, not only did more interruptions occur, but 96 percent of them involved men interrupting women.

From her doctoral research in sociology at the University of California, Santa Barbara, Pamela Fishman concludes, "Both men and women regarded topics introduced by women as tentative [whereas] topics introduced by the men were treated as topics to be pursued. The women . . . did much of the necessary work of interaction, starting conversations and then working to maintain them."

Closely connected to conversational roles is the matter of styles of speech. Linguist Robin Lakoff, of the University of California, Berkeley, along with many other researchers, has pointed to questioning as a distinctive characteristic of women's speech. Specifically, women:

- Ask more questions. Fishman's analysis of tape-recorded conversations between professional couples found that the women asked nearly three times as many questions as the men.

- Make statements in a questioning tone. ("I was walking near that, um, new construction site?") The rising inflection, Lakoff says, suggests that the speaker is seeking confirmation even though she may be the only one who has the necessary information.

- Use more tag questions. Adding a brief question at the end of a sentence (". . . don't you think?") suggests doubt or encourages the listener to respond. Not all studies have confirmed Lakoff's assertion that women use more of these, however.

- Lead off with a question. Starting a conversation this way ("Hey, y' know what?") is intended to ensure a listener's attention. This device and others led West and Zimmerman to note that there are "striking similarities" between the conversations between men and women and those between adults and children.

- Use more "hedges" or qualifiers ("kinda") in their speech and also rely on intensifiers ("really"). The latter, which can refer not only to the choice of words but to the emphasis with which they are pronounced (*"amazing"*), tell the listener "how to react," according to Lakoff. "Since my saying something by itself is not likely to convince you," Lakoff observes, "I'd better use double force to make sure you see what I mean."

The implications of these findings have been the subject of considerable discussion, particularly among feminists. That women express their thoughts more tentatively and work harder to get someone's attention probably says something about their conversational experience with men—experience along the lines of what Derber, Fishman, West and Zimmerman have documented. Moreover, women may have internalized men's assumptions that what they have to say isn't very interesting or intellectually rigorous. This hesitancy then becomes the norm for "proper" feminine speech. Lakoff deplores this situation, noting that "a woman is damned if she does and damned if she doesn't." She is "ostracized as unfeminine by both men and women" if she speaks directly and assertively but dismissed "as someone not to be taken seriously, of dim intelligence, frivolous" if she adopts the traditional style and role.

While it may be a disadvantage in our society, "women's language" has features that many believe should be preserved. Requesting rather than commanding, attending to others' needs in a conversation and listening more effectively are seen by many as valuable social skills. Linguist Sally McConnell-Ginet of Cornell University urges women to adopt a conversational style that doesn't sacrifice sensitivity but "nevertheless doesn't make you sound as if you have less commitment to your beliefs than you have." The issue, she adds, is not just "how women should change the way they speak, but how men should change the way they listen."

In the last few years, researchers have also begun to look at how a particular setting can influence patterns of speech. "There's been a change from looking at discrete elements of language [and toward] interaction — the whole situation," says Cheris Kramarae, professor of speech communication at the University of Illinois. We're "studying language in context."

Viewing language in concrete situations has led some researchers to argue recently that speech is at least as much a function of social status as of gender. Duke University anthropologist William O'Barr pored over 10 weeks' worth of trial transcripts and discovered that a witness's occupation and experience on the stand told more about speech patterns than whether the witness was a man or woman did. "So-called women's language is neither characteristic of all women nor limited only to women," O'Barr writes in his book *Linguistic Evidence*. If women generally use "powerless" language, he adds, this may be due largely "to the greater tendency of women to occupy relatively powerless social positions" in American society.

Occupation — or at least situational context — also proved the dominant factor in a study of day-care workers by psychologist Jean Berko Gleason of Boston University. "Male day-care teachers' speech to young children," she points out, "is more like the language of female day-care teachers than it is like that of fathers at home."

Finally, West spent five years exploring conversational dynamics among male and female physicians and patients at a Southern family-medicine practice. Since physician and patient provide a clear example of a relationship between two people of unequal status, West could determine whether interruptions reflected status or gender. The answer: Both played a part. Overall, physicians interrupted patients more often than the reverse, but female physicians were interrupted more when they had male patients. "It appears," West concludes, "that gender can take precedence over occupational status in conversation."

At the same time, gender differences in speech may simply reflect power relations between men and women in general. Maryann Ayim, who teaches education at the University of Western Ontario, puts it this way: "If females are more polite and less aggressive than males in their language practices, if they are more supportive and less dominant, this is hardly shocking, for it simply reflects the reality in every other sphere of life."

THE AGGRESSORS
Melvin Konner

Melvin Konner, an anthropologist, a physician, and a professor at Emory University, makes the case in this New York Times Magazine *essay for what he views as a fundamental biological difference in aggression between males and females. You might want to compare his arguments with those made on the same issue by the Jo Durden-Smith and Diane DeSimone essay and by the Naomi Weisstein essay elsewhere in this chapter.*

Dr. Dan Olweus knows the bullies in Norway; at least those 8 to 16 years old in a population of 140,000 in 715 public schools. Olweus, a professor of psychology at the University of Bergen, was asked by the Norwegian Government to get a handle on the bullying problem. Concluding his recent study, he estimates that of the 568,000 Norwegian schoolchildren, 41,000, or 7 percent, bully others regularly. The bullies were far more likely to be male: more than 60 percent of the girls and 80 percent of the boys victimized in grades 5 to 7 were bullied by males. The tendency of girls to bully declined with age; in boys, it rose: a twofold difference in the second grade widens to fivefold in the ninth.

Many studies, even of remote, primitive societies, show that males predominate overwhelmingly in physical violence. Pick your behavior: grabbing and scratching in toddlers, wrestling and chasing in nursery-school children, contact sports among teen-agers, violent crime in adulthood, tank maneuvers in real, grown-up wars. In 1986, Alice H. Eagly and Valerie J. Steffen, then of Purdue University, published a survey of 63 psychological studies. They emphasized that no category existed in which women were more aggressive than men, and they said the tendency to produce pain or physical injury was far more pronounced in men. Joining a distinguished line of social and psychological researchers, Eagly and Steffen concluded that these differences "are learned as aspects of gender roles and other social roles."

That belief, a tenacious modern myth, becomes less justified with every passing year: sex difference in the tendency to do physical harm is intrinsic, fundamental, natural—in a word, biological.

Olweus, in a smaller study—one of scores contributing to this new conclusion—selected 58 boys aged 15 through 17, and compared blood levels of testosterone, the male sex hormone, to aggression. He found a strong effect of testosterone on intolerance for frustration and response to provocation. The puzzle of aggression is not yet solved, but it seems increasingly apparent that testosterone is a key. However, it is testosterone circulating not only post-pubertally, as has been commonly thought, but also during early development—specifically, during fetal life, at the stage when the brain is forming. The first clues to this process came from animal studies. In 1973, G. Raisman and P. M. Field reported a significant sex difference in a part of the rat's brain known as the preoptic area—a region that, in females, helps control the reproductive cycle, certain brain cell connections in this area were more numerous in females. Most interestingly, castration of males at birth, or early treatment of females with testosterone, abolished the adult brain difference.

This was the first of many similar studies showing that the differentiation not only of the brain but of behavior—especially sexual and aggressive behavior—depends in part on early testosterone exposure. This has proved to be true of rats, mice, hamsters, rabbits and monkeys, among other species. Clear anatomical differences have been found in the hypothalamus and amygdula regions of the brain as well as the preoptic area.

One ingenious study showed that the tendency to fight in adult mice, although greater by far in males, differs among females, depending on whether they spent their fetal life near males or other females in the womb. Females with males on each side in utero grew up to be fighters, but those with only one adjacent male were less pugnacious as adults. Those flanked by two other females in the womb became the least aggressive adults. Separate evidence indicated that the three groups of females also differed in their degree of exposure to intrauterine testosterone—which had evidently come from the blood of the nearby males.

No experimental evidence is available for humans, of course, but some clinical studies are suggestive. Sometimes human fetuses are exposed to hormones that have effects similar to those of testosterone—for example, synthetic progestins, used to maintain pregnancy. June M. Reinisch, now director of the Kinsey Institute, studied 25 girls and boys with a history of such exposure and found them more aggressive than their same-sex siblings, as indicated by a paper-and-pencil test. This finding was in line with studies of monkeys and other animals exposed to male sex hormones in utero. Females with such exposure engaged in more rough-and-tumble play during development than other females. As in the human study, the differences became apparent before puberty.

Some years ago, there was a bitter controversy over whether men with an extra male-determining Y chromosome—the XYY syndrome—were hypermasculine. One not-so-subtle humorist wrote in to *Science* that it was silly to get so excited over the extremely rare XYY syndrome, when 49 percent of the species was already afflicted with the XY syndrome—an uncontroversial disorder known to cause hyperactivity and learning disabilities in childhood, premature mortality in adulthood and an egregious tendency to irrational violence throughout life. "Testosterone poisoning," a colleague of mine calls it.

Is there no contribution of culture, then, to the consistent male excess in violence? Of course there is; but it acts on an organism already primed for the sex difference. Cultures can dampen it or exaggerate it. The role of modeling in encouraging aggression is well proved. Give a girl a steady diet of Wonder Woman and lady wrestlers while her brother gets Mr. Rogers, and you may well push them past each other on the continuum. But we now have a pretty good answer to Margaret Mead's famous question: What if an average boy and an average girl were raised in exactly similar environments? We don't know, she said. Now we do. The boy would hit, kick, wrestle, scratch, grab, shove and bite more than the girl and be more likely to commit a violent crime later in life.

Mead became famous for her elegant demonstrations of cultural variation in sex roles. Among the Tchambuli, a New Guinea fishing society, the women, "brisk, unadorned, managing and industrious, fish and go to market; the men, decorative and adorned, carve and paint and practice dance steps." Among the Mundugumor, river-dwelling cannibals, also in New Guinea, "the women are as assertive and vigorous as the men; they detest bearing and rearing children, and provide most of the food. . . ." These quotations from her 1949 book "Male and Female" helped provide the basis for the modern conception of the tremendous flexibility of sex roles — as well they should have. But the Tchambuli men, when they finished their dance steps, went headhunting. And note that Mead's own words following her often-cited quote on the Mundugumor are: *"leaving the men free to plot and fight."* In every known society, homicidal violence, whether spontaneous and outlawed or organized and sanctioned for military purposes, is committed overwhelmingly by men.

The conclusion would seem to be that women should run the world. If we can agree that the greatest threat to human survival over the long haul is posed by human violence itself, then the facts of human violence — the sex difference, and its biological basis — can lead nowhere else. But what of Margaret Thatcher, Indira Gandhi, Golda Meir; what of Catherine the Great and Elizabeth I, in earlier eras? They are no use as test cases. All were women who had clambered to the tops of relentlessly male political and military hierarchies. They could scarcely restrain the surges of all those millions of gallons of testosterone continually in flux under their scepters. And again: the categories overlap; the consistent differences are in averages. The gauntlets those five women ran to get to the top and stay there can scarcely be said to have been at the least-aggressive end of the female spectrum. And women in a male world often find themselves outmachoing the men — to gain credibility, to consolidate power, to survive.

Those negative examples notwithstanding, a steady, massive infusion of women into positions of power, in a balanced way, throughout the world, should in fact reduce the risk that irrational factors — "Come on, make my day" sorts of factors — will bring about an end to life on earth. Political scientists and historians often argue as if there were no resemblance between fistfights and war. Anthropologists and biologists know better.

Interestingly, that same Norway that sent Dan Olweus off to study — and try to diminish — bullying, appears to be in the vanguard. Not only the Prime Minister, but 8 of the 18 members of the Cabinet, are currently free of testosterone poisoning. In an almost-all-male, consistently violent world of national governments, this little boat of the Norwegian Cabinet may run into some high seas. But it is a far cry from the Viking ships of yore, and I, for one, am keeping a hopeful eye on its prow.

SUGGESTIONS FOR WRITING

Informal Essays

1. After reading a few essays from this chapter, write an essay in which you describe an athletic confrontation with a member of the opposite sex. Weave a thesis through your essay or include a thesis in your conclusion.

2. Using a single personal experience, show how you were surprised by the behavior of the opposite sex because it failed to conform to your expectations.

3. Argue that the preoccupation with research into sex differences plays into the hands of chauvinists.

Short Documented Papers

1. Write a report on the gains that women have made in athletics.

2. Develop an argument supporting the claim that women will never be able to close the gap between men and women in athletic performance.

3. Write a report in which you describe the differences which researchers have found between male and female attitudes toward sexual intercourse — and then argue that these differences are the result of either (1) biology or (2) social conditioning.

4. Write a paper in which you argue for or against the conclusion that males have a math gene. Bring up and deal with any opposing data or argument.

5. Write an argument in which you attack or defend one of the studies that supports inherent sex differences. Use several additional sources to support your position.

6. Discuss what appears to be genetic differences between men and women in matters of basic health — such differences as life expectancy, immune system efficiency, vulnerability to heart attacks, tendencies toward depression, and others.

Longer Documented Papers

1. Some researchers conclude that differences between the behavior of males and females are partly due to the fact that each is dominated by a different hemisphere of the brain. Explain this theory and describe those male and female strengths and weaknesses which this theory accounts for.

2. Write a research argument in which you dispute the validity (and perhaps even the accuracy) of three or four conclusions made by researchers on sex differences.

3. After a survey of the research, contrast two or three male strengths or weaknesses with two or three female strengths or weaknesses.

4. Discuss three or four sex differences which seem directly attributable to sex hormones.

5. Discuss three or four sex differences which seem directly attributable to male and female physiology.

6. Discuss three or four sex differences which seem to be directly attributable to social conditioning.

BILINGUAL EDUCATION: *Does It Work?*

The sentiments evoked by the Statue of Liberty are central to our national identity. Indeed, we are flattered by Emma Lazarus's words chiseled on its base, and we have long seen our nation — ideally, anyway — as a great melting pot.

Through the years, immigrant parents struggled with the English language in an effort to accommodate themselves to the nation they had determined to call their own, and they were eager to enroll their children in schools, where they would prepare themselves, through an immersion in their new language, to become Americans.

This melting pot ideal was questioned during the 1960s. A rediscovered pride in cultural and ethnic roots and a heightened awareness of civil rights led some people to doubt the effectiveness and validity of forcing immigrant children through such an abrupt cultural transformation. At about the same time, studies showed that the dropout rate of immigrant children was significantly higher than that of their English-speaking counterparts. During this same period, a wave of legal and illegal immigrants from Latin American countries flooded certain American school systems — particularly those in the Southwest.

Finally, in the 1974 *Lau* v. *Nichols* decision, the Supreme Court ruled in favor of Chinese immigrant students in San Francisco who had contended that their civil rights had been violated because, as non-English-speaking students, they were being denied the quality of education received by their English-speaking peers. The high court made no specific recommendations, but the Department of Health, Education and Welfare addressed the problem by requiring that immigrant students be taught basic academic subjects in their native languages.

To many observers, this decision seemed to confer on immigrant children the absolute right to be instructed in their native languages — no matter what those languages might be, and no matter how few pupils in the same school system shared those languages. Congress provided funds for the administration of the HEW mandate, but school systems with sizable immigrant enrollments were faced with the burden of the costs of implementing such a program.

Opponents of the federal government's bilingual education guidelines rankle at the enormous costs of such a program. They also contend that the program dramatically slows immigrant children's mastery of English — and thus impedes their assimilation into their new culture. Indeed, the most pessimistic of the critics see the Southwest becoming Spanish-speaking Quebec.

Most of those in favor of bilingual education don't question the melting pot ideal. On the contrary, they contend that their opponents underestimate the allure of

American culture to immigrants. Most immigrants, the supporters say, are eager to be assimilated into American life — but assimilation is difficult, they add, if the children, forced to sink or swim in a new language, fail in school. Bilingual education, to its supporters, is thus a more efficient and less painful way to see that the immigrant child is able to make his way into the American mainstream.

AGAINST BILINGUAL EDUCATION
Tom Bethell

In this essay Tom Bethell, the longtime Washington editor of Harper's, *traces the inception and early development of federal bilingual education policies, and then he excoriates the self-serving bureaucracy that has been built around them. It was this kind of stinging criticism that prompted the Reagan administration and Congress to reduce the projected funding levels for bilingual programs during the early 1980s.*

This year the United States government, which I am beginning to think is afflicted with a death wish, is spending $150 million on "bilingual education" programs in American classrooms. There is nothing "bi" about it, however. The languages in which instruction is conducted now include: Central Yup'ik, Aleut, Yup'ik, Gwich'in, Athabascan (the foregoing in Alaska), Navajo, Tagalog, Pima, Plaute (I promise I'm not making this up), Ilocano, Cambodian, Yiddish, Chinese, Vietnamese, Punjabi, Greek, Italian, Korean, Polish, French, Haitian, Haitian-French, Portuguese, Arabic, Crow (yes, Virginia . . .), Cree, Keresian, Tewa, Apache, Mohawk, Japanese, Lakota, Choctaw, Samoan, Chamorro, Carolinian, Creek-Seminole, and Russian.

And there are more, such as Trukese, Palauna, Ulithian, Woleian, Marshalles, Kusaian, Ponapean, and, not least, Yapese. And Spanish — how could I have so nearly forgotten it? The bilingual education program is more or less the Hispanic equivalent of affirmative action, creating jobs for thousands of Spanish teachers; by which I mean teachers who speak Spanish, although not necessarily English, it has turned out. One observer has described the HEW-sponsored program as "affirmative ethnicity." Although Spanish is only one of seventy languages in which instruction is carried on (I seem to have missed a good many of them), it accounts for 80 percent of the program.

Bilingual education is an idea that appeals to teachers of Spanish and other tongues, but also to those who never did think that another idea, the United States of America, was a particularly good one to begin with, and that the sooner it is restored to its component "ethnic" parts the better off we shall all be. Such people have been welcomed with open arms into the upper reaches of the federal government in recent years, giving rise to the suspicion of a death wish.

The bilingual education program began in a small way (the way such programs always begin) in 1968, when the Elementary and Secondary Education Act of 1965 was amended (by what is always referred to as "Title VII") to permit the development of "pilot projects" to help *poor* children who were "educationally disadvantaged because of their inability to speak English," and whose parents were either on welfare or earning less than $3,000 a year. At this germinal stage the program cost a mere $7.5 million, and as its sponsors (among them Sen. Alan Cranston of California) later boasted, it was enacted without any public challenge whatever.

Tom Bethell, "Against Bilingual Education," *Harper's* February 1979.

"With practically no one paying heed," Stephen Rosenfeld wrote in the *Washington Post* in 1974 (i.e., six years after the program began),

> Congress has radically altered the traditional way by which immigrants become Americanized. No longer will the public schools be expected to serve largely as a "melting pot," assimilating foreigners to a common culture. Rather, under a substantial new program for "bilingual" education, the schools — in addition to teaching English — are to teach the "home" language and culture to children who speak English poorly.

Rosenfeld raised the important point that "it is not clear how educating children in the language and culture of their ancestral homeland will better equip them for the rigors of contemporary life in the United States." But in response, a withering blast of disapproval was directed at the *Post's* "Letters" column. Hadn't he heard? The melting pot had been removed from the stove.

Bureaucratic imperative (and, I would argue, a surreptitious death wish) dictated that the $7.5 million "pilot program" of 1968 grow into something more luxuriant and permanent. As it happened, the U.S. Supreme Court decision *Lau v. Nichols*, handed down in 1974, provided the stimulus.

In this case, Legal Services attorneys in Chinatown sued a San Francisco school district on behalf of 1,800 Chinese-speaking students, claiming that they had been denied special instruction in English. The contention that these pupils had a *constitutional* right to such instruction (as was implied by filing suit in federal court) was denied both by the federal district court and the appeals court. The Justice Department entered the case when it was heard before the Supreme Court, arguing that the school district was in violation of a 1970 memorandum issued by HEW's Office for Civil Rights. This memorandum in turn was based on the 1964 Civil Rights Act, which decreed (among other things) that the recipients of federal funds cannot be discriminated against on the basis of national origin. The 1970 memorandum defined language as basic to national origin and required schools to take "affirmative steps" to correct English-language deficiencies.

Evidently intimidated by this rhetorical flourishing of "rights," the Supreme Court unanimously affirmed that federally funded schools must "rectify the language deficiency in order to open instruction to students who had 'linguistic deficiencies.'" In effect, the Office for Civil Rights had taken the position that the immigrant's tongue was to be regarded as a right, not an impediment, and the Supreme Court had meekly gone along with the argument.

Armed now with this judicial mandate, HEW's civil-rights militants went on the offensive, threatening widespread funding cutoffs. No longer would the old method of teaching immigrants be countenanced (throwing them into the English language and allowing them to sink or swim). No longer! Now the righteous activists within government had exactly what they are forever searching for: a huddled mass of yearning . . . victims! Discriminated against the moment they arrive at *these* teeming, wretched, racist, ethnocentric shores!

America the Bad . . . One Nation, Full of Victims . . . Divisible. (I have in my hands an odious document, the "Third Annual Report of the National Council on Bilingual Education," which remarks that "Cubans admitted after Castro; and more recently Vietnamese refugees . . . became citizens unintentionally." No doubt they are yearning to be free to return to Ho Chi Minh City and Havana.) That's about the size of it in the 1970s, and so it came to pass that the Office for Civil Rights "targeted" 334 school districts, which would have to start "bilingual-bicultural" classes promptly or risk having their federal funds cut off.

"The OCR [Office for Civil Rights] policy is difficult to explain," Noel Epstein remarked in a thoughtful survey of bilingual education titled "Language, Ethnicity and the Schools" and published recently by the Institute for Educational Leadership. "There is no federal legal requirement for schools to provide bilingual or bicultural education." The Supreme Court had merely said that *some* remedy was needed — not necessarily bilingual education. For example, the Chinese children in the *Lau* case could have been given extra instruction in English, to bring them up to par. But the Office for Civil Rights took the position that they would have to be taught school subjects — mathematics, geography, history, et cetera — in Chinese. And the Court's ruling had said nothing at all about bi*cultural* instruction. (This turns out to mean teaching that in any transaction with the "home" country, America tends to be in the wrong.)

In any event, the bilingual education program was duly expanded by Congress in 1974. It would no longer be just for poor children; all limited-English speakers would qualify; the experimental nature of the program was played down, and there was the important addition of biculturalism, which is summarized in a revealing paragraph in Epstein's booklet:

> Bicultural instruction was elevated to a required component of Title VII programs. The definition of "bilingual" education now meant such instruction had to be given "with appreciation for the cultural heritage of such children. . . ." This underlined the fact that language and culture were not merely being used as vehicles for the transmission of information but as the central sources of ethnic identity. The U.S. Civil Rights Commission had in fact urged the name of the law be changed to "The Bilingual Bicultural Education Act," but key Senate staff members blocked this idea. They feared it would "flag a potentially dangerous issue that might defeat the overall measure," Dr. Susan Gilbert Schneider reports in a valuable dissertation on the making of the 1974 act. Some lobby groups had expressed discomfort about federally sponsored biculturalism. The National Association of School Boards suggested that the legislation could be read as promoting a divisive, Canadian-style biculturalism.

It certainly could. Notice, however, the strong suggestion here that the objection was not so much to the possibility of cutting up the country, as to being *seen* to promote this possibility, which of course might defeat it. As I say, these things are best kept surreptitious — at the level of anonymous "Senate staff members."

At this stage the bilingual seed had indeed taken root. Congressional appropriations had increased from the beggarly $7.5 million to $85 million in fiscal year 1975. The Office for Civil Rights was on the alert. A potential 3.6 million "victimized" children of "limited English-speaking ability" had been identified, and they would furnish the raw material for an almost endless number of bureaucratic experiments. Militant Chicanos, suddenly sought out to fill ethnic teaching quotas, stood on the sidelines, ready to pour a bucket of guilt over any old-fashioned, demurring Yankee who might raise a voice in protest.

Even so, there was a cloud on the horizon — perhaps only a conceptual cloud, but nevertheless an important one, as follows: the idea behind bilingual education was that children would begin to learn school subjects in their native tongue while they were learning English elsewhere—in special English classes, on the playground, through exposure to American society generally. But while they were in this "stage of transition"—learning English—instruction in the home tongue would ensure that they were not needlessly held back academically. Then, when they had a sufficient grasp of English, they could be removed from the bilingual classes and instructed in the normal way. That, at least, was the idea behind bilingual education originally.

But you see the problem, no doubt. At bottom, this is the same old imperialism. It is a "melting pot" solution. The children learn English after all—perhaps fairly rapidly. And at that point there is no reason to keep them in bilingual programs. Moreover, from the point of view of HEW's civil-rights militants, there is rapid improvement by the "victims"—another unfortunate outcome.

The riposte has been predictable—namely, to keep the children in programs of bilingual instruction long after they know English. This has been justified by redefining the problem in the schools as one of "maintenance" of the home tongue, rather than "transition" to the English tongue. You will hear a lot of talk in and around HEW's numerous office buildings in Washington about the relative merits of maintenance versus transition. Of course, Congress originally had "transition" in mind, but "maintenance" is slowly but steadily winning the day.

The issue was debated this year in Congress when Title VII came up for renewal. Some Congressmen, alerted to the fact that children were still being instructed in Spanish, Aleut, or Yapese in the twelfth grade, tried to argue that bilingual instruction should not last for more than two years. But this proposal was roundly criticized by Messrs. Edward Roybal of California, Baltasar Corrada of Puerto Rico, Phillip Burton of California, Paul Simon of Illinois, and others. In the end the language was left vague, giving school boards the discretion to continue "bilingual maintenance" as long as they desired. Currently, fewer than one-third of the 290,000 students enrolled in various bilingual programs are significantly limited in their English-speaking ability.

Then a new cloud appeared on the horizon. If you put a group of children, let's say children from China, in a classroom together in order to teach them English, that's segregation, right? Watch out, then. Here come the civil-rights militants on the rampage once again, ready to demolish the very program that they had done so much to encourage. But there was a simple remedy that would send them trotting tamely homeward. As follows: Put the "Anglos" in with the ethnics. In case you hadn't heard, "Anglo" is the name given these days to Americans who haven't got a drop of ethnicity to their names—the ones who have already been melted down, so to speak.

Putting Anglos into the bilingual program killed two birds with one stone. It circumvented the "segregation" difficulty, and—far more to the point—it meant that the Anglos (just the ones who needed it!) would be exposed to the kind of cultural revisionism that is the covert purpose behind so much of the bilingual program. Put more simply, Mary Beth and Sue Anne would at last learn the new truth: the Indians, not the cowboys, were the good guys, Texas was an ill-gotten gain, and so on.

As Congressman Simon of Illinois put it so delicately, so *surreptitiously:* "I hope that in the conference committee we can get this thing modified as we had it in subcommittee, to make clear that we ought to encourage our English-language students to be in those classes so that you can have the interplay."

As things worked out, up to 40 percent of the classes may permissibly be "Anglo," Congress decreed. And this year there has been another important change: an expanded definition of students who will be eligible for bilingual instruction. No longer will it be confined to those with limited English-*speaking* ability. Now the program will be open to those with "limited English proficiency in understanding, speaking, reading, and writing." This, of course, could be construed as applying to almost anyone in elementary or high school these days.

To accommodate this expansion, future Congressional appropriations for bilingual education will increase in leaps and bounds: $200 million next year, $250 million the year after, and so on in $50 million jumps, until $400 million is spent in 1983, when the program will once again be reviewed by Congress.

Meanwhile, HEW's Office of Education (that is, the *E* of HEW) appears to be getting alarmed at this runaway program. It commissioned a study by the American Institutes for Research in Palo Alto, and this study turned out to be highly critical of bilingual education. The Office of Education then drew attention to this by announcing the findings at a press conference. ("They've got it in for us," someone at the Bilingual Office told me. "Whenever there's an unfavorable study, they call a press conference. Whenever there's a favorable study, they keep quiet about it.")

In any event, the Palo Alto study claimed that children in bilingual classes were doing no better academically, and perhaps were doing slightly worse, than children from similar backgrounds in regular English classes. The study also reported that 85 percent of the students were being kept in bilingual classes after they were capable of learning in English.

There has been very little Congressional opposition to the bilingual programs, thus bearing out what the Washington writer Fred Reed has called the Guppy Law: "When outrageous expenditures are divided finely enough, the public will not have enough stake in any one expenditure to squelch it." (Reed adds, in a brilliant analysis of the problem: "A tactic of the politically crafty is to pose questions in terms of rightful virtue. 'What? You oppose a mere $40 million subsidy of codpiece manufacture by the Nez Percé? So! You are against Indians. . . .' The thudding opprobrium of anti-Indianism outweighs the $40 million guppy bite in the legislators' eyes.")

Risking that opprobrium, John Ashbrook of Ohio tried to cut out the bilingual program altogether. Referring to the evidence that the program wasn't working, but the budget for it was increasing annually, Ashbrook said that "when one rewards failure, one buys failure." On the House floor he added: "The program is actually preventing children from learning English. Someday somebody is going to have to teach those young people to speak English or else they are going to become public charges. Our educational system is finding it increasingly difficult today to teach English-speaking children to read their own language. When children come out of the Spanish-language schools or Choctaw-language schools which call themselves bilingual, how is our educational system going to make them literate in what will still be a completely alien tongue . . . ?"

The answer, of course, is that there will be demands not for literacy in English but for public signs in Spanish (or Choctaw, et cetera), laws promulgated in Spanish, courtroom proceedings in Spanish, and so on. These demands are already being felt—and met, in part. As so often happens, the ill effects of one government program result in the demand for another government program, rather than the abolition of the original one.

This was borne out by what happened next. When the amendment abolishing bilingual education was proposed by Ashbrook (who is usually regarded in Washington as one of those curmudgeons who can be safely ignored), *not one* Congressman rose to support it, which says something about the efficacy of the Guppy Law. Instead, the House was treated to some pusillanimous remarks by Congressman Claude Pepper of Florida—a state in which it is, of course, politically unwise to resist the expenditure of federal money "targeted" for Hispanics. Pepper said: "Now there is something like parity between the population of the United States and Latin America. My information is that by the year 2000 there probably will be 600 million people living in Latin America, and about 300 million people living in the United States."

Perhaps, then, it would be in order for the "Anglos" to retreat even further, before they are entirely overwhelmed. This brings to mind a most interesting remark made by Dr. Josue Gonzalez, the director-designate of the Office of Bilingual Education (the head of the program, in other words), in the course of an interview that he granted me. Actually, Dr. Gonzalez said many interesting things. He suggested a possible cause of the rift with the Office of Education. "Bilingual education was hatched in Congress, not in the bureaucracy," he said. "The constituents [i.e., Hispanics, mostly] talked directly to Congress. Most government programs are generated by so-called administrative proposal—that is, from within the bureaucracies themselves."

He said of regular public education in America: "I've plotted it on a graph: by the year 2010, most college graduates will be mutes!" (No *wonder* the Office of Education isn't too wildly enthusiastic.) And he said that, contrary to what one might imagine, many "Anglo" parents are in fact only too anxious for their children to enroll in a bilingual course. (If Johnny doesn't learn anything else, at least he might as well learn Spanish—that at least is my interpretation.)

The melting-pot idea is dead, Dr. Gonzalez kept reassuring me. Why? I asked him. What was his proof of this? He then made what I felt was a revealing observation, and one that is not normally raised at all, although it exists at the subliminal level. "We must allow for diversity . . . ," he began, then, suddenly veering off: "The counterculture of the 1960s showed that. Even the WASP middle-American showed that the monolithic culture doesn't exist. Within the group, even, they were rejecting their own values."

I imagine that Attila or Alaric, in an expansive and explanatory mood, might have said much the same thing to some sodden Roman senators who were trying to figure out how it was that Rome fell, exactly.

Dr. Gonzalez had me there and he knew it, so he promptly resumed the offensive. "There are those who say that to speak whatever language you speak is a human right," he went on. "The Helsinki Agreements and the President's Commission on Foreign Language Study commit us to the study of foreign languages. Why not our own—domestic—languages?"

Later on I decided to repeat this last comment to George Weber, the associate director of the Council for Basic Education, a somewhat lonely group in Washington. The grandson of German immigrants, Mr. Weber speaks perfect English. "Only in America," he said. "Only in America would someone say a stupid thing like that. Can you imagine a Turk arriving in France and complaining that he was being denied his human rights because he was taught at school in French, not Turkish? What do you think the French would say to that?"

Easing into English

Stan Luxenberg

Stan Luxenberg's essay focuses on the bilingual programs in three different high schools in New York City and in doing so provides concrete examples of the central argument of bilingual education supporters: It works. These specific programs suggest that bilingual education methods can promote a rapid and efficient assimilation of immigrant children into the American mainstream.

Just as they have done for decades, the children of immigrants — from Ecuador, Italy, Vietnam, and dozens of other countries — continue coming into New York City's already crowded high schools, speaking little English but hoping to receive the education that will enable them to improve their lives.

Battered by budget cuts and short of teachers, the city's educational system must nonetheless integrate the steady flow of new students into the American mainstream. In the past, newcomers were simply dropped into classes and left to struggle through as best they could . . . or could not.

Recently, however, in response to federal mandates, New York City has been increasing its high school bilingual program aimed at easing the transition faced by non-English speakers. Immigrants are given special courses in English — called English as a second language (ESL) — while at the same time they take the regular content area courses in their native language. The idea is to allow students to continue their education by increasing their knowledge of content at their own grade levels at the same time they are acquiring English.

"When students come here they're scared stiff because they can't speak English," says Alan Irgang, principal of Franklin D. Roosevelt High School in Brooklyn. "If you mainstream them into regular classrooms they wouldn't last."

Most of these students pick up English in two or three years and then switch to regular classes. In some schools they can continue studying their native language so that they can graduate from high school truly bilingual. While the students attend special homerooms for bilingual assistance where they feel more comfortable at a time such support is critical, they are also encouraged to mix with other students. From the beginning they take music, art, and physical education with American-born students. As soon as they pick up some English, they are sometimes moved into regular math classes.

Before the students go into regular English and social studies classes, their English must be fairly good. History poses the biggest problem. As their English improves they may be able to understand generally what a teacher is saying, but it is difficult for them to grasp ideas quickly enough to take notes and to place the content in some perspective. "Once the time is right, the students are better off getting into the mainstream," says Irgang. "We don't help them by keeping them in the bilingual program."

Stan Luxenberg, "Easing into English," *American Education* January–February 1981.

To teach basic courses in foreign languages, the schools must find textbooks and devise a curriculum suitable for the newcomers. Locating materials in Chinese and Italian is perhaps the most difficult. But the teachers are helped by the Comprehensive High School Bilingual Program's federal funding which provides $563,019 in Title VII money (under the Bilingual Education Act) to supplement staff for the five high schools. The money makes possible curriculum specialists in Chinese, Spanish, and Italian who can develop curriculum. In addition, resource teachers work in the schools helping the regular teachers, developing courses and advising students.

About 675 students are in this high school bilingual program — 180 Chinese, 50 Italian, and the rest Spanish-speaking. The program, begun five years ago, will end this August.

When students first enter the school system, they are tested to determine how much English they know. Those who do poorly have the option of entering the special ESL program, and their parents are notified about the program. If they want their children put into some regular classes, this is possible too.

For Chinese students, learning English is particularly difficult. Accustomed to reading characters rather than an alphabet, the immigrants must make an intense adjustment to master their new language. At Lower East Side Prep, which serves students living in the city's Chinatown, immigrants take special English courses for three periods a day. Although a few more high schools offer courses for Chinese natives, the Chinatown school has a waiting list of over 200 students wanting to enter.

Lower East Side Prep is particularly appealing because it has only 500 students, including 180 Chinese in the special English classes. It is an alternative school designed for recent immigrants and students who have previously dropped out of school. Many of the students are older, ranging from 18 to 21, and are more motivated than younger people.

It is a school with few classrooms. Instead, students meet in large rooms divided only by blackboards. The Chinese youngsters come from a wide range of backgrounds in Hong Kong, Taiwan, and mainland China. More recently have come Vietnamese boat people who speak Chinese. The families — a mixture of poor peasants and sophisticated middle-class families — have left isolated villages and the large cities.

Some arrive knowing virtually no English. Pau Ngok Wan, 19, arrived in the United States in 1979 from Wenchau, a small city in mainland China. He had a ninth grade education. With the help of an interpreter, Wan explains how the special bilingual program is helping him. "My English is very poor," he says. "I wouldn't be able to stay in a regular high school."

The Chinese students who know little English begin with what the school calls ESL level one, basic English vocabulary, with frequent conversation sessions. When they reach level four they take a special transition course, from which most are able to move into regular English classes. "Sometimes students at this level (four) can write better than the average youngster in tenth grade," says Edward Hom, principal at Lower East Side Prep. "The students have been practicing grammar and punctuation. They can find words in the dictionary."

When students first enter the school, they fill out a brief questionnaire telling how long they have been in this country and how much schooling they had in their native countries. Each takes brief math and English exams which the teachers use as an informal basis for placement in the proper levels. Students who advance faster in English than the rest of the class are moved up to another level. Last September, 161 returning students at the school were tested in English to determine if they needed to continue in the special classes. Of these, 67 passed and were mainstreamed into regular classes.

The ESL courses are taught mainly in English, but teachers sometimes use Chinese to make certain everything is understood. "Is a freezer cold or hot?" asked a teacher in a level four class. "Is it freezing today?" Then she began explaining the word "frozen" and, to make certain the class understood, she lapsed into Chinese.

Students, while given credit for courses taken in their native countries, must still take the credits here required for all New York high school graduates. To earn a degree, students must pass required courses and also the New York State Regents competency exams. Students who came to the country after the eighth grade can take the exam in their native language and qualify for the degree. Of the 60 oriental students who graduated last year from the program, 50 went on to colleges and universities — from the city colleges to ivy league schools. . . .

Most students in the bilingual program are Spanish-speaking, and they face less of a problem in mastering English than the Chinese do. At Benjamin Franklin High School in Spanish Harlem there are 120 students from Puerto Rico and other parts of Latin America in ESL classes. They can normally move from the special classes in a year and a half or two, taking two periods a day of English while in the program. The ESL program produces some of the school's best students, said Melvin Taylor, Benjamin Franklin principal. At that high school — as at other comprehensive bilingual schools — attendance by ESL students is 10 to 20 percent higher than that of regular students. A recent valedictorian of the Harlem school started out in bilingual classes. Taylor has found that education holds a special value for those who come from countries where schools are not open to everyone.

Joe Barbarino, who teaches regular and ESL English classes, agrees. "These kids come wanting to learn. Apathy is nonexistent."

Before the current program, immigrant youngsters entering Benjamin Franklin took special language classes but could not take courses in subject areas. Since it would be two years before they could handle regular courses, students would take six years to finish high school — assuming they stayed that long.

Benjamin Franklin is a large inner-city school with 2,000 students and uniformed guards monitoring the halls. Because the ESL pupils are a relatively small group, they have more direct contact with teachers. They know the assistant principal overseeing the program. The school even helps the students get after-school jobs.

Teachers try to run the ESL classes in English as much as possible, but many — as with the Chinese classes at Lower East Side Prep — fall back on Spanish temporarily when the class is having a particularly hard time. "I'd rather have them know what's going on than sitting like zombies," Barbarino says.

In one exercise his students were practicing how to change a sentence from present to past tense. "What is the past tense of can't?" Barbarino asks them. Someone says "couldn't," but not all the students are sure what that means. "*Pudo?*"

one girl questions, wondering if the Spanish verb she understood means the same as the English word. "Right," Barbarino assures her.

By the time the students have finished two years of special classes, their English is far from perfect. But they can keep up in regular English classes. "They feel better about themselves and their ability to cope," explains Barbarino.

Social studies texts present special problems. Resource teachers are constantly searching for appropriate ones. Spanish translations of the standard American textbooks are troublesome for students coming from South America. These students have little background in United States history, while American students were exposed to the subject in fourth and seventh grades, notes Jonathan Houston, the resource teacher coordinator at Benjamin Franklin High School. Students who grew up under dictatorships have little conception of what democracy is. Spanish-language volumes on the subject are aimed at mature scholars. To solve the problem, Houston is developing his own materials. One lesson, for example, emphasizes that many colonists came to the New World to escape persecution, just as many students' families had to flee their homelands.

Finding an appropriate American history text for Italian students is not much easier. The only ones published were written in Italy from a European perspective. According to the Italian author of a text used at Roosevelt High School, George Washington was a poor general and had to rely on Lafayette, the European, for assistance. Even given the European perspective, the material is more difficult for young Italian-born students than for American youngsters. Tony Rutigliano, who teaches the course, must move slowly in order to explain concepts that are foreign to the students. Few have heard, for example, about our war between the states. "I cannot cover what a regular history class would," he noted. "I have to spend time introducing examples of things they understand."

Anna Maria Gallo, assistant principal at Roosevelt in charge of foreign languages, underlines the basic problem of locating suitable books. Most texts, she says, are too hard or too easy. One ESL teacher trained in Spanish and teaching ESL translated Spanish exercises into English for beginners in order to teach Italian students English. "The people who write the books are not in classrooms," says Gallo. "Teachers often have to create their own materials. Everybody's feeling their way through."

Yet it is the teachers' willingness to do more than would be asked in a regular classroom that is making the program work. "They really believe in their students," says Pu-Folkes, "and in giving the youngsters the opportunity to learn in their new country."

AGAINST A CONFUSION OF TONGUES
William A. Henry, III

William A. Henry, III, a writer for Time, *lists four different approaches to educating immigrant children: (1) total immersion in English, (2) short-term bilingual education, (3) a dual curriculum, and (4) language and cultural maintenance. And he then surveys the problems inherent in the latter two extended bilingual education approaches. Henry shares the most grave reservation of most of bilingual education's critics: He fears that language maintenance inevitably becomes cultural maintenance for immigrant children. Critics contend that cultural maintenance not only blocks assimilation into the American mainstream; it also creates a political and social divisiveness that could polarize and divide the nation in the same way that the English and French language and cultural differences polarize and divide Canada.*

"We have room for but one language here, and that is the English language, for we intend to see that the crucible turns our people out as Americans and not as dwellers in a polyglot boarding house."

— Theodore Roosevelt

In the store windows of Los Angeles, gathering place of the world's aspiring peoples, the signs today ought to read, "English spoken here." Supermarket price tags are often written in Korean, restaurant menus in Chinese, employment-office signs in Spanish. In the new city of dreams, where gold can be earned if not found on the sidewalk, there are laborers and businessmen who have lived five, ten, 20 years in America without learning to speak English. English is not the common denominator for many of these new Americans. Disturbingly, some of them insist it need not be.

America's image of itself as a melting pot, enriched by every culture yet subsuming all of them, dates back far beyond the huddled yearning masses at the Baja California border and Ellis Island, beyond the passage in steerage of victims of the potato famine and the high-minded Teutonic settlements in the nascent Midwest. Just months after the Revolution was won, in 1782, French-American Writer Michel Guillaume-Jean de Crèvecoeur said of his adopted land: "Individuals of all nations are melted into a new race of men." Americans embittered by the wars of Europe knew that fusing diversity into unity was more than a poetic ideal, it was a practical necessity. In 1820 future Congressman Edward Everett warned, "From the days of the Tower of Babel, confusion of tongues has ever been one of the most active causes of political misunderstanding."

The successive waves of immigrants did not readily embrace the new culture, even when intimidated by the xenophobia of the know-nothing era or two World Wars. Says Historian James Banks: "Each nationality group tried desperately to remake North America in the image of its native land." When the question arose of making the U.S. multilingual or multicultural in public affairs, however, Congress

William A. Henry, III, "Against a Confusion of Tongues," *Time* 13 June 1983.

stood firm. In the 1790s, 1840s and 1860s, the lawmakers voted down pleas to print Government documents in German. Predominantly French-speaking Louisiana sought statehood in 1812; the state constitution that it submitted for approval specified that its official language would be English. A century later, New Mexico was welcomed into the union, but only after an influx of settlers from the North and East had made English, not Spanish, the majority tongue.

Occasional concentrations of immigrants were able to win local recognition of their language and thereby enforce an early form of affirmative action: by 1899 nearly 18,000 pupils in Cincinnati divided their school time between courses given in German and in English, thus providing employment for 186 German-speaking teachers. In 1917 San Francisco taught German in eight primary schools, Italian in six, French in four and Spanish in two. Yet when most cities consented to teach immigrant children in their native Chinese or Polish or Yiddish or Gujarati, the clearly stated goal was to transform the students as quickly as possible into speakers of English and full participants in society.

Now, however, a new bilingualism and biculturalism is being promulgated that would deliberately fragment the nation into separate, unassimilated groups. The movement seems to take much of its ideology from the black separatism of the 1960s but derives its political force from the unprecedented raw numbers — 15 million or more — of a group linked to a single tongue, Spanish. The new metaphor is not the melting pot but the salad bowl, with each element distinct. The biculturalists seek to use public services, particularly schools, not to Americanize the young but to heighten their consciousness of belonging to another heritage. Contends Tomás A. Arciniega, vice president for academic affairs at California State University at Fresno: "The promotion of cultural differences has to be recognized as a valid and legitimate educational goal." Miguel Gonzalez-Pando, director of the Center for Latino Education at Florida International University in Miami, says: "I speak Spanish at home, my social relations are mostly in Spanish, and I am raising my daughter as a Cuban American. It is a question of freedom of choice." In Gonzalez-Pando's city, where Hispanics outnumber whites, the anti-assimilationist theory has become accepted practice: Miami's youth can take twelve years of bilingual public schooling with no pretense made that the program is transitional toward anything. The potential for separatism is greater in Los Angeles. Philip Hawley, president of the Carter Hawley Hale retail store chain, cautions: "This is the only area in the U.S. that over the next 50 years could have a polarization into two distinct cultures, of the kind that brought about the Quebec situation in Canada." Professor Rodolfo Acuña of California State University at Northridge concurs. Says Acuña: "Talk of secession may come when there are shrinking economic resources and rising expectations among have-not Hispanics."

Already the separatists who resist accepting English have won laws and court cases mandating provision of social services, some government instructions, even election ballots in Spanish. The legitimizing effect of these decisions can be seen in the proliferation of billboards, roadside signs and other public communications posted in Spanish. Acknowledges Professor Ramón Ruiz of the University of California at San Diego: "The separatism question is with us already." The most portentous evidence is in the classrooms. Like its political cousins, equal opportunity and social justice, bilingual education is a catchall term that means what the speaker wishes it to mean.

There are at least four ways for schools to teach students who speak another language at home:

1. Total immersion in English, which relies on the proven ability of children to master new languages. Advocates of bilingual education argue that this approach disorients children and sometimes impedes their progress in other subjects, because those who have already mastered several grades' worth of material in their first language may be compelled to take English-language classes with much younger or slower students.

2. Short-term bilingual education, which may offer a full curriculum but is directed toward moving students into English-language classes as rapidly as possible. In a report last month by a Twentieth Century Fund task force, members who were disillusioned with the performance of elaborate bilingual programs urged diversion of federal funds to the teaching of English. The panel held: "Schoolchildren will never swim in the American mainstream unless they are fluent in English."

3. Dual curriculum, which permits students to spend several years making the transition. This is the method urged by many moderate Hispanic, Chinese and other ethnic minority leaders. Says Historian Ruiz: "The direct approach destroys children's feelings of security. Bilingual education eases them from something they know to something they do not."

4. Language and cultural maintenance, which seeks to enhance students' mastery of their first language while also teaching them English. In Hispanic communities, the language training is often accompanied by courses in ethnic heritage. Argues Miami Attorney Manuel Díaz, a vice chairman of the Spanish American League Against Discrimination: "Cultural diversity makes this country strong. It is not a disease."

The rhetoric of supporters of bilingualism suggests that theirs may be a political solution to an educational problem. Indeed, some of them acknowledge that they view bilingual programs as a source of jobs for Hispanic administrators, teachers and aides. In cities with large minority enrollments, says a Chicago school principal who requested anonymity, "those of us who consider bilingual education ineffective are afraid that if we say so we will lose our jobs." Lawrence Uzzell, president of Learn Inc., a Washington-based research foundation, contends that Hispanic educational activists are cynically protecting their own careers. Says Uzzell: "The more the Hispanic child grows up isolated, the easier it is for politicians to manipulate him as part of an ethnic voting bloc."

The signal political success for bilingualism has been won at the U.S. Department of Education. After the Supreme Court ruled in 1974 that Chinese-speaking students were entitled to some instruction in a language they could understand, the DOE issued "informal" rules that now bind more than 400 school districts. Immersion in English, even rapid transition to English, does not satisfy the DOE; the rules compel school systems to offer a full curriculum to any group of 20 or more students who share a foreign language. The DOE rules have survived three presidencies, although Jesse Soriano, director of the Reagan Administration's $138 million bilingual program, concedes, "This is money that could be spent more effectively." About half of students from Spanish-speaking homes drop out before the end of high school; of the ones who remain, 30% eventually score two or more years below their age group on standardized tests. But it is hard to demonstrate the value of any bilingual approach in aiding those students. In 1982 Iris Rotberg reported in the *Harvard Education Review*: "Research findings have shown that bilingual programs are neither better or worse than other instructional methods." Indeed, the DOE's review found that of all methods for teaching bilingual students English and mathematics, only total immersion in English clearly worked.

One major problem in assessing the worth of bilingual programs is that they often employ teachers who are less than competent in either English or Spanish, or in the specific subjects they teach. In a 1976 test of 136 teachers and aides in bilingual programs in New Mexico, only 13 could read and write Spanish at third-grade level. Says former Boston School Superintendent Robert Wood: "Many bilingual teachers do not have a command of English, and after three years of instruction under them, children also emerge without a command of English." Another complicating factor is the inability of researchers to determine whether the problems of Hispanic students stem more from language difficulty or from their economic class. Many Hispanic children who are unable to speak English have parents with little education who hold unskilled jobs; in school performance, these students are much like poor blacks and whites. Notes Harvard's Nathan Glazer: "If these students do poorly in English, they may be doing poorly in a foreign language."

Even if the educational value of bilingual programs were beyond dispute, there would remain questions about their psychic value to children. Among the sharpest critics of bilingualism is author Richard Rodriquez, who holds a Berkeley Ph.D. in literature and grew up in a Spanish-speaking, working-class household; in his autobiography *Hunger of Memory*, Rodriguez argues that the separation from his family that a Hispanic child feels on becoming fluent in English is necessary to develop a sense of belonging to American society. Writes Rodriguez: "Bilingualists do not seem to realize that there are two ways a person is individualized. While one suffers a diminished sense of private individuality by becoming assimilated into public society, such assimilation makes possible the achievement of public individuality." By Rodriguez's reasoning, the discomfort of giving up the language of home is far less significant than the isolation of being unable to speak the language of the larger world.

The dubious value of bilingualism to students is only part of America's valid concern about how to absorb the Hispanic minority. The U.S., despite its exceptional diversity, has been spared most of the ethnic tensions that beset even such industrialized nations as Belgium and Spain. The rise of a large group, detached from the main population by language and custom, could affect the social stability of the country. Hispanic leaders, moreover, acknowledge that their constituents have been less inclined to become assimilated than previous foreign-language communities, in part because many of them anticipated that after earning and saving, they would return to Puerto Rico, Mexico, South America or Cuba. Says historian Doyce Nunis of the University of Southern California: "For the first time in American experience, a large immigrant group may be electing to bypass the processes of acculturation." Miami Mayor Maurice Ferré, a Puerto Rican, claims that in his city a resident can go from birth through school and working life to death without ever having to speak English. But most Hispanic intellectuals claim that their communities, like other immigrant groups before them, cling together only to combat discrimination.

The disruptive potential of bilingualism and biculturalism is still worrisome: millions of voters cut off from the main sources of information, millions of potential draftees inculcated with dual ethnic loyalties, millions of would-be employees ill at ease in the language of their workmates. Former Senator S.I. Hayakawa of California was laughed at for proposing a constitutional amendment to make English the official language of the U.S. It was a gesture of little practical consequence but great symbolic significance: many Americans mistakenly feel there is something racist, or oppressive, in expecting newcomers to share the nation's language and folkways.

Beyond practical politics and economics, separatism belittles the all-embracing culture that America has embodied for the world. Says writer Irving Howe, a scholar of literature and the Jewish immigrant experience: "The province, the ethnic nest, remains the point from which everything begins, but it must be transcended." That transcendence does not mean disappearance. It is possible to eat a Mexican meal, dance a Polish polka, sing in a Rumanian choir, preserve one's ethnicity however one wishes, and still share fully in the English-speaking common society. Just as American language, food and popular culture reflect the past groups who landed in the U.S., so future American culture will reflect the Hispanics, Asians and many other groups who are replanting their roots. As Author Rodriguez observes after his journey into the mainstream, "Culture survives whether you want it to or not."

BILINGUAL CLASSES:
A BILATERAL CONFLICT

Sally Reed

Sally Reed, a former senior editor of Instructor *magazine, briefly surveys the arguments of those who support bilingual education and summarizes the results of research that has attempted to compare the effectiveness of the bilingual approach to educating immigrant children with more traditional approaches. The defenders of bilingual education Reed quotes insist that the first priority is the rapid assimilation of children into American culture but also insist that these children's native tongues should be maintained and developed throughout their public schooling. Do these seem like contradictory ideas to you, or can you reconcile them without much trouble?*

When 11-year-old Joanna Poniatowski arrived at the Hanson Park Elementary School on [Chicago's] northwest side last year, she had traveled halfway around the world to settle in a country she had never seen at a school where most of the children spoke a language very different from her own. Her parents, who left their native Poland for Austria two days before martial law was declared, ultimately immigrated to Chicago to live in the world's largest Polish community outside of Warsaw.

Hanson Park School, across the street from St. Stanislaus Roman Catholic Church, where mass is said in both Polish and English, and a stone's throw from a Polish bakery where grandmothers converse in their native dialects, is a refuge for Joanna as she makes her transition from one world to another. Here, under the tutelage of Rafaela Mielcarek, a teacher who speaks both English and Polish, Joanna studies English as a second language and until she masters it, pursues science, math and social studies in her native tongue.

"The purpose of the bilingual-education program is to help children who have come from Poland to learn English," Mrs. Mielcarek said, "but they study other subjects in Polish so that they do not lose time acquiring knowledge in those areas."

Joanna's experience is that of many students who enter American schools each year from Poland, Mexico, Vietnam, Haiti, the Dominican Republic and other countries where English is virtually unknown. To assimilate them, the schools resort to two bilingual approaches: the transformational method for transition into English, or the maintenance method, in which students also continue studying their native language. However, a recent national report and proposed Federal legislation have called these strategies into question, with critics charging that students stay in their native languages too long.

The issue has become all the more complex as the largest influx of new immigrants in more than half a century has been accompanied by reduced Federal and state funding for education.

Sally Reed, "Bilingual Classes: A Bilateral Conflict," *The New York Times* 21 August 1983.

And besides other problems, bilingual programs are hobbled by a shortage of qualified teachers. According to a Department of Education study of teacher-training programs in bilingual education, 56,000 more teachers are currently needed nationwide from kindergarten through the 12th grade, but the current graduation rate of such teachers is only 2,000 a year.

Polish is one of 140 languages now spoken in the nation's schools. Spanish is the most often spoken foreign language, and last year Vietnamese replaced Chinese as the second most frequently spoken in federally supported school programs.

Miss Poniatowski is one of 46 Polish-speaking pupils in her school. She is one of 220,000 students across the nation in the federally financed Title VII bilingual program, one of 660,000 nationwide in state-financed programs and one of an estimated 3.5 million students needing such services nationally.

For the last 17 years, under legislative mandate and a Supreme Court ruling, schools have been required to provide such students as Joanna with "the use of two languages, one of which is English, as a medium of instruction." According to Title VII of the Elementary and Secondary Education Act, when a school has between 10 and 20 students who speak the same foreign language, the school must provide a separate bilingual teacher.

Unlike an immersion program, where students are quickly placed in an English environment, the transformational and maintenance approaches assume that the fastest way to English is through the native tongue and that skills learned in one language can be transferred to another.

Gloria Zamora, president of the National Association for Bilingual Education, is among those who believe that the transformation approach is "the law of the land."

"The underlying philosophy is to use the first language as a bridge for the second," she said. "The objective is to move the child into English, after which he never again concentrates on a native language."

In the Los Angeles Unified School District, for example, there are 118,000 students of limited English ability, and Hispanic students now make up 49 percent of the school population. Students are taught English as a second language and take their basic subjects in Spanish until they are ready to enter regular English classes.

"Our purpose in bilingual education is to move youngsters into the mainstream curriculum as soon as possible," said Ignacio DeCarrillo, director of the bilingual program for the Los Angeles schools.

At Hanson Park School in Chicago, which also has bilingual programs in Spanish and Italian as well as Polish, Joanna Poniatowski will make the transition to English classes in approximately two years. But she will also maintain her language skills in Polish through a special maintenance class taught by Mrs. Mielcarek. "The pressure is on learning English," Mrs. Mielcarek said. "But the concern is that the Polish not be lost."

The maintenance of their native language is a critical priority in many ethnic communities. In New York City's bilingual programs there are 70,000 students and 13 language groups in 684 public schools. Seventy percent of the students are in a Spanish program. At Public School 155, for example, children who have achieved proficiency in English maintain their basic skills in Spanish through a special language-arts class.

"The goal is not to be dominant in Spanish," said Sonia Gulardo, director of bilingual education for Community School District 4 in East Harlem. "Our students are learning English. But this country needs bilingual people."

In Milwaukee, the school system recently began a bilingual program for 100 Vietnamese and 290 Laotians, including 140 Hmong, an ethnically distinct Laotian hill tribe. The bilingual Spanish program is aimed not only at maintaining native language skills but also developing them so that by the 12th grade students are proficient in two languages.

Some critics of bilingual education simply object to teaching any language to the foreign-born other than English. Others, including the American Federation of Teachers, argue that maintaining a native language keeps the child from being assimilated into the school and becoming proficient in English.

Other critics contend that schools cannot cope adequately with the linguistic diversity of its student population and that some test scores indicate that the approaches have been ineffective. They point to the most extensive study to date, conducted in the late 1970's, by the American Institute for Research, which found that students in Title VII Spanish programs performed at a lower level in English language arts than did non-Title VII students.

This concern is expressed in "Making the Grade," a recent report on Federal education policy issued by the 20th Century Fund. The report recommends that schools "emphasize the primacy of English" and suggests that funds earmarked for bilingual education be used solely to teach non-English-speaking students to read and write English.

The Bilingual Education Improvement bill now in Congress also reflects a shift in thinking on the Federal level, where the budget for Title VII last year was $134 million. It in effect eliminates the emphasis on native languages by accepting different teaching methods such as immersion and English-as-a-second-language classes not based on students' native language.

Opponents to this thinking argue that native languages must be maintained in bilingual programs for linguistic as well as political and social reasons. "We do believe in the primacy of English, and teaching English is our primary goal," said Mrs. Zamora of the National Association for Bilingual Education. "But we believe it doesn't have to be done at the sacrifice of other languages.

"There is now a large body of research, particularly in linguistics," she said, "that supports what Unesco articulated 15 years ago: that is, no matter what language one may come to use as an adult, there are definite cognitive advantages to being educated in one's native tongue."

Indeed, Joan Friedenberg, associate professor of bilingual education at Florida International University, studied Spanish-speaking students in the third and fourth grades in Dade County, Florida, and found that those who learned to read simultaneously in English and Spanish scored higher on achievement tests than those taught to read English alone. Her conclusion was that schools should not delay in teaching English but not at the expense of the native language.

There are, however, as many studies and conflicting tests scores as there are opinions as to the effectiveness of bilingual education. "There is no consensus in the research community about the best results," said Louise Terry Wilkinson, head of the educational psychology department at the University of Wisconsin. In an attempt to isolate variables that may determine the success of the bilingual programs, the National Institute of Education is currently conducting a three-year study to examine language acquisition, the impact of parental and teacher attitudes and comparison of teaching practices.

While it appears that Congress, administrators and tax-weary communities are in no mood to expand bilingual programs, schools such as Hanson Park are faced with the increasing influx of new students. "Bilingual programs can hold kids back, perhaps, and keep them from assimilating as quickly as they might," said Frank J. DePaul, the Hanson Park principal. "But at their best the programs encourage children to read and write in English and children who do not understand a subject because they don't know the language are no longer labeled slow.

"We claim that we want students to learn foreign languages," he added. "Well, here we have these children coming to our schools with a capacity for dual languages. Not maintaining these skills is a terrible waste of our human resources."

LANGUAGE
James Fallows

James Fallows, the Washington editor for the Atlantic *for well over a decade now, is a former critic of bilingual education who underwent a conversion in the course of his firsthand observation of the program in action. His arguments are the central ones of the program's supporters: (1) When it comes to assimilating immigrant children into the American mainstream, bilingual education simply works — and works surprisingly well; (2) immigrant families are eager to accommodate themselves to American life, and they are acutely aware that mastering English is vital to the successful cultural assimilation they desire.*

. . . A national culture is held together by official rules and informal signals. Through their language, dress, taste, and habits of life, immigrants initially violate the rules and confuse the signals. The United States has prided itself on building a nation out of diverse parts. *E Pluribus Unum* originally referred to the act of political union in which separate colonies became one sovereign state. It now seems more fitting as a token of the cultural adjustments through which immigrant strangers have become Americans. Can the assimilative forces still prevail?

The question arises because most of today's immigrants share one trait: their native language is Spanish. . . .

The term "Hispanic" is in many ways deceiving. It refers to those whose origins can be traced back to Spain (*Hispania*) or Spain's former colonies. It makes a bloc out of Spanish-speaking peoples who otherwise have little in common. The Cuban-Americans, concentrated in Florida, are flush with success. Some of them nurse dreams of political revenge against Castro. They demonstrate little solidarity with such other Hispanics as the Mexican-Americans of Texas, who are much less estranged from their homeland and who have been longtime participants in the culture of the Southwest. The Cuban-Americans tend to be Republicans; most Mexican-Americans and Puerto Ricans are Democrats. The Puerto Ricans, who are U.S. citizens from birth, and who have several generations of contact with American city life behind them, bear little resemblance to the Salvadorans and Guatemalans now pouring northward to get out of the way of war. Economically, the Puerto Ricans of New York City have more in common with American blacks than with most other Hispanic groups. Such contact as Anglo and black residents of Boston and New York have with Hispanic life comes mainly through Puerto Ricans; they may be misled about what to expect from the Mexicans and Central Americans arriving in ever increasing numbers. Along the southern border, Mexican-American children will razz youngsters just in from Mexico. A newcomer is called a "TJ," for Tijuana; it is the equivalent of "hillbilly" or "rube."

Still, "Hispanic" can be a useful word, because it focuses attention on the major question about this group of immigrants: Will their assimilation into an English-speaking culture be any less successful than that of others in the past?

James Fallows, "Language," *The Atlantic* November 1983.

To answer, we must consider what is different now from the circumstances under which the Germans, Poles, and Italians learned English.

The most important difference is that the host country is right next door. The only other non-English-speaking group for which this is true is the French-Canadians. Proximity has predictable consequences. For as long as the Southwest has been part of the United States, there has been a border culture in which, for social and commercial reasons, both languages have been used. There has also been a Mexican-American population accustomed to moving freely across the border, between the cultures, directing its loyalties both ways.

Because it has always been so easy to go home, many Mexicans and Mexican-Americans have displayed the classic sojourner outlook. The more total the break with the mother country, the more pressure immigrants feel to adapt; but for many immigrants from Mexico, whose kin and friends still live across the border and whose dreams center on returning in wealthy splendor to their native villages, the pressure is weak.

Many people have suggested that there is another difference, perhaps more significant than the first. It is a change in the nation's self-confidence. The most familiar critique of bilingual education holds that the nation no longer feels a resolute will to require mastery of the national language. America's most powerful assimilative force, the English language, may therefore be in jeopardy.

It is true that starting in the early 1960s U.S. government policy began to move away from the quick-assimilation approach preferred since the turn of the century. After surveys of Puerto Rican students in New York City and Mexican-Americans in Texas revealed that they were dropping out of school early and generally having a hard time, educational theorists began pushing plans for Spanish-language instruction. The turning point came with *Lau* v. *Nichols*, a case initiated in 1971 by Chinese-speaking students in San Francisco. They sued for "equal protection," on grounds that their unfamiliarity with English denied them an adequate education. In 1974, the Supreme Court ruled in their favor, saying that "those who do not understand English are certain to find their classroom experience wholly incomprehensible and in no way meaningful." The ruling did not say that school systems had to start bilingual programs of the kind that the phrase is now generally understood to mean — that is, classrooms in which both languages are used. The court said that "teaching English to the students . . . who do not speak the language" would be one acceptable solution. But the federal regulations and state laws that implemented the decision obliged many districts to set up the system of "transitional" bilingual education that has since become the focus of furor.

The rules vary from state to state, but they typically require a school district to set up a bilingual program whenever a certain number of students (often twenty) at one grade level are from one language group and do not speak English well. In principle, bilingual programs will enable them to keep up with the content of, say, their math and history courses while preparing them to enter the English-language classroom.

The bilingual system is accused of supporting a cadre of educational consultants while actually retarding the students' progress into the English-speaking mainstream. In this view, bilingual education could even be laying the foundation for a separate Hispanic culture, by extending the students' Spanish-language world from their homes to their schools.

Before I traveled to some of the schools in which bilingual education was applied, I shared the skeptics' view. What good could come of a system that encouraged, to whatever degree, a language other than the national tongue? But after visiting elementary, junior high, and high schools in Miami, Houston, San Antonio, Austin, several parts of Los Angeles, and San Diego, I found little connection between the political debate over bilingual education and what was going on in these schools.

To begin with, one central fact about bilingual education goes largely unreported. It is a *temporary* program. The time a typical student stays in the program varies from place to place — often two years in Miami, three years in Los Angeles — but when that time has passed, the student will normally leave. Why, then, do bilingual programs run through high school? Those classes are usually for students who are new to the district — usually because their parents are new to the country.

There is another fact about bilingual education, more difficult to prove but impressive to me, a hostile observer. Most of the children I saw were unmistakably learning to speak English.

In the elementary schools, where the children have come straight out of all-Spanish environments, the background babble seems to be entirely in Spanish. The kindergarten and first- to third-grade classrooms I saw were festooned with the usual squares and circles cut from colored construction paper, plus posters featuring Big Bird and charts about the weather and the seasons. Most of the schools seemed to keep a rough balance between English and Spanish in the lettering around the room; the most Spanish environment I saw was in one school in East Los Angeles, where about a third of the signs were in English.

The elementary school teachers were mostly Mexican-American women. They prompted the children with a mixture of English and Spanish during the day. While books in both languages are available in the classrooms, most of the first-grade reading drills I saw were in Spanish. In theory, children will learn the phonetic principle of reading more quickly if they are not trying to learn a new language at the same time. Once comfortable as readers, they will theoretically be able to transfer their ability to English.

In a junior high school in Houston, I saw a number of Mexican and Salvadoran students in their "bilingual" biology and math classes. They were drilled entirely in Spanish on the parts of an amoeba and on the difference between a parallelogram and a rhombus. When students enter bilingual programs at this level, the goal is to keep them current with the standard curriculum while introducing them to English. I found my fears of linguistic separatism rekindled by the sight of fourteen-year-olds lectured to in Spanish. I reminded myself that many of the students I was seeing had six months earlier lived in another country.

The usual next stop for students whose time in bilingual education is up is a class in intensive English, lasting one to three hours a day. These students are divided into two or three proficiency levels, from those who speak no English to those nearly ready to forgo special help. In Houston, a teacher drilled two-dozen high-school-age Cambodians, Indians, Cubans, and Mexicans on the crucial difference between the voiced *th* sound of "this" and the voiceless *th* of "thing." In Miami, a class of high school sophomores included youths from Cuba, El Salvador, and

Honduras. They listened as their teacher read a Rockwellesque essay about a student with a crush on his teacher, and then set to work writing an essay of their own, working in words like "garrulous" and "sentimentalize."

One of the students in Miami, a sixteen-year-old from Honduras, said that his twelve-year-old brother had already moved into mainstream classes. Linguists say this is the standard pattern for immigrant children. The oldest children hold on to their first language longest, while their younger sisters and brothers swim quickly into the new language culture.

The more I saw of the classes, the more convinced I became that most of the students were learning English. Therefore, I started to wonder what it is about bilingual education that has made it the focus of such bitter disagreement.

For one thing, most immigrant groups other than Hispanics take a comparatively dim view of bilingual education. Haitians, Vietnamese, and Cambodians are eligible for bilingual education, but in general they are unenthusiastic. In Miami, Haitian boys and girls may learn to read in Creole rather than English. Still, their parents push to keep them moving into English. "A large number of [Haitian] parents come to the PTA meetings, and they don't want interpreters," said the principal of Miami's Edison Park Elementary School last spring. "They want to learn English. They don't want notices coming home in three languages. When they come here, unless there is total noncommunicaton, they will try to get through to us in their broken English. The students learn the language *very* quickly."

Bilingual education is inflammatory in large part because of what it symbolizes, not because of the nuts and bolts of its daily operation. In reality, bilingual programs move students into English with greater or lesser success; in reality, most Spanish-speaking parents understand that mastery of English will be their children's key to mobility. But in the political arena, bilingual education presents a different face. To the Hispanic ideologue, it is a symbol of cultural pride and political power. And once it has been presented that way, with full rhetorical flourish, it naturally strikes other Americans as a threat to the operating rules that have bound the country together.

Once during the months I spoke with and about immigrants I felt utterly exasperated. It was while listening to two Chicano activist lawyers in Houston who demanded to know why their people should be required to learn English at all. "It is unrealistic to think people can learn it that quickly," one lawyer said about the law that requires naturalized citizens to pass a test in English. "*Especially when they used to own this part of the country*, and when Spanish was the *historic language* of this region."

There is a historic claim for Spanish — but by the same logic there is a stronger claim for, say, Navajo as the historic language of the Southwest. The truth is that for more than a century the territory has been American and its national language has been English.

I felt the same irritation welling up when I talked with many bilingual instructors and policy-makers. Their arguments boiled down to: What's so special about English? They talked about the richness of the bilingual experience, the importance of maintaining the children's abilities in Spanish — even though when I watched the instructors in the classroom I could see that they were teaching principally English.

In my exasperation, I started to think that if such symbols of the dignity of language were so provocative to me, a comfortable member of the least-aggrieved ethnic group, it might be worth reflecting on the comparable sensitivities that lie behind the sentiments of the Spanish-speaking.

Consider the cases of Gloria Ramirez and Armandina Flores, who taught last year in the bilingual program at the Guerra Elementary School, in the Edgewood Independent School District, west of San Antonio.

San Antonio has evaded questions about the balance between rich and poor in its school system by carving the city up into independent school districts. Alamo Heights is the winner under this approach, and Edgewood is the loser. The Edgewood School District is perennially ranked as one of the poorest in the state. The residents are almost all Mexican-Americans or Mexicans. It is a settled community, without much to attract immigrants, but many stop there briefly on their way somewhere else, enough to give Edgewood a sizable illegal-immigrant enrollment.

In the middle of a bleak, sunbaked stretch of fields abutting a commercial vegetable farm, and within earshot of Kelly Air Force Base, sits Edgewood's Guerra School. It is an ordinary-looking but well-kept one-story structure that was built during the Johnson Administration. Nearly all the students are Mexican or Mexican-American.

Gloria Ramirez, who teaches first grade, is a compact, attractive woman of thirty-three, a no-nonsense veteran of the activist movements of the 1960s. Armandina Flores, a twenty-seven-year-old kindergarten teacher, is a beauty with dark eyes and long hair. During classroom hours, they deliver "Now, children" explanations of what is about to happen in both Spanish and English, although when the message really must get across, it comes in Spanish.

Both are remarkable teachers. They have that spark often thought to be missing in the public schools. There is no hint that for them this is just a job, perhaps because it symbolizes something very different from the worlds in which they were raised.

Gloria Ramirez was born in Austin, in 1950. Both of her parents are native Texans, as were two of her grandparents, but her family, like many other Mexican-American families, "spoke only Spanish when I was growing up," she says. None of her grandparents went to school at all. Her parents did not go past the third grade. Her father works as an auto-body mechanic; her mother raised the six children, and recently went to work at Austin State Hospital as a cleaner.

Ramirez began learning English when she started school; but the school, on Austin's east side, was overwhelmingly Mexican-American, part of the same culture she'd always known. The big change came when she was eleven. Her family moved to a working-class Anglo area in South Austin. She and her brother were virtually the only Mexican-Americans at the school. There was no more Spanish on the playground, or even at home. "My parents requested that we speak more English to them from then on," she says. "Both of them could speak it, but neither was comfortable."

"Before then, I didn't realize I had an accent. I didn't know until a teacher at the new school pointed it out in a ridiculing manner. I began learning English out of revenge." For six years, she took speech classes. "I worked hard so I could sound — like this," she says in standard American. She went to the University of Texas, where she studied history and philosophy and became involved in the Mexican-

American political movements of the 1970s. She taught bilingual-education classes in Boston briefly before coming home to Texas.

Armandina Flores was born in Cuidad Acuña, Mexico, across the river from Del Rio, Texas. Her mother, who was born in Houston, was an American citizen, but *her* parents had returned to Mexico a few months after her birth, and she had never learned English. Flores's father was a Mexican citizen. When she reached school age, she began commuting across the river to a small Catholic school in Del Rio, where all the other students were Chicano. When she was twelve and about to begin the sixth grade, her family moved to Del Rio and she entered an American public school.

At that time, the sixth grade was divided into tracks, which ran from 6-1 at the bottom to 6-12. Most of the Anglos were at the top; Armandina Flores was initially placed in 6-4. She showed an aptitude for English and was moved up to 6-8. Meanwhile, her older sister, already held back once, was in 6-2. Her parents were proud of Armandina's progress; they began to depend on her English in the family's dealings in the Anglo world. She finished high school in Del Rio, went to Our Lady of the Lake College in San Antonio, and came to Edgewood as an aide in 1978, when she was twenty-two.

Considered one way, these two stories might seem to confirm every charge made by the opponents of bilingual education. Through the trauma of being plucked from her parents' comfortable Spanish-language culture and plunged into the realm of public language, Gloria Ramirez was strengthened, made a cosmopolitan and accomplished person. Her passage recalls the one Richard Rodriguez describes in *Hunger of Memory*, an autobiography that has become the most eloquent text for opponents of bilingual programs.

"Without question, it would have pleased me to hear my teachers address me in Spanish when I entered the classroom," Rodriguez wrote. "I would have felt much less afraid. . . . But I would have delayed — for how long postponed? — having to learn the language of public society."

Gloria Ramirez concedes that the pain of confused ethnicity and lost loyalties among Mexican-Americans is probably very similar to what every other immigrant group has endured. She even admits that she was drawn to bilingual education for political as well as educational reasons. As for Armandina Flores, hers is a calmer story of successful assimilation, accomplished without the crutch of bilingual education.

Yet both of these women insist, with an edge to their voices, that their students are fortunate not to have the same passage awaiting them.

It a was very wasteful process, they say. They swam; many others sank. "You hear about the people who make it, but not about all the others who dropped out, who never really learned," Ramirez says. According to the Mexican-American Legal Defense and Education Fund, 40 percent of Hispanic students drop out before they finish high school, three times as many as among Anglo students.

"Many people around here don't feel comfortable with themselves in either language," Ramirez says. Flores's older sister never became confident in English; "she feels like a lower person for it." She has just had a baby and is anxious that he succeed in English. Ramirez's older brother learned most of his English in the Marines. He is married to a Mexican immigrant and thinks that it is very important that their children learn English. And that is more likely to happen, the teachers say, if they have a transitional moment in Spanish.

Otherwise, "a child must make choices that concern his survival," Ramirez says. "He can choose to learn certain words, only to survive; but it can kill his desire to learn, period. Eventually he may be able to deal in the language, but he won't be educated." If the natural-immersion approach worked, why, they ask, would generation after generation of Chicanos, American citizens living throughout the Southwest, have lived and died without ever fully moving into the English-language mainstream?

These two teachers, and a dozen others with parallel experience, might be wrong in their interpretation of how bilingual education works. If so, they are making the same error as German, Polish, and Italian immigrants. According to the historians hired by the Select Commission, "Immigrants argued, when given the opportunity, that the security provided them by their cultures eased rather than hindered the transition." Still, there is room for reasonable disagreement about the most effective techniques for bringing children into English. A former teacher named Robert Rossier, for example, argues from his experience teaching immigrants that intensive courses in English are more effective than a bilingual transition. Others line up on the other side.

But is this not a question for factual resolution rather than for battles about linguistic and ethnic pride? Perhaps one approach will succeed for certain students in certain situations and the other will be best for others. The choice between bilingual programs and intensive-English courses, then, should be a choice between methods, not ideologies. The wars over bilingual education have had a bitter, symbolic quality. Each side has invested the issue with a meaning the other can barely comprehend. To most Mexican-American parents and children, bilingual education is merely a way of learning English; to Hispanic activists, it is a symbol that they are at last taking their place in the sun. But to many other Americans, it sounds like a threat not to assimilate.

"It is easy for Americans to take for granted, or fail to appreciate, the strength of American culture," says Henry Cisneros, the mayor of San Antonio. Cisneros is the first Mexican-American mayor of the country's most heavily Hispanic major city, a tall, grave man of thirty-six who is as clear a demonstration of the possibilities of ethnic assimilation as John Kennedy was. Cisneros gives speeches in Spanish and in English. Over the door that leads to his chambers, gilt letters spell out "Office of the Mayor" and, underneath, "*Oficina del Alcalde*." "I'm talking about TV programs, McDonald's, automobiles, the Dallas Cowboys. It is very pervasive. Mexican-Americans *like* the American way of life."

"These may sound like just the accouterments," Cisneros says. "I could also have mentioned due process of law; relations with the police; the way supermarkets work; the sense of participation, especially now that more and more Mexican-Americans are in positions of leadership. All of the things that shape the American way of life are indomitable."

In matters of civic culture, many Mexican-Americans, especially in Texas, act as custodians of the values the nation is said to esteem. They emphasize family, church, and patriotism of the most literal sort, expressed through military service.

In the shrinelike position of honor in the sitting room, the same place where black families may have portraits of John F. Kennedy or Martin Luther King, a Mexican-American household in Texas will display a picture of the son or nephew in the Marines. Every time I talked with a Mexican-American about assimilation and separatism, I heard about the Mexican-American heroes and martyrs who have served in the nation's wars.

All the evidence suggests that Hispanics are moving down the path toward assimilation. According to a survey conducted in 1982 by Rodolfo de la Garza and Robert Brischetto for the Southwest Voter Registration Education Project, 11 percent of Chicanos (including a large number of illegal immigrants) were unable to speak English. The younger the people, the more likely they were to speak English. Ninety-four percent of those between the ages of eighteen and twenty-five could speak English, versus 78 percent of those aged sixty-six to eighty-seven. Not surprisingly, the English-speakers were better educated, had better jobs, and were less likely to have two foreign-born parents than the Spanish-speakers.

The details of daily life in Hispanic centers confirm these findings. The first impression of East Los Angeles or Little Havana is of ubiquitous Spanish, on the billboards and in the air. The second glance reveals former Chicano activists, now in their late thirties, bemused that their children have not really learned Spanish, or second-generation Cubans who have lost interest in liberating the motherland or in being Cubans at all.

Ricardo Romo says that when he taught Chicano studies at UCLA, his graduate students would go into the San Antonio *barrio* but could not find their way around, so much had they lost touch with the Spanish language. At a birthday party for a Chicano intellectual in Texas, amid piñatas and plates laden with *fajitas*, a birthday cake from a bakery was unveiled. It said "Happy Birthday" in Spanish — misspelled. There was pathos in that moment, but it was pathos that countless Italians, Poles, and Jews might understand.

With Mexico next door to the United States, the Mexican-American culture will always be different from that of other ethnic groups. Spanish will be a living language in the United States longer than any other alternative to English. But the movement toward English is inescapable.

In only one respect does the Hispanic impulse seem to me to lead in a dangerous direction. Hispanics are more acutely aware than most Anglos that, as a practical reality, English is the national language of commerce, government, and mobility. But some have suggested that, in principle, it should not be this way.

They invoke the long heritage of Mexican-Americans in the Southwest. As "Californios" or "Tejanos," the ancestors of some of these families lived on and owned the territory before the Anglo settlers. Others came across at the turn of the century, at a time of Mexican upheaval; still others came during the forties and fifties, as workers. They have paid taxes, fought in wars, been an inseparable part of the region's culture. Yet they were also subject to a form of discrimination more casual than the segregation of the Old South, but having one of the same effects. Because of poverty or prejudice or gerrymandered school districts, many Mexican-Americans were, in effect, denied education. One result is that many now in their fifties and sixties do not speak English well. Still, they are citizens, with the right of citizens to vote. How are they to exercise their right if to do so requires learning English? Do they not deserve a ballot printed in a language they can understand?

In the early seventies, the issue came before the courts, and several decisions held that if voters otherwise eligible could not understand English, they must have voting materials prepared in a more convenient language. In 1975, the Voting Rights Act amendments said that there must be bilingual ballots if more than 5 percent of the voters in a district were members of a "language minority group." The only "language minority groups" eligible under this ruling were American Indians, Alaskan natives, Asian-Americans (most significantly, Chinese and Filipinos), and Spanish-speakers. A related case extracted from the Sixth Circuit Court of Appeals the judgment that "the national language of the United States is English."

So it is that ballots in parts of the country are printed in Spanish, or Chinese, or Tagalog, along with English. This is true even though anyone applying for naturalization must still pass an English-proficiency test, which consists of questions such as "What are the three branches of government?" and "How long are the terms of a U.S. Senator and member of Congress?" The apparent inconsistency reflects the linguistic reality that many native-born citizens have not learned the national language.

By most accounts, the bilingual ballot is purely a symbol. The native-born citizens who can't read English often can't read Spanish, either. As a symbol, it points in the wrong direction, away from a single national language in which the public business will be done. Its only justification is the older generation, which was excluded from the schools. In principle, then, it should be phased out in several years.

But there are those who feel that even the present arrangement is too onerous. Rose Matsui Ochi, an assistant to the mayor of Los Angeles, who served on the Select Commission, dissented from the commission's recommendation to keep the English-language requirement for citizenship. She wrote in her minority opinion, "Abolishing the requirement recognizes the inability of certain individuals to learn English." Cruz Reynoso, the first Mexican-American appointee to the California Supreme Court, was also on the Select Commission, and he too dissented. "America is a *political* union — not a cultural, linguistic, religious or racial union," he wrote. "Of course, we as individuals would urge all to learn English, for that is the language used by most Americans, as well as the language of the marketplace. But we should no more demand English-language skills for citizenship than we should demand uniformity of religion. That a person wants to become a citizen and will make a good citizen is more than enough."

Some Chicano activists make the same point in less temperate terms. Twice I found myself in shouting matches with Mexican-Americans who asked me who I thought I was to tell them — after all the homeboys who had died in combat, after all the insults they'd endured on the playground for speaking Spanish — what language they "should" speak.

That these arguments were conducted in English suggests the theoretical nature of the debate. Still, in questions like this, symbolism can be crucial. "I have sympathy for the position that the integrating mechanism of a society is language," Henry Cisneros says. "The U.S. has been able to impose fewer such integrating mechanisms on its people than other countries, but it needs some tie to hold these diverse people, Irish, Jews, Czechs, together as a nation. Therefore, I favor people learning English and being able to conduct business in the official language of the country."

"The *unum* demands only certain things of the *pluribus*," Lawrence Fuchs says. "It demands very little. It demands that we believe in the political ideals of the republic, which allows people to preserve their ethnic identity. Most immigrants come from repressive regimes; we say, we're asking you to believe that government should *not* oppress you. Then it only asks one other thing: that in the wider marketplace and in the civic culture, you use the official language. No other society asks so little.

"English is not just an instrument of mobility. It is a sign that you really are committed. If you've been here five years, which you must to be a citizen, and if you are reasonably young, you should be able to learn English in that time. The rest of us are entitled to that."

Most of the young people I met — the rank and file, not the intellectuals who espouse a bilingual society — seemed fully willing to give what in Fuchs's view the nation asks. I remember in particular one husky Puerto Rican athlete at Miami Senior High School who planned to join the Navy after he got his diploma. I talked to him in a bilingual classroom, heard his story, and asked his name. He told me, and I wrote "*Ramón*." He came around behind me and looked at my pad. "No, no!" he told me. "You should have put R-A-Y-M-O-N-D."

A Second Look at Bilingual Education

Lucia Solorzano

In this U.S. News & World Report *article, Lucia Solorzano surveys several school districts that have turned away from bilingual education to experiment with the traditional immersion approach. These school districts have been prompted in their efforts by two forces: (1) Immigrant parents were dissatisfied with their children's progress in English mastery under the bilingual program, and (2) school districts were having problems staffing classrooms with qualified bilingual teachers due to an influx of large numbers of immigrant children. One conclusion derived from these experiments: Children highly literate in their native tongues do well in immersion programs, but the same cannot be said for immigrant children who have poor educational backgrounds.*

When Spanish-speaking children in Belen Rodriguez's kindergarten class in Miami say, "*Baño*, teacher, *baño*," Rodriguez makes her pupils use English.

Says Rodriguez: "If the kids know they can lean on my ability to speak Spanish, they will never learn English. So I reply, 'I don't understand what you're saying,' and they immediately say, 'Bathroom, teacher, bathroom.'"

Such scenes are increasingly common in classrooms from Washington, D.C., to Houston as educators challenge the most widely used method of teaching 3.6 million schoolchildren who speak little or no English: Bilingual education.

Now even the parents of some immigrant children are backing moves to plunge them into classes conducted in English only — similar to the immersion process of past decades when waves of newcomers flocked to America and rapidly joined the mainstream.

In bilingual instruction, billed not long ago as most effective for children who do not speak English, subjects such as math and science are taught in native tongues while students learn English in separate classes.

Recently, critics have attacked that approach, arguing that young people grasp the language faster if they are immersed fully — all of their courses taught in English. Others counter that many young people are traumatized by immersion and that bilingual education should be continued.

Studies Under Way

Among lawmaking and administrative bodies wrestling with the issue:

- Schools in Dade County, Fla., including Miami, have started a three-year pilot project to assess whether students who speak little or no English learn subjects better using their home language or English only.

Lucia Solorzano, "A Second Look at Bilingual Education," U.S. News & World Report 11 June 1984.

- The District of Columbia is facing such a rapid influx of poorly educated refugees from Central America that it must push students into English-only classes as quickly as possible to make room for newcomers who even more desperately need bilingual support.
- Congress is considering a broadening of the Bilingual Education Act to include funds for courses taught in English only as well as for those given in both English and another tongue.

Reflecting demands for change, the federal office of Bilingual Education and Minority Languages Affairs, which under previous administrations pushed dual-language instruction, is conducting a study of English-immersion techniques. Says Jesse Soriano, the director: "We have never said there is only one way to teach math or social studies, so why should we say bilingual education is the only way?"

Fears Voiced

Many Hispanics and members of other ethnic groups are opposed to returning to the wholesale immersion that was blamed for high dropout rates among children who were unable to learn through that method.

Warns Norma Cantu, head of educational programs for the Mexican American Legal Defense and Educational Fund: "We don't want to turn back the clock and head in that direction again."

Educators trying out intensified English programs say that their efforts differ greatly from the old "sink or swim" approach. In Houston, where eight elementary schools are testing an English-only approach, all instructors have had special training in teaching students who speak another language.

Students participating in Miami's pilot program receive 30 minutes of instruction daily in the language arts of their native tongues. Explains Ralph Robinett, director of Dade County's Department of Bilingual/Foreign-Language Education: "Developing good communications skills in the students' home language helps them to more rapidly translate these skills into learning English."

Educators find that English-immersion programs are most successful with younger children from families that speak and write their native language with sophistication. Such programs fall short, however, for a recent wave of newcomers — teenagers from rural villages in Central America who read and write their native language poorly.

Since last fall, District of Columbia public schools have received 2,000 students from Central America, and 15 to 20 more arrive each week. Teaching English and other subjects is a cultural and educational struggle because most students cannot relate words such as *traffic light* to familiar concepts from their rural homes.

Sixty teenagers from El Salvador, their ages 13 to 19, are enrolled at Washington's Francis Junior High School. About six years ago, the school switched from teaching courses such as science in Spanish. A major reason: Parents complained that their children were not learning English fast enough.

The school has since reintroduced a special bilingual program, and now 30 new Salvadoran refugees are learning subject matter in Spanish at the same time they are studying English. Notes teacher Bertha Lastre: "These students can hardly read and write Spanish, which makes the transition into English that much more difficult."

A typical problem at Francis: Many of the newcomers cannot find the subject in a sentence written in Spanish. But with home-language support, the math skills of one 18-year-old rose in a single semester from a third-grade to a seventh-grade level.

Educators are a long way from consensus on what approach is the most effective for equipping people who don't speak English for a productive life in the United States.

Many, however, are convinced that there may be no single solution — that using a variety of methods may turn out to be best.

GENERATIONS APART
Cynthia Gorney

Cynthia Gorney, a Washington Post *staff writer, briefly summarizes a study which concludes that bilingual critics' praise for the traditional immersion method of teaching immigrant students used widely throughout the nation's history is largely undeserved — that it did a poor job of facilitating the assimilation of immigrant children into the American mainstream. You might want to compare this conclusion with the similar conclusions of the two Texas teachers, themselves successful products of the immersion method, who were interviewed by James Fallows in his essay earlier in this chapter.*

What about the generations who never heard their own languages spoken in school? Much of the argument against bilingual education comes from people remembering their own immigrant relatives — or from people like American Federation of Teachers President Albert Shanker, who entered school as a Yiddish speaker and believes, for all the pain that caused him, that classes in Yiddish would probably have kept him from learning English as well as he did.

"Surely, the exacerbation of the generation gap among immigrants through shame and guilt, in the name of Americanization, cannot be considered a successful outcome of schooling," California Department of Education consultant Dennis Parker argued in a 1984 paper titled "The Great School Myth: Everybody's Grandfather Made It — and Without Bilingual Education." Citing historians who have examined turn-of-the-century school records, Parker observed that every immigrant group's dropout rates were in fact exceedingly high in those years. If that generation's immigrants "made it" without bilingual education, Parker wrote, they did so because an exploding and far more industrial American economy welcomed them even without fluent English or a high school education.

And even though many bilingual-education advocates are often articulate, successful professionals who were forced in school to speak nothing but English, they uniformly insist that any benefits of the forced English were far outweighed by the damage it did to other children.

"For every one of the people I know who made it, as I did, I know at least five or 10 who didn't," said Lily Wong Fillmore, a University of California linguistics professor who spoke only Chinese when she first began school in a heavily Hispanic town on the California coast. Fillmore's English is flawless, but she says she is simply one of the lucky ones. "I run into some of them now when I go back to Watsonville. They're old before their time, because their lives have been spent in farm work. The ones who hit the big time ended up in the canneries."

Cynthia Gorney, "Generations Apart," *The Washington Post* 7 July 1985.

For Teachers, Ten Years of Trial and Error

Cynthia Gorney

Washington Post staff writer Cynthia Gorney, on assignment in California school districts with high concentrations of immigrant children, discusses the overwhelming logistical problems with staffing these districts have faced in their efforts to carry out bilingual programs and the onerous burdens the programs have imposed upon many teachers.

OAKLAND—On March 1, nine years after state officials first began requiring bilingual education for children who speak another language more fluently than they speak English, the California State Education Code finally caught up with Franklin Elementary School.

Spurred by an Oakland parent's lawsuit demanding improved bilingual classes citywide, a judge ordered the city's schools into compliance with the state guidelines that map out the largest bilingual education effort in the nation. In California, if an elementary school has one grade with at least 10 limited-English students from a particular language group, the school has to offer a bilingual class just for them.

Inside Franklin, which sits in the midst of inexpensive rental housing that attracts new immigrants, 14 languages are spoken in the course of a normal school day. According to state regulations, the school was supposed to offer bilingual classes in Cantonese, Spanish, Vietnamese, Laotian, the Cambodian language Khmer and the Ethiopian language Tigrinya.

So this is what happened at Franklin:

Priscilla McClendon, a fifth-grade teacher who jokes that she finds challenge aplenty in just mastering English, was assigned a group of fourth- and fifth-grade Cambodians and told to promise in writing that she would learn Khmer.

Francesca Ferrari was assigned a collection of first- to third-grade Ethiopians and told to promise in writing that she would learn Tigrinya. Since state law requires at least one-third of the children in a bilingual class to be native English speakers, she got some of those, too—eight black American children and one Hispanic girl whose mother had just pulled her out of a Spanish bilingual class because she thought her daughter wasn't learning enough English.

Pat Eimerl lost her Cambodian-Vietnamese-Ethiopian-Thai-Hispanic sixth grade, which on the books had been labeled a Cambodian bilingual class, since Eimerl had earlier promised in writing to learn Khmer. Her new students, all of whom filed in one afternoon carrying the contents of their former desks, are Cantonese-speaking Vietnamese. Eimerl was told to promise she would learn Cantonese, since this was now supposed to be a Chinese bilingual class, but for weeks she refused to sign the promise.

"See, with Cambodian I'm safe, because there aren't any classes," Eimerl said (she meant language classes for teachers) on the morning of the class shift. She was

Cynthia Gorney, "For Teachers, Ten Years of Trial and Error," *The Washington Post* 8 July 1985.

standing in the hallway, watching 11-year-old Asian boys wander back and forth in search of the right classrooms, and she was so angry her voice shook. "But there are Chinese classes. I've got three kids. I'm 40 years old. I'm not about to go try to learn Chinese."

'WHO'S BEING SERVED?'

Ten years ago, when federal officials began their unprecedented push for bilingual education in public schools across the country, grand hopes and promising research armed them against their critics. High school dropout rates for Hispanics were far higher than those for white students, they observed; here, they argued, was a possible remedy. Theory and their own convictions convinced them that students who learned at least part time in their native language had a much better chance in the schools: they would keep up academically, they would maintain their self-esteem, and they might in the end become literate and articulate in two languages.

A decade later, with half a million children enrolled in what their schools describe as bilingual programs, much of the whole enterprise has dismayed both its longtime critics and some of the people who most ardently believe in bilingual education. National Hispanic high school dropout rates, although not reliably monitored, are as high as ever: just under 40 percent, according to estimates by the Washington-based National Hispanic Policy Development Project. Teachers from San Francisco to Providence can be heard complaining that bilingual classes hold students back or keep them away from English. A U.S. Department of Education study, published in 1983 to vehement criticism from many bilingual educators, found "no consistent evidence" that dual-language instruction improved students' academic progress.

And bilingual advocates say schools are slapping the "bilingual" label on classes that have almost nothing to do with dual-language teaching. They also say that because some states don't require bilingual education and some schools ignore their own state requirements, more than three-quarters of the limited-English-speaking children in this country are receiving no dual-language instruction at all.

"What's going on in 90 percent of the classrooms in this country is a joke in respect to what bilingual education ought to be," said Duane Campbell, a Spanish-English bilingual teacher who now works in the bilingual teacher training program at California State University at Sacramento. "And if you're going to tell me that doesn't work, I'll agree with you. It doesn't work."

Campbell, an Iowa-born Anglo, sounds a little more embittered than many of his colleagues. Franklin is in more linguistic turmoil than most neighborhood schools. But a Washington Post inquiry into public school bilingual education found similar heat and frustration among teachers, parents, administrators and researchers — many of whom are still at odds about the classroom efforts public schools are calling bilingual education.

There is nothing simple about this. Like many broad public school programs, the term "bilingual education" covers such vast territory — gifted teachers and dreadful teachers, imaginative new workshops and rote learning in overcrowded classrooms — that it defies the kind of generalizations people seem to want when such a controversial idea is proposed as public policy. So complex is the argument that critics and advocates cannot even agree on how many children in this country come to school with what the jargon calls "limited English proficiency"; the estimates range from 1.5 million to 3.5 million.

But a look at the problems in this massive undertaking, the business of helping immigrant schoolchildren in their own language, might begin at Franklin Elementary, or Franklin Year-Round, as the school is now officially named: its side-by-side buildings now hold children in a schedule that has eliminated the summer break. Down the long hallways, the bulletin boards all acolor with spring tulips and construction paper Humpty-Dumptys, doorways frame bright classrooms crowded desk to desk with the children of the new immigration. *Phumpuang Phaisan, Khadihaj Muhammed, Phonevil Pomsouvanh, Kai-Phong Mack, Alejandro Esparza* — the names, in careful block lettering, fill pink and green class lists on the desk of Franklin's harried bilingual coordinator, and next to each name the numerical code for the language the child brought to school: Khmer, Tigrinya, Laotian, Cantonese, Spanish.

"If you figure just the amount of time, money and education disruption . . . the fact that English speakers have zero rights . . . this has been costly as hell," said Martha Muller, the coordinator who for the last three months has been shuffling and reshuffling names into lists that will comply with California state education laws. "The law is not meant for this kind of school. It is meant for a nice, neat, orderly Spanish-English population, or a Chinese-English population, or something. But it's not meant for a multilanguage school."

"Now that we're in compliance, it's just as ridiculous as when we were out of compliance," said Michael Phillips, who teaches his combined fourth- and fifth-grade class in both English and the Vietnamese he learned in preparation for a year's special military assignment in Vietnam. "So all my English-speaking kids have to sit there and wait while I'm translating for the Vietnamese. Now who's being served there?"

As chaotic as it is at this school, with nearly every morning bringing new immigrants to the front office to enroll their children, bilingual education at Franklin is in some of the same trouble that has plagued schools across the country for the last decade. It begins with California state law — a law, similar to those in some of the 22 states that mandate or permit bilingual classes, that lay out the number of speakers of any single language that is supposed to trigger a bilingual class.

It was violations of that requirement, among many other complaints, that moved a group of Oakland parents last fall to bring what turned into a bitterly argued lawsuit that accused the city school board of causing "irreparable injury" to thousands of students by failing to offer them bilingual classes. The documentation listed Franklin as one of the worst offenders: the school was missing teachers or aides in five languages, including Laotian and Tigrinya.

How does a school find candidates for a job like that? School officials actually interviewed a few people, Franklin principal Jay Cleckner said, although lawyers for the parents' group insisted Oakland had done far too little recruiting and hiring. But almost nobody qualified as an American classroom teacher, Cleckner said. And if a few spoke English well enough to work as classroom aides, he said, he could not keep them in part-time jobs that paid about $5 an hour and offered no benefits. "I have interviewed for aides and for teachers, people who are very qualified," Clecker said. "But they can go back to work for four times what I can pay them, and I tell them, 'Go. Take care of yourself.'"

The national shortage of qualified teachers has for some years been one of bilingual education's major problems. There is not a single Khmer- or Hmong-speaking credentialed teacher in California, which has the nation's highest numbers of refugees from Cambodia and the part of Laos that was home to the Hmong people. Even qualified teachers who speak fluent Spanish are in short supply in many states; when Houston bilingual administrator Delia Pompa was presented this year with the revised Texas mandates for bilingual education through fifth grade, she calculated that even with extensive recruiting and $1,500 bonuses for the mostly Spanish-speaking dual-language teachers, conventional teaching patterns were going to leave the district short 400 teachers qualified to work in two languages.

"Before, when Hispanics went to college, they went into teaching," said Pompa, who plans to accommodate the shortage by classroom rearrangements like teacher pairing. "Hispanics are starting to go into other professions. . . . Teaching, and education in general, is going through a low period. Teaching isn't looked at as a real respected profession. You're looking at a lot of problems."

Hardly anybody seriously expects Franklin's elementary school teachers to learn Khmer or Laotian in their spare time. But one of the ways many areas have adapted to the shortage is by asking teachers to sign up for courses in languages that seem more manageable to learn. In California, state figures show that fully half the "bilingual" teachers are regular teachers who have pledged to learn dual-language teaching methods and become fluent in a second language (usually Spanish, but occasionally English) while a bilingual aide helps them with the children.

That leads to a whole new set of problems. How well those teachers are actually learning both the language and the complicated business of dual-language teaching varies wildly from school to school, particularly since many principals are dubious about the idea to begin with. One elementary school will house an after-hours class for teachers genuinely committed to learning Spanish, and usually doing so on their own time; a second will sign up "bilingual" teachers who plainly have little interest in ever learning more than a few words of the language. Even when they do try, bilingual advocates sometimes wonder what comes of their efforts: a Hispanic attorney tells of the newly trained Texas teacher who stood before a parents' group and began, "Damas y caballos," which is a salutation of sorts, it means "Ladies and horses."

And the proceedings inside the dual-language class are only as effective as the teacher who runs it. In visits this spring to more than 20 bilingual classrooms, a reporter watched one bilingual teacher review long division in English scarcely intelligible through his Spanish accent, and another teacher who spoke no Spanish and left all the Spanish business to an aide she clearly distrusted: "I don't even think she's graduated from high school," the teacher confided.

Here were teachers translating right through history and arithmetic lessons, despite linguists' warnings that simultaneous translation is the least effective bilingual teaching method because it lets the student listen to the language he knows best. Here were teachers frustrated by school systems that hurried children into full-time English so fast that, as the teachers saw it, some of the point of bilingual education was being lost — the idea that children's English work will be stronger and more confident if they are allowed to fully develop and work in their own language at least part time for more than a year or two.

Here were teachers so tired of the whole bilingual effort—of juggling multiple two-language reading groups, battling supervisors and watching children's confusion when a school offered them dual language at one grade but then abruptly not at another—that the teachers had finally bailed out. "You go crazy—that's why a lot of bilingual teachers go out of the program, because they can't handle it," said Erlinda Griffin, a quadrilingual Filipina who left bilingual teaching seven years ago for a school supervisorial job in the central California farm city of Fresno. Griffin believes bilingual education theory, and she has seen programs that seem to her to use it successfully. "But unfortunately, they were in the minority—there were so few of them."

And here, too, were teachers, nearly all of them monolingual English speakers, convinced that the bilingual classes they had seen were in large part misguided efforts that held a lot of children back. An Arizona teacher remembered Geme, her Navaho student who had sat through five years of bilingual classes before somebody realized the boy was having trouble because he had spoken scarcely a word of Navaho before he came to school. A suburban San Francisco teacher remembered Spanish-speaking children who never seemed to make the promised transition into English. A Rhode Island counselor remembered the Puerto Rican boy, bewildered by his referral to bilingual classes, who told the counselor in flawless English that he had grown up and gone to school in Lawrence, Mass.

"This is the stuff that goes on all the time," the counselor said. "I think a lot of kids are kept in those programs simply to build up the numbers and justify the programs. We've got kids in those programs who are fluent in English."

If anybody does belong in bilingual classes, who is it to be? To this day that generates argument and still another set of complaints. Some states reserve bilingual classes only for children who speak Spanish or some other language, prompting complaints about ethnic and linguistic segregation. California requires them whenever possible to be in classes with native English speakers so the children won't be segregated and will have role models to help them learn the language.

But that doesn't satisfy everybody either. Because most bilingual classes are designed as remedial programs, aimed at moving children into English as rapidly as possible, English-speaking parents have often been disappointed when they allow their children into bilingual classes in the hope that they will learn Spanish. And in towns like Fillmore, a heavily Hispanic southern California farming community where the expansion of bilingual classes set off an angry Anglo protest this spring, English-speaking parents say their children waste time in a class taught partly in another language.

"Who's going to meet my daughter's needs?" demanded Judy Collins, a Fillmore parent whose husband recently proposed a controversial city council-adopted resolution making English the "official language" of Fillmore. "The amount of time that teacher is speaking Spanish is time that my child is not getting English instruction," Collins said.

It is complaints like these that have complicated the response to a generally unenthusiastic 1983 bilingual-education report by two federal Department of Education researchers. At the request of a White House policy review group, the researchers examined several hundred studies on bilingual education, many of which concluded that the classes had improved students' academic performance, and found only 39 to be "methodologically acceptable." After analyzing those 39 studies, the researchers reported bilingual education producing only mixed results.

"Sometimes kids did better," said Department of Education analyst Keith Baker, the report's coauthor. "Sometimes it had no effect. And sometimes it had negative effects."

Baker and his partner, who have been criticized for their own methodology, suggested in the report that although limited-English-speaking children clearly needed some special attention, education officials might rethink their reliance on classes using native languages — that full-time intensive English programs, for example, might be more effective in some cases.

Would Franklin Elementary's Francesca Ferrari, facing her tiny Ellis Island of a classroom earlier this year, have done any of her students a greater service by using their own language?

"This I do not know," she said.

"I do not know what I really think about bilingual education," Ferrari said.

When the Oakland parents' lawsuit was settled in May, with school officials committing themselves to a considerable expansion of the bilingual staff, the central office finally found some qualified teachers' aides for Franklin; a Tigrinya-speaking Ethiopian man now helps in Ferrari's classroom for 80 minutes a day. And she welcomes his presence, she said. He makes things easier for her. Last month they were working on *sq* words, and Ferrari did not have to go into contortions or bring lemons into class to explain *squirt* and *squint* and *squid*.

These are ideas the children would have grasped without translation, Ferrari said. Demonstrations, in her experience, are sometimes even more vivid than translation. But she is happy to have the aide anyway — "grateful," Ferrari said. "I think it's a sense of security for the children to have him there, I really do."

Her class no longer includes the Spanish-speaking child; it is now all Ethiopian and native English-speaking children, and in March, as a welcoming gesture, Ferrari put up an Ethiopian market poster and wrote the Tigrinya words for "How are you?" in big bright letters on a poster she taped to the classroom door. *Camilla Ha.*

Some weeks later, in discreet messages conveyed through the principal's office, Ferrari was told that this had distressed the Ethiopian families. Parents of all but three of her Ethiopian students indicated on signed forms that they wished their children taught exclusively in English, so Ferrari need no longer abide by her implausible promise to learn Tigrinya.

"They don't want their culture brought in," Ferrari said. "They feel they can take care of that at home." She took the poster down and pulled *Camilla Ha* off the classroom door.

FOR LEARNING OR ETHNIC PRIDE?

Ezra Bowen

Time *reporter Ezra Bowen gives a brief, thoughtful overview of the bilingual education controversy, citing the arguments and concerns of both the program's advocates and its critics. You would do well to read this essay near the outset of your perusal of the readings in this chapter.*

Judy Collins, a mother who lives in Ventura County, Calif., is fighting mad. "They are teaching kids the Pledge of Allegiance in Spanish," she says, of bilingual classes at San Cayetano Elementary School, which her daughter attends. "It's a United States flag," she adds indignantly. "They need to learn that in English."

Collins' exasperation reflects the feelings of millions of Americans on one side of an inflammatory issue: bilingual education in America's public schools. More than 1.3 million students whose primary language is not English are enrolled in federal, state or local study programs that provide instruction in their native tongues. These programs have their roots in the federal Bilingual Education Act, passed as a noble experiment in 1968. Its original aim was to generate optional instruction that would help immigrant youngsters and native-born Hispanic-American children learn English quickly. Meanwhile, they were to move ahead in their schoolwork by using their own language as much as necessary. That at least is what Congress thought it was doing.

Proponents of bilingual learning, however, see it not only as a way to help students with limited English proficiency (LEP) make the transition into the mainstream of American classrooms but as a means for preserving the students' native language and culture. Today bilingual programs are conducted in a gallimaufry of around 80 tongues, ranging from Spanish to Lithuanian to Micronesian Yapese. Some of these courses are designed to maintain a student's original language indefinitely, bolstering the language with enrichment studies in indigenous art, music, literature and history. The annual cost is well over $350 million.

Supporters argue that instruction in children's native tongues is essential to providing them with an adequate education. "The Federal Government has a profound responsibility to these children," says James Lyons, chief lobbyist for the National Association for Bilingual Education. But critics hotly question whether such expenditures are worthwhile. They also challenge the role of the Federal Government in favoring or heavily funding any particular method of instruction, much less sponsoring cultural-maintenance studies. "The intent of bilingual education has been distorted into a vehicle for a bicultural approach to education," says Robert Sweet, a member of the White House Office of Policy Development.

Bilingual learning, no longer just an optional classroom service, has become a fundamental issue of public policy. "It's cultural, it's social, it's political," says Robert Calfee, professor of education and psychology at Stanford University. Nationally, by some estimates, 3.6 million school-age youngsters are rated as LEPs, 80% of them Hispanic. The voting bloc represented by their parents has generated congressional

Ezra Bowen, "For Learning or Ethnic Pride?" *Time* 8 July 1985.

support for expanding bilingualism into cultural maintenance. Even the White House is gun-shy about attacking the concept too vehemently, although the Administration considers it both inappropriate and wasteful.

Some see bilingual education as potentially worse than that. Former California Senator S.I. Hayakawa believes the result of language maintenance could be to foster divisiveness like that of the French-speaking separatist movement in Canada that peaked in the 1970s. As an intended antidote, he introduced and still lobbies for a constitutional amendment that would make English the official U.S. language for government affairs.

Backers of bilingual education embrace it as a legal right in a dozen states. Federal guidelines specify only that school districts with more than 5% minority nationals among their pupils provide LEPs with effective English instruction. Moreover, the Supreme Court, in a 1974 decision involving 1,800 Chinese students in San Francisco, confirmed that the district had to provide for the education of the English-deficient students: but the court did not say how. "Teaching English to the students of Chinese ancestry who do not speak the language is one choice" in the method of instruction, wrote Justice William Douglas in the court's unanimous decision. "Giving instructions to this group in Chinese is another. There may be others."

Indeed there are, for if ever a law has come to mean different things to different people, it has been the Bilingual Education Act and its derivative edicts.

- To Ivan Quintanilla, 9, who just finished fourth grade in Miami, bilingual education has meant learning flawless English in the two years since he arrived from Cuba. He has also been able to keep up to grade level in his courses through a mix of his native tongue and English. "When we are in the Spanish part of our studies we all speak Spanish," says Ivan. "But when we are in the English part or in recess no one speaks Spanish." He concludes, "You must speak English if you want to have friends and be happy."

- To slim, smiling Quoc Cong Tran, 16, who arrived at a San Francisco high school from Vietnam six months ago, language instruction means a minimum of short-term help in classroom Vietnamese, while he loads up on English in courses called English as a second language. "My future, I choose American," says Quoc.

- To Benjamin Viera, 37, a native New Yorker married to a Puerto Rican wife who speaks Spanish around the house, bilingual education used to mean trouble in communicating with his son, now going into eighth grade. Six years ago Viera switched the boy out of a bilingual program and into regular classes. "I'd talk to him in English at home, and he couldn't understand me," complains Viera. "He'd go and ask his mother what I said. His teacher was giving him Spanish all day and very little English."

- To Jackie Gutierrez, 8, of the Santa Clara pueblo in New Mexico, bilingual learning has meant sitting in a twice-a-week class listening and responding to Leon Baca, a teacher of the ancient Tewa language. During a recent session, Baca grunted, "*Nyaemangeri!*" The students replied, "Left side!" "*Haa* [yes]," intoned Baca; then "*Ko'ringeri!*" The children shouted, "Right side!" Asked later what the enrichment class was all about, Jackie replied, "We're learning to speak Indian."

To advocates, the learning experiences of Jackie Gutierrez and Ivan Quintanilla are what the bilingual programs are all about: easing the transition to English or holding on to one's ethnic heritage, or both. "It is very important to us that kids take pride in their own culture," says Ligaya Avenida, director of bilingual programs for the San Francisco unified school district, where some 44 languages are spoken. "In the process of acquiring English you have to develop their cognitive abilities without losing their self-image."

Others disagree vehemently. Says Cuban-born Carol Pendás Whitten, head of the Department of Education's Office of Bilingual Education: "If parents want to preserve the native language, that's fine, but I do not think it should be the role of the school." Another opponent is Bill Honig, California's superintendent of public instruction, who insists such instruction "should be transitional . . . Bilingual education is not going to be used as a cultural isolation program."

Significantly, no one has proved beyond doubt that LEP youngsters learn faster or better through bilingual instruction than by any other methods, including old-fashioned "submersion," i.e., going cold turkey into regular classrooms where only English is spoken. Says Adriana de Kanter, one of the authors of a controversial 1981 study sponsored by the Department of Education: "Basically we found that sometimes [bilingualism] worked, and sometimes it didn't, and that most of the time, it made no difference at all."

Meanwhile, dedicated teachers are laboring to lead their LEPs into the mainstream, either with strict bilingual methods or with broad variations on them. In El Paso, public secondary schools are using the High Intensity Language Training program that emphasizes training in English as a second language. Until 1982, many of El Paso's Hispanic high schoolers either failed or dropped out. Today HILT students regularly appear on the honor roll; many are members of the National Honor Society and several have graduated at the top of their classes.

At Brooklyn's P.S. 189, Principal Josephine Bruno runs her school on a bilingual basis, switching back and forth so that students take one class in English and another in their native tongue. Whatever language they use, Bruno's charges are getting the message: 86% of her 1,130 students read English at grade level. Such results prompt Bruno, and thousands like her, to brush aside the furor over bilingual education. "If the kids are learning," she asks, "who cares?"

Unfortunately, this neglects the bigger question: Are they learning because of bilingual studies or in spite of them? Nearly 20 years and hundreds of millions of dollars have gone by, but the question remains.

An Alternative to Bilingualism
Joan Keefe

Joan Keefe is a member of the National Advisory and Coordinating Council on Bilingual Education of the Department of Education. She is also a teacher of French and English as a Second Language (ESL) in the Washington, D.C., area. In this essay she expresses some familiar reservations about bilingual education, and she argues that ESL programs for immigrant children are far more effective than bilingual programs as a means of assimilating them into our education system.

WASHINGTON — It is not surprising that Secretary of Education William J. Bennett, in a speech on bilingual education, asked whether American schools should "continue down the same failed path on which we have been traveling." No convincing evidence has emerged that the 17-year federal experiment with bilingual education has worked.

Even less surprising is the ensuing outrage voiced by bilingual education interest groups, who have transformed the program into a powerful political steamroller. Bilingual education is a faith that bureaucrats, administrators, teachers, researchers and clerks protect, preserve, and propagate: It provides lucrative rewards to entrenched job-holders.

The program requires that children be taught academic subjects in the foreign language used at home, with some part of the day given to learning English. Often, those lessons in English constitute no more than two hours a week. In addition, the students are taught their own ethnic culture. In 1984, taxpayers spent $138 million to teach only 182,000 students. Although at least 15 percent of the programs are in Spanish, educators have been required to teach subjects in many languages, including Eskimo and American Indians' tribal languages.

Most students in bilingual programs are not immigrants but American-born citizens. Current testing practices even bring second- and third-generation children into the programs. This provokes critics to charge administrators with trying to expand and perpetuate what was originally a temporary program.

Do American-born children need bilingual instruction? If it had existed earlier in the century, some of today's leading educators, scholars and entertainers would have been placed in classes in languages their immigrant parents spoke. Would they have gained their present prominence — or have stagnated in cultural and linguistic ghettos?

Nobody denies that children born abroad need special help. No one proposes that they be allowed to "sink or swim." One solution is English as a second language, a method of teaching in English to non-English speakers that has succeeded in schools and colleges for years. Unfortunately, students in bilingual programs are permitted only a few hours of English as a second language each week. But children who take English as a second language for most of their day can learn it well enough to participate in mainstream classes in 12 to 18 months. It is far less expensive and

Joan Keefe, "An Alternative to Bilingualism," *The New York Times* 24 October 1985.

easier to provide than bilingual education because it is offered exclusively in English to students of different language groups in a single classroom.

This method and other alternatives have been almost suppressed by the bilingual establishment, including Hispanic interest groups with clout in Congress. Only 4 percent of the $176 million that law authorizes can be used for English as a second language or for any other method.

In 1980, a Carter Administration study by Dr. Keith Baker and Adrienne de Kanter of the Education Department found that transitional bilingual education had worked in some settings but had been ineffective, even harmful, in others. In some school districts, English as a second language and structured English immersion programs had worked. The study, disputed by Hispanic interest groups, concluded that transitional bilingual education was only one of several useful approaches. The Harvard Educational Review published similar findings in 1982.

Mr. Bennett has, reasonably, asked legislators to amend Federal laws requiring local educators to use a single method of education. Let schools have bilingual programs if they wish but return to them the freedom to choose English as a second language or other structured approaches. Alas, the bilingual education lobby has repeatedly squashed this solution in Congress.

Members of Congress who wish to end Federal imposition of a single educational method on local districts have the Administration's full weight behind them. They need to act and to be given full public support. At stake is the future of many young citizens.

Educating the Melting Pot
Lucia Solorzano

U.S. News & World Report journalist Lucia Solorzano gives readers an idea of the diverse range of bilingual programs and alternatives being tried across the nation by describing the programs operating in four different school districts in areas with large immigrant populations. You might want to compare these programs to the four approaches William Henry, III, identifies in his essay earlier in the chapter. Can you see evidence for both bilingual education's critics and for its advocates in this essay?

What is the best way to teach children who speak little or no English?

Since 1968, the federal government's answer has been bilingual education—instruction in all subjects given in a child's native language while he or she learns English.

In the current school year, $139 million in federal dollars is serving fewer than 210,000 students—a small portion of the estimated 1.2 million to 1.7 million who speak little or no English.

It's a situation that has drawn sharp criticism from Secretary of Education William Bennett, who last fall launched an attack against bilingual education, charging that "after $1.7 billion of federal funding, we have no evidence that the children whom we sought to help . . . have benefited."

Bennett wants changes in the law that would allow federal money to be used for a wider variety of teaching methods than traditional bilingual education.

Opposing Bennett are Hispanic leaders, who argue that dual-language instruction is needed to insure that language-deficient students do not stumble in other subjects while studying English.

While the national debate goes on, some school districts have adopted bilingual-education programs with great success. Others, relying chiefly on state and local funds, have found alternatives better suited to their needs. A look at the range of programs being tried—

Classic bilingual
San Francisco

The longstanding method of teaching language-deficient children, which Secretary Bennett is challenging, can be found at Spring Valley Elementary School in Chinatown. Here the cacophony of Chinese mingles with the steady beat of phonetic English.

"K, as in kite," May Chung, one of 12 bilingual teachers, pronounces slowly. "Gee yew," she adds in Chinese. The children nod knowingly.

All subjects are taught in Chinese until a child has mastered sufficient English to join a regular class. "Children learn in any language," says Principal Lonnie Chin. "If it is a science lesson, the purpose may be to find out the chemical reaction when you burn sugar, and you don't learn it any better in English."

Lucia Solorzano, "Educating the Melting Pot," *U.S. News & World Report 31 March 1986.*

Three fourths of the school's 580 pupils speak little or no English. As many as 85 percent come from homes where no English is spoken. A number come from families barely literate in Chinese.

Such disparity between home life and school demands this type of instruction, says Chin. "It is incumbent on schools to bridge that gap, and that is the real purpose of bilingual education."

Once a child can function in English, native-language support is ended. Many kindergartners can make themselves verbally understood within a year. Older students may need two years or longer. But native-language support is continued for as long as it takes to insure that these students complete grade-level work while studying English. Legaya Avenida, director of the city's bilingual program, insists that the method follows sound educational philosophy. "It begins with what the child knows and develops that knowledge to the point where the child can function in society."

Coping with 55 languages
Falls Church, Va.

English as a second language (ESL) is one method of instruction endorsed by Secretary Bennett because of its strong emphasis on English. It also is the method of choice at Graham Road Elementary School in Fairfax County. An afternoon spent in Joseph Branscomb's classroom explains why.

Hung, fresh from Vietnam, joined "Mr. B's" fourth-through-sixth-grade class just this school year. Classmates Paris and Marjan are from Iran; Elena from Greece. Chunly Mon is from Cambodia. Nuria and Dany are Salvadoran. Endad is from Bangladesh.

"With five or more languages within a classroom, bilingual education would not work," says Branscomb, who speaks only English. "My goal is to teach everything in English so they learn to use English to express themselves."

In Fairfax County, more than 55 languages are spoken. Diplomats' well-educated children mix with youngsters from war-torn nations who have not been to school for years. Newcomers arrive weekly. ESL helps cope with the diversity. At Graham Road Elementary, children with limited English skills spend half days in a regular classroom taking courses like math and music that require little English. Says fourth-grade teacher Floy Houser: "This gives them a chance to be around American children and hear them talk. They learn a lot from each other."

During reading and social studies, which demand better English skills, pupils who need help go to their own classes. In Branscomb's room, the emphasis is on listening, then speaking to help children absorb the rhythm of English. Pupils click their fingers and recite jazz chants to understand verb tenses.

When a boy whispers in his native tongue, Branscomb asks, "Do you like to speak English today?" He explains: "I don't want to prohibit use of their language; I want to get across that it's more important they use English."

Immersion — not submersion
McAllen, Tex.

The teaching method known as English "immersion," which also draws applause from administration officials, is a sensitive topic in this part of the country. Many

Hispanics remember the days before bilingual education when the English "submersion" method held sway. Then, students were punished for speaking Spanish and were expected to pick up English simply by being with English-speaking people.

But English immersion, as it is being tried in a five-year pilot program at Sam Houston Elementary here, is vastly different. Pupils are taught all subjects in English by teachers who know their native language but use it only when students do not understand. Children with problems can ask questions in their language, which will be answered.

When Thelma Lanfranco's kindergarten class entered school last fall, none of the 22 students spoke or read English. Their favorite television programs were beamed out of Mexico. After seven months, the pupils are reading in English and watching Saturday-morning cartoons in both languages.

"Working in two languages slowed them down," says Lanfranco. "It is hard at the beginning for these kids, but it becomes routine."

Adds fellow teacher Diana Lozano: "If a child prefers Spanish, he can speak it. This is nothing like we or our parents went through."

Test scores in a similar Houston program found immersion students scoring about the same as bilingual students in reading, language development and vocabulary.

Still, parents such as Eva and Raul Alavez not only back the approach but find that their two children can teach them English as well. "These are just little kids," says Mrs. Alavez, "but it's important for them to know English."

Preserving the native tongue
Hamtramck, Mich.

Bilingual education, according to the Department of Education's emphasis, should use native-language instruction only until a child has mastered sufficient English to pick up his studies. But within the Arab community in this working-class city near Detroit, an experiment is under way that challenges Secretary Bennett's goal of mastery of English above all else. First and second graders here learn Arabic and English, looking to strengthen the native tongue while English is being learned.

At Holbrook Elementary, Arab immigrants spend half days in a classroom where only English is spoken. For the other half, the Arab students move to a room in which subjects are taught only in Arabic, with added instruction in Arabic-language skills.

While pupils such as 7-year-old Fath Almawri from Yemen sing "Home on the Range" in English, English-speaking pupils, like Tommy Taylor, can join their Arab classmates in learning the days of the week in Arabic. "Outside the classroom, the Arabic students speak English," says teacher Mohammed Hussein. "They help Tommy with Arabic, and he helps them with English."

Concerned that the strong emphasis on Arabic might cause students to lag in their proficiency in English, the district tested the Arab students' performances against those of native English speakers. At the end of a year's instruction, scores for students who had studied Arabic were higher in reading, math and English-language skills than those for non-participants, though the students' scores had been lower when school began.

With so many different teaching methods in use—and strong advocates for each—the question of which is best promises to spark continued debate both in Washington and at the local level. But as these four communities found, the key to success may not be the method but the caring and commitment given to the progress of every student.

Official English or English Only?

James C. Stalker

James C. Stalker, a University of Michigan professor, vigorously disputes the dominant concern of bilingual education critics — the fear that such programs will promote a cultural divisiveness which will ultimately undermine the social and political stability of the nation. His well-developed arguments conclude that such fears are exaggerated and essentially misguided. Contrast his arguments with those made by Tom Bethell and William A. Henry, III, earlier in this chapter.

CLARIFICATION OF THE ISSUES

. . . . One of the primary expressed reasons for the call for an official English centers on bilingual programs and on Hispanic and Asian immigrants. The most common statement is that the Hispanic and Asian populations prefer not to assimilate into mainstream American culture, that they do not want to learn English or adopt traditional, mainstream cultural norms, and that bilingual programs support their desire for separateness by enabling them to maintain their native language under the guise of learning English. The emotional reactions to such a position by many people who regard themselves as "traditional, mainstream" Americans is all too predictable. Those immigrants who are different and wish to remain different should go back where they came from, go back to the culture which they hold as more valuable and dear to them than "our" culture. They should go back where they are comfortable and everyone speaks their language.

There are really three issues here: (1) the legitimacy of cultural maintenance, (2) the intention and effectiveness of bilingual programs, and (3) simple communication. For the first of these issues, we can say the obvious: that we are all culturally different in some way or another; that each of us very probably values and wishes to maintain or obtain some part of our native heritage, whatever it is; that we are all immigrants, except for Amerindians; and that we expect others to be tolerant and accepting of our Scots, Polish, Russian, or African heritage. (During periods of high immigration, claims that assimilation is not happening seem to be more prevalent [see e.g., Whitney, *Literary Digest*, Chen and Henderson]). We must also remember that as a nation, we at least give lip service to the notion that our cultural diversity is one of the factors which separates the United States from many other countries in the world, one of the factors that has enabled the US to maintain an open society in the face of political, economic, and social strains which prevent other countries from realizing their full potential. We have been coping with political and cultural diversity since before the Revolution and engaging in cultural maintenance for at least that long.

The second issue, that of the intention and effectiveness of bilingual programs, should be handled as a separate problem. If bilingual programs are ineffective in

James C. Stalker, "Official English or English Only?," *English Journal* March 1988.

teaching children English, then something should be done about the programs themselves. Passing a law directed at the official status of English is relatively unlikely to make the bilingual programs better. Outlawing the programs through an English-only law is even less likely to improve the English of the children and adults now in those programs.

The focus on bilingual programs is in part prompted by an often unarticulated fear that we will become a nation which will need interpreters in the legislature. It is a concern over communication, a concern that we might be able to deal with somewhat more objectively than the problem of cultural and political difference.

HISTORICAL BACKGROUND

Language diversity was already an issue before the Revolution. As early as 1753, in a letter to a friend, Benjamin Franklin expressed the fear that German would be so prevalent in Pennsylvania that the legislature would need interpreters. He noted that a good many of the street signs in Philadelphia were in German, without an English translation (Mencken 140). By 1745 there were approximately 45,000 German speakers in the colonies, and by 1790 there were some 200,000, nine per cent of the population (Anderson 80). Enough of them settled in Pennsylvania to cause Franklin to envisage the possibility of that colony's becoming a German-speaking region. In 1795, the Germans of Virginia (not Pennsylvania) petitioned Congress to print laws in German for those immigrants in Virginia who had not yet learned English. The subcommittee turned in a favorable report on the petition, but it was tabled. A later request that same year also received a favorable review in committee but was defeated on the floor of Congress by a vote of 42 to 41 (Mencken 139).

Even with such a rebuff, the German speakers did not go away or learn English. Rather, their numbers increased: 1.5 million arrived between 1830 and 1860, and another 1.5 million arrived during the decade of the 1880s. In 1900 the German immigrants and their children numbered approximately 8 million compared to the 2.5 million English immigrants and their children (Anderson 80). These latter arrivals were no more eager to abandon their native language than were their cultural ancestors. As a consequence, there were German bilingual schools in Pennsylvania during the latter half of the nineteenth century; German newspapers were common in New York and Pennsylvania, down the Ohio River valley, into Missouri and Texas.

We can get some retrospective idea of how substantial the influence of the German immigrants would have been throughout nineteenth- and early twentieth-century America, linguistically and culturally, by consulting the 1980 census, in which the number of people who reported themselves as being of German heritage was only slightly less than the number reporting themselves as being of English heritage — 49.6 million English to 49.2 million German. Scottish and Irish heritage people add another 50.2 million, but many of those immigrants did not think of themselves as English, nor did they speak the same dialect ("The Melting Pot" 30).

Other language groups desired to maintain their native languages when they came to the United States, and a look into our history turns up some interesting results of that desire. The Louisiana constitution allowed the publication of laws in French, and they were so published until about seventy years ago. California (1849) and Texas allowed the publication of laws in Spanish, and New Mexico still maintained Spanish and English as official languages of the state until 1941. In 1842 Texas required the publication of its laws in German as well as Spanish and English and added Norwegian in 1858 (Mencken 141). After the Civil War, several states required the use of English as the language of instruction in the public schools, but several allowed the use of other languages in one way or another. In Louisiana, French could be used in those parishes where the French language was spoken. Hawaii allowed the use of other languages by petition. Minnesota required books in English, but explanations could be in other languages (Ruppenthal). What all of this tells us is that we have never been absolutely certain that we need to or should require that everyone speak and read and write English. On the other hand, there has been a rather constant pressure to maintain a common language, and that language has been English. German had the strongest chance to displace English; in fact, it had nearly two hundred years to do so, but it did not succeed. The conclusion that we can draw is that English is probably not seriously threatened. It has maintained its position as the common language and likely will continue to do so.

THE STATUS OF SPANISH: PRESENT AND FUTURE

The assumption that Spanish will succeed in displacing English where German did not is probably unfounded, but we must recognize that the possibility exists. However, certain conditions must prevail for that eventuality to take place. The Spanish speakers must not only want to maintain Spanish, but they must also refuse to learn any English at all. Even in those sections of the country in which there are large Spanish-speaking populations, it does not seem to be economically possible for all Spanish immigrants to remain monolingual. In fact, the evidence points to the opposite conclusion. Results from a 1976 study indicate that of 2.5 million people who spoke Spanish as their native language, 1.6 million adopted English as their principal language (Veltman 14). Fifty per cent of the population switched from Spanish to English as their principal language. In order to offset this large loss of native speakers, Veltman calculates that Spanish-speaking women would need to produce 4.5 children each, but the average Chicano woman has only 2.9 children. A 1985 Rand Corporation study found that "more than 95 percent of first-generation Mexican-Americans born in the United States are proficient in English and that more than half the second generation speaks no Spanish at all" (Nunberg). Another study found that 98 per cent of Hispanic parents in Miami felt it essential that their children read and write English perfectly (Trasvina). In other words, Spanish speakers in the United States show a strong tendency to become English speakers, and as a result we are unlikely to become a Spanish-speaking country.

The loss of native speakers might be offset by the immigration of new Spanish speakers, but the evidence is that 50 per cent of Spanish speakers who immigrate to the US already speak some English (Chen and Henderson). They obviously are not Spanish-only speakers and can be reasonably expected to learn more English. It is simply maladaptive and dysfunctional not to do so. If the only way to prevent the maintenance of Spanish among a particular part of the population is to control immigration, then we must take the bull by his horns rather than his tail. We must control immigration through restrictive immigration laws rather than by trying to control immigration through a constitutional amendment mandating English as the official language. Would such an amendment then enable us to control immigration by preventing anyone who does not speak English from migrating to the US? That would be a very interesting law indeed.

To be complete, we need to consider the possibility that the statistics I have given are inaccurate — that Spanish speakers are not learning English at any great rate, that Spanish speakers will pour into the country in such large numbers that their number will equal or exceed the number of speakers of English, and that as a consequence, we will become a country with two major languages. If that should happen, the US could also become a country socially, politically, and linguistically divided, like Canada or Sri Lanka or any of several African countries. Countries which are composed of two largely monolingual groups do seem to have more tensions that tend to pull the nation apart rather than aid it in retaining unity. It is not generally politically wise for a nation to possess two major, equally important languages, especially when each group attaches great emotional value to its own language and culture and becomes xenophobic about the other language and culture. Will passing a law declaring English as the official language prevent the rise of a second major language? Only if we also pass a set of restrictive laws, among them a law which limits immigration to those people who already speak English, and a law which prohibits the use of any language other than English.

LEGISLATION: EFFECTS AND ALTERNATIVES

We have to question the effectiveness of these two additional laws. Limiting immigration might indeed work, if we are willing to build an eight-foot concrete wall along the Mexican-American border and convert a significant portion of our defense budget (or perhaps that portion of our education budgets now devoted to bilingual education) to patrolling our Southern borders. We have not been very effective in enforcing the immigration restrictions that we already have, and a new, more restrictive law is unlikely to accomplish any more than the current laws do.

The money for massive enforcement of current or new immigration restrictions is unlikely to materialize, so let's consider the ramifications of the other major possibility, prohibition of the use of any language other than English. If any language group, Spanish or other, chooses to maintain its language, there is precious little that we can do about it, legally or otherwise, and still maintain that we are a free country. We cannot legislate the language of the home, the street, the bar, the club, unless we are willing to violate the privacy of our people, unless we are willing to set up a cadre of language police who will ticket and arrest us if we speak something other than English. What we can do is disenfranchise all of those who have not yet learned or cannot learn English. We can exclude them from the possibility of taking part in our political system and from our schools, and because they will be uneducated, we can prevent them from benefiting from the economic system. We can insure a new oppressed minority. If that minority becomes a majority, through immigration (legal or illegal) and through birth, we will live with the consequences of our actions.

I dwelt on the German immigration into our country in the eighteenth and nineteenth centuries because that group very deliberately maintained its language and culture. Thus, those parts of the Spanish and Asian populations which are reluctant to abandon their culture and language because they had to abandon their countries for political and economic reasons are not unique to the United States. This is not a new problem. The Germans, for the most part, have eventually become users of English, not because of repressive linguistic policies or legislation, but for that most effective reason of all—utility. People learn a new language or dialect if they see that that language or dialect has high potential value for them, not because they are legally required to. The very fact that our current evidence says that more Spanish speakers are learning English than are retaining their own language is a pretty good indication that a good many of them believe English to be more useful and therefore more valuable than Spanish. English enables them to gain more than they have, to partake in the political and economic life of the United States more fully than Spanish (or Vietnamese or Chinese) does.

Our need is not to insure that everyone in the United States be a monolingual speaker of English but rather to insure that our country continues to hold its own politically and economically in the world at large. To accomplish this task, all Americans must be less provincial and less linguistically ethnocentric. English is now the predominant world language, especially in business, technology, and education, the mainstays of traditional, mainstream American culture. Because of the world-wide importance of English as an international language, it is unlikely that the United States will lose English as its common language at a time when other countries are seeking more speakers of English and teaching their own populations English. However, we will need people who can speak the languages of other countries. For the United States to continue to be an important economic and political power in the world, Americans of whatever variety will need two languages—their first language and English, or English and a second language. English is indeed a world language, but as every international tourist or business traveler learns, not everyone in the world speaks English. Rather than eliminate the second language of our immigrants, we need to help them learn English and maintain that valuable resource they already have, the use of a second language, and we need to teach our native English speakers a second language.

The United States has always been a polyglot country. It is part of our strength. It is unlikely that nonnative speakers of English, be they immigrants or born here, will remain monolingual, because they need English to talk with other Americans whose native language is not English and with other people in the world who do not speak Vietnamese or Spanish or French or Arabic or whatever. Multilingualism in a country is potentially dangerous only if it becomes the rallying point for cultural divisiveness. Otherwise, it is a benefit of great economic and political value.

Aside from the purely utilitarian economic value of knowing more than one language, there is evidence that knowing a second language increases our abilities to use our first language. People who know two languages generally perform better on tests of verbal ability administered in their native language than do monolingual speakers. That is to say, if your native language is English, and you learn Japanese, you will perform better on tests which measure your knowledge of and abilities in English (Hakuta). Parents who know and accept the research that shows that "bilingual youngsters are more imaginative, better with abstract notions and more flexible in their thinking" are enrolling their children in private language programs to give them the advantage that bilingual programs give other groups of children (Wells).

CONCLUSION

Neither our Congress nor any other national legislature has ever had much success in legislating morals or beliefs. Making English the official or only language of the United States will not alter my personal beliefs about the value of my language or my beliefs about yours. Rather than taking the path of linguistic legislation, we are much more likely to be successful in maintaining a common language in the United States by pursuing the American tradition of persuasion and demonstration. The very fact that English speakers (whether English is their first or second language) are economically and politically more powerful than non-English speakers is a better argument for learning English than an argument based on the fact that English is the official or only language of the United States. (See Carlin for a similar argument from the viewpoint of politics.)

I have tried to point out some distinctions here, perhaps the most important of which is that *official, only,* and *common* are not synonymous when coupled with *English.* A great many of us wish to maintain English as the *common* language of the United States, but that goal need not, and probably should not, entail legislating English as the *only* language or the official language. The problems that we have as a multilingual society have been with us since at least 1753 when Benjamin Franklin noted them, and we have managed to overcome them or turn them to our advantage without depriving anyone of the freedom of speech that we value so highly. There are distinct advantages for our culture, for our children, and for each of us individually to be multilingual, especially if we all share a language in common. If we are concerned about the quality and intent of bilingual programs or about the effects of our immigration policies, let's be direct and honest and focus on those and not pretend that legislating language choice will improve or change bilingual programs or slow immigration.

Works Cited

Anderson, Charles. *White Protestant Americans.* Englewood Cliffs, NJ: Prentice Hall, 1970.

Carlin, David R., Jr. "Charm and the English Language Amendment." *The Christian Century.* 101.27 (1984): 822–23.

Chen, Edward M., and Wade Henderson. "New 'English-only' Movement Reflects Old Fear of Immigrants." *Civil Liberties* No. 358 (1986): 8.

"Charting The Great Melting Pot." *U. S. News & World Report* 7 July 1986: 30.

Hakuta, Kenji. *The Mirror of Language: The Debate on Bilingualism.* New York: Basic, 1986.

"Immigrants Who Don't." *Literary Digest* 88.11 (1926): 50.

"Is English the Only Language for Government?" *New York Times* 26 Oct. 1986, late ed., sec. 4: 6.

Mencken, H. L. *The American Language: Supplement I.* New York: Knopf, 1945.

Nunberg, Geoffrey. "An 'Official Language' for California?" *New York Times* 2 Oct. 1986, late ed., sec. 3: 23.

Ruppenthal, J. C. "The Legal Status of the English Language in the American School System." *School and Society* 10 (1919): 658–66.

Trasvina. John D. "'Official' English Means Discrimination." *U. S. A. Today* 25 July 1986: 10A.

Veltman, Calvin. *Language Shift in the United States.* The Hague: Mouton, 1983.

Wells, Stacy. "Bilingualism: The Accent Is on Youth." *U. S. News & World Report* 28 July 1986: 60.

Whitney, Parkhurst. "They Want to Know What Their Children Are Saying." *Collier's Magazine* 14 July 1923: 13, 21.

SUGGESTIONS FOR WRITING

Informal Essays

1. If you belong to a family outside the white Anglo-Saxon Protestant mainstream, write an essay on the ease or difficulty of your own cultural assimilation. Use a quote or two from a couple of the essays in this chapter.
2. If you know of the experiences of an immigrant family or student, use those experiences as an example to make a point about bilingualism.
3. If you have had experience in a bilingual classroom, describe your experiences.

Short Documented Papers

1. Contrast the ideas expressed by those on opposing sides of a single point in the controversy over bilingualism.
2. Contrast the statistical support that the critics and defenders of bilingual education use to support their views.
3. Contrast the historical precedents that each side uses to support its views.
4. After determining two of the weakest points made by either the critics or the defenders of bilingual education, show their vulnerability.
5. Develop two or three of the most convincing points made by either side of the controversy.

Longer Documented Papers

1. In a research argument, make the case for or against bilingual education.
2. In a research report, contrast three or four of the most important points made by both the critics and the defenders of bilingual education.
3. Determine the weakest points made by both sides of the controversy and demonstrate their vulnerability.

JOYCE CAROL OATES'S
"Where Are You Going, Where Have You Been?"
What's Going on in This Story?

Although Joyce Carol Oates is a quiet, unpretentious woman, the product of a rural working-class western-New York upbringing, she is also something of a workhorse. In fact, if you were to look over the offerings of American fiction over the last three decades, you would find yourself standing in a long shadow cast by the towering stack of novels, short stories, and poetry of Joyce Carol Oates. Although she has spent most of her adult life teaching college English, she has somehow also found the time, since the appearance of her first book in 1964, to publish nearly twenty novels, fifteen volumes of short stories, and numerous collections of poetry and literary criticism.

Although it might seem that Oates's prodigious output would thin the quality of her fiction, that's not the case at all. In fact, by almost anyone's ranking, Oates is one of the most highly respected American writers to have appeared since World War II.

"Where Are You Going, Where Have You Been?" is one of her best stories. It was first published in the literary magazine *Epoch* in 1966, then appeared in Oates's collection of short stories *The Wheel of Love* in 1970, and has since been anthologized in scores of college literature textbooks. In 1986 it was made into a film, *Smooth Talk*, by the feminist director Joyce Chopra. In short, "Where Are You Going, Where Have You Been?" has become one of America's classic modern short stories.

It's not surprising that the story has been so widely praised. Oates describes the world of modern adolescence with such careful attention to detail — the world of shopping malls, movie theaters, and rock music — that we seem to be able to see into the heads of her teenage characters.

But Oates seems to have larger things in mind than a portrait of American teenagers. In fact, just as we are settling in to the story's realistic tone, it turns into something else before our eyes. Indeed, the story turns almost surrealistic. There's just something wrong, out of plumb, with Arnold Friend, the glib and threatening young man who shows up unexpectedly on Connie's doorstep. "Who the hell do you think you are?," Connie asks. The stranger's answer, "Don't you know who I am?," along with other intriguing and seemingly contradictory hints, has led critics a merry chase. Who is this Arnold Friend, and where *has* he been?

Readers most certainly have been guessing. In the essays following the story, you will find a variety of ideas about the story. That's not surprising. It's one of those stories that suggests more than it says. When the eerie Arnold Friend shows up, the words on the page seem to tell only part of what's going on. Like listening to a whisper on the other side of a door, what we can't hear seems more important than what we can hear. In fact, there's probably enough evidence left over in the story, and enough ambiguity, to support your own interpretation — or, at the least, a permutation of one that has already been offered up.

But no matter what conclusions you draw about "Where Are You Going, Where Have You Been?," we think that you will like the story. Like all really good stories, the more you know about it, the more you like it.

"WHERE ARE YOU GOING, WHERE HAVE YOU BEEN?"

Joyce Carol Oates

Here is the text of "Where Are You Going, Where Have You Been?," one of Joyce Carol Oates's most highly regarded and widely read stories. The setting is comfortably familiar: the teen hangouts, burger joints, and shopping malls of middle America. But there is a decidedly eerie character lurking around this familiar setting, the ominous figure of Arnold Friend.

Even as you read the story for the first time, you might try to answer some of the questions the story poses: What is the significance of the background rock music to which fifteen-year-old Connie frequently responds? (At one point, she insists it is "like music at a church service—always something to depend upon.") What is the significance of Arnold Friend's name and of his question "Don't you know who I am?" What is the significance of the title? Is it related to Friend's insistence that "The place where you came from ain't there any more, and where you had in mind to go is cancelled out"? Why does Friend seem virtually omniscient? Is he merely a product of Connie's fantasies or is he horrifyingly real? Is he an embodiment of everything Connie values or is he an allegorical embodiment of satanic evil? Just what is going on here?

FOR BOB DYLAN

Her name was Connie. She was fifteen and she had a quick, nervous giggling habit of craning her neck to glance into mirrors or checking other people's faces to make sure her own was all right. Her mother, who noticed everything and knew everything and who hadn't much reason any longer to look at her own face, always scolded Connie about it. "Stop gawking at yourself. Who are you? You think you're so pretty?" she would say. Connie would raise her eyebrows at these familiar old complaints and look right through her mother, into a shadowy vision of herself as she was right at that moment: she knew she was pretty and that was everything. Her mother had been pretty once too, if you could believe those old snapshots in the album, but now her looks were gone and that was why she was always after Connie.

"Why don't you keep your room clean like your sister? How've you got your hair fixed—what the hell stinks? Hair spray? You don't see your sister using that junk."

Her sister June was twenty-four and still lived at home. She was a secretary in the high school Connie attended, and if that wasn't bad enough—with her in the same building—she was so plain and chunky and steady that Connie had to hear her praised all the time by her mother and her mother's sisters. June did this, June did that, she saved money and helped clean the house and cooked and Connie couldn't do a thing, her mind was all filled with trashy daydreams. Their father was

Joyce Carol Oates, "Where Are You Going, Where Have You Been?," *The Wheel of Love* (New York: The Vanguard Press, 1970).

away at work most of the time and when he came home he wanted supper and he read the newspaper at supper and after supper he went to bed. He didn't bother talking much to them, but around his bent head Connie's mother kept picking at her until Connie wished her mother was dead and she herself was dead and it was all over. "She makes me want to throw up sometimes," she complained to her friends. She had a high, breathless, amused voice that made everything she said sound a little forced, whether it was sincere or not.

There was one good thing: June went places with girl friends of hers, girls who were just as plain and steady as she, and so when Connie wanted to do that her mother had no objections. The father of Connie's best girl friend drove the girls the three miles to town and left them at a shopping plaza so they could walk through the stores or go to a movie, and when he came to pick them up again at eleven he never bothered to ask what they had done.

They must have been familiar sights, walking around the shopping plaza in their shorts and flat ballerina slippers that always scuffed the sidewalk, with charm bracelets jingling on their thin wrists; they would lean together to whisper and laugh secretly if someone passed who amused or interested them. Connie had long dark blond hair that drew anyone's eye to it, and she wore part of it pulled up on her head and puffed out and the rest of it she let fall down her back. She wore a pull-over jersey blouse that looked one way when she was at home and another way when she was away from home. Everything about her had two sides to it, one for home and one for anywhere that was not home: her walk, which could be childlike and bobbing, or languid enough to make anyone think she was hearing music in her head; her mouth, which was pale and smirking most of the time, but bright and pink on these evenings out; her laugh, which was cynical and drawling at home — "Ha, ha, very funny," — but high-pitched and nervous anywhere else, like the jingling of the charms on her bracelet.

Sometimes they did go shopping or to a movie, but sometimes they went across the highway, ducking fast across the busy road, to a drive-in restaurant where older kids hung out. The restaurant was shaped like a big bottle, though squatter than a real bottle, and on its cap was a revolving figure of a grinning boy holding a hamburger aloft. One night in midsummer they ran across, breathless with daring, and right away someone leaned out a car window and invited them over, but it was just a boy from high school they didn't like. It made them feel good to be able to ignore him. They went up through the maze of parked and cruising cars to the bright-lit, fly-infested restaurant, their faces pleased and expectant as if they were entering a sacred building that loomed up out of the night to give them what haven and blessing they yearned for. They sat at the counter and crossed their legs at the ankles, their thin shoulders rigid with excitement, and listened to the music that made everything so good: the music was always in the background, like music at a church service; it was something to depend upon.

A boy named Eddie came in to talk with them. He sat backwards on his stool, turning himself jerkily around in semicircles and then stopping and turning back again, and after a while he asked Connie if she would like something to eat. She said she would and so she tapped her friend's arm on her way out — her friend pulled her face up into a brave, droll look — and Connie said she would meet her at eleven, across the way. "I just hate to leave her like that," Connie said earnestly, but the boy said that she wouldn't be alone for long. So they went out to his car, and on the way Connie couldn't help but let her eyes wander over the windshields and faces all around her, her face gleaming with a joy that had nothing to do with Eddie or even this place; it might have been the music. She drew her shoulders up and sucked in her breath with the pure pleasure of being alive, and just at that moment she happened to glance at a face just a few feet from hers. It was a boy with shaggy black hair, in a convertible jalopy painted gold. He stared at her and then his lips widened into a grin. Connie slit her eyes at him and turned away, but she couldn't help glancing back and there he was, still watching her. He wagged a finger and laughed and said, "Gonna get you, baby," and Connie turned away again without Eddie noticing anything.

She spent three hours with him, at the restaurant where they ate hamburgers and drank Cokes in wax cups that were always sweating, and then down an alley a mile or so away, and when he left her off at five to eleven only the movie house was still open at the plaza. Her girl friend was there, talking with a boy. When Connie came up, the two girls smiled at each other and Connie said, "How was the movie?" and the girl said, "*You* should know." They rode off with the girl's father, sleepy and pleased, and Connie couldn't help but look back at the darkened shopping plaza with its big empty parking lot and its signs that were faded and ghostly now, and over at the drive-in restaurant where cars were still circling tirelessly. She couldn't hear the music at this distance.

Next morning June asked her how the movie was and Connie said, "So-so."

She and that girl and occasionally another girl went out several times a week, and the rest of the time Connie spent around the house — it was summer vacation — getting in her mother's way and thinking, dreaming about the boys she met. But all the boys fell back and dissolved into a single face that was not even a face but an idea, a feeling, mixed up with the urgent insistent pounding of the music and the humid night air of July. Connie's mother kept dragging her back to the daylight by finding things for her to do or saying suddenly, "What's this about the Pettinger girl?"

And Connie would say nervously, "Oh, her. That dope." She always drew thick clear lines between herself and such girls, and her mother was simple and kind enough to believe it. Her mother was so simple, Connie thought, that it was maybe cruel to fool her so much. Her mother went scuffling around the house in old bedroom slippers and complained over the telephone to one sister about the other, then the other called up and the two of them complained about the third one. If June's name was mentioned her mother's tone was approving, and if Connie's name was mentioned it was disapproving. This did not really mean she disliked Connie, and actually Connie thought that her mother preferred her to June just because she was prettier, but the two of them kept up a pretense of exasperation, a sense that they were tugging and struggling over something of little value to either of them. Sometimes, over coffee, they were almost friends, but something would come up — some vexation that was like a fly buzzing suddenly around their heads — and their faces went hard with contempt.

One Sunday Connie got up at eleven — none of them bothered with church — and washed her hair so that it could dry all day long in the sun. Her parents and sister were going to a barbecue at an aunt's house and Connie said no, she wasn't interested, rolling her eyes to let her mother know just what she thought of it. "Stay home alone then," her mother said sharply. Connie sat out back in a lawn chair and watched them drive away, her father quiet and bald, hunched around so that he could back the car out, her mother with a look that was still angry and not at all softened through the windshield, and in the back seat poor old June, all dressed up as if she didn't know what a barbecue was, with all the running yelling kids and the flies. Connie sat with her eyes closed in the sun, dreaming and dazed with the warmth about her as if this were a kind of love, the caresses of love, and her mind slipped over onto thoughts of the boy she had been with the night before and how nice he had been, how sweet it always was, not the way someone like June would suppose but sweet, gentle, the way it was in movies and promised in songs; and when she opened her eyes she hardly knew where she was, the back yard ran off into weeds and a fence-like line of trees and behind it the sky was perfectly blue and still. The asbestos "ranch house" that was now three years old startled her — it looked small. She shook her head as if to get awake.

It was too hot. She went inside the house and turned on the radio to drown out the quiet. She sat on the edge of her bed, barefoot, and listened for an hour and a half to a program called XYZ Sunday Jamboree, record after record of hard, fast, shrieking songs she sang along with, interspersed by exclamations from "Bobby King": "An' look here, you girls at Napoleon's — Son and Charley want you to pay real close attention to this song coming up!"

And Connie paid close attention herself, bathed in a glow of slow-pulsed joy that seemed to rise mysteriously out of the music itself and lay languidly about the airless little room, breathed in and breathed out with each gentle rise and fall of her chest.

After a while she heard a car coming up the drive. She sat up at once, startled, because it couldn't be her father so soon. The gravel kept crunching all the way in from the road — the driveway was long — and Connie ran to the window. It was a car she didn't know. It was an open jalopy, painted a bright gold that caught the sunlight opaquely. Her heart began to pound and her fingers snatched at her hair, checking it, and she whispered, "Christ. Christ," wondering how bad she looked. The car came to a stop at the side door and the horn sounded four short taps, as if this were a signal Connie knew.

She went into the kitchen and approached the door slowly, then hung out the screen door, her bare toes curling down off the step. There were two boys in the car and now she recognized the driver: he had shaggy, shabby black hair that looked crazy as a wig and he was grinning at her.

"I ain't late, am I?" he said.

"Who the hell do you think you are?" Connie said.

"Toldja I'd be out, didn't I?"

"I don't even know who you are."

She spoke sullenly, careful to show no interest or pleasure, and he spoke in a fast, bright monotone. Connie looked past him to the other boy, taking her time. He had fair brown hair, with a lock that fell onto his forehead. His sideburns gave him a fierce, embarrassed look, but so far he hadn't even bothered to glance at her. Both boys wore sunglasses. The driver's glasses were metallic and mirrored everything in miniature.

"You wanta come for a ride?" he said.

Connie smirked and let her hair fall loose over one shoulder.

"Don'tcha like my car? New paint job," he said. "Hey."

"What?"

"You're cute."

She pretended to fidget, chasing flies away from the door.

"Don'tcha believe me, or what?" he said.

"Look, I don't even know who you are," Connie said in disgust.

"Hey, Ellie's got a radio, see. Mine broke down." He lifted his friend's arm and showed her the little transistor radio the boy was holding, and now Connie began to hear the music. It was the same program that was playing inside the house.

"Bobby King?" she said.

"I listen to him all the time. I think he's great."

"He's kind of great," Connie said reluctantly.

"Listen, that guy's *great*. He knows where the action is."

Connie blushed a little, because the glasses made it impossible for her to see just what this boy was looking at. She couldn't decide if she liked him or if he was just a jerk, and so she dawdled in the doorway and wouldn't come down or go back inside. She said, "What's all that stuff painted on your car?"

"Can'tcha read it?" He opened the door very carefully, as if he were afraid it might fall off. He slid out just as carefully, planting his feet firmly on the ground, the tiny metallic world in his glasses slowing down like gelatine hardening, and in the midst of it Connie's bright green blouse. "This here is my name, to begin with," he said. ARNOLD FRIEND was written in tarlike black letters on the side, with a drawing of a round, grinning face that reminded Connie of a pumpkin, except it wore sunglasses. "I wanta introduce myself, I'm Arnold Friend and that's my real name and I'm gonna be your friend, honey, and inside the car's Ellie Oscar, he's kinda shy." Ellie brought his transistor radio up to his shoulder and balanced it there. "Now, these numbers are a secret code, honey," Arnold Friend explained. He read off the numbers 33, 19, 17 and raised his eyebrows at her to see what she thought of that, but she didn't think much of it. The left rear fender had been smashed and around it was written, on the gleaming gold background: DONE BY CRAZY WOMAN DRIVER. Connie had to laugh at that. Arnold Friend was pleased at her laughter and looked up at her. "Around the other side's a lot more — you wanta come and see them?"

"No."

"Why not?"

"Why should I?"

"Don'tcha wanta see what's on the car? Don'tcha wanta go for a ride?"

"I don't know."

"Why not?"

"I got things to do."

"Like what?"

"Things."

He laughed as if she had said something funny. He slapped his thighs. He was standing in a strange way, leaning back against the car as if he were balancing himself. He wasn't tall, only an inch or so taller than she would be if she came down to him. Connie liked the way he was dressed, which was the way all of them dressed: tight faded jeans stuffed into black, scuffed boots, a belt that pulled his waist in and showed how lean he was, and a white pull-over shirt that was a little soiled and showed the hard small muscles of his arms and shoulders. He looked as if he probably did hard work, lifting and carrying things. Even his neck looked muscular. And his face was a familiar face, somehow: the jaw and chin and cheeks slightly darkened because he hadn't shaved for a day or two, and the nose long and hawklike, sniffing as if she were a treat he was going to gobble up and it was all a joke.

"Connie, you ain't telling the truth. This is your day set aside for a ride with me and you know it," he said, still laughing. The way he straightened and recovered from his fit of laughing showed that it had been all fake.

"How do you know what my name is?" she said suspiciously.

"It's Connie."

"Maybe and maybe not."

"I know my Connie," he said, wagging his finger. Now she remembered him even better, back at the restaurant, and her cheeks warmed at the thought of how she had sucked in her breath just at the moment she passed him — how she must have looked to him. And he had remembered her. "Ellie and I come out here especially for you," he said. "Ellie can sit in back. How about it?"

"Where?"

"Where what?"

"Where're we going?"

He looked at her. He took off the sunglasses and she saw how pale the skin around his eyes was, like holes that were not in shadow but instead in light. His eyes were like chips of broken glass that catch the light in an amiable way. He smiled. It was as if the idea of going for a ride somewhere, to someplace, was a new idea to him.

"Just for a ride, Connie sweetheart."

"I never said my name was Connie," she said.

"But I know what it is. I know your name and all about you, lots of things," Arnold Friend said. He had not moved yet but stood still leaning back against the side of his jalopy. "I took a special interest in you, such a pretty girl, and found out all about you — like I know your parents and sister are gone somewheres and I know where and how long they're going to be gone, and I know who you were with last night, and your best girl friend's name is Betty. Right?"

He spoke in a simple lilting voice, exactly as if he were reciting the words to a song. His smile assured her that everything was fine. In the car Ellie turned up the volume on his radio and did not bother to look around at them.

"Ellie can sit in the back seat," Arnold Friend said. He indicated his friend with a casual jerk of his chin, as if Ellie did not count and she should not bother with him.

"How'd you find out all that stuff?" Connie said.

"Listen: Betty Schultz and Tony Fitch and Jimmy Pettinger and Nancy Pettinger," he said in a chant. "Raymond Stanley and Bob Hunter — "

"Do you know all those kids?"

"I know everybody."

"Look, you're kidding. You're not from around here."

"Sure."

"But — how come we never saw you before?"

"Sure you saw me before," he said. He looked down at his boots, as if he were a little offended. "You just don't remember."

"I guess I'd remember you," Connie said.

"Yeah?" He looked up at this, beaming. He was pleased. He began to mark time with the music from Ellie's radio, tapping his fists lightly together. Connie looked away from his smile to the car, which was painted so bright it almost hurt her eyes to look at it. She looked at that name, ARNOLD FRIEND. And up at the front fender was an expression that was familiar — MAN THE FLYING SAUCERS. It was an expression kids had used the year before but didn't use this year. She looked at it for a while as if the words meant something to her that she did not yet know.

"What're you thinking about? Huh?" Arnold Friend demanded. "Not worried about your hair blowing around in the car, are you?"

"No."

"Think I maybe can't drive good?"

"How do I know?"

"You're a hard girl to handle. How come?" he said. "Don't you know I'm your friend? Didn't you see me put my sign in the air when you walked by?"

"What sign?"

"My sign." And he drew an X in the air, leaning out toward her. They were maybe ten feet apart. After his hand fell back to his side the X was still in the air, almost visible. Connie let the screen door close and stood perfectly still inside it, listening to the music from her radio and the boy's blend together. She stared at Arnold Friend. He stood there so stiffly relaxed, pretending to be relaxed, with one hand idly on the door handle as if he were keeping himself up that way and had no intention of ever moving again. She recognized most things about him, the tight jeans that showed his thighs and buttocks and the greasy leather boots and the tight shirt, and even that slippery friendly smile of his, that sleepy dreamy smile that all the boys used to get across ideas they didn't want to put into words. She recognized all this and also the singsong way he talked, slightly mocking, kidding, but serious and a little melancholy, and she recognized the way he tapped one fist against the other in homage to the perpetual music behind him. But all these things did not come together.

She said suddenly, "Hey, how old are you?"

His smiled faded. She could see then that he wasn't a kid, he was much older — thirty, maybe more. At this knowledge her heart began to pound faster.

"That's a crazy thing to ask. Can'tcha see I'm your own age?"

"Like hell you are."

"Or maybe a coupla years older. I'm eighteen."

"Eighteen?" she said doubtfully.

He grinned to reassure her and lines appeared at the corners of his mouth. His teeth were big and white. He grinned so broadly his eyes became slits and she saw how thick the lashes were, thick and black as if painted with a black tarlike material. Then, abruptly, he seemed to become embarrassed and looked over his shoulder at Ellie. 'Him, he's crazy," he said. "Ain't he a riot? He's a nut, a real character." Ellie was still listening to the music. His sunglasses told nothing about what he was thinking. He wore a bright orange shirt unbuttoned halfway to show his chest, which was a pale, bluish chest and not muscular like Arnold Friend's. His shirt collar was turned up all around and the very tips of the collar pointed out past his chin as if they were protecting him. He was pressing the transistor radio up against his ear and sat there in a kind of daze, right in the sun.

"He's kinda strange," Connie said.

"Hey, she says you're kinda strange! Kinda strange!" Arnold Friend cried. He pounded on the car to get Ellie's attention. Ellie turned for the first time and Connie saw with shock that he wasn't a kid either—he had a fair, hairless face, cheeks reddened slightly as if the veins grew too close to the surface of his skin, the face of a forty-year-old baby. Connie felt a wave of dizziness rise in her at this sight and she stared at him as if waiting for something to change the shock of the moment, make it all right again. Ellie's lips kept shaping words, mumbling along with the words blasting in his ear.

"Maybe you two better go away," Connie said faintly.

"What? How come?" Arnold Friend cried. "We come out here to take you for a ride. It's Sunday." He had the voice of the man on the radio now. It was the same voice, Connie thought. "Don'tcha know it's Sunday all day? And honey, no matter who you were with last night, today you're with Arnold Friend and don't you forget it! Maybe you better step out here," he said, and this last was in a different voice. It was a little flatter, as if the heat was finally getting to him.

"No. I got things to do."

"Hey."

"You two better leave."

"We ain't leaving until you come with us."

"Like hell I am—"

"Connie, don't fool around with me. I mean—I mean, don't fool *around*," he said, shaking his head. He laughed incredulously. He placed his sunglasses on top of his head, carefully, as if he were indeed wearing a wig, and brought the stems down behind his ears. Connie stared at him, another wave of dizziness and fear rising in her so that for a moment he wasn't even in focus but was just a blur standing there against his gold car, and she had the idea that he had driven up the driveway all right but had come from nowhere before that and belonged nowhere and that everything about him and even about the music that was so familiar to her was only half real.

"If my father comes and sees you—"

"He ain't coming. He's at a barbecue."

"How do you know that?"

"Aunt Tillie's. Right now they're—uh—they're drinking. Sitting around," he said vaguely, squinting as if he were staring all the way to town and over to Aunt Tillie's back yard. Then the vision seemed to get clear and he nodded energetically. "Yeah. Sitting around. There's your sister in a blue dress, huh? And high heels, the poor sad bitch—nothing like you, sweetheart! And your mother's helping some fat woman with the corn, they're cleaning the corn—husking the corn—"

"What fat woman?" Connie cried.

"How do I know what fat woman, I don't know every goddamn fat woman in the world!" Arnold Friend laughed.

"Oh, that's Mrs. Hornsby. . . . Who invited her?" Connie said. She felt a little lightheaded. Her breath was coming quickly.

"She's too fat. I don't like them fat. I like them the way you are, honey," he said, smiling sleepily at her. They stared at each other for a while through the screen door. He said softly, "Now, what you're going to do is this: you're going to come out that door. You're going to sit up front with me and Ellie's going to sit in the back, the hell with Ellie, right? This isn't Ellie's date. You're my date. I'm your lover, honey."

"What? You're crazy—"

"Yes, I'm your lover. You don't know what that is but you will," he said. "I know that too. I know all about you. But look: it's real nice and you couldn't ask for nobody better than me, or more polite. I always keep my word. I'll tell you how it is, I'm always nice at first, the first time. I'll hold you so tight you won't think you have to try to get away or pretend anything because you'll know you can't. And I'll come inside you where it's all secret and you'll give in to me and you'll love me—"

"Shut up! You're crazy!" Connie said. She backed away from the door. She put her hands up against her ears as if she'd heard something terrible, something not meant for her. "People don't talk like that, you're crazy," she muttered. Her heart was almost too big now for her chest and its pumping made sweat break out all over her. She looked out to see Arnold Friend pause and then take a step toward the porch, lurching. He almost fell. But, like a clever drunken man, he managed to catch his balance. He wobbled in his high boots and grabbed hold of one of the porch posts.

"Honey?" he said. "You still listening?"

"Get the hell out of here!"

"Be nice, honey. Listen."

"I'm going to call the police—"

He wobbled again and out of the side of his mouth came a fast spat curse, an aside not meant for her to hear. But even this "Christ!" sounded forced. Then he began to smile again. She watched this smile come, awkward as if he were smiling from inside a mask. His whole face was a mask, she thought wildly, tanned down to his throat but then running out as if he had plastered make-up on his face but had forgotten about his throat.

"Honey—? Listen, here's how it is. I always tell the truth and I promise you this: I ain't coming in that house after you."

"You better not! I'm going to call the police if you—if you don't—"

"Honey," he said, talking right through her voice, "honey, I'm not coming in there but you are coming out here. You know why?"

She was panting. The kitchen looked like a place she had never seen before, some room she had run inside but that wasn't good enough, wasn't going to help her. The kitchen window had never had a curtain, after three years, and there were dishes in the sink for her to do—probably—and if you ran your hand across the table you'd probably feel something sticky there.

"You listening, honey? Hey?"

"—going to call the police—"

"Soon as you touch the phone I don't need to keep my promise and can come inside. You won't want that."

She rushed forward and tried to lock the door. Her fingers were shaking. "But why lock it," Arnold Friend said gently, talking right into her face. "It's just a screen door. It's just nothing." One of his boots was at a strange angle, as if his foot wasn't in it. It pointed out to the left, bent at the ankle. "I mean, anybody can break through a screen door and glass and wood and iron or anything else if he needs to, anybody at all, and specially Arnold Friend. If the place got lit up with a fire, honey, you'd come runnin' out into my arms, right into my arms an' safe at home — like you knew I was your lover and'd stopped fooling around. I don't mind a nice shy girl but I don't like no fooling around." Part of those words were spoken with a slight rhythmic lilt, and Connie somehow recognized them — the echo of a song from last year, about a girl rushing into her boy friend's arms and coming home again —

Connie stood barefoot on the linoleum floor, staring at him. "What do you want?" she whispered.

"I want you," he said.

"What?"

"Seen you that night and thought, that's the one, yes sir. I never needed to look anymore."

"But my father's coming back. He's coming to get me. I had to wash my hair first —" She spoke in a dry, rapid voice, hardly raising it for him to hear.

"No, your daddy is not coming and yes, you had to wash your hair and you washed it for me. It's nice and shining and all for me. I thank you sweetheart," he said with a mock bow, but again he almost lost his balance. He had to bend and adjust his boots. Evidently his feet did not go all the way down; the boots must have been stuffed with something so that he would seem taller. Connie stared out at him and behind him at Ellie in the car, who seemed to be looking off toward Connie's right, into nothing. This Ellie said, pulling the words out of the air one after another as if he were just discovering them, "You want me to pull out the phone?"

"Shut your mouth and keep it shut," Arnold Friend said, his face red from bending over or maybe from embarrassment because Connie had seen his boots. "This ain't none of your business."

"What — what are you doing? What do you want?" Connie said. "If I call the police they'll get you, they'll arrest you —"

"Promise was not to come in unless you touch that phone, and I'll keep that promise," he said. He resumed his erect position and tried to force his shoulders back. He sounded like a hero in a movie, declaring something important. But he spoke too loudly and it was as if he were speaking to someone behind Connie. "I ain't made plans for coming in that house where I don't belong but just for you to come out to me, the way you should. Don't you know who I am?"

"You're crazy," she whispered. She backed away from the door but did not want to go into another part of the house, as if this would give him permission to come through the door. "What do you . . . you're crazy, you. . . ."

"Huh? What're you saying, honey?"

Her eyes darted everywhere in the kitchen. She could not remember what it was, this room.

"This is how it is, honey: you come out and we'll drive away, have a nice ride. But if you don't come out we're gonna wait till your people come home and then they're all going to get it."

"You want that telephone pulled out?" Ellie said. He held the radio away from his ear and grimaced, as if without the radio the air was too much for him.

"I toldja shut up, Ellie," Arnold Friend said, "you're deaf, get a hearing aid, right? Fix yourself up. This little girl's no trouble and's gonna be nice to me, so Ellie keep to yourself, this ain't your date — right? Don't hem in on me, don't hog, don't crush, don't bird dog, don't trail me," he said in a rapid, meaningless voice, as if he were running through all the expressions he'd learned but was no longer sure which of them was in style, then rushing on to new ones, making them up with his eyes closed. "Don't crawl under my fence, don't squeeze in my chipmunk hole, don't sniff my glue, suck my popsicle, keep your own greasy fingers on yourself!" He shaded his eyes and peered in at Connie, who was backed against the kitchen table. "Don't mind him, honey, he's just a creep. He's a dope. Right? I'm the boy for you and like I said, you come out here nice like a lady and give me your hand, and nobody else gets hurt, I mean, your nice old bald-headed daddy and your mummy and your sister in her high heels. Because listen: why bring them in this?"

"Leave me alone," Connie whispered.

"Hey, you know that old woman down the road, the one with the chickens and stuff — you know her?"

"She's dead!"

"Dead? What? You know her?" Arnold Friend said.

"She's dead — "

"Don't you like her?"

"She's dead — she's — she isn't here any more — "

"But don't you like her, I mean, you got something against her? Some grudge or something?" Then his voice dipped as if he were conscious of a rudeness. He touched the sunglasses perched up on top of his head as if to make sure they were still there. "Now, you be a good girl."

"What are you going to do?"

"Just two things, or maybe three," Arnold Friend said. "But I promise it won't last long and you'll like me the way you get to like people you're close to. You will. It's all over for you here, so come on out. You don't want your people in any trouble, do you?"

She turned and bumped against a chair or something, hurting her leg, but she ran into the back room and picked up the telephone. Something roared in her ear, a tiny roaring, and she was so sick with fear that she could do nothing but listen to it — the telephone was clammy and very heavy and her fingers groped down to the dial but were too weak to touch it. She began to scream into the phone, into the roaring. She cried out, she cried for her mother, she felt her breath start jerking back and forth in her lungs as if it were something Arnold Friend was stabbing her with again and again with no tenderness. A noisy sorrowful wailing rose all about her and she was locked inside it the way she was locked inside this house.

After a while she could hear again. She was sitting on the floor with her wet back against the wall.

Arnold Friend was saying from the door, "That's a good girl. Put the phone back."

She kicked the phone away from her.

"No honey. Pick it up. Put it back right."

She picked it up and put it back. The dial tone stopped.

"That's a good girl. Now, you come outside."

She was hollow with what had been fear but what was now just an emptiness. All that screaming had blasted it out of her. She sat, one leg cramped under her, and deep inside her brain was something like a pinpoint of light that kept going and would not let her relax. She thought, I'm not going to see my mother again. She thought, I'm not going to sleep in my bed again. Her bright green blouse was all wet.

Arnold Friend said, in a gentle-loud voice that was like a stage voice, "The place where you came from ain't there any more, and where you had in mind to go is cancelled out. This place you are now — inside your daddy's house — is nothing but a cardboard box I can knock down any time. You know that and always did know it. You hear me?"

She thought, I have got to think. I have got to know what to do.

"We'll go out to a nice field, out in the country here where it smells so nice and it's sunny," Arnold Friend said. "I'll have my arms tight around you so you won't need to try to get away and I'll show you what love is like, what it does. The hell with this house! It looks solid all right," he said. He ran a fingernail down the screen and the noise did not make Connie shiver, as it would have the day before. "Now, put your hand on your heart, honey. Feel that? That feels solid too but we know better. Be nice to me, be sweet like you can because what else is there for a girl like you but to be sweet and pretty and give in? — and get away before her people come back?"

She felt her pounding heart. Her hand seemed to enclose it. She thought for the first time in her life that it was nothing that was hers, that belonged to her, but just a pounding, living thing inside this body that wasn't really hers either.

"You don't want them to get hurt," Arnold Friend went on. "Now, get up, honey. Get up all by yourself."

She stood.

"Now, turn this way. That's right. Come over here to me. — Ellie, put that away, didn't I tell you? You dope. You miserable creepy dope," Arnold Friend said. His words were not angry but only part of an incantation. The incantation was kindly. "Now, come out through the kitchen to me, honey, and let's see a smile, try it, you're a brave, sweet little girl and now they're eating corn and hot dogs cooked to bursting over an outdoor fire, and they don't know one thing about you and never did and honey, you're better than them because not a one of them would have done this for you."

Connie felt the linoleum under her feet; it was cool. She brushed her hair back out of her eyes. Arnold Friend let go of the post tentatively and opened his arms for her, his elbows pointing in toward each other and his wrists limp, to show that this was an embarrassed embrace and a little mocking, he didn't want to make her self-conscious.

She put out her hand against the screen. She watched herself push the door slowly open as if she were back safe somewhere in the other doorway, watching this body and this head of long hair moving out into the sunlight where Arnold Friend waited.

"My sweet little blue-eyed girl," he said in a half-sung sigh that had nothing to do with her brown eyes but was taken up just the same by the vast sunlit reaches of the land behind him and on all sides of him — so much land that Connie had never seen before and did not recognize except to know that she was going to it.

Preface to "Where Are You Going, Where Have You Been?"

Joyce Carol Oates

"Where Are You Going, Where Have You Been?" first appeared in Epoch *in 1966 and then was published with other Oates stories in* The Wheel of Love *in 1970. In 1974 several of Oates's most popular stories were selected to be published in a paperback edition with "Where Are You Going, Where Have You Been?" as its title story. In her brief preface to this book, Oates makes several generalizations about her purpose in writing stories that involve youthful characters. You might want to carefully reconsider the story you have just read in light of these observations. Does the story, for example, contain evidence supporting her assertion that a common struggle among young Americans consists of "the attempt to rescue spiritual values from a society constantly in the process of devaluing itself"? And does this story, as Oates insists, "deal with human beings struggling heroically to define personal identity in the face of incredible opposition, even in the face of death itself"? As you can see, Oates's observations will provide you with a number of different perspectives on "Where Are You Going, Where Have You Been?"*

If we could live inside one another's heads for a single day, for even a single hour, so much would become clear — so many puzzling differences, so many ostensible reasons for "estrangement," would vanish. Are we not, each of us, the center of the universe? — yet we were born into a culture that assumes that some people are the center, some few individuals are *absolute*, and their decrees, their beliefs, their ways of life must be accepted by all, no matter how destructive they are. There are cultures in which divinity is spread out equally, energizing everyone and everything; there are other cultures — unfortunately, ours is one of them — in which the concept of "divinity" was snatched up by a political/economic order, and the democratic essence of divinity denied.

Though it has been denied, this essence of divinity has not been destroyed, and we are witnessing in our time its re-emergence, its evolution back into consciousness. Already we have had terrible psychic upsets, breaks between generations, heroic struggles wrongly called "rebellious acts," and, most tragic of all, casualties among those who sense that their society is an unhealthy one but who have no idea of how to transcend it, how to create a counter-magic to negate it. We have experienced countless manifestations of the struggle I believe to be common to most young Americans today: the attempt to rescue spiritual values from a society constantly in the process of devaluing itself.

I know from personal experience, as a writer, that a barrier of some kind does exist between one way of thinking and another, one "consciousness" and another. Yet it is intangible, inexplicable. Stories of mine like "Where Are You Going, Where Have You Been?" and "Happy Onion" and "Boy and Girl" have been constantly misunderstood by one generation, and intuitively understood by another. A

Joyce Carol Oates, Preface, *Where Are You Going, Where Have You Been?* (New York: Fawcett Publications, 1974).

large number of readers seem to see in such stories morbidity, absurdity, and a sense that life is meaningless; younger readers — who write to me, or whom I meet while visiting college campuses — seem to understand that these stories deal with human beings struggling heroically to define personal identity in the face of incredible opposition, even in the face of death itself. (And I believe a new, healthier, saner concept of the experience of death is also evolving in our time.) Where some adult readers see ugliness, because they call "ugly" anything that offends a certain fixed concept of morality, other readers may see a kind of beauty. A new morality is emerging in America, in fact on the North American continent generally, which may appear to be opposed to the old but which is in fact a higher form of the old — the democratization of the spirit, the experiencing of life as meaningful in itself, without divisions into "good" or "bad," "beautiful" or "ugly," "moral" or "immoral."

What seemed to be dead — the world-matter surrounding us — has been discovered to be living, intensely alive. What seemed to be dead — the concept of "God" — is waking up, returning to consciousness. Because we are living in transformational years, our lives cannot be eventless. Some of us will be very frustrated, some of us will survive beautifully; some of us — perhaps the very youngest — will experience the turmoil as if it were quite natural and the acceleration of change in our time nothing extraordinary.

The stories in this collection are all realistic, and the mode in which I write is, if it must be given a name, that of psychological realism. Some tend toward the symbolic, but they are also realistic. "Year of Wonders," which concludes the volume, is set largely upon one of those centers of the universe a mystic knows to be a "mandala," though most people see it as the shopping plaza out by the expressway. Is one vision correct, and the other incorrect? Does the mystic know something the realist can't quite express? But the visions are not antithetical; they are complementary. Both are required. We come by both naturally, and should not reject one in favor of the other.

"Don't You Know Who I Am?" The Grotesque in Oates's "Where Are You Going, Where Have You Been?"

Joyce M. Wegs

According to Joyce M. Wegs, the questions in Oates's title are the very questions Connie's sources of authority, her parents, should, but never do, ask her. Subject to no traditional sense of moral discipline or purpose, Connie has made a religion of her adolescent preoccupations. Arnold Friend, Wegs concludes, is "the incarnation of Connie's unconscious desires and dreams, but in an uncontrollable nightmare form"; hence, "Connie discovers that her dream love-god also wears the face of lust, evil, and death." Friend, however, is not merely Connie's unwelcome fantasy fulfillment; Wegs argues that his name is a variation on Arch Fiend — that he "has all the traditional sinister traits of that arch-deceiver and source of grotesque terror, the devil." In short, Wegs will give you a number of specific ideas to try out on Oates's story.

Joyce Carol Oates's ability to absorb and then to transmit in her fiction the terror which is often a part of living in America today has been frequently noted and admired. For instance, Walter Sullivan praises her skill by noting that "horror resides in the transformation of what we know best, the intimate and comfortable details of our lives made suddenly threatening."[1] Although he does not identify it as such, Sullivan's comment aptly describes a classic instance of a grotesque intrusion: a familiar world suddenly appears alien. Oates frequently evokes the grotesque in her fiction, drawing upon both its traditional or demonic and its contemporary or psychological manifestations.[2] In the prize-winning short story, "Where Are You Going, Where Have You Been?", Oates utilizes the grotesque in many of its forms to achieve a highly skillful integration of the multiple levels of the story and, in so doing, to suggest a transcendent reality which reaches beyond surface realism to evoke the simultaneous mystery and reality of the contradictions of the human heart. Full of puzzling and perverse longings, the heart persists in mixing lust and love, life and death, good and evil. Oates's teenage protagonist, Connie, discovers that her dream love-god also wears the face of lust, evil and death.

Centering the narrative on the world of popular teenage music and culture, Oates depicts the tawdry world of drive-in restaurants and shopping plazas blaring with music with a careful eye for authentic surface detail. However, her use of popular music as a thematic referent is typical also of her frequent illumination of the illusions and grotesquely false values which may arise from excessive devotion to such aspects of popular culture as rock music, movies, and romance magazines.

Joyce M. Wegs, "'Don't You Know Who I Am?' The Grotesque in Oates's 'Where Are You Going, Where Have You Been?,'" *Journal of Narrative Technique* 5 (1975).

In all of her fiction as in this story, she frequently employs a debased religious imagery to suggest the gods which modern society has substituted for conventional religion. Oates delineates the moral poverty of Connie, her fifteen-year-old protagonist, by imaging a typical evening Connie spends at a drive-in restaurant as a grotesquely parodied religious pilgrimage. Left by her friend's father to stroll at the shopping center or go to a movie, Connie and her girlfriend immediately cross the highway to the restaurant frequented by older teenagers. A grotesque parody of a church, the building is bottle-shaped and has a grinning boy holding a hamburger aloft on top of it. Unconscious of any ludicrousness, Connie and her friend enter it as if going into a "sacred building"[3] which will give them "what haven and blessing they yearned for." It is the music which is "always in the background, like music at a church service" that has invested this "bright-lit, fly-infested" place with such significance. Indeed, throughout the story the music is given an almost mystical character, for it evokes in Connie a mysterious pleasure, a "glow of slow-pulsed joy that seemed to rise mysteriously out of the music itself."

Although the story undoubtedly has a moral dimension,[4] Oates does not take a judgmental attitude toward Connie. In fact, much of the terror of the story comes from the recognition that there must be thousands of Connies. By carefully including telltale phrases, Oates demonstrates in an understated fashion why Connies exist. Connie's parents, who seem quite typical, have disqualified themselves as moral guides for her. At first reading, the reader may believe Connie's mother to be concerned about her daughter's habits, views, and friends; but basically their arguments are little more than a "pretense of exasperation, a sense that they . . . [are] tugging and struggling over something of little value to either of them." Connie herself is uncertain of her mother's motives for constantly picking at her; she alternates between a view that her mother's harping proceeds from jealousy of Connie's good looks now that her own have faded and a feeling that her mother really prefers her over her plain older sister June because she is prettier. In other words, to Connie and her mother, real value lies in beauty. Connie's father plays a small role in her life, but by paralleling repeated phrases, Oates suggests that this is precisely the problem. Because he does not "bother talking much" to his family, he can hardly ask the crucial parental questions, "Where are you going?" or "Where have you been?" The moral indifference of the entire adult society is underscored by Oates's parallel description of the father of Connie's friend, who also "never . . . [bothers] to ask" what they did when he picks up the pair at the end of one of their evenings out. Similarly, on Sunday morning, "none of them bothered with church," not even that supposed paragon, June.

Since her elders do not bother about her, Connie is left defenseless against the temptations represented by Arnold Friend. A repeated key phrase emphasizes her helplessness. As she walks through the parking lot of the restaurant with Eddie, she can not "help but" look about happily, full of joy in a life characterized by casual pickups and constant music. When she sees Arnold in a nearby car, she looks away, but her instinctive flirtatiousness triumphs and she can not "help but" look back. Later, like Lot's wife leaving Sodom and Gomorrah, she cannot "help but look back" at the plaza and drive-in as her friend's father drives them home. In Connie's case, the consequences of the actions she can not seem to help are less biblically swift to occur and can not be simply labeled divine retribution.

E
CA
Go

Like Joyce V
chaste yet
Connie play
version in u
her heartbea
young perso
Connie's fat
arrival of A1
that her hea
inside this b
even literary
discuss "the
Bobby King,

Fifteen-yea
tion is an appr
Have You Bee
allegory. Many
Samuel J. Pic
fault.[1] Most, h
O'Connor, bu
the intent of
framework of
contemporary
with externall

The first pa
"She knew she
fresh desirable
life. When she
an undesirable

From the c
powerlessness
attractive, so t
at work, is wea
as moral allego
study, howeve

Marie M. O. Urba
You Been?," *Studi*

proje
to ge
blunt

C
her u
make
same
threa
noisy
was l
with
poun
her b
self is
back
hair i

O
consi
the q
both
one.
of mi
conve
As do
it." H
home
query
Then
she b
Arno
simpl
how
she w
identi
of th
conce
lost a
ignor
is tota

De
Oates
helple
the c
level,
Dylan
does i

Since music is Connie's religion, its values are hers also. Oates does not include the lyrics to any popular songs here, for any observer of contemporary America could surely discern the obvious link between Connie's high esteem for romantic love and youthful beauty and the lyrics of scores of hit tunes. The superficiality of Connie's values becomes terrifyingly apparent when Arnold Friend, the external embodiment of the teenage ideal celebrated in popular songs, appears at Connie's home in the country one Sunday afternoon when she is home alone, listening to music and drying her hair. It is no accident that Arnold's clothes, car, speech, and taste in music reflect current teenage chic almost exactly, for they constitute part of a careful disguise intended to reflect Arnold's self-image as an accomplished youthful lover.

Suspense mounts in the story as the reader realizes along with Connie that Arnold is not a teenager and is really thirty or more. Each part of his disguise is gradually revealed to be grotesquely distorted in some way. His shaggy black hair, "crazy as a wig," is evidently really a wig. That mask-like appearance of his face has been created by applying a thick coat of makeup; however, he has carelessly omitted his throat. Even his eyelashes appear to be made-up, but with some tarlike material. In his clothing, his disguise appears more successful, for Connie approves of the way he dresses, as "all of them dressed," in tight jeans, boots, and pullover. When he walks, however, Connie realizes that the runty Arnold, conscious that the ideal teenage dream lover is tall, has stuffed his boots; the result is, however, that he can hardly walk and staggers ludicrously. Attempting to bow, he almost falls. Similarly, the gold jalopy covered with teenage slang phrases seems authentic until Connie notices that one of them is no longer in vogue. Even his speech is not his own, for it recalls lines borrowed from disc jockeys, teenage slang, and lines from popular songs. Arnold's strange companion, Ellie Oscar, is just as grotesque as Arnold. Almost totally absorbed in listening to music and interrupting this activity only to offer threatening assistance to Arnold, Ellie is no youth either; he has the "face of a forty-year-old baby." Although Arnold has worked out his disguise with great care, he soon loses all subtlety in letting Connie know of his evil intentions; he is not simply crazy but a criminal with plans to rape and probably to murder Connie.

However, Arnold is far more than a grotesque portrait of a psychopathic killer masquerading as a teenager; he also has all the traditional sinister traits of that arch-deceiver and source of grotesque terror, the devil. As is usual with Satan, he is in disguise; the distortions in his appearance and behavior suggest not only that his identity is faked but also hint at his real self. Equating Arnold and Satan is not simply a gratuitous connection designed to exploit traditional demonic terror, for the early pages of the story explicitly prepare for this linking by portraying popular music and its values as Connie's perverted version of religion. When Arnold comes up the drive, her first glance makes Connie believe that a teenage boy with his jalopy, the central figure of her religion, has arrived; therefore, she murmurs "Christ, Christ" as she wonders about how her newly-washed hair looks. When the car—a parodied golden chariot?—stops, a horn sounds "as if this were a signal Connie knew." On one level, the horn honks to announce the "second coming" of Arnold, a demonic Day of Judgment. Although Connie never specifically recognizes Arnold as Satan, her first comment to him both hints at his infernal origins and faithfully reproduces teenage idiom: "Who the *hell* do you think you are?" (emphasis

Dylan ba
the ritual
between
Oates doe
complete
and her s

Notes

[1] Walter Su
The Ho

[2] Joyce Ma
Ken Ke

[3] Joyce Car
(1970;

[4] See Walt
Itself,"

[5] Andrew I
26, qu
newspa

[6] Linda Ku

allegory. It seems evident that members of Connie's family embody much of the same resigned acceptance of "excluded alternatives" as do the characters in *A Garden*. Burwell argues that each of the major characters in *A Garden* realizes that he is "part of a drama whose outcome has largely been determined but remains unknown."[3] Thus, in refusing to attend a family picnic, Connie is rejecting not only her family's company, but the settled order of their existence — in which recognition of "excluded alternatives" is tantamount to acceptance of their lives.

The popular music which permeates "Where Are You Going . . ." is at the same time the narrative's *zeitgeist* and *leitmotiv*, serving as the former in order to maintain plausible realism, and the latter to establish allegorical significance. The recurring music then, while ostensibly innocuous realistic detail, is in fact, the vehicle of Connie's seduction and because of its intangibility, not immediately recognizable as such. Attesting to the significance of the *zeitgeist* in this narrative, "Where Are You Going . . ." is dedicated to Bob Dylan, who contributed to making music almost religious in dimension among the youth. It is music — instead of an apple — which lures Connie, quickens her heartbeat; and popular lyrics which constitute Friend's conversation and cadence — his promises, threats, and the careless confidence with which he seduces her.

Connie fuses unexplored sexuality with the mystery of the music when, at home, she thinks about her encounters: "But all the boys fell back and dissolved into a single face that was not even a face but an idea, a feeling mixed up with the urgent insistent pounding of the music."

Before Friend arrives, Connie is bored and perhaps regrets not having gone to the cook-out with her family, so she goes in the house and turns on the radio "to drown out the quiet." Friend understands that music is sexual currency by pointing out his companion's radio when he invites her for a ride. And he succeeds in breaking her conversational ice by discussing the merits of a commonly admired singer.

Oates employs musical metaphor in her description of Friend. "He spoke in a simple lilting voice, exactly as if he were reciting the words to a song." Intrinsic to Friend's function is the fact that he himself is a record. While waiting for Connie to accept his ride offer, "he began to mark time with the music from Ellie's radio." Even their union is presaged by the sexually pointed observation of Connie listening "to the music from her radio and the boy's blend together."

The images which overtly suggest religious allegory while more subtly supporting the existential theme, are interspersed throughout the work. When Connie and her girl friend first enter the local "hang-out" where the girls and boys meet, they feel "as if they were entering a sacred building" where background music seems like that of a "church service." The day of the cook-out, which is significant both because it is the day of her defiance of her parents and the day of her capitulation to Friend, is a Sunday. "None of them bothered with church" identifies her spiritual vacuity. When Connie first hears Friend's car enter the driveway, she whispers "Christ," as later Friend evokes the name of Christ with a curse when she threatens to call the police.

Friend is a strange syncretism of O'Connor's Bible-pedaling Manley Pointer in manner, and Satan in appearance. When Connie first observes Friend, she notices his "shaggy black hair," his "jalopy painted gold,"[4] and his broad grin. As the narrative progresses, his features appear more ominous, his hair like a wig, his slitted eyes "like chips of broken glass" with "thick black tarlike" lashes when not covered by mirrored, but masking sunglasses; and he looks older. Like Milton's Satan "crested aloft and Carbuncle his Eyes with burnished Neck of verdant Gold, erect,"[5] Friend posited atop his golden jalopy, has a muscular neck which suggests the reptilian, as does the fact that he "slid" rather than stepped out of the car. His feet resemble the devil's cloven hooves: "One of his boots was at a strange angle, as if his foot wasn't in it."

Friend's mesmeric influence on Connie further supports my contention that he represents a superhuman force. "Don't you know who I am?" he asks in an eery fashion, as if she had encountered him before, as one does evil. She is unable to make a telephone call for help because he is watching her; she bumps against a piece of furniture in a familiar room; and when he commands her to do what would otherwise seem an irrational act, to place her hand on her heart to understand its flaccidity, she readily obeys. His directives culminate when he convinces her, "What else is there for a girl like you but to be sweet and pretty and give in."

The recurring use of a twentieth-century symbol of irony—the false smile—further veils the existential meaning in realistic narrative. Over the student drive-in hangs a "revolving figure of a grinning boy holding a hamburger aloft." And Friend intersperses smiles with threats. "'Connie, don't fool around with me. I mean—I mean, don't fool *around*,' he said shaking his head. He laughed incredulously." Friend demands a smile from his conquest as well: "Now come out through the kitchen with me, honey, and let's see a smile."

In the end, Oates makes it clear that Connie, in capitulating to Friend, is not simply surrendering her virginal innocence, but bowing to absolute forces which her youthful coquetry cannot direct—absolute forces over which she has no control. At this point she thinks for the first time in her life that her heart "was nothing that was hers . . . but just a pounding, living thing inside this body that wasn't really hers either."

In the seduction which Friend engineers, Connie is merely the personification of the female he wishes to dominate, to be taller than, to despoil. The phrases he delivers from his musical repertoire are not even tailored to Connie: "'My sweet little blue-eyed girl' he said in a half-sung sigh that had nothing to do with her brown eyes."

In the presentation of this complex narrative, the major characters represent two distinct personifications in the dual levels of the allegory. It is apparent that Friend represents the devil who tempts the chaste yet morally vacuous girl-victim. Yet upon closer analysis, it appears that Connie takes the active part as *Everyman* experiencing the inevitable realization of her insignificance and powerlessness while Friend, who personifies the Erinyes, is merely the catalyst.

Although Oates uses the trappings of a realist to craft plausible characters—a dreamy teenaged girl, a hypnotic Manson-like man—and renders a facsimile of awkward adolescent behavior and speech, with contemporary youth's devotion to popular music as a convincing *zeitgeist*, this must not obscure her design. She presents an allegory which applies existential initiation rites to the Biblical seduction myth to represent *Everyman's* transition from the illusion of free will to the realization of externally determined fate.

Notes

[1] "The Short Stories of Joyce Carol Oates," *Georgia Review*, 28 (1974) 218–226.

[2] In *The Wheel of Love and Other Stories* (New York: Vanguard, 1972).

[3] Rose Marie Burwell, "Joyce Carol Oates and an Old Master," *Critique: Studies in Modern Fiction*, 15 (1973), 48–57.

[4] This also seems to be a parody of the Cinderella tale. Painted on the golden car is a "drawing of a round, grinning face that reminded Connie of a pumpkin" (p. 35).

[5] John Milton, *Paradise Lost*, IX, 500–501.

THE MYTH OF THE ISOLATED ARTIST
Joanne V. Creighton

The following essay consists of excerpts from the opening chapter of a book-length study on Oates. In it Joanne V. Creighton discusses Oates's biographical background and its influence on her writing, her own perception of her role and purpose as a writer, and kinships that she has sensed with particular past writers — which she calls "spiritual marriage." Creighton will arm you with several additional perspectives from which to consider "Where Are You Going, Where Have You Been?"

Joyce Carol Oates claims that much of her fiction is personal, "but distorted a little, made into fiction. What excites me about writing is the uses I can make of myself, of various small adventures, errors, miscalculations, stunning discoveries, near-disasters, and occasional reversals of everything, but so worked into a fictional structure that no one could guess how autobiographical it all is."[1] Indeed, no one could. She lives what appears to be a quiet, serene life, cut off from the violence, brutality, and emotional duress which typifies her fiction. Oates also says that she likes to combine herself with another person to form a "third person, a 'fictional' person." She playfully warns her interviewer "that with the least provocation (a few hints of your personal life, let's say, your appearance, your house and setting), I could 'go into' your personality and try to imagine it, try to find a way of dramatizing it. I am fascinated by people I meet, or don't meet, people I only correspond with, or read about; and I hope my interest in them isn't vampiristic, because I don't want to take life from them, but only to honor the life in them, to give some permanent form to their personalities."[2] While Oates has transformed into fiction many of the people she has known, most of the places she has lived, and many of the news events — major and minor — of our time, her disarming modesty and graciousness keep private all but the baldest facts about her personal life.

She was born June 16, 1938, the eldest of three children of Caroline and Frederick Oates, and lived until she was seventeen in Erie County, outside of Lockport in western New York State, a locale that undoubtedly inspired the creation of Oates's own fictional Eden County, the setting of a number of her volumes. Similarly, her Catholic, working-class, rural origins give a sense of authenticity to the characterization in her early fiction. Although Oates has mentioned cryptically that "terrible things happened" during her childhood,[3] she does not go into detail. Furthermore, while emotionally charged familial relationships are at the heart of her fiction, she gives no clues about how much of her considerable insight into parent-child and sibling relationships is based on personal experience. With characteristic privacy, she makes only generous comments about her parents. For example, in one interview she mentions their innate artistic talent: her father, a tool-and-die designer, who had to quit school at about the seventh grade to go to work, has "always been able to play the violin and the piano — *instinctively*"; her mother is creative with flowers and the house: "if I have any artistic talent, I think I inherited

Joanne V. Creighton, "The Myth of the Isolated Artist," *Joyce Carol Oates* (Boston: G. K. Hall, 1979).

it from them." She does point out the importance of her life in the country—on her maternal grandparents' farm—in shaping her character: "The real clue to me is that I'm like certain people who are not really understood—Jung and Heidegger are good examples—people of peasant stock, from the country, who then come into a world of literature and philosophy. Part of us is very intellectual, wanting to read all the books in the library—or even wanting to *write* all the books in the library. Then there's the other side of us, which is sheer silence, inarticulate—the silence of nature, of the sky, of pure being."[4]

Oates claims that as a child she was not exposed to much "art," but one book she did have which profoundly affected her was *Alice in Wonderland and Through the Looking-Glass*, an influence which one can trace imagistically in her fiction. More important, though, are the psychological implications of the text which she says have "worked their way into the very fiber of my being." She explains them as follows:

> A child triumphs.—The Child in us, which may be called our instincts or intuitive powers, is always superior to the snarls of the rational mind, and if we have faith in it and attempt to establish a rapport with it, we will always triumph.
>
> Salvation is assured. All the animals win: The pawn becomes a queen.—Whether through our own strenuous activity or through what used to be called "grace," we will transcend the present; our personalities are layers upon layers, moving toward a kind of completion.
>
> "You're nothing but a pack of cards."—A profound recognition, the declaration of the Child when confronted with the enormous ego-centered complexities of the so-called adult world.
>
> "It's a huge game of chess that's being played—all over the world—if this is the world at all, you know. Oh, what fun it is! How I *wish* I was one of them! . . ." Alice exclaims.—She is, once again, profoundly right. A novelist recognizes this truth every day: Though one can be detached from the activities of life, seeing them as no more than games, it is necessary to get down there in the game as well, to play it with as much enthusiasm as possible. Everyone is playing and no one is left out. The game is *being played* and we are participants, not really controlling the game, but fulfilling it in some existential, mysterious way. In any case, a victory of some kind is assured.[5]

The valuing of the instinctual and intuitive, the belief in the possibility of transcendence of the ego, and the need to be involved in the "game"—the existential reality of life—are truths which lie at the heart of her fiction. Equally important, however, are the nightmarish aspects of Carroll's world which are echoed in Oates's, especially in her novel *Wonderland*.

She attended a one-room schoolhouse where the education, she observes, was not particularly good. After junior high in Lockport, she took a bus to high school outside of Buffalo, where she was fortunate, she says, to receive a sound education. She isolates Henry David Thoreau's *Walden* and Fyodor Dostoevsky's *The Brothers Karamazov* as having "a powerful effect" on her at this time. It was at Syracuse University, which she entered at age seventeen, however, where the excitement of the world of books took tenacious hold of Joyce Carol Oates. Here she read William Faulkner, a significant influence on her writing, who she claimed "bowled" her over. "Then Kafka. . . . Later, Freud, Nietzsche, Mann—they're almost real personalities in my life. And Dostoevsky and Melville."[6] She became then and remains today a voracious reader of literature, philosophy, and psychology. "I like to write, but I really love to read: that must be the greatest pleasure of civilization."[7] A recipient of a New York State Regents' Scholarship and a Syracuse scholarship, she was an outstanding student, valedictorian of her 1960 class with a B.A. in English and a minor in philosophy. In fact, her creative-writing professor, Donald A. Dike, says quite unequivocally that "she was the most brilliant student we've ever had here." During her college years she won the first of her many awards, first prize in *Mademoiselle* magazine's college fiction contest for her story "In the Old World." Professor Dike, commenting amusingly upon her creative productivity, claims that while she wrote mostly stories, "about once a term she'd drop a 400-page novel on my desk."[8]

In 1960 Oates attended the University of Wisconsin in Madison, completing an M.A. in English in 1961. At a faculty tea she met fellow graduate student Raymond Smith, whom she married a short time later: "It was very romantic," Oates observes.[9] She moved with her husband to his first teaching job in Beaumont, Texas, and she commuted briefly to Rice University in Houston where she began a Ph.D. in English. But the story she tells about this experience is that while browsing in the library, quite by accident, she came across one of her stories in Martha Foley's *Best American Short Stories* and decided then to become a professional writer. In 1962 the Smiths moved to Detroit where Oates was employed as an English instructor at the University of Detroit, while her husband taught English at Wayne State University. She skillfully evokes the city of Detroit as a setting for many of her stories and two novels, *them* and *Do With Me What You Will*. A small Catholic university, similar to the University of Detroit, is the setting for some of her stories, most notably "The Dead."

In 1966 Raymond Smith took a position in the English Department at the University of Windsor in Ontario; the following year he was joined by his wife. Frequent courses taught by Mrs. Smith, as she is called there, include literature and psychology, modern world literature, and creative writing. She has commented often upon how much she enjoys the give-and-take of teaching and the academic environment itself. Her academic satires, many collected in *The Hungry Ghosts*, also attest to her awareness of the fears, phobias, and pretensions of that world. Moreover, her sensitivity to the tensions, rewards, and disappointments of the special relationship of teacher-student is evident in many of her works. The Smiths are landed immigrants in Canada who retain their American citizenship and do not consider themselves to be Canadian. So far, at least, Oates's work has been set in American experience; only her academic satires and a recent collection, *Crossing the Border*, take place in Canada, and they focus largely on Americans who have crossed the border.

Seemingly contented with the life she leads, Joyce Carol Oates does admit to one period of personal crisis, in 1971, when she felt bogged down with social commitments and close to collapse. But fortunately her husband took a sabbatical leave that year and while in London, England, for the year, she had a chance to rest and to work out her problem. She mentions that the story "Plot" was written out of that personal distress, and she sees it as a kind of triumphant demonstration of the ability of the artist to use art therapeutically. "I found a fabric of some kind to absorb the various emotions that were drawing me under."[10] "So I feel that literature is wonderfully optimistic, instructive, because it so often demonstrates how human beings get through things, maneuver themselves through chaos, and then *write about it*."[11] That she was thirty-three at this time of crisis in her life she carefully notes, and adds that she believes that many people have such a turning point in their lives at approximately that age. Now she claims that she has restructured her life so that she no longer does anything she does not want to do. A large part of her contentment comes from a professed detachment from the "ego personality," a remark which is illuminated by a consideration of her public self, the Joyce Carol Oates who sees herself as a "voice" of the "communal consciousness" of our culture.[12]. . .

Oates's monistic philosophy shapes her conception of herself as an artist. Since she feels that the intellect is as "natural" to man as the instincts are, she does not scorn civilization, intelligence, "Faustian" control. Indeed, she has said repeatedly that she identifies as an artist with Mann's Adrian Leverkühn. She does not feel that the artist can be "too intellectual":

> In our time, in the Seventies, we are chided for being too intellectual, too clinical, if we do not surrender to the tyranny of the Present. Our art, if it is careful, if it makes a rational and even calculated point, is considered a betrayal of the spontaneous joy of life—living—which is always non-rational or anti-rational, as if only the more primitive levels of our brains are truly human. All of this is a mistake. More than that, it is a waste: it is a waste that intelligent people should earnestly deny their intelligence, extolling the impulsive and the sensuous and the "original" . . . and though I believe that the basis of ʳhe writing of fiction is the unconscious, the oceanic, ungovernable, unfathomable reservoir of human energy, it is still my deepest certainty that art, if not life, requires intelligence and discretion and transcendence.[13]

But Oates does feel that the myth of the isolated artist has been perpetuated too long, damaging both the creative writers who subscribe to it and the criticism predicated upon it. Oates insists that the artist does not create in isolation, out of his ego, but rather that his art grows out of and is a part of his culture. Like the scientist who acknowledges his debt to others, who knows that his findings are dependent upon the investigations which have come before his, the artist, too, is an individual who attempts "to give voice to many voices," who attempts "to synthesize and explore and analyze." His work should be looked upon as a "communal effort": "If I were to suggest, in utter seriousness, that my fiction is the creation of thousands upon thousands of processes of consciousness, synthesized somehow in me, I would be greeted with astonishment or disbelief, or dismissed as being 'too modest.' In civilization, no one can be 'too modest.'"[14]

What has been thought of by some as feigned modesty or coy disingenuousness is, I think, Oates's genuine respect for both the artist's nurturing by his culture and the inexplicable nature of the creative process. For Oates the artist is both a personal human being and "an impersonal creative process." His talent is a mystery: "why does his era require *him* to give shape to these shapeless dreams?—Why not someone else? A question not to be answered."[15] His inspiration, his consciousness, like that of any man, "is not the private possession of the individual . . . but belongs to his culture."[16] It is not surprising, I think, for a writer of such extraordinary productivity as Oates to be in awe of the creative process. She sees herself, indeed all artists, as a kind of medium who takes in and gives shape to stimuli from her culture. The writer, she feels, is not totally responsible for what he writes about: he must insist upon "the sanctity of the world. . . . It may be his role, his function, is to articulate the very worst, to force into consciousness the most perverse and terrifying possibilities of the epoch, so that they can be dealt with and not simply feared."[17] But because there "is a pernicious symbiotic relationship between writers and critics," critics may "condition their subjects," Oates fears, to write against their own inspiration, to cut themselves off from the nourishing communal "reservoir of energy" which infuses their work.[18] Now, although one may sense a defensive plea for immunity from criticism here, nonetheless, this respect for the sanctity of the artist's world is consistent with Oates's view of the artist as voice and synthesizer of his culture's consciousness.

Oates argues that just as a writer is part and product of his culture, he is recipient of its literary and intellectual traditions. Like T. S. Eliot, she sees the individual talent existing within a "strong tradition": "I just see myself as standing in a very strong tradition and my debt to other writers is very obvious. I couldn't exist without them."[19] Oates eclectically absorbs images and ideas from other writers as well as from experiential reality. Profusely interspersed throughout her books are quotations from and allusions to other writers' works. Even her titles are often literary allusions. A number of her stories are rewritings of well-known short-story masterpieces such as Henry James's "Turn of the Screw," Kafka's "The Metamorphosis," Joyce's "The Dead," and Chekhov's "The Lady with the Pet Dog." She characterizes these stories as "spiritual marriages" between herself and these literary masters, a tribute to her "kinship" and her "love and extreme devotion to these other writers."[20] She even gives credit to an imaginary author, "Ferandes," whose stories she claims to have "translated" from the Portuguese in *The Poisoned Kiss*. This alleged "possession" by an alien, imaginary author whose stories are quite antithetical to her own is Oates's strangest account of her extraordinary receptivity to stimuli from outside her conscious self. She is reluctant to isolate influences, claiming, "I've been influenced in many ways by nearly everyone I've read, and I've read nearly everyone."[21] Intellectually, she is nurtured by diverse currents in modern thought.

Oates then is a writer especially sensitive to how much of the creative process is outside of the conscious control of the artist, how much is drawn from beyond his own ego. As she would bring the writer down from his elitist ivory tower, she is impatient with an art-for-art's sake mentality, an overemphasis on craftsmanship to the exclusion of "felt life." While Oates admires careful craftsmanship, she also values the writer like D. H. Lawrence whose intense need "to convey the emotions of one man to his fellows" makes his work uneven.[22] In advice to novice writers in an article entitled "Building Tension in a Short Story," Oates argues:

> It isn't "words" or "style" that make a scene, but the context behind the words, and the increase of tension as characters come into conflict with one another. "Words" themselves are relatively unimportant, since there are countless ways of saying the same thing.
>
> A final suggestion: be daring, take on anything. Don't labor over little cameo works in which every word is to be perfect. Technique holds a reader from sentence to sentence, but only content will stay in his mind.[23]

Indeed, perhaps the most common charge against her is that she doesn't spend enough time worrying about "words," perfecting her craft. Statements like the above, coupled with her amazing productivity, have created the impression that she does not revise, and although she insists that she does—painstakingly—her style is often not finely honed.

Oates clearly stresses the rhetorical nature of fiction over its value as crafted art: "all the books published under my name in the past 10 years have been formalized, complex propositions about the nature of personality and its relationship to a specific culture (contemporary America). The propositions are meant to be hypothetical and exploratory, inviting responses that are not simple, thalamic praise/abuse, but some demonstration that there is an audience that participates in the creation of art."[24] For her, as well as for D. H. Lawrence, the novel is the "one bright book of life," or, as she calls it, "the most human of all art forms,"[25] which expresses truths as no other medium can. Just as writers should not overly invest their egos in their works, their works should not be viewed as "crimes for which they are on perpetual trial."[26] One senses Oates's impatience with the often unsympathetic reception her works have received and her exasperation that they have not elicited the kind of participatory readership that she would like. Her fictional inquiry focuses obsessively upon the nature of the "self" and its relationship to "the other." Although Oates's published canon does not yet span much time, a continuum can be discerned in it, a continual reformulation and reassessment of the problems of selfhood, which shows her characters groping toward the liberating oneness which underlies their creator's vision.

Notes

[1]"Transformations of Self: An Interview with Joyce Carol Oates," *Ohio Review*, 15, i (1973), 54.

[2]Joe David Bellamy, "The Dark Lady of American Letters," *Atlantic*, 229 (February 1972), 67.

[3]Walter Clemons, "Joyce Carol Oates: Love and Violence," *Newsweek*, December 11, 1972, p. 73.

[4]Ibid., pp. 72–73.

[5]"Other Celebrity Voices: How Art Has Touched Our Lives," *Today's Health*, 52 (May 1974), 31.

[6]R. M. Adams, "Joyce Carol Oates at Home," *New York Times Book Review*, September 28, 1969, p. 48.

[7]Bellamy, p. 66.

[8]Clemons, p. 73.

[9]Ibid., p. 74.

[10]Letter to the author, February 23, 1976.

[11]"Transformations of Self," p. 55.

[12]Interview with the author, May 25, 1976.

[13]"The Short Story," *Southern Humanities Review*, 5 (Summer 1971), 213–14.

[14]"The Myth of the Isolated Artist," *Psychology Today*, 6 (May 1973), 74–75.

[15]"New Heaven and New Earth," *Saturday Review*, November 4, 1972, p. 284.

[16]"The Myth of the Isolated Artist."

[17]*New Heaven, New Earth*, p. 7.

[18]"The Myth of the Isolated Artist."

[19]Clemons, p. 73.

[20]Bellamy, p. 64.

[21]Letter to the author, October 22, 1975.

[22]*New Heaven, New Earth*, pp. 37–81.

[23]*Writer*, June 1966, 44.

[24]"The Myth of the Isolated Artist."

[25]"New Heaven and New Earth," p. 54.

[26]*New Heaven, New Earth*, p. 46.

"Where Are You Going, Where Have You Been?": Seduction, Space, and a Fictional Mode

Christina M. Gillis

*Like Marie Urbanski, Christina Gillis sees Connie and Arnold Friend as charac-
ters in a religious allegory of the temptation of Eve, but Gillis also focuses on the
modes of "interior space" implied in Friend's sexual threats: "Gonna get you, baby"
and "I'll come inside you where it's all secret and you'll give in to me and you'll love
me." Gillis contends that Arnold is trying to invade other interior spaces of Connie's
besides the obvious sexual one: "the domestic space, the state of childhood associated
with home, and, of course, the individual consciousness." Gillis demonstrates her
interpretation with a discussion of Connie's changing perceptions of the familiar
surroundings of her kitchen as Friend stands outside her door. Connie's surroundings
grow less and less familiar to her until she reaches the point where, as Arnold
insists, the place where she came from "ain't there any more." Gillis, incidentally,
makes numerous allusions to such literary works as John Milton's* Paradise Lost,
Fanny Burney's Evelina, *Samuel Richardson's* Clarissa, *Mark Twain's* Huckleberry Finn, *Henry James's* The Portrait of a Lady, *and F. Scott Fitzgerald's* The
Great Gatsby. *You may want to ask your instructor to comment on and to explain
the elements in these works that Gillis feels Oates's story echoes.*

Joyce Carol Oates' "Where Are You Going, Where Have You Been?" is a story
about beginnings and passage points; and it is a story about endings: the end of
childhood, the end of innocence.[1] The account of fifteen-year-old Connie's encounter with a mysterious stranger named Arnold Friend, a man who leads his victim
not to a promising new world, but, rather, to a violent sexual assault, is a tale of
initiation depicted in grotesque relief.

But "Where Are You Going" is also a story where spatial limitations are of crucial
concern, and to this degree it provides a commentary on stories and story-telling.
As Oates transforms elements of fairy tale and dream into a chilling description of
temptation, seduction, and probable rape, we are forced to consider the distinctions
between fairy tale and seduction narrative, to note particularly that in "Where Are
You Going" seduction involves the invasion of personal, interior space: ". . . his
words, replete with guile,/Into her heart too easy entrance won," Milton says of
Satan's meeting with Eve (*Paradise Lost*, IX, 732-780). Women are vulnerable to
seduction, and of course rape, Susan Brownmiller has reminded us, for what at first
may be seen as purely physiological reasons,[2] and there is little doubt of physical
violence when Arnold Friend croons to Connie, "I'll come inside you where it's all
secret"; but the seduction motif functions so successfully in "Where Are You Going"
because the delineation of interior space figured in the female body analogizes

Christina M. Gillis, "'Where Are You Going, Where Have You Been?': Seduction, Space, and a
Fictional Mode," *Studies in Short Fiction* 18 (Winter 1981).

invasion at several levels: the domestic space, the state of childhood associated with the home, and, of course, the individual consciousness.

Following the example of the eighteenth-century seduction tale, Oates takes us *within* in her story, pointing up one direction which fiction has taken for some two hundred years. In the transformation of romance into sentimental narrative, the seduction of the inexperienced young woman depends in part upon the demarcation of interior space and the importance of maintaining it intact. More specifically, too, private space is congruent with the domestic. In painting, the conversation piece shows us the family unit within its drawing room, closed off from an outside world; sentimental drama draws us within to witness the distresses of private persons in familial surroundings; and seduction narratives which stress the strength of the virtuous daughter in warding off the dangerous rake similarly suggest the importance of protecting both the physical body and the nuclear family.[3] In this sense, we may speak of the domestication or privatization of sin in eighteenth-century literature: in a world which historian Lawrence Stone has described as ever more conscious of private space we are not surprised to find fictions turning toward the exploration of private zones and evil represented as that which threatens the privacy of self and the family unit.[4] Readers may now penetrate the locus of private, familial activity, the consciousness of the fictionalized character, and the pages of the text they are reading. The theme of the young lady's "entering the world" (to quote Fanny Burney's *Evelina* and a score of so-called "female" fictions) — or perhaps, like Clarissa Harlowe, her seduction into the "world" — provides a context within which we may consider how Oates' Connie is "invaded" and where she may indeed be going.

At the outset we may identify "Where Are You Going" as an American "coming of age" tale, the main character Connie joining that cast of characters which includes Huckleberry Finn, Isabel Archer, and Jay Gatsby. But while the poles of Oates' story are innocence and experience, the focus of attention is the process of seduction, or the threshold between the two states. The lines are clear, the threshold visually realized. Connie belongs to a tradition of domesticated Eves; for them, Satan's entrance into the garden is replaced by the invasion of a rake like Lovelace (in Richardson's *Clarissa*) into one's private chamber — or ultimately, in the twentieth century, by the approach of the cowboy-booted Arnold Friend to the kitchen door of an asbestos-covered ranch house. The physical world shrinks in this fiction; unlike Eden, the perimeter of a private room, or body, lends itself to specific accounting. Within a described locus, space itself is at issue, the fiction setting up a tension whereby the private is open to both attack and transformation.

Spatial limits are increasingly important in "Where Are You Going." If the threshold of the kitchen door ultimately receives the burden of tension in the tale, Oates carefully prepares us for the climactic scene by setting up, at the outset, contrasting *loci*. The very title of the story calls attention to duality: a future (where you are going) and a past (where you have been). The tale catches its main character at a passage point where, it is implied, the future may depend precipitously on the past. More specifically, the two major locations of the tale are the home and family unit it signifies, and the outside world represented first in the drive-in hamburger joint, later in Arnold Friend himself. Connie herself lives in two worlds, even dressing appropriately for each: she "wore a pull over jersey blouse that looked one way when she was at home and another way when she was away from home.

Everything about her had two sides to it, one for home and one for anywhere that was not home." Home is the daylight world, a known, established order where so-called parental wisdom would seem to negate the dreams and desires of youth. Connie is, then, constantly at odds with her family, ever looking forward to her excursions to the drive-in, the night-time world, the "bright-lit, fly-infested restaurant" which she and her friend approach, "their faces pleased and expectant as if they were entering a sacred building that loomed up out of the night to give them what haven and blessing they yearned for." A mood of expectation pervades Connie's night-time world. Like the light on Daisy Buchanan's pier that promised romance to Jay Gatsby, the bright-lit hamburger joint also holds out new worlds within its "sacred" precincts: cars, music, boys, experience.

Even when the initial meeting with a boy named Eddie — the experience "down the alley a mile or so away" — is over, when the clock has struck eleven and the Cinderella land fades back into the night, a "big empty parking lot [with] signs that were faded and ghostly," even then, the mood of expectation is only temporarily broken. There will be other nights in this midsummer dream-time. Eddie and his like, all the boys, Oates tells us, "fell back and dissolved into a single face that was not even a face but an idea, a feeling, mixed up with the urgent insistent pounding of the music and humid air of July." No wonder that Connie resists being "dragged back to the daylight" by her mother's too-insistent voice. The mother who had once been pretty ("but now her looks were gone and that was why she was always after Connie") sees in Connie a dim outline of her own former self; but the dream perception seems long faded, and Connie's sister June, the only other female family member, is a plain, stalwart sort who has clearly never had much to do with dreams.

But mother and sister are not the villains here, of course, Connie no Cinderella for whom a night-time dream becomes daylight reality. Rather, dream becomes nightmare when Connie first meets at the drive-in Arnold Friend, no Prince Charming, but a man with metallic, cold eyes, driving a bright gold jalopy. And Arnold Friend only pretends to be young. Later, with the discovery of Arnold's true age, Connie will feel her heart pound faster; the bizarre realization that Friend's companion has the face of a "forty year old baby" will cause the teenager to experience a "wave of dizziness." And we are shocked too: there is no fairy tale world here, no romance after all. Friend's first muttered threat, "Gonna get you, baby," is to be played out not in a dream, but in the daylight hours and within a domestic space.

Even before Arnold Friend's entrance into the driveway of Connie's home, reality and dream are beginning to clash dangerously. Connie sits in the sun "dreaming and dazed with the warmth about her as if this were a kind of love, the caresses of love"; but when she opens her eyes she sees only a "back yard that ran off into weeds" and a house that looked small. Arnold's appearance in Connie's driveway on the Sunday morning when her family have gone off to a barbecue only underlines the confused merging of two worlds Connie has always kept apart. She approaches the kitchen door slowly, hangs out the screen door, "her bare toes curling down off the step." Connie is not yet ready to make the step outside.

With Arnold's arrival the significance of separate locations in "Where Are You Going" acquires new intensity, and the delineation of space becomes a matter of crucial concern. Connie's refusal to move down off the step bespeaks her clinging to a notion that walls and exact locations offer the protection of the familial order.

Now, with Friend's initial invitation to join him and his friend in the car, and with his assertion that he has placed his "sign" upon her, Connie moves further back into the kitchen: she "let the screen door close and stood perfectly still inside it." From the familiar kitchen space, she attempts to make sense of her experience. But the mirror sunglasses make it impossible for the girl to see what Friend is looking at; the enigmatic smile tells nothing; and even as she attempts to amass assorted physical data on her visitor, she finds that "all these things did not come together."

Then the familiar and the private begin to give way to the unexpected visitor. Having realized the true age of the two intruders and being told that they will not leave until she agrees to go along with them, Connie has the sense that Friend "had driven up the driveway all right but had come from nowhere before and belonged nowhere . . . everything that was so familiar to her was only half real." The drawing of the magical sign, a sign of ownership over her, suggests control over her own private consciousness. Connie wonders how Friend knows her name; but later, much more troubling, is his knowledge that her father is not coming back soon, that the family is at the picnic. Connie finds herself sharing a perhaps imaginary, perhaps real, view of the barbecue. Friend refers to a "fat woman" at the barbecue:

> "What fat woman?" Connie cried.
> "How do I know what fat woman. I don't know every goddamn fat woman in the world!" Arnold Friend laughed.
> "Oh, that's Mrs. Hornsby. . . . Who invited her?" Connie said. She felt a little lightheaded. Her breath was coming quickly.

And penetration of consciousness is only the preamble to penetration in a sexual sense: "And I'll come inside you where it's all secret and you'll give in to me and you'll love me—" says Friend. The disorder implied in Friend's knowing too much, more than can be rationally explained, is now to be played out in trespassing upon the body itself. A limit has been passed. Connie does not want to hear these words; she "backed away from the door. She put her hand up against her ears as if she'd heard something terrible."

Connie retreats further within the kitchen, but the space of the room also loses familiarity as interior worlds break down. Just as earlier in the morning the adolescent has begun to see her own home as small, now the kitchen looked "like a place she had never seen before, some room she had run inside but that wasn't good enough, wasn't going to help her." Doors too become meaningless. "But why lock [the door]?" Friend taunts; "it's just a screen door, It's just nothing." Friend is still articulating spatial limits—"[I] promise not to come in unless you touch the phone"—but such limits no longer have meaning. The statement, "I want you," the words of the teen-ager's love song, now connote a world where the limits around self are not viable. The breaking of a limitation and the opening of a door (here is the language which Richardson used in reference to the rape of Clarissa Harlowe, and here are Richardson's issues too) destroy both individual innocence and the order of the innocent's world. "It's all over for you here," Friend tells Connie. Crying out for the mother that will not come, Connie feels not the protective parental embrace, but rather a feeling in her lungs as if Friend "was stabbing her . . . with no tenderness." And then the horrible statement muttered in a stage voice, the statement which spells the end of a world: "The place where you came from ain't there any more, and where you had in mind to go is cancelled out. This place you are now — inside your daddy's house — is nothing but a cardboard box I can knock down any time."

Obliteration through violent assault is multi-dimensional in "Where Are You Going." The domestic space, a house as the nurturing place of childhood, yields to attack from outside no less than the body, consciousness, even "heart" of the girl is forced to give way. Observing that the house looks solid, Friend tells Connie, "Now, put your hand on your heart, honey. . . . That feels solid too but we know better." And when Connie feels her own pounding heart, "she thought for the first time in her life that it was nothing that was hers, that belonged to her." If "Where Are You Going" is the story of the end of childhood, the end of romance, the invasion and probable destruction of private and self-contained space provide one important definition of the end of innocence. Friend's taking over the "heart" of the young girl so that "it was nothing that was hers" spells a conquest of both space and will: his intimation that he will wait for and then kill the family if Connie does not go with him is the more terrible because of Connie's own ambivalent feelings about her family, the breaking in the child's trust in her parents. Finally, the satanic visitor's incantation, "We'll go out to a nice field, out in the country where it smells so nice and it's sunny," represents not only a chilling perversion of pastoral — for the words of Satan can lead not toward, but only away from, Eden — but a ritualized statement that all of the walls defining an individual self have been destroyed. Connie's pushing open the screen door to go off with Arnold Friend, the ultimate yielding, signifies that indeed the place she came from "ain't there any more."

Notes

[1] Joyce Carol Oates, "Where Are You Going, Where Have You Been?" *The Wheel of Love* (New York: Vanguard, 1970).

[2] Susan Brownmiller, *Against Our Will* (New York: Simon and Schuster, 1975), p. 14.

[3] Mario Praz, *Conversation Pieces: A Survey of the Informal Group Portrait in Europe and America* (University Park, Pa.: Pennsylvania State University Press, 1971), 68–70. Praz discusses Hogarth in particular, noting the latter's interest in viewing his family groups as characters in a drama. For an analysis of the image of the chaste maiden in eighteenth-century fiction, see Marlene LeGates, "The Cult of Womanhood in Eighteenth-Century Thought," *Eighteenth Century Studies* 10 (Fall 1976), 21–39. The motif of seduction in the literature of sentiment is treated particularly in R. F. Brissenden, *Virtue in Distress* (New York: Barnes and Noble, 1974).

[4] Lawrence Stone has explored privacy as an aspect of the "closed domesticated nuclear family" in *The Family, Sex, and Marriage in England 1500–1800* (New York: Harper and Row, 1977), p. 253. The subject has been provocatively treated in Richard Sennett, *The Fall of Public Man* (New York: Knopf, 1977), but Sennett does not fully appreciate the tension between private and public in sentimental literature.

A Source for "Where Are You Going, Where Have You Been?"

Tom Quirk

The essays of Joyce Wegs, Marie Urbanski, and Christina Gillis all treat "Where Are You Going, Where Have You Been?" as a religious or moral allegory of one sort or another. Tom Quirk, by contrast, emphasizes the story's real-life underpinnings by demonstrating the many similarities between the characteristics of Arnold Friend and story's plot and the characteristics of Charles Howard Schmid and his widely publicized murders of three adolescent girls in Tucson, Arizona, in 1965 (the year before the story was published). For Quirk, the close resemblance between Oates's highly imaginative treatment of her characters and the historical facts of the Schmid case makes the story's indictment of the souring American Dream even more damning.

One of Joyce Carol Oates's most familiar and most disturbing short stories—
"Where Are You Going, Where Have You Been?"—is so richly symbolic and her characters are so improbably dressed and motivated that one is tempted to see it exclusively as a play of primal forces rather than as a fiction derived from and responsive to life itself. One critic, in fact, has argued that the story is an allegory.[1] And, indeed, the characters in the story seem larger than life. Her villains (and there is no mistaking that they are villains) are actuated by raw emotions, or none at all, outfitted in the most unlikely and sinister ways, and possessed of an unaccountable knowledge of the doings of the victim and her family. The victim herself is a freshly washed, blond, blue-eyed picture of innocence. But however attractive a view it may be to imagine Ms. Oates conceiving of a modern "tale" in the tradition of Hawthorne and Poe which freely mingles the marvelous with the psychologically true, it is contrary to the overwhelming evidence that the author drew her inspiration for her story from a real event publicized in popular national magazines. This view also injures the story itself for it diverts our attention from the fact that the evil she portrays is all too real and renders ineffective the pointed criticism Oates makes of the American Dream, which is the larger purpose of her story. Rather, Oates modelled her story after real people and real events—though she did, as any gifted writer does, imaginatively transform the actual into a fiction of dramatic power. It is my purpose here, then, to identify the parallels between her story and the magazine reports of a real criminal and a real crime which seem to have had a germinal effect upon Oates's creative imagination and to suggest how her theme of the death of the American Dream may have been prompted by these magazines.

The source of and inspiration for Oates's fiend, Arnold Friend, is not nearly so mysterious as the almost supernatural attributes of this character might suggest. Oates's character, as I shall demonstrate, was derived from the exploits, widely

Tom Quirk, "A Source for 'Where Are You Going, Where Have You Been?,'" *Studies in Short Fiction 18* (Fall 1981).

publicized by *Time*, *Life*, and *Newsweek* magazines during the winter of 1965-66, of a real killer from Tucson, Arizona.[2] Moreover, the publication date of "Where Are You Going, Where Have You Been?" in *Epoch* (Fall 1966) suggests this influence, though the more accessible appearance of the story later in her collection of short stories, *The Wheel of Love* (1970), tends to obscure the implication that she probably wrote the story soon after her acquaintance with the grisly details of the three murders committed by a young man named Charles Howard Schmid and nick-named by the author of the *Life* piece about him as the "Pied Piper of Tucson."

Oddly enough, those very details which, by their peculiarity, tend to mark Arnold Friend as an inhuman, perhaps superhuman avatar of undiluted evil are derivative rather than invented. Charles Schmid, an extremely short and muscular man, was a mere five feet three inches tall but nevertheless had been a state champion in gymnastics during his high school years. After being suspended from high school for stealing tools from the auto shop, he continued to inhabit well beyond his teen years such high school haunts as drive-in restaurants, bowling alleys, and the public swimming pool. He was, in fact, twenty-three years old when he was arrested for the murders of Gretchen and Wendy Fritz, aged 17 and 13, in the fall of 1965 and while an earlier third murder of Alleen Rowe, 15, was still being investi-gated. To compensate for his shortness and to disguise the fact that he was a good deal older than the teen-aged girls to whom he was attracted, Schmid went to bizarre and rather stagey extremes. As all the national magazines pointed out, Schmid stuffed rags and folded tin cans into his black leather boots to appear a few inches taller. And he dyed his hair raven black, often wore pancake make-up, pale cream lipstick, and mascara. He sometimes darkened his face to a "tan" with make-up and painted a beauty mark on his cheek.

His behavior was as audacious as his appearance. He drove a gold colored car, in which he "cruised" Tucson's Speedway Boulevard. And he was known to tell tall-tales about how he came into the money he habitually flourished — to his male admirers he suggested that he trafficked in drugs; to the females he bragged that he had been paid by women whom he had taught "100 ways to make love." He was also inclined to introduce himself by a number of aliases, his favorite being "Angel Rodriguez."

The parallels in "Where Are You Going?" to the reports of the Schmid case are too clear-cut to have been accidental. The young victim of Arnold Friend's atten-tion, Connie, notices that he, like Schmid, is quite short: "He wasn't tall, only an inch or so taller than she would be if she came down to him."[3] But he, like the gymnast Schmid, is muscular as well. He wore a "belt that pulled his waist in and showed how lean he was, and a white pull-over shirt that was a little soiled and showed the hard, small muscles of his arms and shoulders. He looked as if he probably did hard work, lifting and carrying things. Even his neck looked muscular." And Arnold Friend totters and wobbles on his black, leather boots and eventually almost loses his balance. This draws Connie's attention to his feet: "He had to bend and adjust his boots. Evidently his feet did not go all the way down; the boots must have been stuffed with something so that he would seem taller."

Oates's description of Friend's face was probably derived from the several photo-graphs reprinted in national magazines. One photo in particular may have been influential for it showed Schmid, as Oates had described Friend, with "cheeks slightly darkened because he hadn't shaved for a day or two, and the nose long and hawklike." And Schmid's dark eyes in this photograph may well have impressed her as "chips of broken glass that catch the light in an amiable way." But more concretely, Friend also wears make-up, as did Schmid. His eye lashes are extremely dark, "as if painted with a black tarlike material." And he may even be wearing a wig. Connie notes Friend's fascinating but dangerous smile, "as if he were smiling from inside a mask." "His whole face was a mask, she thought wildly, tanned down to his throat but then running out as if he had plastered make-up on his face but had forgotten about his throat."

In incidental ways, too, Arnold Friend recalls Charles Schmid. Friend also drives a gold car, apparently older than the gold car Schmid owned, but newly painted. He is older than the boys with whom Connie is familiar; though Oates makes his age a question, Connie thinks he may be thirty, even older. And Arnold Friend is characterized by the same sort of compensating braggadocio Schmid's friends remembered of him in the magazine articles: "He sounded like a hero in a movie, declaring something important. But he spoke too loudly and it was as if he were speaking to someone behind Connie." Moreover, the shocking and confident sexual directness of Friend contrasts sharply with the "caresses of love" Connie dreamed of before Friend pulled into her drive, "sweet, gentle, the way it was in the movies and promised in songs." Schmid's habitual brag to teen-aged girls that he knew "100 ways to make love" is only slightly less direct than Friend's brag to Connie: "I'll hold you so tight you won't think you have to get away or pretend anything because you'll know you can't. And I'll come inside you where it's all secret and you'll give in to me and you'll love me." "People don't talk like that," says Connie, but of course some people do, and Charles Schmid apparently did. Finally, even the name of Oates's villain may have been suggested by the *Life* article. For, whatever other symbolic suggestion the name may have, the irony of a young man who had once tied a string to the tail of his pet cat and had beaten it against the wall until it was a bloody mass but nevertheless assumed the alias "Angel" could hardly have been lost upon Oates's artistic sensibility. Surely she intended to the same sort of irony in naming her demoniac character "Friend."

For the violent crime implied in "Where Are You Going?" — the rape and subsequent murder of Connie — which is not dramatized but is a sure eventuality, Oates also seems to have drawn upon the story of Charles Schmid, but she made certain alterations in the details of it. Alleen Rowe was, like Connie, fifteen years old at the time of her assault, and she too had washed her hair just before her assailants arrived. Rowe's rape and murder also involved accomplices with an apparent knowledge of her parents' habits. Friend, it will be remembered, knows Connie's name, that her family is gone to a barbecue, and how long they will be gone. Arnold Friend is accompanied by Ellie, a rather passive if not oblivious accomplice to be sure, but Schmid's violent crime involved a young man, John Saunders, and a young woman, Mary French. Apparently on the spur of the moment, these three wondered whether they might kill someone and get away with it.[4] Because she had once "stood up" John Saunders, they decided upon Alleen Rowe and went to her house the same evening. Perhaps by a "fortunate" coincidence, or perhaps aware that Alleen's mother worked nights, they found Alleen home alone. Mary French tapped on Alleen's window and eventually persuaded her to go for a drive with them. In the desert, the two men raped her and then beat her to death, and the three buried her in the sand.

The rape of the Rowe girl was, according to the *Newsweek* account of the murder, an afterthought. The *Newsweek* article is entitled "Killing for Kicks" and it portrays the real criminal act as very nearly motiveless and unaccountable. In fact, *Life, Time* and *Newsweek* all preferred to lay the blame on a generation of indulgent, cruising teenagers and their unmindful parents. But Ms. Oates modified the details of the actual event in significant ways. For one thing, she has Connie's seduction conducted in broad daylight while her family is away at a family barbecue and has Arnold Friend display intimate, even satanic knowledge of her family's doings. Also, she chose to downplay Saunder's part in the murder and eliminated the role of Mary French altogether. It is Friend, rather than his accomplice, who is apparently offended by the casual snub he receives at a drive-in restaurant and says to Connie, "Gonna get you, baby." And she seems to have combined Schmid's reputation as a "pied piper" with Mary French's inducements to Alleen to leave her house in the character of Arnold Friend. Thus, she gave to her story an unsettling tension by locating the evil in a single character whose motive was even slighter than John Saunder's and who was not afraid to tempt her in the daytime.

Oates also seems to have combined Schmid's three victims into one, or perhaps two characters. The murder of Wendy Fritz had been the result of her having accompanied her older sister Gretchen to the desert with Schmid. Oates suggests at least the unintentional complicity of Connie's older sister June, whom Connie resents because her mother continually reminds Connie what a model daughter June is. But Connie's parents allow her to go out at night with her friends because June does the same; and it is this freedom that brings Connie into the orbit of Arnold Friend. But Connie also resembles Alleen Rowe in her age, her freshly washed hair, her love for rock and roll music, and as *Life* described it, a susceptible, romantic mentality.

Thus far our discussion of Oates's reaction to an actual incident has focused upon the particular ways she took suggestions from the documented reports of Schmid's violent crimes and dramatized them in her story. But, more significantly, she seems also to have taken her cues from these magazine reports in more general ways which may account for the related thematic elements of seductive rock and roll and violently extinguished innocence which permeate her story.

One cannot help but pause and ponder Oates's dedication of this story to Bob Dylan. However, it is a mistake, I think, to conclude with Urbanski that the dedication is perjorative because Dylan made music "almost religious in dimension among youth."[5] Rather, it is honorific because the history and effect of Bob Dylan's music had been to draw youth away from the romantic promises and frantic strains of a brand of music sung by Buddy Holley, Chuck Berry, Elvis Presley and others. It was Bob Dylan, after all, who told us that the "times they are a changin'," and one of Oates's aims in her short story is to show that they have already changed. It is the gyrating, hip-grinding music of people like Elvis Presley, whom Schmid identified as his "idol," which emanates from Ellie's transistor radio, the "hard, fast, shrieking" songs played by the disc jockey "Bobby King" rather than the cryptic, atonal folk music of Bob Dylan.

Both Connie and Arnold Friend are enthusiastic about "Bobby King" and psychologically linked to one another by an appreciation of the rhythmic beat of the music he plays. Connie observes that Ellie's radio is tuned to the same station as her radio in the house, and when Arnold Friend says that King is "great," Connie concedes, "He's kind of great." Arnold counters, "Listen, that guy is *great*. He knows where the action is" (p. 41). Friend's statement of enthusiasm recalls the quotation that introduces the *Life* essay on Charles Schmid:

> "Hey, c'mon babe, follow me,
> I'm the Pied Piper, follow me,
> I'm the Pied Piper
> And I'll show you where it's at.
> — Popular song,
> Tucson, winter 1965

Arnold Friend does, indeed, show Connie "where it's at," and he draws her from the house with his alternating blandishments and threats much as a pied piper. Moreover, Connie's ultimate, mindless decision to go with Friend is meant to recall the beckoning tempo of rock and roll: "She cried out, she cried for her mother, she felt her breath start jerking back and forth in her lungs as if it were something Arnold Friend was stabbing her with again and again with no tenderness. A noisy, sorrowful wailing rose all about her and she was locked inside the way she was locked inside the house."

When Connie kicks the telephone away and opens the screen door to go with Friend, there can be little question where she is going nor where she has been. She is going to her death, and her fate is largely the result of a consciousness shaped by the frantic life of cruising in fast cars, sipping cokes out of sweating paper cups with anonymous boys, a consciousness epitomized by the frantic music she listens to.

But it is naive to suppose that this story is about the dangerous effects of rock and roll; rather, the music is emblematic of the tempo of American life generally. And the questions in the title — where are you going, where have you been? — are addressed to America itself. The author of the *Life* article asked sarcastically, "Isn't Tucson — out there in the Golden West, in the grand setting where the skies are not cloudy all day — supposed to be a flowering of the American Dream?" Oates's short story is her withering, disturbing reply, and her story is very nearly a suspenseful parody of the mythic promises of the West and "Home on the Range." For Connie's house is distant from any others and the "encouraging words" Arnold Friend speaks are hypnotic enough to lure her out of doors beneath a perfectly blue, cloudless sky.

Insofar as this story has a setting, it is set in the West. Connie's parents leave for a family "barbeque," and their daughter day dreams in the summer heat ("It was too hot," she thinks), under the sky "perfectly blue and still." She stares from her "asbestos 'ranch house'" to the limitless expanse of land outside it. Her house seems small to her, and Arnold reminds her that the walls of her house do not provide a citadel: "The place where you came from ain't there any more, and where you had in mind to go is cancelled out. This place you are now — inside your daddy's house —

is nothing but a cardboard box I can knock down any time. You know that and always did know it. You hear me?" Her "asbestos" house is no protection from the devilish forces embodied in Arnold Friend, nor from his fiery passion and never has been. If there were a fire inside, Friend tells her, "If the place got lit up with a fire, honey, you'd come runnin' out into my arms an' safe at home."

Of course there is a fire inside, a fire inside Connie's brain. The pounding of her heart is simply "a pounding, living thing inside this body that really wasn't really hers either." Arnold's "incantation" draws her out, but those values generally associated with the American Dream, of hearth and home and innocent youth, are by this time a dim flicker in her mind. Thoughts of "Aunt Tillie's" barbeque, hot dogs and corn on the cob, tender flirtations, the lovely promises of songs are now remote, almost as though they had never been. As she steps out to Arnold Friend, she sees the land: "the vast sunlit reaches of the land behind him and on all sides of him — so much land that Connie had never seen before and did not recognize except to know that she was going to it."

When one knows that Charles Schmid buried his victims in the desert, the dictum of the American Dream that one ought to return to the land, that nature speaks to us in lasting and benevolent ways, takes on a singularly sinister connotation. The American Dream is quite extinct here, and Connie's parents and sister are as much dreamers as she. Ultimately, the questions which Oates chose as a title for her story might be asked about America itself as well as about Connie's life, and asked more effectively in the slang idiom of Connie's generation: "Where *are you* going? Where *have you* been?" For they address a society which, by tradition, has preferred its agrarian dreams and promises to harsher realities and aggressive evils and is therefore dangerously blind to them. Our antique values, says Oates, are not proof against the seductions of the piper's song.

Notes

[1] Marie Mitchell Olesen Urbanski, "Existential Allegory: Joyce Carol Oates's 'Where Are You Going, Where Have You Been?'" *Studies in Short Fiction*, 15 (Spring 1978), 200–203.

[2] "Secrets in the Sand," *Time*, 26 November 1965, p. 28; Dan Moser, "The Pied Piper of Tucson," *Life*, 4 March 1966, pp. 18–24, 80C f; "Growing Up in Tucson: Death Sentence," *Time*, 11 March 1966, p. 28; and "Killing for Kicks" *Newsweek*, 14 March 1966, pp. 35–36.

Since some of the parallels between the Oates short story and the national magazine coverage of the Charles Schmid case occur only in the *Life* essay — for example, the fact that the real victim, Alleen Rowe, and Oates's fictional victim, Connie, both washed their hair shortly before the arrival of their assailant — it seems likely that this essay was the primary, if not the sole source of Oates's familiarity with the story. Therefore, all the information about the murder case has been taken from the *Life* piece unless otherwise indicated in the text or by footnote.

[3] "Where Are You Going, Where Have You Been?," rpt. in *The Wheel of Love* (New York: The Vanguard Press, 1970).

[4] "Killing for Kicks," *Newsweek*, 14 March 1966, pp. 35–36.

[5] Urbanski, p. 202.

WHO IS ARNOLD FRIEND? THE OTHER SELF IN JOYCE CAROL OATES'S "WHERE ARE YOU GOING, WHERE HAVE YOU BEEN?"

G. J. Weinberger

As ominously threatening as Arnold Friend may seem to Connie, G. J. Weinberger argues that he is not a satanic figure, as other writers in this chapter assert. On the contrary, Weinberger insists, Friend does not really exist, except in the sense that "fantasy is a mode of experience." Rather, Friend is a manifestation of Connie's alter ego, her double—an embodiment of her fearful "insights into the violence and sexuality of adulthood." Such an interpretation, Weinberger notes, accounts for Connie's state of romantic reverie just before Friend appears at her door; it also explains Arnold's uncanny familiarity with the details of Connie's private life. Friend's psychological role is to usher Connie into the world of adult maturity she both longs for and fears. The alternative is a state of perpetual adolescence repre- sented by Connie's sister June in her real world and Ellie in her fantasy. For Weinberger, then, the story's conclusion is not an unhappy one: "Realizing then . . . that each person must undergo the rites of passage alone, with only one's other self to help, Connie . . . crosses the threshold and goes out into the sunlight, into the vast, threatening adult world."

When Connie faces Arnold Friend, she faces her other self, in Oates's treatment of the *Doppelgänger* motif, which informs such well-known works as Poe's "William Wilson," Melville's "Bartleby the Scrivener," Crane's "The Bride Comes to Yellow Sky," and Conrad's "The Secret Sharer," among many others. The principal outward difference between these and Oates's version, Connie's *alter ego* being of the opposite sex and extremely threatening, results from Arnold Friend's representing not only a protagonist's mythic, irrational side (one of several characteristics he shares with his literary forerunners), but also a cluster of insights into the violence and sexuality of adulthood. His indeterminate age, somewhere between eighteen and thirty, empha- sizes the transition which Connie must undergo, one reflected in the future-past duality inherent in the title of the story (Gillis 67).

We first see Connie at home, an ordinary middle-class setting, complete with a mother who runs the household and nags, an older "maiden" sister, and an unin- volved father who appears only to work, eat, read the newspaper, and sleep. To- gether, these people drive away, out of the story, to a conventional Sunday barbecue. Connie's father, like her friend's father who chauffeurs the girls to the shopping plaza, "never bothered to ask what they had done." The father's lack of involvement allows Connie a relative degree of freedom. No one ever asks, "Where are you going, Where have you been?"

G. J. Weinberger, "Who Is Arnold Friend? The Other Self in Joyce Carol Oates's 'Where Are You Going, Where Have You Been?,'" *American Imago* 45 (Summer 1988).

The house and the domestic environment represent the known, the rationally apprehendable, much like the law in "Bartleby." Within this environment, Connie is a conventional adolescent girl. She is vain and messy, and bears herself differently at home and abroad. She and her mother share the occasional good moment as a reprieve from the usual arguments, which also serve to set limits for Connie.

She may tell a fib here and there but she gets home shortly after 11 P.M. Connie is additionally controlled by her mother's constantly comparing her to her sister June and by June's working at her high school. But while she may have little power at home, Connie certainly does have some — over boys. This too is conventional, especially in view of the relative maturation of the sexes, and represents her first tentative experiments with adulthood. Connie is on the threshold: her hair and her walk both attract attention and she is willing to assume risks, "ducking fast across the busy road" to the hamburger drive-in "where the older kids hung out." On the night Connie meets Eddie, she and her friend run across the highway "breathless with daring," to a world of bright lights and music.

There is popular music everywhere in this story. Music is the medium through which adolescents attempt to derive the meaning of life and it is in a music-induced trance-like state that Connie later sees Arnold Friend. Music takes on an almost religious significance — "the music that made everything so good: the music was always in the background, like music at a church service; it was something to depend upon" (36) — and Wegs sees a grotesque religious parody in the entire drive-in episode. But Bob Dylan, to whom the story is dedicated, and whom Urbanski acknowledges as one "who contributed to making music almost religious in dimension among the youth" (201), does not write typically adolescent music. His work often deals with types of evil ("Blowin' in the Wind," "The Masters of War"), sexuality ("Lay Lady Lay"), or change ("The Times They Are a' Changing"). Thematically, then, the music points at the serious world beyond adolescence, even if the drive-in crowd listens merely to amplified sound. In its loudness, accompanied by bright lights, it has elements of orgiastic abandon. After the drive-in episode, when she is back at the plaza, amid shops (symbols of commerce, of order), Connie is too far away to hear the music.

The function of the drive-in episode is not limited to introducing the music and bright lights and the almost cinematic effect of unreality which results. More important is Connie's seeing the shaggy-haired boy who later reappears as Arnold Friend, just as the vacuous smile of the hamburger boy atop the bottle-shaped drive-in building reappears as Arnold Friend's dangerous smile. The black-haired boy is merely a boy uttering an adolescent, would-be *macho* remark, but he provides the impetus to the rest of the story, involving Connie's trance, wherein she has her vision of the evil and often irrational world of adulthood to which she crosses over. To put it in R. D. Laing's terms, her "earliest phantasies are experienced in sensation: later, they take the form of plastic images and dramatic representations" (4).

Significantly, when the boy in the golden car tells Connie, "Gonna get you, baby," Eddie, Connie's companion, does not notice. Eddie's being presented as an individual promising no particularly perceptive gifts — "He sat backwards on his stool, turning himself jerkily around in semi-circles and then stopping and turning again, and after a while he asked Connie if she would like something to eat" — is important because it leaves Connie as the only person who notices the boy and hears his remark; this accords with the element of private vision shared by many protagonists in *Doppelgänger* stories. Thus, for instance, William Wilson is surprised that the officials at his school remain unaware of his double's designs (171); the lawyer in "Bartleby" must consult his assistants to validate his perceptions of his recalcitrant copyist (32, 34–35); and Conrad's captain wonders if Leggatt is visible only to him (130).

Arnold Friend does not exist—which makes him no less "real," since "phantasy is a mode of experience" (Laing 3, 24). "He" is simply Connie's projected other self, depicted in Oates's way, with a heavy emphasis on evil, violence, and the threat of rape (if not death) which Connie must acknowledge.[1] As Arnold Friend tells her, "This is your day set aside for a ride with me and you know it." The cost of refusal is failure to attain adulthood, as illustrated by the twenty-four-year-old June who works as a school secretary, still lives at home, and who obediently, and inappropriately dressed, goes to the family barbecue.[2] To warn Connie against such a refusal is the function of Ellie Oscar. With his radio and sunglasses, and his readiness to employ violence, Ellie is an extension of Arnold Friend, but he also represents the alternative to him. His clothes, for example, and his general vapidity attest to a forty-year-old perpetual adolescence which is underscored by the sexlessness of his neuter name. His status is illustrated by Arnold Friend's telling Connie that Ellie will sit in the back seat during their ride, in the role of child *vis-a-vis* the two "adults." Ellie apparently understands only when spoken to in adolescent clichés. In the extraordinary paragraph near the end of the story, when Arnold tells him off with an extensive series of clichés, there appears a further purpose: a kind of exorcism of these phrases for the benefit of Connie, who is leaving behind the world where they are commonly heard.

Connie's refusal to participate in the family barbecue shows her growing sense of power and independence and, more important, leaves her at home alone, a situation emphasized by her mother's "Stay home alone then." Of course, it also leaves her more vulnerable: ". . . at adolescence we observe relative ego weakness due to the intensification of the drives, as well as absolute ego weakness due to the adolescent rejection of parental ego support" (Blos, *The Adolescent Passage* 144). The daydreams, the music, and all the rest follow—

> Connie sat with her eyes closed in the sun, dreaming and dazed with the warmth about her as if this were a kind of love, the caresses of love, and her mind slipped over onto thoughts of the boy she had been with the night before and how nice he had been, how sweet it always was, not the way someone like June would suppose but sweet, gentle, the way it was in movies and promised in songs; and when she opened her eyes she hardly knew where she was, the back yard ran off into the weeds and a fence-like line of trees and behind it the sky was perfectly blue and still. The asbestos "ranch house" that was now three years old startled her—it looked small. She shook her head as if to get awake.

Then, after turning on the radio, "to drown out the quiet," and paying close attention to the music, as instructed by the disc jockey, she

> bathed in a glow of slow-pulsed joy that seemed to rise mysteriously out of the music itself and lay languidly about the airless little room, breathed in and breathed out with each gentle rise and fall of her chest.

Her entry into her trance — or her dream (Rubin 58–59) — is followed immediately by the car coming up the driveway.

The ambiguity of the passage where Connie enters her trance, which leaves room for other interpretations of this story (such as Wegs's and Urbanski's), is strongly reminiscent of the questions Hawthorne leaves us with regarding the consciousness of Young Goodman Brown in the forest (see also Winslow 268). More important, however, is that Connie is alone, a prerequisite for facing one's other self. Thus, William Wilson and his double speak to each other only when they are alone together; the lawyer ensconces Bartleby on his side of the folding doors in his office (28); the captain takes the unusual step of going on watch and is therefore alone to receive Leggatt (95–97); and Crane's Potter, who in the company of his new bride comes upon the rampaging Scratchy Wilson, "exhibited an instinct to at once loosen his arm from the woman's grip" (119).

The creation of Arnold Friend in Connie's mind is made possible by her reaching the appropriate time in her life. In this regard, Arnold Friend's name — "a friend" — as a common slang expression for the menstrual period, supports the theme of impending adulthood. Arnold's form, as noted earlier, is borrowed from the shaggy-haired boy in the drive-in; however, unlike the boys she knows, Arnold Friend, who is not a boy, is beyond Connie's control, although, because of his "source," he looks conventional enough.

> She recognized most things about him, the tight jeans that showed his thighs and buttocks and the greasy leather boots and the tight shirt, and even that slippery friendly smile of his, that sleepy dreamy smile that all the boys used to get across ideas they didn't want to put into words.

The adolescent boy's conventionally displayed sexuality here is serious beyond anything in Connie's prior experience. She recognizes no pattern: ". . . all these things did not come together." Arnold Friend does not stop at slippery smiles. He is all too willing to put the matter into words; and, unlike Bartleby, Scratchy Wilson, or Leggatt, he is not affected by the world of order. As Connie soon learns, he is beyond the control of police or parents.

Arnold is unable to enter the house which represents Connie's old environment as well as order, like the shops at the plaza, but only for as long as Connie does not attempt to use the telephone. Besides, he does not have to enter: "I ain't made plans for coming in that house where I don't belong but just for you to come out to me, the way you should" (50). In other words, Connie is expected to step into adulthood voluntarily. Certainly, her merely material home (she has lived in it only during her adolescence, between the ages of twelve and fifteen) is no match for the forces of adulthood: "I mean, anybody can break through a screen door and glass and wood and iron or anything else if he needs to, anybody at all, and specially Arnold Friend."

The kinship between this "friend" and Connie — her name signifies constancy to the process of growth to adulthood — is actually established early in the story. The curious phrasing of Connie's mother's chiding her daughter, "Stop gawking at yourself. Who are you?" (34), is directly related to Connie's first words to Arnold: "Who the hell do you think you are?"; both depict attempts to discover an emerging or new identity, in acknowledgment that adolescence "is essentially a time of personal discovery" (Winnicott 145). Likewise, Connie's wishing her mother dead and her telling friends that her mother sometimes makes her want to throw up (35), represents not only conventional adolescent jargon and escapism, but also her preparing to leave her childhood (and her dependence on her mother) behind. Arnold Friend's threat later in the story that her family may be harmed reflects her adolescent hostility and symbolizes her unconscious knowledge that in her passage to adulthood the old ties must become as dead for her. This is underlined shortly thereafter in Connie's realization, "I'm not going to see my mother again. . . . I'm not going to sleep in my bed again."

Connie's appearance early on also foreshadows her transition from adolescence to adulthood: "She wore a pull-over jersey blouse that looked one way when she was at home and another way when she was away from home. Everything about her had two sides to it, one for home and one for everywhere that was not home. . . ." Moreover, her "trashy daydreams" which her mother complains about hail from a realm of feeling and darkness with which Connie is as yet unacquainted:

> But all the boys fell back and dissolved into a single face that was not even a face but an idea, a feeling, mixed up with the urgent insistent pounding of the music and the humid night air of July. Connie's mother kept dragging her back to the daylight by finding things for her to do. . . .

In a similar passage, when Connie agrees to spend the evening with Eddie, she goes with him, "her face gleaming with a joy that had nothing to do with Eddie or even this place; it might have been the music."[3]

The "tiny metallic world" of Arnold Friend's sunglasses which mirror everything in miniature, and in which Connie sees her blouse reflected, is related to the mirror at the end of "William Wilson" and to the place in "The Secret Sharer" where the captain and Leggatt rest on opposite ends of the skylight, creating a mirror image of each other (103). At first inscrutable, Arnold Friend without his sunglasses is spectral, qualities designed to heighten the sense of unreality—"he came from nowhere and belonged nowhere" (like Bartleby)—which in turn is supported by references to the possibility of his wearing a wig and by our being told unequivocally that "His whole face was a mask."

Because Connie is not an initiate into the secrets of the world which Arnold Friend represents, she appears briefly unable to read what is clearly written on his car: his name, the numerological "secret code," and, around a dent on the left rear fender, "DONE BY A CRAZY WOMAN DRIVER." This last inscription is important because it hints at the essentially anti-woman attitude of the adult world. Women are not, and are not allowed to be, in control. They are its quintessential victims, even if the violence is occasionally masked (see Walker 59, Gillis 65ff.). As Arnold Friend tells Connie, "I am always nice at first, the first time"; but later, when she is unable to call her mother, Connie "felt her breath jerking back and forth in her lungs as if it were something Arnold Friend were stabbing her with again and again with no tenderness." When she looks at the car again, she notices on the front fender the inscription "MAN THE FLYING SAUCERS," an obsolete adolescent expression, clearly pointing to Connie's leaving the world she has known. Significantly, she looks at the inscription "for a while as if the words meant something to her that she did not yet know."

Connie's formal initiation begins when Arnold Friend draws his X-sign in her direction, at which moment the music from inside the house and from the car blend together. As the encounter proceeds, it becomes more and more apparent that Arnold exists only in Connie's imagination. She never turns down his invitation to go for a ride: she gives no answer the first time and says "I don't know" the second. At first, Arnold appears to be an inch or two taller than Connie, but it becomes evident that later that they are of equal height. He knows everything about Connie — her name, her friends' names, who she was with the night before, where her family is, what they are wearing, what they are doing — because he is she. Thus, while it is tempting to think of Arnold Friend as Satan (Wegs 69, Creighton 381), unable to cross the threshold uninvited, Connie is actually face to face with a part of herself (Winslow 264). Potential adulthood has always been part of Connie's make-up, as it is of every adolescent: Arnold Friend tells her, "Sure you saw me before. . . . You just don't remember," and, "I know everybody." After the blending of the music, and after his voice, orchestrated by Connie, has, in fact, become the voice of the disc jockey, she becomes dizzy, sees him in a blur, and "had the idea that he had driven up the driveway all right but had come from nowhere before that and belonged nowhere and that everything about him and even about the music that was so familiar to her was only half real."

Arnold Friend's voice, at various times monotone, lilting, or chanting, is related to music; and like music, it serves to link adolescent pop culture in general with the threatening adult world. Thus, when he asks her, "Don't you know who I am?" she hears him sound like "a hero in a movie" speaking too loudly. Soon after, when Connie has begun to accept the inevitability of her change of world, he uses "a gentle-loud voice that was like a stage voice" to tell her, "This place you are now — inside your daddy's house — is nothing but a cardboard box I can knock down any time. You know that and always did know it."

This decisive insight on Connie's part — since she *is* Arnold Friend — follows closely Arnold's telling her "It's all over for you here," her necessarily fruitless attempt to cry out for and phone her mother — what could she possibly say to her? — and her dawning awareness: ". . . deep inside her brain was something like a pinpoint of light that kept going and would not let her relax." The change is immediate — when Arnold Friend runs his fingernail down the screen the noise does not make Connie shiver, "as it would have the day before" — and leads to Arnold's penultimate voice:

> His words were not angry but only part of an incantation. The incantation was kindly. "Now, come out through the kitchen to me, honey, and let's see a smile, try it, you're a brave, sweet little girl and now they're eating corn and hot dogs cooked to bursting over an outdoor fire, and they don't know one thing about you and never did and honey, you're better than them because not a one of them would have done this for you."

Realizing then, if only in a hazy way, that each person must undergo the rites of passage alone, with only one's other self to help, Connie, brushing the hair out of her eyes in order to see more clearly, crosses the threshold and goes out into the sunlight, into the vast, threatening adult world. The last paragraph in the story reiterates the uncaring nature of the world. As soon as it becomes apparent that

Connie is leaving the house, Arnold Friend falls back on a cliché, "My sweet little blue-eyed girl," mouthing it with "a half-sung sigh that had nothing to do with her brown eyes."

Notes

[1] According to Laing, "The firm distinction between self and other, between the whole of a person and parts of a person, do not hold for phantasy" (26).

[2] In the adolescent girl, "Forerunners of romantic love are to be observed, as well as all sorts of beautifications, in an attempt to speed up artificially the maturational schedule. The defensive reversal of these trends, as in asceticism, only highlights their conflictual nature" (Blos, *The Young Adolescent* 115).

[3] Blos has found that the "physical separateness from the parent or polarization of the past through change in social role, style of dress and grooming, special interests, and moral choices often represents the only means by which the adolescent can maintain his psychological integrity during some critical stage of the individuation process" (*The Adolescent Passage* 147–148).

References

Blos, Peter. *The Adolescent Passage*. New York: International Universities Press, 1979.

———. *The Young Adolescent*. New York: The Free Press, 1970.

Conrad, Joseph. "The Secret Sharer," in *'Twixt Land and Sea*. Edinburgh, and London, 1925.

Crane, Stephen. "The Bride Comes to Yellow Sky," in *The Works of Stephen Crane*, vol. IV. Charlottesville, 1970.

Creighton, Joanne V. "Joyce Carol Oates's Craftsmanship in *The Wheel of Love*." *Studies in Short Fiction*, 15 (1978): 375–84.

Gillis, Christina M. "'Where Are You Going, Where Have You Been?': Seduction, Space, and a Fictional Mode." *Studies in Short Fiction*, 18 (1981): 65–70.

Hawthorne, Nathaniel. "Young Goodman Brown," in *Mosses From an Old Manse*. Boston and New York, 1882.

Laing, R. D. *The Self and Others*. Chicago: Quadrangle, 1962.

Melville, Herman. "Bartleby the Scrivener," in *The Piazza Tales*. New York, 1963.

Oates, Joyce Carol. "Where Are You Going, Where Have You Been?" in *The Wheel of Love and Other Stories*. New York, 1970.

Poe, Edgar Allen. "William Wilson," in *The Tales and Poems of Edgar Allan Poe*. New York: "New Fordham Edition," n.d.

Rubin, Larry. "Oates's 'Where Are You Going, Where Have You Been?'" *Explicator*, 42.4 (1984): 57–59.

Urbanski, Marie. "Existential Allegory: Joyce Carol Oates's 'Where Are You Going, Where Have You Been?'" *Studies in Short Fiction*, 15 (1978): 200–203.

Walker, Carolyn. "Fear, Love, and Art in Oates' 'Plot.'" *Critique: Studies in Modern Fiction*, 15 (1973): 59–70.

Wegs, Joyce M. "'Don't You Know Who I Am?': The Grotesque in Oates's 'Where Are You Going, Where Have You Been?'" *Journal of Narrative Technique*, 5 (1975): 66–72.

Winnicott, D. W. *Deprivation and Delinquency*. Ed. Clare Winnicott, et al. London and New York: Tavistock, 1984.

Winslow, Joan D. "The Stranger Within: Two Stories by Oates and Hawthorne." *Studies in Short Fiction*, 17 (1980): 263–268.

SUGGESTIONS FOR WRITING

Informal Essays

1. Write an essay in which you discuss and demonstrate two or three things you like or dislike about Joyce Carol Oates's "Where Are You Going, Where Have You Been?"

2. Do you think that Connie's experience with Arnold Friend is real or merely a fantasy? Discuss your conclusion at length.

3. Are you aware of any convicted felon (or personal acquaintance) besides the one described in Tom Quirk's essay who reminds you of Arnold Friend? Identify this male and discuss the resemblances between him and the character in "Where Are You Going, Where Have You Been?"

4. Have you ever had any Connies among your female acquaintances? Write an essay in which you answer this question. Refer to the story as you develop your essay.

Short Documented Papers

1. Write an essay in which you demonstrate how convincing (or unconvincing) you think Joyce Carol Oates's presentation of Connie's adolescent world is.

2. Discuss Connie's perception of males in the opening pages of "Where Are You Going, Where Have You Been?" *before* Arnold Friend's arrival on her doorstep. Include a discussion of her attitude toward her father as well as toward Eddie. Include also her general impressions of young males during the shopping-plaza episode.

3. Discuss the character and the thematic function of Ellie, Arnold Friend's sidekick.

4. Discuss the significance of rock music in "Where Are You Going, Where Have You Been?" Demonstrate how it functions in the story's theme.

5. Discuss Connie's perception of the world that her mother and her sister June represent to her.

6. Discuss the significance of the appearance of Arnold Friend's car.

7. Discuss the meaning of the title of Oates's "Where Are You Going, Where Have You Been?"

Longer Documented Papers

1. When Arnold Friend shows up on Connie's doorstep, she reacts with surprise and annoyance: "Who in the hell do you think you are?" Who does Oates think he is? After reading the essays of Joyce Wegs and G. J. Weinberger, write a paper in which you discuss Arnold Friend's role in Oates's story.

2. Demonstrate the validity of one or two of the observations Oates makes about American youth or contemporary American society in her preface (the second essay in this chapter) with specific details from "Where Are You Going, Where Have You Been?"

3. Select two or three of the observations Joanne V. Creighton makes about Oates's girlhood in upstate New York or about her views of the function of a fiction writer and relate these observations to her concerns in "Where Are You Going, Where Have You Been?"

4. Discuss Connie's experience with Arnold Friend as an adolescent rite of passage, an initiation into her great source of fear and fascination, adulthood.

5. Discuss Connie's experience with Arnold Friend as the jarring, traumatic fulfillment of her dreamy, sentimental, rock music-accompanied sexual fantasies.

6. Discuss "Where Are You Going, Where Have You Been?" as a moral allegory of a culture that has lost any sense of moral or transcendent purpose.

7. Identify and carefully trace two or three motifs (patterns of images) in "Where Are You Going, Where Have You Been?"

OBSCENITY: *To Censor or Not?*

According to Mary Ellen Ross ("Censorship or Education"), pornography has mush-roomed into a seven-billion- to ten-billion-dollar-a-year industry. Moreover, sexually explicit material is no longer confined to rundown areas in large cities. It's now as close as your local video rental store, your telephone system's 900 numbers, and your cable television channels.

The controversy that swirls around the issue of the censorship of obscenity settles on a few simple questions: (1) What is it? If obscenity is not possible to define with any precision, we might end up censoring serious literature and art along with hard-core pornography. (2) What is its effect? If its effect is harmful, is the answer to the problem censorship or education? If its effect is benign or beneficent, perhaps it should be distributed freely. (3) Should it be protected under the First Amendment to the Constitution?

It's not surprising that such difficult questions often end up being debated in U.S. courts. In fact, the essays in this chapter so often contain allusions to famous obscenity trials that the best help we can offer here is to describe a few of these trials.

The first trial didn't occur in the United States at all. In the eighteenth and nineteenth centuries, U.S. judges had the habit of going back to English law to look for precedents. One of these precedents was the case known as *Queen* v. *Hicklin* (1868). In Wolverhampton, England, a local magistrate, Justice Benjamin Hicklin, declared that an anti-Catholic pamphlet ("The Confessional Unmasked; shewing the depravity of the Romish priesthood . . .") was legally obscene. The Hicklin decision established two important precedents for U.S. obscenity trials before the early 1930s: (1) Tests for obscenity could be based on whether the material would tend to corrupt anyone who might come in contact with it, including children, and (2) obscenity could override other values, such as a book's literary, scientific, or artistic merits.

Not until the 1930s did U.S. courts begin to move away from the *Hicklin* defini-tion of what is legally obscene. In a famous 1934 obscenity trial, *United States* v. *One Book Entitled* Ulysses, Judge John Woolsey ignored *Hicklin* entirely when he ruled that James Joyce's novel *Ulysses* was not obscene.

Until the *Ulysses* trial, books were banned on the basis of isolated passages; Woolsey ruled that a book could be ruled obscene only on the effect of the entire book. Before the *Ulysses* trial, the law took into account the effect that obscene materials might have on children; Woolsey declared that a book's effect on adults with "average sex instincts" was what counted, not its effect on children. (He also concluded that *Ulysses* is an "emetic" rather than an "aphrodisiac," a conclusion that James Joyce probably wouldn't have appreciated.)

In *Roth* v. *United States* (1957), Sam Roth was convicted of sending pornography through the mails. In this case the Supreme Court defined obscene material as that which "deals with sex in a manner appealing to the prurient interest" and which offends "the common conscience of the community by present-day standards." The Court also ruled that obscenity is not protected by the "freedom of speech" safeguards in the First Amendment, though justices Hugo Black and William Douglas dissented. Both argued that the First Amendment protected all published material, including obscenity.

Douglas's and Black's literal reading of the First Amendment opened up a hornet's nest of controversy about its applicability to sexually explicit material. Indeed, medieval Jewish scholars never expended as much intellectual energy on analyzing the Torah as lawyers, judges, civil libertarians, and conservatives have expended — especially in the last couple of decades — on analyzing the few words of the First Amendment:

Congress shall make no law . . . abridging the freedom of speech, or of the press.

The three problems connected with obscenity and the First Amendment are these: (1) Did Congress intend those words to cover sexually explicit photographs and words as well as political speeches and writing? (2) If Congress did not intend the First Amendment to protect obscenity from censorship, should the amendment be used now to protect it? (3) Finally, if Congress cannot censor sexually explicit materials, can the states do it?

Back to our history. The definition of obscenity that came out of *Memoirs* v. *Massachusetts* (1966) made it almost impossible for the federal courts to rule that writing (as opposed to photographs and live shows) is obscene. In its consideration of the famous eighteenth-century underground novel *Fanny Hill*, the Supreme Court declared that written material is obscene only if "(1) . . . the dominant theme of the material as a whole appeals to a prurient interest in sex; (2) . . . the material is patently offensive . . . ; (3) . . . the material is utterly without redeeming social value." Using that definition, the Supreme Court declared that *Fanny Hill* was not obscene.

In the Supreme Court's most recent significant ruling on obscenity, *Miller* v. *California* (1973), the justices determined by a 5–4 vote that the "common conscience of the community" (see *Roth* v. *United States*, above) need not be national. That is, the community of Murray, Kentucky, might find obscene what New York City doesn't. In 1990, *The Guide to American Law Supplement* says that *Miller* v. *California* defines obscenity as "something that the average person, applying contemporary community standards and taking the work as a whole, would find appeals to the prurient interest; depicts or describes sexual conduct in a patently offensive way; and lacks serious literary, artistic, political, or scientific value."

And that is basically where it stands. *Miller* v. *California* has been refined and sharpened slightly, but it remains the last significant statement on obscenity by the Supreme Court. Since *Miller* v. *California*, of course, other obscenity cases have come before the Supreme Court. In 1984 Indianapolis, Indiana, no doubt encouraged by *Miller* v. *California*, passed a stringent antipornography law that was later struck down by the U.S. Court of Appeals. In 1989 Carlin Communications sued Mountain Bell Telephone for refusing to provide telephone lines to companies who wanted to deliver pornographic messages through 900 numbers. The U.S. Court of Appeals for the Ninth Circuit upheld Mountain Bell Telephone's ban on "Dial-a-Porn" services. When the case was appealed, the Supreme Court denied hearing arguments on the case, thus approving Mountain Bell's ban.

Blushes and Leers as Guides to Crime

Robert W. Haney

This excerpt from Robert Haney's book Comstockery in America: Patterns of Censorship and Control *(1960) is the oldest work in this chapter, and we therefore begin with it. But there is a better reason for placing it first: It can serve as an introduction to the subject itself because it is a brief and entertaining history of censorship of the obscene, from the sixteenth through the twentieth centuries.*

> **O, forfend it God,**
> **That in a Christian climate, souls refined**
> **Should show so heinous, black, obscene a deed!**
>
> **William Shakespeare, *Richard II***

Shakespeare's Bishop of Carlisle would seem to be lamenting the presence in England of a shocking book, describing and illustrating the most abhorrent activities conceivable by man. . . . Perhaps some gruesome new method of torturing human beings has been discovered, and the author has thoughtfully provided hauntingly repulsive, full-page woodcuts to show the reader how he can test the new discovery for himself by combining his talents as a carpenter with those of an appropriate victim. . . .

Unfortunately, Shakespeare deprives us of the pleasure of speculating on what is so obscene, for we are informed that what the Bishop is actually speaking about is the horrible idea of a subject's judging his king! Such, at one time, was an activity to which the adjective "obscene" could be attached. Since Shakespeare's epoch the word has been limited almost exclusively to nonpolitical uses. It has, in the process, become more vague.

The word "obscene" comes from the latin *obscenus*, which originally meant inauspicious and ill-omened. Later, *obscenus* came to mean filthy, abominable, indecent. In its English usage, "obscene" has the two standard meanings of (1) "offensive to the senses or to taste or refinement" (disgusting, repulsive, etc.) and (2) "offensive to modesty or decency; expressing or suggesting unchaste or lustful ideas: impure, indecent, lewd." However, "obscene" is not defined by these terms; the word has its true meaning in the undertones and connotations that surround it. And these implicit values vary so widely from person to person that the word can never be clearly defined. Almost everyone agrees that obscene material should not be circulated in society, but there is no consensus — the claims of the Legion of Decency and the National Office for Decent Literature notwithstanding — concerning what is and what is not obscene.

There will be ample opportunity to discuss this problem more fully in a later chapter. For the present, we must keep the elusive quality of the word carefully in

Robert W. Haney, "Blushes and Leers as Guides to Crime," *Comstockery in America: Patterns of Censorship and Control* (Boston: Beacon Press, 1960).

mind as we turn briefly to the historical record. No story offers better materials for a study of the varieties of human folly and the intransigence of human pride.

Like the first American Sedition Act, the edict of the Star Chamber issued in 1586 was political in its intention. It was designed to make sure that no statements hostile to the government were circulated in Great Britain. This was also the purpose of the later licensing and censorship laws directed against books and newspapers. In 1695, however, the last Licensing Act expired and was not renewed. This lapse apparently occurred, not from any zeal on the part of the government to advance the cause of freedom of the press, but because the Act was vexatious in its procedures.[1] In any case, it gave printing a great incentive to expand.

Some people expected that this new freedom from prior restraints would result in a vast outpouring of harsh criticism directed against William III, but they were proved wrong. The new journals and unlicensed books were remarkably reserved. Macaulay attributes this decorum to the renewed literary activities of those men who, being moderate and law-abiding, had been ill-disposed to violate the censorship statutes. The laws had, instead, only evoked the attacks of the naturally lawless and immoderate. Macaulay's analysis of what happened deserves wide circulation:

> Some weak men had imagined that religion and morality stood in need of the protection of the licenser. The event signally proved that they were in error. In truth the censorship had scarcely put any restraint on licentiousness or profaneness. The Paradise Lost had narrowly escaped mutilation: for the Paradise Lost was the work of a man whose politics were hateful to the government. But Etherege's She Would If She Could, Wycherley's Country Wife, Dryden's Translations from the Fourth Book of Lucretius, obtained the Imprimatur without difficulty: for Etherege, Wycherley and Dryden were courtiers. From the day on which the emancipation of our literature was accomplished, the purification of our literature began. That purification was effected, not by the intervention of senates or magistrates, but by the opinion of the great body of educated Englishmen, before whom good and evil were set, and who were left free to make their choice. During a hundred and sixty years the liberty of our press has been constantly becoming more and more entire; and during those hundred and sixty years the restraint imposed on writers by the general feeling of readers has been constantly becoming more and more strict. At length even that class of works in which it was formerly thought that a voluptuous imagination was privileged to disport itself, love songs, comedies, novels, have become more decorous than the sermons of the seventeenth century.[2]

Shortly before the removal of prior restrictions on the press, the foundations were laid for nonpolitical censorship. Obscenity became an offense in the sight of the law. Oddly enough, the first reported case dealing with obscenity as such, dated 1663, deals not with obscene literature or pictures but with the obscene behavior of a ribald poet. Sir Charles Sedley, in an inebriated and nude state, had exhibited himself from a balcony overlooking London's Covent Garden, had hurled bottles of "offensive liquor" at the assembled onlookers, and had indulged himself in blasphemous language. "From this merry prank, perversely enough, was conceived our present obscenity law, with the sparkling figure of Sir Charles its innocent and unwitting progenitor."[3]

The number of applications of the obscenity law in Great Britain was almost negligible. Before 1727 the Common Law did not hold obscene literature subject to indictment. Even after that date, there was generally great freedom for pre-Victorian poets and novelists. In the middle of the nineteenth century, however, all this was changed, for in 1857 the Obscene Publications Act was passed. The House of Lords was disturbed by the legislation, but was reassured by Lord Chief Justice Campbell that "the measure was intended to apply exclusively to works written for the single purpose of corrupting the morals of youth, and of a nature calculated to shock the common feelings of decency in any well-regulated mind."[4]

In 1868, Lord Chief Justice Cockburn applied Campbell's law in such a way that all of Campbell's reassurances became dead letters. In dealing with a pamphlet sensationally entitled *The Confessional Unmasked*, Cockburn declared in *Regina* v. *Hicklin*:

> The test of obscenity is this, whether the tendency of the matter charged as obscenity is to deprave and corrupt those whose minds are open to such immoral influences and into whose hands a publication of this sort may fall.[5]

This guide to determining whether or not a written work is obscene thereafter became the standard for all obscenity decisions in Great Britain and, later, in the United States. It should be noted that the Hicklin rule went far beyond the supposed concern of the original Act with the morals of the young. It made the test of obscenity the effect which the material in question would allegedly have upon those who were predisposed to being influenced by such material. It determined obscenity, in short, by the reactions, not of average people, but of people for whom any obscene matter would acquire great significance.

In the United States, censorship has had an erratic but long history. Several of the colonies, notably Virginia, did not welcome new ideas, but none were so vigorous in their attack upon them as were the inhabitants of Massachusetts Bay. In that tightly knit theocracy, anyone who displayed a unique inclination of the mind was likely to find himself the recipient of an invitation to move. Professor Thomas J. Wertenbaker tells the story of attorney Thomas Lechford, who wrote a book entitled *Of Prophesie* and made the mistake of asking a friend to read it. The friend was incensed by the book's contents and immediately forwarded it to Governor Winthrop, with the strong recommendation that it be burned instead of printed. The book may have achieved neither distinction, but Lechford was made as uncomfortable as possible.[6]

Although no formal censorship laws existed, censorship was practiced wherever someone sufficiently outraged the theocracy. In 1650, William Pynchon's *The Meritorious Price of Our Redemption* was condemned by the Massachusetts General Court (the legislative body), and Boston's executioner was ordered to burn it in the market place. In 1654 the General Court commanded all citizens to surrender to the authorities certain books teaching the beliefs of the Quakers; the books were to be burned. In 1669, before Thomas à Kempis' *Imitation of Christ* could be reprinted, the General Court had it revised to suit its own tastes. One of the saddest days for the New England clergy occurred in 1686 when Edmund Andros arrived in Boston to take over his duties as royal governor. On that day, the power of the theocracy to control the press was ended.

Great Britain continued to impose restrictions upon freedom of the press in her colonies, even though restraints had been ended in the mother country. But even these restrictions ceased to operate in 1725. Thereafter, there were a number of prosecutions against printers and publishers for seditious libel, the most famous being the case of the New York newspaperman John Peter Zenger.[7] We have already noted that, following the Revolution, the Sedition Act of 1798 imposed severe restraints upon the freedom of citizens of the newly established country. These restraints were ended, however, as soon as Jefferson became President. Political censorship was not to be revived until the two world wars.

Cultural censorship, on the other hand, was just beginning. The first prosecutions of books on the charge of obscenity took place in Pennsylvania (*Commonwealth v. Sharpless*, 1815) and in Massachusetts (*Commonwealth v. Holmes*, 1821). In the latter case, involving a book called *Memoirs of a Woman of Pleasure*, the court decided that obscene libel is a Common Law offense. There were, however, very few prosecutions for obscenity until after the Civil War. In 1842 Congress forbade the importation of obscene books, and in 1865 it declared illegal the mailing of obscene goods within the United States. A complete, comprehensive obscenity law was passed eight years later at the instigation of Anthony Comstock.[8]

Anthony Comstock is surely one of the most colorful and influential figures in the history of censorship. It might be said that he was the somber American counterpart of Thomas Bowdler, the British censor of Shakespeare and Gibbon, whose standard was: "If any word or expression is of such a nature that the first impression it excites is an impression of obscenity, that word ought not to be spoken nor written or printed; and if printed, it ought to be erased."[9]

Comstock was born in 1844, when state and federal governments were just beginning to take a few, ineffective steps against obscene literature. He was a deeply religious man with a strong sense of personal sin. His diary is full of cries of despair concerning his depraved nature, as in this passage from 1864:

> Sin, sin. Oh how much peace and happiness is sacrificed on thy altar. Seemed as though Devil had full sway over me today, went right into temptation, and then, Oh such love, Jesus snatched it away out of my reach. How good is he, how sinful am I. . . . O I deplore my sinful weak nature so much. If I could but live without sin, I should be the happiest soul living: but Sin, that foe that is ever lurking, stealing happiness from me. What a day will it be when the roaring Lion shall be bound & his wanderings cease, then will we have rest, the glorious rest free from sin.[10]

Comstock's life was without joy, although it assuredly had its moments of pleasure. He was appalled by what others would call the beauty of the Roman Catholic service of worship, which he deemed mere frivolity. During the Civil War he attended his first Mass and "soon became disgusted. Do not think it right to spend Sunday morn. in such manner. Seemed much like Theater."[11] His philosophy of life was summed up crisply: "I hate this milk and water system. Give me a man who dares to do right and one ready at *all times* to discharge his duty to the community and to God."[12]

Comstock's duty, as he understood it, was to attempt to improve the morals of other people by rendering obscene literature and photographs inaccessible. For years he was the secretary of the New York Society for the Suppression of Vice. He also inspired the founding of the Watch and Ward Society in Boston. Ever on the alert for dangers to public manners and morals, he attacked the dime novels which were so popular in the late nineteenth and early twentieth centuries as "devil-traps for the young."[13] He acquired his greatest fame, however, by prodding Congress into passing what came to be called the Comstock Law, which attempted to provide effective controls over the circulation of obscene materials in the mails. Comstock even had himself appointed a special postal agent in order to aid more directly in the suppression of obscenity. He was able to boast that he had destroyed more than fifty tons of indecent books, 28,425 pounds of plates for the printing of such books, almost four million obscene pictures, and 16,900 negatives for such pictures. He also credited himself with the dubious distinction of having driven fifteen people to suicide.[14]

Margaret Leech has said of him:

> Anthony Comstock was adapted to the folkways of his time and place. Often in the fight against obscenity he stood alone. Always he was in the van. But somewhere behind him an army of Puritans was solidly massed. For this reason, he was feared and hated—because he was so strong. Had his crusade run counter to the *mores* of his people, he would have been a pitiful figure, a martyr to his lonely ideal. But in him people cursed the spirit of enforced righteousness made palpable—fleshly and menacing, with ginger-colored whiskers and a warrant and a Post Office badge. He was the apotheosis, the fine flower of Puritanism.

When D. M. Bennett was tried in New York for the circulation of obscene literature, the assistant district attorney, William P. Fiero, made it clear that Comstock was well supported:

> This case is not entitled "Anthony Comstock against D. M. Bennett"; this case is not entitled "The Society for the Suppression of Vice against D. M. Bennett." Yes, it is. It is the United States against D. M. Bennett, and the United States is one great society for the suppression of vice.[15]

The aggressive pattern which Comstock set was followed by other moral reformers throughout the country, both during his lifetime and after it. Their cry was that of the niece of Don Quixote, who, eyeing the volumes of chivalric lore on her uncle's shelves, declared, "You must not pardon any of them, for they are all to blame. It would be better to toss them out of the window into the courtyard, make a heap of them, and then set fire to it; or else you can take them out to the stable yard and make a bonfire there where the smoke will not annoy anyone."[16]

For all his strength, Comstock met his match in a man whom he never knew personally—and probably never wanted to know. In 1905 George Bernard Shaw, erroneously assuming that Comstock had been responsible for the New York Public Library's decision to move the copy of his play *Man and Superman* into its reserved section, lashed out against Comstock with characteristic sarcasm: "Comstockery is the world's standing joke at the expense of the United States. Europe likes to hear of such things. It confirms the deep-seated conviction of the Old World that America is a provincial place, a second-rate country-town civilization after all."[17] Comstock retaliated several weeks later by suggesting to the police that Shaw's play about prostitution, *Mrs. Warren's Profession*, be suppressed. The police followed his advice, but the Court of Special Sessions decided that the play could not be banned.

Comstock's followers were not impressed by Shaw's objections. Adopting the procedures used so successfully by their hero, they sought out and had prosecuted under existing obscenity statutes a number of significant books. Since Boston and New York were the centers of the book publishing industry, they became the centers of the book banning industry. Before 1933, Arthur Schnitzler's *Reigin*, Theodore Dreiser's *The Genius* and *An American Tragedy*, Sherwood Anderson's *Dark Laughter*, Upton Sinclair's *Oil!*, and James Branch Cabell's *Jurgen* were condemned. All of Trotsky's works, Sinclair Lewis' *Elmer Gantry*, Radclyffe Hall's *The Well of Loneliness*, Aldous Huxley's *Antic Hay*, Ernest Hemingway's *The Sun Also Rises*, and Erich Maria Remarque's *All Quiet on the Western Front* were banned in one or more localities. Even the sale of Bertrand Russell's *What I Believe* was prohibited. The criterion of judgment was usually whether or not sex was discussed in an offensive manner. This was carried to such an extreme that Lenin's *State and Revolution* was seized in Boston in 1927 as *obscene!*

The protectors of the public's morals were, on occasion, more sensitive about their own reputations than they were about obscenity. *The American Mercury* for September, 1925, contained a hostile article about the Rev. J. Frank Chase, a Methodist minister and the secretary of Boston's Watch and Ward Society. Mr. Chase retaliated the following year by banning the April issue because of Herbert Asbury's "Hatrack," a story about a small-town prostitute which Chase found to be "immoral" and "full of filthy and degrading descriptions." The indomitable H. L. Mencken, editor of the magazine, decided to fight this attack and went to Boston to violate the ban. In a dramatic display of showmanship, he sold a copy of the April issue to Mr. Chase on "Brimstone Corner," whereupon Mencken was arrested. He won his case, however, and was also able to secure an injunction restricting the activities of the Watch and Ward Society.

The federal government, meanwhile, through its control of customs and the mails, was actively engaged in censoring literature. Adhering to the spirit of the Comstock Law, it excluded such works as Boccaccio's *Decameron*, Voltaire's *Candide*, and the complete works of Rabelais. It even succumbed to the complaints of the defeated Mr. Chase and banned the April issue of *The American Mercury* from the mails. Like local censors, however, the federal government was embarrassed from time to time by not having its left hand aware of what its right hand was doing. Thus, while the Post Office Department was lighting its bonfires for the warming of obscene books, those very books were being admitted through customs, and other books banned by customs were allowed to circulate freely through the mails. The power of customs was restricted in 1930 when a new Tariff Act deprived customs officials of their absolute authority; the Act required a jury trial in a federal court whenever a seizure was contested.[18]

The censors who followed Comstock's example were mostly private citizens. They had the support, however, of federal state, and local governments. Frequently their procedure was to enter a bookstore, buy a book that they deemed obscene, and then call in a policeman who was standing conveniently just outside the door. These censors were a kind of auxiliary police force or special squad in charge of the locality's morals. They depended entirely upon existing statutes for the success of their work. Hence, when the courts began to interpret obscenity laws more rigidly, these citizens received as great a setback as did the official censors.

Legal setbacks, at first infrequent, eventually crushed most of the censors under a landslide. In 1922 the New York Supreme Court decided, in a case involving Théophile Gautier's *Mademoiselle de Maupin*, that classics cannot be judged by the standards used for ordinary books. In a trial that resulted from the banning of Theodore Dreiser's *An American Tragedy* in Boston, only the so-called obscene parts of the book were placed before the court. This led to a change in the state law: after 1930, Massachusetts courts could prohibit the public sale, not of any book "containing obscene, indecent language," but only of "a book which is obscene." A book had to be read and judged as a whole.

The Hicklin rule had been adopted by United States courts in 1879, but it was not always regarded as infallible. In 1913, in the United States District Court of Southern New York, Judge Learned Hand expressed a dislike for the rule—a dislike which was later to be echoed by many others. Because the rule had become normative in American law, however, Judge Hand believed that he should follow it:

> I hope it is not improper for me to say that the rule as laid down, however consonant it may be with mid-Victorian morals, does not seem to me to answer to the understanding and morality of the present time. . . . I question whether in the end men will regard that as obscene which is honestly relevant to the adequate expression of innocent ideas, and whether they will not believe that truth and beauty are too precious to society at large to be mutilated in the interests of those most likely to pervert them to base uses. Indeed, it seems hardly likely that we are even today so lukewarm in our interest in letters or serious discussion as to be content to reduce our treatment of sex to the standard of a child's library in the supposed interest of a salacious few, or that shame will long prevent us from adequate portrayal of some of the most serious and beautiful sides of human nature. . . .
>
> Yet, if the time is not yet when men think innocent all that which is honestly germane to a pure subject, however little it may mince its words, still I scarcely think that they would forbid all which might corrupt the most corruptible, or that society is prepared to accept for its own limitations those which may perhaps be necessary to the weakest of its members. If there be no abstract definition, such as I have suggested, should not the word "obscene" be allowed to indicate the present critical point in the compromise between candor and shame at which the community may have arrived here and now? . . . To put thought in leash to the average conscience of the time is perhaps tolerable, but to fetter it by the necessities of the lowest and least capable seems a fatal policy.[19]

Twenty years later, Judge Hand's thoughts were embodied in a new rule for obscenity cases.

Notes

[1] Winston S. Churchill, *A History of the English-Speaking Peoples* (New York, Dodd, Mead 1957), vol. III, p. 168. For a very thorough and illuminating history of censorship in Britain down to the time of the American Revolution, see Frederick Seaton Siebert, *Freedom of the Press in England, 1476–1776* (Urbana, University of Illinois, 1952). For the story of the end of licensing, see Charles R. Gillett, *Burned Books; Neglected Chapters in British History and Literature* (New York, Columbia, 1932), vol. II, pp. 549–58.

[2] Thomas Babington Macaulay, *The History of England from the Accession of James II* (New York, Williams, n.d.) vol. IV, ch. xxi, p. 422.

[3]Leo M. Alpert, "Judicial Censorship of Obscene Literature," *Harvard Law Review*, Nov., 1938, p. 41. Earlier there had been a few cases, probably numbering not more than a dozen, involving prosecutions against books and pamphlets containing "lascivious" and "scurrilous" matter. A work by a nephew of John Milton faced such a charge. See Gillett, *op. cit.*, vol. I, pp. 90–93, 263–64.

[4]Quoted by Huntington Cairns, "Freedom of Expression in Literature," *The Annals of the American Academy of Political and Social Science*, Nov., 1938, p. 81.

[5]Quoted, *ibid.*

[6]Thomas J. Wertenbaker, *The First Americans 1607–1690* (New York, Macmillan, 1927), pp. 238–39; see also Isabel M. Calder, "Thomas Lechford (fl. 1629–1642)," *Dictionary of American Biography* (New York, Scribner, 1933), vol. XI, p. 87.

[7]See Arthur M. Schlesinger, Sr., *Prelude to Independence, the Newspaper War on Britain, 1764–1776* (New York, Knopf, 1957), pp. 61–65 *et passim*.

[8]Norman St. John-Stevas, *Obscenity and the Law* (London, Secker & Warburg, 1956), p. 160. See also Cairns, *op. cit.*, p. 81; Gillett, *op. cit.*, vol. I, pp. 256–59, and Thomas B. Leary and J. Roger Noall, "Entertainment: Public Pressures and the Law," *Harvard Law Review*, Dec., 1957, p. 347, note 150.

[9]Quoted by Richard Hanser, "Shakespeare, Sex . . . and Dr. Bowdler," *The Saturday Review*, Apr. 23, 1955, p. 50.

[10]Quoted by Heywood Broun and Margaret Leech, *Anthony Comstock, Roundsman of the Lord* (New York, Boni, 1927), pp. 55–56.

[11]*Ibid.*, p. 38.

[12]*Ibid.*, p. 69.

[13]Mary Noel, "Dime Novels," *American Heritage*, Feb., 1956, p. 55.

[14]Alpert, *op. cit.*, p. 57; Mark Van Doren, "Anthony Comstock (1844–1915)," *Dictionary of American Biography* (New York, Scribner, 1930), vol. IV, p. 331.

[15]Broun and Leech, *op cit.*, pp. 88–89.

[16]Miguel de Cervantes, *Don Quixote de la Mancha*, trans. Samuel Putnam (New York, Viking, 1949), I:6, p. 52.

[17]Quoted by Morris L. Ernst and Alexander Lindey, *The Censor Marches On* (New York, Doubleday, Doran, 1940), p. 60. See also Broun and Leech, *op. cit.*, pp. 229–36.

[18]For an interesting list of volumes which the censors have not liked, see Anne Lyon Haight, *Banned Books* (New York, Bowker, 1955). Note also Ernst and Lindey, *op. cit.*, ch. i, and Edgar Kemler, *The Irreverent Mr. Mencken* (Boston, Little, Brown, 1950), ch. xiii.

[19]*U.S. v. Kennerley*, 209 Fed. 119 (Southern District, New York), quoted by St. John-Stevas, *op, cit.*, p. 161. At this point, a comment by Heywood Broun on Anthony Comstock seems relevant: "Anthony Comstock may have been entirely correct in his assumption that the division of living creatures into male and female was a vulgar mistake, but a conspiracy of silence about the matter will hardly alter the facts." Broun and Leech, *op. cit.*, p. 274.

WOMEN FIGHT BACK

Susan Brownmiller

In Against Our Will: Men, Women and Rape *(1975), Susan Brownmiller became an early and effective advocate for those women who have felt that members of the women's movement are wrong to side with liberals who resist legal efforts to censor pornography. In the following excerpt from* Against Our Will, *Brownmiller argues her central point: that "Pornography, like rape, is a male invention, designed to dehumanize women, to reduce the female to an object of sexual access, not to free sensuality from moralistic or parental inhibition."*

The theory of aggressive male domination over women as a natural right is so deeply embedded in our cultural value system that all recent attempts to expose it — in movies, television commercials or even in children's textbooks — have barely managed to scratch the surface. As I see it, the problem is not that polarized role playing (man as doer; woman as bystander) and exaggerated portrayals of the female body as passive sex object are simply "demeaning" to women's dignity and self-conception, or that such portrayals fail to provide positive role models for young girls, but that cultural sexism is a conscious form of female degradation designed to boost the male ego by offering "proof" of his native superiority (and of female inferiority) everywhere he looks.

Critics of the women's movement, when they are not faulting us for being slovenly, straggly-haired, construction-booted, whiny sore losers who refuse to accept our female responsibilities, often profess to see a certain inexplicable Victorian primness and anti-sexual prudery in our attitudes and responses. "Come on, gals," they say in essence, "don't you know that your battle for female liberation is part of our larger battle for sexual liberation? Free yourselves from all your old hang-ups! Stop pretending that you are actually offended by those four-letter words and animal noises we grunt in your direction on the street in appreciation of your womanly charms. When we plaster your faceless naked body on the cover of our slick magazines, which sell millions of copies, we do it in sensual obeisance to your timeless beauty — which, by our estimation, ceases to be timeless at age twenty or thereabouts. If we feel the need for a little fun and go out and rent the body of a prostitute for a half hour or so, we are merely engaging in a mutual act between two consenting adults, and what's it got to do with you? When we turn our movie theaters into showcases for pornographic films and convert our bookstores to outlets for mass-produced obscene smut, not only should you marvel at the wonders of our free-enterprise system, but you should applaud us for pushing back the barriers of repressive middle-class morality, and for our strenuous defense of all the civil liberties you hold so dear, because we have made obscenity the new frontier in defense of freedom of speech, that noble liberal tradition. And surely you're not against civil liberties and freedom of speech, now, are you?"

Susan Brownmiller, "Women Fight Back," *Against Our Will: Men, Women and Rape* (New York: Simon & Schuster, 1975).

The case against pornography and the case against toleration of prostitution are central to the fight against rape, and if it angers a large part of the liberal population to be so informed, then I would question in turn the political understanding of such liberals and their true concern for the rights of women. Or to put it more gently, a feminist analysis approaches all prior assumptions, including those of the great, unquestioned liberal tradition, with a certain open-minded suspicion, for all prior traditions have worked against the cause of women and no set of values, including that of tolerant liberals, is above review or challenge. After all, the liberal *politik* has had less input from the feminist perspective than from any other modern source; it does not by its own considerable virtue embody a perfection of ideals, it has no special claim on goodness, rather, it is most receptive to those values to which it has been made sensitive by others. . . .

Pornography has been so thickly glossed over with the patina of chic these days in the name of verbal freedom and sophistication that important distinctions between freedom of political expression (a democratic necessity), honest sex education for children (a societal good) and ugly smut (the deliberate devaluation of the role of women through obscene, distorted depictions) have been hopelessly confused. Part of the problem is that those who traditionally have been the most vigorous opponents of porn are often those same people who shudder at the explicit mention of any sexual subject. Under their watchful, vigilante eyes, frank and free dissemination of educational materials relating to abortion, contraception, the act of birth, and female biology in general is also dangerous, subversive and dirty. (I am not unmindful that a frank and free discussion of rape, "the unspeakable crime," might well give these righteous vigilantes further cause to shudder.) Because the battle lines were falsely drawn a long time ago, before there was a vocal women's movement, the anti-pornography forces appear to be, for the most part, religious, Southern, conservative and right-wing, while the pro-porn forces are identified as Eastern, atheistic and liberal.

But a woman's perspective demands a totally new alignment, or at least a fresh appraisal. The majority report of the President's Commission on Obscenity and Pornography (1970), a report that argued strongly for the removal of all legal restrictions on pornography, soft and hard, made plain that 90 percent of all pornographic material is geared to the male heterosexual market (the other 10 percent is geared to the male homosexual taste), that buyers of porn are "predominantly white, middle-class, middle-aged married males" and that the graphic depictions, the meat and potatoes of porn, are of the naked female body and of the multiplicity of acts done to that body.

Discussing the content of stag films, "a familiar and firmly established part of the American scene," the commission report dutifully, if foggily, explained, "Because pornography historically has been thought to be primarily a masculine interest, the emphasis in stag films seems to represent the preferences of the middle-class American male. Thus male homosexuality and bestiality are relatively rare, while lesbianism is rather common."

The commissioners in this instance had merely verified what purveyors of porn have always known: hard-core pornography is not a celebration of sexual freedom; it is a cynical exploitation of female sexual activity through the device of making all such activity, and consequently all females, "dirty." Heterosexual male consumers of pornography are frankly turned on by watching lesbians in action (although never in the final scenes, but always as a curtain raiser); they are turned off with the sudden swiftness of a water faucet by watching naked men act upon each other. One study quoted in the commission report came to the unastounding conclusion that "seeing a stag film in the presence of male peers bolsters masculine esteem." Indeed. The men in groups who watch the films, it is important to note, are *not* naked.

When male response to pornography is compared to female response, a pronounced difference in attitude emerges. According to the commission, "Males report being more highly aroused by depictions of nude females, and show more interest in depictions of nude females than [do] females." Quoting the figures of Alfred Kinsey, the commission noted that a majority of males (77 percent) were "aroused" by visual depictions of explicit sex while a majority of females (68 percent) were not aroused. Further, "females more often than males reported 'disgust' and 'offense.'"

From whence comes this female disgust and offense? Are females sexually backward or more conservative by nature? The gut distaste that a majority of women feel when we look at pornography, a distaste that, incredibly, it is no longer fashionable to admit, comes, I think, from the gut knowledge that we and our bodies are being stripped, exposed and contorted for the purpose of ridicule to bolster that "masculine esteem" which gets its kick and sense of power from viewing females as anonymous, panting playthings, adult toys, dehumanized objects to be used, abused, broken and discarded.

This, of course, is also the philosophy of rape. It is no accident (for what else could be its purpose?) that females in the pornographic genre are depicted in two cleanly delineated roles: as virgins who are caught and "banged" or as nymphomaniacs who are never sated. The most popular and prevalent pornographic fantasy combines the two: an innocent, untutored female is raped and "subjected to unnatural practices" that turn her into a raving, slobbering nymphomaniac, a dependent sexual slave who can never get enough of the big, male cock.

There can be no "equality" in porn, no female equivalent, no turning of the tables in the name of bawdy fun. Pornography, like rape, is a male invention, designed to dehumanize women, to reduce the female to an object of sexual access, not to free sensuality from moralistic or parental inhibition. The staple of porn will always be the naked female body, breasts and genitals exposed, because as man devised it, her naked body is the female's "shame," her private parts the private property of man, while his are the ancient, holy, universal, patriarchal instrument of his power, his rule by force over *her*.

Pornography is the undiluted essence of anti-female propaganda. Yet the very same liberals who were so quick to understand the method and purpose behind the mighty propaganda machine of Hitler's Third Reich, the consciously spewed-out anti-Semitic caricatures and obscenities that gave an ideological base to the Holocaust and the Final Solution, the very same liberals who, enlightened by blacks, searched their own conscience and came to understand that their tolerance of "nigger" jokes and portrayals of shuffling, rolling-eyed servants in movies perpetuated the degrading myths of black inferiority and gave an ideological base to the continuation of black oppression — these very same liberals now fervidly maintain that the hatred and contempt for women that find expression in four-letter words used as expletives and in what are quaintly called "adult" or "erotic" books and movies are a valid extension of freedom of speech that must be preserved as a Constitutional right.

To defend the right of a lone, crazed American Nazi to grind out propaganda calling for the extermination of all Jews, as the ACLU has done in the name of free speech, is, after all, a self-righteous and not particularly courageous stand, for American Jewry is not currently threatened by storm troopers, concentration camps and imminent extermination, but I wonder if the ACLU's position might change if, come tomorrow morning, the bookstores and movie theaters lining Forty-second Street in New York City were devoted not to the humiliation of women by rape and torture, as they currently are, but to a systematized, commercially successful propaganda machine depicting the sadistic pleasures of gassing Jews or lynching blacks?

Is this analogy extreme? Not if you are a woman who is conscious of the ever-present threat of rape and the proliferation of a cultural ideology that makes it sound like "liberated" fun. The majority report of the President's Commission on Obscenity and Pornography tried to pooh-pooh the opinion of law enforcement agencies around the country that claimed their own concrete experience with offenders who were caught with the stuff led them to conclude that pornographic material is a causative factor in crimes of sexual violence. The commission maintained that it was not possible at this time to scientifically prove or disprove such a connection.

But does one need scientific methodology in order to conclude that the anti-female propaganda that permeates our nation's cultural output promotes a climate in which acts of sexual hostility directed against women are not only tolerated but ideologically encouraged? A similar debate has raged for many years over whether or not the extensive glorification of violence (the gangster as hero; the loving treatment accorded bloody shoot-'em-ups in movies, books and on TV) has a causal effect, a direct relationship to the rising rate of crime, particularly among youth. Interestingly enough, in this area — nonsexual and not specifically related to abuses against women — public opinion seems to be swinging to the position that explicit violence in the entertainment media does have a deleterious effect; it makes violence commonplace, numbingly routine and no longer morally shocking.

More to the point, those who call for a curtailment of scenes of violence in movies and on television in the name of sensitivity, good taste and what's best for our children are not accused of being pro-censorship or against freedom of speech. Similarly, minority group organizations, black, Hispanic, Japanese, Italian, Jewish, or American Indian, that campaign against ethnic slurs and demeaning portrayals in movies, on television shows and in commercials are perceived as waging a just political fight, for if a minority group claims to be offended by a specific portrayal, be it Little Black Sambo or the Frito Bandido, and relates it to a history of ridicule and oppression, few liberals would dare to trot out a Constitutional argument in theoretical opposition, not if they wish to maintain their liberal credentials. Yet when it comes to the treatment of women, the liberal consciousness remains fiercely obdurate, refusing to be budged, for the sin of appearing square or prissy in the age of the so-called sexual revolution has become the worst offense of all.

A law that reflects the female reality and a social system that no longer shuts women out of its enforcement and does not promote a masculine ideology of rape will go a long way toward the elimination of crimes of sexual violence, but the last line of defense shall always be our female bodies and our female minds. In making rape a *speakable* crime, not a matter of shame, the women's movement has already fired the first retaliatory shots in a war as ancient as civilization. . . .

What Is a Civil Libertarian to Do When Pornography Becomes So Bold?

Moderated by *Walter Goodman*

This debate is between Ernest van den Haag, a conservative professor of social philosophy at New York University, and Gay Talese, the liberal author of Thy Neighbor's Wife, *a description and analysis of sexual attitudes and practices in the United States.*

As pornography has proliferated across the land, from centers of sexual technology such as New York and Los Angeles to less advanced communities, a suspicion that something may be awry has begun to nag at even that enlightened vanguard which once strove to save Lady Chatterley from the philistines. Having opened the door to sex for art's sake, they have found that it is no longer possible to close it against sex for profit's sake.

Where does duty lie today for the dutiful civil libertarian confronted by efforts around the country to prosecute the purveyors of porn? One may wish that Al Goldstein, an avant-garde publisher of the stuff, would go away, but no civil libertarian can cheer the efforts by lawmen in Wichita, Kansas, to have him put away. One might doubt that Harry Reems, who has filled many X-rated screens, is contributing much to the art of the cinema, yet no civil libertarian wants the assistant U.S. Attorney in Memphis, Tennessee, to clap him in irons. What to do?

To grapple with this matter, I brought together two figures known to have provocative—and sharply conflicting—views on the subject: author Gay Talese, whose ongoing research for a book about sex in America includes the management of two New York City massage parlors, and psychoanalyst Ernest van den Haag, adjunct professor of social philosophy at New York University and a favorite "expert witness" of pornography prosecutors everywhere.

Our conversation began with an effort by Professor van den Haag to identify the animal which he believes ought to be locked up:

VAN DEN HAAG: I would call pornographic whatever is blatantly offensive to the standards of the community.

TALESE: But does the public have the right to ban *Ulysses* because some people find it offensive?

VAN DEN HAAG: I think anyone who reads *Ulysses* for the sake of pornographic interests ought to get a medal! The characteristic focus of pornography is precisely that it leaves out all human context and reduces the action to interaction between organs and orifices—and that I find obscene, degrading to sex and dehumanizing to its audiences.

"What Is a Civil Libertarian to Do When Pornography Becomes So Bold?" Moderated by Walter Goodman. *The New York Times*, 21 November 1976.

TALESE:	So if you have a picture of a girl, including the genitals, then that is pornographic.
VAN DEN HAAG:	Not necessarily.
TALESE:	But if she's making love it would be?
VAN DEN HAAG:	I'm not even opposed to that altogether. But, if the lovemaking picture focuses on the operation of the genitals . . .
TALESE:	You mean if it shows the genitals while the love-making is going on?
VAN DEN HAAG:	If the genitals are shown incidentally, that does not greatly disturb me. But if it is clearly focused on the operation of the genitals and the persons are only shown incidentally, then I think the stuff is pornographic.
TALESE:	There's no agreement on a definition at all, even by the people who want to ban it. Obscenity is the *one* crime that cannot be defined. Unlike murder, burglary, forgery, the word means different things to different people — to judges, to newspaper editors, to pornographic film-makers.
VAN DEN HAAG:	That's why we have courts of law and lawyers.
TALESE:	And it means different things to different lawyers — it's the most imprecise of crimes.
VAN DEN HAAG:	Gay, if you were to see a man walking down the street, fully clothed except that his genitals were exposed, would you regard that as obscene?
TALESE:	On the issue of whether the cop on the beat has the right to stop public behavior that is unseemly and offensive we have no quarrel. But no policeman ought to have the right to stop two homosexuals in a Holiday Inn in Teaneck, New Jersey, from doing whatever they want together. They have that right, and I have the right to see a film or a play even if it is considered offensive by Sidney Baumgarten of the Mayor's Midtown Enforcement Project. I don't want policemen to tell me what is moral or immoral in my private life. I think we have too much government and where sex is concerned, I want next to no government.
VAN DEN HAAG:	I certainly agree, Gay, that you or I should be allowed to indulge in sexual acts in our homes. That's our business. I am not in the least disturbed about that. But when anyone can see the spectacle we are no longer dealing with a private matter, but with a public matter.
TALESE:	If I want to pay five dollars to go into a theater to go see "Deep Throat," that's a private matter.
VAN DEN HAAG:	Then you regard a public spectacle as a private act.
TALESE:	How about buying a book?
VAN DEN HAAG:	If it is publicly available to anyone who pays the price, it's a public matter.
TALESE:	So, according to you, I have the right to read *Ulysses* or *The Story of O* or *The Sex Life of a Cop* in my home — only I shouldn't be allowed to get it into my home in the first place.

VAN DEN HAAG:	The police should not come into your home and check what you're reading — but the police can accuse a seller of selling something pornographic. The matter can then be brought up before a jury and if the jury feels that what the seller sold publicly is pornography, then the seller can be convicted.
TALESE:	So you'd ban such magazines as *Playboy* or *Oui* or *Screw*?
VAN DEN HAAG:	I have testified against *Screw* and I am in favor of banning it. As for *Playboy* and so on, I would leave those to juries in particular communities. If I'm invited as an expert to testify about the effects they will have on a particular community, I will testify that these effects are deleterious, but it is not for me to decide whether they should be prohibited or not.
GOODMAN:	Ernest, why should it be any more the business of a jury what Gay likes to read or watch than it is what he likes to do in bed?
VAN DEN HAAG:	Gay's view — one that is widespread — is that society consists of individuals, each independent of each other, and that the task of the government is merely to protect one individual from interference by others. That is not my view. My view is that no society can survive unless there are bonds among its members, unless its members identify with each other, recognize each other as humans and do not think of each other simply as sources of pleasure or unpleasure. For once they do, then they may come to think of people as kinds of insects. If one disturbs you, you kill it. Once you no longer recognize that a person is fully human, like yourself, you can do what the Germans did to the Jews — use the gold in their teeth. Human solidarity is based on our ability to think of each other not purely as means, but as ends in ourselves. Now the point of all pornography, in my opinion, is that it invites us to regard the other person purely as a subject of exploitation for sexual pleasure.
GOODMAN:	Gay, am I right in assuming that you don't agree that pornography has such dire consequences?
TALESE:	Government interference in these areas is usually justified on the grounds that obscenity is harmful to the morals of society, harmful to family life, harmful to juveniles. But in fact there is no proof that exposure to pornography leads to anti-social behavior. There is no proof that watching a pornographic movie leads anybody to go out and commit rape.
VAN DEN HAAG:	You're not getting my point. I do not maintain that reading pornography leads to an increase in crime. It may, but I don't think there's conclusive evidence either way. I feel that the main damage pornography does is not to the individual but to the social climate.
TALESE:	Tell me how.
VAN DEN HAAG:	You and I both write books, and our books are somehow meant to influence what people feel and think. Sexual mores, you certainly will agree, have changed over the past century. Why

have they changed? Basically because of the ideas of people who write books, make movies, produce things. The biology of sex hasn't changed. What has changed is our perception of it and our reaction to it. So I don't think it can be denied that books do have an influence. If that is so, we come to the question of whether the government has the right or duty to limit it. Here my point is a very simple one. Every community has a right to protect what it regards as its important shared values. In India, I would vote for the prohibition against the raising of pigs for slaughter. In the United States, where a certain amount of sexual reticence has been a central value of traditional culture, I would vote for the rights of communities to protect their sexual reticence.

TALESE: And I'm saying that the government should not have the right to deal with this "crime" that it cannot define. The Supreme Court has never been able to define what is obscene to the satisfaction of most Americans. If you are going to give government the power to tell us what is obscene and to restrict our freedom to read books, see films or look at pictures, if you give government that kind of power over the individual, you are not going to maintain a democracy.

VAN DEN HAAG: I am for freedom, too, but you ignore the fact that freedom can be used for good or bad. For instance, if the Weimar Republic had banned its political pornographers such as Hitler, then perhaps six million Jews would not have been killed. The dogmatic insistence on freedom as the only value to be protected by the government disregards such things as survival and community traditions which are essential to survival.

TALESE: But you seem to forget that Hitler himself opposed pornography. Almost the first thing he did on taking power was to ban *Ideal Marriage*, a classic work on sex and marriage.

GOODMAN: Would you put any limits at all on individual liberties in this area, Gay?

TALESE: I believe there should be censorship — in the home. I have two daughters, and in my home I do exercise censorship. I subscribe to magazines and newspapers that I do not leave on the coffee table. But I do not want government to tell me what I can have in my house or what I can have my daughters read.

VAN DEN HAAG: I congratulate you on having this family that you describe. Let me point out that many American families are not so structured. Not all parents are able to exercise such parental discipline.

GOODMAN: But isn't Gay's response to government intrusions into family life in accord with your own principles as a conservative?

VAN DEN HAAG: In an ideal society, things that we now regulate by law, would be regulated by custom and by the authority of parents. We don't live in this ideal society. The authority of parents has been undermined by all kinds of things, starting with progres-

	sive education. If we could strengthen the hand of parents and integrate families more, that would be much better. I have found no way of doing so for the time being.
TALESE:	So you're willing to give this power to a policeman.
VAN DEN HAAG:	I am not proposing that we trust the government with the power of censorship. I'm opposed to censorship, opposed to prior restraint which is unconstitutional. I am in favor of traditional American legislation. Whereby each state, and more recently each community, may determine for itself what it wishes and what it does not wish to be publicly sold. In each case, Ralph Ginzburg or Al Goldstein or you or anyone can publish whatever he wishes. Until the bounds have been exceeded . . .
TALESE:	What bounds? It's all so hypocritical. One night these people have been at an American Legion smoker enjoying hard-core porn and the next day they are deciding to put a pornographer in jail. What a member of the jury is likely to say in public has nothing to do with the way he behaves in private. That seems to me socially unhealthy. Many of the people who would go on record to have Times Square closed down because it has too many massage parlors patronize the places. We're dealing here with something very private — sexual desires. Very private.
GOODMAN:	But is the expression of these desires around an area such as Times Square really all that private? It seems pretty public to me.
TALESE:	Sure, Times Square has always been a center of public entertainment. What some people can't stand is that it is today a center of entertainment for the working class instead of for the elite. There are two kinds of pornography. You have the pornography for the working man, like the 42nd Street peep shows, and you have the "legitimate theater," where the elite can see "Let My People Come," "Oh, Calcutta!" or the works of Edward Albee or Arthur Miller or Tennessee Williams. The government does not as readily interfere with the pornography of the elite as it does with the pornography of the man who buys his magazine at the corner newsstand, which is the museum of the man in the street, or the man who pays 25 cents to see copulating couples in a coin-operated machine. Pornography is primarily denied to the blue collar classes. That has always been the case. Strong government tries always to control the masses — just as much in China and Cuba as in Times Square. The people who get their pleasure from going to an art gallery to look at Goya's "The Naked Maja" aren't bothered by government.
GOODMAN:	Ernest, under your definition of pornography, is there any difference between a picture of a copulating couple on a museum wall and in the centerfold of a girly magazine?
VAN DEN HAAG:	Yes, effect and intent are different, and I think the courts are

correct in taking the context into consideration. That is, if Hugh Hefner had put "The Naked Maja" in Playboy a few years ago, it might have become pornographic in that context though Goya had not intended it that way.

TALESE: So pornography is all right for the elite, but not for the working man.

VAN DEN HAAG: It may appear that way, but the reason, as you yourself pointed out, is that the working man gets his pornography in a more public way. A theater at which you've made a reservation and paid $10 is much less public than the 25-cent arcade; therefore, there is more justification, if you are against pornography, to intervene against one than against the other.

GOODMAN: You don't deny, Gay, that Times Square has in fact become a place of public pornography.

TALESE: Yes, our sensibilities are assaulted. I wish the 42nd Street pornographer would be more subtle. But people have as much right to put a quarter in a machine as to pay $5 for "Deep Throat" or $10 for "Let My People Come." I do not want to give to law enforcement officials the right to clean up Times Square, to deny pornography to those who want it. If crimes are being committed, people being mugged, that should be prevented. But nobody is forced to go into a peep show or a massage parlor or to pay for sex with a prostitute.

GOODMAN: I take it you're opposed to laws against prostitution.

TALESE: I would really like to see prostitution legalized, but I know that would be the worst thing for prostitution, because it would mean that women would have to be fingerprinted.

VAN DEN HAAG: You would simply decriminalize it.

TALESE: I would like to see that happen.

GOODMAN: And you, Ernest?

VAN DEN HAAG: For call girls yes; for street prostitution no.

GOODMAN: Isn't that a trifle elitist, as Gay terms it?

VAN DEN HAAG: No. A call girl is an entirely private proposition. You call her. In the case of the street prostitute, the initiative must come from the soliciting girl, and that makes a difference.

TALESE: Have you ever been assaulted by a prostitute on the street? All the girls do is ask a question.

VAN DEN HAAG: There's more to it than that. In the United States, for some reason, prostitution has always been connected with crime. The sort of thing that exists around Times Square attracts not only prostitutes and their customers, but people who prey on prostitutes and customers and make the whole area unsafe. I believe that crime must not only be prosecuted; it must also be prevented.

TALESE: What offends the white New Yorker, the customer on his way to the bus terminal, about Times Square is that he walks through the neighborhood and sees the great number of blacks there — the black prostitutes and black pimps. That's what makes people fearful. There is more crime all over the country today, but it has nothing to do with prostitutes working Eighth Avenue. You see, I don't think it's a crime to have sex with a person. The prostitutes are there, on the street in great numbers, because men — not the children Ernest is legitimately concerned about but middle class married white men — want them. For some reason, they find prostitutes necessary. That's their private affair. I don't want to have Times Square become acceptable to Franco Spain. I don't want government to clean it up.

VAN DEN HAAG: You're saying that people should be allowed to have what they want. But should people be forced to have what they don't want? Suppose that a town in Ohio votes that it doesn't want prostitutes on its streets or pornographic movies? You are in favor of pornography in principle, regardless of what the majority wants.

TALESE: I am in favor of freedom of expression.

VAN DEN HAAG: The men who wrote Article I of the Bill of Rights intended to make sure that the government would not suppress opposition. They did not intend to include such things as pornography.

TALESE: They wrote that Congress shall make no law abridging freedom of speech or the press; they didn't add, "except when it comes to sexual expression."

GOODMAN: Gentlemen, I am not sure how much light we have shed on pornography but your respective positions are clear as day. And I thank you.

FIRST AMENDMENT PIXILLATION
William Buckley

William Buckley is the founder of National Review, *a conservative magazine, and the moderator of* Firing Line, *a television discussion show. The point of Buckley's short essay, which originally appeared in* National Review, *is simple: The First Amendment was never intended to protect obscenity, nor should it now be "stretched" to protect it. In fact, Buckley says, until recently no one ever suggested that the First Amendment was supposed to protect obscenity.*

Freedom of the press is in mortal peril again, this time out in Kansas, where pseudonymous postal officials tricked New York pornographer Al Goldstein into mailing them his brainchildren, *Screw* and *Smut.* Civil libertarians are swarming to the defense of Goldstein and his former partner, one James Buckley (don't even ask), who are now on trial on federal charges of mailing obscene materials. "*Screw* is a despicable publication," says Harvard's Alan Dershowitz, "but that's what the First Amendment was designed to protect." False. That's what the First Amendment is currently *used* to protect, but . . . well, class, let's have a short review.

Until very recently nobody suggested that the First Amendment had been intended to protect obscenity. Or that it should be *stretched* to protect it. As for the first point, the record is clear: obscenity, like incitement to riot, has traditionally been illegal. And the intentions of the Framers are limned with shocking clarity in Leonard Levy's *Legacy of Suppression.* Judge Wolsey's famous ruling in *Ulysses,* let it be recalled, denied that *Ulysses* was obscene simply as a matter of fact (more emetic than aphrodisiac, he sniffed), without faintly suggesting that nothing was obscene, or that the law should not take cognizance of — and punish — obscene publications. As a matter of fact, the U.S. struggled along for almost two centuries uninundated by the likes of *Screw,* and is it suggested that during those years American thought was stultified? As for the contention that the First Amendment should be stretched, well, that is incompatible with the principle of the rule of law. Let those who want it changed get another Amendment. Of course they can't: their whole case depends heavily on forging a phony constitutional pedigree for their libertarianism, and only deludes people because they have succeeded in intimating that the Constitution has already committed us, whether we like it or not, to . . . *Screw.*

Yet here is Geoffrey Stone of the University of Chicago: "If a publisher wants to play it safe, he has to attempt to figure out what is the most restrictive, conservative notion of obscenity in the country and not publish anything that violates that standard. The net effect is that the rights of citizens in every other location are impaired." And Dershowitz: "Any community can act as the censor of any other community — that's small-town censorship." If *Screw* is illegal in Paw Paw, Michigan, you see, it will be impossible or unprofitable to publish it in New York, and the mind of every American is manacled. One might as well argue that the remaining dry counties in Kansas inexorably will bring Prohibition back to New York. Actually

William Buckley, "First Amendment Pixillation," *National Review* 29 (1977).

it is the "libertarian" forces who are battling to impose a single rule everywhere—and who, in the name of "individual" rights, would deny citizens the right to act as a community for certain purposes. As usual, their demand for "freedom" is for a kind of freedom that in fact must come at the expense of a structural principle of real freedom: the principle of federalism.

By all means *do* shed a tear for the First Amendment—not because it is threatened in Kansas, but because it is expounded in the nation's top law schools by such minds as those of Messrs. Stone and Dershowitz.

Research on How Women Experience the Impact of Pornography

Diana E. H. Russell

Diana Russell's research goes to the heart of the most important question in the controversy over pornography: its effects. Through the years, those who do not want pornography censored have often argued (1) that it is impossible to trace the effects of pornography on behavior, (2) that pornography has no effect, or (3) that it has a good effect. Russell thinks that all three of these conclusions are wrong. In her research on the effects of pornography, Diana Russell asked a sampling of 933 San Francisco women: "Have you ever been upset by anyone trying to get you to do what they'd seen in pornographic pictures, movies, or books?" Obviously, Russell's statistical and (X-rated) anecdotal summary of the responses to the question will be useful to you if you are attempting to build a case for pornography's negative effects on men and women or if you intend to argue that we ought to censor it.

Research on how women experience the impact of pornography has so far been of little interest to male researchers. I would therefore like to present some preliminary results from my own research.

Nine hundred thirty-three women 18 years and older, who were living in San Francisco during the summer of 1978, were interviewed to ascertain the prevalence of sexual assault in that city. These women were drawn from a random-household sample obtained by a San Francisco public-opinion polling firm — Field Research Associates. The women in the study were asked the following question: "Have you ever been upset by anyone trying to get you to do what they'd seen in pornographic pictures, movies, or books?" Of the 929 women who answered this question, 89 (10 percent) said they had been upset by such an experience at least once, while 840 (90 percent) said they had no such experience. Since the sample is a representative one, one can predict from this finding that 10 percent of the adult female population in San Francisco would say that they have been upset by men having seen something in pornography and then trying to get the women to do what they'd seen. Of course, it is possible that the women may be wrong in thinking that the men were inspired by what they had seen in the pornographic pictures, movies, or books. On the other hand, there are apt to be many instances of upsetting sexual contact in which the woman was unaware that the man's idea came from having viewed pornography; these instances would not get picked up by this question.

Those who answered "yes" to the question were then asked to describe the experience that upset them the most. As will be noted in some of the replies quoted below, although most of the women were able to avoid doing what was asked

Diana E. H. Russell, "Research on How Women Experience the Impact of Pornography," *Pornography and Censorship*, eds. David Copp and Susan Wendell (Buffalo, N.Y.: Prometheus Books, 1983).

or demanded of them, others were not so fortunate. And even in cases where the behavior was avoided, the woman often ended up feeling harassed and/or humiliated.

SELECTED ANSWERS TO PORNOGRAPHY QUESTIONS:

Have you ever been upset by anyone trying to get you to do what they'd seen in pornographic pictures, movies, or books? IF YES: Could you tell me briefly about the experience that upset you the most?

Ms. A:	Urinating in someone's mouth.
Ms. B:	It was a three-girls-and-him situation. We had sex. I was really young—like fourteen.
Ms. C:	He was a lover. He'd go to porno movies, then he'd come home and say, "I saw this in a movie. Let's try it." I felt really exploited, like I was being put in a mold.
Ms. D:	I was staying at this guy's house. He tried to make me have oral sex with him. He said he'd seen far-out stuff in movies, and that it would be fun to mentally and physically torture a woman.
Ms. E:	It was physical slapping and hitting. It wasn't a turn-on; it was more a feeling of being used as an object. What was most upsetting was that he thought it would be a turn-on.
Ms. F:	He'd read something in a pornographic book, and then he wanted to live it out. It was too violent for me to do something like that. It was basically getting dressed up and spanking. Him spanking me. I refused to do it.
Ms. G:	He forced me to have oral sex with him when I had no desire to do it.
Ms. H:	This couple who had just read a porno book wanted to try the groupie number with four people. They tried to persuade my boyfriend to persuade me. They were running around naked, and I felt really uncomfortable.
Ms. I:	It was S & M stuff. I was asked if I would participate in being beaten up. It was a proposition, it never happened. I didn't like the idea of it.
INTERVIEWER:	Did anything else upset you?
Ms. I:	Anal intercourse. I have been asked to do that, but I don't enjoy it at all. I have *had* to do it, *very* occasionally.
Ms. J:	My husband enjoys pornographic movies. He tries to get me to do things he finds exciting in movies. They include twosomes and threesomes. I always refuse.
	Also, I was always upset with his ideas about putting objects in my vagina, until I learned this is not as deviant as I used to think. He used to force me or put whatever he enjoyed into me.
Ms. K:	He forced me to go down on him. He said he'd been going to porno movies. He'd seen this and wanted me to do it. He also

wanted to pour champagne on my vagina. I got beat up because I didn't want to do it. He pulled my hair and slapped me around. After that I went ahead and did it, but there was no feeling in it.

Ms. L: I was newly divorced when this date talked about S & M and I said, "You've got to be nuts. Learning to experience pleasure through pain! But it's your pleasure and my pain!" I was very upset. The whole idea that someone thought I would want to sacrifice myself and have pain and bruises. It's a sick mentality. This was when I first realized there were many men out there who believe this.

Ms. M: Anal sex. First he attempted gentle persuasion, I guess. He was somebody I'd been dating a while and we'd gone to bed a few times. Once he tried to persuade me to go along with anal sex, first verbally, then by touching me. When I said "No," he did it anyway — much to my pain. It hurt like hell.

Ms. N: This guy had seen a movie where a woman was being made love to by dogs. He suggested that some of his friends had a dog and we should have a party and set the dog loose on the women. He wanted me to put a muzzle on the dog and put some sort of stuff on my vagina so that the dog would lick there.

Ms. O: My old man and I went to a show that had lots of tying up and anal intercourse. We came home and proceeded to make love. He went out and got two belts. He tied my feet together with one, and with the other he kinda beat me. I was in the spirit, I went along with it. But when he tried to penetrate me anally, I couldn't take it, it was too painful. I managed to convey to him verbally to quit it. He did stop, but not soon enough to suit me.

Then one time, he branded me. I still have a scar on my butt. He put a little wax initial thing on a hot plate and then stuck it on my ass when I was unaware.

Ms. P: My boyfriend and I saw a movie in which there was masochism. After that he wanted to gag me and tie me up. He was stoned. I was not. I was really shocked at his behavior. I was nervous and uptight. He literally tried to force me, after gagging me first. He snuck up behind me with a scarf. He was hurting me with it and I started getting upset. Then I realized it wasn't a joke. He grabbed me and shook me by my shoulders and brought out some ropes, and told me to relax, and that I would enjoy it. Then he started putting me down about my feelings about sex and my inhibitedness. I started crying and struggling with him, got loose, and kicked him in the testicles, which forced him down on the couch. I ran out of the house. Next day he called and apologized, but that was the end of him.

As may be clear from some of the quotations cited, there was often insufficient probing by the interviewers to determine the exact nature of the unwanted sexual experience. This means that the number of clear-cut cases of forced intercourse (i.e., rapes) reported in answer to this question is likely to be a considerable underestimate (see Table 1).

Table 1	Sexual Assaults Reported in Answer to Question:

Have you ever been upset by anyone trying to get you to do what they'd seen in pronographic pictures, movies or books?

SEXUAL ASSAULT	NUMBER
Completed vaginal intercourse with force	4
Completed oral, anal, or vaginal intercourse with foreign object, with force	10
Attempted oral, anal, vaginal intercourse with foreign object, with force	1
TOTAL	15

While it cannot be concluded from these data that pornography is *causing* the behavior described, I think one can conclude that at minimum it *does* have some effect. The most notable is that 10 percent of the women interviewed felt they had been personally victimized by pornography. Regarding the men's behavior, at the very least it appears that some attempt to use pornography to get women to do what they want.[1] It also seems likely that some pornography may have reinforced and legitimized these acts, including the assaultive behavior, in those men's minds. In some cases the actual *idea* of doing certain acts appears to have come from viewing pornography — as in the suggestion that a dog be used on a woman, and in some of the S & M proposals.

Millions of dollars were spent on the research conducted by the Commission on Obscenity and Pornography, which came up with the false conclusions that pornography is harmless. Just the few questions cited here, included in a survey on another topic, are sufficient to refute their irresponsible conclusion.

Note

[1] Note Donald Mosher's finding that 16 percent of a sample of 256 male college students had "shown a girl pornography, or taken a girl to a sexy movie to induce her to have intercourse." Donald Mosher, "Sex Callousness toward Women," *Technical Reports of the Commission on Obscenity and Pornography*, Vol. 8, 1971, p. 314.

Pornography, Obscenity, and the Case for Censorship

Irving Kristol

Irving Kristol, once the liberal editor of Commentary *(1947–1952), is now one of America's leading "neoconservatives." He is the author of* Reflections of a Neoconservative: Looking Back, Looking Ahead *(1983), from which this excerpt is taken.*

Kristol raises an interesting question. Critics of censorship laws usually argue that these laws censor the good along with the bad. The broad net of pornography laws, the critics say, restrict the sale of Henry Miller along with hard-core girlie magazines. Kristol argues just the opposite: It's legalized pornography that drives out good art; operating under Gresham's law, pornography establishes the debased and drives out the good.

Pornography, Kristol argues, is "inherently and purposefully subversive of civilization and its institutions." Pornography, Kristol says, debases those who view it. What should be censored will always be a difficult and troubling question, but the question is far too important to ignore.

Being frustrated is disagreeable, but the real disasters in life begin when you get what you want. For almost a century now, a great many intelligent, well-meaning, and articulate people — of a kind generally called liberal or intellectual, or both — have argued eloquently against any kind of censorship of art and/or entertainment. And within the past ten years, the courts and the legislatures of most Western nations have found these arguments persuasive — so persuasive that hardly a man is now alive who clearly remembers what the answers to these arguments were. Today, in the United States and other democracies, censorship has to all intents and purposes ceased to exist.

Is there a sense of triumphant exhilaration in the land? Hardly. There is, on the contrary, a rapidly growing unease and disquiet. Somehow, things have not worked out as they were supposed to, and many notable civil libertarians have gone on record as saying this was not what they meant at all. They wanted a world in which *Desire under the Elms* could be produced, or *Ulysses* published, without interference by philistine busybodies holding public office. They have got that, of course; but they have also got a world in which homosexual rape takes place on the stage, in which the public flocks during lunch hours to witness varieties of professional fornication, in which Times Square has become little more than a hideous market for the sale and distribution of printed filth that panders to all known (and some fanciful) sexual perversions.

But disagreeable as this may be, does it really matter? Might not our unease and disquiet be merely a cultural hangover — a "hang-up," as they say? What reason is there to think that anyone was ever corrupted by a book?

Irving Kristol, "Pornography, Obscenity, and the Case for Censorship," *Reflections of a Neoconservative: Looking Back, Looking Ahead* (New York: Basic Books, 1983).

This last question, oddly enough, is asked by the very same people who seem convinced that advertisements in magazines or displays of violence on television do indeed have the power to corrupt. It is also asked, incredibly enough and in all sincerity, by people — for example, university professors and schoolteachers — whose very lives provide all the answers one could want. After all, if you believe that no one was ever corrupted by a book, you have also to believe that no one was ever improved by a book (or a play or a movie). You have to believe, in other words, that all art is morally trivial and that, consequently, all education is morally irrelevant. No one, not even a university professor, really believes that.

To be sure, it is extremely difficult, as social scientists tell us, to trace the effects of any single book (or play or movie) on an individual reader or any class of readers. But we all know, and social scientists know it too, that the ways in which we use our minds and imaginations do shape our characters and help define us as persons. That those who certainly know this are nevertheless moved to deny it merely indicates how a dogmatic resistance to the idea of censorship can — like most dogmatism — result in a mindless insistence on the absurd.

I have used these harsh terms — "dogmatism" and "mindless" — advisedly. I might also have added "hypocritical." For the plain fact is that none of us is a complete civil libertarian. We all believe that there is some point at which the public authorities ought to step in to limit the "self-expression" of an individual or a group, even where this might be seriously intended as a form of artistic expression, and even where the artistic transaction is between consenting adults. A playwright or theatrical director might, in this crazy world of ours, find someone willing to commit suicide on the stage, as called for by the script. We would not allow that — any more than we would permit scenes of real physical torture on the stage, even if the victim were a willing masochist. And I know of no one, no matter how free in spirit, who argues that we ought to permit gladiatorial contests in Yankee Stadium, similar to those once performed in the Colosseum at Rome — even if only consenting adults were involved.

The basic point that emerges is one that Walter Berns has powerfully argued: No society can be utterly indifferent to the ways its citizens publicly entertain themselves. Bearbaiting and cockfighting are prohibited only in part out of compassion for the suffering animals; the main reason they were abolished was because it was felt that they debased and brutalized the citizenry who flocked to witness such spectacles. And the question we face with regard to pornography and obscenity is whether, now that they have such strong legal protection from the Supreme Court, they can or will brutalize and debase our citizenry. We are, after all, not dealing with one passing incident — one book, or one play, or one movie. We are dealing with a general tendency that is suffusing our entire culture.

I say pornography *and* obscenity because, though they have different dictionary definitions and are frequently distinguishable as "artistic" genres, they are nevertheless in the end identical in effect. Pornography is not objectionable simply because it arouses sexual desire or lust or prurience in the mind of the reader or spectator; this is a silly Victorian notion. A great many nonpornographic works — including some parts of the Bible — excite sexual desire very successfully. What is distinctive about pornography is that, in the words of D. H. Lawrence, it attempts "to do dirt on [sex] . . . [It is an] insult to a vital human relationship."

In other words, pornography differs from erotic art in that its whole purpose is to treat human beings obscenely, to deprive human beings of their specifically human dimension. That is what obscenity is all about. It is light years removed from any kind of carefree sensuality — there is no continuum between Fielding's *Tom Jones* and the Marquis de Sade's *Justine*. These works have quite opposite intentions. To quote Susan Sontag: "What pornographic literature does is precisely to drive a wedge between one's existence as a full human being and one's existence as a sexual being — while in ordinary life a healthy person is one who prevents such a gap from opening up." This definition occurs in an essay *defending* pornography — Miss Sontag is a candid as well as gifted critic — so the definition, which I accept, is neither tendentious nor censorious.

Along these same lines, one can point out — as C. S. Lewis pointed out some years back — that it is no accident that in the history of all literatures obscene words, the so-called four-letter words, have always been the vocabulary of farce or vituperation. The reason is clear; they reduce men and women to some of their mere bodily functions — they reduce man to his animal component, and such a reduction is an essential purpose of farce or vituperation.

Similarly, Lewis also suggested that it is not an accident that we have no offhand, colloquial, neutral terms — not in any Western European language at any rate — for our most private parts. The words we do use are either (1) nursery terms, (2) archaisms, (3) scientific terms, or (4) a term from the gutter (i.e., a demeaning term). Here I think the genius of language is telling us something important about man. It is telling us that man is an animal with a difference: He has a unique sense of privacy, and a unique capacity for shame when this privacy is violated. Our "private parts" are indeed private, and not merely because convention prescribes it. This particular convention is indigenous to the human race. In practically all primitive tribes, men and women cover their private parts; and in practically all primitive tribes, men and women do not copulate in public.

It may well be that Western society, in the latter half of the twentieth century, is experiencing a drastic change in sexual mores and sexual relationships. We have had many such "sexual revolutions" in the past — the bourgeois family and bourgeois ideas of sexual propriety were themselves established in the course of a revolution against eighteenth-century "licentiousness" — and we shall doubtless have others in the future. It is, however, highly improbable (to put it mildly) that what we are witnessing is the Final Revolution which will make sexual relations utterly unproblematic, permit us to dispense with any kind of ordered relationships between the sexes, and allow us freely to redefine the human condition. And so long as humanity has not reached that utopia, obscenity will remain a problem.

One of the reasons it will remain a problem is that obscenity is not merely about sex, any more than science fiction is about science. Science fiction, as every student of the genre knows, is a peculiar vision of power: What it is really about is politics. And obscenity is a peculiar vision of humanity: What it is really about is ethics and metaphysics.

Imagine a man — a well-known man, much in the public eye — in a hospital ward, dying an agonizing death. He is not in control of his bodily functions, so that his bladder and his bowels empty themselves of their own accord. His consciousness is overwhelmed and extinguished by pain, so that he cannot communicate with us, nor we with him. Now, it would be, technically, the easiest thing in the world to put a television camera in his hospital room and let the whole world witness this spectacle. We do not do it — at least we do not do it as yet — because we regard this as an *obscene* invasion of privacy. And what would make the spectacle obscene is that we would be witnessing the extinguishing of humanity in a human animal.

Incidentally, in the past our humanitarian crusaders against capital punishment understood this point very well. The abolitionist literature goes into great physical detail about what happens to a man when he is hanged or electrocuted or gassed. And their argument was — and is — that what happens is shockingly obscene, and that no civilized society should be responsible for perpetrating such obscenities, particularly since in the nature of the case there must be spectators to ascertain that this horror was indeed being perpetrated in fulfillment of the law.

Sex — like death — is an activity that is both animal and human. There are human sentiments and human ideals involved in this animal activity. But when sex is public, the viewer does not see — cannot see — the sentiments and the ideals. He can only see the animal coupling. And that is why, when men and women make love, as we say, they prefer to be alone — because it is only when you are alone that you can make love, as distinct from merely copulating in an animal and casual way. And that, too, is why those who are voyeurs, if they are not irredeemably sick, also feel ashamed at what they are witnessing. When sex is a public spectacle, a human relationship has been debased into a mere animal connection.

It is also worth noting that this making of sex into an obscenity is not a mutual and equal transaction but rather an act of exploitation by one of the partners — the male partner. I do not wish to get into the complicated question as to what, if any, are the essential differences — as distinct from conventional and cultural differences — between male and female. I do not claim to know the answer to that. But I do know — and I take it as a sign that has meaning — that pornography is, and always has been, a man's work; that women rarely write pornography; and that women tend to be indifferent consumers of pornography. My own guess, by way of explanation, is that a woman's sexual experience is ordinarily more suffused with human emotion than is man's, that men are more easily satisfied with autoerotic activities, and that men can therefore more easily take a more "technocratic" view of sex and its pleasures. Perhaps this is not correct. But whatever the explanation, there can be no question that pornography is a form of "sexism," as the women's liberation movement calls it, and that the instinct of women's liberation has been unerring in perceiving that when pornography is perpetrated, it is perpetrated against them, as part of a conspiracy to deprive them of their full humanity.

But even if all this is granted, it might be said — and doubtless will be said — that I really ought not to be unduly concerned. Free competition in the cultural market-place — it is argued by people who have never otherwise had a kind word to say for laissez-faire — will automatically dispose of the problem. The present fad for pornography and obscenity, it will be asserted, is just that, a fad. It will spend itself in the course of time; people will get bored with it, will be able to take it or leave it alone in a casual way, in a "mature way," and, in sum, I am being unnecessarily distressed about the whole business. The *New York Times*, in an editorial, concludes hopefully in this vein.

> In the end . . . the insensate pursuit of the urge to shock, carried from one excess to a more abysmal one, is bound to achieve its own antidote in total boredom. When there is no lower depth to descend to, ennui will erase the problem.

I would like to be able to go along with this line of reasoning, but I cannot. I think it is false, and for two reasons, the first psychological, the second political.

The basic psychological fact about pornography and obscenity is that it appeals to and provokes a kind of sexual regression. The sexual pleasure one gets from pornography and obscenity is autoerotic and infantile; put bluntly, it is a masturbatory exercise of the imagination, when it is not masturbation pure and simple. Now, people who masturbate do not get bored with masturbation, just as sadists do not get bored with sadism, and voyeurs do not get bored with voyeurism.

In other words, infantile sexuality is not only a permanent temptation for the adolescent or even the adult — it can quite easily become a permanent, self-reinforcing neurosis. It is because of an awareness of this possibility of regression toward the infantile condition, a regression which is always open to us, that all the codes of sexual conduct ever devised by the human race take such a dim view of autoerotic activities and try to discourage autoerotic fantasies. Masturbation is indeed a perfectly natural autoerotic activity, as so many sexologists blandly assure us today. And it is precisely because it is so perfectly natural that it can be so dangerous to the mature or maturing person, if it is not controlled or sublimated in some way. That is the true meaning of Portnoy's complaint. Portnoy, you will recall, grows up to be a man who is incapable of having an adult sexual relationship with a woman; his sexuality remains fixed in an infantile mode, the prisoner of his autoerotic fantasies. Inevitably, Portnoy comes to think, in a perfectly *infantile* way, that it was all his mother's fault.

It is true that, in our time, some quite brilliant minds have come to the conclusion that a reversion to infantile sexuality is the ultimate mission and secret destiny of the human race. I am thinking in particular of Norman O. Brown, for whose writings I have the deepest respect. One of the reasons I respect them so deeply is that Mr. Brown is a serious thinker who is unafraid to face up to the radical consequences of his radical theories. Thus, Mr. Brown knows and says that for his kind of salvation to be achieved, humanity must annul the civilization it has created — not merely the civilization we have today, but all civilization — so as to be able to make the long descent backward into animal innocence.

And that is the point. What is at stake is civilization and humanity, nothing less. The idea that "everything is permitted," as Nietzsche put it, rests on the premise of nihilism and has nihilistic implications. I will not pretend that the case against nihilism and for civilization is an easy one to make. We are here confronting the most fundamental of philosophical questions, on the deepest levels. In short, the matter of pornography and obscenity is not a trivial one, and only superficial minds can take a bland and untroubled view of it.

In this connection, I must also point out, those who are primarily against censorship on liberal grounds tell us not to take pornography or obscenity seriously, while those who are for pornography and obscenity on radical grounds take it very seriously indeed. I believe the radicals — writers like Susan Sontag, Herbert Marcuse, Norman O. Brown, and even Jerry Rubin — are right, and the liberals are wrong. I also believe that those young radicals at Berkeley, some seven years ago, who provoked a major confrontation over the public use of obscene words, showed a brilliant political instinct. And once Mark Rudd could publicly ascribe to the president of Columbia a notoriously obscene relationship to his mother, without provoking any kind of reaction, the SDS [Students for a Democratic Society] had already won the day. The occupation of Columbia's buildings merely ratified their victory. Men who show themselves unwilling to defend civilization against nihilism are not going to be either resolute or effective in defending the university against anything.

I am already touching upon a political aspect of pornography when I suggest that it is inherently and purposefully subversive of civilization and its institutions. But there is another and more specifically political aspect, which has to do with the relationship of pornography and/or obscenity to democracy, and especially to the quality of public life on which democratic government ultimately rests.

Though the phrase "the quality of life" trips easily from so many lips these days, it tends to be one of those clichés with many trivial meanings and no large, serious one. Sometimes it merely refers to such externals as the enjoyment of cleaner air, cleaner water, cleaner streets. At other times it refers to the merely private enjoyment of music, painting, or literature. Rarely does it have anything to do with the way the citizen in a democracy views himself — his obligations, his intentions, his ultimate self-definition.

Instead, what I would call the "managerial" conception of democracy is the predominant opinion among political scientists, sociologists, and economists, and has, through the untiring efforts of these scholars, become the conventional journalistic opinion as well. The root idea behind this managerial conception is that democracy is a "political system" (as they say) which can be adequately defined in terms of — can be fully reduced to — its mechanical arrangements. Democracy is then seen as a set of rules and procedures, and *nothing but* a set of rules and procedures, whereby majority rule and minority rights are reconciled into a state of equilibrium. If everyone follows these rules and procedures, then a democracy is in working order. I think this is a fair description of the democratic idea that currently prevails in academia. One can also fairly say that it is now the liberal idea of democracy par excellence.

I cannot help but feel that there is something ridiculous about being this kind of a democrat, and I must further confess to having a sneaking sympathy for those of our young radicals who also find it ridiculous. The absurdity is the absurdity of idolatry — of taking the symbolic for the real, the means for the end. The purpose of democracy cannot possibly be the endless functioning of its own political machin-ery. The purpose of any political regime is to achieve some version of the good life and the good society. It is not at all difficult to imagine a perfectly functioning democracy which answers all questions except one — namely, why should anyone of intelligence and spirit care a fig for it?

There is, however, an older idea of democracy — one which was fairly common until about the beginning of this century — for which the conception of the quality of public life is absolutely crucial. This idea starts from the proposition that democracy is a form of self-government, and that if you want it to be a meritorious polity, you have to care about what kind of people govern it. Indeed, it puts the matter more strongly and declares that if you want self-government, you are only entitled to it if that "self" is worthy of governing. There is no inherent right to self-government if it means that such government is vicious, mean, squalid, and debased. Only a dogmatist and a fanatic, an idolater of democratic machinery, could approve of self-government under such conditions.

And because the desirability of self-government depends on the character of the people who govern, the older idea of democracy was very solicitious of the condition of this character. It was solicitous of the individual self, and felt an obligation to educate it into what used to be called "republican virtue." And it was solicitous of that collective self which we call public opinion and which, in a democracy, governs us collectively. Perhaps in some respects it was nervously oversolicitous — that would not be surprising. But the main thing is that it cared, cared not merely about the machinery of democracy but about the quality of life that this machinery might generate.

And because it cared, this older idea of democracy had no problem in principle with pornography and/or obscenity. It censored them — and it did so with a perfect clarity of mind and a perfectly clear conscience. It was not about to permit people capriciously to corrupt themselves. Or, to put it more precisely: In this version of democracy, the people took some care not to let themselves be governed by the more infantile and irrational parts of themselves.

I have, it may be noticed, uttered that dreadful word censorship. And I am not about to back away from it. If you think pornography and/or obscenity is a serious problem, you have to be for censorship. I will go even further and say that if you want to prevent pornography and/or obscenity from becoming a problem, you have to be for censorship. And lest there be any misunderstanding as to what I am saying, I will put it as bluntly as possible: If you care for the quality of life in our American democracy, then you have to be for censorship.

But can a liberal be for censorship? Unless one assumes that being a liberal *must* mean being indifferent to the quality of American life, then the answer has to be yes, a liberal can be for censorship — but he ought to favor a liberal form of censorship.

Is that a contradiction in terms? I do not think so. We have no problem in contrasting *repressive* laws governing alcohol and drugs and tobacco with laws *regulating* (i.e., discouraging the sale of) alcohol and drugs and tobacco. Laws encouraging temperance are not the same thing as laws that have as their goal prohibition or abolition. We have not made the smoking of cigarettes a criminal offense. We have, however, and with good liberal conscience, prohibited cigarette advertising on television, and may yet, again with good liberal conscience, prohibit it in newspapers and magazines. The idea of restricting individual freedom, in a liberal way, is not at all unfamiliar to us.

I therefore see no reason why we should not be able to distinguish repressive censorship from liberal censorship of the written and spoken word. In Britain, until a few years ago, you could perform almost any play you wished, but certain plays, judged to be obscene, had to be performed in private theatrical clubs, which were deemed to have a "serious" interest in theater. In the United States, all of us who grew up using public libraries are familiar with the circumstances under which certain books could be circulated only to adults, while still other books had to be read in the library reading room, under the librarian's skeptical eye. In both cases, a small minority that was willing to make a serious effort to see an obscene play or read an obscene book could do so. But the impact of obscenity was circumscribed and the quality of public life was only marginally affected.

I am not saying it is easy in practice to sustain a distinction between liberal and repressive censorship, especially in the public realm of a democracy, where popular opinion is so vulnerable to demagoguery. Moreover, an acceptable system of liberal censorship is likely to be exceedingly difficult to devise in the United States today, because our educated classes, upon whose judgment a liberal censorship must rest, are so convinced that there is no such thing as a problem of obscenity, or even that there is no such thing as obscenity at all. But, to counterbalance this, there is the further, fortunate truth that the tolerable margin for error is quite large, and single mistakes or single injustices are not all that important.

This possibility of error, of course, occasions much distress among artists and academics. It is a fact, one that cannot and should not be denied, that any system of censorship is bound, upon occasion, to treat unjustly a particular work of art — to find pornography where there is only gentle eroticism, to find obscenity where none really exists, or to find both where its existence ought to be tolerated because it serves a larger moral purpose. Though most works of art are not obscene, and though most obscenity has nothing to do with art, there are some few works of art that are, at least in part, pornographic and/or obscene. There are also some few works of art that are in the special category of the comic-ironic "bawdy" (Boccaccio, Rabelais). It is such works of art that are likely to suffer at the hands of the censor. That is the price one has to be prepared to pay for censorship — even liberal censorship.

But just how high is this price? If you believe, as so many artists seem to believe today, that art is the only sacrosanct activity in our profane and vulgar world — that any man who designates himself an artist thereby acquires a sacred office — then obviously censorship is an intolerable form of sacrilege. But for those of us who do not subscribe to this religion of art, the costs of censorship do not seem so high at all.

If you look at the history of American or English literature, there is precious little damage you can point to as a consequence of the censorship that prevailed throughout most of that history. Very few works of literature — of real literary merit, I mean — ever were suppressed; and those that were, were not suppressed for long. Nor have I noticed, now that censorship of the written word has to all intents and purposes ceased in this country, that hitherto suppressed or repressed masterpieces are flooding the market. Yes, we can now read *Fanny Hill* and the Marquis de Sade. Or, to be more exact, we can now openly purchase them, since many people were able to read them even though they were publicly banned, which is as it should be under a liberal censorship. So how much have literature and the arts gained from the fact that we can all now buy them over the counter, that, indeed, we are all now encouraged to buy them over the counter? They have not gained much that I can see.

And one might also ask a question that is almost never raised: How much has literature lost from the fact that everything is now permitted? It has lost quite a bit, I should say. In a free market, Gresham's Law can work for books or theater as efficiently as it does for coinage — driving out the good, establishing the debased. The cultural market in the United States today is being preempted by dirty books, dirty movies, dirty theater. A pornographic novel has a far better chance of being published today than a nonpornographic one, and quite a few pretty good novels are not being published at all simply because they are not pornographic, and are therefore less likely to sell. Our cultural condition has not improved as a result of the new freedom. American cultural life was not much to brag about twenty years ago; today one feels ashamed for it.

Just one last point, which I dare not leave untouched. If we start censoring pornography or obscenity, shall we not inevitably end up censoring political opinion? A lot of people seem to think this would be the case — which only shows the power of doctrinaire thinking over reality. We had censorship of pornography and obscenity for 150 years, until almost yesterday, and I am not aware that freedom of opinion in this country was in any way diminished as a consequence of this fact. Fortunately for those of us who are liberal, freedom is not indivisible. If it were, the case for liberalism would be indistinguishable from the case for anarchy; and they are two very different things.

But I must repeat and emphasize: What kinds of laws we pass governing pornography and obscenity, what kind of censorship — or, since we are still a federal nation, what kinds of censorship — we institute in our various localities may indeed be difficult matters to cope with; nevertheless the real issue is one of principle. I myself subscribe to a liberal view of the enforcement problem: I think that pornography should be illegal *and* available to anyone who wants it so badly as to make a pretty strenuous effort to get it. We have lived with under-the-counter pornography for centuries now, in a fairly comfortable way. But the issue of principle, of whether it should be over or under the counter, has to be settled before we can reflect on the advantages and disadvantages of alternative modes of censorship. I think the settlement we are living under now, in which obscenity and democracy are regarded as equals, is wrong; I believe it is inherently unstable; I think it will, in the long run, be incompatible with any authentic concern for the quality of life in our democracy.

DIRT AND DEMOCRACY
Alan Wolfe

In this essay, Alan Wolfe, a professor of sociology at Queens College and author of Whose Keeper?: Social Science and Moral Obligation, *reviews five books on pornography and censorship. Because he quotes the authors of these books and discusses their ideas, you will need to keep the five works in mind: For Adult Users Only: The Dilemma of Violent Pornography, edited by Susan Bubar and Joan Hoff; Pornography: Men Possessing Women by Andrea Dworkin; The New Politics of Pornography by Donald Alexander Downs; Hard Core: Power, Pleasure, and the "Frenzy of the Visible" by Linda Williams; and Freedom and Taboo: Pornography and the Politics of a Self Divided by Richard S. Randall.*

Wolfe's essay is particularly valuable because it offers an overview of the dilemmas and complexities of both sides of the censorship argument.

Pornography exists where sex and politics meet. Since few other activities are as fascinating as these two pleasures, it is no wonder that questions involving pornography have been with us so long.

Sex is, or at least is supposed to be, intimate, caring, invisible to others: the very definition of private. Politics is, or is supposed to be, open, debatable, a spectacle: the essence of public. A world in which sex and its representations were of no concern to others could not, by force of definition, contain pornography. A world in which politics regulated all sexual activities and their representation could not, by force of police, contain pornography either. To discuss pornography is always to discuss a matter of balance.

Our politics — the way we balance public and private things — are those of liberal democracy. As Richard Randall stresses in his comprehensive treatment of the subject, both liberalism and democracy are intimately linked to the pornographic inclination, even if that link is troubling and contradictory. Liberalism respects a private sphere within which government — that is, other people — ought not to find itself. Although the founders of liberalism might be unable to imagine their arguments for freedom of expression used in defense of the prurient, pornography could not exist without the two most fundamental props of the liberal world order: a market that efficiently responds to supply and demand, with little concern for the morality of what is traded; and a legal system that places a premium on individual rights.

Yet if liberalism is inclined to protect the pornographic, democracy is inclined to forbid it. Randall is correct to emphasize that it is the elite that seeks to defend the right of pornographic expression and the majority that seeks to curtail it. Politicians never run for office in favor of pornography. Unmoved by appeals to artistic expression, little concerned for constitutional subtleties, worried about the vulnerability of their children, Americans would gladly give up this one liberal right if they could be guaranteed that in return they would be rid of unwanted ugliness.

Alan Wolfe, "Dirt and Democracy," *The New Republic* 19 February 1990.

Legislatures and city councils, responsive to democratic demands, regularly try to control pornography; courts, undemocratic in principle and liberal in practice, try to stop them.

In the past 20 years, liberalism and democracy have both expanded in scope. Pornographers have shared, surely disproportionately, in the expansion of liberal rights that has defined American judicial practice since the Warren Court. The rise of the Moral Majority and other censorial movements, on the other hand, is one of the byproducts of increasingly plebiscitary democratic urges. The result of these simultaneous developments is what Donald Downs calls a "new politics of pornography" in which few of the older images, alliances, positions, and judicial standards make sense. Three developments since around 1970 have set the stage for the new politics of pornography.

First, the form of pornography has changed beyond recognition. Any images men may have in their heads about stag films — any leftover memories of fraternity bashes of the 1950s — have nothing to do with what pornography represents now. The sex is far more explicit; today's hard core is tomorrow's R-rated movie, or, to put it another way, yesterday's illegality is today's television commercial. In addition, the "quality" has improved. As Linda Williams points out, plots have been added, full-length feature status is now the norm, and efforts at credibility have been introduced. The symbol of these changes, of course, is video; most people now watch pornography at home in living color, not in grungy inner-city arcades. And high-definition television, once the Japanese get around to supplying it, is next.

Second, nearly all legal efforts used by local communities to control pornography in recent years have failed. The Supreme Court's 1957 decision in *Roth v. United States* — despite its famous language banning material that "appeals to the prurient interest" — effectively opened the door to previously forbidden sexual expression: 31 obscenity convictions were reversed between 1967 and 1973. The ability of pornographers to use courts and the First Amendment to their advantage (Downs notes that in Minneapolis the MCLU offices were in a building owned by its leading pornographic client, presumably rent-free) led local police to give up even trying to win convictions. Even a town as conservative as Indianapolis was able to initiate only two obscenity cases between 1979 and 1985. During the 1970s and early 1980s, in short, pornography grew increasingly worse as the ability to regulate it declined proportionately.

Third, our awareness that pornography involves violence against women has increased. Of the three developments, this is the most controversial, because there is no absolute proof — nor will there ever be — that pornography *definitely* results in harm to women. (Based on the Danish experience with legalization, the opposite case is equally as plausible: pornography may also be an excuse for men to masturbate and be done, and thus protect women.) Still, the images contained in pornography, brutal toward all, are most brutal toward women. Pornography is, to some degree, a feminist issue. How much it is a feminist issue is the most passionately debated question in the current writing on the subject.

If questions involving pornography always involve matters of balance, the rise of a new politics of pornography has placed in doubt what ought to be balanced with what. Under the rules of the "old" politics of pornography, the right to free expression stood on one side and the ability of a community to protect itself from untoward sexuality stood on the other. Under the new politics of pornography, violence against women is defined as what we need protection against, whereas what pornography might stand for is not completely clear.

The new politics of pornography crested with the report of the Meese Commission in 1986, which concluded that pornography (including the violent kind) had increased to the point of being out of control. What was most striking about the Meese Commission was not its conclusions, but the way it reached them. For the commission focused specifically on the insult and injury to women involved in pornography, even to the extent of quoting, without attribution, Robin Morgan's fighting words: "Pornography is the theory; rape is the practice." The feminist critique of pornography had arrived.

That critique was the product of the meeting of two minds: legal theorist Catherine MacKinnon and essayist Andrea Dworkin. Dworkin expounded her ideas in *Pornography: Men Possessing Women*, recently republished with a new introduction. In Dworkin's view, sex is power, nothing else; and all the power belongs to the man. Every man is a beast, every woman an innocent and (remarkably, for a feminist) passive victim. Pornography, like heterosexual sex in general, is merely an extreme form by which men exercise power over women.

The philosophy in Dworkin's bedroom is the philosophy of Hobbes. She tells me, for example, that I have refrained from raping my son not because I love him, but because of the fear that when he grows up, he might rape me back. Dworkin, in that sense, is really not all that interested in pornography as such; the chapter of that name in her book is four pages long, whereas the one called "Force" is 70. (Brutal treatments of gay men or animals would not, presumably, bother her.) Let Dworkin herself speak:

> In the male system, women are sex; sex is the whore. The whore is porné, the lowest whore, the whore who belongs to *all* male citizens: the slut, the cunt. Buying her is buying pornography. Having her is having pornography. Seeing her is seeing pornography. Seeing her sex, especially her genitals, is seeing pornography. Seeing her in sex is seeing the whore in sex. Using her is using pornography. Wanting her means wanting pornography. Being her means being pornography.

Dworkin believes that what men do to women in pornography is *worse* than what Nazis did to Jews in concentration camps: "The Jews didn't do it to themselves and they didn't orgasm. . . . No one, not even Goebbels, said that the Jews liked it." Dworkin does Robin Morgan one better: sex is the theory and extermination the practice. Women, though, unlike the Jews in the camps, are fighting back. (Totally passive, they suddenly found a voice.) Her advice to them is: "know the bastard on top of you." Men are scared. The women they have treated pornographically all their lives are massed to castrate them, and Dworkin is wielding the biggest knife.

This kind of analysis would hardly seem the stuff of local ordinances — especially in the American Midwest. But, as Downs recounts in his illuminating history of these events, one of Dworkin's readers was Catherine MacKinnon, by all accounts a brilliant political strategist. In 1983 MacKinnon invited Dworkin to teach a class with her at the University of Minnesota School of Law. Two essential conclusions were quickly reached in the seminar: first, that pornography is not a question of free speech, because women cannot speak; and second, that pornography, because it harms women, does not extend civil liberties, it violates civil rights.

The resulting Minnesota ordinance was a first in American law. Pornography — not, as in most judicial decisions since *Roth*, the narrower notion of obscenity — was defined as discrimination against women. Finding herself depicted in what she believed to be pornographic fashion by any image — nine definitions of such depictions were given in the ordinance — any woman could lodge a complaint with the local Civil Rights Commission and, after a series of steps were followed, could win the right to a hearing. The Minnesota ordinance was eventually declared unconstitutional in 1985. Still, we may hear more from the feminist anti-pornographers. Given a censorial mood on campus, which makes it against university policy to say anything derogatory against women, minorities, gays, Native Americans, and the handicapped, we may soon see efforts to ban pornographic films from campus facilities or pornographers from rostrums. There is no way around it. Since the threat of an anti-discrimination suit is designed to stop the practice of depicting women pornographically *before* it occurs, the issue raised by Dworkin and MacKinnon is censorship. Is the harm to women represented in pornography so great that we are justified in using our democratic powers to stop it?

The first reaction to the rise of a feminist movement for censorship was to argue on empirical grounds that the harm done to women by pornography is not as great as feared. It has been said that pornography has targets other than women; that women make and enjoy pornography themselves; that no harm against women from pornography can be proved. Although in a narrow and technical sense these arguments are accurate, they miss the point. When a political position has as much popularity as the desire to control pornography, we ought to give those who hold it credit for their views, not dismiss them as know-nothings, anti-intellectual philistines, or (as Randall unfortunately does) people repressing the pornographic within. When the rage of women is eloquent and dramatic, we ought not let Dworkin's absurd rhetoric deny an important point. Pornography is demeaning, women are its primary targets, and even if we cannot prove that it causes violence, it certainly offends the sensibility of some very engaged citizens.

At this point, a second line of defense against censorship enters: even though pornography demeans women, it serves positive goals that are more important. Whether or not pornography has value, one form of this argument runs, liberty clearly does. Hence pornography can be bad, but what it symbolizes — free speech — is good. Pornography, therefore, has redeeming value in spite of itself. A similar response to the Dworkin-MacKinnon position has arisen among feminists who, objecting strenuously to their depiction of the passivity of women, argue that free sex has as much value as free speech. Did it ever occur to Dworkin and others like her, these thinkers have asked, that women like sex? It was hardly the intent of the feminist movement, after all, to turn all women into Puritans. (For similar reasons, gays objected vehemently to the Minneapolis ordinance.) Revisionist feminists — if they may be called that — also find indirect value in pornography. We have libidos.

They need outlets. Free speech and free sex both make a certain toleration of pornography necessary.

Both of these arguments are trying to balance the way that the new politics of pornography defines harm with the way that the old politics of pornography defined freedom. It is not easy to do. Harm is concrete, sensate, unambiguous. Rights are abstract and intellectualized, at least one remove away from immediate experience. Weigh the two, and the argument against harm will win, at least with the popular majorities that decide such things. Similarly, the argument for sexual freedom is unhelpful in this debate. Its images of sex correspond exactly to ACLU images of rights: free speech and free sex are private matters, not the business of anyone else. The age of AIDS should teach us otherwise: so long as tax monies are used to save lives, there *is* a public interest in private sex. The state may not be the best regulator, the regulation itself can often misfire, but a community cannot take a position of moral neutrality toward the libido. Most people recognize, in short, that your sexuality is at least partly my concern. Some sexual freedom is clearly necessary to discover the self. Some regulation is clearly necessary to protect the society without which there can be no selves.

Pornography has little redeeming social value. By artistic criteria, it is close to worthless. Heroic attempts to defend the pornographic imagination by Angela Carter and Simone de Beauvoir (in the case of Sade) or Susan Sontag (in the case of Georges Bataille and Pauline Réage) treat a rarefied aspect of the genre that has little to do with the predictability and the sheer mediocrity of much of the pornographic expression. By criteria of psychological development, moreover, pornography fails again. It infantilizes people, mostly men, locking them into a stage in which limits do not exist, all desires can be satisfied, and every complexity avoided. By the Kantian criterion of respect for persons, furthermore, pornography fails a third time, treating women as things available for the whimsical pleasures of men; pornography in that sense is also without redeeming moral value.

By civic criteria, finally, pornography flunks most severely. Although free speech gives much to pornography, pornography gives almost nothing to free speech. It does not enhance our capacity to act as citizens. It does not cause us to reflect on rights and responsibilities. It does not encourage participation in the life of the community. Pornographers are free riders on the liberties of everyone else. If a human activity with so little value is balanced against even a slight possibility that it may cause rape and mayhem, the feminist case for censorship would seem to win.

Still, for all that, the bad taste that censorship leaves in the mouth cannot be easily washed away. The question of pornography raises a host of complex moral and symbolic issues that cannot be resolved by banishing the problem's manifestations. On moral grounds, for example, the case for censorship and the case for unrestricted rights to pornography are quite similar — and similarly without nuance. Feminists like Dworkin, who would regulate all the fine details of private life, believe that there is no morality to speak of when discussing pornography; everything is power. Civil libertarians, on the other hand, ruling private behavior beyond the pale of public scrutiny, also believe that there is no morality at issue; everything is principle. The moral neutrality of both positions can hardly win a hearing among most people, who believe that pornography, which is obviously about sex, is also about morality.

Pornography raises issues about the nature of the self, moreover, that cannot be addressed either by banning pornography or by celebrating it. One of the unanticipated benefits of the feminist case for censorship has been to sharpen the sense of what we are in danger of losing if the urge to censor gets out of hand. It is not individual freedom to do or say anything one wants with little regard for the sensitivity of the community. The loss would be deeper, for pornography symbolizes fundamental human needs without which we would not be fully human. Two of them are the need to be aware of the dark side of sexuality and the need to make sense out of multiple realities. If we have learned anything about texts at all in this century, it is that the more readers, the more interpretations — that reality, in short, is never simply one unambiguous thing.

Those who would censor pornography have complete epistemological confidence that they know exactly what it is. Reflecting on the experience in Minneapolis, Dworkin writes: "For women who are hurt by pornography, this law simply describes reality; it is a map of the real world." None of the contingencies and ambiguities of language, representation, and meaning that one finds in thinkers like Derrida or Rorty have made it into the consciousness of feminist censors. For example, Joan Hoff, who frequently cites Foucault on the social contingency of knowledge, argues that we know what pornography is, even though no history of it is available to us. When that history is written, she already knows what it will say. What is at stake is not whether her unwritten history is correct but that such certainty about historical development is the exact opposite of what Foucault teaches us about genealogies. In Hoff's view — and in the view of many of the contributors to the book that she edited with Susan Gubar — there is only one representation in any pornographic work, the one that brutalizes women.

Linda William's book *Hard Core* is a brilliant demolition of the position that pornography represents one thing only. Arguing against the feminist case for censorship, Williams urges that we take pornography seriously, which does not mean that we like it, or that we believe it is art. Remarkably non-evaluative in her description of pornographic films since the invention of moving pictures (she offers a negative assessment only once, on the quality of the music in *Deep Throat*), Williams wants us to learn the rules of the pornographic genre.

All forms of representation have genre rules, and Williams turns to musical comedies to help understand pornography: like hard-core porno films, they regularly break narrative to introduce numbers. (She might also have looked at operas. They, too, have numbers, and one of the greatest works of art written in any genre at any time is about a man who lusts uncontrollably, indeed pornographically, after women. *Don Giovanni* would surely have been actionable under the Dworkin-MacKinnon ordinance.) The rules of the pornographic genre are defined by a fundamental contradiction: if a man enjoys pleasure inside a woman, generally viewed by men as the most satisfying way to experience sexual pleasure, the physical evidence of his pleasure is invisible. The conventions of pornography follow from efforts to capture what the trade calls a "money shot": proving visibly that the man has satisfied himself.

Pornography cannot mean one thing, and one thing only, because genre conventions, instead of confining all reality within pre-established frames, enable multiple interpretations of reality to exist simultaneously. That is why pornography is not, as Dworkin claims, *only* about men brutalizing women. It may equally be the case that what men want to see in pornographic movies is not the naked woman, since most men, in the course of their lives, get to see that with some frequency, but the image of another man enjoying himself visibly, which most men never get to see. We do not know, of course, whether this interpretation is correct. But William's subtle and fascinating explications suggest that, in not knowing, we are best off allowing pornographic representations to exist. Despite what Hoff says, the history, or at least a history, of pornography has been written, and it does not show what she thought it would.

If the feminist censor's conviction that pornography reflects an unambiguous map of reality is naive, so is her conviction that, knowing the single-minded evil it represents, we can abolish it by force of law. Randall makes a convincing case that such an optimistic view of the powers of law is not justified. It is, in his view, the dark side of pornography that makes it important. Humans are the "pornographic" animal, fascinated and appalled by their sexuality. The pornography that we see out there is a reflection of the pornographic deep within our selves. Since pornography is part of what we are, we harm only ourselves by regulating it too severely. At the same time, however, since "complete sexual freedom is a contradiction of the human condition," we will need to control our sexual impulses in some way. Neither censors nor civil libertarians, Randall argues, understand "the paradoxical, mutually supportive relationship between pornography and censorship." We will have to live with various efforts to reconcile sexuality and its control, none of which will ever solve the problem.

The recognition that pornography speaks to needs within the self — its need to interpret as well as its need to express itself sexually — is a much firmer guide for sorting out the new politics of pornography than the purely libertarian notion of individual freedom. For one thing, the issue is not the abstract right of shady businessmen to sell dirty pictures, or the equally abstract right of sexual pleasure-seekers to purchase them — rights that in both cases apply to minorities. Pornography is important, rather, because in speaking to the self, it is speaking to a universal: we all have an interest in the many ways in which fundamental human conflicts are represented in print and in film.

In addition, both the free speech and the free sex argument, reflecting the optimism of liberal rationality, claim that our thoughts and our libidos if left free to roam will, like prices in an equally anarchic market, be guided by invisible hands into public benefits. Liberals, adherents to an all-too-optimistic faith, do not want to peek too closely into private spaces. They fear what they will find there.

Imperfect creatures growing to adulthood with sexual conflicts unresolved, many of us (surprisingly many, by most sociological accounts) need outlets for our imaginations, relying on our power to give meaning to representations of fantasies buried deep within the self, even if the pictorial representations of those fantasies involve, on the surface, harm to others. A case against censorship ought to argue not that we can discover some redeeming virtue in pornographic expression, but that we cannot.

Considering how rapidly the terrain has shifted in the debate over pornography we are a long way from developing legal standards that will help us keep in balance the needs pornography obviously serves with the offensiveness it obviously entails. Until such a standard is developed, the debate over pornography will be social, not legal, and its participants will be intellectuals and academics, not lawyers. What we have a right to expect in the debate is honesty. Such an objective is not helped by politicizing pornography as exclusively a women's issue, as if women should compete with other oppressed groups in demonstrating how submissive they really are. The category of woman is both too broad and too narrow to make much sense in this debate.

Two political scientists among the authors reviewed here, Donald Downs and Richard Randall, ought to be commended for trying to develop standards, even though neither is successful. Randall argues that we should make offensiveness, not harm, the crucial offense, a position that would restrict expression far more than any current standard—given how offensive people like Dworkin find loving and intimate sex, let alone what most people mean by pornography. Downs has a better proposal. He would extend the definition of obscenity to include violence, an attempt he recognizes as largely symbolic but still important in responding to concerns about abuse of women. Downs is essentially arguing that the best course is to have laws on the books against certain representations but not to enforce them. Such an approach makes sense to the degree that it is sensitive to all the contradictions of pornography, but it also is a recipe for disaster in fueling paranoia.

It is no wonder that none of the standards we have established for balancing the concerns involved in pornographic expression—including those tried, valiantly, by the Supreme Court—seems any longer to work. In concerning themselves with freedom on the one hand and community standards on the other, they are balancing the wrong things. We need a standard for pornography capable of putting into balance what we know about the self and what we know about potential harm to others. The feminist case against pornography is powerful and eloquent. But it establishes a border for the public debate, it does not resolve it. Moral philosophers long ago demonstrated convincingly that harm, though a tragedy, does not settle the question of what is morally permissible.

CENSORSHIP OR EDUCATION?
FEMINIST VIEWS ON PORNOGRAPHY
Mary Ellen Ross

Mary Ellen Ross, an assistant professor of religion at Trinity University, discusses the disagreements which have developed within religious groups and within feminist groups in America over the issue of censorship of pornography. As Ross observes, Catholics and fundamentalist Protestants tend to favor censorship, while mainline Protestants tend to favor combating pornography with education and "consciousness-raising." A similar schism exists within feminist groups, as Ross demonstrates in her summary of the arguments of feminist supporters and critics of the controversial 1984 Indianapolis Anti-Pornography Ordinance (which was later struck down by the U. S. Court of Appeals). Ross finally sides with those who favor education over censorship and suggests forms such an approach to the problem may take.

Pornographic images have been proliferating at a remarkable rate. What was a $5 million-a-year enterprise merely 25 years ago has boomed to a $7 billion to $10 billion-a-year industry today. Pornography turns a larger profit than the conventional film and music industries combined. This surge is due in part to the discovery of new markets. While adult bookstores, peepshows and movie theaters still thrive, the fastest growing sectors of the industry are pornographic video cassettes, cable television, and phone sex. Pornography is no longer confined to the seedier sections of town. It is readily available to all, including children, and in the privacy of our own homes. It reflects not only the increasing privatization and fragmentation of our culture, but also our ambivalence about sexuality.

To the religious, no images are neutral. Liberal and conservative churches have sought to reverse the proliferation of explicit and degrading depictions of human sexuality. But their approaches have varied considerably. Groups on the religious right have focused on the sexually explicit and sexually arousing characteristics of pornography, which they denounce as obscene. The Catholic Church, drawing on natural law theology, has condemned pornography as undermining human dignity and subverting the common social good. In its most recent resolution on the subject, the Episcopal Church declared in July 1988 that hard-core pornography abuses the self-images of women, children and men, and urged congregations to support then–Attorney General Edwin Meese's report with its call for stricter and tougher enforcement of already existing laws against pornography.

Some denominations, such as the Southern Baptist Convention, the Evangelical Lutheran Church in America and the United Methodist Church, have expressed special outrage over child pornography and have also called for telephone and television companies to do more to restrict access to pornographic materials. The Presbyterian Church (U.S.A.), in an exhaustive and exemplary report on the subject in June 1988 ("Pornography: Far from 'The Song of Songs'"), condemned the

Mary Ellen Ross, "Censorship or Education? Feminist Views on Pornography," *The Christian Century* 7 March 1990.

proliferation of sexually explicit materials that demean men and women. Unlike religious right groups and the Catholic Church, which insist that freedom of expression is not absolute and that human dignity is a greater good than the right of the pornographers to freedom of speech, the mainline Protestant churches have shied away from efforts to restrict expression, tending to recommend that church members register their objections with distributors of pornographic material (boycotting them, if necessary) and stressing the importance of education. Both mainline Protestant and Catholic churches have been addressing the degradation of human sexuality and especially of women that pornography entails rather than emphasizing as the religious right groups do the inherent objectionableness of sexually explicit and sexually stimulating material.

The traditional definition of pornography — material that is sexually arousing or appeals to prurient interests — is no longer satisfactory. The critical feature of all pornography is not that it deals with sexual themes, but that it eroticizes violence, humiliation, degradation and other explicit forms of abuse. Churches disagree widely over how we might best cope with the rapid and relentless growth of the pornography industry. One possibility, suggested by religious right groups and the Catholics, is censorship. The mainline Protestant churches, by contrast, have urged education and consciousness-raising.

The debate over the appropriate response to pornography is not limited to the churches. Since women are the most frequent victims of pornography, feminists, too, have debated how to respond to it. The churches can learn from their discussions.

The objection that much of pornography is demeaning to women surfaced early in the contemporary feminist movement, particularly in Kate Millett's 1970 book *Sexual Politics*, which analyzed some of Henry Miller's limited and negative portrayals of women. The antipornography fight gained its greatest momentum in 1975 with the appearance of "snuff" films in the U.S. Claiming to depict the actual killing and dismembering of female actors during explicitly sexual scenes, these films highlighted the link between sex and violence that frequently characterizes pornography. The antipornography movement that flourished in this climate reached its most stringent form when feminist activists Andrea Dworkin and Catherine MacKinnon drafted the Indianapolis Anti-Pornography Ordinance in 1984.

This ordinance defined pornography as anything that presents women as sexual objects, as enjoying pain, humiliation or rape, or as being physical harmed. It also identified as pornography material that depicts women in "scenarios of degradation, injury, abasement, or torture" and as "filthy or inferior, bleeding, bruised, or hurt in a context that makes these conditions sexual." Underlying the ordinance is the assumption that pornography plays an important role in causing rape and domestic violence, and therefore is not only demeaning but constitutes an overt physical threat to women. The ordinance would have permitted any woman who felt degraded or victimized by a piece of pornographic literature or pornographic film to have a court injunction issued against the booksellers, theater owners, publishers and distributors to prevent the marketing of the offending material. The ordinance, which the city government passed and the mayor approved, was opposed by a group of book publishers, distributors and sellers. The resulting court case (*Hudnut v. the American Booksellers Association*) went as far as the U.S. Court of Appeals, which ruled in favor of the booksellers. The U.S. Supreme Court, by refusing to review the case, confirmed the lower court's decision. But both MacKinnon and Dworkin have stated they will continue their campaign against pornography through all available channels. Thus the Indianapolis ordinance remains a live issue.

The efforts of MacKinnon and Dworkin have helped us recognize the inadequacy of the "sexual arousal" definitions of pornography; they have made us aware of the profound misogyny in pornography, and revealed how extensive pornographic images are in our culture. Because it called for a form of censorship, however, the Indianapolis ordinance raised a red flag before publishing houses and a number of feminists. One such group of feminists fears that the censoring of sexually explicit materials would violate the constitutional guarantee of freedom of speech and backfire on women by permitting the censorship of feminist speech. Some lesbians have objected to the ordinance out of fear that it would serve to permit certain expressions of sexuality and discourage others. Eventually, the discomfort over the Indianapolis ordinance gave birth to FACT (Feminist Anti-Censorship Taskforce), which filed an *amicus curiae* brief with the court on behalf of the book publishers opposed to the ordinance.

FACT argued that the ordinance reinforced the prevailing prejudices that women are not interested in sexual expression, that sexually explicit materials are degrading to women, and that women cannot make choices about sexual matters for themselves but need the paternalistic protection of the law. We do not have to look far for examples of these assumptions, FACT contended; for example, a number of states until recently restricted the circulation of birth-control information on the grounds that it fostered immorality and undermined the family, and statutory rape laws still assume that young men are responsible for their sexual behavior and young women are not.

FACT argued that very little social-scientific evidence substantiates the assertion that pornography causes violence. Misogynist images exist everywhere in our society, it noted; we cannot possibly control all of them. It pointed out that violence itself is the problem, not just violence linked to sex. Therefore, to be consistent, the ordinance should have tried to censor all displays of violence.

FACT claimed that the Indianapolis ordinance perpetuated gender stereotypes by implying that women are helpless victims who don't enjoy sex and that men cannot control their sexual urges and can be incited to violent action by the mere sight of pornography. These stereotypes are precisely what feminists should be fighting, FACT insisted.

Finally, FACT argued that the ordinance could not be effective because sexual meanings are generally determined in relation to a context, and because sexual messages are notoriously complex and ambiguous. For instance, feminists disagree on the interpretation of *Swept Away*, a Lina Wertmuller film that portrays an upperclass woman who is sexually dominated by her servant and who eventually begins to enjoy the domination. Some feminists find this theme objectionable, whereas other feminists find illuminating the movie's exhaustive examination of a relationship of domination and submission. Terms in the ordinance such as "sex object" and "subordination" are vague, FACT asserted, and could be interpreted in a number of ways.

In essence, FACT has called for the protection of sexually explicit speech. It argues that an author could portray, for example, a rape scene — even a scene in which a woman enjoys rape — in constructing a story that it ultimately and thoroughly feminist. It believes that the stifling of erotic imagery would ultimately deter the feminist imaginations and voices that strive to remove female sexuality from patriarchal control.

The FACT brief reveals that censorship creates far more difficulties than it solves. And yet the problem remains: women's bodies are used to sell everything from whiskey to tractor parts; heavy-metal rock-and-roll bands sing songs glorifying sexual violence; and hard-core pornography depicts virtually every form of torture and mutilation imaginable. The FACT stance seems to downplay the fact that as members of our society none of us avoids being affected by prevailing images. While it may be impossible to prove that a particular pornographic image or text has actually caused a rape, the proliferation of such images certainly helps create a climate in which rape gains a certain level of acceptability. (By portraying gang rape as entertainment *Hustler* diminishes for its readers some of the horror of this crime.) FACT appears to support the call to assert one's autonomy from cultural images, but its assumption that we are completely unaffected by cultural images is as incorrect as assuming, with Dworkin and MacKinnon, that we are completely at the mercy of such images. Therefore, while I share FACT's opposition to censorship, I nonetheless believe we must recognize pornography's destructive influence, and that it runs counter to the foundational Christian feminist understanding that men and women are created equal and that both sexes were made in the image of God. Christians and feminists believe that pornography calls for concrete response.

Action against pornography can take many forms and still steer clear of censorship. It is certainly appropriate for churches to boycott and demonstrate against objectionable films and images. Churches can urge phone companies and video stores to make it difficult for minors to use phone sex and X-rated films. They can lobby for restrictive zoning to curtail the spread of pornography into residential areas. All congregations should support rape crisis centers and battered women's shelters that assist the ultimate victims of our pornography-ridden society.

I would warn Christian feminists that it would be a strategic mistake to forge an alliance with groups on the religious or political right simply because they, too, oppose pornography. Although they have used feminist language at times, their opposition to pornography stems much more from their nostalgia for a "purer" America, and they disagree with feminists on crucial issues such as sex education and day care.

My own experience suggests that the most effective means of attacking pornography is education. In ethics classes, in which most of the students are in their first or second year of college, I first show (after giving advance warning and making it clear that attendance is optional) the Canadian Film Board's documentary *Not a Love Story*, which portrays some of the most violent and degrading pornography available. I show the film not for its shock value but to alert my students to the extremes of misogyny represented in the pornography industry. Before seeing the film, most of my students define pornography as material that is merely sexually explicit. Afterward they find this equation questionable. After viewing and discussing the film, we analyze images from a much milder source, *Playboy* magazine. Again, almost all the students have considered the pictures in *Playboy* objectionable only because of the nudity. But once they have examined the models' poses, the contexts in which the models appear and the overall format of the magazine, they recognize that pornography does in fact degrade women, that it invariably shows women and not men in positions of submission and weakness. I conclude by having the class scrutinize images in advertising, fiction, the conventional film industry and other conventional media for more subtle portrayals of pornographic themes. My students' remarks suggest that as a result of this analysis they are less likely to become consumers of pornography or of products that are advertised with pornographic themes. Churches may wish to follow this approach.

To construct a precise and effective critique of pornography, we must also have a clear idea of what we consider normative sexual expression. Unfortunately, throughout much of its history the church's views of sexuality have differed little from those of contemporary pornographers. Many Christian thinkers have expressed contempt for human physicality and for women, a contempt that pornographers clearly share. But Christianity contains more positive attitudes as well, including biblical affirmations of the human body—evident in the creation story, the concept of the incarnation and the Roman Catholic notion of the unitive purposes of sexuality. This social and communal understanding of erotic life is totally absent in the privatized world of pornography. Churches, in their teachings about sexuality, must resist the isolation and fragmentation that pornography represents. A sound theology of the body must not only celebrate male and female physicality but also acknowledge that sexuality is meant to help unite individuals, and ultimately communities.

Censorship and the Fear
of Sexuality
Marty Klein

Marty Klein, a licensed marriage counselor and sex therapist (and the author of
Your Sexual Secrets: When to Keep Them, How to Share Them) *claims that*
those who favor the censorship of sexually explicit materials are, in fact, doing so
because they have unresolved psychological problems concerning their own sexuality.
In the course of this discussion, Klein makes a case for pornography's positive and
psychologically therapeutic effects.

In 1986, Ronald Reagan created the Meese Commission with the express purpose
of destroying the pornography industry. It was widely expected that the commission
would issue a report linking pornography to sexual violence. As often happened
during the Reagan Administration, however, things did not go exactly as planned.
The Meese Commission could find no causal link between sexually explicit materials
and sexually aggressive behavior. To its surprise, the commission also found that less
than one percent of the imagery in the most popular porn magazines was of "force,
violence, or weapons." And yet, despite these and other well-known findings, a
surprising number of people — many of them otherwise staunch defenders of our
First Amendment rights — wish to censor pornography in the interests of some
greater social good.

I will not address the pornography issue from the standpoint of civil liberties,
although there is overwhelming evidence from this point of view that the censorship
of sexually explicit materials is harmful. Nor will I address the argument that
pornography degrades women. Proponents of censorship almost invariably want to
suppress pornography by and for lesbians and gay men as well — which shows that,
although some censors may sincerely wish to uphold the dignity of women, this is
not their real motive.

Finally, I will not discuss the dangerous way that censorship strengthens the hand
of America's political and religious right wing. Conservatives such as Citizens
Against Pornography candidly admit that they also want to criminalize abortion,
restore prayer in school, and destroy anti-discrimination programs. Humanists and
feminists who align themselves with these people are making a profound mistake.

Instead, I wish to address the psychological issues that typically lie behind the
desire to censor sexually explicit materials.

What does every child learn about sex? Simple: sex is bad. We all learn this as
children when we are rudely discouraged from touching ourselves, when we are
forbidden to play "doctor," when we are punished for asking certain questions, or
when we experience our parents' discomfort while bathing us.

So, although no one ever explains *why* sex is bad, we come to believe that it is.
But we also know that we are sexual beings — which makes *us* bad. All children
know that their sexual feelings and behavior put them in constant danger of being

Marty Klein, "Censorship and the Fear of Sexuality," *The Humanist* July–August 1990.

punished, leading inescapably to the fear that their sexuality will cause them to be rejected or even abandoned by their parents. This is what Freud's "latency period" is really about: children hiding their sexuality to avoid punishment, rejection, and abandonment.

This early terror of sex stays with us, and the fear of sexuality getting out of control becomes a part of every adult's unconscious. The fear that "bad" sexuality can lead to destruction or abandonment means that trusting one's own sexuality or the sexuality of others feels *very* dangerous. And this is what a lot of the desire to censor pornography is: an expression of our fear of "dangerous" sexuality.

Our basic, archaic fear, then, is that our sexual impulses will invite punishment and destroy others. This is an irrational fear that people do not admit to themselves, much less talk about with each other. Thus, both individuals and the society they constitute develop myths that are taken as fact, myths that are easier to deal with than the irrational fear. Jimmy Swaggart, for example, could not accept the reality of his own sexual desires, and so instead spent a lot of time decrying the "perversions" of others. Pornography, of course, does not depict *real* sex — only fantasy. But some people want to censor it because pornography is a *symbol* of the "bad" sexuality that we unconsciously fear.

What distinguishes this kind of sexuality? First, it is pleasure-centered. Second, it does not feel constrained to conform to roles or polite rules. Third, it is not bound or controlled by notions of "love." And fourth, it places value on losing control (although within a secure environment).

This kind of sexuality admits to being a form of self-expression, self-exploration, and self-healing. From this perspective, sex is the most personal of art forms. And, as a way of plugging into the cosmic battery, it can be intensely spiritual, because it allows people to interface with the universe directly, instead of through a person, ritual, or institution.

Yet, because our culture has traditionally depicted sex as beyond our control and therefore dangerous, anything which threatens our ability to maintain that control is also seen as dangerous. And pornography, since it is designed to be sexually arousing, does exactly that. Moreover, the sexuality it depicts is itself frequently out of control (that is, driven by passion instead of reason), which can be frightening. Censorship, then, is an attempt to reestablish some crucial sense of control over sexuality.

There are many ways in which pornography triggers people's fear of losing control of sexuality. Pornography depicts sex outside the context of love — which, in our culture, is the most important boundary separating "bad," uncivilized sex from "good," sane sex. As depicted in romance novels and other media, love conquers sexuality, making it wholesome and restoring control to its wild, unpredictable expression.

When sex is separated from love, a wide range of choices suddenly appears. These choices include multiple partners, sex with those of "inappropriate" age, class, or race, sex that is (consensually) rough rather than gentle, and sex for pleasure rather than intimacy.

In other activities, such as shopping and eating, a high degree of choice is considered positive rather than problematic. But in the context of our sexual fears and our desire for sexual simplicity, a high degree of choice is threatening. For example, many men unconsciously fear that exposure to homosexuals and homosexual culture will seduce them away from heterosexuality. That is, people fear that even something as profoundly basic as their sexual identity is not safe from intrusion and unwanted change. Therefore, according to this "reasoning," controlling the influences on one's sexuality is critical.

Pornography is also an invitation to get in touch with one's fantasies and desires. Since most people fear that their desires are weird (or worse), this invitation is frightening. Many people look at their mates and think, "If you *really* knew me, you couldn't love me." Therefore, some people desire to remove the temptation of pornography so they can stay hidden—from themselves as well as their mates.

Interestingly, our culture suggests that the "wrong" kind of sexual experience will undermine people's *nonsexual* values and "morality." Our culture fears that sexual pleasure-seeking will be so rewarding that it will soon overwhelm us, destroying our ability to defer it. Sexual pleasure is thus seen as something that must not get a foothold in our consciousness.

There is much truth to the fear that the unfettered pursuit of sexual pleasure will force us to examine our choices and our reality. This does not mean, however, that we will subordinate everything else in our lives to the quest for sexual gratification. In reality, when people accept their desire to seek pleasure, they can also leave it at will and return to it when appropriate. As proof, look at an extreme: in even the most "immoral" pleasure-seeking activity—extra-marital affairs—people *do* go back to work, remain with their families, and so on. The illicit sex doesn't necessarily control them.

Finally, censorship often appeals to people who were sexually abused as children. Being molested is an experience of powerlessness for a child, and depictions of sex without the conventional constraints of love and politeness can trigger fear, shame, anger, or traumatic memories for these people. Some claim that the child molester is "motivated" or "instructed" by pornography. We know, however, that this is rarely true; as even the FBI admits, most child molesters are into power, not pedophilia.

The unconscious fear of punishment can also lead to the desire to limit "bad" sexuality. Most of us are or have been ashamed that we masturbate and associate the activity with the possibility or experience of punishment. Since pornography is primarily designed to enhance masturbation, it feels to many like dangerous stuff.

Some of us also experience an unconscious feeling of shame or fear over the voyeurism involved in consuming pornography. People who had no privacy as children may overidentify with porn actors being "violated" by the viewing public, forgetting that filmmaking is a consensual business arrangement. And people with voyeuristic fantasies they can't acknowledge may react by condemning pornography especially harshly. Psychodynamically, sexuality can be seen as the dangerous, "child" part of the self, while the censor is the "parent" reassuring the child that everything is under control—whether it actually is or not.

Virtually no one has enough accurate, judgment-free information about sex. We don't watch other people do it, we can't find many accurate representations of it in the media, and few of us talk honestly about it with each other. It's almost impossible to know the full range of sexual thoughts and behavior of the people around us—and, therefore, impossible to know how much we have in common.

This is difficult enough to handle, but much of American advertising is based upon exploiting this fact. Its message is: "Are you sexually adequate or normal? Why take a chance that you're not? Buy this product and feel secure." Of course, religion, government, and medicine are also involved in persuading people that their sexuality may not be "normal" or "acceptable" in some abstract, theoretical sense. As a result, people learn to distrust their own sexuality and to trust only those with the "authority" to judge it. The fear of sexual abnormality easily leads to censorship — to suppressing that abnormal sexuality out *there*.

We Americans like things neat and tidy; the problem is, real sex isn't. Nor is sex clean and wholesome. Pornography holds up a mirror of what sex is like on a broad level — not in terms of the content (which is an exaggeration of common experience, just like major league sports and PBS cooking shows), but in terms of the passion and the willingness to relinquish control. It shows a part of the reality of sex that many of us wish to avoid.

By portraying lust as acceptable, pornography also increases some people's fears about aggression: "Will I lose control of my lust and hurt myself? Will I 'use' someone and later regret it?" Some censors complain that pornography cheapens sex — that is, shows it without love or "meaning." But what's wrong with "meaningless" sex if both partners agree to it? There is no reason that sex cannot or should not express our ignoble side: aggression, lust, greed, selfishness, hedonism (all with the consent of one's partner, of course). Sex is the most harmless arena of all in which to play out, express, and investigate this side of being human. Sexuality can be our sandbox, if we simply set down some basic ground rules.

These same critics also tend to attack pornography because it treats people as sexual objects. So long as this is done with the consent of both viewer and viewed, this is a reasonable activity as well. Unfortunately, some people fear that they won't be adequate sex objects. They don't understand that *just being emotionally present* makes one sexually adequate.

Our culture depends on a symbiotic system of male-female sexual incapacity and miscommunication; the authentic sexuality represented by pornography transcends and shatters this unholy alliance.

The idea of female sexual power being unblocked (that is, not bound by love, commitment, or the need of a male's expertise) is frightening to both men and women; our society clearly fears that this power will be expressed by voracious female sexual appetites, the abandonment of the family, or the judgment of some men as simply not good enough. Contrast, for example, the way a woman with a strong sexual appetite is called a "nympho" — someone out of control — while a man with a similar appetite is called a "stud" — someone who is skilled and selective, clearly in control. The portrayals of female lust and sexual enthusiasm in pornography confront us with our modern double standard: seeing women as competent, powerful equals in the workplace, but as weak, vulnerable creatures needing protection and guidance in the bedroom.

Thus, pornography is the symbol of a threatening kind of sexuality that places value on losing control and separates sex from love. We can also describe this as "authentic" sexuality — sex valued for its own sake, with its own subjective logic.

To the extent that we are attached to the status quo, the fear of this kind of sex *is* rational. Authentic sexuality is ultimately revolutionary. It challenges gender roles by depicting women as lusty without being bad. It enfranchises us all as sexual beings — but for who we are, not for what we do. It returns to us the right and means to own and evaluate our own sexuality, rather than referring us to social definitions of what is "normal." It challenges the role of monogamy and the nuclear family as the exclusive source of emotional comfort. It undermines traditional religions by refusing to make procreation the primary purpose of sex. It also challenges the basis of advertising, which creates sexual insecurity in order to sell products. It trusts people to take care of themselves and others during sexual encounters. Finally, it sees sex as a positive force we can use to explore and expand our human horizons, rather than as a negative force we must control and restrict to protect ourselves.

Contrast this with the kind of sexual expression that is *not* generally subject to censorship — the kind that connects sex with either love or guilt and punishment. Clearly, these forms of sexual expression pose no threat to the status quo. Examples include teen magazines featuring male heartthrobs, Barbie and Ken dolls, romance novels ("women's pornography" that routinely depicts rape leading to love), sexually titillating yet moralistic television shows like *Dynasty*, and even sexual harassment in the workplace. Of course, would-be censors do not admit that fear motivates them. No one says, "Sex scares me," because such a statement would not be considered a valid foundation for public policy (nor should it be). Instead, people hide behind social fables about the supposedly "objective" dangers of uncontrolled sexuality such as rape and child molestation.

What can be done about the dangerous, anti-democratic censorship that stems from the fear of sexuality? We can affirm that many people are afraid of sex and empower them to find the solution to their fear. We can work to separate this fear from valid public policy considerations. While acknowledging the difficulties in changing such deeply rooted attitudes, we must remind people that they already know how to handle their anger and fear without acting it out in their significant relationships. We also need to identify and develop programs dealing with sexuality in a positive light, programs which the public can support. These may include educating young women about date rape; teaching young men to use condoms; providing accurate sexual information through respected figures like Ann Landers; training medical students in sexuality; and teaching people how to discuss sexual values and anxieties with their children.

Two thousand years ago, the Roman senate considered a law requiring slaves to wear distinctive clothing. "This is a bad idea," protested one citizen. "They may look around and realize just how large their numbers are." If only enough people had the courage to wear X-rated hat pins or armbands — because the reality is that millions and millions of Americans consume various kinds of sexually explicit materials every month. If you're one of them, know that your numbers are large — and that your rights are under attack in virtually every segment of society.

Now, more than ever, it is time — emotionally and spiritually — to just say yes.

Is Pornography a Matter of Free Expression?

Patty McEntee

Patty McEntee is a member of Morality in Media, which describes itself as a "non-profit, interfaith national organization working to stop the traffic in pornography constitutionally." Perhaps more than any other author in this chapter, McEntee expresses the concerns of everyday, usually "silent," Americans about pornography. McEntee uses the Supreme Court's Miller v. Miller *decision to call people to action. "Since the obscenity law is grounded in contemporary standards," McEntee says, "it is vital that communities loudly and clearly protest against the invasion of there homes and neighborhoods by illegal pornography. If they do not, their silences may be misinterpreted as acceptance."*

On a typical day in New York City, my senses are assaulted by pornographic material almost continuously. On my way to work, I pass newsstands with racks of porn magazines, one more explicit than the next. I pick up a newspaper and flip past advertisements for dial-a-porn "services," erotic dancing clubs and video stores with "adult" sections. Small cards advertising dial-a-porn are occasionally scattered all over the sidewalk or placed on car windshields. When I turn on the television, I may come across a talk show host respectfully interviewing porn movie "actresses" or the producers of the homemade porn movies that are now on the shelves of my local video store. Every so often, the mailman delivers an unsolicited envelope of full-color ads for the latest porn videos that are now available through the mail.

While not all this material is available in every neighborhood, hi-tech advances have made it almost impossible to shield oneself completely from the pornography industry and its products. What's more, newscasts regularly interview distributors who claim it is their right to display and promote the sale of these items. But whose rights are at stake here? Most Americans get only one side of the story and are repeatedly fed the clichés and distortions of the very people profiting from pornography. So, let's take a look at "censorship," the First Amendment, pornography and obscenity.

If I refuse to shop in my neighborhood stationery store because it sells pornographic magazines, am I a "censor"? If Morality In Media (MIM) encourages citizens to urge their district attorney to enforce their state's obscenity law, is it guilty of "censorship"? Although it may surprise some people, the answer is no. The word censorship has been misused ad nauseam. Censorship is *prior* restraint *by government* of freedom of speech or the press.

Although civil libertarians may not like to say so, the First Amendment is not without limits. Obscenity, slander, libel, perjury, inciting a riot and false advertising are not within the area of constitutionally protected speech or freedom of the press.

"Pornography" is a generic term that includes both hardcore and softcore porn. "Obscenity" is the legal term for "hardcore" pornography, and obscenity is not

Patty McEntee. "Is Pornography a Matter of Free Expression?," *America* 10 August 1991.

protected by the First Amendment. Another legal term is "indecency," and it is prohibited in broadcasting (radio and television). The Federal Communications Commission (F.C.C.) has defined indecency as "language or material that depicts or describes, in terms patently offensive as measured by contemporary community standards for the broadcast medium, sexual or excretory activities or organs."

The F.C.C. has also imposed fines on those who broadcast indecency. This 24-hour ban on indecency is, however, currently being challenged in the Federal Court of Appeals in Washington, D.C., by the American Civil Liberties Union, People for the American Way, the television networks and a group ironically calling itself "Action for Children's Television." Morality In Media believes, on the contrary, that the potential flow of indecent broadcasts into the nation's living rooms is a great threat to the country's moral well-being. If the 24-hour indecency ban is struck down, television depictions of oral sex, sodomy, orgies, sadomasochism and bestiality could become commonplace by the turn of the century.

According to the U.S. Supreme Court, materials or performances are "obscene" if: a) taken as a whole, they appeal to the prurient interest; b) depict or describe in a patently offensive manner sexual conduct specifically defined, or c) taken as a whole, lack serious literary, artistic, political and scientific value. Obscenity may apply to magazines, videos, dial-a-porn, cableporn or live performances.

Throughout our history, the Supreme Court, no matter whether characterized as conservative, moderate or liberal, has held that obscenity is not protected by the First Amendment. In 1973, the Court stated: "We hold that there are legitimate state interests at stake in stemming the tide of commercialized obscenity. . . . These include the interest of the public in the quality of life and the total community environment, . . . and, possibly, the public safety itself. . . . There is a 'right of the nation and the states to maintain a decent society.' . . . The sum of experience, including that of the past two decades, affords an ample basis for legislatures to conclude that a sensitive, key relationship of human existence, central to family life, community welfare and the development of the human personality, can be debased and distorted by crass commercial exploitation of sex."

In recent years, Federal law enforcement against illegal pornography (obscenity) has increased substantially. Major law enforcement efforts are still needed, however, at the state or local (district attorney) level. Nor are these the only effective measures that can be taken. Meetings with store owners, picketing, public seminars to educate the community and counseling groups for pornography addicts and their wives are also useful. These efforts may be labeled "censorship" by those who don't know what censorship is or who want to confuse the public. But does not our freedom as persons and citizens include the right to try to influence others for good, the right to rebel against total decadence and the right to preserve our cherished Judeo-Christian values? Is it not our *right* to protect our children from sexual abuse and exploitation? Have we not the *right* to try to create safer and more decent communities for these children? It sometimes seems, however, that the right to raise children has taken a back seat to the so-called "right" to distribute hardcore pornography despite a local community's protests.

Studies indicate that porn addicts are 40 percent more likely to commit a sex crime than non-addicts, but these are not the only damages that pornography inflicts on our society. Men addicted to porn lose faith in marriage and commitment and are more likely to have extramarital affairs or to visit prostitutes. They think convicted rapists should be given lighter sentences and they persuade themselves that sexual perversions are more common than is the fact ("Everyone's doing it"). Not surprisingly, the marriages of these men often end in divorce.

Attorney General Richard Thornburgh said that enforcement of pornography laws would be one of his top five priorities, but the battle continues. Pornography is still a business that makes from $9 billion to $10 billion annually in the United States. It is the third largest profit maker for organized crime after drugs and gambling. As Federal Judge Jose Gonzales remarked in the recent obscenity trial of the 2 Live Crew rap group: "This is a case between two ancient enemies: 'anything goes' and 'enough already!'"

That conviction of "enough already" is now widespread. Common sense perceives that pornography is related to sex crimes, promiscuity and the devaluation of committed marriages and family life. Citizens everywhere are tired of the pornographic assault. Since the obscenity law is grounded in contemporary community standards, it is vital that communities loudly and clearly protest against the invasion of their homes and neighborhoods by illegal pornography. If they do not, their silence may be misinterpreted as acceptance.

Protests of this sort have grown stronger each year with the Morality In Media-sponsored White Ribbon Against Pornography (WRAP) Campaign.

In 1987, a woman named Norma Norris sat in St. Paul's Roman Catholic Church in Butler, Pa., and listened to her pastor, Msgr. Francis Glenn, lament the pornography epidemic. He said that the local district attorney actually thought people didn't care because he rarely received a complaint. As Norma Norris thought of her 2,000 fellow-parishioners, she concluded, "That can't be — they must care!" She decided then and there to come up with a way to express the community's true standard. Thus was born the WRAP Campaign. It was a huge success that first year in Butler, and it was launched nationally by MIM in 1988.

Last year's WRAP Campaign enrolled over five million participants from all 50 states in activities such as letter-writing campaigns; the display of a white ribbon in porn-free stores; proclamations from governors and mayors; motorcades flying the ribbon from car antennas; presentations of white bows to district attorneys who support obscenity-law enforcement and public seminars in which citizens heard the testimonies of pornography's victims, including reformed porn addicts and former porn actresses. The WRAP campaign continues to expand and is now promoted by groups in Australia, Canada, France and Switzerland. The 1991 WRAP Campaign, Oct. 27–Nov. 3, promises to be the largest yet.

From time immemorial, symbols have conveyed crucial messages. During the Persian Gulf War, support for U.S. troops was symbolized by a yellow ribbon. The white ribbon symbolizes a battle still being fought here at home — the battle against the dehumanizing forces of pornography that strike at the soul of America. Morality In Media urges every citizen to join this moral struggle by taking part in the WRAP Campaign against illegal hardcore pornography.

SUGGESTIONS FOR WRITING

Informal Essays

1. After reading a few of the essays in this chapter, write a paper in which you discuss a personal experience you have had with censorship. Perhaps you were a member of a high school or college newspaper staff that ran into a censorship problem. As you look back now, do you feel the same? Is the issue as clear as it was then? Is censorship of a high school newspaper the same as government censorship of a national magazine? In what way is it the same? In what way is it different? Should high school publications be covered by the First Amendment?

2. Write a humorous paper on your first contact with pornography. Devise your own thesis.

3. Write a paper in which you attack or defend the current rating system for movies (G, PG, PG 13, R, NC 17, and X).

4. If there has been a controversy in your town over censorship, describe it.

Short Documented Papers

1. Contrast the positions taken by Ernest van den Haag and Gay Talese in the debate transcribed in "What Is the Civil Libertarian to Do When Pornography Becomes So Bold?"

2. After reading the summary of the *Miller v. California* decision (1973) in the introduction to this chapter and the interview with Alexander Bickel ("Pornography, Censorship and Common Sense"), attack or defend the Supreme Court's decision that states or localities should be able to decide what is the "common conscience of the community."

3. After reading a few of the definitions of pornography given in the introduction to this chapter and a few in the articles reprinted in this chapter, see if you can come up with a better definition than those you have read.

4. Discuss the harmful (or benign) effects of pornography.

5. Discuss the two different responses — censorship and education — which some feminists (and traditional Christians) make to the harmful effects of pornography. Side with one of the two responses.

6. After reading the essays by Brownmiller, Ross, and McEntee, describe the points some feminists and some Christians have in common in their responses to pornography.

Longer Documented Papers

1. Attack or defend the idea that obscene materials should be protected under First Amendment rights. See in particular the articles by Buckley, Kristol, Wolfe, and the dissenting comments by justices Douglas and

Black in response to *Roth* v. *United States* (in the introduction to this chapter).

2. Write a report that sums up the main arguments on both sides of the censorship controversy.

3. Argue the anticensorship case.

4. Argue the procensorship case.

5. Argue that pornography has either a harmful (or benign) influence on society. Argue, too, what might be the most appropriate response to the issue.

6. Describe and discuss the differences of opinion feminists express in their attitudes toward pornography. (You might also want to include within that paper an analysis of the different Christian perspectives on pornography.)

JAPANESE INTERNMENT: *Wartime Necessity or Tragic Mistake?*

Wartime passions and anti-Japanese sentiment were running high in the United States in 1942, particularly on the West Coast. It was widely assumed, for instance, that the attack on Pearl Harbor in December 1941 had been aided by a large network of Japanese informers living on the Hawaiian Islands.

Then early in 1942, the Japanese bombed other Allied bases and cities, including Hong Kong, Manila, and colonies along the Malaysian Peninsula. Fear of an imminent Japanese invasion gripped California citizens, and rumors of resident Japanese complicity with the enemy curculated widely. Such rumors were stoked by a real scare — the shelling of the coast near Santa Barbara by a Japanese submarine — and by a host of false alarms.

Fueled by these fears, West Coast politicians, newspaper editorial writers, and civic groups exerted a great deal of pressure on the federal government to round up the Japanese living on the West Coast and send them to internment camps.

It's not surprising that a nation at war would have worried about the inhabitants of Japanese ancestry in their midst, many of whom had not been assimilated into the mainstream of U.S. society. In fact, the Issei, consisting of Japanese immigrants, most of them farmers and fishermen, had been prohibited by the 1924 Immigration Act from becoming naturalized citizens. A second group, the Nisei, consisted of the children of the Issei. American citizens by birth and education, the Nisei were sometimes required by their parents to attend Japanese-language schools, and many Californians assumed that the Niseis' family loyalties might well be stronger than their national ties. The third and smallest group, the Kibei, were more worrisome. Like the Nisei, they were American citizens by birth, but they had been sent by their Issei parents to Japan for their education — an education that many Americans believed included heavy political indoctrination.

Rather than try to sort out this culturally diverse group, a process that might have taken years, on February 19, 1942, Franklin D. Roosevelt signed an executive order that sent all 110,00 Japanese living on the West Coast to "relocation camps," where most remained for the duration of the war.

There were many Americans at the time who protested that Roosevelt's executive order was unconstitutional, and many Americans today look back at what we did with shame. The internment, the critics say, was simply the result of prejudice heightened by wartime hysteria, and Pearl Harbor simply contributed a veneer of credibility to the longstanding attempts of the Hearst press, the American Legion, and various conservative and agricultural groups to vilify the Japanese living in their midst.

The issue of the Japanese internment may well seem less complicated than other issues in this book. With the luxury of historical hindsight, few of us today, especially those of us too young to have experienced the acute, compelling sense of national peril that gripped people in those times, would be inclined to support that 1942 decision to intern the West Coast Japanese. The essays in this chapter nevertheless contain ample supporting evidence for a historical justification of the way our government, under crisis conditions, chose to handle a difficult problem.

A brief history of events leading to the internment of the Japanese in 1942 is contained in "The Activation of the Stereotype" by Jacobus ten Broek and others.

The Civil Liberties Act of 1987 formally apologized for the federal governent's "fundamental violations of the basic civil liberties and constitutional rights" of those people of Japanese descent who were interned from 1942 to 1945. The act also provided $20,000 in compensation for each surviving camp internee. More recently, on December 7, 1991, at the Honolulu, Hawaii, ceremony commemorating the fiftieth anniversary of the Japanese attack on Pearl Harbor, President George Bush once again expressed the nation's deep regret over the wartime internments and extended the nation's apology for them.

How to Tell Your Friends from the Japs

This Time *essay, written only days after the Japanese Pearl Harbor attack, provides a telling example of how widespread and intense the national anti-Japanese hysteria was in those dark days of late 1941. You might also want to look up a similar article in the* Life *magazine of the same date, which comes complete with diagrams of Japanese and Chinese facial features and applies such phrases as* inscrutable malice *to the Japanese character.*

There is no infallible way of telling them [the Chinese and the Japanese] apart, because the same racial strains are mixed in both. Even an anthropologist, with calipers and plenty of time to measure heads, noses, shoulders, hips, is sometimes stumped. A few rules of thumb — not always reliable:

- Some Chinese are tall (average: 5 ft. 5 in.). Virtually all Japanese are short (average: 5 ft. 2½ in.).
- Japanese are likely to be stockier and broader-hipped than short Chinese.
- Japanese — except for wrestlers — are seldom fat; they often dry up and grow lean as they age. The Chinese often put on weight, particularly if they are prosperous (in China, with its frequent famines, being fat is esteemed as a sign of being a solid citizen).
- Chinese, not as hairy as Japanese, seldom grow an impressive mustache.
- Most Chinese avoid horn-rimmed spectacles.
- Although both have the typical epicanthic fold of the upper eyelid (which makes them look almond-eyed), Japanese eyes are usually set closer together.
- Those who know them best often rely on facial expression to tell them apart: the Chinese expression is likely to be more placid, kindly, open; the Japanese more positive, dogmatic, arrogant.

  In Washington, last week, Correspondent Joseph Chiang made things much easier by pinning on his lapel a large badge reading "Chinese Reporter — NOT *Japanese* — Please."
- Some aristocratic Japanese have thin, aquiline noses, narrow faces and, except for their eyes, look like Caucasians.
- Japanese are hesitant, nervous in conversation, laugh loudly at the wrong time.
- Japanese walk stiffly erect, hard-heeled. Chinese, more relaxed, have an easy gait, sometimes shuffle.

"How to Tell Your Friends from the Japs," *Time* 22 December 1941.

Japanese Saboteurs in Our Midst
Stanley High

Like the preceding Time essay, Stanley High's article was an immediate reaction to the Pearl Harbor attack. It provides a good, comprehensive summary of the circumstantial evidence that at the time led many West Coast citizens to seriously question the loyalties of those of Japanese descent who were living in their midst. Reader's Digest, by the way, deleted this essay from the back issues of the magazine they sold to libraries after World War II.

At the time he wrote this article, High was a senior editor for Reader's Digest.

Japan is ready, in case of war, to hit us hard—from the inside. Japanese on the West Coast are well prepared for the event. They have assembled detailed data on our vital Pacific defenses. They possess the bases, the equipment and the disciplined personnel with which to strike either through sabotage or open acts of war.

Evidence of the thoroughness and extent of Japanese machinations has been dug up through six months of hard work by undercover men set upon the trail by Congress. Neither in war nor in peace would any other nation on earth be so careless of its security as to tolerate the situation which exists at the harbor of Los Angeles, for example.

Los Angeles harbor is one of America's vital defense areas. It is one of the nation's six naval operating bases and usually there are important units of the Pacific fleet at anchor inside its breakwater.

Close to the harbor are 150 producing oil wells. Along its shoreline are tank farms estimated to contain 8,000,000 barrels of oil—enough to flood the surface of the harbor with an inflammable blanket eight inches thick.

Near the center of the harbor, Terminal Island bulges with shipyards, drydocks, storage tanks of oil and aviation gasoline, half a billion dollars' worth of defense projects and Reeves Field, naval flying base.

Here in the midst of this naval stronghold the United States keeps open house for its potential enemies.

On the island is a community of 3500 to 5000 Japanese, most of them fishermen or cannery hands. How many of them are aliens, the authorities have not ascertained—not at least with complete accuracy—but one estimate is 3000 in the whole harbor area. "Little Tokyo" is squalid, but it seems to attract Japanese visitors. Japanese consular officers visit it frequently; officers and men from Japanese vessels seek its hospitality. Groups come from San Diego, Bakersfield and San Francisco.

In the Japanese fishing fleet, obligingly allowed to share harbor space here with the U.S. Navy, there are 250 vessels. Many of them, perhaps 90 percent, are manned by reservist officers and sailors of the Japanese navy. Inshore they fly the Stars and Stripes, as required by law. At sea they frequently run up the flag of the Rising Sun, as the government has photographs to prove.

They are extraordinary fishing boats. They are Diesel-powered with engines that give them a 6000-mile cruising range—say to Panama and back. They have short-wave radio capable of working direct with Japan. Some have radio telephones, sonic depth-finders, million candlepower Sperry searchlights, electrically driven air compressors and winches.

What the Navy thinks of these boats is summed up in the fact that it recently bought 32 of them for conversion into minesweepers and patrol boats. They are likewise convertible on short notice into minelayers and torpedo boats. Bait boxes are built so that they could conceal a pair of surface torpedo tubes with self-propelling torpedoes. Between the bait boxes and the gunwales is room for two more torpedoes. Or the boat could carry 30 mines with anchors, or 90 without anchors. Its winch could handle an 1800-pound mine.

This potentially dangerous fleet still plies unhampered among our naval vessels and defense plants and up and down our coastline. What they would do in case of war, only war will tell, but a strong hint has been revealed.

Last winter two retired Japanese officers—one for the army and one for the navy—toured our West Coast states to stir Japan's agents to renewed activity. They carried with them a secret document entitled *The Triple Alliance and the Japanese-American War.* One copy got into American hands.

This textbook has much to say about Japan's "surprise fleet," with its "minelayers capable of carrying a heavy load of mines for distribution in American sea routes of merchantmen and battleships." "We can then," the booklet continues, "strike the enemy fleet at a most opportune time and cut off communication lines as well as merchantmen."

Meanwhile, wherever the U.S. fleet is maneuvering, fishing must almost always be good, for the Japanese boats turn up—not forgetting their telescopic cameras. Recently they turned up for the Navy's maneuvers in the Caribbean. West Coast fishermen had never fished those waters before.

Japan has already profited from these operations at sea and ashore. Our coastline—including the remote bays and harbors of Alaska—is more familiar to Japan and to the Japanese reservists in the West Coast fishing fleet, who have painstakingly photographed, mapped and charted it, than to our own sailors. Helped along by our American laxity, they appear to have done the same job on the U.S. Navy.

A few weeks ago, in this defense area, government investigators came into possession of two documents. The first, printed by the Japanese navy, was purloined from a Japanese naval reservist on Terminal Island. It is a several-hundred-page, ship-by-ship description of the important units of the U.S. fleet—complete with photographs and scale drawings for each. It is up to date, including several ships launched last summer.

The second document is a map, likewise printed in Japan—an overall key to our Pacific naval defenses including Hawaii. Most startling item on it is a diagram showing in accurate detail the battle formation of our Pacific fleet, presumably a well-guarded secret.

Almost as important as the fishing fleet are the Japanese farmers. A government investigator pointed out—two years ago—that there was not a single flying field on the entire West Coast which did not have Japanese farmers nearby.

They seem curiously indifferent about soil fertility. The Kettleman Hills area is poor farm land. But it contains one of the nation's most valuable oil fields. In the adjacent San Joaquin Valley plenty of fertile land is available. But Kettleman Hills, nonetheless, has a thriving community of Japanese truck gardeners.

Recently two Japanese rented—for truck gardening—the 1300-acre Conroy Ranch, most of it too dry to be farmed at all. But the ranch is traversed by the huge aqueduct which carries water to the city of Los Angeles. The ranch house is adjacent to the Water Patrol Road and the aqueduct's casually protected inspection gate.

Of the loyalty to the United States of thousands of our West Coast Japanese, particularly the Nisei, or American-born, there is and can be no question. In fact they have supplied much of the information our government has.

But pressure to serve the Emperor is too strong for many to resist, and over the years Japan has made every effort to keep its hold on the Japanese in America.

At birth Japanese parents register their children with the consul. Those who hesitate are subjected by the Japanese organization to various forms of pressure ranging from social cold-shouldering through business boycott to blunt threats— familiar Axis technique. The registration makes the child a citizen of Japan as well as of the United States—and this is the status of more than 60 percent of California's American-born Japanese.

At kindergarten age, Japan reaches for the child again and he is sent—each day after public school—to one of the 248 Japanese-language schools in California. Almost all the teachers are either alien Japanese or educated in Japan. Many of them are Shinto priests, trained in the religion of Japanese nationalism. Until last spring, when a threatened investigation put them momentarily on the shelf, the textbooks used in these schools were published by the Japanese Imperial Board of Education.

Lesson 30 of the Junior High School Reader declares: "The objective of Japanese education, no matter in what country it may be, is to teach the people never to be ashamed of their Japanese citizenship. We must never forget—not even for a moment—that we are Japanese."

Lesson one in Grade Five begins: "Our heavenly ruler has governed our Empire for ages past and we are his subjects. . . . There is no other country with such a royal lineage. Be thankful you are a Japanese and worship the Imperial Family."

"Hawaii is known as a possession of the United States of America," says the eighth grade reader, "but here the Japanese language is spoken just as you hear it in Yokohama. . . . Hawaii's development to its present stage is due to the Japanese."

After this yearly indoctrination, Japan's helping hand is extended into a network of some 60 useful and potentially useful adult organizations. Every Japanese community of any size has Buddhist temples—over the altars, the inscription: "Now let us worship the Emperor every morning." Shinto—even more undisguised in its propagandist teachings—is also well represented. In Los Angeles there are 16 Shinto temples.

Almost every Japanese family in the U.S. is a member of a "Ken," or clan. Headquarters for each Ken is Japan—in the prefecture from which the family originated. The Ken's aim is to maintain the family tie with Japan. There are 57 Kens in Los Angeles alone. They are linked in an association; its hidden control is in the hands of one of Japan's top-flight spies.

Most potent of all organizations among the Japanese is the Japanese Association. Wherever so much as a handful of Japanese are gathered, an Association is forthwith formed. It serves the community in numerous worthy ways. Control of these Associations—according to the testimony of Japanese—is almost wholly in the hands of aliens. Behind the scenes the strings are pulled by the Japanese consul. The Associations enable the consuls to keep a record of comings and goings of every Japanese, to transmit messages, launch propaganda and, when pressure is required, put on the screws.

Thus the Japanese community — more than any other in the United States — is a fertile field for the purposeful machinations of a foreign power. With the generous support of the government of the United States the field is being cultivated.

The book which the two Japanese officers carried on their last winter's tour comes to this conclusion: "Should America become involved in war she would be subjected to gigantic, united attack from Japan, Germany and Italy. Only the flag of the sun would fly in the Pacific. In the Atlantic, the swastika, which also symbolizes the sun and life, will be active with might. In addition, the meaningful flag of Italy would flash. In the face of all this, if America comes against Japan and tries to block her it would be no more than a pin prick."

It is doubtful whether Japan's spies and saboteurs inside the United States were in need of any such sales talk. Driven by their own well-nurtured patriotism and apparently unmolested by the government they are plotting against, their part in the anticipated triumph appears to be well prepared.

THE DIES REPORT

This brief Newsweek *article describes an old Japanese plot to invade the United States. That plot was unearthed (along with other evidence that suggested the existence of a network of Japanese saboteurs living in the United States) by the House Committee on Un-American Activities chaired by Texas congressman Martin Dies. You can understand how these kinds of revelations, which might be dismissed as merely rumor and hearsay during peacetime, would help fan widespread fear and distrust, especially among citizens along the Pacific coast, after the Japanese Pearl Harbor attack.*

Baron Gen. Giichi Tanaka, Japanese Premier known as the "Machiavelli of Nippon," called on Emperor Hirohito July 25, 1927, with a 10,000 word document. It was his advice to the new Emperor, who had ascended to the throne on Christmas Day, 1926, and it contained a plan for the conquest of Manchuria and the rest of China, India, Asia Minor, Central Asia, and even Europe by the Japanese. But Tanaka pointed out that Japan must first crush the United States before she could carry out the rest of the program.

Excerpts from the famous Tanaka Memorial were published by the Chinese five days after Japan invaded Manchuria in September 1931 and by the Russian newspaper Pravda on Nov. 5, 1931. The Chinese claimed to have got it from a Korean clerk who stole a copy and the Russians from a clerk who photostated it. The Japanese began a barrage of official denials, which were widely accepted.

On Feb. 27 Rep. Martin Dies of Texas, chairman of the House committee to investigate un-American activities, which is seeking a continuing appropriation of $100,000, made public a 285-page report on Japanese plans and plots which he said was based on a mass of evidence, including the Tanaka Memorial. He had planned public hearings on them last September but waited at the request of Attorney General Francis Biddle.

The Dies report included a secret Japanese "invasion map" of the United States as well as a supplement to the Tanaka Memorial by Lt. Gen. Kiyokatsu Sato urging that Japan capture Hawaii, destroy the Panama Canal from the air, and land troops on the West Coast of the United States to destroy cities and ports. Building a line of defense along the Rocky Mountains, the Japanese, according to Sato, would then take the offensive toward the East Coast.

To further plans for conquest of America, the Dies report revealed, the Japanese Government used thousands of Japanese residents of the United States and its possessions to obtain detailed information about the American Fleet, Hawaii, the Panama Canal, and even the Los Angeles water supply. Code devices included necklaces, matches cut at various lengths, dental plates, the notching of postage stamps, and a copy of George Bernard Shaw's "The Devil's Disciple," certain words of which were underlined in invisible ink.

"The Dies Report" [our title], Newsweek 9 March 1942.

The report was made public a day before the deadline for re-registration of all enemy aliens in the United States and as the Army and Department of Justice were preparing to move all Japanese, citizens as well as aliens, out of Pacific Coast "combat zones." Residents of Coast communities were more anxious than ever to get rid of their aliens after rumors that signal lights were seen before the submarine attack near Santa Barbara on Feb. 23 and the air-raid alarm over Los Angeles on Feb. 25.

LIFE IN A CALIFORNIA
CONCENTRATION CAMP

This letter, published in The Nation, *contains a former University of California home economics major's chilling firsthand account of life in the assembly center in which she had been interned. Notice that, like most of her young Nisei counterparts, the woman is by no means an immigrant speaking in Pidgin English. She is an American citizen who was born and educated in this country, as were two-thirds of those who were evacuated and interned in relocation camps. What is sobering about this essay (and Ted Nakashima's account, which follows this one) the writer's poignantly human concerns.*

Dear Sirs: I inclose excerpts from a letter to a member of my household written by a Japanese student, American-born, registered at the University of California in the Department of Home Economics, who for the last year and half has lived in my home.

Since I do not know how the neighboring American citizens would be disposed toward Japanese criticism of their local "Assembly Center" I feel that it might be inadvisable for you to identify the writer or the camp.

MARION RANDALL PARSONS
Berkeley, Cal., May 26

[The excerpts follow.]

We are now in our "apartment" in _____ Assembly Center, having arrived here yesterday after a heavy shower. _____ is famous for black clayey soil; so you can imagine what the mud was like. Lunch was a horrid affair—one frankfurter, a mess of overboiled cabbage, white bread, pasty rice, and canned cherries. All the workers are volunteers from the camp, and the cooks are quite inexperienced or else rusty with disuse, since many of the farmers from our vicinity were house boys and cooks some thirty years ago. Dinner was better—canned carrots and peas, one slab of canned pork, lettuce salad, apricots, and plenty of milk. There is a great shortage of waiters and common laborers. My brother was asked to help, but upon hearing that they are paid 70 cents a day and that board and room is subtracted from that, he said no!

The "apartments" are rooms with four, six, and eight beds. Usually they assign one "apartment" to a family. The rooms have screened windows, concrete or wooden floors, and a door that may or may not fit. Some doors are at least two inches too small for the doorway. When we first saw our living quarters we were so sick we couldn't eat or talk—couldn't even cry till later. Since they will not allow less than four in one room my two brothers are living with H— and me. We have put up canvas partitions. These things are tolerable, but you should see the latrines! Ten

"Life in a California Concentration Camp," *The Nation* 154 (1942).

seats lined up; hard, fresh-sawed, unsandpapered wood; automatic flushing about every fifteen minutes.

My parents feel humiliated but are quite resigned. I admire their stoicism or whatever it is that enables them to hold up under so much. P— is in the hospital, one of the many that filled up the temporary wards as soon as they entered. . . .

I have been offered a job as dietician! Was busy till 10 p.m. yesterday. There is no regular dietician we can work under. Another girl and I have had our hands full helping with the mess halls, planning menus, even cooking. There is great need for trained nurses and decent hospital equipment. The only fresh fruit we can get is bananas and the only fresh vegetable is cabbage. Many people need special diet — allergies, diabetes, stomach ulcer, high blood pressure. V— and I feel overloaded, especially because we don't know a thing about planning menus from equations, balancing calories, weighing out grams, etc.

Three-fourths of the population loaf all day while the mess-hall boys and girls and the hospital staff work like horses. Right now the nurses are on duty twelve or fourteen hours a day. We greenhorn dieticians on ten hours can't complain.

We are slowly getting adapted to the diet, lack of privacy, etc., but every time we think of the white plastered walls, sunny rooms, and green gardens we left behind we again drop into depression. . . .

Last night it rained — for many people on their beds. Our head nurse says she cries every night when she thinks of the old folks, many of whom will most likely die here very soon, and of the children, who don't understand why they can't leave this horrid place.

Thanks, millions and millions, for those books. They are life-savers, especially for H—, who feels there's hardly anything left to live for except books.

I have been giving you the worst side of life here — the side most obvious. There is another side to the picture too. Some of the boys play all day, stopping only to sleep and eat. Some of the formerly busy mothers have time to look after their babies and chat with the neighbors. For many this is a long vacation in somewhat drab surroundings.

One man says he has a new slogan. Instead of "Remember Pearl Harbor" it is "Remember the Concentration Camp."

Until our dying day we'll not forget.

Concentration Camp: U.S. Style

Ted Nakashima

*Like the anonymous University of California coed who wrote the preceding essay,
Ted Nakashima, in this letter to* The New Republic, *gives another tormented,
firsthand account of life inside an assembly center—in this case, Camp Harmony
in Pullayap, Washington. Notice that Nakashima is at pains to give the reader his
solidly American middle-class credentials: his parents are forty-year residents of the
U.S.; one brother is an MIT-trained architect, the other an MD. He himself was
an architectural draftsman for the Army before his internment. His obvious frustration and bitterness are not difficult to understand.*

Unfortunately in this land of liberty, I was born of Japanese parents; born in
Seattle of a mother and father who have been in this country since 1901. Fine
parents, who brought up their children in the best American way of life. My mother
served with the Volunteer Red Cross Service in the last war—my father, an editor,
has spoken and written Americanism for forty years.

Our family is almost typical of the other unfortunates here at the camp. The
oldest son, a licensed architect, was educated at the University of Washington, has
a master's degree from the Massachusetts Institute of Technology and is a scholarship graduate of the American School of Fine Arts in Fontainebleau, France. He is
now in camp in Oregon with his wife and three-months-old child. He had just
completed designing a much needed defense housing project at Vancouver,
Washington.

The second son is an M.D. He served his internship in a New York hospital, is
married and has two fine sons. The folks banked on him, because he was the
smartest of us three boys. The army took him a month after he opened his office.
He is now a lieutenant in the Medical Corps, somewhere in the South.

I am the third son, the dumbest of the lot, but still smart enough to hold down
a job as an architectural draftsman. I have just finished building a new home and
had lived in it three weeks. My desk was just cleared of work done for the Army
Engineers, another stack of 391 defense houses was waiting (a rush job), when the
order came to pack up and leave for this resettlement center called "Camp
Harmony."

Mary, the only girl in the family, and her year-old son, "Butch," are with our
parents—interned in the stables of the Livestock Exposition Buildings in Portland.

Now that you can picture our thoroughly American background, let me describe
our new home.

The resettlement center is actually a penitentiary—armed guards in towers with
spotlights and deadly tommy guns, fifteen feet of barbed-wire fences, everyone
confined to quarters at nine, lights out at ten o'clock. The guards are ordered to
shoot anyone who approaches within twenty feet of the fences. No one is allowed
to take the two-block-long hike to the latrines after nine, under any circumstances.

Ted Nakashima, "Concentration Camp: U.S. Style," *The New Republic* 106 (1942).

The apartments, as the army calls them, are two-block-long stables, with windows on one side. Floors are shiplaps on two-by-fours laid directly on the mud, which is everywhere. The stalls are about eighteen by twenty-one feet; some contain families of six or seven persons. Partitions are seven feet high, leaving a four-foot opening above. The rooms aren't too bad, almost fit to live in for a short while.

The food and sanitation problems are the worst. We have had absolutely no fresh meat, vegetables or butter since we came here. Mealtime queues extend for blocks; standing in a rainswept line, feet in the mud, waiting for the scant portions of canned wieners and boiled potatoes, hash for breakfast or canned wieners and beans for dinner. Milk only for the kids. Coffee or tea dosed with saltpeter and stale bread are the adults' staples. Dirty, unwiped dishes, greasy silver, a starchy diet, no butter, no milk, bawling kids, mud, wet mud that stinks when it dries, no vegetables—a sad thing for the people who raised them in such abundance. Memories of a crisp head of lettuce with our special olive oil, vinegar, garlic and cheese dressing.

Today one of the surface sewage-disposal pipes broke and the sewage flowed down the streets. Kids play in the water. Shower baths without hot water. Stinking mud and slops everywhere.

Can this be the same America we left a few weeks ago?

As I write, I can remember our little bathroom—light coral walls. My wife painting them, and the spilled paint in her hair. The open towel shelving and the pretty shower curtains which we put up the day before we left. How sanitary and clean we left it for the airlines pilot and his young wife who are now enjoying the fruits of our labor.

It all seems so futile, struggling, trying to live our old lives under this useless, regimented life. The senselessness of all the inactive manpower. Electricians, plumbers, draftsmen, mechanics, carpenters, painters, farmers—every trade—men who are able and willing to do all they can to lick the Axis. Thousands of men and women in these camps, energetic, quick, alert, eager for hard, constructive work, waiting for the army to do something for us, an army that won't give us butter.

I can't take it! I have 391 defense houses to be drawn. I left a fine American home which we built with our own hands. I left a life, highballs with our American friends on week-ends, a carpenter, laundry-truck driver, architect, airlines pilot—good friends, friends who would swear by us. I don't have enough of that Japanese heritage "ga-man"—a code of silent suffering and ability to stand pain.

Oddly enough I still have a bit of faith in army promises of good treatment and Mrs. Roosevelt's pledge of a future worthy of good American citizens. I'm banking another $67 of income tax on the future. Sometimes I want to spend the money I have set aside for income tax on a bit of butter or ice cream or something good that I might have smuggled through the gates, but I can't do it when I think that every dollar I can put into "the fight to lick the Japs," the sooner I will be home again. I must forget my stomach.

What really hurts most is the constant reference to us evacués as "Japs." "Japs" are the guys we are fighting. We're on this side and we want to help.

Why won't America let us?

Outcast Americans
William Robinson

William Robinson was a reporter for American Magazine, *a general-interest periodical that ceased circulation during the early 1950s. In "Outcast Americans,"
Robinson discusses the fear, social isolation and the somewhat ambiguous loyalties
of those of Japanese descent who were confronted first with the increasing fear and
hostility of Americans living around them. Robinson also summarizes his observations of the actual evacuation and of life at Camp Manzanar in the Mojave Desert,
based on his two visits there. Be sure to watch for the poignant vignette that closes
his essay.*

Doc was scared. And you couldn't blame him.

There he was, at thirty-nine, an American, born and reared; taxpayer, voter,
clubman; honor alumnus of a famous university; authority on intricate phases of
surgery. He was dapper, chipper, proud; a well-tailored little man who had lifted
himself by his bootstraps.

And his world was crumbling.

Ten days earlier his California-born wife had taken their two sons and fled to
friends in Utah. That left Doc where I found him — in San Francisco, disconsolate,
bewildered, in the ruins of his life. Now Uncle Sam had given him just 48 hours to
wind up his affairs and prepare to get out of town. The notice was nailed to a
telephone pole outside his office door. He didn't know where he was going, nor
when, nor how.

Doc is a Japanese-American.

He had been caught up in a fantastic backswirl of the maelstrom of war. With
72,000 other American citizens of Japanese ancestry — men, women, children, and
infants — he was being evacuated from the Pacific Coast, now become a theater of
military operations, to join 42,000 alien Japanese in exile for the duration.

In Doc's office, I sat on the operating table, Doc on a white stool, endlessly
toying with a pair of bright forceps. He was trying to bluff it through, laugh it off,
but he kept coming back to personal perplexities. Would they keep him behind
barbed wire? Would they confiscate his money? Could he practice his profession in
camp? That made him think of the patients he was leaving.

"What can I do about Mrs. Tayama? I had her slated for an operation next week.
And little Taki, with that infected arm." He named others and their ailments. He
looked searchingly at me. "Say, do you suppose the Government would make an
exception in my case? I'm needed here!"

"Why don't you ask them?" I suggested.

"By George," he said impulsively, "I will! I'll go see them right now."

William Robinson, "Outcast Americans," *American Magazine* September 1942.

We emerged into Japtown's principal business street, already more than half deserted. Doc got into his car and started the motor, and then, leaning out, he said, as though it were an afterthought:

"By the way, I've been wondering whether families will be permitted to live together in the camps . . ." His voice trailed off. Japs usually hide their sentiments. Sometimes you wonder if they have any.

I told him what Army officials had told me — that every effort would be made to keep families together. He nodded absently. "Oh, well, I just wondered. Give me a ring tomorrow and I'll tell you what happens." He drove away.

Five days later I got around to calling Doc's number. "I'm sorry," said the operator impersonally, "that number has been disconnected." . . .

As simply, as inexorably as that, Japanese vanished from our Western seaboard. In late March, fifteen weeks after Pearl Harbor, they were still doing business as usual from Vancouver to San Diego. By June 1 they were gone, swallowed up into stockades, reception camps, and resettlement areas established far back from the military emplacements along the coast.

Behind this monstrous mass migration lies a baffling problem in human justice. Doubtless, many of the Japanese are loyal, trustworthy Americans. But strange things have happened on the West Coast. Investigators have picked up irregular radio signals; a wireless set was discovered in a fishermen's truck; in a Jap home, agents found a searchlight cunningly concealed in a chimney; strange lights have flashed out to sea, possibly to pass on information to enemy submarines. The Government is acting generously and kindly toward the Jap thousands along the West Coast; but because this is total war, intelligence authorities are taking no chances. They have no intention of jeopardizing the safety and security of the entire West Coast by allowing a few hundred or even a few dozen Jap fifth columnists to remain and carry out their work of treason and sabotage.

Japanese born in Japan, or elsewhere outside the United States, are forbidden the right to become American citizens. But their children, born in America, are American citizens. Thus, about two thirds of all persons of Japanese ancestry in the United States are Americans by birthright, subject to all the rights, privileges, and duties of any other American. But are they truly Americans? Is their allegiance unquestionable?

Military and civil authorities in California, Washington, and Oregon frankly don't know. Japanese children customarily attended language schools where they learned the mysticism of Nippon. Every Japanese child is taught to obey its parents unswervingly until they die. Since many of the elders to whom American citizenship is denied are bitter about the discrimination, it is reasonable to assume this also rankles in their offspring.

Authorities know, too, that many American-born Japanese have a personal problem of divided citizenship. By birth, they are Americans under our laws. But — and here's the catch — if the birth of a child was registered with a Japanese consul, the child is entitled also to the citizenship of Japan, under Japanese laws.

In the first excitement after Pearl Harbor, some West Coast legislators debated the advisability of amending our law so that a child of foreign parentage would be required at maturity to produce evidence that he had resided most of his life in the

United States and conducted himself in a manner that would demonstrate his fitness for citizenship.

The motion was sidetracked and eventually forgotten, on the ground that no Caucasian could hope to plumb the depths of Oriental minds. Also, it was impossible to determine which American-born Japanese had been registered with the consulates; the busy Japs burned all records in the first moments of the war.

Of course, if you wanted to be naïve about it, you could ask each American Japanese to take an oath of allegiance. But authorities had a hunch it wouldn't amount to much. Two California-born and American-educated Japanese — Hideo Okusako and Charles Hiasao Yoshii — had sworn allegiance to the Stars and Stripes during every year of their schooling, and are now blatting Japanese propaganda to America from radio stations in Tokyo.

Today many mature American Japanese don't know where their own sympathies lie. I am convinced of that, after talking with hundreds of them. All their friendships and contacts are in America. Many don't know either the customs or the language of Japan. Yet, so thorough was their home training, they would feel themselves traitors if they aided America in a war against Japan.

America has never assimilated them. During business hours they associated with white Americans, but after dark they lived in huddled colonies. When they moved into a district, whether in a city or a countryside, Caucasians moved away. Their neighbors were other Orientals or dark-skinned peoples.

Their dual nationality was reflected in their homes. The food usually was an eerie blending of East and West. One Jap family proudly served me strawberry shortcake covered with a gooey, dark brown sauce containing chopped almonds. It was good, but hard to eat with chopsticks, which many Japanese families prefer to knives and forks.

Their confusion extended to their religions. About half of all the Japanese in America are Buddhists, according to official surveys. The others are scattered through all the Christian faiths. Denominations never seemed to make much difference to the Japanese themselves; they went where they were welcomed. In an upper-caste Japanese home one evening, I saw a rosary and a copy of Science and Health with Key to the Scriptures, lying on a teakwood table in front of a pot-bellied image of Buddha.

What cast the die against these strange people was the fact that they had, intentionally or by chance, clustered around important military objectives in the West. One Army airfield was surrounded to the depth of a mile or more by Japanese truck gardens. A Navy base near Los Angeles was flanked by a colony of Japanese fishermen. Near Seattle, Japanese populated an island where movements of ships could hardly be missed. Literally scores of miles of strategic highways along which military columns had to roll were fringed by Japanese-held properties. Military men shudder to think what might have happened in an emergency if those highways had been dynamited or blocked by wrecks of Japanese trucks.

Yet it is characteristically American and democratic that, at first, the Japs were given a chance to leave the coast voluntarily. About 1,000 did. Since many of their elders had been quietly gathered in at the outbreak of the war, a fiery little priest, the Rev. F. J. Caffery, of Los Angeles, became their shepherd. He led a grotesque flock that day late in March — a 10-mile-long procession of automobiles in all stages of decrepitude, over 300 weary miles of meadow and mountain and desert, into oblivion. I went along.

We started at dawn from a park in Pasadena. As the ragtag column started chugging forward, soldiers materialized from somewhere and took places in the line. At the end came an army mechanical unit, complete with tins of gasoline and tow car. They hauled more than one of those jallopies up the mountains before the day was over.

Civilians hardly looked up from their chores as the weird parade went by, although one farmer had erected a sign in his front yard: "Good-by, Japs. See you in Hell." Another had rigged up a signpost with an arrow pointing to: "Tokyo, 6,874 miles."

After hours of desert travel, we entered flat, dusty Owens Valley. Gaunt mountains rose in the west; beyond them lay the waste of Death Valley. Eastward, close by, towered the snow-clad Sierra Nevadas. In the last light we passed the foot of Mt. Whitney, highest peak in the continental United States. Just at dark we came to Manzanar. Soldiers stood guard at the gate.

Then the camp consisted of two dozen long, barracklike, low buildings, sheeted with tar paper and slats. Each building was divided into four compartments, and each compartment held 16 steel cots. An enormous ditching machine was roaring and snorting in the middle of the street, cutting a sewer trench. Under floodlights, hundreds of workmen were building new barracks.

Through this bedlam wandered the new arrivals like wan ghosts, each with his bundle of bedding. I watched an old man peering into the rooms. At the first three he shook his head, but he went in the fourth and dropped his bundle on a cot. I went over to see what had attracted him, but couldn't tell; to me, they all looked alike.

Up the line, somebody began hammering lustily on a dishpan. Th crowd surged that way. I found myself wedged against a slender young Japanese in United States Army uniform, except for insignia. He said his name was Iijima, he had enlisted at St. Louis, Mo., in September, and been mustered out with honor in February. "Why?" I asked. He shook his head. "Search me," he said. "I guess they don't want us in the Army."

The dishpan was being hammered at the door of the communal dining hall. When 1,000 of us crowded in, the walls were bulging. I found myself facing a tall, prim young Japanese girl. Her name, it developed, was Oko Murata. A private secretary in Los Angeles, she had volunteered to do office work in the camp. "I knew I'd have to come sooner or later, so I thought it might as well be sooner," she smiled casually. There were 20 other American-born girls in camp, all aiding in organization.

After a time I walked back down the street. Near the ditching machine I came across a wiry, middle-aged Jap crouching and sifting dirt through his fingers.

"Me," he said, "I'm gardener. Damn' good gardener. Best in Beverly Hills, you bet. This, damn' good dirt. Plenty thing grow here. You watch see." He got up and looked up and down the street, measuring with squinted eyes.

"Here I'm go plant begonia," he said. "There, maybe good cineraria. Make nice border lantana. Fix up middle street like parkway, maybe, with plenty nice flower shrub." He fell silent, busy with his plans. Finally he said, "Yes. Very good. I'm make this little bit of heaven. You watch see." . . .

I went back to Manzanar in early summer. More than 10,000 Japanese were there. The snow line had moved far up the mountains and the gullies were chuckling brooks. The tar-paper shacks were still squat and ugly, but no uglier and much more orderly than many Western desert camps.

Kids were playing ball on a diamond at the edge of town. Girls in slacks and gay print dresses were sitting on the side lines, calling shrill advice. Tall, prim Oko was at her desk in the Administration Building, yawning over columns of figures. She had spring fever, she said. She gave me the gossip.

Three of her girl-friends had met and married young evacuees. One was already expecting. Some of the boys had organized a swing band. A mimeograph newspaper, the *Manzanar Free Crest*, had made its appearance, full of good-natured gags. The police—all Japanese evacuees—had raided three prosperous crap games. Almost $1,000 worth of war bonds and stamps had been sold through the camp post office.

The schools were running full time, using the standard California educational system and textbooks. Several nurseries were operating for the convenience of mothers. A town council, called the Advisory Board, had been formed to work on administrative matters with the army-civilian management set up by the Government. Several church services were held weekly and meetings were always crowded. The hospital was going great guns, momentarily expecting a rush of maternity cases. Young Dr. James Goto, its chief, had finished inoculating evacuees for typhoid and smallpox and was busy with $100,000 worth of equipment and supplies.

I couldn't find my ambitious little gardener friend, but I saw his handiwork everywhere. There were "flower shrub" in tidy parkways and clusters of blossoms in gardens. And on the north side, in the lush, warm shade, cinerarias were taking root.

After that first voluntary evacuation in March, the gloved fist of the Army closed down on Japanese who hadn't gone. From the Presidio of San Francisco, Lieut. Gen. John L. DeWitt, commanding all military operations in the western United States, had issued crisp orders.

First, all Japanese still at liberty were "frozen"—prohibited from traveling more than 5 miles from their homes, never after dark. Next, evacuation zones were set up, bounded by streets in cities or township lines in rural areas. Finally, one after another, the zones were evacuated.

Each person was permitted to take bedding and linens, but no mattress; toilet articles, extra clothing, and essential personal effects. No family could take more than its members could carry. No pets could be taken. No personal items or household goods could be shipped to the assembly center. The Government provided for the storage of heavy household effects such as pianos and refrigerators. On the appointed day, fleets of military trucks rolled into the zone. Soldiers supervised the loading of the evacuees and their bundles. At a signal, the caravans rolled away, leaving whole square blocks of cities and square miles of farm land tenantless.

Economically, the departure of the Japs presented no particular problem in the cities, although bank clearances fell off temporarily in some localities and house servants were hard to get. But it was different in the country. Japs had owned or controlled 11,030 farms valued at $70,000,000. They had provided virtually all the artichokes, early cantaloupes, green peppers, and late tomatoes, and most of the early asparagus. They owned or controlled the majority of the wholesale produce markets and thousands of retail vegetable stands.

When they disappeared, the flow of vegetables stopped. Retail prices went up. Many vegetables vanished entirely. There were rumors of a food shortage. Into this situation plunged dynamic Larry Hewes, regional director of the Farm Security Administration and agricultural member of General DeWitt's Wartime Civil Control Administration. He ranged the farms night and day, cajoling the Japs to keep planting up to the final minute and recruiting white farmers to take over their lands when they had gone. He insisted upon fair prices or equitable share-cropping agreements, and by mid-summer the West's agriculture was rolling along as though nothing had happened. . . .

Now that the Japs have been rounded up and tucked away for the duration, what shall we do with them afterward?

There is one answer, although it doesn't take a long-range view.

At four isolated points in the West, workmen are now constructing new camps to be known as Resettlement Areas. One is in western Oregon, in a great flat, treeless sink known as Tule Lake. Another is on the desolate Colorado desert, on the California — Arizona boundary. There will be others later farther inland, in Utah, Colorado, Idaho, and New Mexico, if the Government is able to overcome the vehement protests of the officials and people of those states.

All of the land to be used for resettlement belongs to the Government; most of it is controlled by the Indian Bureau. It is planned — although rather nebulously — to put the Japanese evacuees onto this land and encourage them to develop its latent agricultural resources.

They will be paid for their work. Secretary of War Stimson has set wages for a 44-hour week at from $8 to $16 a month, plus free food, shelter, medical care, and hospitalization. Free clothing will be issued "when and if necessary." In addition, all evacuees will receive coupon books to buy items at the camp canteens. No family may have a total of more than $7.50 in coupons in any month.

"Naturally," a spokesman for the Wartime Civil Control Administration told me, "the land will revert back to the Government after the war, with all improvements."

"But what about the Japs themselves?" I persisted. "What will happen to them?"

He shook his head slowly. "We can't see that far ahead," he replied. . . .

Two things keep recurring to me as I write this report. The first is the well-scrubbed, moon-shaped face of tiny Kiku, who used to be our housemaid. Her father, an immigrant, was my gardener. He brought up a bottle of saki the night she was born and we drank a toast to the new arrival.

Kiku came to my study the other evening to say good-by. Next morning, she said, they'd come for her.

Searching for words and trying to be bluff and hearty, I said, "Well, have a good time. Where will you be?"

She stood in the doorway like a timid little mouse, her face expressionless. "I don't know, sir. They don't tell us."

I cleared my throat. "No, of course not. Well, take care of yourself."

She turned, and with her back to me she said, "I hope you will think of me. I shall think of you all."

I said, still fumbling awkwardly, "Sure; you bet. Well, so long."

She didn't answer. The door closed and she was gone. I don't know where she is now.

The other thing I keep thinking about is the poignant inscription on the Statue of Liberty. You'll find these words down toward the bottom, serenely untouched by the howling storms of more than half a century:

"Give me your tired, your poor, your huddled masses yearning to be free; the wretched refuse of your teeming shores. Send these, the homeless, tempest-tossed, to me. I lift my lamp beside the Golden Door."

Conditions at Camp Harmony

The U.S. Army, stung by Ted Nakashima's indictment of Camp Harmony in The New Republic, *invited the magazine to send one of its reporters to the camp to draw his or her own conclusions about Nakashima's criticisms. This is the visiting reporter's account. You will want to compare this account closely with Nakashima's, which appears earlier in the chapter, and draw your own conclusions from these two contradictory versions of camp life. Do you see, by the way, anything ironic about the comparison which the reporter draws at the article's conlusion?*

Some months ago *The New Republic* published an article by Ted Nakashima, an American of the Japanese race who was at the time an inmate of an assembly center. Although his article did not say so, it was Camp Harmony, Puyallup, Washington. Mr. Nakashima's main point was that he is a loyal American, who was engaged on important war work (as an architect drawing plans for houses to be occupied by defenseplant workers) and that he strongly resented being obliged to go and live instead in the virtual idleness of an assembly center. Incidentally, he complained of some of the physical conditions at the center.

The United States Army took exception to certain of these statements made by Mr. Nakashima. At the army's request, *The New Republic* sent a special investigator to Camp Harmony to check Mr. Nakashima's statements. We publish herewith summaries of the criticisms and of the facts as reported by our investigator.

Mr. Nakashima said the inmates of Camp Harmony are confined to quarters at nine and that lights must be out at ten.

Comment: The regulations on this matter have varied from time to time and from camp to camp. When our investigator visited Camp Harmony, the curfew was at ten o'clock and lights must be out at ten-thirty. This seems not unreasonable in a camp with many old people and small children.

Mr. Nakashima said there were no fresh meats, vegetables or butter, that the evacués had to stand in line for meals in the rain and mud, that dishes and silverware were dirty, and there was milk only for children.

Comment: For a short time at the beginning, certainly not more than a month, the evacués got the United States Army "B" ration. They had small quantities of fresh meat, green vegetables and butter. Thereafter they got the army "A" ration, with plenty of all these things. Some of the older Japanese Americans objected to the American food, because they wanted rice. There seems no doubt that the conditions of which Mr. Nakashima complains were temporary and unimportant.

If dishes and silverware were dirty, this was a reflection on the evacués, and not on the American authorities, since the evacués were in charge of dishwashing.

The charge was made that a broken sewer was insanitary and unpleasant.

Comment: A sewer line did break, but was repaired as soon as possible and there have been no further accidents of this kind.

Mr. Nakashima complained that the camp was guarded by men armed with machine guns, with orders to shoot if the evacués came too close to the barbed wire.

Comment: It is true there are armed guards and barbed wire. It is also true that the evacués were ordered not to walk on the grass within ten feet of the barbed-wire fences. There are not, however, any orders to shoot, and the rule about keeping off the grass is widely disobeyed without penalty.

In general it may be said that some of Mr. Nakashima's criticisms were exaggerated, and that those that were true referred to temporary conditions which were ameliorated shortly after Mr. Nakashima wrote his article (but not as a result of his writing, so far as we know). Conditions at this camp, except for the first few weeks, have been as good as could reasonably be expected by anyone. While the problem of what to do about the Japanese Americans in the long run remains unsolved, the army's part in setting up and maintaining proper conditions in the camps has been carried out satisfactorily. Certainly there can be no doubt that our treatment of persons of the Japanese race has been infinitely better than has been the case with Americans who have been captured or interned by the Japanese.

Issei, Nisei, Kibei

It is ironic that this essay, one of the earliest comprehensive and sweeping criticisms of U.S. policy regarding the evacuation and internment of people of Japanese descent in the Western states to appear in a national periodical, appeared not in a liberal journal like The Nation *or* The New Republic, *but in* Fortune, *a conservative business magazine. This essay will provide you with your best overview of the actual evacuation procedures and of conditions in both the temporary assembly centers and, later, in the permanent relocation camps. This account also describes the loyalty test administered to camp inhabitants during late 1943, and it discusses the mixed motives of the small minority of those who failed this loyalty oath.*

When the facts about Japanese brutality to the soldier prisoners from Bataan were made known, Americans were more outraged than they had been since December 7, 1941. Instinctively they contrasted that frightfulness with our treatment of Japanese held in this country; and, without being told, Americans knew that prisoners in the U.S. were fed three meals a day and had not been clubbed or kicked or otherwise brutalized. Too few, however, realize what persistent and effective use Japan has been able to make, throughout the entire Far East, of U.S. imprisonment of persons of Japanese descent. This propaganda concerns itself less with how the U.S. treats the people imprisoned than who was imprisoned. By pointing out, again and again, that the U.S. put behind fences well over 100,000 people of Japanese blood, the majority of them citizens of the U.S., Japan describes to her Far Eastern radio audiences one more instance of American racial discrimination. To convince all Orientals that the war in the Pacific is a crusade against the white man's racial oppression, the enemy shrewdly notes every occurrence in the U.S. that suggests injustice to racial minorities, from the Negroes to the Mexicans and Japanese.

The enemy, of course, deliberately refrains from making distinctions among the various kinds of detention we have worked out for those of Japanese blood in this country. Unfortunately, Americans themselves are almost as confused as the Japanese radio about what has happened to the Japanese minority in this country—one-tenth of 1 percent of the nation's total population. There are three different types of barbed-wire enclosures for persons of Japanese ancestry. First there are the Department of Justice camps, which hold 3,000 Japanese aliens considered by the F.B.I. potentially dangerous to the U.S. These alone are true internment camps.

Second, there are ten other barbed-wire enclosed centers in the U.S., into which, in 1942, the government put 110,000 persons of Japanese descent (out of a total population in continental U.S. of 127,000). Two-thirds of them were citizens, born in the U.S.; one-third aliens, forbidden by law to be citizens. No charges were brought against them. When the war broke out, all these 110,000 were resident in the Pacific Coast states—the majority in California. They were put behind fences when the Army decided that for "military necessity" all people of Japanese ancestry, citizen or alien, must be removed from the West Coast military zone.

Within the last year the 110,000 people evicted from the West Coast have been subdivided into two separate groups. Those who have professed loyalty to Japan or an unwillingness to defend the U.S. have been placed, with their children, in one of the ten camps called a "segregation center" (the third type of imprisonment). Of the remainder in the nine "loyal camps," 17,000 have moved to eastern states to take jobs. The rest wait behind the fence, an awkward problem for the U.S. if for no other reason than that the Constitution and the Bill of Rights were severely stretched if not breached when U.S. citizens were put in prison.

Back in December, 1941, there was understandable nervousness over the tight little Japanese communities scattered along the West Coast. The long coast line seemed naked and undefended. There were colonies of Japanese fishermen in the port areas, farmlands operated by Japanese close to war plants, and little Tokyos in the heart of the big coastal cities. There were suspected spies among the Japanese concentrations and there was fear of sabotage. Californians were urged to keep calm and let the authorities take care of the problem. In the first two weeks the Department of Justice scooped up about 1500 suspects. A few weeks later all enemy aliens and citizens alike were removed from certain strategic areas such as Terminal Islands in Los Angeles harbor, and spots near war plants, power stations, and bridges. But Californians did not completely trust the authorities. While the F.B.I. was picking up its suspects, civilian authorities were besieged with telephone calls from citizens reporting suspicious behavior of their Oriental neighbors. Although California's Attorney General Warren (now governor) stated on February 21, 1942, that "we have had no sabotage and no fifth-column activity since the beginning of the war," hysteria by then had begun to spread all along the coast. Every rumor of Japanese air and naval operations offshore, and every tale of fifth-column activity in Hawaii, helped to raise to panic proportions California's ancient and deep antagonism toward the Japanese Americans.

For decades the Hearst press had campaigned against the Yellow Peril within the state (1 percent of the population) as well as the Yellow Peril across the seas that would one day make war. When that war prophecy came true, the newspapers' campaign of hate and fear broke all bounds. And, when Hearst called for the removal of all people of Japanese ancestry, he had as allies many pressure groups who had for years resented the presence of Japanese in this country.

The American Legion, since its founding in 1919, has never once failed to pass an annual resolution against the Japanese-Americans. The Associated Farmers in California had competitive reasons for wanting to get rid of the Japanese-Americans who grew vegetables at low cost on $70 million worth of California land. California's land laws could not prevent the citizen-son of the Japanese alien from buying or renting the land. In the cities, as the little Tokyos grew, a sizable commercial business came into Japanese-American hands — vegetable commission houses, retail and wholesale enterprises of all kinds. It did not require a war to make the farmers, the Legion, the Native Sons and Daughters of the Golden West, and politicians resent and hate the Japanese-Americans. The records of legislation and press for many years indicate that the antagonism was there and growing. War turned the antagonism into fear, and made possible what California had clearly wanted for decades — to get rid of its minority.

By early February both the Hearst press and the pressure groups were loudly demanding the eviction of all people of Japanese blood — to protect the state from the enemy, and to protect the minority from violence at the hands of Filipinos and other neighbors. A few cases of violence had, indeed, occurred, and spy talk ran up and down the coast. On February 13, a group of Pacific Coast Congressmen urged President Roosevelt to permit an evacuation; a week later the President gave that authority to the Army. On February 23, a Japanese submarine shelled the coast near Santa Barbara. Lieutenant General John I. DeWitt, on March 2, issued the order that all persons of Japanese descent, aliens and citizens, old and young, women and children, be removed from most of California, western Oregon and Washington and southern Arizona. The greatest forced migration in U.S. history resulted.

At first the movement inland of the 110,000 people within the prohibited zone was to be voluntary. The Japanese-Americans were merely told to get out. Within three weeks 8,000 people had packed up, hastily closed out their business affairs, sold their possessions or left them with neighbors, and set forth obediently toward the east. But Arizona remembered all too well how California had turned back the Okies in the past, and many Japanese-Americans were intercepted at this border. Kansas patrolmen stopped them. Nevada and Wyoming protested that they did not want to receive people found too dangerous in California. About 4,000 got as far as Colorado and Utah. It became apparent that the random migration of so many unwanted people could result only in spreading chaos. By March 29 voluntary evacuation was forbidden, and the Army made its own plans to control the movement.

The *évacués* reported to local control stations where they registered and were given a number and instructions on what they could take (hand luggage only) and when they should proceed to the first camps, called assembly centers. Although they were offered government help in straightening out their property problems, many thousands, in their haste and confusion, and in their understandable distrust of government, quickly did what they could for themselves. They sold, leased, stored, or lent their homes, lands, personal belongings, tractors, and cars. Their financial losses are incalculable.

The Army, in twenty-eight days, rigged up primitive barracks in fifteen assembly centers to provide temporary quarters for 110,000. Each *évacué* made his own mattress of straw, took his place in the crowded barracks, and tried to adjust to his new life. By August 10 everyone of Japanese descent (except those confined to insane asylums and other safe institutions) was behind a fence in "protective custody." They were held here (still within the forbidden military zone) until a newly created civilian agency, the War Relocation Authority, could establish other refuges farther inland. WRA's job was to hold the people until they could be resettled in orderly fashion.

WRA appealed to the governors of ten nearby western states. With one exception, Colorado's Governor Carr, they protested that they did not want the Japanese-Americans to settle in their domain, nor did they want any relocation center erected within their borders unless it was well guarded by the Army. Finally nine remote inland sites were found, all of them on federally owned land. (One assembly center in eastern California became a relocation camp.) Most of them were located, for lack of better acreage, on desolate, but irrigable desert tracts. More tar-papered barracks were thrown up, more wire fences built, and once more the people moved.

By November, 1942, all the *évacués* had packed up their miserably few possessions, had been herded onto trains and deposited behind WRA's soldier-guarded fences, in crowded barrack villages of between 7,000 and 18,000 people.

They felt bitterness and anger over their loss of land and home and money and freedom. They knew that German and Italian aliens — and indeed, Japanese aliens in other parts of the U.S. — had been interned only when the F.B.I. had reason to suspect them. Second-generation citizens of German and Italian origin were not evacuated from California; nor were the second-generation citizens of Japanese descent elsewhere in the U.S. put behind fences.

Although the *évacués'* resentment at regimentation within WRA's little Tokyos is deep, it is seldom expressed violently. Considering the emotional strains, the uprooting, and the crowding, no one can deny that the record of restraint has been remarkable. Only twice have the soldiers been asked to come within a WRA fence to restore order.

But WRA and its director, Dillon Myer, have been under almost continual attack by congressional committees in Washington and by a whole long list of badgering groups and individuals on the West Coast. The Dies Committee goes after WRA and the Japanese minority at frequent intervals. Even Hedda Hopper, the movie gossip, prattles innuendoes. Not wishing to "imply anything," she noted last December that "we've had more than our share of explosions, train wrecks, fires, and serious accidents" since WRA has released so many of the *évacués*. Actually, not one of the 17,000 has been convicted of anti-American activity.

WRA has usually been criticized for the wrong reasons. It has been accused of turning loose, for resettlement, "dangerous Japs." The implication usually is that no Japanese-American should be released, although from the very beginning WRA's prescribed purpose was to help the *évacués* to find some place to live outside the prohibited zone. Again and again, the pressure groups and California Congressmen have urged that WRA's ten centers be turned over to the Army. (In February the President, instead, dropped WRA intact, with its Director Dillon Myer, into the Department of Interior.) Most frequently Mr. Myer has been charged with pampering the Japanese-Americans. Almost every day the Hearst papers fling the word "coddling," with the clear implication that all persons of Japanese descent, citizen or no, women and infants, should be treated strictly as prisoners of war, which of course they are not.

No one who has visited a relocation center and seen the living space, eaten the food, or merely kept his eyes open could honestly apply the word "coddling" to WRA's administration of the camps. The people are jammed together in frame barracks. A family of six or seven is customarily allotted an "apartment" measuring about twenty by twenty-five feet. It is a bare room, without partitions. The only privacy possible is achieved by hanging flimsy cotton curtains between the crowded beds.

Furniture is improvised from bits of scrap lumber: a box for a table, three short ends of board made into a backless chair. The family's clothing and few personal possessions are somehow stuffed neatly away, on shelves, if scrap lumber — a priceless commodity in all camps — is available. Otherwise, they are stuffed away under the beds. The quarters are usually neat. There are no cooking facilities and no running water in the barracks, unless the *évacué* has brought his own electric plate or had a friend "on the outside" send one in. As in Army camps, each block of twelve or fourteen barracks (250 to 300 people) has its central mess hall, laundry building, public latrines, and showers.

With faithful regularity, irresponsible yarns are circulated that the évacués are getting more and better food than other Americans. Actually, the food cost per day is held below 45 cents per person. For 15 cents a meal the food is possibly adequate, but close to the edge of decent nutrition. In most camps, located far from dairy districts, milk is provided only for small children, nursing and expectant mothers, and special dietary cases. There are two meatless days a week and a heavy emphasis on starches. Nearly a third of the food requirements are grown on the irrigated fields of the camp itself. This reduces the actual cash outlay for food to 31 cents per person.

Practically everyone who wants a job can work, and most of the able bodied do. They plant and till the camp's vegetable acreage, prepare the food in the mess halls, do stenographic work for the Caucasian staff, work in the cooperative store. In some centers they make furniture for the administration building or cotton mattresses to take the place of the hard straw pallets. Some are barbers and cobblers for the community, doctors in the hospital, scrubwomen in the latrines, garbage collectors. The maximum wage (a doctor, for instance) is $19 a month; the minimum, $12; the average, $16. In addition, those who work get a clothing allowance for themselves and their dependents — at the most, $3.75 a month for an adult in the northernmost center.

Individual enterprise is forbidden. To set up one's own dress-making service within the community, or to sell shell jewelry or anything else to the outside is prohibited. In order to keep the center wage uniform, all economic activities must be conducted through the community cooperative, which pays its barbers and other workers the standard stipend. With their small monthly wage, and by dipping into their prewar savings, most évacués buy extras to eat, but they can get only nonrationed food, since they possess no ration books. They send to the mail-order houses for some of their clothes, buy shoes, yard goods, and clothing at the cooperative store. Their children go to school in the barracks village, and when they are sick, to the center hospital.

Thus the pampering and thus the humiliation. A doctor distinguished in his profession, who lived with grace and charm in a decently comfortable home before the war, is today huddled in a small room with all his family. He practices his profession for $19 a month at the center hospital, serving under a Caucasian of lesser accomplishments, hired for considerably more money. A man who spent twenty years building up his own florist business or commission house, or who operated a large vegetable farm in one of California's valleys, is merely "stoop labor" on the center's acreage.

The record of Japanese-Americans during the depression indicated that they did not take to public relief. They were too proud. They stuck together, helped each other, and almost never appeared on WPA or home-relief lists. To virtually all of them it is now galling to be distrusted wards of the nation, their meager lodging and food a scanty handout, the payment for their labor somewhat the same.

They have always been an isolated, discarded, and therefore ingrown people. Today this is more true than ever. The barracks village as a rule is literally isolated.

At Manzanar, California, for example, the center is but a tiny square in a vast and lonely desert valley, between two great mountain ranges. Spiritually the people are just as isolated as that. Thrown together in a compact racial island of their own frustrated people, they grow in upon themselves and each other; they become almost completely detached from American life, the war, the world. Their small children speak more Japanese than they would if they competed daily with other American school children. The teen-age boys and girls are ostentatiously American in clothes, slang, and behavior. It is as if they were trying too hard to convince themselves that they *are* Americans. They know that they must and will go out the gate soon.

The adults think about themselves, and about the past they left. With time and distance, California's farm valleys, towns, and cities become more golden-hued than ever to the *évacués*. They brood vaguely and fearfully on the future; the war, sometimes, seems like a vague abstraction, the cause of their troubles. And they think about rumors — which they often trust more than they do printed, official announcements. It may be a rumor that the Army will take over. Or that the *évacués* in this center will all be transported to another. This is the most nightmarish rumor of all to people who have moved so much in the past two years.

They think, too, about the endless details of their camp life. Each group of 250 or so *évacués* has a block manager who gets $16 a month for listening to their complaints and, if possible, straightening out innumerable daily problems. The food in the mess hall is badly prepared; there is no toilet paper in the ladies latrine; the neighbors play the radio too late and too loud; the roof of No. 29 barracks has a small leak.

Finally, there are gossip and politics. The Japanese-Americans back in California went their way without much participation in politics as most American citizens know it. In the barracks village of WRA there is little real self-government. Most of the centers have a Council made up of block representatives or managers. But there is only a slight area within which such a congress can make community decisions. Usually at the meeting of the Council the members do little more than listen to new rules; new plans of WRA, handed down from Washington or the local director. The block representatives are expected to pass on this information to all the people.

Originally WRA ruled that citizens alone could hold office in the centers, but this proved to be unwise. Two-thirds of the *évacués* are citizens but most of these American-born Nisei are from eighteen to twenty-eight years of age — too young to take on such responsible jobs as the block manager's. Beside, among the Japanese-Americans born here are hundreds of Kibei — young men who were sent to Japan for part of their education. Not all — but a large percentage of them — are pro-Japan, particularly those who gained the latter part of their education in Japan. Disliked by the Nisei majority, outnumbered and maladjusted, the Kibei often have become a nuisance, creating little areas of disaffection in the center.

Thus it turned out that the Issei, the aliens, parents of the Nisei and Kibei could best provide the authority, stability, and seasoned wisdom needed in a block manager. They possessed a tradition of family and community leadership, and had commanded respect in the past. Above all they usually have an earnest desire to make the block of 230 or more people in which they live function in an orderly and quiet fashion. They are aliens primarily because U.S. law forbade them to become citizens. Many of them have a real loyalty to the U.S. not because the U.S. has invited their loyalty, but because they look to their children's American future for their own security.

Politics in the centers has nothing to do with office or votes or *apparent* power. But it *is* power, the power of demagoguery, of spreading the infection of bitterness, exaggerating an instance or affront into an issue that may even get to the point of a small strike against WRA. The leaders have not invariably been pro-Japan. Some, both aliens and citizens, who had been good Americans became indignant at their loss of freedom and their right to participate in the life of their nation.

It may be that the administration was not willing to permit a big funeral for a man accidentally killed when a work truck overturned; it may be that three or four of the Caucasian staff displayed signs of race discrimination; it may be a rumor more plausible than fact. The "politicians" take any one of these, or a series, and worry it into a big camp issue. How great an issue it becomes depends most of all on the degree of confidence the center as a whole has in its director and the coolness and fairness with which he customarily handles his people. Too often the administration is out of touch with the main issues and grievances within the camp. WRA suffers, like every other agency, from the manpower shortage. Competent center directors and minor personnel are scarce. Often enough the director finds his Caucasian staff more of a problem than the *évacués*.

The two so-called "riots," which brought the Army over the fence, arose from the accumulation of small grievances, whipped up to a crisis by groups struggling for power and eager to put the administration on the spot. There was, in each instance, a strike. Actually a strike in a relocation center is self-defeating since almost all labor in the community works to provide goods and services for the *évacués* themselves; no more than a handful work in the staff mess and office building. Only when violence occurred, and the director thought he needed help in maintaining order was the Army invited in.

But trouble rarely reaches either the strike stage or violence. The people in the Pacific Coast's little Tokyos rarely appeared on police blotters in the past, and now the crime record of WRA centers compares favorably with that of any small cities of their size, or, indeed, with any Army camp. Most of the policing is done by the *évacués* themselves appointed to the "internal security" staff of each center.

Policing should be simpler than ever from now on. The ideological air has been cleared; the pro-Japan people have been moved out. The process of sifting the communities, separating the loyal and the disloyal, is virtually complete. The "disloyal" have been sent to a segregation center in northeastern California, leaving the other nine centers populated only by the loyal.

To all the *évacués*, the two words, registration and segregation, are almost as charged with emotion as that disturbing term evacuation. Quite simply the two nouns mean that a questionnaire was submitted to all adults in the centers to determine their loyalty or disloyalty. On the basis of this, plus F.B.I. records and in some instances special hearings, WRA granted or denied the *évacués* "leave clearance," the right to go East and find a job. The same information was used as a basis for segregating the "disloyal" in a separate center. About 18,000 (the "disloyal" and all their dependents) will sit out the war at Tule Lake, within a high, manproof, barbed-wire enclosure, unless Japan shows more enthusiasm than she has to date for their repatriation. (These 18,000 must not be confused with the few thousand interned by the Department of Justice.)

But separating the loyal and the disloyal is not so simple a job as it might seem. Loyalty is difficult to measure accurately on any scales, and the sifting of the *évacués* was clumsily handled. The process began in February, 1943, when the Army decided to recruit a combat unit of Japanese-Americans. A registration form was printed containing twenty-eight questions to determine loyalty and willingness to fight. It was to be filled out by all men of military age. Someone realized that it would be well to have just such records on all adults in the centers. Plans were suddenly changed and everyone from seventeen years of age up was given the twenty-eight questions.

Nothing is more disastrous in a rumor-ridden, distrustful, neurotic community like a relocation center than to make one explanation of purpose today and a quite different one tomorrow. The people, newly arrived in the WRA centers, were still stunned by their evacuation, loss of property and freedom, and were acutely conscious of their stigma as "enemy." There was misunderstanding about the purpose of registration at most of the centers. The questionnaire was so carelessly framed, its wording had to be changed during the process of registration. A few thousand refused to fill out the form at all. Others, remembering that they had lost business, home, and their civil rights, wrote angry ("disloyal") answers. They had no enthusiasm for defending a democratic America that had imprisoned them for no crime and without trial.

WRA, in an effort to be fair, has granted hearings in recent months for those who wished to explain the answers they made in anger or confusion. Pride made a few people stick to what they first wrote. There is little question that the majority of adults sent to Tule Lake feel loyalty to Japan, but there are also behind Tule's fences a few thousand who are not disloyal.

Most of the Issei who chose Tule Lake are there because of firm ties of loyalty to Japan or strong ties of family relationships. Some Issei were afraid of bringing reprisals upon their relatives in Japan by affirming loyalty to the U.S. The parents who chose Tule Lake usually have taken all their children with them. Only a few sons and daughters over seventeen, who had the right to choose for themselves, could resist strong family pressure. It is ironic and revealing that at the high school at Tule Lake, civics and American history are popular elected courses.

Japan, however, makes no legal claims of protective interest in the Nisei or Kibei. When the Spanish consul visits Tule to report conditions of Japan, he is legally concerned only with the welfare of Issei, the nationals of Japan. And, under U.S. law, the Nisei and Kibei cannot abrogate their American citizenship during wartime, even if they want to. Their expatriation, and even the repatriation of most of the Issei to Japan, during the war, is unlikely. Negotiations for the exchange of civilian war prisoners have been slow, and the delay is due to Japan, not to the U.S. State Department.

To a minority living at Tule Lake, Japan's unwillingness to arrange frequent exchange of prisoners is not disheartening. This minority does not want to set sail for Japan; it wants to stay in the U.S. People are at Tule Lake for many complicated reasons besides "disloyalty" and family relationships. There is evidence, for example, that some chose this kind of imprisonment for reasons of security and weariness. This is indicated by the percentages of people in the various centers who said they wanted to be segregated. When the decision was made last fall to turn the Tule Lake camp into a segregation center, nearly 6,000 out of 13,000 residents of that center decided to stay put. This high percentage of "disloyal," the highest in any center, is explained in part by unwillingness to be uprooted and moved again. In the Minidoka relocation center in Idaho, only 225 people out of 7,000 chose to go to Tule.

There are a few tired and discouraged people from other WRA centers who went to Tule Lake because they knew that the barbed wire fences in that camp would stand permanently throughout the war. They reasoned that they would have certain refuge for the duration while the other centers, according to *évacué* rumor, might be abruptly closed, and everyone turned loose without resources.

Some chose Tule Lake imprisonment as a gesture against what they consider the broken promises of democracy. For example, there is a young Nisei who enlisted in California early in 1941 because he felt strongly about fascism. He was abruptly thrown out of his country's army after Japan attacked the U.S. and put behind the fences along with all the other *évacués*. In February, 1943, when he was handed a questionnaire on loyalty and his willingness to defend the U.S., he was too angry to prove his "loyalty" that way; he had already amply demonstrated it. He is at Tule Lake, not because of his love for Japan, but as a protest to the government he honestly wanted to serve back in 1941.

There is the Japanese-American who fought in the last war in the U.S. Army, and is a member of the American Legion. When the Japanese struck Pearl Harbor, he offered his services to the Army and to industry in California. He was turned down. Sent to a relocation center he became a "troublemaker," with the slogan, "If you think you are an American, try walking out the gate." He was packed off to an "isolation center," and finally wound up at Tule Lake. Last year the U.S. Treasury received a check from him, mailed from behind Tule's barbed wire. It was a sum in excess of $100 and represented his income tax for the calendar year, 1942, when he had received belated payment for his 1941 services as navigator on a Portuguese ship. He insisted on paying his tax, as usual. He has, of course, no wish to go to Japan. He too sits out the war at Tule Lake in protest against the failure of democracy.

The minority who are in Tule for reasons of weariness or protest are not important numerically. But they show what can happen to people who are confused, discouraged, or justifiably angry. They reveal some ugly scars inflicted by our society. It is too early to speculate about what will happen to these 18,000 prisoners. A few thousand, at the most, may get aboard the *Gripsholm*. Will all the rest be shipped finally to a defeated Japan? Or will they be a postwar U.S. problem?

When the Tule Lake prisoners will end their days is less important to consider than what is to become of those "loyal" *évacués* who are still in the nine other centers. Everyone deemed loyal, by the sifting process of registration and hearings, has been granted "leave clearance." Fortified with a handful of official papers, a numbered identification card bearing his picture and fingerprints, an *évacué* can set forth to the East. He gets his railroad fare, $3 a day travel money, and if he has no savings, $25 in cash.

During the last twelve months, 17,000 *évacués* have had the courage to go "outside." They are with rare exceptions, young and single, or married but childless. A Nisei has to master considerable courage to go out into the society that rejected him two years ago. From behind the fence "the outside" has become vague, enormous and fearful. The huddling together, which is resented, is nonetheless a cohesive, protective force, hard to overcome. As he leaves the soldier-guarded gate, the young Nisei is about as lonely as any human being could be; he faces even more prejudice than his father did as immigrant contract labor.

The most powerful magnets to draw him out are letters from friends who have already gone east. Those who have made the plunge usually report back to their friends enthusiastically. The people who have started a new life — most of them from eighteen to thirty years old — are the pioneers. In the factories and in the restaurants and hotels, in the offices and in the kitchens where they work, they are building a future not merely for themselves, but for those who may follow. When they write back, "We can eat in *any* restaurant in New York" they spread a little hope. Or, "I attracted very little attention on the train." Or "In Chicago, nobody seems to care that I have a Japanese face." They tell of the church groups who are almost alone in providing some kind of organized social protection for those who relocate in cities like Chicago.

They are being sent "outside" wherever a not-too-prejudiced community provides opportunity. Seven WRA regional officers have staffs scouting for job prospects, talking to employers and, in general, smoothing the way. Illinois has taken more relocated American Japanese than any other state — 4,000. Most of these have found jobs in and around Chicago. Winnetka housewives compete for Nisei servants, and even the Chicago *Tribune* has been calm. Only Hearst howls.

Ohio's industrial cities have taken about 1,500 from the relocation centers. Although special clearances have been needed for the eastern defense area, a few hundred have already gone to New York City, and the stream to the northeastern states will increase steadily. Scattered throughout midwestern states like Wisconsin, Montana, and Iowa are hundreds more.

There are, of course, areas of resistance. Antagonism to WRA's *évacués* is apt to increase not diminish when the European war ends and the casualty lists come only from the Pacific. Utah has taken about 2,000 *évacués* — mostly in Ogden and Salt Lake City where at first they were quietly absorbed. But last month the state A.F. of L. petitioned Salt Lake City authorities to deny business licenses to people of Japanese ancestry. Two thousand have gone to Colorado, but recent campaigns, like Hearst's in the Denver *Post* and proposed new discriminatory legislation keep the state aroused. Wayne W. Hill, a state representative in Colorado, wearing the uniform of a sergeant in the U.S. Army, got emergency leave from his camp last month to beg the Colorado Legislature not to pass a bill barring Japanese aliens from owning land. About to be discharged from the Army, he said, "I am just as willing to die a political death as I am to die in battle to preserve American freedom." He was warmly applauded, but the House passed the bill; the Senate turned it down fifteen to twelve.

Arizona has had such a spree of race hating in the last year that WRA does not try to place people of Japanese ancestry there. A year ago the governor signed a bill making it impossible to sell anything — even a pack of cigarettes — to a person of Japanese descent without first publishing in the newspaper, days in advance, one's intention to do so, and filing documents with the governor. The law was declared unconstitutional after a few months' operation. It was not aimed merely at the new

WRA settlers who number fifty-seven. It was intended to strangle Arizona's prewar Japanese-American population (632), many of whom make a good living in the highly competitive business of vegetable farming.

With only 17,000 young, unencumbered, and fairly bold Nisei out on their own, the biggest and hardest job of resettlement remains. The supply of young people without dependents is not unlimited. Early this year the Army, which had previously accepted only volunteers, decided to draft the Nisei, like Negroes, for segregated units. This new turn of events will draw off a few thousand *évacués*. But the most difficult problems are obviously the large families and the older people. Depending heavily on the well-known tightness of the family unit of its *évacués*, WRA believes that many of the young men and women already relocated will soon bring their parents and small sisters and brothers out. Perhaps these Nisei who are so aggressively American themselves will not want their families held behind the fences.

However, in WRA centers there are hundreds of families with several young children, none old enough to leave alone. He is a courageous father who dares to start a new life with these responsibilities when, at the center, food, shelter, education, medical care, $16 a month, and clothing are provided. Farm families are often afraid to go to the Midwest to try a totally new kind of agriculture. And many feel that they are too old to start again as day laborers. There are the men who had retail, export, import, wholesale, commission businesses. The concentrated little Tokyos in California make possible a whole commercial structure in which the Japanese provided goods and services for each other. Presumably there will be no more little Tokyos to serve.

Even if the *évacués* were allowed back on the Pacific Coast tomorrow, they could not readily establish themselves in the old pattern. Quite apart from race prejudice, the gap they left has closed in two years. Except for the few who own land, they would have to build in California as patiently as they now do in the East. They have been more thoroughly dislocated than they realize as they think nostalgically about California.

No one can gauge how soon the prewar unwillingness to accept charity or government relief deteriorates into a not-unpleasant habit of security. It is too much to expect of any people that their pride be unbreakable. Some of the old farm women who were "stoop labor" all their lives, even after their Nisei sons' landholdings or leased acres became sizable, have had the first rest in their history. Most of the old bachelors who had always been day laborers frankly enjoy the security of the centers.

If the war lasts two more years, and if WRA has succeeded in finding places for 25,000 more Japanese-Americans in the next twenty-four months (and WRA hopes to better that figure), it will be a job well done. That would leave some 45,000 in the relocation centers, as continuing public wards, not to mention over 20,000 at Tule Lake and the Department of Justice internment camps. Whatever the final residue, 25,000 or 45,000, it is certain that the "protective custody" of 1942 and 1943 cannot end otherwise than in a kind of Indian reservation, to plague the conscience of Americans for many years to come.

Meanwhile in the coming months, and perhaps years, a series of cases testing the constitutionality of evacuation and detention, even suits for recovery of property will come before the higher courts. Verdicts of "unconstitutional," or even eventual settlement of property claims cannot undo the record. It is written not only in military orders, in American Legion resolutions, Hearst headlines, and Supreme Court archives. It is written into the lives of thousands of human beings, most of them citizens of the U.S.

When future historians review the record, they may have difficulty reconciling the Army's policy in California with that pursued in Hawaii. People of Japanese blood make up more than one-third of the Hawaiian Islands' population, yet no large-scale evacuation was ordered after Pearl Harbor and Hickam Field became a shambles. Martial law was declared; certain important constitutional rights of everyone were suspended. The Department of Justice and the military authorities went about their business, rounded up a few thousand suspects. In Hawaii, unlike California, there was no strong political or economic pressure demanding evacuation of the Japanese-Americans. Indeed, had they been removed, the very foundation of peacetime Hawaiian life, sugar and pineapple growing, would have been wrecked. General Delos C. Emmons, who commanded the Hawaiian district in 1942, has said of the Japanese-Americans there: "They added materially to the strength of the area."

For two full years the West Coast "military necessity" order of March, 1942, has remained in force — and unprecedented quasi-martial law, suspending a small minority's constitutional rights of personal liberty and freedom of action. Those loyal *évacués* who can take jobs in war plants in the East have reason to ask why they are forbidden to return to California to plant cabbages. Mr. Stimson and Mr. Knox have assured the nation that the Japanese enemy is *not* coming to our shores. The Pacific Coast is now a "defense command," no longer "a theatre of operations," in the Army's own terminology. Each month the March, 1942, order seems more unreasonable.

Perhaps the Army forbids the *évacués* to return home less for military reasons than because of strong California pressures and threats. The Hearst papers on the Pacific Coast promise pogroms, if any Japanese citizen of alien descent is permitted to come home. New groups like the Home Front Commandos of Sacramento have risen to cry: "They must stay out — or else." The Associated Farmers and the California Grange, the American Legion and the Sons and Daughters of the Golden West reiterate the theme of *or else*. Politicians listen and publicly urge that the despised minority be kept out of California for the duration.

There are Californians who care about civil liberties and human justice and see the grave danger of continued quasi-martial law, but they have difficulty getting their side heard. The California C.I.O., the League of Women Voters, and segments of the church are all putting up a fight against continued "protective security." They work side by side with the Committee on American Principles and Fair Play, a group that includes such distinguished Californians as President Robert G. Sproul of the University of California, Ray Lyman Wilbur, and Maurice E. Harrison.

Lieutenant General John L. DeWitt, who ordered the evacuation of 1942, encouraged California's racist pressure groups when he said, "I don't care what they do with the Japs as long as they don't send them back here. A Jap is a Jap." General Delos C. Emmons, who succeeded DeWitt on the West Coast last September, says very little. He is the same General Emmons who decided *not* to order wholesale evacuation of the Japanese from Hawaii.

The longer the Army permits California and the rest of the Pacific Coast to be closed to everyone of Japanese descent, the more time is given the Hearst papers and their allies to convince Californians that they will indeed yield to lawlessness if the unwanted minority is permitted to return. By continuing to keep American citizens in "protective custody," the U.S. is holding to a policy as ominous as it is new. The American custom in the past has been to lock up the citizen who commits violence, not the victims of his threats and blows. The doctrine of "protective custody" could prove altogether too convenient a weapon in many other situations. In California, a state with a long history of race hatred and vigilanteism, antagonism is already building against the Negroes who have come in for war jobs. What is to prevent their removal to jails, to "protect them" from riots? Or Negroes in Detroit, Jews in Boston, Mexicans in Texas? The possibilities of "protective custody" are endless, as the Nazis have amply proved.

THE JAPANESE-AMERICANS
Homer A. Harris

Homer A. Harris was the secretary-manager of the Associated Produce Dealers and Brokers of Los Angeles when he wrote this response to "Issei, Nisei, Kibei," the preceding essay. He voices the widespread suspicion among produce growers about collusion among produce growers and wholesalers of Japanese descent. His exaggerated notion of the number of kibei among the nisei and his certainty that a Japanese air raid on Los Angeles really took place, but was covered up by the state and federal governments, were probably shared at the time by many of his fellow citizens on the Pacific coast.

To the Editors:

The April issue of *Fortune* [on Japan and the Japanese] is most interesting and despite the handicaps of wartime you have surpassed the September, 1936 issue. . . .

It is most regrettable that the same commendation cannot be extended to the article "Issei, Nisei, Kibei," which has treated this extremely vital, though controversial subject, from a rather superficial and sentimental viewpoint.

The article shows only the Japanese side of the problem, and fails to inquire into the reasons for "a policy as ominous as it is new." It must have occurred to you that the entire West Coast population and the U.S. Army had not become hysterical over the war or were so prejudiced as to waive every consideration except to remove the Japanese from the Pacific Coast. . . .

No other government has ever attempted to control its nationals in this country to the same degree. Every Japanese who came to this country was registered with the consulate, their children were registered at birth, retaining their Japanese citizenship along with their American citizenship. As [the child] grew up he made daily obeisance to the picture of the Emperor. After attendance at the public school each day he was bundled off to a Japanese language school, where under the tutelage of an alien-born teacher, usually a Shinto priest, he was taught the Japanese Language and the worship of the Emperor of Japan. Then at the age of twelve or thereabouts, he was sent in shiploads to Japan to be educated, indoctrinated, and trained as a Japanese, body, heart, and soul. Incidentally he put in his compulsory three years' service in the Army or Navy and returned to this country to claim his American citizenship.

More than two-thirds of the Japanese boys were given this training, according to a well-known Japanese American, who has been accepted by agencies of our government as representative of the Japanese citizens. Yet your article speaks of the Kibei as a noisy but unimportant minority among the Nisei. . . .

We know that there were some loyal citizens among the Nisei, knew that they were a minority, but not even the Japanese could or would distinguish between loyal and disloyal.

Homer A. Harris, "The Japanese-Americans," *Fortune* July 1944.

The coast was under military attack, the details of which probably will not be disclosed until after the war. We knew that submarines were being sunk off the coast long before the shelling of the Santa Barbara coast. The air raid in March, 1942 was not a false alarm as officially reported but a bombing raid with bombs dropped and enemy planes shot down.

The citizens expected a hit-and-run raid on war plants and then, and only then, did they expect sabotage and aid to the enemy from the disloyal Japanese. After such a raid it is probable that reprisal en masse against all Japanese would have followed. These were the reasons the citizens of the Coast petitioned for the removal of the Japanese. . . .

I cannot overlook the inference in your article that the opposition to the Japanese on the Coast from farmers is based on the fact that the white growers cannot meet Japanese competition. This is true but not in the way you infer. The competition from the Japanese was distinctly unfair and contrary to American principles and law. Japanese control of vegetable production was based on a vertical-trust idea. The Japanese grower employed Japanese truckmen to haul to market to Japanese commission merchants, who sold to Japanese retailers. Preference was given at all times to fellow countrymen. If control of an area was desired, the elaborate series of associations, all stemming back into the Japanese Consulate, were put on the job. The white growers were crowded out of the Santa Maria Valley by Japanese paying landowners more rent than anyone, even themselves, could recover from the production of crops. If a commission merchant were to be eliminated it was easy for the Japanese competitor to pay the growers more than the merchandise sold for. In the case of the retailer the Japanese would undersell him regardless of losses. Through the associations their competitive losses were spread over all the members of a group, or passed on to another group or in some cases subsidized from an outside source. Only a few months before Pearl Harbor the State Department of Agriculture required eighteen Japanese commission merchants to disgorge thousands of dollars they had withheld from growers in one district and overpaid to growers in another district where there was keen competition with Caucasian merchants.

All things considered, the people on the Coast have shown surprisingly little prejudice on the Japanese question. They realize that we have citizens of Japanese extraction, a majority of whom are citizens in name only, and that when the military need has passed these citizens must be given the same privileges as any other. Yet they know that if the Japanese in this country continue to be dominated by the Japanese Government after the war as in the past it will only mean that within a generation we will be at war again.

*　　*　　*　　*　　*

Fortune thanks Mr. Harris, secretary manager of the Associated Produce Dealers and Brokers of Los Angeles, for an earnest statement of his viewpoint. The editors, however, can find no verification of the March, 1942 "bombing," and they cannot accept Mr. Harris's interpretation of Japanese-American citizenships. According to the Department of Justice (director of Alien Enemy Control Unit), registering American-born children as dual citizens is a common practice by aliens from all countries. But many American-born children of Japanese later renounced their unsought Japanese citizenship; and many more refused to take such action because they refused to dignify the notion of supposed allegiance to Japan. As for the Kibei, best government figures available indicate that no more than 20,000 out of 70,000 American-born Japanese have ever visited Japan. How many of the 20,000 became indoctrinated as servants of the Emperor, no man can say. *Fortune* rests on its estimate that they are a minority among the 70,000, and more of a nuisance than a menace. In conclusion, *Fortune* gladly meets Mr. Harris on a basic area of agreement: that loyal U.S. citizens, of Japanese or any other extraction, "must be given the same privileges as any other."

The Editors

RACISM ON THE WEST COAST
Carey McWilliams

Carey McWilliams served as editor of The New Republic *from 1955 until 1975 and wrote such books as* Prejudice: Japanese Americans, Symbol of Racial Intolerance *(1944). McWilliams reports, in the following essay, on the racism that dominated the Gannon Committee hearings in the California state legislature in 1943 and 1944 as well as on the racism that charged the atmosphere in California nearly two years after those of Japanese descent had been interned in camps.*

The West Coast's new campaign to prevent the release of any persons of Japanese ancestry from relocation centers for the duration of the war began in December, 1942, with the appointment by the American Legion, California Department, of a five-man committee to conduct "an impartial investigation of all Japanese Relocation Areas in the State of California." Among the members of this impartial committee were Harper L. Knowles (of La Follette Committee fame); H. J. McClatchy of the California Joint Immigration Committee; and State Senator Jack Tenney of Los Angeles County. Tenney heads the "Little Dies Committee" of the state legislature. Shortly after the committee had been appointed, Tenney announced that it would take over the investigation for the American Legion.

Within the next two months, literally hundreds of West Coast organizations "went on record" by the adoption of a series of stock resolutions on the "Japanese question." I have examined scores of these resolutions and have yet to see one that by its form or content would indicate that it had been offered *by the members* of the particular organization; invariably these resolutions were presented *for concurrence* by one or another of the groups mentioned. With the newspapers featuring this organized activity, feeling began to mount throughout California. The city of Gardena omitted from its honor roll of citizens in the service the names of seventeen Japanese Americans; the American Legion summarily revoked the charters of the Townsend Harris and Commodore Perry Posts (made up of Japanese American veterans of the First World War). In Portland, Oregon, the Legion protested when local citizens sought to provide some volunteer care for a Japanese cemetery. Vigilante groups were formed in Salinas "to prevent the return of the Japanese." The California Federation of Women's Clubs expressed grave concern for their "sisters" in the East and Middle West whose safety, and presumably whose virtue, were being endangered by the release of evacuees from the centers.

The moment the legislature convened in January, 1943, a spate of anti-evacuee bills, resolutions and memorials were introduced. In debating these measures, mass evacuation was cited *as proof* of the disloyal character of the evacuees by the very individuals who had urged mass evacuation *for the protection* of the evacuees against mob violence. Statements and chants were hurled at the evacuees that no one had dreamed of during the period immediately after Pearl Harbor. Throughout the year legislative investigations, state and federal, were carefully spaced in such a manner

Carey McWilliams, "Racism on the West Coast," *The New Republic 110* (1944).

as to provide an endless stream of newspaper headlines. First the Tenney investigation; then the farcical investigation conducted by Senator Chandler of Kentucky (which was really directed by Ray Richards of The Los Angeles Examiner); then the Dies Committee investigation in June, 1943; then an investigation by still another committee of the California Assembly; and, finally, yet another investigation by the Dies Committee.

Before the Dies Committee had conducted any investigation whatever, Representative J. Parnell Thomas, from a room in the Biltmore Hotel in Los Angeles, began to release a barrage of sensational stories about the War Relocation Authority and the evacuees. Calling "smear" witnesses to the stand, the committee tried its best to prevent the WRA from refuting their baseless charges. Some 35 factual misstatements were pointed out in the testimony of one witness. At these hearings, witnesses were openly encouraged to threaten the evacuees with mob violence. Public officials charged with the duty of law enforcement were given a pat on the back when they predicted "free murder," "violence" and "bloodshed" if a single evacuee were permitted to return to the West Coast.

At the hearings of the Gannon Committee (of the state legislature), Mrs. Maynard Force Thayer of Pasadena — stanch Republican, an outstanding clubwoman, a pillar of the community — was browbeaten by the chairman of the committee in a manner that finally evoked a murmur of protest from The Los Angeles Times. Mrs. Thayer was asked, for example, if she had ever "smelled the inside of a Japanese home"; she was asked if she wanted the government "to protect a people who farm their wives out to another man to procreate his name"; and she was queried as to her opinion about a "people where different sexes do nude bathing together." When Mrs. Thayer tried to get in a word about the Bill of Rights, she was rebuked by Mr. Gannon as follows: "The Bill of Rights is not such a sacred thing . . . don't you know that at the time the Bill of Rights was written we had 150,000 slaves in the United States? What did the Bill of Rights do about that?" While this fantastic and obscene circus was being conducted, The Los Angeles Examiner, in one day, devoted 62 inches of space to the hearings. In being haled before these committees, I was questioned, not about the evacuees of the WRA program, but about my views on "racial integrity," "mongrelization," "mixed marriages," "miscegenation statutes" and similar fancy topics.

At the time of the so-called "riot" at Tule Lake, the real riot occurred, not in the center, but in the pages of the California newspapers. Newspaper stories appeared charging that "bombs, knives, guns and various lethal weapons" had been found among the evacuees; that a Japanese evacuee had "pushed his way into" the bedchamber of a "white woman"; that the personnel of the center was "intermingling" with the evacuees; that the evacuees were being "coddled" and "pampered" (on a food allowance of 43 cents per person per day). Mr. Ray Richards of the Hearst press even suggested that Dillon Myer had knowingly failed to confiscate "lethal weapons" and that he had been a party to the "manufacture" of such weapons (see The San Francisco Call-Bulletin, December 21, 1943). With unblushing mendacity, The Los Angeles Herald-Express carried a headline reading: "Bare Deadly Peril as Armed Japanese Stream into California." Representative John Costello went so far as to announce, on December 9, 1943, that "hundreds of Japanese Americans and alien Japanese" were being permitted to return to California. Needless to say, there was no semblance of truth in these charges. Later The Los Angeles Times, in fancy headlines, charges that "450 Cases of Whiskey Go to Tule Lake" and, again, "Whiskey Flows to Tule Lake." The whiskey in question was consigned to the *town* of Tule Lake, not to the relocation center. "These Japs," wrote a columnist in The Times (referring not to the Japanese in Japan but to some 70,000 American citizens of Japanese ancestry), "are a depraved breed who can't be dealt with like mischievous boys . . . . We should wake up to the fact that protection of Americans from these degraded brutes is of more importance than the Little Tokyo Knitting and Brotherly Love Club." Only the fact that the Japanese government, in November, 1943, canceled further negotiations for the exchange of nationals, finally brought about some moderation in this frenzied campaign.

A section of the West Coast press systematically deflects hatred of Japan against the evacuees and uses hatred of the evacuees to justify its contention that the war in the Pacific is primarily racial in character. The consistent theme of the Hearst press is that "the war in the Pacific is the World War, the War of Oriental Races against Occidental Races for the Domination of the World" (The Los Angeles Examiner, March 23, 1943). Here is another characteristic statement from The San Francisco Examiner of January 25, 1943 (italics mine):

> Bad as the situation is in Europe, the war there is between European Occidental nations, *between white races*. Antagonisms, hatreds and jealousies, no matter how violent, cannot obscure the fact that the warring nations of Europe stem from common *racial*, cultural, linguistic and social roots. *It is a family affair*, in which the possibility of ultimate agreement and constructive harmony has not been dismissed even by the most determined opponents.

There can be no question but that anti-evacuee agitation in California is being cultivated for partisan political purposes. The hearings mentioned were, in large part, aimed at "smearing" the administration and building up a wall of reactionary feeling by stimulating racial hatred. To some extent this agitation has unquestionably been effective. Political officials in California have been cowed into silence; even those who are inclined to be fair do not dare to speak out on this issue. Just as Senators Hill and Pepper have been forced to disavow any interest in racial equality, so even the fair-minded members of the California delegation in Congress have been coerced on this thoroughly bogus "Japanese problem." Not one of these men dares to state publicly his real views on the evacuee problem.

No more serious mistake could be made than to encourage the belief that these groups can be handled quietly or that, by tactful diplomacy, they can be induced to forget the "Japanese issue." The aggressions of race bigots in California are of the same character as the insulting attacks made in Congress on the Negro minority by the white-supremacy advocates from the Deep South. Race bigotry in California can never be appeased. Every concession made to bigotry on the West Coast (and mass evacuation was such a concession) only encourages bolder aggression. As Representative Eberharter said, in his courageous minority report as a member of the Dies Committee, these recurrent investigations in California have "fostered a type of racial thinking which is already producing ugly manifestations and which seems to be growing in intensity. Unless this trend is checked, it may eventually lead to ill advised actions that will constitute an everlastingly shameful blot on our national record." Recent flare-ups against the evacuees in other sections of the country show that, in the absence of a strong affirmative federal policy and program on the race question, California bigots stand a good chance of spreading their particular version of the white-supremacy doctrine throughout the nation.

The military situation in the Pacific has changed since mass evacuation was ordered. The Japanese have been forced out of the Aleutians; Hawaii has been converted into one of the great fortresses of the world (and martial law has been modified); the Japanese are on the defensive throughout the Pacific. Various emergency measures adopted after Pearl Harbor have been relaxed on the West Coast and the general situation has so changed in our favor as to warrant the military in lifting the ban against the return of the evacuees. As long as the ban exists, race bigots in California will have an issue about which they will continue to conduct ever more fantastic and increasingly violent campaigns. If the ban is lifted, there will be no mass return of the evacuees and the freely predicted "murder" and "bloodshed" will not occur. There is a respectable opinion in California today that favors lifting the ban. The organizations I have mentioned create, rather than reflect, public opinion on the West Coast.

Issues of great importance are involved in this question. In default of an affirmative federal policy and program on race relations, race-minded groups in California will continue, in effect, to dictate our policy as a nation toward the peoples of the Orient. By taking advantage of this latent weakness in the federal government, California since 1882 has forced the Washington authorities to adopt a series of measures each of which has seriously jeopardized our national interests in the Far East: the exclusion of Chinese immigration; the passage of the 1924 immigration law; the mass evacuation of the resident Japanese. It requires no insight to predict that this same situation will continue until the American people realize that local areas should not be permitted to force the federal government into the position of having to adopt their particular attitudes on race relations.

AMERICAN FAIR PLAY?

This brief Time *essay details some of the racist activities of certain posts of the American Legion during the war as well as the difficulties faced by many of those of Japanese descent as they attempted to return to their home areas after being released from relocation camps by the War Relocation Authority. (The* Fortune *essay earlier in the chapter points out that after the WRA had administered a loyalty test to the relocation camp population, the 18,000 who failed the loyalty test were segregated in the Tule Lake, California camp. The remaining 70,000-plus inhabitants of the other camps were allowed to leave the camps and live in areas outside the West Coast. As of early 1944, only 17,000 had attempted to do so. As this essay indicates, the number of those who had left the camps had grown to 33,000 by early 1945.)*

For 13 weeks the Hood River (Ore.) Post of the American Legion persisted in its shameful pre-eminence — its members had struck the names of 16 Japanese-American soldiers from a public honor roll, had steadfastly refused to restore them. The Legion's embarrassed national commander had sent a "recommendation" which sounded like an order: put the names back. Some 500 of Hood River County's 11,580 citizens signed a full-page newspaper advertisement headed: "So Sorry Please. Japs Are Not Wanted in Hood River." Hood River's Legion Post replied to the national organization: ". . . inadvisable at this time. . . ."

But last week, after digesting some strong hints that their charter might be in danger, Hood River's legionnaires finally voted to restore 15 of the 16 names.

Relieved, National Commander Edward N. Scheiberling whipped out a press release: ". . . source of gratification to the American Legion everywhere . . . sound sense of American fair play. . . ." Said the New York *Times,* "The Hood River Post is to be congratulated on having the courage to admit its mistake."

But racial intolerance on the West Coast had abated not a whit:

- Hood River, still as anti-Japanese as ever, mouthed a rumor — white servicemen would demand the removal of their names if those of the Japanese-Americans went back. At week's end the honor roll was still bare of Nisei names.
- In Seattle, Tetel Takayoshi, graduate of the University of Washington and prewar teaching supervisor at King County's Harborview Hospital, returned to her old job. "I'm glad to be back," she reassured her friends. "I was born here — this is my home." But after eleven days of snubs and silences she quietly packed her bags, headed back to Denver.
- In Portland, Ore., R. Tsubota, a truck farmer, brought a truckload of vegetables to the Portland Farmers' Market, found himself virtually boycotted. At nearby Gresham, citizens circulated a petition asking that all persons of Japanese blood be deported to a Pacific island.

"American Fair Play?" *Time* 19 March 1945.

- Sam Takeda, a San José, Calif. farmer, awakened with a start one night last week — the front of his house had been soused with gasoline, set afire. After he beat out the flames, someone fired a shot at him.

The Nisei were not friendless on the Pacific Coast — many openly welcomed them and hundreds deplored acts of violence. In Woodinville, Wash., Kametaro Funai, just out of a relocation camp, ran up against the manpower shortage. Promptly, some University of Washington students came out to help him on his farm.

But whether the nation liked it or not, the Japanese-haters' methods were proving exceedingly effective. Of 33,000 Japanese and Nisei who had left war relocation centers, only 1,640 had returned to the West Coast. Of 60,397 still in WRA camps, only 1,938 had announced any intention of going back to their old homes. The rest, bewildered by the ways of their erstwhile neighbors and friends, made plans to go to other parts of the country, or just waited, wondering what to do.

Postwar Exports

This brief Time essay confirms the fact that some 6,000 inhabitants among the segregated group at Tule Lake, California, had at best divided loyalties during the war. The question, of course, remains how many of these who desired to return to Japan were driven to renounce the United States by their outrage over their nearly three years of incarceration.

They were born in the U.S. and, until Pearl Harbor, had therefore enjoyed all the blessings of citizenship. They had gone to the public schools, voted, earned a living. Some of them had friends or relatives in the U.S. armed forces. But last week these 6,000-odd U.S. Japanese were busy renouncing their citizenship to swear allegiance to Emperor Hirohito.

By & large, they were the fanatical, trouble-making variety of Nisei segregated at Tule Lake, Calif., for disloyalty. Until a year ago change of allegiance was so difficult to achieve that a Nisei had to commit treason or desert from the armed forces to make it. Now, thanks to a recent act of Congress, anybody can renounce his U.S. citizenship if the U.S. Attorney General finds it is not contrary to the national defense.

Some of the Nisei who have got or are getting a chance at renunciation are afraid that to be returned to the hostile Pacific Coast would be worse than being reinterned as aliens. But the majority of them dearly want to go back to Japan — even though they can see from their newspapers how their future homeland is being devastated by the U.S., how close it is to defeat. After the war is over they will be sent back to what is left of the land few of them have ever seen.

"Postwar Exports," *Time* 2 April 1945.

Our Worst Wartime Mistake

Eugene V. Rostow

At the time he wrote this essay, Eugene V. Rostow was dean of the Yale Law School. He later served as undersecretary of state for political affairs in the Johnson administration. This Harper's essay is one of the early sobering reassessments of the evacuation and relocation policy which many had viewed as a grim wartime necessity only three years earlier. Notice Rostow's comparison of the federal government's treatment of people of Japanese descent on the West Coast with its treatment of other potentially dangerous immigrant groups in other parts of the country. The government, for instance, interned only a small number of the multitudes of those of Japanese descent living in Hawaii (who constituted one-third of the total Hawaiian population). Notice too that the federal government's evacuation and relocation policies were upheld by Supreme Court decisions late in the war.

Time is often needed for us to recognize the great miscarriages of justice. The Dreyfus case had lasted four years before public opinion was fully aroused. The trials of Sacco and Vanzetti endured six years. As time passes, it becomes more and more plain that our wartime treatment of the Japanese and the Japanese-Americans on the West Coast was a tragic and dangerous mistake. That mistake is a threat to society, and to all men. Its motivation and its impact on our system of law deny every value of democracy.

In the perspective of our legal tradition, the facts are almost incredible.

During the bleak spring of 1942, the Japanese and the Japanese-Americans who lived on the West Coast of the United States were taken into custody and removed to camps in the interior. More than one hundred thousand men, women, and children were thus exiled and imprisoned. More than two-thirds of them were American citizens.

These people were taken into custody as a military measure on the ground that espionage and sabotage were especially to be feared from persons of Japanese blood. The whole group was removed from the West Coast because the military authorities thought it would take too long to conduct individual investigation on the spot. They were arrested without warrants and were held without indictment or a statement of charges, although the courts were open and freely functioning. They were transported to camps far from their homes, and kept there under prison conditions, pending investigations of their "loyalty." Despite the good intentions of the chief relocation officers, the centers were little better than concentration camps.

If the evacuees were found "loyal," they were released only if they could find a job and a place to live, in a community where no hoodlums would come out at night to chalk up anti-Japanese slogans, break windows, or threaten riot. If found "disloyal" in their attitude to the war, they were kept in the camps indefinitely — although sympathy with the enemy is no crime in the United States (for white people at least) so long as it is not translated into deeds or the visible threat of deeds. On May 1, 1945, three years after the program was begun, about 70,000

Eugene V. Rostow, "Our Worst Wartime Mistake," *Harper's 191* (1945).

persons were still in camps. While it is hoped to have all these people either free, or in more orthodox confinement, by January 1, 1946, what is euphemistically called the Japanese "relocation" program will not be a closed book for many years.

The original program of "relocation" was an injustice, in no way required or justified by the circumstances of the war. But the Supreme Court, in three extraordinary decisions, has upheld its main features as constitutional. This fact converts a piece of wartime folly into national policy—a permanent part of the law—a doctrine enlarging the power of the military in relation to civil authority. It is having a sinister impact on the minority problem in every part of the country. It is giving aid to reactionary politicians who use social division and racial prejudice as their tools. The precedent is being used to encourage attacks on the civil rights of both citizens and aliens. As Mr. Justice Jackson has said, the principle of these decisions "lies about like a loaded weapon ready for the hand of any authority that can bring forward a plausible claim of an urgent need." All in all, the case of the Japanese-Americans is the worst blow our liberties have sustained in many years. Unless repudiated, it may support devastating and unforeseen social and political conflicts.

What was done in the name of military precaution on the West Coast was quite different from the security measures taken in Hawaii or on the East Coast, although both places were active theaters of war in 1942.

On the East Coast enemy aliens were controlled without mass arrests or evacuations, despite their heavy concentration in and near shipping and manufacturing centers. Aliens had been registered, and the police had compiled information about fascist sympathizers, both aliens and citizens. "On the night of December 7, 1941," Attorney General Biddle reported, "the most dangerous of the persons in this group were taken into custody; in the following weeks a number of others were apprehended. Each arrest was made on the basis of information concerning the specific alien taken into custody. We have used no dragnet techniques and have conducted no indiscriminate, large-scale raids." General regulations were issued, somewhat restricting the freedom of all enemy aliens over fourteen years of age. They were forbidden to enter military areas; they had to get the District Attorney's permission before traveling; they were forbidden to own or use firearms, cameras, short-wave radio sets, codes, ciphers, or invisible ink. This control plan kept security officers informed, but otherwise allowed the aliens almost their normal share in the work and life of the community.

Enemy aliens under suspicion, and those who violated the regulations, were subject to summary arrest, and were then promptly examined by one of the special Alien Enemy Hearing Boards. These boards could recommend that the individual alien be interned, paroled, or released unconditionally. The examinations were smoothly conducted, and they did nothing to lower prevailing standards of justice. Of the 1,100,000 enemy aliens in the country, 9,080 had been examined by the end of June 1943, about 4,000 of them being then interned. By June 30, 1944, the number interned had been reduced to approximately 2,500.

In Hawaii a different procedure was followed, but one less drastic than the evacuation program pursued on the West Coast, although Hawaii was certainly a more active theater of war. Immediately after Pearl Harbor, martial law was installed in Hawaii, and the commanding general assumed the role of military governor. Yet, although about one-third the population of Hawaii is of Japanese descent, and although the tension was great after the Pearl Harbor raid, there was no mass roundup on the islands. Fewer than 800 Japanese aliens were sent to the mainland for internment, and fewer than 1,000 persons of Japanese ancestry, 912 of them being citizens, were sent to relocation centers on the mainland. Many of the latter group were families of interned aliens, transferred voluntarily. Those arrested in Hawaii were taken into custody on the basis of individual suspicion, resting on previous examination or observed behavior. Even under a regime of martial law, men were arrested as individuals, and not because of the color of their skins. Safety was assured without mass arrests, or needless hardship.

On the West Coast the security program was something else again. Immediately after Pearl Harbor there were no special regulations for persons of Japanese extraction. Known enemy sympathizers among the Japanese, like white traitors and enemy agents, were arrested. There was no sabotage by persons of Japanese ancestry. There was no reason to suppose that the 112,000 persons of Japanese descent on the West Coast, less than 2 per cent of the population, constituted a greater menace than such persons in Hawaii, where they were 32 percent of the population.

After a month's silence, the organized minority whose business it has been to exploit racial tensions on the West Coast went to work. They had strong support in the Hearst press and its equivalents. Politicians, fearful of an unknown public opinion, spoke out for white supremacy. West Coast Congressional delegations led by Senator Hiram Johnson, urged the administration to exclude all persons of Japanese blood from the coast states. Anti-Oriental spokesmen appeared before special hearings of the Tolan Committee, and explained the situation as they conceived it to Lieutenant General J. L. DeWitt, commanding the Western Defense Command. Tension was intensified, and doubters, worried about the risks of another Pearl Harbor, remained silent, preferring too much caution to too little. An opinion crystallized in favor of evacuating the Japanese.

After some hesitation, General DeWitt proposed the policy of exclusion on grounds of military need. The War Department backed him up. No one in the government took the responsibility for opposing or overruling him.

Despite the nature of the emergency, the Army's lawyers wanted more legal authority before action was taken. The President issued an Executive Order in February 1942, and in March Congress passed a statute, authorizing military commanders to designate "military areas" and to prescribe the terms on which any persons could enter, leave, or remain in such areas. A policy of encouraging the Japanese to move away individually had shown signs of producing confusion. It was therefore decided to establish a compulsory system of detention in camps, to simplify the process of resettlement, and to afford the fullest measure of security.

The history of law affords nothing more fantastic than the evidence which is supposed to justify this program. General DeWitt's final recommendation to the Secretary of War, dated February 14, 1942, but not made public until early in 1944, explains the basis of his decision.

"In the war in which we are now engaged," he said, "racial affinities are not severed by migration. The Japanese race is an enemy race and while many second and third generation Japanese born on United States soil, possessed of United States citizenship, have become 'Americanized,' the racial strains are undiluted." From the premise of a war of "races," the general had no difficulty reaching his conclusion. There is "no ground for assuming," he said, that Japanese-Americans will not turn against the United States. So much for the idea that men are presumed innocent until proved guilty, and that American citizens stand on an equal footing before the law without regard for race, color, or previous condition of servitude! "It therefore follows," the general added, "that along the vital Pacific Coast over 112,000 potential enemies, of Japanese extraction, are at large today. There are disturbing indications that these are organized and ready for concerted action at a favorable opportunity. The very fact that no sabotage has taken place to date is a disturbing and confirming indication that such action will be taken."

There was somewhat more evidence than the absence of sabotage to prove its special danger. The Japanese lived closely together, often concentrated around harbors and other strategic areas. Japanese clubs and religious institutions played an important part in their segregated social life. Japanese language schools existed, to preserve for the American born something of the cultural heritage of Japan. The Japanese government, like that of many other countries, asserted a doctrine of nationality different from our own, which gave rise to possible claims of dual citizenship. Thus a long-standing conflict in international law, involving many countries other than Japan, was invoked to cast special doubt on the loyalty of American citizens of Japanese descent.

Much of the suspicion inferentially based on these statements disappears on closer examination. In many instances the concentration of Japanese homes around strategic areas had come about years before, and for entirely innocent reasons. Japanese cannery workers, for example, had had to live on the waterfront in order to be near the plants in which they worked. Japanese truck gardeners had rented land in the industrial outskirts of large cities to be close to their markets. They had rented land for gardening under high tension lines — regarded as a very suspicious circumstance — because the company could not use the land for other purposes; the initiative in starting this practice had come from the utility companies, not from the Japanese.

Despite discrimination against the Japanese, many had done well in America. They were substantial property owners. Their children participated normally and actively in the schools and universities of the West Coast. Their unions and social organizations had passed resolutions of loyalty in great number, before and after Pearl Harbor. It is difficult to find real evidence that either religious or social institutions among the Japanese had successfully fostered Japanese militarism or other dangerous sentiments. The Japanese language schools, which the Japanese-Americans themselves had long sought to put under state control, seem to represent little more than the familiar desire of many immigrant groups to keep alive the language and tradition of the "old country"; in the case of Japanese-Americans, knowledge of the Japanese language was of particular economic importance, since so much of their working life was spent with other Japanese on the West Coast.

Some elements among the Japanese were, of course, suspect. They were known to the authorities, who had for several years been checking on the Japanese-American population. Many had been individually arrested immediately after Pearl Harbor, and the others were under constant surveillance.

It is also true that a considerable percentage of the evacuees later gave negative answers to loyalty questions in the questionnaires they were asked to fill out while in camps. Many of those answers were expressly based upon the treatment the individuals had received; the same shock of evacuation and confinement undoubtedly was responsible indirectly for many more. Basically, however, the issue of abstract loyalty is irrelevant. Disloyalty, even in the aggravated form of enthusiastic verbal support for the Axis cause, is not a crime in the United States. At most, it is a possible ground for interning enemy aliens. Citizens must do more than talk or think disloyal thoughts before being arrested and jailed.

Apart from the members of the group known to be under suspicion, there was no evidence beyond the vaguest fear to connect the Japanese on the West Coast with the unfavorable military events of 1941 and 1942. Both at Pearl Harbor and in sporadic attacks on the West Coast the enemy had shown that he had knowledge of our dispositions. There was some signaling to enemy ships at sea, both by radio and by lights, along the West Coast. There were several episodes of shelling the coast by submarine—although two of the three such cases mentioned by General DeWitt as tending to create suspicion of the Japanese-Americans took place *after* their removal from the coast. (These were the only such items in his report which were not identified by date.) And those subsequently arrested as Japanese agents in the Pearl Harbor area were all white men.

The most striking comment on the quality of the evidence produced by General DeWitt to support his proposal was made by Solicitor General Fahy, whose job it was to defend the general's plan before the Supreme Court. He relied upon the general's report "only to the extent that it relates" statistics and other details concerning the actual evacuation and the events which took place after it. But the briefs that he himself presented were identical in the substance of their argument. The Japanese-Americans were an unknown, unknowable, foreign group, living together, and moving in mysterious ways, inscrutable to puzzled white men. Therefore, let them be imprisoned; let their property be taken into custody, sold off at bargain prices, dissipated, and lost; let their roots be torn up, let their children suffer the irreparable shock of life in a concentration camp; let their relation to society be distorted by the searing memory of humiliation, rejection, and punishment.

The evidence supports one conclusion only: the dominant element in the development of our relocation policy was race prejudice, not a military estimate of a military problem.

By the time the issues raised by this program reached the Supreme Court, the crisis which was supposed to justify it had passed. The first cases came up in June 1943, the second and third in December 1944. The course of the war had changed completely; the Japanese were no longer prowling off California, but fighting defensively among the islands of the Western Pacific.

The problem presented to the Supreme Court was thus completely different from that which confronted worried soldiers, legislators, and executive officials in the melancholy months after Pearl Harbor. Invalidation of the relocation scheme would do no possible harm to the prosecution of the war. The Supreme Court could afford to view the issues in perspective, giving full weight to its own special responsibilities for the development of constitutional law as a whole.

Moreover, the issue for the court was infinitely more complex than that which faced General DeWitt in 1942. The court had to decide not only whether General DeWitt had acted within the scope of his permissible authority, but whether it should validate what had been done. As many episodes in our constitutional history attest, those are different issues. The court could not escape the fact that it was the Supreme Court, arbiter of a vast system of customs, rules, habits, and relationships. Its decision inevitably would have far-reaching effects — on the power of the military, on our developing law of emergencies, on the future of those demagogues and political groups which live by attacking minorities, and on the future decision of cases in lower courts and police stations, involving the rights of citizens and aliens, the availability of habeas corpus, and like questions.

The question of how and on what grounds the Supreme Court should dispose of the cases also was one of broad political policy. Would a repudiation of Congress, the President, and the military in one aspect of their conduct of the war affect the people's will to fight? Would it create a campaign issue for 1944? Would it affect the power and prestige of the Supreme Court as a political institution?

In a bewildering and unimpressive series of opinions, relieved only by the dissents of Justice Roberts and Justice Murphy in one of the three cases — *Korematsu v. United States* — the court chose to assume that the main issues did not exist. In avoiding the risks of overruling the government on an issue of war policy, it weakened society's control over military power — one of the controls on which the whole organization of our society depends. It failed to uphold the most ordinary rights of citizenship, making Japanese-Americans into second-class citizens, who stand before the courts on a different legal footing from other Americans. It accepted and gave the prestige of its support to dangerous racial myths about a minority group, in arguments which can easily be applied to any other minority in our society.

The reasoning of the court was simple and direct. The problem was the scope of the war power of the national government. Both Congress and the executive seemed to have decided that special measures were required because espionage and sabotage were especially to be feared from persons of Japanese descent on the West Coast in the spring of 1942. It was not the job of the Supreme Court to decide such questions for itself. Its task was that of judicial review — to uphold the judgment of the officers directly responsible for fighting the war if, the court said, there was "any substantial basis" in fact for the conclusion that protective measures were necessary.

Two propositions which the court accepted as "facts" were held to afford a sufficiently "rational basis" for military decision. The first was that in time of war "residents having ethnic affiliations with an invading enemy may be a greater source of danger than those of different ancestry" — a doctrine which belongs with the race theories of the Nazis and, moreover, is contrary to the experience of American society in both our World Wars. (The weight of scientific evidence is that the most important driving urge of such minority groups is to conform, not to rebel.) The second was that on the West Coast in 1942 there was no time to isolate and examine the suspected Japanese on an individual basis — although of the 110,000 persons subject to the exclusion orders, 43 percent were over fifty or under fifteen years old; they had lived in California without committing sabotage for five months after Pearl Harbor; in the country as a whole, thousands of aliens were examined individually without substantial delay; and in Britain 74,000 enemy aliens were checked in a few months.

By accepting the military judgment on these two points, without any evidence in the record to back it up, without requiring any testimony from the military, and even without adequate discussion by the court itself, the court has taken "judicial notice" of doubtful and controversial propositions of fact, as if they were as well-established as the census statistics or the tide tables. The court could have sent the cases back for a full trial on the justification for General DeWitt's decision. Instead, it upheld his ruling. Thus it created a profound question as to the position of the military power in our public life. . . .

The Japanese exclusion program rests on five propositions of the utmost potential menace:

1. Protective custody, extending over three or four years, is a permitted form of imprisonment in the United States.

2. Political opinions, not criminal acts, may contain enough danger to justify such imprisonment.

3. Men, women, and children of a given racial group, both Americans and resident aliens, can be presumed to possess the kind of dangerous ideas which require their imprisonment.

4. In time of war or emergency the military — perhaps without even the concurrence of the legislature — can decide what political opinions require imprisonment, and which groups are infected with them.

5. The decision of the military can be carried out without indictment, trial, examination, jury, the confrontation of witnesses, counsel for the defense, the privilege against self-incrimination, or any of the other safeguards of the Bill of Rights.

The idea of punishment only for individual criminal behavior is basic to all systems of civilized law. A great principle was never lost so casually. Mr. Justice Black's comment was weak to the point of impotence: "Hardships are a part of war, and war is an aggregation of hardships." It was an answer in the spirit of cliché: "Don't you know there's a war going on?" It ignores the rights of citizenship, and the safeguards of trial practice which have been the historical attributes of liberty.

We believe that the German people bear a common political responsibility for outrages secretly committed by the Gestapo and the SS. What are we to think of our own part in a program which violates every principle of our common life, yet has been approved by the President, Congress, and the Supreme Court?

Three chief forms of reparation are available, and should be pursued. The first is the inescapable obligation of the federal government to protect the civil rights of Japanese-Americans against organized and unorganized hooliganism. If local law enforcement fails, federal prosecutions under the national Civil Rights Act should be undertaken.

Secondly, generous financial indemnity should be sought. Apart from the sufferings of their imprisonment, the Japanese-Americans have sustained heavy property losses from their evacuation.

Finally, the basic issues should be presented to the Supreme Court again, in an effort to obtain a prompt reversal of these wartime cases. The Supreme Court has often corrected its own errors in the past, especially when that error was occasioned by the excitement of a tense moment. After the end of the Civil War, several earlier decisions were reversed by *Ex Parte Milligan.* The famous flag-salute case of 1940 has recently been overruled in the decision of *West Virginia* v. *Barnett.* Similar public expiation in the case of the Japanese-Americans would be good for the court, and for the country.

THE NISEI COME HOME
Victor Boesen

Throughout the war, War Relocation Authority spokesmen and others refused to speculate about what would happen to relocation camp inhabitants after the war's end. Given the widespread racist hostility that McWilliams and a Time reporter described in earlier essays in the chapter, the return of these people to their former homes along the Pacific Coast looked virtually impossible. As Boesen suggests in this New Republic essay, however, after the war repatriation took place with remarkable speed and with, all things considered, relatively little hostility.

Yoshimatsu Masuda works two days a week in a fish cannery near Long Beach, California. It is no job for an old fisherman who spent 20 years of his life pulling his livelihood out of the Pacific, but it's the best Masuda can do under the circumstances. California has a law prohibiting alien Japanese from owning commercial fishing licenses.

Some day, Masuda hopes, the law will be revoked and he can go back to his old business. He has faith in his neighbors. "California people all right," he says warmly. "It's state guv'ment causes trouble." As far as California's attitude to its alien Japanese and its citizens of Japanese ancestry is concerned, the old fisherman is correct on both counts.

After many years of persecution because of their race, dating back to the 1890's, the Japanese are beginning to feel they really have a home in California. Returning from wartime relocation centers in other states, they discover that the old hostility has lessened perceptibly and that both Japanese aliens and Nisei (second-generation Japanese born in the US) have been encouraged to take up their old occupations.

Most of the animosity that still persists stems, as old Masuda puts it, from the state government's continued efforts to keep the Nisei in a sort of second-class-citizen category. Discriminatory laws such as the fishing-license ban that beached Masuda and the state's Alien Land Law still remain on the books. An occasional legislator like State Senator Jack Tenney, head of California's "Little Un-American Activities Committee," embarks on anti-Japanese tirades; Attorney General Fred N. Howser has tried, unsuccessfully, to deprive Japanese aliens of their landholdings, but their efforts have evoked little approval from the average Californian. And although the Hearst newspapers and the ultra-conservative Native Sons of the Golden West still bait the Japanese, their antics arouse less and less enthusiasm.

There is nothing miraculous in this change of attitude. Californians have not undergone a sudden spiritual catharsis which has divested them of deep-seated moral prejudices. Moral or anthropological considerations have little to do with it; many Californians have simply learned that the people they used to regard as "interlopers" are actually useful, conscientious citizens—and as such are to be valued highly.

The war decisively banished any doubts as to the courage or patriotism of Japanese Americans. At the very time California businessmen and farmers were taking

Victor Boesen, "The Nisei Come Home," *The New Republic 118* (1948).

over the properties of Japanese who had been evacuated to relocation centers, the nation's newspapers were carrying glowing accounts of the heroic 442nd Nisei Infantry Battalion in Italy. And despite the efforts of state officials, various freelance Japanophobes and anti-Japanese sections of the press (Hearst papers and the Sacramento *Bee*) to make it appear otherwise at the time, the Japanese committed no known act of disloyalty to this country, as attested by the FBI, the Army's Western Defense Command and the Navy.

In addition, the war indirectly created a new respect for the multitudes of Japanese truck farmers and gardeners who had to leave the area for alleged security reasons. While these people sweated out the war in relocation centers, the Californians discovered, by trying it themselves, that their erstwhile neighbors had done a superb job in cultivating and reclaiming the land and raising produce for sale at attractive prices.

There are other less utilitarian reasons why Californians are not rallying much to the tom-toms in Sacramento, and why, for instance, townspeople boycotted a barber who put up a "No Japs Wanted" sign in his window. The Nisei are intelligent and well behaved; they have an extremely low crime rate and boast the highest percentage of college graduates of any racial group in the country. The 442nd Infantry's IQ was among the best in the Army.

The feelings of many Californians about the return of the Japanese were expressed by a Negro who had moved into Los Angeles' "Little Tokyo" during the war. "Now that they've returned," he declared, "it's only right they should get their places back, because this is their home." And the Negro moved out.

The Nisei are pleased at the clearing atmosphere. One of them gives the typical report that Japanese are increasingly finding their way into the Caucasian business world, that they are being accepted both as employees and as fellow businessmen. To Nisei war vets, this atones in part for the wartime seizures of Japanese fruit, vegetable and produce industries, which have yet to be regained.

Agents of the War Relocation Authority, who conceived a healthy respect for the Japanese during the internment period, have helped persuade Caucasian employers to give the Nisei a try at office jobs, hitherto closed to them. The results have been excellent. When a presentable, efficient Nisei girl places herself as a typist or secretary, she usually creates a demand for more.

Jimmy Yahiro, proprietor of the Nisei Employment Agency in Los Angeles, says he has "no trouble in placing the girls in all kinds of office jobs"; the pastor of a Japanese church remarks, "The girls and women are getting lots of positions in stores on Broadway, in Beverly Hills and in country and city offices. I placed several in an exclusive Beverly Hills dress shop at $10 a day."

The men who get a chance make good just as quickly as the girls. One 442nd vet was refused a chemist's job. "Try the back door," counseled a Nisei attorney. "Take any kind of work they hire. Show them what kind of fellow you are." The boy followed his advice; today he is a chemist for an oil company.

To help break down dying prejudice, Nisei who are accepted into "white" employment practise a discipline not always found among other workers. Several hundred have gone into the hot, unpleasant work of pressing records in the phonograph-recording industry. One such worker, a college graduate, said, "Many Nisei dropped off as soon as they found they had to go through the training period at low wages.

Some of us older men felt that this created a bad impression, and now we have set an unwritten policy that no Nisei is to take a job unless he will stick. . . ."

Many Nisei, discovering the community's growing willingness to accept Japanese, are going into business for the first time. Patronage of a Japanese establishment in a Caucasian neighborhood may be sparse at first, but it soon grows. Take the experience of the Nisei who opened a service station.

"My first Caucasian customers would drive away when they saw I was Japanese," he declared. "Then a few began stopping and found that I gave prewar service. Once they came in, they became regular customers."

Meanwhile, those business and professional men who haven't yet picked up where they left off during the war, are resorting to gardening. Today, in the Los Angeles area alone, more than 3,000 Japanese, a third more than were similarly employed in 1941, are tending the district's yards and estates, grown unkempt while they were away. Angelenos are so happy to have them back that they are paying them up to $600 a month, compared to $125 before the war. Some of the more industrious gardeners, juggling six or seven lawns at a time, have earned as much as $50 a day. What the clients don't know is that very often the little man clipping the hedge is a college graduate in one of the professions or an ex-businessman with more money in the bank than his employer.

For those able immediately to resume operations at their old stands in such Japanese specialties as flower markets, flower farms and wholesale fish markets, business is brisk. Such resistance as Caucasian interlopers put up at the start quickly faded or is working out to the advantage of the Japanese.

The first Nisei to return to Los Angeles, co-owner with his father and two brothers of a flower market on the edge of Little Tokyo which had been operated for them by Caucasian managers, found signs on the wall reading, "No Japs Allowed Between 7th and 8th." He kept out of sight all day, and that evening asked his Caucasian manager about the signs. The next day he found police posted around the market, with a radio car standing by. "You have nothing to be afraid of," they told him.

The only unpleasant incident to occur in the store came when a man proclaimed in loud tones: "I wouldn't spend a dime in a place run by Japs!" No one seemed interested. Some time later, this same man, who runs a flower shop in connection with a funeral home, phoned to ask if he could buy some flowers. The original returnee took the call. His brothers, both back by now, suggested that the man be told to go to hell. This was vetoed, however, and today his monthly account averages $1,400.

Soon after his first order, he came around and apologized for his earlier conduct. "I made a fool of myself," he kept repeating. Now he and his wife exchange dinner invitations with the brothers and their families, and go fishing together.

George Endow, a San Fernando Valley flower grower, who also runs the Sugar Bowl Café in Little Tokyo, estimates that there has been a 60-percent comeback among Japanese flower growers — largely because the Caucasians who took over in their absence were amateurs and unable to compete on the basis of quality production. To offset this disadvantage, the Caucasians boycotted those wholesalers who bought from Japanese growers, which merely drove more wholesalers to the Japanese owners.

Another Japanese comeback has been made in fish wholesaling. A typical example is furnished by Frank Tsuchiya, of the Pacific California Fish Company. His firm, which did a million-dollar-a-year business before the war, not only has all its old customers back but has expanded its operations by 35 percent.

[All of this] is encouraging, but it is only a symptom of something bigger. That something bigger is the growing realization of the people of California that Nisei make good neighbors.

Arguments in Favor of Evacuation

Morton Grodzins

Morton Grodzins was a member of the research team that conducted the Japanese American and Evacuation and Resettlement Study at the University of California from 1942 to 1948. His book Americans Betrayed *(1949) was one of the earliest book-length postwar indictments of the federal government's wartime internment policy. The following selection is taken from the appendix of Grodzins's book. It simply lists and discusses the pretexts and justifications for the internment Grodzins and his fellow researchers heard from individuals and institutions in the Pacific Coast states.*

SABOTAGE, ESPIONAGE, AND THE FIFTH COLUMN

The sabotage, espionage, and fifth-column argument started in the largest number of instances from what was believed to have taken place on December 7, 1941. Stories of "what happened at Pearl Harbor" did not begin to circulate generally until the very end of December. Once the style was set, these stories became endless. The form resolution passed by eleven California county boards of supervisors noted that "during the attack on Pearl Harbor . . . the Japanese were aided and abetted by fifth columnists of the Japanese race." The same point about Pearl Harbor was made in Congress at least ten times between January 20 and February 18, 1942. Pearl Harbor was a partial foundation for the first demand of the California Joint Immigration Committee in favor of evacuation and a prominent reason for evacuation advanced by American Legion groups. Pearl Harbor formed the basis of the anonymous chain letters circulated in southern California during January and February and was mentioned frequently, and sometimes hysterically, in letters received by Attorney-General Biddle. Newspaper stories sometimes made the Pearl Harbor stories very precise, and on one occasion the moderate *San Francisco Chronicle* printed drawings by a staff artist illustrating the exact manner in which Japanese blocked roads with overturned trucks and signaled attacking planes with flashlights.

It was a short step between what was alleged to have happened at Pearl Harbor and what might happen on the Pacific Coast. Californians were in general agreement with Attorney-General Earl Warren that the state presented "the most likely objective in the Nation" for sabotage and espionage activities. Mayor Bowron of Los Angeles, the city managers of Oakland and Alameda in the San Francisco region, the governors of Washington and Oregon, and the mayors of the largest cities in those states all expressed similar views.

An important variation of the argument was the thesis of *concerted sabotage*. Attorney-General Warren of California was its chief exponent. On February 2 Mr. Warren asserted it was "significant" that there had been no reports of sabotage and

Morton Grodzins, "Arguments in Favor of Evacuation" *Americans Betrayed* (Chicago: University of Chicago Press, 1949).

fifth-column activities in the state. This, he said, looked "very much" as if it were "a studied effort not to have any until the zero hour arrives." The California attorney-general made the most elaborate presentation of this argument in his testimony before the Tolan Committee. His remarks at this point were confined to the Japanese alone:

"To assume that the enemy has not planned fifth column activities for us in a wave of sabotage is simply to live in a fool's paradise.

"Unfortunately, however, many of our people and some of our authorities . . . are of the opinion that because we have had no sabotage and no fifth column activities in this State since the beginning of the war, that means that none have been planned for us. *But I take the view that that is the most ominous sign in our whole situation. It convinces me more than perhaps any other factor that the sabotage that we are to get, the fifth column activities that we are to get, are timed just like Pearl Harbor was timed and just like the invasion of France, and of Denmark, and of Norway, and all of those other countries.*

". . . *Our day of reckoning is bound to come. . . . When, nobody knows, of course, but we are approaching an invisible deadline.*"

This stand received the widest concurrence. And the argument was used by Congressman Tolan; Mayor Riley of Portland, Oregon; Mayor Millikin of Seattle; Mayor Bowron of Los Angeles; the Korean "espionage agent," Kilsoo K. Haan; columnists Walter Lippmann and Westbrook Pegler; several editorial writers; a number of correspondents of Attorney-General Biddle; and, not least of all, by General DeWitt in his recommendation for mass evacuation.

Direct evidence of sabotage intent or sabotage practice was cited in a number of instances. Immediately after Pearl Harbor it was reported that ground glass had been found in shrimp canned by Japanese workers and that Japanese saboteurs had sprayed overdoses of arsenic poison on vegetables. Japanese residents allegedly set up a number of unusual signaling devices similar to those which had been reported at Hawaii: "A beautiful field of flowers on the property of a Japanese farmer" near Ventura, California, had been plowed up because "it seems the Jap was a fifth columnist and had grown his flowers in a way that when viewed from a plane formed an arrow pointing the direction to the airport. The chief of police of Los Angeles charged that on December 8 and 9 "a large amount of loose hay was piled in the shape of an arrow pointing to one of our major aviation plants." The district attorney of Tulare County said that "Jap truck farmers of the Ivanhoe district had planted tomatoes so they form a crude arrow pointing to an air training field."

By far the most damaging claims of sabotage intent came to the public attention as the result of numerous raids by the Federal Bureau of Investigation. After the promulgation of the contraband orders in January sensational mass raids were made. The newspaper headlines were large and the stories shocking. On February 6, for example, a two-line, eight-column streamer headline on page 1 of the *San Francisco Chronicle* announced raids on what FBI agents "feared to be a deadly nest of saboteurs on the edge of the huge Mare Island Navy Yard." With the searches still continuing, it was revealed that contraband goods had been seized that included a "complete set of US Navy signal flags, at least five illegal radios, at least two guns, at least two illegal cameras." Five days later contraband material seized in the search of a hundred homes and business establishments near Monterey Bay uncovered "more than 60,000 rounds of rifle ammunition, 14,900 rounds of shotgun ammunition, 378 pistol bullets, eleven still cameras," and a large amount of additional contraband material. Revelations of this kind were made at almost daily intervals for more than a month, with pictures of the contraband goods and the arrested aliens appearing frequently.

The cumulative effect of the claims and alleged proofs of the sabotage, espionage, fifth-column dangers showed itself in many of the letters urging evacuation that came to national legislators and administrative officials. The same considerations had a great weight in swinging editorial opinion in favor of evacuation, the statement of the *Stockton Record* of February 21 being typical in this regard:

"In recent days FBI agents have operated in many parts of California and uncovered caches of arms and contraband. . . . The circumstances smack strongly of those which contributed to the tragedy of Pearl Harbor. . . . The United States cannot afford to take chances. . . . The Pacific coast is in danger."

PUBLIC MORALE

Quantitatively of little importance, the public morale argument was put succinctly by Governor Olson of California when he said that if evacuation were carried out "everyone would feel much safer about the alien and the Japanese population." The loss of the sense of security resulting from the continued presence of Japanese Americans was set forth by the State Personnel Board as one justification for suspending all Japanese American employees of California. To the Department of Justice came letters demanding more rapid action on the part of officials in removing Japanese, whose very presence on the coast was described as undermining public morale and hampering the war effort. The following was a representative complaint: "Here on the west coast your snail-like action in dealing with the Japs has come in for much criticism almost to the point of creating a don't give a dam [sic] attitude."

HUMANITARIANISM

Two categories of this argument were differentiated, one dealing with the danger to resident Japanese if they were not taken into custody, the other dwelling upon the humane manner with which the evacuation would be carried out.

a) Vigilantism and race riots. —The statement that evacuation was necessary in order to insure "the safety of the people who are moved as well as the safety of all the rest of the population" became a catch phrase of the pre-evacuation period. Citizens writing to President Roosevelt (whose mail on the subject came to Attorney-General Biddle) set the proposition in its shortest threatening form: "Unless you remove all Japanese, alien and American born, from California, we the people will slaughter them."

As early as January 16 an officer of a powerful agricultural marketing group wrote his congressman that "in the Imperial Valley a group of Filipinos met and were drawing names of individual Japanese out of a box to be 'taken care of' by those drawing the names. . . . It would not take very much of a 'match' to start a terrific conflagration." This fear was echoed on several occasions in the halls of Congress, and Congressman Voorhis, one of the three moderates of the western bloc, based his approval of mass evacuation on his fear of what might happen to the Japanese.

Local law-enforcement officers of California expressed the greatest concern over the possibility of vigilante action, regarding it as a prime reason for the necessity of evacuation. The sheriff of Merced said that he heard "rumblings of vigilante activity"; the chief of police of Huntington Beach described anti-Japanese sentiment "at fever heat"; the police chief of Watsonville wrote that "racial hatred is mounting higher and higher" and that Filipinos were "arming themselves and going out looking for an argument with Japanese." Attorney-General Warren himself expressed a similar view, and the mayor of Olympia, Washington, wrote that unless all Japanese, "irrespective of citizenship," were removed from the entire coastal region, "there will be a recurrence of the old time vigilante action that will effect a removal in its own peculiar way."

b) Humane evacuation. — The second type of humanitarian argument not only held that mass evacuation could be carried out without undue economic, physical, and moral hardship but also adduced positive values to that movement. At times the issue was put negatively: "No one wants to see them suffer. I have lots of very nice Japanese friends and I like them." Congressman Leland Ford went one step further and said that mass evacuation was a "very humanitarian" device, since it would avoid separating families, which might occur if only alien enemies were moved. A resolution of the Pacific League, a conservative civic organization of Los Angeles, took exactly the same line.

APPROVAL OF JAPANESE MILITARISM

A large portion of the public argument in favor of evacuation attempted to prove that all Japanese were of particular danger to the nation's safety. The first category of these proofs dwelt upon the active (or passive) approval of Japanese military aggression on the part of American residents of Japanese ancestry.

In some cases this allegation was made in the broadest terms, a correspondent of the *Sacramento Bee* writing: "It is not logical to think that very many are loyal to us. They cannot help but sympathize with their own country." Californians writing to national officials emphasized the same point: "There are no Japs that would do anything for us, even though second generation and American citizens, they all have and are at this moment working for their country."

In its most damaging aspect, this symbol of identification was wielded in a specific fashion. On many occasions the allegation was made that approval of Japanese militarism on the part of Japanese Americans was demonstrated by the fact that no resident Japanese ever gave information to law-enforcement officers about the subversive activities of other members of the group. This declaration was made by Attorney-General Warren and by at least five other persons before the Tolan Committee alone, including two California police chiefs. It was later given credence by a high-ranking military officer.

A similar type of issue was made over the claim that Japanese Americans knew about Pearl Harbor in advance. As one person wrote to President Roosevelt, "Surely some of the many '100% Loyal Japanese Americans' knew what was going to take place there [Hawaii]. Why didn't *one* of them step forward and forewarn us if they are so 'loyal.'" The city manager of Alameda, California, made the same charge, and Mayor Bowron of Los Angeles said that a "large number" of resident Japanese "knew what was coming" and "overplayed their hand" in the year before the war by going "out of their way" to demonstrate American patriotism.

More tangible evidence of the support of Japanese militarism by American Japanese was presented by Attorney-General Warren to the Tolan Committee. The attorney-general put into the record several pages of quotations from vernacular newspapers of the United States describing contributions of tinfoil, clothing, other materials, and cash made to the Japanese government by Japanese residents in the United States between 1938 and 1941. He quoted items to prove the interest of Japanese Americans in the welfare of Japanese military leaders.

INFLUENCE OF THE JAPANESE GOVERNMENT

The second argument designed to prove the special danger of Japanese Americans was based on the influence the Japanese government allegedly wielded over the Japanese American community. It was held that this influence was made effective through propaganda, financial subsidy, or physical coercion (usually by Japanese consular agents) through the media of the prefectoral organizations, the language schools, or the Buddhist (and Shinto) church. The dual-citizenship status of the Nisei was held up as the symbol of the imperial government's power.

The releases issued by the California Joint Immigration Committee emphasized these points. A correspondent of the Attorney-General declared that the Japanese Americans had been "well instructed" by agents of the emperor, while another wrote that "pressure brought to bear on them by the Japanese government" would make it "almost impossible for them to remain loyal to the United States government." Governor Olson stated that the language schools taught allegiance to Japan and asserted that the "schools have been conducted through the aid and abetment of the Japanese consulates." He also said that the consuls had promoted "fifth column activities" by "insisting that the entire Japanese population really belonged to Japan. Attorney-General Warren described at length the "agricultural, commercial, educational, social, religious, and patriotic associations," which blanketed every Japanese community. At the top of the pyramid of the many associations were the Japanese Association of America in northern California and the Japanese Central Association in southern California. The attorney-general pointed out that one or another of the associations had sent gifts to the Japanese government, instilled "the Japanese military code of boshido," encouraged Japanese Americans to return to Japan for their education, and persuaded those educated in Japan to return to America.

The issue of dual citizenship was raised on many occasions. It was the starting point that led to the eventual dismissal of all Americans of Japanese ancestry employed by the state of California and a frequently utilized argument of military officials.

MIGRATION AND DISTRIBUTION

Those who urged the course of mass evacuation pointed to the manner in which resident Japanese were congregated in the vicinity of strategic industrial and military installations. In many cases the attempt was made to show that the distribution was not accidental but rather that it had taken place by means of fraudulent immigration or planned internal migration.

Attorney-General Earl Warren of California made this argument in its most complete form, and his presentation had the greatest influence on the military officers in whom discretion for evacuation rested.

Newspaper correspondents and editorialists took up the geographic issue with enthusiasm. The *San Diego Union*, for example, commented: "Maps showing the strongest concentration of Japanese, both aliens and citizens, along the Pacific Coast reveal that almost without exception they are settled in the vital strategic military points, factories, reservoirs and beachlands. No group of 200,000 or so persons could have completely surrounded such vital areas had they not planned it carefully in advance, which probably is precisely what they did."

THE RACIAL ARGUMENT

Distrust of the Japanese race as such was implicit in a large part of all the arguments in favor of evacuation. That distrust was put explicitly on many occasions, by all types of persons and in a variety of ways.

Congressman Rankin put the racial argument in its most sweeping form when he told the Congress that "once a Jap, always a Jap" and that "you cannot regenerate a Jap, convert him, and make him the same as a white man any more than you can reverse the laws of nature." Persons writing to the Attorney-General developed the same theme: "They are the most cunning and unreliable of any class living. A Jap is a Jap. The only one you can trust is a dead one." Those contributing letters to newspapers were equally inclusive, e.g., "They are treacherous and barbarous by nature."

Officials of the three western states were inclined to admit that some proportion of the resident Japanese were loyal to America but professed a complete inability to distinguish loyal from disloyal. The governor and attorney-general of California, the attorney-general of Washington, and the mayors of Los Angeles, Seattle, and Portland, among many others, took this view. All thought it "difficult" or "impossible" to segregate the good Japanese from the bad, whereas, in the words of Attorney-General Warren, "when we are dealing with the Caucasian race [German and Italian aliens] we have methods that will test the loyalty of them." Mayor Bowron thought many Japanese Americans might "intend to be loyal" but asked, "When the final test comes, who can say but that 'blood will tell'?" Lesser law-enforcement officers of California supported mass evacuation for substantially the same reason.

The racial argument sometimes held that Japanese all looked alike, sometimes that their thought-processes were inscrutable to Caucasians. These themes were occasionally supplemented with the statement (by the Native Sons of the Golden West, for example) that the high birth rate of resident Japanese was a mark of their special danger and, by extension, a reason for evacuation.

CULTURAL FACTORS

The last, and least frequently used, of the arguments purporting to prove the special danger of Japanese Americans was based on the cultural habits of the group.

The lag making for nonallegiance was noted in religion, education, language, and familial patterns.

A spokesman for the California Joint Immigration Committee put great emphasis on Japanese cultural patterns making for poor Americanism. Many American citizens of Japanese ancestry, he said, were sent to Japan for an education which "for all intents and purposes" made them Japanese. Language schools in America tended to accomplish the same purpose. The religion of emperor worship similarly led people away from Americanism.

This last point was apparently a reference to Shintoism. An Oregon state senator extended the danger classification to Buddhists, stating that "the Buddhist religion is looked on as a national Japanese custom," and "even among the children there isn't much social mixing between the Buddhist and the Christian children." A California club leader was more absolute: "Persons of Japanese ancestry cannot safely be treated as American citizens until at least three generations have been reared in this country. It takes that long to get a group of nationals who believe in both emperor and ancestor worship, and who are most rigidly bound down by family ties, to really break loose and become Americans."

These allegations received general support from a number of political leaders, and the State Personnel Board of California utilized the cultural patterns of Japanese Americans as one reason for discharging them from state employment.

ECONOMIC ASPECTS

The importance of Japanese Americans to the economic life of the western states became inextricably involved in the determination of evacuation as public policy. Experts were not lacking who testified to the substantial contribution of Japanese Americans to the economy of the country, especially in the production of vegetables. The necessity of meeting the extraordinary quotas of the "Food for Victory" program gave added point to these statements. On the other hand, a chorus of voices affirmed that Japanese Americans were either not important to the nation's economy or actually detrimental to it. A secondary economic argument held that whatever economic losses might be suffered as a result of evacuation would be offset by the useful productive work of Japanese Americans in areas of concentration.

Those most insistent upon the economic unimportance of Japanese American farmers were themselves farmers. The Western Growers Protective Association and its allied organization, the Grower-Shipper Vegetable Association, produced numerous statements to demonstrate that a movement of Japanese would cause "no dislocation of food commodities." In their own publications and in communications to state and national political leaders, these groups pressed home this point. Various units of the California Farm Bureau Federation and a leader of the Associated Farmers took substantially the same stand. Political leaders, including Governor Olson, contributed supporting views.

The principal economic theme dwelt on the small contribution made to total farm production by resident Japanese farm operators. Opinion was more divided with respect to the effect of evacuation on the supply of farm laborers. The farm bureau federations, which were quick to deny the importance of Japanese entrepreneurs, were among the first to suggest that the labor loss could be negated by using

Japanese as field hands under Army guard. This idea was also expressed by many others.

A number of persons testified that the only production losses as the result of evacuation would be in so-called nonessential, "specialty" crops. A substantial minority, however, denied the possibility of even this minor loss and saw only positive economic advantages in the movement. The latter viewpoint was expressed by a Seattle lawyer who asserted that "Japanese standards of living and working conditions" had eliminated white gardeners. This had brought about "an unhealthy economic condition," and "no greater service can be rendered the country than to restore the former condition."

THE APPEAL TO PATRIOTISM

One of the earliest and most persistent of the symbols manipulated in favor of evacuation maintained that loyal Japanese should co-operate in the evacuation movement and stamped those who refused to co-operate as disloyal. Congressman Leland Ford wrote in this vein as early as January 16, asserting that a patriotic Japanese could make his contribution to the safety of the country "by permitting himself to be placed in a concentration camp." If American citizens of Japanese ancestry were not "loyal enough" to volunteer for internment, then "they ought to be placed in a camp anyhow." The logic of this point of view apparently appealed to many political leaders, including the governor of California, the mayor of Los Angeles, and the city managers of Oakland and Alameda. Correspondents of Attorney-General Biddle and a number of newspaper editorialists utilized the same argument. A spokesman for the Los Angeles County Defense Council acknowledged that the council's appeal to patriotism was an effort to circumvent the legal obstacles of forced movements. "We have considered and realized the limitation of the committee in dealing with the American citizens of Japanese descent from a constitutional point of view and we are seeking to overcome that by inviting them to participate in the war effort here by joining their relatives outside of the prescribed areas."

NECESSITY FOR DRASTIC MEASURES

Some persons felt so strongly about the Japanese problem that they urged the most extreme action, without regard for legal limitations and without recourse to any specific reason except "something drastic has to be done."

A California congressman put the matter: "Let's move these Japanese out and talk about it afterwards." The mayor of a California City was even more specific when he wrote to Congressman Tolan that "the Constitution can go overboard, if necessary." The same views were held by California law-enforcement officers. The district attorney of Madera County, for example, wrote: "We must forget such things as the writ of habeas corpus, and the prohibition against unreasonable searches and seizures. The right of self-defense, self-preservation . . . is higher than the Bill of Rights."

More intemperate statements were not lacking. Persons writing to the Justice Department seethed: "Francis Biddle and other Washington officials are hypnotized by the constitutional niceties. . . . Like Pegler, I say 'To hell with habeas corpus'"; asserted: "We can't trust them and must take off the kid gloves and play the game the Axis way"; and demanded that the Attorney-General be replaced by "a hard boiled gentleman, one who is not afraid of doubtful constitutional rights of traitors." Others wrote that "a good dose of toughness and not politics is what we and our allies need. . . . It is time to see some drastic action on our part"; that it was necessary to "give these vermin the treatment they deserve"; and that, if injustice were done, "we could smile about it, and, in their own vernacular say 'So sorry.' Let's get tough, for heaven's sake. . . . Let's get tough with everybody."

THE ACTIVATION OF THE STEREOTYPE

Jacobus ten Broek, Edward N. Barnhart, and Floyd W. Matson

Jacobus ten Broek, a professor at the University of California, was authorized by the directors of the Japanese American Evacuation and Resettlement Study to summarize the voluminous data amassed by those involved in the project. He did so in Prejudice, War, and the Constitution *(1954) with the help of two University of California colleagues, Edward N. Barnhart and Floyd W. Matson. This chapter of ten Broek's book traces the significant role members of the press and politicians at federal, state, and local levels played in fueling the hysteria and racism that urged President Roosevelt to sign the executive order to intern those of Japanese descent who lived on the West Coast.*

The Japanese attack on Pearl Harbor came as a profound shock, if not a complete surprise, to residents of the Pacific Coast states. Although for many years most citizens had been aware that war was a possibility, many refused to believe the first reports from Honolulu and were convinced only by repeated broadcasts and ubiquitous black headlines. But the full import of the news soon became apparent as all service personnel was ordered to report to stations, as jeeps and convoys in war regalia appeared on the streets, and military aircraft began to roar overhead. By midafternoon of December 7, 1941, thousands of citizens were rushing to recruiting stations to enlist or offering their services in any capacity.

Before they could recover from the initial shock, West Coast residents were confronted with more bad news. Coincident with the Pearl Harbor attack enemy forces had struck with disastrous effect at Hong Kong, Manila, Thailand, Singapore, Midway, Wake, and Guam. Japanese bombers had at a single blow destroyed the air defenses of Hong Kong, and within a few days occupied Kowloon peninsula and placed the British crown colony in jeopardy. On December 10 the "impregnable" British warships *Repulse* and *Prince of Wales* were sunk by Japanese planes, thus upsetting the balance of naval power in the far Pacific. The little kingdom of Thailand had surrendered on December 8, and the enemy began a swift southward movement through the British Malay States toward Singapore. Other Japanese troops landed in the Philippines on December 10 and were converging on Manila. Guam was captured on December 11, the fate of Wake Island appeared sealed (it fell on December 23), and Midway was imperiled by an enemy task force. Meanwhile, dispatches which had filtered through censorship suggested that American losses at Pearl Harbor were far worse than at first indicated. It was freely predicted that Alaska and the Pacific Coast itself were next in line for Japanese attack and even attempted invasion.

People everywhere were frightened, and their fear was heightened by a feeling of helplessness. The threat of bombings and invasion, plus the absence of precise

Jacobus ten Broek, Edward N. Barnhart, and Floyd W. Matson, "The Activation of the Stereotype," *Prejudice, War, and the Constitution* (Berkeley: University of California Press, 1954).

information as to events in Hawaii, quickly bred rumors of total disaster. It was whispered that the entire Pacific fleet had been destroyed; that every reinforcing ship sent out from the mainland had been sunk off the coast by Japanese submarines.

Almost at once rumors about the resident Japanese began. Japanese gardeners were said to be equipped with short-wave transmitters hidden in garden hose; Japanese servants and laborers who failed to appear for work on December 7 (a Sunday) were accused of prior knowledge of the Hawaii attack. Japanese farmers were charged with smuggling poison into vegetables bound for market, and cans of seafood imported from Japan were said to contain particles of ground glass. Signaling devices similar to those reported found in Hawaii were alleged to have been set up in coastal areas. A number of anxious Californians, according to one report, went so far as to plow up "a beautiful field of flowers on the property of a Japanese farmer," because "it seems the Jap was a fifth columnist and had grown his flowers in a way that when viewed from a plane formed an arrow pointing the direction to the airport."

These rumors and accusations arose largely as a result of the stories of fifth-column activity at Pearl Harbor which were rapidly accumulating in the press. After an inspection of the Pacific base, Secretary of the Navy Knox was quoted as saying that sabotage at Pearl Harbor constituted "the most effective fifth-column work that's come out of this war, except in Norway." Newspaper headlines on the Knox report generally stressed this aspect: "Secretary of Navy Blames Fifth Columnists for the Raid," "Fifth Column Prepared Attack," "Fifth Column Treachery Told." Other stories told of secret signaling and faked air-raid alerts by Hawaiian Japanese at the time of the attack, of arrows cut in the cane fields to aid enemy pilots, and roadblocks improvised to tie up military traffic.

In opposition to the rumors and scare stories was a succession of official assurances that all dangerous enemy aliens had been apprehended, that necessary precautions had already been taken, and that Japanese Americans as a whole were loyal to the United States. This viewpoint was, moreover, echoed in the editorials of most California newspapers during the first days of war. Despite these assurances, however, Americans became increasingly restive as the prospect of Japanese attack or invasion grew more plausible. For half a century they had heard of the treachery and deceitfulness of resident Japanese—of how the "Japs" were concentrated in strategic areas of the state; of how by "peaceful invasion" they hoped to take over first California and ultimately the nation; of how they formed a network of spies and soldiers in disguise, patiently awaiting the Imperial signal to rise against the white man.

The news from the battle-fronts, recording new Allied losses almost daily, made the most alarmist forebodings seem realistic. Charges of fifth-column plots multiplied rapidly and broadened· in scope, soon including the mainland as well as Hawaii, and possible future actions as well as past events. It was reported, for example, that a Los Angeles naval sentry had seen signal lights in a Japanese waterfront colony; that the suicide of a Japanese doctor had uncovered a spy ring in the same area; that members of the notorious Black Dragon Society had been planted in cities and fishing communities; that the fifth-column character of Japanese schools in America had been exposed. The halls of Congress echoed with such exposures; Senator Guy Gillette of Iowa warned that "Japanese groups in this country planned sabotage and subversive moves," and Congressman Martin Dies of Texas announced the discovery of a book revealing Japanese plans to attack the United States.

Meanwhile the war was being brought steadily closer to home. On December 20 it was announced that Japanese submarines were attacking West Coast shipping; and on the same day two tankers were reportedly torpedoed off California. Two days later newspapers told of the shelling of a freighter by an enemy sub near Santa Barbara; the next day two more tankers were said to have been attacked off the California coast. Residents of the coastal states began to feel that their shores were under virtual blockade by enemy submarines.

The refugees from Hawaii, arriving in late December, brought new rumors of sabotage by island Japanese on December 7. It was said that Japanese had placed obstructions on the road to Pearl Harbor to keep reinforcements from getting through; that they had sabotaged the planes on the landing fields; that one group had entered Hickam Field in a milk truck, let down the sides and turned machine guns on American pilots as they ran to their planes.

Impressive "confirmation" of these rumors was contained in a sensational dispatch by a United Press correspondent, Wallace Carroll, who visited Honolulu shortly after the attack. Repeating with an air of authority most of the charges made by Honolulu refugees, the report declared that numbers of Hawaii Japanese had had advance knowledge of the bombing, and that Japanese produce merchants delivering to warships had been able to report on United States fleet movements. Carroll speculated that newspaper advertisements placed by Japanese firms may have been coded messages, and asserted that the enemy raiders had been aided by improvised roadblocks and arrows cut in the cane fields. The hands of Japanese pilots shot down during the assault were, he said, adorned with the rings of Honolulu high schools and of Oregon State University. The dispatch continued:

> Japanese of American nationality infiltrated into the Police Departments and obtained jobs as road supervisors, sanitary inspectors or minor government officials. Many went to work in the postoffice and telephone service, ideal posts for spies. . . .
>
> An American resident, who had studied Japanese methods in Manchuria and North China, told me that the Japanese fifth column and espionage organizations in the islands were similar to those which had been used to undermine the Chinese.

Accounts such as this, together with reports of new Allied reverses and tales of atrocities in the Philippines, goaded some Filipino Americans into direct retaliation against their Japanese neighbors. On December 23 a Japanese American, honorably discharged from the United States Army, was found stabbed to death on a Los Angeles sidewalk; his assailants were reported to be Filipinos. On Christmas Day in Stockton, windows of numerous Japanese business houses were smashed, assertedly by gangs of Filipinos. The next day in the same city an alien Japanese garage attendant was shot to death by a Filipino; newspapers prominently featured the incident, under such headlines as "Jap, Filipino District Under Guard; 1 Slain," "Stockton Jap Killed by Filipino; Riots Feared; Area Under Guard." By the end of December similar incidents were publicized almost daily. On December 29, a Japanese waiter was shot to death by a Filipino in Chicago. On December 30 an alien Japanese was shot and wounded in Sacramento; on New Year's Day a Japanese and his wife were murdered in the Imperial Valley. Other cases were reported from Gilroy and Livermore, and even from Utah.

Thus, within the first three weeks of war, the familiar Japanese stereotype was again visible on the Pacific Coast, and aroused individuals and groups were militantly reacting to it. The surprise attack of December 7, occurring in the midst of peace negotiations, seemed a definite confirmation of the old remembered tales of Japanese deceitfulness. Although for a time many citizens were reluctant to blame resident Japanese for the actions of Japan, and newspaper comment frequently was on the side of tolerance, the accumulating "evidence" of sabotage and espionage gradually put an end to toleration. Popular anger and apprehension rose in proportion to the continuing successes of the enemy, and by the end of 1941 suspicion and animosity were the most frequently expressed attitudes toward the Japanese Americans.

January was another month of disasters for the Allies and frustrations for the people at home. Manila fell to the Japanese on January 2, and an outnumbered American garrison began its struggle at Bataan and on Corregidor, with little hope of reinforcement. Japanese troops were advancing through Malay jungles to the crucial port of Singapore. Borneo was invaded and the entire East Indies came under attack. The scattered islands of the far Pacific were falling before the enemy with incredible rapidity; there were landings in New Guinea, and Australia was directly menaced. At home, reports continued of West Coast shipping attacked by enemy submarines; and off the eastern coast the Germans were rapidly intensifying their U-boat warfare and had torpedoed several Allied vessels.

In this atmosphere of frustration, fear, and anger, popular sentiment on the West Coast in the first month of 1942 was concentrated more and more against resident Japanese. Although the official restrictions on enemy-alien activity had been directed impartially at Germans, Italians, and Japanese, in the popular mind the Japanese were special targets of suspicion. Their Oriental appearance marked them inescapably in an area whose greatest danger was from the Far Eastern end of the Axis. Acts of violence against Japanese Americans continued to be reported in the press from such widely separate areas as Seattle, Fresno, Sacramento, and Santa Maria. Front-page attention was given FBI raids and arrests of Japanese allegedly possessing contraband. Popular tensions were increased by the charge in the Roberts Committee report that espionage in Hawaii had centered in the Japanese consulate, and that through its intelligence service the Japanese had obtained complete information on Pearl Harbor. The principal effect of such disclosures, however they were intended, was strongly to support the rumors of disloyalty among Japanese in Hawaii and to cast further doubt upon the loyalty of Japanese along the coast.

Early in January prominent voices began to call for more vigorous steps to control the resident Japanese, including their mass removal from the West Coast. News commentators, editorial writers, and public officials expressed displeasure at the "indecision and inaction" of the Department of Justice and urged drastic measures. John B. Hughes, a Los Angeles commentator for the Mutual Broadcasting Company, gained prominence as the first widely heard newsman to press the subject of evacuation. In the first of a month-long series of anti-Japanese broadcasts, Hughes compared the treatment of local Japanese with that of Americans captured by Japanese armies and warned that the failure to adopt strong measures would result in "disaster to the Pacific Coast." In subsequent commentaries he lent his support to rumors of espionage and fifth-column activities, charging that United States Japanese had contributed funds to Japan's war chest and hinting that the control of California's vegetable output was part of the over-all Japanese war plan.

Hughes also entered into a correspondence with Attorney General Biddle in which he urged the internment of both aliens and citizens of Japanese ancestry. "Persons who know the Japanese on the west coast," he wrote, "will estimate that ninety percent or more of American-born Japanese are primarily loyal to Japan." The commentator's justification for this indictment was the old yellow peril thesis of race: "Their organization and patient preparation and obedience to unified control could never be possible among the nationals of any Caucasian people. The Japanese are a far greater menace in our midst than any other axis patriots. They will die joyously for the honor of Japan." As a clincher, a justification was offered which was to be frequently advanced by proponents of evacuation: "There was an old law in the West, the law of the Vigilantes. Its whole code was: Shoot first and argue later. That code will be invoked, I'm afraid, unless authorities formulate a policy, an adequate policy, and put it into effect."

The calculated purpose of the Hughes campaign, like others which followed it in the press and on the air, was to persuade the public to demand a policy of action toward the local Japanese: specifically that of rounding them up and removing them from the coast. This policy of exclusion, frequently urged in conjunction with demands for internment, had a threefold appeal: first, in the light of what the public feared from the Japanese (espionage and sabotage) it seemed a perfect remedy; second, it offered an outlet for the public's antipathy toward the resident Japanese by urging forceful action against them; and finally it offered an opportunity for action, a chance to "do something," to a population fretting to strike back against Japan but so far offered no chance for direct action.

Hughes was not long in finding company among newspapermen. By the end of January a radical shift had taken place in the editorial position of California newspapers. During the first month of war these journals had for the most part been tolerant if not sympathetic toward the Japanese in America; but in the following three weeks unfavorable comment gradually increased to the point where it equalled expressions of tolerance. In the last days of January the trend suddenly accelerated and pro-Japanese utterances were lost in a barrage of denunciation — which centered on charges of Japanese disloyalty, demands for strict control measures, and growing sentiment for mass evacuation.

The keynote of the evacuation demands was sounded by the San Diego *Union*, one of the first major journals to press the issue, which opened a sustained editorial campaign on January 20 with arguments drawn largely from fifth-column rumors:

> In Hawaii and in the Philippines treachery by residents, who although of Japanese ancestry had been regarded as loyal, has played an important part in the success of Japanese attacks. . . .
>
> Every Japanese — for the protection of those who are loyal to us and for our protection against those who are not — should be moved out of the coastal area and to a point of safety far enough inland to nullify any inclinations they may have to tamper with our safety here.

In subsequent editorials the *Union* dwelt on the evils of Japanese citizenship, maintained that there was no way of determining the loyalty of "our so-called American citizens of Japanese ancestry," and exclaimed: "We are confronted on both sides by enemies who have devoted their entire careers to development of treachery, deceit, and sabotage. We can afford to be neither soft-headed nor soft-hearted in dealing with them or their agents."

The Hearst newspapers on the Pacific Coast, which in earlier years had led in the agitation against resident Japanese, did not conspicuously join the editorial clamor for evacuation — although news articles frequently were slanted against the Japanese. But it was in the Hearst press that the first of numerous syndicated columns condemning the Japanese minority was published. On January 29, Henry McLemore, a former sports reporter, wrote from Los Angeles:

> The only Japanese apprehended have been the ones the FBI actually had something on. The rest of them, so help me, are free as birds. There isn't an airport in California that isn't flanked by Japanese farms. There is hardly an air field where the same situation doesn't exist. . . .
>
> I know this is the melting pot of the world and all men are created equal and there must be no such thing as race or creed hatred, but do those things go when a country is fighting for its life? Not in my book. No country has ever won a war because of courtesy and I trust and pray we won't be the first because of the lovely, gracious spirit. . . .
>
> I am for immediate removal of every Japanese on the West Coast to a point deep in the interior. I don't mean a nice part of the interior either. Herd 'em up, pack 'em off and give 'em the inside room in the badlands. Let 'em be pinched, hurt, hungry and dead up against it. . . .
>
> Personally, I hate the Japanese. And that goes for all of them.

The mood of the McLemore attack was not widely evident in editorial comment prior to February. But the "Letters to the Editor" columns of many newspapers in the last weeks of January showed a rising tide of anti-Japanese feeling along the coast. In these informal communications, more graphically than elsewhere, the myths and slanders of bygone years were dusted off and put on display. The Sacramento *Bee* printed a letter from one of its readers who invoked the ancient battle-cry "America for Americans," and complained that Japanese were "forcing other races off the land, including whites from pioneer families." A letter in the Santa Rosa *Press Democrat* asked: "Biologically and economically, is the Jap fitted to mingle in American life?" and asserted that "when our trouble is over they must be returned to their rising sun." Another Sacramento reader declared that Japanese American citizens would "betray the land of their birth . . . simply because they are treacherous and barbarous by nature." A Native Daughter of the Golden West asked: "Did God make the Jap as He did the snake, did you hear the hiss before the words left his mouth? Were his eyes made slanting and the hiss put between his lips to warn us to be on our guard?" A San Francisco reader urged the authorities to "put all the Japs in camps . . . . First thing you know they will be pulling another surprise on us."

On January 17, the California senate also passed without dissent a measure aimed at Japanese employees of the state. Claiming that numbers of state workers appeared to "possess dual citizenship," the bill called upon the State Personnel Board to prevent the employment of anyone "who is not loyal to the United States and to . . . provide for the dismissal from the [state civil] service of such persons as may be proved to be disloyal to the United States." Although Japanese were not directly named in the bill, all the lawmakers who spoke on the proposal referred openly to the need for examining the loyalty of Japanese American employees. Senators Jack Metzger and John Harold Swan, coauthors of the bill, produced a photostatic copy of a payroll sheet of the State Motor Vehicle Department which contained only Japanese names, and Senator Swan purported to see in this "a systematic plot to get Japanese on the state payroll and allow them to bore from within." Senator Metzger contributed to the fifth-column rumors by charging that "Japanese fifth columnists in milk wagons drew machine guns instead of milk bottles out of twenty-one wagons in Honolulu the morning of December 7 and turned them on Pearl Harbor barracks." Later the same senator was reported as saying: "I don't believe there is a single Japanese in the world who is not pulling for Japan. They will spy, commit sabotage, or die if necessary."

In the national capital, outcries against the Japanese Americans began to be heard from West Coast congressmen late in January. As in other circles, congressional discussion during the first six weeks of war had generally shown confidence in the loyalty and integrity of resident Japanese. An early harbinger of changing attitudes among West Coast congressmen was the insertion into the *Congressional Record* by Congressman Leland Ford of Los Angeles of an anti-Japanese telegram from movie actor Leo Carillo, which read in part: "Why wait until [the Japanese] pull something before we act. . . . Let's get them off the coast into the interior. . . . May I urge you in behalf of the safety of the people of California to start action at once."

The decision to evacuate all Japanese Americans from the West Coast, which came during February, was reached in a context of gathering fear, suspicion, and anger on the part of the American public — a mood occasioned by the unanticipated disasters in the Pacific. Had the United States fleet not been decimated at Pearl Harbor, but steamed off intact to meet and destroy the Japanese navy, as most Americans had been certain it would; had the Japanese armies been turned back at Singapore by the land and sea defenses which had been thought invincible; in short, had the Allies taken the initiative at the outset and shown promise of checking the Japanese advance, it is doubtful that American opinion — public and private, official and unofficial — could have been mobilized in support of evacuation. Assured of ultimate victory and sustained by a diet of war successes, a secure and confident America might well have fulfilled its democratic ideal of tolerance and hospitality toward the Japanese minority in its midst.

But the war did not go that way, and Americans were given no prospect of security or gleam of optimism. In mid-February, only seventy days after the first attack on Malaya, "impregnable" Singapore surrendered unconditionally to the Japanese, in what Winston Churchill was to call "the greatest disaster to British arms which history records." The capitulation forced an Allied withdrawal to the Dutch East Indies, and the way not lay open for an enemy attack upon Burma and India. The Japanese, in fact, had entered Burma a week before to cut the Burma Road and isolate China. The Indies were sealed off and their fate ordained by the fall of Sumatra, Borneo, and Celebes; and in a series of sea engagements during February the Japanese first split and then methodically destroyed American and Allied naval forces. Enemy penetration of the southwest Pacific was equally rapid and decisive. In January Japanese forces had leveled the centers of defense in the Solomons; from these positions they now struck west at New Guinea, bombing Salamaua and Port Moresby and even neutralizing Port Darwin on the Australian coast. By the end of February an invasion of Australia seemed imminent; the final fall of the beleaguered Philippine garrison was virtually assured; the surrender of Java and the complete conquest of the rich Indies was only days away; and the great subcontinent of India was threatened with assault. Nothing had occurred to indicate that the bewildering tide of conquest might soon be stemmed, and not a few Americans wondered when their turn would come in the Japanese schedule of invasion.

Early in the month, meanwhile, in conjunction with its program of alien evacuation from prohibited areas, the Justice Department began a series of "spot raids" to uncover contraband and counter anticipated sabotage. FBI agents, together with state and local officers, descended without warning or warrant upon a number of localities and searched the homes of Japanese. Large amounts of "contraband" were found, and numbers of alien Japanese were apprehended. Each of these surprise raids received attention from California newspapers, usually beneath black banner headlines. Particular stress was placed upon the lists of contraband seized. One search, for example, was reported to have uncovered "11 cameras, 14 short wave radio sets, 12 binoculars, a telescope, nine rifles, six revolvers, many thousands of rounds of ammunition, 84 knives, a large searchlight, four floodlights, four telescope gun sights, a box of sulphuric acid, Japanese maps and three sets of maps and charts of the Monterey Bay area." The Japanese operator of a sporting goods store was said to possess "70,000 rounds of rifle and shotgun ammunition, 12 rifles and shotguns, a public address system, cameras and film, books of Japanese propaganda and a radio operator's handbook."

The effect of these accounts in augmenting public suspicions may be glimpsed in a letter to Attorney General Biddle from a San Diego resident: "How much longer are we going to let these traitorous barbarians strut among us seeking every means of destroying us, storing arms and ammunition right under our noses and within stone's throw of our war industries, just because hasty action on our part might be impolite or offend the one out of every hundred Japs who is not conspiring against us?" Editorial writers also were influenced by the apparent findings of the anti-Japanese raids. A typical comment in the Stockton *Record* declared that "in recent days FBI agents have operated in many parts of California and uncovered caches of arms and contraband. . . . The circumstances smack strongly of those who contributed to the tragedy of Pearl Harbor. . . . The Pacific Coast is in danger."

The inevitable effect of the arrests and spot raids, dramatically pointed up by the press, was to confirm the traditional image of the Japanese handed down from earlier generations and revived upon the outbreak of war. The rising tide of popular feeling is shown by the frequent appeals of the Department of Justice—and especially of Attorney General Francis Biddle—asking the public to forego vigilantism and maintain tolerance toward the Japanese Americans. But such appeals did little to check the rise of anti-Japanese sentiment. In fact, the control measures adopted by the Department of Justice seemed to many only a further confirmation of their fears: the creation of prohibited and restricted zones, the establishment of a curfew, the dramatic searches and seizures—all appeared to justify the deepening public suspicions of the Japanese, both citizens and aliens, as actually or potentially disloyal and dangerous.

The aggravated state of public opinion was also reflected during February in the words and actions of prominent politicians and political bodies. The boards of supervisors of eleven California counties joined in a solemn declaration that "during the attack on Pearl Harbor . . . the Japanese were aided and abetted by fifth columnists of the Japanese." State Attorney General Earl Warren had first proclaimed his attitude on January 30, when a press dispatch quoted him as saying that the Japanese situation in the state "may well be the Achilles heel of the entire civilian defense effort. Unless something is done it may bring about a repetition of Pearl Harbor." On February 2, Warren revealed to a private conference of sheriffs and district attorneys his intense suspicion of resident Japanese — which was so profound that the very absence of sabotage seemed to him a sure sign of its future occurrence: "It seems to me that it is quite significant that in this great state of ours we have had no fifth column activities and no sabotage reported. It looks very much to me as though it is a studied effort not to have any until the zero hour arrives." He concluded that "every alien Japanese should be considered in the light of a potential fifth columnist," and urged that the Alien Land Law be enforced to remove all Japanese from areas near vital installations. (It should be emphasized, however, that the public report of the conference called only for removal of enemy aliens — *not* of all Japanese Americans.)

In subsequent days Attorney General Warren produced a variety of arguments purporting to show that resident Japanese were not only dangerous but much more of a threat than resident Germans or Italians. His arguments constitute a resumé of anti-Japanese cliches which had been accumulating for over half a century. There was, he said, no way to determine the loyalty of Japanese Americans. It was impossible for Americans to comprehend Oriental ways; the alien culture was diffused through religion, language schools, and the practice of sending children to Japan for education. In Japan "they are indoctrinated with the idea of Japanese imperialism. They receive their religious instruction which tied up their religion with their Emperor, and they come back here imbued with the ideas and policies of Imperial Japan." Warren alleged that Japanese in America generally approved of Japan's military conquests, implying that they would also favor the conquest of America; and he declared that the Japanese government exerted a broad control over the activities of all Japanese in this country.

Equally vigorous in his opposition to the Japanese, and in his contributions to the stereotype, was Mayor Fletcher Bowron of Los Angeles. In a radio address of February 5, Bowron warned of the danger of leaving the California Japanese at liberty. Among the Nisei there were "a number who are doubtless loyal to Japan, waiting probably, with full instructions as to what to do, to play their part when the time comes." The next day the mayor was quoted as denouncing the "sickly sentimentality" of Americans who feared injustices to the Japanese. The control "measures taken so far are so ineffectual as to be ridiculous." On Lincoln's birthday he again devoted his weekly radio address to the Japanese problem, arguing that if Lincoln were living he would round up "the people born on American soil who have secret loyalty to the Japanese Emperor." On still another occasion he disclaimed "any racial or other prejudice," but declared that "I know of no rule, no way to separate those who say they are patriotic and are, in fact, loyal at heart, and those who say they are patriotic and in fact at heart are loyal to Japan."

The shift in public sentiment, visible in late January, from comparative tolerance to general hostility toward the Japanese minority, was accurately mirrored in the Pacific Coast press. The ratio of unfavorable to favorable editorials was nineteen to one in the five days between January 22 and 26; hostile letters to the editor, chiefly demands for mass evacuation, attained their peak between February 1 and 5. By February, also, news stories favorable to the Japanese Americans were reduced from a December high of 22 percent to less than 3 percent, and during the thirty-day period from January 12 to February 10, fifteen times more news space was given to unfriendly items than to favorable copy. News stories devoted to evacuation demands reached their peak in the five days from February 6 to 10; these stories alone occupied seven times the space taken by all favorable news copy in the month from January 12 to February 10.

Editorial pressure in early February centered chiefly on the danger of a West Coast "Pearl Harbor." There was general agreement with the opinion of the Sacramento *Bee* that "the experience with the fifth column in Hawaii is overwhelming evidence that . . . the authorities must take no chances with possible Jap or Axis sympathizers." Newspapers pointed frequently to contraband seized by the FBI as sufficient evidence of Japanese disloyalty, and much attention was given to the growing number of evacuation demands by politicians, officials, and organizations. The activities of the Western congressional bloc were widely featured, often with speculation that federal action approving Japanese removal was soon to be taken.

Editorial writers voiced increasing opposition during February to the nonevacuation policy of the Department of Justice. Equally noteworthy were the exhortations of several widely syndicated columnists who added their voices to the cry for mass removal. Henry McLemore, whose personal campaign had begun late in January, continued to press his attack against the Department of Justice. Observing that aliens had been allowed weeks in which to evacuate the prohibited zones and would have "time to perfect their time bombs, complete their infernal machines," McLemore charged the Attorney General with handling the Japanese threat "with all the severity of Lord Fauntleroy playing squat tag with his maiden aunt."

Walter Lippmann, one of the most influential political columnists, added his name in mid-February to the list of those opposing federal policy and urging stronger measures. Subsequently Westbrook Pegler, then a Scripps-Howard columnist, translated the Lippmann argument into his own idiom, declaring on February 16 that "the Japanese in California should be under guard to the last man and woman right now and to hell with *habeas corpus* until the danger is over." Pegler went on:

> Do you get what [Lippmann] says? . . . The enemy has been scouting our coast . . . . The Japs ashore are communicating with the enemy offshore and . . . on the basis of "what is known to be taking place" there are signs that a well-organized blow is being withheld only until it can do the most damage. . . .
>
> We are so dumb and considerate of the minute constitutional rights and even of the political feelings and influence of people whom we have every reason to anticipate with preventive action!

Under the prodding of public opinion and the press, members of Congress from the West Coast states intensified their efforts toward the formulation of a severe control program aimed at the Japanese. On February 10 a committee set up by the joint Pacific Coast delegation approved a resolution recommending total evacuation of all Japanese from the coastal area. The recommendation was made despite advice from Army and Navy authorities that a sustained Japanese attack on the coast was "impossible" and that even enemy raids, although possible, "would be sporadic and would have little, if any, bearing on the course of the war." The reasons for disregarding this advice, as given in a letter to the President from the joint delegation, were plainly the exploded myth of sabotage at Pearl Harbor and the stereotyped belief in disloyalty and treachery among Japanese Americans. The letter pointed to "the seriousness of the Japanese menace along the entire Pacific Coast" which had evoked "insistent demands for prompt action," and asserted that "the critical nature of the situation and its latent subversive potentialities are so compelling as to justify the taking of extreme and drastic measures."

The mounting anger and suspicion of many citizens was expressed during February in the demands of various officials that the government act against the Japanese Americans without regard to legal or constitutional restraints. The mayor of one California city advised Congressman Tolan that "the Constitution can go overboard, if necessary"; should evacuation prove awkward in constitutional terms, "then we must win the war by dictatorship methods." A California congressman put the case more succinctly: "Let's move these Japanese out and talk about it afterwards." And the district attorney of Madera County declared that "we must forget such things as the right of *habeas corpus* and the prohibition against unreasonable searches and seizures. The right of self-defense, self-preservation . . . is higher than the Bill of Rights."

The opening days of March found the Japanese ordered away from the coast in the so-called "voluntary evacuation" program instituted by General DeWitt and the Western Defense Command. At the end of the month is "voluntary" program gave way to forced evacuation and internment. But public hostility remained; although newspaper columnists and editorialists turned most of their attention to other issues and policies, attacks against the Japanese continued. For the most part the trouble centered in Tulare and Fresno counties, where open vigilante action continued as the weeks passed and local Japanese still remained in residence. During March an attempt was made to burn down a Japanese-owned hotel at Sultana. On April 13 at Del Ray five evacuees were involved in a brawl with the local constable — following which a crowd of white residents, some armed with shotguns, threatened violence to a nearby camp of Japanese Americans. On succeeding nights the windows of four Japanese stores were smashed, and similar incidents occurred in Fresno. In northern Tulare County, a group known as the "Bald Eagles" — described by one observer as "a guerilla army of nearly 1,000 farmers" — armed themselves for the announced purpose of "guarding" the Japanese in case of emergency. A similar organization was formed in the southeast part of the county, where a large number of evacuees were concentrated.

Pilgrimage to Manzanar

Sadae Iwataki

Sadae Iwataki was one of the Nisei (the children of Japanese immigrants, American citizens by birth) evacuated and interned during World War II. When Congress passed the Civil Liberties Act of 1987, Iwataki, with numerous other Nisei, was prompted to make a pilgrimage to the camp where she had spent part of her childhood. As you will see in this Christian Science Monitor essay, nearly fifty years later she is still "trying hard to forgive and forget." Her response to questions of how it could have happened seems especially sobering.

On Sept. 16, 36 members of my family made a pilgrimage to the site of the Manzanar Relocation Center in southeast California. In the spring of 1942, the United States government unceremoniously deposited thousands of Japanese-American men, women, and children in this internment camp during World War II. I was one of them.

For this trip back, our guide was Shi Nomura, Manzanar curator for the Eastern California Museum in Independence, Calif. He has made the camp his personal crusade for over 17 years and knows more about it than any other person living.

Manzanar was a remote place in my consciousness. I had pushed it back in my mind until recent years when the camp began to make the news headlines. Somehow I felt a stigma attached to my Manzanar connection. I was not alone. "Death Valley," a niece responded when someone asked her about her place of birth.

Over the years I had sped by on Highway 395 with my husband, taking our children on fishing trips to the Sierras. As we passed the little town of Lone Pine, I'd begin searching the desolate brush-covered terrain, with Mt. Whitney as a magnificently incongruous backdrop, and wonder, "This is where I lived?"

For "this" was not even a ghost town. Aside from two weather-beaten guardhouses, ther was absolutely no sign that we had once made this barren land our home.

I first saw these guardhouses as our buses rolled in through the gates in May 1942, after a long, anxiety-ridden train and bus ride from Los Angeles. The "civilian exclusion order" that we had received six days earlier gave our family only a few frantic days to dispose of our businesses, homes, and treasured belongings.

We then reported to our evacuation point as instructed with bedding, clothing, and personal possessions—only what we could carry. Armed soldiers assigned the families numbers and herded us onto the trains. These are memories that have been hard to erase.

On the day of my return to Manzanar, gray clouds shed intermittent rain, eventually giving way to a blistering hot sun. And then the wind came up, that pervasive, gusty, stinging wind, unmercifully shooting pellets of gravel. It was enough to bridge the 45 years that had passed since I lived here.

Sadae Iwataki, "Pilgrimage to Manzanar," *The Christian Science Monitor* 20 December 1989.

Our 11-car caravan drove past the guardhouses to the camp grounds. It was a wilderness to me: I wanted to know where I had lived. Where our barracks had stood. Uncle Shi led me over to our Block 21. There was our clothesline pole foundation, where the family laundry used to flap in the wind. "That's where the women's latrine was, and there the men's," he pointed out.

Memories came rushing back. The humiliating lack of privacy in the communal latrine/bathhouses. The constant struggle with the sand seeping through the walls and the floors of our tar-papered barracks. The armed sentry towers edging the camp.

I picked up a sliver of wood with a nail stuck in it. Wherever I stepped, there were nails. Thousands and thousands of nails. Once the internees were released in the summer of 1945, the barracks had outlived their usefulness, Uncle Shi told me. They had to be disposed of. Lumber was in much demand and eager buyers plentiful. So the barracks were torn apart, plank by plank.

We made a last stop outside the perimeter of the camp, a mile off the highway. Here was the graveyard. Watched over by a solemn white monument that my people erected in 1943, on which "Memorial to the Dead" was inscribed in Japanese. With a pang I recalled the death of my aunt only two months after we arrived.

On Aug. 10, 1988, President Reagan signed into law the Civil Liberties Act of 1987 providing former internees restitution and an apology "for . . . fundamental violations of the basic civil liberties and constitutional rights. . . ."

The burden of shame has been officially lifted and I am trying hard to forgive and forget. "How could it have happened?" demand the *Sansei* (third generation in this country) and *Yonsei* (fourth generation). The *Nisei* (second generation), having experienced California life in the 1920s, '30s, and '40s, reply, "Easily."

Fifteen former internees made this pilgrimage, including one born in camp.

Gone now were the *Issei* (first generation). The *Nisei* had become the elders. Others in the group were our *Sansei* and *Yonsei* children and grandchildren, and spouses. Over 120,000 Japanese-Americans from all along the Pacific Coast were sent to 10 inland war relocation centers in 1942.

MAKING AMENDS

The words of fomer U.S. Attorney General Richard Thornburgh in an October 1990 Justice Department ceremony provide a fitting conclusion for our readings in this chapter.

In a quiet Justice Department ceremony last week, nine elderly Japanese Americans received checks for $20,000 each. They were the first of more than $1.25 billion in reparations payments the United States will give Americans of Japanese ancestry who were forcibly relocated and interned during World War II. In handing out the payments, which were authorized by Congress in 1988, Atty. Gen. Dick Thornburgh apologized for one of the most egregious government actions of this century:

Your struggle for redress and the events that led to today are the finest examples of what our country is about and of what we have pledged to protect and defend. Your efforts have strengthened the nation's Constitution by reaffirming the inalienability of our civil rights.

We enjoy a precious system of government that is unsurpassed by any in the world. Even when that system failed you, you never lost your faith in it. On the contrary, you believed that through that system you could achieve the justice which you had been denied. By finally admitting a wrong, a nation does not destroy its integrity but, rather, reinforces the sincerity of its commitment to the Constitution and hence to its people. In forcing us to re-examine our history, you have made us only stronger and more proud. For that, all Americans are indebted to you. I am not unmindful of the historic role this Department of Justice played in the internment. It is somehow entirely fitting that it is here we now celebrate redress.

"Making Amends," *U.S. News & World Report* 22 October 1990.

SUGGESTIONS FOR WRITING

Informal Essays

1. Write a short essay with this thesis: The United States's decision to relocate West Coast Japanese-Americans was heavily influenced by wartime hysteria. Use two or three examples to support your thesis.

2. For the sake of argument, let's say that the wartime hysteria concerning Japanese-Americans is merely a dramatic example of similar irrational episodes that have occurred throughout United States history. Argue that the hysteria which fueled this incident was not a singular episode in U.S. history and could happen again.

Short Documented Papers

1. Discuss and analyze — probably through classification — individual Japanese reactions to their incarceration and internment.

2. Argue the case that Roosevelt's executive order to intern Japanese had little or nothing to do with national security.

3. Write a report on anti-Japanese hysteria in the months following the Pearl Harbor attack within one of the following groups: (1) California newspapers, (2) California politicians, (3) California civic and agricultural organizations.

4. Discuss the extent to which the rumors of an imminent Japanese invasion were substantiated by fact, or discuss the extent to which such rumors were groundless.

Longer Documented Papers

1. Write an argument that justifies the federal government's decision to evacuate Japanese-Americans from the West Coast and intern them in camps during most of World War II.

2. Argue that the internment of Japanese-Americans was prompted primarily by racism and hysteria.

3. Argue that Roosevelt's executive order was a mistake.

4. Write a report on anti-Japanese sentiment in the United States from 1941 to 1945.

5. Write a report on Japanese-American relocation camps during World War II. Try to do justice to the War Relocation Authority's and the Japanese-Americans' points of view. Remember, this is a report, not an argument, so you'll have to remain objective and disinterested — which may not be easy.

6. Argue that the West Coast press and politicians fueled the racism and hysteria that led to the internment of Japanese-Americans.

A RESEARCH WRITER'S HANDBOOK

WHAT IS A RESEARCH PAPER?

Ideally, a research paper begins when you are curious or angry about something. You might, for instance, want to know about how those huge statues on Easter Island were shaped and erected. Or you might want to gather your ideas — and the ideas of others — to show us why we should keep gory fairy tales out of the hands of small children.

To support your ideas, you search out books, articles, and other writings. Then, using the facts and ideas you find in them, you write an original work. What makes it a source, or research, paper is the fact that your work also includes a record of the books, articles, and newspapers (your sources) that you used to write it. What makes it original is that no one has ever combined the ideas and evidence from those diverse sources in such a way before.

The Research Report

One kind of research paper is the research report, which is an impartial presentation of an idea. When you write a research report you say, in essence, "I am going to illustrate, not argue, an idea." Naturally, when you write a report about a controversy, your purpose is only to explain and describe what the controversy is about, not to persuade the reader that one of the sides is the correct one.

The Research Argument

Another kind of research paper is the research argument. In this kind of research paper, you try to persuade your readers that one side of an argument — your side, of course — is the right one. What you are saying, in effect, is this: "I have already taken a position. As I go along, I will fill you in on what the controversy is about, but my real purpose is to show you why my position is right and why the other position is wrong."

You aren't detached. Indeed, you may argue a side vigorously. But you should remain reasonable and fair.

WRITING A RESEARCH PAPER BASED ONLY ON THE ARTICLES IN THIS BOOK

Toward the end of this chapter we have included a sample research paper that one of our students, Victoria Herndon, wrote using the essays in Chapter 4, "Advertising: Is It More Than Harmless Puffery?" To make the advice in this section a bit more concrete, the general advice about how to put together a research paper is followed by bracketed comments about Herndon's problems and progress as she worked her way through her paper.

Some of the advice may seem more trouble than it's worth (in particular, the advice about bibliography cards and note cards). But it's probably a good idea that the steps you follow as you write a short research paper based on the essays in this book ought to resemble the steps you would follow if you were going to write a longer paper based on library research.

Preliminary Reading

1. Do some preliminary reading in an assigned chapter, starting with the introduction to the chapter. Now skim a few of the essays before sitting down to read one or two of the essays that seem to be balanced or overview articles. Even if you've already decided what side of an argument you're going to take, try to do this preliminary reading with an open mind. You might find that the arguments on the other side are so good that you'll want to switch sides.

[Victoria Herndon was assigned a paper on the essays in Chapter 4: "Advertising: Is It More Than Harmless Puffery?" Her instructor told the students that they could either choose a topic at the end of the chapter or come up with a topic of their own. After reading the introduction to the chapter, Herndon needed to know more before she could make up her mind about a thesis, so she browsed through the titles of the essays in the chapter, stopping occasionally to sample an introductory paragraph. She finally decided to skim two essays, one on each side of the broad controversy: Vance Packard's ". . . and the Hooks Are Lowered" and Harold Edwards's "The Dour Critics of Advertising."]

The Topic

2. Choose a topic from the list of suggestions for writing (at the end of each chapter) or work on a topic that your instructor assigns.

[After listening to a discussion in class on the chapter, Victoria Herndon went to her instructor and talked over her idea: a broad defense of advertising. Her instructor liked the idea and encouraged her to pursue it.]

The Preliminary Outline

3. Prepare a preliminary outline. Even if you don't know a whole lot about your topic at this point, you should know enough to prepare a preliminary outline. For instance, if you're going to argue, you no doubt already have in mind some reasons

for your position. If you're going to write a report, no doubt you already have ideas about how it can be broken down into segments. Take the time to list those on a sheet of paper. While you're at it, see if you can think of any more.

We can't emphasize this enough: Spend some time here thinking through your outline. The more work you put into your outline, the more time you'll save when you begin your research.

[When Herndon sat down to write a sketchy outline, she knew she was going to have to revise it later. She just didn't know enough about the topic to write a very good outline at this point. But she also knew that having any kind of outline was better than having nothing. Her reading would have been aimless if she hadn't written an outline to give it direction. You can see the outline she finally ended up with, after many a revision, on p. 553.]

Further Reading

4. Read more deeply into the articles than you did in Step 1. Scan all the articles in your chapter. Read titles and introductory paragraphs, looking for the authors' theses, and perhaps scan topic sentences and conclusions. Now you have a better idea of the essays that are the most relevant to your thesis.

[Now that Herndon had an outline, no matter how sketchy it was, her reading became more focused, and she began to see which articles she would want to read and which articles she could ignore. Even at this early stage, she was able to refine her outline a bit.]

Working Bibliography

5. Prepare a working bibliography. This list of works, your working bibliography, will provide full bibliographic information (author's name, date the work was published, page numbers, and so forth) so that when you take notes from each work you won't have to repeat the bibliographic information on each notecard.

There are two ways of creating this working bibliography. For a research paper as short as the one you're going to write, you can merely write a list of your sources on a piece of paper and alphabetize the list later when you make up your finished Works Cited page. But there's an even easier way: Most researchers write down each source on a separate 3-by-5-inch or 4-by-6-inch notecard. This method enables you to quickly realphabetize your cards when you add or take away sources from your bibliography.

Whatever method you choose, put the information down according to the format you will be using when you hand in your finished paper. You will eventually be preparing a formated list of work on your Works Cited page, so you might as well use that format now as you prepare your working bibliography. You will find the Works Cited page formats on p. 549.

[Herndon used 3-by-5-inch notecards to copy the bibliographic information of each work that she read and thought she was going to use.]

Reading and Note-taking

6. Now do your serious reading, taking notes as you go. An easy way to take notes is to use notecards. (Most researchers prefer 4-by-6-inch cards because they are large enough to get a lot of notes on.) With notecards, you can easily discard needless information; you can sort information as you work; and you can write your first draft based on a final arrangement of your cards.

Since you already have a working bibliography (either as a list on a sheet of paper or on separate notecards) the only source identification you'll need on each 4-by-6-inch card is the author's last name in the upper left-hand corner of your card. In the upper right-hand corner, write a main heading from your preliminary outline that this particular notecard addresses.

Most of your notecards will be made up of paraphrases; you might want to review the sections on summarizing and paraphrasing in Chapter 1 before you proceed with your note-taking. You will, however, want to quote your source every time he or she is particularly forceful, especially if the forceful statement is uttered by a widely recognized authority. (Read pp. 7–8 in Chapter 1 if you are unsure of yourself here.) You won't use all the quotes you copy, but at this stage you don't know exactly what you'll be quoting, so it's better to have more material available than you'll eventually need.

In the left-hand margin next to each paraphrase and quotation, write the page number where you found it. If you fail to do this, you will end up thumbing through essays looking for page numbers when it comes time to write your paper.

A single notecard contains evidence from one source on a particular idea; that is, every time your source shifts to a new idea, you should begin a new notecard. If you do this, you will be able to organize your notecards in exactly the same order that you will be using them in your final paper.

[Even after Herndon had listened to her instructor's reasons for using the 4-by-6-inch cards — that it was a research *method* they were learning — she thought that writing her notes on 4-by-6-inch cards was kind of silly (she preferred writing her notes on regular paper), but, conscientious student that she was, she followed her instructor's advice and used the 4-by-6-inch cards. Later in her research she began to see the method in her instructor's apparent madness.]

The Revised Outline

7. Revise your outline. As you read more deeply into your subject, you will probably have to revise your outline. In fact, you may want to spend some time at this point in constructing a revised outline, making it as detailed as you can. That new outline will help as you write your first draft, the next step.

[Herndon had serious trouble with this stage. In her reading, she had come across a lot of interesting information that she hated to part with. Unfortunately, rather than throw out the material, she tried to see where it might be forcibly inserted in her paper. She was beginning to let her material control her outline rather than the other way around. Finally, after three or four attempts at a revised outline, she bit the bullet and threw the extraneous material into the trash can.]

First Draft

8. Write a first draft. Arrange your notecards according to your outline and write your first draft from the material you have on your notecards. As you write, record the author's last name and the page number of the quotation or summary in a parenthesis following each quotation or paraphrase. (See pp. 546–548, later in this chapter, for a fuller description of what goes in these parentheses.)

By the way, it's a good idea to leave plenty of white space in this first draft to allow for revisions. It's also a good idea to let your first draft cool for a day or two. At any rate, you'll need to reread your first draft and make as many improvements as you can by writing over, under, and through your words. You might find at this point that you need to go back to your sources—or even find new sources—to further develop certain ideas that are sketchy in your first draft.

[Herndon had no problems to speak of here. Since she had spent a lot of time fine-tuning her outline, and because she had thrown out extraneous material in the last stage, she was able to write her first draft quickly.]

Second Draft

9. If you have time, write out a second draft based on the revisions to the first draft, and continue to improve your paper as you write. Work hard at making your prose clear and concise. In particular, make sure that all paraphrases and quotations are introduced properly. (Source introductions are discussed at length in Chapter 1.)

[Although Herndon didn't particularly like revising, she didn't want to ruin her paper by not following through. She *certainly* didn't want the time she had spent up till this point to be wasted. So she rewrote her thesis statement to make it clearer; she inserted a topic sentence into a paragraph that lacked one; and she identified one of the sources that she had forgotten to identify. She broke one sentence into two; she sharpened her diction by looking up some words in a thesaurus; and she threw out one whole paragraph. In short, she revised her paper to make it clear, smooth, and concise.]

Final Version

10. If your revised draft is in good shape, polish it, proofread it, and then type a final version of your paper.

[Herndon's instructor had warned her not to confuse editing (rewriting awkward and unclear sentences, improving topic sentences and transitions, and other editing chores) with proofreading (looking for typographical errors, misspellings, omissions, and so on). So after she had typed her paper, Herndon proofread it carefully.]

Finishing Touches

11. Finally, prepare a title page, a final outline, a note page (if you need one), and a Works Cited page. Since you already have a list of works, in their proper

formats, all you have to do to put together a Works Cited page is to type in each item. (The formats for all of these sections are described later in this chapter.)

[Because Herndon had followed instructions, her outline and bibliography (she used no note page) were ready to type, so this stage took her only a few minutes to prepare. Justice and hard work prevailed. Herndon got an A on her paper.]

WRITING A RESEARCH PAPER BASED ON LIBRARY RESEARCH

Thesis

1. Discover a thesis. Your instructor may want you to discover a thesis on your own. If that's the case, begin with a general topic that interests you. Let's say you've long been interested in the idea of evolution, and your biology class has whetted your interest even more. You might like to begin, then, with the general topic of evolution. You can narrow your general topic in a variety of ways. You might, for instance, sit down with a piece of paper and brainstorm, perhaps by asking questions that come to your mind, like these:

> How does evolution operate on the cellular level?
> Is there more than one theory about its operation?
> Were there any evolutionists before Darwin?
> How was Darwin treated when people began to realize the implications of his theory?
> Are there any controversies among evolution's advocates?
> Does evolution only mean "survival of the fittest"?
> What is "sexual selection"?

You see the idea, don't you? By asking questions, you are in effect narrowing your broad topic. You may have to narrow even further, but you now have a start toward an acceptable thesis.

Or you can go about the narrowing process more formally, like this:

> evolution
> the process of evolution
> the rate of evolution
> controversies about the rate of human evolution

There's another way of narrowing a topic. You might go to the library with your broad topic in hand and consult the *Readers' Guide to Periodical Literature*, an index to the articles in more than a hundred periodicals (more about that research tool later). Starting with the most recent edition of the *Readers' Guide*, look up your broad topic, Evolution, and read the titles of the articles. These titles might suggest a topic you can write on. For instance, you might find an article with a title that seems to suggest that a controversy is going on among the evolutionists. Read the article. Let's say that it argues that humans emerged from their fellow primates only 500,000 years ago, not the million years that most other evolutionists claim. Somewhere in the article, you will probably find the author brings up (and probably documents) his or her opponent's argument. Look up the opponent's article and read it. You're on your way toward a paper thast describes a controversy among the evolutionists.

Working Outline

2. Prepare a working outline based on what you have learned thus far about your thesis. Using what you have learned thus far and your common sense, break down your thesis to logical parts. For instance, for the paper on the controversy among the evolutionists, you could make a simple outline, even at this stage. Begin with your tentative thesis:

There is a controversy raging among evolutionists about the date of human emergence.

Then break it down to logical parts.

1. Those who say that humans emerged two million years ago.
2. Those who say that humans emerged one million years ago.
3. Those who say that humans emerged 500,000 years ago.

This plan may not hold up. In fact, you may discover, as you read, that the topic should be broken down by the different *reasons* given by the evolutionists.

That's probably all you can do right now. You will no doubt refine that outline — or even change it, as we describe above, as you learn more about your thesis. But at least now you have a starting place when you begin your serious research. You'll have to take our word for it that a preliminary outline will save you a lot of time in the library.

Research Sources

3. Begin your research in earnest. Following are some of the sources that you will probably want to consult as you search for information.

The card catalog

The card catalog is an index to all the books your library contains. As you probably know, it contains author cards, book title cards, and subject cards. But since you probably don't know any authors or book titles yet, you will probably only use the subject cards at this point.

Before you pull open a catalog drawer, however, you will save time by consulting *The Library of Congress List of Subject Headings*, a two-volume reference work usually located near the card catalog. Your library very likely uses this subject-heading system, and you will find working with these two volumes to find appropriate subject headings much easier than shuffling through card-catalog drawers.

As you search for your subject headings, begin with some of the exact words in your thesis. The Library of Congress list is surprisingly specific. Only if you fail to find your specific words should you try more general ones. Once you have spent twenty minutes or so finding your subject headings, you can begin looking them up in the card catalog.

If you find a book that covers your thesis thoroughly, you'll have to narrow your thesis further or find a new one. A research paper can be justified only if it requires evidence from a variety of works. If the information you need can be found in a single source, you're not really writing a research paper.

If you're lucky (or unlucky, depending upon your point of view), the card catalogue in your library may have been replaced by a microfilm catalogue or a computer catalogue. In fact, the library we use is now in the process of switching from a traditional card catalogue to computer terminals. If all goes well, in the next semester or two we will press a few keys on a computer terminal and the information that was once on little 3-by-5-inch cards in the wooden drawers will come to the screen. The system promises to be quicker than the traditional card catalogue. (For information on other computer databases, see Computer Databases, later in this section.)

The Readers' Guide to Periodical Literature

This multivolumed set contains bibliographic information that will lead you to articles that were published in over one hundred of the widest-circulation magazines in the United States.

The *RGPL* is also easy to use. The volumes are arranged by years (the first volume is dated 1900–1904). In each volume you can find entries under an author's name, the title of an article, or the subject of an article.

For your topic, you would probably want to work backward, starting with the most recent year. Once again, look under key words that you think might lead you to magazine articles.

When you find an article listed, you will also find information specifying when and in what periodical the article was published. Before you go to the stacks to try to locate the magazine, check the index of the periodicals your library has. (That index is sometimes called a circular file.)

The New York Times Index and other newspaper indexes

The volumes in these indexes are arranged by years. Thus, if you wanted to look up initial reactions to the stock market crash of 1929, you would go immediately to the 1929 volume. There you would find bibliographic information that will lead you to news articles and editorials that appeared in *The New York Times* on the crash of the market. If you wanted later commentaries on the crash, you might start with the most recent volume and work your way backward to 1929. (By the way, since *The New York Times* is on microfilm, you'll have to learn to use the microfilm reader. But as we've said, librarians are inevitably a helpful lot, and they'll be glad to show you how.)

Specialized indexes

There are hundreds of other indexes to periodicals in addition to the *Readers' Guide to Periodical Literature*. For instance, for indexes that are somewhat more specialized, you might consult the *Humanities Index* or the *Social Sciences Index*. Specialized indexes contain articles on fields as diverse as archeology, gerontology, juvenile delinquency, and semantics.

If you need articles in a more specialized field, such as art, applied science, biology, business, political science, your library is likely to have an index that lists articles within those fields. If, for instance, you were researching Picasso's Blue Period, you would certainly want to consult the *Art Index*, which lists articles in art journals from 1929 to the present. For the 1929 stock market crash, you would want to consult the *Business Periodicals Index*.

Computer databases

Some libraries have computer terminals that can search a variety of sources of information — usually indexes to articles in magazines and journals. (In fact, some lucky students can search their library's databases by using the personal computer in their dorms.)

To start you on your search of these computerized sources of information, all you need to know is a few key words. If you want to find articles on owls in the Northwest, type in *owls* and the computer will show a list of all the articles on owls that it has in it database. Naturally, begin with the most precise key words that you can. If you begin with a key word that is too general, the computer will come up with more sources than you can handle. Most of the computer database systems can print out, in just a few seconds, the information that you have found.

Other reference works

In addition to these main sources of information discussed, you might want to use other reference books, also usually located in the reference room. There are, for instance, specialized dictionaries. If you wanted to begin your paper with a quotation, all you do is look up your subject in the *Oxford Dictionary of Quotations* or some other quotation dictionary. If you wanted to see how a word was used in 1856, you could look up the word in the thirteen-volume *Oxford English Dictionary*.

General encyclopedias like the *Encyclopaedia Brittanica* and the *Encyclopedia Americana* are handy, especially at the beginning of your research when you want an overview of the subject. (The articles are usually followed by short bibliographies.) Later on in your research, you might want to use a specialized encyclopedia. If you were writing on the origin in France of existentialism, for instance, you might want to consult the *Encyclopedia of Philosophy*.

Finally, there are atlases, yearbooks, almanacs, who's whos, plot digests, and hundreds of other reference works to help you write a documented paper.

One more suggestion: When all else fails, see your librarians. We've never met one who wasn't full of helpful advice about where to locate something in the library.

Now you will follow the steps already described in writing a research paper, based on the articles in this book (see pp. 538–542.) That is, now that you've completed your preliminary reading and research, you will scan your sources, prepare a preliminary bibliography, take extensive notes, revise your preliminary outline, write your drafts, and prepare your final version.

We now turn to special problems in writing the research paper.

DOCUMENTING YOUR SOURCES

Documenting Quotations

Except for famous quotations used incidentally, all quotations have to be documented. That is, when you use a quotation, you also have to tell the reader where you found it.

Documenting Paraphrases and Summaries

Summaries and paraphrases (like quotations) have to be documented. That is, you have to tell the reader, in a citation, *exactly* where you found your borrowing, right down to the page number.

You don't, however, have to document common facts. For instance, you wouldn't have to tell your reader where you found the fact that the stock market crashed in 1929. That fact is not arguable, and it can be found in all books that take the trouble to mention it. As you might expect, much of the information found in a general encyclopedia doesn't need to be documented. Encyclopedias generally deal with information about ideas, people, and events that is neither arguable nor unique. (But then you will seldom use encyclopedias as sources in a research paper anyway.) However, you do have to document specific numbers. For instance, if you were to mention in your paper that there were twenty thousand prostitutes at work in Paris in the mid-eighteenth century, you would need to document where you found that number — even if you found that same number in a number of other sources.

The best advice we can give you on this problem of when to document is this: Keep your readers in mind. If you think they might question your information or might wonder about your source, go ahead and document it. Your rule of thumb should be this: When in doubt, document.

But you don't need to stop after every sentence to document the information in that sentence. Think in terms of paragraphs. That is, if you are writing a paragraph that is composed of paraphrases or quotations from a single source, wait until you get to the end of the paragraph before you stop to document it. The reader knows, then, that the entire paragraph is indebted to the source that he finds documented at its end. If, however, your paragraph is composed of a variety of sources, you'll have to stop to document each one immediately after you use it.

FORMATS

In this section we're going to discuss various standard formats that you'll need to follow as you write your research paper. Your instructor may prefer the American

Psychological Association (APA) documentation method; you can find formats for that kind of a paper in the appendix.

Formats for In-Text Documentation

The latest stylebook of The Modern Language Association, bless its heart, simplifies the whole process of citing sources. For one thing, you can almost forget about footnotes. Now when you borrow someone else's ideas, you only need to follow the borrowing with the page number of the article or book that you borrowed from. (Use the page numbers in this text as if they were the page numbers of the original sources.) These brief acknowledgments direct your reader to a separate page called Works Cited, which is located at the end of your paper. There the reader — if he or she wishes — can go to find the complete bibliographic information about your source. Here then is what a citation within the text looks like:

> Peter Quennell claims that *Marriage à-la Mode* is William Hogarth's "best painting and most imaginative" of all the moral series and that it in fact is a "true poetic tragedy" (Quennell 171).

Now your reader knows to look up "Quennell" in the alphabetized list of works that you've used to write your paper. (Some writers leave out the name of the author in the parenthesis when the author has been introduced a line or two above, but we recommend that you include the author's name, as well as the page number, in that parenthesis.)

Of course, if you don't mention the author's name within your text, you'll *have* to put his or her name in the parenthesis. Otherwise your reader wouldn't know which of the items in your Works Cited page number in your text belongs to.

Other Exceptions

1. If you use more than one work by Quennell in your paper, you'll have to add the name of the work you are referring to: (Quennell, *Hogarth's Progress* 171). Now when your readers go to your Works Cited page, they'll find the specific work you're citing.
2. If you cite two authors with the same last name, you'll have to include their first and last names within their respective parentheses. Otherwise your reader might go to your Works Cited page and not know which of the two Smiths you have cited.
3. If you are referring to an anonymous work, put the name of the article in parenthesis: ("Annual Report" 23).
4. If a title is long, use a shortened version, but be certain that the shortened version begins with the same word in the title that is alphabetized in your Works Cited.
5. When your borrowing comes from a work that consists of more than one volume, you'll have to include the volume number and page number

within the parenthesis: (Hibbard 3:12). Now the reader knows to go to the third volume of Hibbard's work and then to page 12.

6. When you refer to a play, put in the act and scene: (*Macbeth* III, i). Of course, if you mention the play in your text, you needn't repeat it in the parenthesis.

And that's about it. No more footnote format problems. No more footnote information that has to be repeated in your bibliography. No more running out of room at the bottom of the page before you can type your footnote in. Usually all you have to do is put a page number in parentheses immediately following your quotation or paraphrase.

Format for a Notes Page

If you use the parenthetical documentation method that we've just been discussing, there is a separate Notes page for supplementary information that might be helpful to your reader. Of course, if you don't feel the need to make these supplementary comments, you don't need a Notes page at all. But if you do, merely put a superscript number where you want the reader to leave the text and go to your page called Notes. (To put in a superscript number, roll up your paper half a notch and type in the number.) Here's what your text will look like when you use a note number.

> Of course, not all Hispanics are eager to have their children go through a bilingual program.[1]

That number 1 directs your readers to a Notes page, where they will find a section located between your last page of text and your Works Cited page. Here's the format for that Notes page:

```
                    NOTES
     [1]Richard  Rodriguez's  autobiography  tells
of  his  schoolboy  experiences  as  a  Hispanic
in  a  school  in  which  the  vast  majority  of
teachers  and  students  were  Anglos.  He  con-
cludes  that  his  immersion  in  English -- as
painful  as  it  might  have  been -- was  the
best  thing  that  could  have  happened  to  him
(13).
     [2]For  a  further  discussion  of  Hispanic
parents'  ambivalence  concerning  their  chil-
dren's  education,  see  Smyth  24-35.
```

As you see, each item is indented five spaces and begins with a superscript number. The author's name, Smyth, mentioned in note 2 refers your reader to the alphabetical listing in Works Cited. Note 1 needs only a page number because the author's name, Rodriguez, is mentioned in the note itself. The reader thus knows to look up *Rodriguez* in the Works Cited page.

Formats for Entries in a Works Cited Page

Now we can go on to the formats for the individual entries in that "Works Cited" page. If none of the following model entries matches the kind of entry you've come up with, use the model that is closest to your entry. Or combine formats from different entries. Let's say you need to acknowledge an idea from a pamphlet that has two editors. First follow the general format for pamphlets. Then follow the format for two book authors (under "Books"). And then add the word "eds." (plural of ed.) in the proper location. That proper spot can be found by looking under the heading "Book with an Editor." And who said research wasn't creative? Here's what you've come up with:

George, Marie and Joe Fulsome, eds. *Saving the Tigers*. Pamphlet. Los Angeles: Save the Beasts Association, 1985.

BOOKS

BOOKS WITH A SINGLE AUTHOR

Hendin, David. *Death as a Fact of Life*. New York: Norton, 1973.

BOOKS WITH TWO AUTHORS

Funk, Wilfred, and Norman Lewis. *30 Days to a More Powerful Vocabulary*. New York: Pocket Books, 1970.

BOOK WITH MORE THAN TWO AUTHORS

Baugh, Albert C., and others. *A Literary History of England*. New York: Appleton-Century Crofts, 1948.

BOOK WITH CORPORATE AUTHOR

American Health Society. *Heart Disease*. Garden City, New York: American Health Society, 1981

A WORK IN MORE THAN ONE VOLUME

Sandburg, Carl. *Abraham Lincoln: The War Years*. 4 vols. New York: Harcourt Brace, 1939.

AN EDITION OF A BOOK AFTER THE FIRST EDITION

Gould, James A. Classic Philosophic Questions. 6th ed. Columbus, Ohio: Merrill Publishing, 1989.

AN ARTICLE OR STORY IN AN EDITED BOOK

Kramer, Samuel. "Sumerian Literature and the Bible." In The Bible in Its Literary Milieu. Eds. John Maier and Vincent Tollers. Grand Rapids: William B. Eerdmans, 1979. 272-284.

MAGAZINES AND NEWSPAPERS

SIGNED ARTICLE IN A MAGAZINE WITH SEPARATE PAGINATION IN EACH ISSUE

Wideman, John Edgar. "Michael Jordan Leaps the Great Divide." Esquire Nov. 1990: 138-145, 210-216.

UNSIGNED ARTICLE IN A MAGAZINE WITH SEPARATE PAGINATION IN EACH ISSUE

"I Pulled the Plug." Family Health July/August 1980: 30-33.

ARTICLE IN A MAGAZINE WITH CONTINUOUS PAGINATION THROUGHOUT A VOLUME OF ISSUES

Anderson, George M. "American Imprisonment Today." America 46 (1982), 354-356.

NEWSPAPER

Ivins, Molly. "New Environmental Fight Looms over Developing Coal-Rich Utah Area." The New York Times 12 March 1979, sec. A: 14.

BOOK REVIEW

Goatley, David. "Saving the Waves." Rev. of Golden Caves by Angie Davis. West Coast Review 3 March 1979: 41-42.

ENCYCLOPEDIAS, PAMPHLETS, AND OTHERS

ENCYCLOPEDIA

Goedicke, Hans. "Sphnix in Art and Mythology." Encyclopedia Americana. 1971 ed.

ALMANAC

"Nobel Prize Winners." Reader's Digest Almanac and Yearbook. 1980 ed.

PAMPHLET

Automobile Safety. Pamphlet. Detroit: National Consumer's Association, 1972.

RADIO OR TELEVISION NEWSCAST

News story on NBC Nightly News. NBC, 12 March 1985.

SAMPLE MLA RESEARCH PAPER

Finally, here is a finished product of the process we have been discussing in this chapter. In this case the writer, Victoria Herndon, was one of our students who wrote a paper on the articles in Chapter 4: "Advertising: Is It More Than Harmless Puffery?" Although her paper is based on the first edition of this book, all but one of the sources she uses remain in this second edition. (Robert Heilbroner's "Advertising as Agitprop" does not appear in this edition.) So you can follow her as she uses the sources in this book. The page numbers in her citations refer to the second edition.

Pay particular attention to how Herndon introduces and states her thesis, how she painstakingly unifies her paper by frequently tying the evidence she presents back in with the topic sentences, how she handles and documents the ideas of her sources, and how she summarizes her conclusions at the end of her paper.

ADVERTISING:
THROUGH THE LOOKING GLASS

by Victoria Herndon

English 102-03
November 10, 1991

OUTLINE: ADVERTISING: THROUGH THE LOOKING
GLASS

Thesis statement: The critics of advertising
exaggerate its defects and ignore its
benefits.

    I. Critics insist that advertising is in-
sidiously powerful and that consumers are
gullible. These criticisms are largely
inaccurate.

        A. The consumer's choice of products
is based on many factors besides
advertising.

        B. Consumers are not overwhelmed by
the power of advertising.

            a. Advertising is largely a pro-
ducer's reaction defensive reac-
tion to the advertising of rival
producers.

            2. Polls and studies indicate
that consumers seldom remember or
respond to particular advertisements.

    II. Critics claim that advertising is de-
ceitful. In fact, advertising is generally accurate and its motives are above
board.

        A. For the most part, advertisements
merely convey specific information
about products.

        B. When exaggerated claims do occur,
consumers seldom take such claims
seriously.

C. The motives of advertisers are more forthright than those of politicians and essayists, who manipulate language in similar ways.

III. Critics fail to recognize that advertising plays a vital role in the democratic system of free enterprise.

A. Advertising plays an important role in providing consumers with freedom of choice.

B. Advertising, like other forms of expression, is protected by the First Amendment of the Constitution, and suspending First Amendment rights of advertisers could endanger the First Amendment rights of everyone.

IV. Critics insist that advertising corrupts cultural values by encouraging materialism. In fact, advertising merely encourages rather than causes materialistic values. Paradoxically, in doing so, it promotes higher cultural values.

A. While advertising may influence materialism, it certainly doesn't create it.

B. As history demonstrates, the most consistent sponsors of higher cultural values have been the very affluent, materialistic societies that advertising promotes.

V. Advertising is a reflection of the free choices that people make in a democratic society.

VI. Critics, in their attempts to vilify advertising, ignore its many benefits.

A. Advertising is informative.

B. Advertising motivates producers to improve product quality.
C. Advertising helps to create jobs and reduce production costs.

ADVERTISING: THROUGH THE LOOKING GLASS

In the words of Robert Louis Stevenson, "Everyone lives by selling something." As business has progressed through the years, so has the business of advertising. With the enormous increase of products available on the market, a greater value has been placed on the importance of advertising to persuade the public to choose a particular product. It is not surprising that advertising is also the center of a growing controversy. Critics of advertising say that the public is "seduced" by images and manipulative language. They contend that the public is virtually powerless against the deceptive practices of advertising: exaggerated claims and numerous qualifiers that disguise the true nature of the products. Critics also insist that the seductive images of advertising encourage materialism ("Advertising: Is It More Than Harmless Puffery?" 151-152). Critics of advertising, however, fail to recognize these important facts: advertising is seldom as powerful as they claim; it is generally accurate; its motives are clear, and it reflects a central principle in a democratic society--freedom of choice. In their attacks on advertising, critics also ignore the valuable function of advertising in today's world: advertising maintains, if not improves, the quality of brand-name products while reducing selling costs.

Critics of advertising insist that advertising is an insidiously powerful influence on society. Samm Sinclair Baker, who has worked as an advertising copy writer and consultant, strongly disagrees. According to Baker, "the advertiser is 'not' in the driver's seat." In fact, in a large chain grocery store, there might be 22 different types of baked beans. There is plenty of opportunity for the unadvertised labels to be chosen by the consumer (Baker 170-174).

Moreover, John Crichton, the former president of the American Association of Advertising Agencies, points out that research reveals that "experience with and opinions about products may be formed from many influences other than advertising." These opinions may be formed from personal experience, conversations with family and friends who have used the product, and by reading an analysis of the product and its reliability in such publications as Consumer Reports. Crichton also points out that because people are bombarded with so many ads, they have learned to tune out most of them. If consumers find an advertising campaign unappealing, they quickly become "bored and inattentive" (Crichton 189-191). Advertising can not possibly be effective if it can not command the attention of consumers.

Robert Heilbroner, an economist and a professor at the New York School of Social Research, cites further evidence that consumers are not overwhelmed by the appeals of advertisers. He points out that, for most businesses, advertising is a defensive reaction to rival companies' advertising campaigns. When all cigarette ads were banned from television, for example, sales were not affected. But if one company does not advertise while its competitor does, the competitor has a distinct advantage. Moreover, Heilbroner notes, "The failure rate of ad campaigns is much greater than the success rate." For example, sales of Lady Gillette products, Pringles potato chips, and Stetson hats were not very successful despite elaborate and expensive ad campaigns. Heilbroner states that there are approximately 28,000 nationally advertised name-brand products on the market today in the United States. Heilbroner notes that in a study cited by Stephen Fox in his book The Mirror Makers, the "average family" is exposed to 1,600 advertisements every day. The 1984 edition of the Statistical Abstract of the United States reveals that 27 percent of the $67 billion spent on advertising went for newspaper ads, with 21 percent spent on TV ads. Of the 1,600 ads a family is exposed to each day, only 80 are really noticed by these consumers, and only 12, according to Stephen Fox, actually "provoke a reaction." It is clear from these figures that advertising is largely ineffective. Heilbroner points to a 1963 newspaper survey for further evidence of this ineffectiveness. This survey indicated that 23 percent of TV viewers "could identify the product in the last commercial they had seen," while a 1981 study revealed that the percentage of TV viewers who could accomplish this task had narrowed to a mere 7 percent (Heilbroner 169-172). It is obvious that advertising is only one of many factors influencing a consumer's product choice. Advertising has become increasingly ineffective because consumers have been bombarded with so many ads that they have come to ignore them.

Critics also insist that advertising is deceitful. In fact, the majority of ads are accurate and, above all, the motives of the advertisers are crystal clear: they want to sell their products. Baker points out that advertising is used on a small scale as well as on a large one. Advertising not only involves television; it can take the form of a message scrawled on a 3" by 5" notecard tacked to the bulletin board in Wal-mart. Baker points out that this type of advertising is purely informative (Baker 170-174). Crichton agrees with Baker: "The dress one sees advertised in the newspaper is available in the sizes and colors listed, and at the price advertised. The headache remedy will alleviate headache pain." Most research indicates that the public does not translate the language of advertising literally. People realize that buying the dress pictured in the ad will not make a woman look just like the slim girl in the ad, unless of course the women looked like the model in the first place (Crichton 190).

Exaggerated claims by advertisers are not necessarily deceitful. These "exaggerations" that the critics get so exercised about are almost always either conventional hyperboles

that consumers recognize as hyperboles. Or
they are exaggerations in the service of humor. As Harold Edwards points out in a recent essay, when an actor in an ad is
surrounded by beautiful girls and says something like "Girls love the smell of Brut,"
the viewer does not seriously believe that
buying the product will mesmerize girls into
following him like zombies. Such advertising
is basically harmless, but critics imply
that viewers are taken in by such advertising. Edwards states that "a number of critics of advertising believe that we are too
weak to resist the appeals of the adman."
Edwards cites Jeffrey Schrank, for example,
who describes consumers as being "rendered
defenseless" to the "attacks" of advertising.
"What a high opinion of the power of advertising. And what a low opinion of mankind,"
observes Edwards. Critics of advertising
give people very little credit for having
intelligence. These critics seem to have a
holier-than-thou attitude, believing that
they can see through the manipulation of advertising, while we ordinary people are deceived (Edwards 202). These critics greatly
underestimate the intelligence of the viewers, and, in doing so, credit advertising
with a level of power that it simply does
not have.

One of the most effective answers to the
critics' argument that advertising is deceptive is that the motives of advertisers are
undeniably clear. Edwards points out that
all language, not just that used in advertising, is manipulated to influence people.

Adwriters, newspapers columnists, essayists, and politicians manipulate the language constantly. Edwards makes another important point: the motives of advertisers are clear, while the motives of politicians, essayists, and columnists often are not. The advertisers' goals are straightforward: to present their products in the most appealing manner possible in order to sell the greatest volume of the products. Edwards states that advertising is really nothing more than the "art of persuasion," a science which the Greeks called rhetoric. Edwards finds the difference in attitudes toward advertisers and essayists, who use the same technique, highly ironic: "When a careful essayist qualifies his statement, we are told he is being logical. When advertisers qualify their statements, we are told they are using 'weasel' words." When an advertiser claims that a product "helps control dandruff," critics accuse the advertiser of using "weasel" words to deceive the consumer. On the other hand, if the advertiser had said the product "controls dandruff," critics would have accused the advertiser of making false claims about the product. When a politician or columnist uses language eloquently to convey his message, he is admired for his use of language to evoke emotional responses. When advertisers attempt this same technique, critics say they "are being unfair by seducing our unconscious" (Edwards 202-205). Theodore Levitt, a marketing and economic consultant, agrees that the advertiser's motives are crystal clear. He as-

ters and institutions of the mind and spirit" (Crichton 190-191). Theodore Levitt also points out that culture thrives in affluent societies, not in primitive ones. Crichton refers to the Churchills, the Huxleys, the Rockefellers, and the Adamses as proof that affluence opens the door to creativity. From these wealthy families have come great statesmen, writers, poets, and business leaders (Leavitt 161). It is obvious that only when men and women do not have to spend all their time struggling to survive, can they find leisure time to concentrate on the "higher," more sophisticated pursuits of art, literature, and philosophy.

Critics blame advertising for the emphasis on material goods in our society, but Crichton observes that advertising should not be blamed for the choices of the individual: "If it appears to critics that the motivations are inferior, and that the rewards are vulgar, it must be remembered that at least the people have their own choice of what those rewards will be, and observation tells us that they spend their money quite differently" (Crichton 191). Democracy is based on the promise of freedom of choice. It is not fair to generalize by implying that the entire society is obsessed with material goods. People spend their money differently. Some may choose to surround themselves with expensive material goods, while others may buy the necessities and contribute to charities. The key to this system is not advertising; it is choice. Professor John W. Crawford, in a lecture at Michigan State

University, observed, "Advertising is an instrument in the hands of the people who use
it. If evil men use advertising for base
purposes, then evil can result. If honest
men use advertising to sell an honest product with honest enthusiasm, then positive
good for our kind of capitalistic society
can result" (Baker 170). Stephen Fox also
believes that advertising reflects the values
of society rather than creates them. Fox
considers blaming advertising for the immoral
values of Americans to be "a matter of killing the messenger instead of dealing with
the bad news" (Heilbroner 174). It is clear
that advertising is a reflection of democratic society. Strictly regulating advertising would hinder the process of freedom
of choice as well as freedom of expression.

The critics also ignore the fact that
advertising can be highly beneficial for
consumers. Advertising maintains, if not
improves, the quaity of brand-name products
while reducing selling costs. Advertising is
very informative. It notifies the public of
new and improved products available on the
market. Heilbroner describes advertising as
"the great information machine of a capitalist economy" (Heilbroner 173).

Advertising also improves the quality of
products by exposing the quality of the advertised goods, thereby creating immense
pressure on producers to keep the quality of
the products high. Effective advertising attracts more customers. If the product is of
inferior quality, then those customers will
tell their friends and thereby ruin the com-

pany's business. Thus, if a company adver-
tises an inferior product, then the company
will be worse off than it would be without
advertising. Essentially, the company would
be just inviting more people to discover how
poor their product actually is. As Baker
puts it, "Nothing fails faster than a poor
product that has been boosted by heavy advertising." Baker also observes that producers of advertised brand-name products feel
pressure to improve quality more than unadvertised generic-label producers do. Brand-
name products have built up a reputation.
They have everything on the line. Unpopular
"x-label" products can simply be sold under
another label. Brand-name producers, however, must keep up the quality of their
products in order to stay in business.
Baker observes that consumers are likely to
try brand-name, well advertised products as
well as unadvertised, cheaper products in
order to compare the quality of both types
of products. If consumers find that the unadvertised product is just as good as the
brand-name product, they will continue buying
it and save money. As Baker concludes, "Not
$1 billion spent on advertising could force"
a consumer to buy a well advertised product
against his will. "If the product is bad,
each ad dollar added will kill it quicker"
(Baker 173-174).

Advertising also creates jobs and reduces
the price of products. Cost reduction is
achieved when sales increase due to effective advertising. To quote Baker again:
"With increased sales, production goes up,

cost per unit goes down," and the consumer usually benefits by reduced prices. According to Advertising Publications, Incorporated, in one year the total amount spent by the top five auto companies on advertising increased 5.6 percent, while sales rose 8.7 percent. As a result, advertising cost per car dropped 2.8 percent, translating into savings for the consumer. During one particular year in the early 1950s, although Chevrolet actually spent far more (65 million dollars) for its advertising than Studebaker (35 million dollars), Chevrolet's advertising outlay only amounted to 30 dollars a car. Studebaker sold 65,000 cars and their advertising costs came to 85 dollars a car. Studebaker's lack of advertising may have contributed to their downfall. Small wonder that an editorial in Life magazine describes advertising as a "vital part of 'the engine of the American economy'" which makes possible the superior methods of manufacturing, distribution, and marketing which contribute to the production of the standard of living of the U.S., "the highest standard of living in the world" (Baker 170-174).

It is clear that the good aspects of advertising outweigh the bad ones. Advertising is a tool in the hands of producers. Like any tool, it can be misused, but it is not logical to blame the tool for the actions and intentions of the ones using it. Critics of advertising fail to recognize this important fact; instead they prefer to view the public as helpless children who need to be led around by the hand to have the truth pointed out to them. Critics ignore the fact that even children recognize that advertisers' only motive is to sell products. Critics exaggerate the materialistic and "immoral" aspects of advertising, and they advocate strict regulation of advertising to eliminate these pernicious influences. Once again, however, these critics fail to realize that, in a sense, advertising regulates itself. If the consumers find the product unsatisfactory, they will spread the word to others. The result will be a dramatic loss of business--a loss suffered by both advertisers and businessmen. Critics do not seem to realize that the alternative is perhaps even scarier than letting advertising regulate itself through competition and consumer choice. The expansion of Federal Trade Commission regulations would threaten not only advertisers' freedom of expression, but also the cornerstone of democracy: freedom of choice. The fact that we don't always like the image we see in the mirror doesn't mean that we should break the mirror.

WORKS CITED

"Advertising: Is It More Than Harmless Puffery?" In Point Counterpoint: Eight Cases for Composition. 2nd ed. Eds. Thayle Anderson and Kent Forrester. San Diego: Harcourt Brace Jovanovich, Publishers, 1987. 151-152.

Baker, Samm Sinclair. "Should Advertising Be Eliminated?" In The Permissible Lie: The Inside Truth About Advertising. New York: World Publishing, 1968. 170-174.

Crichton, John. "Myths About Advertising." In Ethics, Morality, and the Media. Ed. Lee Thayer. New York: Hastings House, 1980. 189-191.

Edwards, Harold. "The Dour Critics of Advertising." In Point Counterpoint: Eight Cases for Composition. Eds. Thayle Anderson and Kent Forrester. San Diego: Harcourt Brace Jovanovich, Publishers, 1987. 202-206.

Heilbroner, Robert L. "Advertising as Agitprop: Puncturing the Myths about Hype." Harper's January 1985: 169-175. [Note: Remember, this source doesn't appear in your book.]

Levitt, Theodore. "Are Advertising and Marketing Corrupting Society? It's Not Your Worry." Advertising Age 6 October 1958: 158-162.

APPENDIX:
THE APA DOCUMENTATION METHOD:

———

The American Psychological Association (APA) uses an alternative method to the MLA documentation method we've used in this chapter. For those who prefer the APA method, we offer this appendix.

Like the MLA, the APA uses parentheses to insert brief citations. Here, then, is what a typical APA parenthetical citation looks like.

> During carnival time in 18th-century Paris, Frenchmen tortured cats (Darnton, 1984, p. 83).

Now your reader knows this: The information immediately preceding the parenthesis can be found on page 83 in a 1984 work by the author, Darnton. If your readers need more information about the Darnton source, they can go to a References page in the back of the paper, where they will find in an alphabetized list of authors, including Darnton, Robert, followed by further bibliographical details about the Darnton source.

Variations on the Basic Pattern

If you mention the author's name in the text, you need only put the date in the parenthesis, like this:

> According to Darnton, during carnival time in 18th-century Paris, Frenchmen tortured cats (1984, p. 83).

If you mention the author *and* the date of publication in the text, everything the reader needs is already there, so naturally you need nothing at the end of the citation except the page number:

> In 1984 Darnton noted that during carnival time in 18th-century Paris, Frenchmen tortured cats (p. 83).

If you use more than one publication by the same author, you need to note that fact in the parenthesis by adding the letter *a* for the first publication, *b* for the second, and so on.

> Tuchman notes that an anonymous poem in the Middle Ages called the medieval knight a "terrible worm in a cocoon" (1978a, p. 88).

If a source has two authors, list both, separated by an ampersand (&), not an *and*, and name both authors each time you use the source in your text. However, if a source has more than two authors, mention all authors' names the first time you use the source in your text. From then on merely name the first author's name, followed by the words *et al.* (which means *and others*). Notice that you don't need to underline et al., but you do need to put a period after *al.*

Formats for a Reference Page in an APA-formatted Paper

A References section at the rear of your paper provides your readers with more information about your sources than they get in the brief information within your text. Notice that the first line of each entry is flush with the left margin, and the following lines are indented three spaces.

If you use more than one work by the same author, list the works by that author by their date of publication. Also, repeat the name of the author for each entry. That is, don't use *ibid* or a dash to tell the reader that the item is another work by the same author.

A Book by a Single Author

```
Tuchman,  B.   (1978).    A   distant   mirror:   The
     calamitous  14th  century.   New  York:  Alfred  A.
     Knopf.
```

[Comment: Notice that the author's first name is represented by initials and only the first letter of the title and subtitle are capitalized. Note, too, that the author's name is followed by period and two spaces, the parentheses that encloses the date is also followed by a period and two spaces, and the title of the work is followed by a period and two spaces. The colon following the city is followed by only a single space.]

A Book by Two or More Authors

```
Lorayne,  H.  &  Lucas,  J.  (1974).   The   memory  book.
     New  York:  Ballantine  Books.
```

[Comment: In AP style, you don't use et al. to represent the names of authors beyond the second. You give credit to each author of the work, even if there are, let's say, six authors. Notice that you use an ampersand, the symbol for *and*, to join the authors' names.]

An Edited Book When You Are Referring to Ideas by the Editor

```
Cantor,  N.  &  Werthman,  M.  (Eds.).  (1968).   The
     history  of  popular  culture.   New  York:  Collier-
     Macmillan.
```

[Comment: If you are referring to an article within the book, see the next item.]

An Edited Book When You Are Referring to One of the Works Included

Brooks, J. (1966). The income revolution. In N. Cantor and M. Werthman (Eds.), <u>The history of popular culture</u> (pp. 684-85). New York: Collier-Macmillan.

[Comment: Note that the date following the author's name is the date the article was published, not the date that the book was published. Compare this item to the previous one.]

A Chapter Within a Book

Gould, S. (1983). The guano ring. In <u>Hen's teeth and horse's toes</u> (pp. 46-55). New York: Norton.

An Article in a Journal That Numbers Its Pages Separately in Each Issue and Then Collects Those Issues in an Annual Volume.

Berg, H. C. 1975. How bacteria swim. <u>Scientific American</u> 229 (6): 24-37.

[Comment: The number 229 following the title of the journal is the volume number; the number 6 within parentheses refers to the particular issue within that volume. Without the issue number, your reader wouldn't know what issue in the volume your page numbers referred to. Note that the volume number is underlined with the title.]

An Article in a Journal That Numbers Its Pages Consecutively Throughout the Year and Then Collects Those Issues in an Annual Volume

Ralls, K. 1976. Mammals in which females are larger than males. <u>Quarterly Review of Biology</u> 51: 245-76.

[Comment: Since the pages in the volume are numbered consecutively throughout the volume, you no longer need to tell your reader the issue within that volume.]

An Article in a Weekly or Biweekly Magazine

Roger, M. (1989, Sept. 18). In Alaska, the future is now. <u>Newsweek</u>, pp. 63-64.

[Comment: Note that proper nouns like Alaska are capitalized when they occur within the title.]

An Article in a Monthly or Bimonthly Magazine

Bethell, T. (1979, February). Against Bilingual
    Education. <u>Harper's</u>, pp. 30-33.

An Article in a Newspaper

Gorney, C. (1985, July 7). Generations apart. <u>The
    Washington Post</u>, p. A 13.

[Comment: Notice that you use the abbreviation for pages (pp.) only for magazines
and newspapers, not for journals.]

Acknowledgments
of Permission

EDWARD ABBEY, "Polemic: Industrial Tourism and the National Parks," from DESERT SOLITAIRE by Edward Abbey, published by McGraw-Hill. Copyright © 1968 by Edward Abbey. Reprinted by permission of Don Congdon Associates, Inc.

SAMM SINCLAIR BAKER, "Should Advertising Be Eliminated?" from THE PERMISSIBLE LIE, published by World Publishing Company July 24, 1968. Copyright © 1968 by Samm Sinclair Baker. Reprinted by permission of Curtis Brown, Ltd.

SID BERNSTEIN, "Is Puffery Flummery?" from ADVERTISING AGE, October 2, 1972. Copyright © 1972 by Crain Communications Inc. Reprinted by permission of ADVERTISING AGE.

TOM BETHELL, "Against Bilingual Education." Copyright © 1979 by HARPER'S. All rights reserved. Reprinted from the February 1979 issue with special permission.

BRUCE BOWER, "Grave Misunderstandings," from SCIENCE NEWS, Vol. 136 (1989). Copyright 1989 by Science Service, Inc. Reprinted with permission from SCIENCE NEWS, the weekly newsmagazine of science.

SUSAN BROWNMILLER, from "Women Fight Back," in AGAINST OUR WILL: MEN, WOMEN AND RAPE. Copyright © 1984 by Susan Brownmiller. Reprinted by permission of Linden Press, a division of Simon & Schuster, Inc.

WILLIAM BUCKLEY, "First Amendment Pixillation," by William Buckley from NATIONAL REVIEW, Vol. 29, 1977. Reprinted by permission of Universal Press Syndicate.

JAMES COATES, "A Forest of Manmade Threats Descends on Yellowstone," from THE CHICAGO TRIBUNE, May 19, 1985. Copyright © 1985 by THE CHICAGO TRIBUNE. Reprinted by permission of THE CHICAGO TRIBUNE.

JAMES LINCOLN COLLIER, "It Is Different for Women," by James Lincoln Collier from READER'S DIGEST, January 1982. Reprinted by permission of the author.

JOANNE V. CREIGHTON, from "The Myth of the Isolated Artist," by Joanne V. Creighton in JOYCE CAROL OATES (Twayne's U.S. Authors Series). Copyright © 1979 by G.K. Hall & Co. Reprinted with permission of Twayne Publishers, an imprint of Macmillan Publishing Company.

JOHN CRICHTON, "Myths About Advertising?" from ETHICS, MORALITY, AND THE MEDIA, ed. Lee Thayer. Copyright © 1980 by Hastings House. Reprinted by permission of the publisher.

JO DURDEN-SMITH AND DIANE DESIMONE, "The Perils of Paul, the Pangs of Pauline," from PLAYBOY, May 1982. Copyright © 1982 by Jo Durden-Smith and Diane deSimone. Reprinted by permission of RLR Associates, Ltd.

HAROLD EDWARDS, "The Dour Critics of Advertising," by Harold Edwards; used by permission of the author.

STUART EWEN, from "The Social Crises of the Mass Culture," in CAPTAINS OF CONSCIOUSNESS: ADVERTISING AND THE SOCIAL ROOTS OF THE CONSUMER CULTURE. Copyright © 1977 by Stuart Ewen. Reprinted by permission of McGraw-Hill, Inc.

James Fallows, "Language," by James Fallows from THE ATLANTIC MONTHLY, November 1983. Reprinted by permission of the author.

FORTUNE, "Issei, Nisei, Kibei," from FORTUNE, April 1944. Copyright © 1944 by Time Inc. All Rights Reserved. Reprinted by permission of FORTUNE.

Christina Marsden Gillis, "'Where Are You Going, Where Have You Been?': Seduction, Space, and a Fictional Mode," from STUDIES IN SHORT FICTION 18 (1981): 65–70. Copyright by Newberry College. Reprinted by permission.

Walter Goodman, "What Is a Civil Libertarian to Do When Pornography Becomes So Bold?" from THE NEW YORK TIMES, November 21, 1976. Copyright © 1976 by The New York Times Company. Reprinted by permission.

Cynthia Gorney, "Generations Apart," from THE WASHINGTON POST, July 7, 1985. Copyright © 1985 The Washington Post.

George Griffin, "Laissez-Faire Advertising," from GRAPHIC ARTS MONTHLY October 1985. Copyright © 1991 by Cahners Publishing Company. Reprinted by permission of Cahners Reprint Services.

Morton Grodzins, "Arguments in Favor of Evacuation," from AMERICANS BETRAYED. Copyright 1949 by The University of Chicago Press. Reprinted by permission of the publisher.

C. Ray Hall, "The Last Person Who Will Ever Touch You," from THE LOUISVILLE COURIER JOURNAL MAGAZINE, October 28, 1990. Copyright © 1990 by the Courier-Journal & Louisville Times Co. Reprinted with permission.

Robert Haney, "Blushes and Leers as Guides to Crime," from COMSTOCKERY IN AMERICA. Copyright © 1960 by Robert Haney. Reprinted by permission of Beacon Press.

Ruth Mulvey Harmer, "Requiem for Everyman," from THE HIGH COST OF DYING, published by Collier-Macmillan, 1963. Copyright by Ruth Harmer Carew. Reprinted by permission of the author.

Victoria Herndon, "Advertising: Through the Looking Glass" (not previously published). Copyright Victoria Herndon. Reprinted by permission of the author.

Stanley High, "Japanese Saboteurs in Our Midst," from READER'S DIGEST, January 1942. Copyright © 1941 by The Reader's Digest Assn., Inc. Reprinted with permission from the January 1942 READER'S DIGEST.

C. Holden, "Female Math Anxiety on the Wane," from SCIENCE, May 8, 1987, Volume 236, beginning page 660. Copyright © 1987 by the AAAS. Reprinted by permission of the American Association for the Advancement of Science.

Paul E. Irion, "The Perspective of Theology," from THE FUNERAL: VESTIGE OR VALUE? by Paul E. Irion, published by Abingdon Press 1966. Copyright Paul E. Irion. Reprinted by permission of the author.

Sadae Iwataki, "Pilgrimage to Manzanar," from THE CHRISTIAN SCIENCE MONITOR, December 20, 1989. Reprinted by permission of K.E. Iwataki.

Eric Julber, "Let's Open Up Our Wilderness," by Eric Julber from READER'S DIGEST, May 1972. Copyright © by Eric Julber. Reprinted by permission of the author.

Joan Keefe, "An Alternative to Bilingualism," from THE NEW YORK TIMES, October 24, 1985. Copyright © 1985 by The New York Times Company. Reprinted by permission.

Marty Klein, "Censorship and the Fear of Sexuality," first appeared in the July/August 1990 issue of THE HUMANIST. Reprinted by permission of THE HUMANIST.

Alfie Kohn, "Girl Talk — Guy Talk," from PSYCHOLOGY TODAY, February 1988. Copyright 1988 by Alfie Kohn. Reprinted from PSYCHOLOGY TODAY with the permission of the author.

Melvin Konner, "The Aggressors," from THE NEW YORK TIMES, August 14, 1988. Copyright © 1988 by The New York Times Company. Reprinted by permission.

IRVING KRISTOL, "Pornography, Obscenity, and the Case for Censorship," from REFLECTIONS OF A NEOCONSERVATIVE by Irving Kristol. Copyright © 1983 by Basic Books, Inc. Reprinted by permission of Basic Books, a division of HarperCollins Publishers, Inc.

JOSEPH WOOD KRUTCH, "Conservation Is Not Enough," from THE VOICE OF THE DESERT by Joseph Wood Krutch. Copyright © 1954, 1955 by Joseph Wood Krutch; renewed 1992 by Marcella Krutch. Reprinted by permission of William Morrow & Company, Inc.

WILLIAM M. LAMERS, JR., "Funerals Are Good for People," from MEDICAL ECONOMICS, June 23, 1969. Copyright © 1969 by Medical Economics Publishing. Reprinted by permission from MEDICAL ECONOMICS Magazine.

THEODORE LEVITT, "Are Advertising and Marketing Corrupting Society? It's Not Your Worry," from ADVERTISING AGE, October 8, 1958. Copyright © 1958 by Crain Communications Inc. Reprinted by permission of ADVERTISING AGE.

ELEANOR EMMONS MACCOBY AND CAROL NAGY JACKLIN, from THE PSYCHOLOGY OF SEX DIFFERENCES. © 1974 by the Board of Trustees of the Leland Stanford Junior University. Reprinted with the permission of the publishers, Stanford University Press.

PATTY MCENTEE, "Is Pornography a Matter of Free Expression?" from AMERICA, August 10, 1991. Reprinted with permission of AMERICA Press, Inc., 106 West 56th Street, New York, NY 10019. Copyright © 1991. All Rights Reserved.

PETER METCALF AND RICHARD HUNTINGTON, "The Role of the Mortician" (our title), from CELEBRATIONS OF DEATH, 2nd edition, pp. 198–200. Copyright © 1991 Cambridge University Press. Reprinted with the permission of Cambridge University Press.

JOSEPHINE MILES, "Government Injunction Restraining Harlem Cosmetic Co.," from POEMS 1930–1960, by Josephine Miles. Reprinted by permission.

JESSICA MITFORD, "Fashions in Funerals," from THE AMERICAN WAY OF DEATH. Copyright © 1963, 1978 by Jessica Mitford. All rights reserved. Reprinted by permission of Jessica Mitford.

AL MORGAN, "The Bier Barons," by Al Morgan from PLAYBOY, June 1960. Copyright Al Morgan. Reprinted by permission of the author.

FRANK H. MURKOWSKI, "We Can Have Both Oil and Wildlife Protection," from THE CHRISTIAN SCIENCE MONITOR, March 17, 1987. Copyright Frank H. Murkowski. Reprinted by permission of the author.

THE NATION, "Life in a California Concentration Camp," from THE NATION, Volume 154, 1942. Reprinted by permission of THE NATION.

NEWSWEEK, "The Dies Report," from NEWSWEEK, March 9, 1942. Copyright © 1942 by Newsweek Inc.; "In Sports, 'Lions' vs 'Tigers,'" from NEWSWEEK, May 18, 1981. Copyright © 1981 by Newsweek Inc.; "Just How the Sexes Differ," from NEWSWEEK May 18, 1981. Copyright © 1981 by Newsweek Inc.; "In Alaska, The Future Is Now," from NEWSWEEK, September 18, 1989. Copyright © 1989 by Newsweek Inc. All rights reserved. Reprinted by permission.

JOHN NICHOLSON, from MEN AND WOMEN: HOW DIFFERENT ARE THEY? Copyright © 1984 by John Nicholson. Reprinted by permission of Oxford University Press, London.

JOYCE CAROL OATES, "Preface" to WHERE ARE YOU GOING, WHERE HAVE YOU BEEN? Copyright by Joyce Carol Oates. Reprinted by permission of the author.

JOYCE CAROL OATES, "Where Are You Going, Where Have You Been?" from THE WHEEL OF LOVE by Joyce Carol Oates, published by Vanguard Press 1970. Copyright © 1970 Joyce Carol Oates. Reprinted by permission of John Hawkins & Associates, Inc.

VANCE PACKARD, ". . . And the Hooks Are Lowered," from THE HIDDEN PERSUADERS by Vance Packard. Copyright © 1981 by Little, Brown and Company. Reprinted by permission of the author.

CHARLES F. PARK, JR., "Conservation and the Environmental Crisis," from EARTHBOUND: MINERALS, ENERGY, AND MAN'S FUTURE by Charles F. Park, Jr. Copyright © 1975 by Freeman, Cooper and Company. Reprinted by permission of the author.

MARGE PIERCY, "Barbie Doll," from CIRCLES ON THE WATER. Copyright © 1982 by Marge Piercy. Reprinted by permission of Alfred A. Knopf, Inc.

J. H. PLUMB, "De Mortuis," from HORIZON, Spring 1967.

IVAN PRESTON, "Puffery is Deception," from THE GREAT AMERICAN BLOWUP. Copyright © 1975 by Ivan Preston. Reprinted by permission of The University of Wisconsin Press.

TOM QUIRK, "A Source for 'Where Are You Going, Where Have You Been?'" from STUDIES IN SHORT FICTION 18 (1981): 413–19. Copyright by Newberry College. Reprinted by permission.

SALLY REED, "The New Pluralism, Bilingual Classes: A Bilateral Conflict," from THE NEW YORK TIMES, August 21, 1983. Copyright © 1983 by The New York Times Company. Reprinted by permission.

CYNTHIA RIGGS, "Access to Public Lands: A National Necessity," from EXXON USA, Second Quarter, 1984. Reprinted by permission of Exxon Company, U.S.A.

MARY ELLEN ROSS, "Censorship or Education? Feminist Views on Pornography," from THE CHRISTIAN CENTURY, March 7, 1990. Copyright © 1990 Christian Century Foundation. Reprinted by permission of The Christian Century.

EUGENE V. ROSTOW, "Our Worst Wartime Mistake." Copyright © 1945 by HARPER'S. All rights reserved. Reprinted from Volume 191 with special permission.

DIANA E. H. RUSSELL, "Research on How Women Experience the Impact of Pornography," from PORNOGRAPHY AND CENSORSHIP, published by Prometheus Books, 1983. Copyright by Diana E. H. Russell. Reprinted by permission of the author.

JEFFREY SCHRANK, "The Language of Advertising Claims," from TEACHING ABOUT DOUBLESPEAK, published by the NCTE, 1976. Copyright 1976 by Jeffrey Schrank. Reprinted by permission of the author.

MICHAEL SCHUDSON, "Advertising as Capitalist Realism," from ADVERTISING: THE UNEASY PERSUASION by Michael Schudson. Copyright © 1986 by Michael Schudson. Reprinted by permission of Basic Books, a division of HarperCollins Publishers Inc.

JOSEPH L. SELDIN, from THE GOLDEN FLEECE: SELLING THE GOOD LIFE TO AMERICANS, published by Macmillan Publishing Company 1963. Copyright © 1963 by Joseph L. Seldin. Reprinted with the permission of Macmillan Publishing Company.

MICHAEL SPECTER, "Hot Tombs," from THE NEW REPUBLIC, September 11, 1989. Copyright © 1989 by THE NEW REPUBLIC, INC. Reprinted by permission of The New Republic.

JAMES C. STALKER, "Official English or English Only?" from ENGLISH JOURNAL, March 1988. Copyright 1988 by the National Council of Teachers of English. Reprinted with permission.

WALLACE STEGNER, "Wilderness Letter," from THE SOUND OF MOUNTAIN WATER by Wallace Stegner. Copyright © 1969 by Wallace Stegner. Used by permission of Doubleday, a division of Bantam Doubleday Dell Publishing Group, Inc.

CAROL TAVRIS and CAROLE OFFIR, excerpts from THE LONGEST WAR: SEX DIFFERENCES IN PERSPECTIVE. Copyright © 1977 by Harcourt Brace Jovanovich, Inc. Reprinted by permission of the publisher.

JACOBUS TENBROEK ET ALIA, "The Activation of the Stereotype," from PREJUDICE, WAR, AND THE CONSTITUTION. Copyright © 1954 renewed 1982 Edward Barnhart, Hazel tenBroek. Reprinted by permission of the University of California Press.

TIME, "American Fair Play?" from TIME, March 19, 1945. Copyright 1945 Time Warner Inc.; "Postwar Exports" from TIME, April 2, 1945. Copyright 1945 Time Warner Inc.; "Against a Confusion of Tongues" from TIME, June 13, 1983. Copyright 1983 Time Warner Inc.; "For Learning or Ethnic Pride?" from TIME, July 8, 1985. Copyright 1985 Time Warner Inc.; "How to Tell Your Friends From The Japs" from TIME, December 22, 1941. Copyright 1941 Time Warner Inc. All reprinted by permission.

WILLIAM TUCKER, "Is Nature Too Good for Us?" Copyright © 1982 by HARPER'S. All rights reserved. Reprinted from the March 1982 issue with special permission.

ROUL TUNLEY, "Can You Afford to Die?" from THE SATURDAY EVENING POST, June 17, 1961. Copyright © 1961 by THE SATURDAY EVENING POST. Reprinted by permission.

GRAHAM TURNER, "The Lost Art of Dying," from THE SUNDAY TELEGRAPH, February 26, 1989. Copyright Graham Turner, a British journalist. Reprinted by permission of the author.

MORRIS K. UDALL, "Close the Arctic National Refuge to Oilmen," from THE CHRISTIAN SCIENCE MONITOR, March 17, 1987. Reprinted by permission of Morris K. Udall.

MARIE MITCHELL OLESEN URBANSKI, "Existential Allegory: Joyce Carol Oates's 'Where Are You Going, Where Have You Been?'" from STUDIES IN SHORT FICTION 15 (1978): 200–03. Copyright by Newberry College. Reprinted by permission.

U.S. NEWS & WORLD REPORT, "Making Amends" from U.S. NEWS & WORLD REPORT, October 22, 1990. Copyright 1990 U.S. News & World Report; "Educating the Melting Pot" from U.S. NEWS & WORLD REPORT March 31, 1986. Copyright 1986 U.S. News & World Report; "A Second Look At Bilingual Education" from U.S. NEWS & WORLD REPORT June 11, 1985. Copyright 1985 U.S. News & World Report; "The Battle for the Wilderness" from U.S. NEWS & WORLD REPORT, July 3, 1989. Copyright 1989 U.S. News & World Report. All reprinted by permission.

THE WASHINGTON POST, "For Teachers, Ten Years of Trial and Error," from THE WASHINGTON POST, July 8, 1985. Copyright © 1985 The Washington Post. Reprinted by permission.

JOYCE M. WEGS, "'Don't You Know Who I Am?' The Grotesque in Oates's 'Where Are You Going, Where Have You Been?'" First printed in the JOURNAL OF NARRATIVE TECHNIQUE, Vol. 5 (1975). Reprinted by permission of the *Journal of Narrative Technique.*

G. J. WEINBERGER, "Who Is Arnold Friend?" The Other Self in Joyce Carol Oates's 'Where Are You Going, Where Have You Been?'" from AMERICAN IMAGO, Vol. 45, pp. 205–215. Reprinted by permission of the author and The Johns Hopkins University Press.

NAOMI WEISSTEIN, "Tired of Arguing about Biological Inferiority?" by Naomi Weisstein from MS. Magazine, November 1982. Reprinted by permission of the author.

ALAN WOLFE, "Dirt and Democracy," from THE NEW REPUBLIC, February 19, 1990. Copyright © 1990 by THE NEW REPUBLIC, INC. Reprinted by permission of The New Republic.

Author-Title Index